高等学校新形态教材
供本科护理学类专业用

Community Nursing
社区护理学

汉英对照

主　编　倪　平

副主编　侯小妮　杨莉莉

参编人员（以姓氏笔画为序）

邓文芳　长江大学医学部护理系

朱雪娇　杭州师范大学公共卫生与护理学院

杨莉莉　浙江中医药大学护理学院

吴　凡　武汉轻工大学医学与健康学院

张晓楠　天津医科大学护理学院

林蓓蕾　郑州大学护理与健康学院

侯小妮　北京中医药大学护理学院

倪　平　华中科技大学同济医学院护理学院

董玉静　南京中医药大学护理学院

温桂敏　锦州医科大学护理学院

人民卫生出版社
·北京·

图书在版编目（CIP）数据

社区护理学 = Community Nursing：汉英对照 / 倪平主编 . -- 北京：人民卫生出版社，2025. 6. -- ISBN 978-7-117-38182-6

Ⅰ. R473. 2

中国国家版本馆 CIP 数据核字第 20251RJ562 号

人卫智网	www.ipmph.com	医学教育、学术、考试、健康，购书智慧智能综合服务平台
人卫官网	www.pmph.com	人卫官方资讯发布平台

社区护理学（汉英对照）
Community Nursing

主　　编：倪　平
出版发行：人民卫生出版社（中继线 010-59780011）
地　　址：北京市朝阳区潘家园南里 19 号
邮　　编：100021
E - mail：pmph @ pmph.com
购书热线：010-59787592　010-59787584　010-65264830
印　　刷：三河市宏达印刷有限公司
经　　销：新华书店
开　　本：850×1168　1/16　　印张：31
字　　数：853 千字
版　　次：2025 年 6 月第 1 版
印　　次：2025 年 9 月第 1 次印刷
标准书号：ISBN 978-7-117-38182-6
定　　价：129.00 元

打击盗版举报电话：**010-59787491**　E-mail：**WQ @ pmph.com**
质量问题联系电话：**010-59787234**　E-mail：**zhiliang @ pmph.com**
数字融合服务电话：**4001118166**　E-mail：**zengzhi @ pmph.com**

前 言
PREFACE

在当今全球化不断深入的时代背景下，医疗保健领域也呈现出日益国际化与多元化的发展趋势。社区护理学作为一门促进和维护社区人群健康的综合学科，正肩负着为广大社区居民提供全面、连续、个性化、多元化且经济有效的健康服务的重任，它是公共卫生体系的重要组成部分，在促进全民健康素养提升和疾病预防控制方面发挥着不可或缺的基石作用。本教材以健康促进为目标，以人群健康管理为中心，分别从社区、家庭及个体的护理功能出发，介绍疾病防治、康复和管理等内容，实现公共卫生学与护理学理论、方法与技能的有机融合。

《社区护理学（双语）》旨在为护理专业的学生以及从事社区护理工作的专业人员搭建一座跨越语言和专业知识的桥梁。本教材通过双语的呈现形式，一方面，帮助读者拓宽国际视野，深入了解国外先进的社区护理理念、模式与实践经验，与国际社区护理前沿接轨，更好地参与国际交流与合作；另一方面，为培养具备双语能力、能够适应多元文化护理环境的高素质社区护理人才提供有力的支持。

在编写过程中，我们秉持科学性、系统性、实用性与前沿性相结合的原则，从社区护理的基础理论出发，详细阐述了社区卫生服务体系与模式，社区健康促进与健康教育，社区家庭健康管理，社区儿童、青少年、女性、老年人群的保健，社区慢性病患者护理，社区伤残患者康复护理，社区安宁疗护以及社区突发公共卫生事件管理等核心内容。每章均精心筛选具有代表性的双语案例，阐释专业术语，并清晰呈现实际操作步骤，力求使读者在掌握专业知识的基础上，能熟练运用英语进行相关的学术交流和开展实践操作。同时，本教材提供精心设计的案例微课、丰富的知识拓展、各章常用单词，以及中英文测试等数字资源，激发学生跳出传统思维的局限，辅助学生自主学习，拓宽知识体系，为学生未来应对复杂多变的学习与工作挑战打下坚实的基础。

在本书的编写过程中，我们得到了长江大学医学部护理系、杭州师范大学公共卫生与护理学院、浙江中医药大学护理学院、武汉轻工大学医学与健康学院、天津医科大学护理学院、郑州大学护理与健康学院、北京中医药大学护理学院、华中科技大学同济医学院护理学院、南京中医药大学护理学院、锦州医科大学护理学院的大力支持和帮助，特此感谢！

由于水平有限，难免有疏漏和不足之处，恳请读者赐教指正！

倪 平

2025 年 6 月

目 录
TABLE OF CONTENTS
URSING

Chapter 1

Overview

第一章

概述

Learning Objectives

Knowledge Objectives

1. Accurately explain the concepts of community and community nursing; the characteristics of community nursing; the work content of community nurses; the roles and competency requirements of community nurses; and the basic philosophy of community nursing.

2. Correctly describe the classification, components and functions of a community; the functions and roles of community nursing; relevant policies, regulations

学习目标

知识目标

1. 正确叙述社区、社区护理的概念；社区护理的特点；社区护士的工作内容；社区护士的角色和能力要求；社区护理的基本理念。

2. 正确描述社区的分类、构成要素和功能；社区护理的功能和作用；社区护理的相关政策法规和伦理规范；社区护士的基本条件。

and ethical standards of community nursing; and the basic qualifications of community nurses.

Ability Objectives

1. Apply knowledge and principles of community health management to develop a personalized health promotion plan for community residents.
2. Conduct physical and mental health assessments for community residents and create a community health care plan for them.
3. Design a health education and promotion activity plan based on the health needs of community residents.

Quality Objectives

1. Promote the spirit of scientific inquiry, focus on individual needs, and develop personalized health plans for residents by utilizing the available resources within the community.
2. Cultivate compassion, responsibility, and empathy, provide genuine care for vulnerable groups in the community, and help them to obtain timely and effective health support and protection.
3. Foster a spirit of understanding and inclusivity, respect the needs of residents from diverse cultural backgrounds, and organize health education and scientific knowledge popularization activities to improve the health literacy of the community residents.

能力目标

1. 运用社区健康管理相关知识与原理，为社区居民制订一份个性化健康促进计划。
2. 对社区居民进行身、心状态评估，为其制订一份社区健康保健计划。
3. 根据社区居民健康需求，为其制订一份健康教育和健康促进活动计划。

素质目标

1. 倡导科学精神，关注个体需求，结合社区实际资源为居民制订个体化健康方案。
2. 培养关爱、责任感和共情能力，切实关怀社区弱势群体，帮助他们获得及时有效的健康支持与保障。
3. 树立理解、包容精神，尊重不同文化背景的居民需求，组织健康教育活动和科普宣传，提升社区居民健康素养。

With the changes in the health care system and the promotion of community health services, the social demand for community nursing services has been on the rise. Community nursing plays an increasingly important role in national health and the construction of a healthy China. Therefore, nursing staff need to correctly understand the

随着医疗体系的变革和社区卫生服务的推进，社会对社区护理服务的需求不断上升。社区护理在全民健康和健康中国建设中发挥着越来越重要的作用。因此，护理人员需要正确理解社区健康管理在基本公共卫生服务和基本医疗服务中的作用，掌握公共卫生和社区卫生服务的基本知识，明确社区护士应具备的核心能

role of community health management in basic public health services and basic medical services, master the basic knowledge of public health and community health services, and clarify the core competencies that community nurses should possess to play an important role in enhancing the health of the whole population and the whole life cycle in the community.

力，以在提升社区全人群和全生命周期的健康水平方面发挥重要作用。

Section 1 Community and Health

I. Concept and Classification of Community

i. The Concept of Community

The word "community" comes from the Latin word, meaning group or collective. In the 1880s, the German sociologist Ferdinand Tönnies first introduced the concept of "community" into sociology and defined it as "a humane social group composed of a homogeneous population with consistent values, close relationships, mutual interaction and mutual support". The World Health Organization (WHO), at its international conference on primary health care, held in Almaty in 1978, defined the community as "a group of people united in some form of social organization or association".

In the 1930s, Mr. Fei Xiaotong, a famous sociologist, introduced the concept of "community" into China, taking into account the characteristics of Chinese society, defined it as "a community is a large group of social groups (e.g. families, clans) or social organizations (e.g. institutions, groups) gathered in a specific geographical area to form a large collective of interrelated lives." The community is the basic unit of society, closely related to people's life and health, and the main place for community nurses to carry out community nursing services.

第一节 社区与健康

一、社区的概念与分类

（一）社区的概念

"社区（community）"一词源自拉丁语，原意为团体或共同体。19世纪80年代，德国社会学家斐迪南·滕尼斯（Ferdinand Tönnies）首次将"社区"这一概念引入社会学，并将其定义为"由同质人口构成的，价值观一致、关系密切、相互往来和守望相助的富有人情味的社会群体"。世界卫生组织（World Health Organization，WHO）于1978年在阿拉木图举行的基层保健医疗国际会议中，将社区定义为"以某种形式之社会组织或团体结合在一起的一群人"。

20世纪30年代，著名社会学家费孝通先生将"社区"这一概念引入中国，并结合中国社会的特点，将其定义为"社区是若干社会群体（如家庭、氏族）或社会组织（如机关、团体）在特定地域内聚集形成的一个生活上相互关联的大集体"。社区是构成社会的基本单位，与人们的生活和健康密切相关，也是社区护士开展社区护理服务的主要场所。

ii. Classification of Community

Communities can be categorized into various types according to different division criteria.

1. Divided by Geographical Characteristics Communities can be categorized into urban, rural and town communities, which is the most common and universal division criteria.

(1) Urban communities are communities located in urban areas, characterized by non-agricultural production activities and with a relatively concentrated population.

(2) Rural communities are communities located in rural areas, characterized mainly by agricultural production activities and with a relatively dispersed population.

(3) Town communities are smaller, less concentrated communities with a predominantly non-agricultural production activity that serve to connect urban and rural communities.

Dividing communities according to geographical characteristics facilitates health assessment and implementation of health interventions based on the specific characteristics of various communities. Organizing and mobilizing community groups to implement preventive and intervention measures oriented to the needs of the community can be supported by local authorities and make full use of existing resources for health promotion activities.

2. Divided by Functional Objectives Communities can be divided into living communities and functional communities.

(1) Living communities are communities whose main purpose is the residence and daily life of the residents.

(2) Functional communities are communities with specific purposes and functions, such as school communities and factory communities. Functional communities are places where youth and workforce populations congregate, and these populations may live centrally or dispersed, but come together within a specific time to achieve common goals. Functional communities are

（二）社区的分类

根据不同的划分标准，社区可以分为多种类型。

1. 按照地域特点划分　社区可以分为城市社区、农村社区和城镇社区，这是最常见、最通用的划分标准。

（1）城市社区是位于城市地区，以非农业生产活动为主要特征，人口相对集中的社区。

（2）农村社区是位于农村地区，以农业生产活动为主要特征，人口相对分散的社区。

（3）城镇社区是规模较小、人口集中程度较低，以非农业生产活动为主的社区，起到连接城市社区和农村社区的作用。

按照地域特点对社区进行划分，有助于根据各类社区的具体特点进行健康评估和实施健康干预。以社区需求为导向，组织和动员社区群体实施预防和干预措施，可以得到当地权威人士的支持，并充分利用现有资源开展健康促进活动。

2. 按照功能目标划分　社区可以分为生活社区和功能性社区。

（1）生活社区是以居民居住和日常生活为主要目的的社区。

（2）功能性社区是具有特定目的和功能的社区，例如学校社区和工厂社区。功能性社区是青少年和劳动力人群聚集的地方，这些人群可能集中居住，也可能分散居住，但在特定时间内会聚集在一起以实现共同目标。功能性社区也是社区护理服务的重要对象。

also an important target for community nursing services.

II. Components and Functions of Community

i. Constituent Elements of a Community

The main constituent elements of a community include the geographical element, the demographic element, the interactive element and the homogeneous element.

1. Geographical Elements A certain range of territory and living space is a prerequisite for the existence and development of a community, and it is an important environmental foundation that constitutes a community. Geographical factors determine the nature and future direction of a community.

2. Demographic Elements People are at the heart of community life and constitute the necessary prerequisites and main elements of a community. Demographic factors cover the quantity, quality, composition and distribution of the population of a community, reflecting the demographic relations and overall appearance within the community. Population quantity refers to the number of people in the community. Population quality (or the competence of the population) includes the comprehensive performance of physical, cultural and ideological qualities, reflecting the population's overall ability to perceive and transform the world. Physical quality refers to health status and life expectancy; cultural quality refers to cultural and scientific level and labor skills; and ideological quality refers to political thought and moral character. These three aspects of population quality are closely interrelated. Physical quality is the natural condition base of population quality, and cultural and ideological quality is the main criterion of population quality. Improvement of cultural and ideological qualities contributes to the enhancement of physical qualities. The improvement of physical quality also provides favorable conditions for improved cultural and

二、社区的构成要素和功能

（一）社区的构成要素

社区的主要构成要素包括地域要素、人口要素、互动要素和同质要素。

1. 地域要素 一定范围的地域和生活空间是社区存在和发展的前提条件，是构成社区的重要环境基础。地域因素决定了社区的性质和未来发展方向。

2. 人口要素 人是社区生活的核心，是构成社区的必要前提和主体要素。人口要素涵盖社区人口的数量、质量、构成和分布，反映社区内部的人口关系和整体面貌。人口数量指社区内人口的多少。人口质量（或称人口素质）是社区成员身体素质、文化素质和思想素质的综合表现，体现了社区成员对世界的认知和改造能力。身体素质主要指健康状况和预期寿命，文化素质指文化科学水平和劳动技能，思想素质指政治思想和道德品质。人口质量的 3 个方面紧密相连。身体素质是人口质量的自然条件基础，文化和思想素质是衡量人口质量的主要标准。提高文化和思想素质有助于增强身体素质，而身体素质的提高也为文化和思想素质的提升提供了良好条件。人口构成涉及社区内不同类型人口的特征，包括生物构成（如性别、年龄、种族等）和社会构成（如社会阶层、职业、文化水平、宗教信仰等），反映了社区内部的人口关系，不同的人口关系表现出不同的社区面貌。人口分布则是指社区人口及其活动在空间上的分布，包括人口密度等。

ideological quality. Population composition involves the characteristics of different types of population within a community, including biological composition (e.g. gender, age, race, etc.) and social composition (e.g. class, occupation, literacy level, religion, etc.), and reflects the demographic relationships within the community, with different demographic relationships manifesting different aspects of the community. Population distribution, on the other hand, refers to the spatial distribution of the community's population and its activities, including population density.

3. Interactive Elements   These include the community's living service facilities, living systems and management organizations. Living service facilities are the material conditions necessary for the production and living of community members, and the links between them, including schools, medical institutions, commercial outlets, banks, pharmacies, supermarkets, transportation facilities and recreational venues. The living systems and management institutions are the guarantee for the normal operation of the community. For example, the domestic waste management system belongs to the living system, and the property, neighborhood committee and police station belong to the management institutions. Appropriate living systems and management institutions can work together to regulate the behavior of community members, coordinate various social relationships, and ensure that the community becomes an orderly social life community. The element of interaction is the basic condition for promoting interaction between people and people, and between people and the environment in the community, and for ensuring the functioning of the community.

4. Homogeneous Elements   These include cultural background, behavioral habits, sense of identity and values, which involve all aspects of people's social life. People living in the same community usually have similar social

3. 互动要素　包括社区的生活服务设施、生活制度及管理机构等。生活服务设施既是社区成员生产和生活所需的物质条件，也是联系社区成员的纽带，主要包括学校、医疗机构、商业服务网点、银行、药店、超市、交通设施和娱乐场所等。生活制度和管理机构是社区正常运作的保障。例如，生活垃圾管理制度属于生活制度，物业、居委会和派出所等属于管理机构。适当的生活制度和管理机构可以共同规范社区成员的行为，协调各种社会关系，确保社区成为一个有序的社会生活共同体。互动要素是促进社区中人与人、人与环境之间互动，保障社区运转的基本条件。

4. 同质要素　包括文化背景、行为习惯、认同意识和价值观念等，涉及人们社会生活的各个方面。生活在同一个社区的人们通常会有相似的社会意识、行为规范、生活方式和文化氛围。这些共同点使社区成员团结起来，共同促

consciousness, behavioral norms, lifestyles and cultural atmosphere. These commonalities unite community members and jointly promote the development of the whole community. The element of homogeneity is the intrinsic foundation of community survival and development.

ii . Functions of the Community

The community has the function of meeting the needs of residents and carrying out management. The full utilization of community functions helps to tap community resources and develop community health services. Community functions can be summarized as follows:

1. Management Function　The community management organization manages residents' social life affairs and regulates their behavior through codes of conduct and regulations, such as setting up a property management system.

2. Service Function　Mobilizing and organizing community forces, through a variety of social services, provides local, direct and timely help to the elderly, children, the sick, the disabled, pregnant women and other vulnerable groups in the community, so as to solve various difficulties that cannot be solved by families and individuals. For example, nursing homes, home help societies and community health services have been set up to meet the needs of residents.

3. Support and Guarantee Function When community residents face illnesses or difficulties, the community provides support and guarantee. The community can contact the local civil affairs department or relevant medical organizations according to the needs of the residents to provide appropriate support and protection to meet the needs of the residents.

4. Educational Function　Operate and co-construct a public space for community education through the establishment of community education and cultural centers and the organization of educational science lectures, etc., to enhance the civilized quality and health literacy of community members, so that the recipients can establish

进整个社区的发展。同质要素是社区生存和发展的内在基础。

（二）社区的功能

社区具有满足居民需求和进行管理的功能。充分发挥社区功能有助于挖掘社区资源并开展社区卫生服务。社区功能可以概括为以下几个方面：

1. **管理功能**　社区的管理机构通过行为规范和规章制度来管理居民的社会生活事务，规范社区居民的行为，例如设立物业管理系统。

2. **服务功能**　动员和组织社区力量，通过多种社会服务，为社区内的老年人、儿童、患者、残疾人、孕妇等弱势群体提供就地、直接、及时的帮助，以解决家庭和个人无法解决的各种困难。例如，设立养老院、家政服务社和社区卫生服务机构等，以满足居民的需求。

3. **支持保障功能**　当社区居民面临疾病或困难时，社区提供支持和保障。社区可以根据居民的需求与当地民政部门或相关医疗机构联系，提供相应的支持和保障，满足居民的需求。

4. **教育功能**　通过设立社区教育文化中心，组织教育科普讲座等活动，运营共建社区教育公共空间，提升社区成员的文明素质和健康素养，使受教育者树立健康意识，自觉改正不良行为，建立有益于健康的行为和生活方式。

a sense of health, consciously improve their undesirable behaviors, and establish behaviors and lifestyles that are beneficial to health.

5. Socialization Function   Individuals grow up and socialize in the community, influencing each other and forming the cultural ecosystem and values of the community. These unique cultures further influence the community residents.

6. Social Participation Function   The community establishes various public service facilities and activity venues, such as libraries, youth activity stations, senior activity stations and cultural activity centers, etc., so that residents can participate in and democratically manage the public affairs of the community, and cultivate a healthy sense of community and the spirit of public welfare. Through the organization of various activities, it promotes interaction among residents, enhances the care and emotional exchange among community residents, unites community strength and creates a sense of belonging.

7. Security and Stabilization Function The community establishes committees for people's mediation, public security and public health through the neighborhood committee to deal with public affairs and public welfare in the community, mediate civil disputes, maintain community security and stability, and reflect the opinions and demands of the public to the government and make suggestions.

III. Community Health

i. Health

Health is a relative, dynamic and individual concept, covering four aspects: physical, psychological, social and moral. As times change and medical paradigms shift, people's understanding of health continues to improve and the meaning of health continues to expand.

In 1948, the World Health Organization (WHO) defined health as "Health is a state of complete physical, mental and social well-being

5. 社会化功能   个体在社区中成长并实现社会化，彼此影响，形成社区特有的文化生态和价值观。这些特有的文化又进一步影响社区居民。

6. 社会参与功能   社区设立各种公共服务设施与活动场所，如图书馆、青少年活动站、老年活动站和文化活动中心等，居民可以参与社区公共事务的民主管理，培养健康的社区意识和公益精神。通过举办各种活动，促进居民互动，增强社区居民之间的关怀和情感交流，凝聚社区力量，产生归属感。

7. 安全稳定功能   社区通过居委会设立人民调解、治安保卫和公共卫生等委员会，处理本社区的公共事务和公益事业，调解民间纠纷，维护社区安全稳定，并向政府反映群众的意见和要求，提出建议。

三、社区健康

（一）健康

健康是一个相对的、动态的、具有个体性的概念，涵盖生理、心理、社会和道德 4 个方面。随着时代的变迁和医学模式的转变，人们对健康的认识不断提高，健康的含义也在不断扩展。

1948 年，WHO 将健康定义为："健康不仅仅是没有疾病和身体缺陷，还应包括完整的生理、心理状态以及良好的社会适应能力"。1986 年，

and not merely the absence of disease or infirmity." In 1986, the WHO updated the definition of health, stating that "to achieve a state of complete physical, mental and social well-being, people need to have the ability to recognize and realize their aspirations, satisfy their needs, and adapt to or improve their environment." In 1989, WHO again put forward a new concept of health, namely, "health is not only the absence of disease, but also includes physical health, mental health, good social adjustment and moral health", reflecting the four-dimensional view of physical, mental, social and moral health and emphasizing that, from the point of view of social public morality, everyone has the responsibility to safeguard the health of human beings; not only to be responsible for one's health, but also to take responsibility for the health of the social group. In 2016, the 9th Global Conference on Health Promotion, held in Shanghai, reaffirmed that health is a universal right, a basic resource for daily life, and a social goal and political priority strategy shared by all countries. Thus, health is both a state and a resource, and that the understanding of health by care recipients changes in response to changes in their life circumstances, culture, values and social norms.

ii. Community Health

Community health refers to the overall health status of a specific group of people—community residents—and the comprehensive health environment created for the health of community residents. Community health is not only one of the important goals of community development, but also an important indicator of the comprehensive strength of the community, it is relative and dynamic. There is an interaction between individuals, families and the community as a whole, and changes in the environment in which they live will also directly affect their health behaviors. The family is the basic unit of the community, and the family consists of individuals, whose health directly affects the health of the family. For example, a family's strengths, resources, and latent abilities can

WHO 对健康的定义进行了更新,认为"要实现身体、心理和社会幸福的完好状态,人们需要具备识别和实现愿望、满足需求以及适应或改善环境的能力"。1989 年,WHO 再次提出了新的健康概念,即"健康不仅指没有疾病,还包括躯体健康、心理健康、社会适应良好和道德健康",体现了生理、心理、社会和道德四维健康观,强调从社会公共道德出发,每个人都有责任维护人类健康;不仅要对自己的健康负责,还要为社会群体的健康承担责任。2016 年,在上海召开的第九届全球健康促进大会,再次强调健康作为一项普遍权利,是日常生活的基本资源,是所有国家共享的社会目标和政治优先策略。由此可见,健康既是一种状态,也是一种资源,而护理服务对象对健康的理解会随着其生活环境、文化、价值观和社会规范的变化而变化。

(二)社区健康

社区健康指的是特定群体——社区居民的整体健康状况以及为社区居民健康所营造的综合健康环境。社区健康不仅是社区发展的重要目标之一,也是衡量社区综合实力的重要标志,具有相对性和动态性。社区的个体、家庭与整个社区之间存在相互影响,其所处的环境变化也会直接影响他们的健康行为。家庭是社区的基本单元,而家庭由个体组成,个体健康直接影响家庭健康。例如,一个家庭的优势、资源和潜在能力可以促进家庭健康。保障社区每个家庭健康的基础是一个健康的社区环境。因此,有必要定期评估社区健康,调动社区内部力量和居民积极参与健康相关的决策,及时解决社区健康问题,促进社区的健康发展。健康社区是指拥有健康的物质环境、人文环境和健康居民的社区,包括社区的健康政策、健康管理、健康

contribute to family health. The basis for ensuring the health of every family in a community is a healthy community environment. Therefore, it is necessary to assess community health regularly, to mobilize the internal forces of the community and the active participation of residents in health-related decision-making, and to solve community health problems in a timely manner, so as to promote the healthy development of the community. A healthy community has a healthy physical and human environment and healthy residents, including community health policy, community health management, community healthy environment and community healthy people. To promote community health, it should take the community as the scope, the family as the unit and the residents as the target, improve the health literacy of the residents, encourage all community members to actively participate in disease prevention and health promotion activities, build up a health belief, cultivate a sense of health and create a healthy community environment.

iii. Factors Affecting Health

The main factors affecting health include four major categories: behavioral lifestyle factors, environmental factors, biological factors and health service system factors.

1. Behavioral and Lifestyle Factors

Individuals' unhealthy behaviors and lifestyles can have a negative impact on health, directly or indirectly. Epidemiological studies have shown that human behaviors and lifestyles are closely related to most non-communicable diseases, and that improving behaviors and lifestyles can help control the onset and progression of these diseases. For example, three risk factors of tobacco use, irrational diet and physical inactivity contribute to the development of coronary heart disease, malignant tumor, type 2 diabetes and lung diseases, and approximately 50% of global deaths are associated with these diseases. Effective intervention in these three risk factors can prevent

环境和健康人群。要促进社区健康,应该以社区为范围、家庭为单位、居民为对象,提高居民的健康素养,鼓励全体社区成员积极参与疾病预防和健康促进活动,建立健康信念,培养健康意识,营造健康的社区环境。

（三）健康的影响因素

影响健康的主要因素可分为 4 大类:行为和生活方式因素、环境因素、生物学因素和卫生服务体系因素。

1. 行为和生活方式因素　个体的不良行为和生活方式能够直接或间接地对健康产生负面影响。流行病学研究表明,人类的行为和生活方式与大多数慢性非传染性疾病密切相关,改善行为和生活方式有助于控制这些疾病的发生和发展。例如,吸烟、不合理的饮食和缺乏体力活动这 3 种危险因素会导致冠心病、恶性肿瘤、2 型糖尿病和肺部疾患,而全球约 50% 的死亡病例与这些疾病相关。有效干预这 3 种危险因素可以预防 80% 的心血管疾病、2 型糖尿病和40% 的肿瘤。常见的不良行为和生活方式包括吸烟、不合理饮食、缺乏体力活动、酗酒、药物滥用和网络成瘾等。

80% of cardiovascular diseases, type 2 diabetes and 40% of tumors. Common undesirable behaviors and lifestyles include smoking, irrational diet, lack of physical activity, indulging in excessive drinking, drug abuse and internet addiction.

2. Environmental Factors Environmental factors include the natural environment and social environment.

(1) Natural Environment: The natural environment, including sunlight, air, water, soil, climate, geography, etc., is the material basis for human survival. A polluted environment is bound to cause harm to human health. For example, severe haze pollution can lead to an increase in the incidence of respiratory symptoms (such as coughing, expectoration, gasping, etc.) in the population, impairing the normal development of children's lung function; increasing the incidence of cardiovascular system events such as myocardial ischemia, myocardial infarction, arrhythmia, atherosclerosis, and so on in the population; increasing the rate of cardiovascular disease emergencies, hospitalization rates and mortality rates; causing a decrease in the immune system function of the organism; affecting the development of children's immune system; damaging the reproductive system, reducing fertility, causing fetal malformation, etc. Excessive or insufficient amounts of certain chemical elements in drinking water or soil may cause disorders in human physiology, leading to the occurrence of diseases. For example, iodine deficiency can cause iodine deficiency disease, and high fluorine can lead to fluorosis of bone, etc.

(2) Social Environment: This includes the political system, economic conditions, laws, culture, education, population, ethnicity, occupation, customs and habits, and social development. Because social environmental factors have an influence on health, WHO put forward the concept of "social determinants of health", which refers to the factors that affect health beyond those that directly lead to disease, caused by the basic structure and social

2. 环境因素 包括自然环境与社会环境。

（1）自然环境：包括阳光、空气、水、土壤、气候、地理等，是人类赖以生存的物质基础。污染的环境必然对人体健康造成危害。例如，严重雾霾污染能导致人群呼吸系统症状（如咳嗽、咳痰、喘息等）发生率增加，损害儿童肺功能正常发育；增加人群心肌缺血、心肌梗死、心律失常、动脉粥样硬化等心血管系统事件的发生；增加心血管疾病急诊率、住院率和死亡率；引起机体免疫功能降低；影响儿童免疫系统的发育；损害生殖系统、降低生育能力、引起胎儿畸形等。饮用水或土壤中某些化学元素过量或不足可能引起人体生理功能紊乱，从而导致疾病的发生。如缺碘引起的碘缺乏病、高氟引起的氟骨症等。

（2）社会环境：包括政治制度、经济条件、法律、文化、教育、人口、民族、职业、风俗习惯、社会发展等。正是由于社会环境因素对健康的影响，WHO提出了"健康的社会决定因素"这一概念，即在那些直接导致疾病的因素之外，由人们居住和工作环境中社会分层的基本结构和社会条件不同所产生的影响健康的因素，包括贫穷、社会排斥、居住条件、工作环境及全球化等。许多国家的经验表明，健康的社会决定因

conditions of social stratification in people's living and working environments, including poverty, social exclusion, living conditions, working environments, and globalization. Experience in many countries has shown that the social determinants of health are the "cause of the causes" of disease and are at the root of many health problems.

3. Biological Factors Biological factors include pathogenic microorganisms, genetics, individual biology, growth and development, and aging. Pathogenic microorganisms are the main causative factors of infectious diseases, which can cause different degrees of pathological changes in the body, thus affecting human health. For example, schistosome and bladder cancer, Epstein-Barr virus and lymphoma, hepatitis B virus and liver cancer, HPV and cervical cancer, Helicobacter pylori and stomach cancer. Genetic factors primarily influence an individual's predisposition to develop certain diseases and often influence the development of many non-communicable diseases. Biological characteristics include age, gender, and health status, etc.

4. Health Service System Health service is a process of activities in which health institutions and health professionals utilize health resources and various means to provide necessary services to individuals, groups and society in a planned and purposeful manner, and it is an important guarantee to prevent and treat diseases and to maintain and promote health. Its content includes measures such as health education for the population, prophylactic immunization, maternal and child health care, regular medical check-ups and the provision of basic therapeutic drugs to the public. Effective, accessible and affordable health services can protect and promote public health. Community health service organizations are the important sectors that provide health care services. The level of health services directly affects the health level of the population.

素是导致疾病"病因的病因",是许多健康问题的根源。

3．生物学因素 生物学因素包括病原微生物、遗传、个体生物学特征、生长发育、衰老等。病原微生物是传染病的主要致病因素,可引起机体不同程度的病理变化,从而影响人体的健康。如血吸虫与膀胱癌、EB病毒与淋巴瘤、乙肝病毒与肝癌、HPV与宫颈癌、幽门螺杆菌与胃癌等。遗传因素主要影响个体在某些疾病上的发病倾向,常影响许多慢性非传染性疾病的发生。生物学特征包括年龄、性别、健康状态等。

4．卫生服务体系 卫生服务是卫生机构和卫生专业人员运用卫生资源和各种手段,有计划、有目的地向个人、群体和社会提供必要服务的活动过程,是防治疾病、维护和促进健康的重要保障。其内容包括对人群进行健康教育,开展预防接种、妇幼保健、定期体检,向公众提供基本的治疗药物等措施。有效、可及、可负担的卫生服务能够保护和促进公众健康。社区卫生服务机构是提供卫生保健服务的重要部门。卫生保健服务水平的高低直接影响人群的健康水平。

Section 2　Community Nursing

Ⅰ. Concept and Characteristics of Community Nursing

ⅰ. The Concept of Community Nursing

According to the American Nurses Association (ANA), "Community nursing is a comprehensive discipline that combines the theories of nursing and public health to promote and maintain the health of community populations". According to the characteristics of the current development of community health services in China, community nursing is defined as "the comprehensive application of the theories and techniques of nursing and public health, community-based, population-oriented, service-centered, integrating medical treatment, prevention, health care, rehabilitation, health education, family planning, etc. into nursing, and with the ultimate purpose of promoting and maintaining the health of the population, providing continuous, dynamic, and comprehensive nursing services". Community nursing emphasizes a health-centered approach that focuses not only on individual health, but also on the health of the community population as a whole, and is committed to providing a wide range of continuous nursing activities so as to maintain and promote community health, prevent diseases, reduce disability, and ultimately achieve the goal of improving the quality of life and health of the community population.

Community nursing consists of basic public health services and basic medical care. In the nursing service of basic public health services, community nurses identify the health conditions of individuals, families and groups in the community that need to be improved through community diagnosis, and carry out health maintenance and health promotion. In the nursing service focusing on basic medical care, the main focus is to

第二节　社区护理

一、社区护理的概念及特点

（一）社区护理的概念

美国护士协会（American Nurses Association，ANA）指出："社区护理学是一门将护理学与公共卫生学理论相结合，用以促进和维护社区人群健康的综合学科"。根据我国当前社区卫生服务发展的特点，社区护理被定义为"综合应用护理学和公共卫生学的理论与技术，以社区为基础、以人群为对象、以服务为中心，将医疗、预防、保健、康复、健康教育、计划生育等融入护理学中，并以促进和维护人群健康为最终目的，提供连续性、动态性和综合性的护理服务"。社区护理强调以健康为中心，不仅关注个人健康，还重视社区整体人群的健康，致力于提供广泛而持续的护理活动，从而维持和促进社区健康、预防疾病、减少残障，最终实现提高社区人群生活质量和健康水平的目标。

社区护理包括以基本公共卫生服务为主和以基本医疗为主的两方面护理服务。在以基本公共卫生服务为主的护理服务中，社区护士通过社区诊断，识别社区内个人、家庭及群体需要改善的健康状况，并开展健康维护和健康促进。而在以基本医疗为主的护理服务中，主要提供围绕个人及整个家庭生命周期的"疾病护理"，实施社区急性和慢性健康问题的管理，以及以家庭为中心的疾病照护。在实际护理服务中，

provide "disease care" throughout the life cycle of individual and the whole family, to implement the management of acute and chronic health problems in the community, as well as family-centered disease care. In actual care services, the two are not entirely separate, but the focus of the services is different.

ⅱ. The Characteristics of Community Nursing

1. The scope of service targets is broad, involving individuals, families, groups and people with different health conditions, different age stages and different social strata. It emphasizes the community population as the service object and focuses on health management on a population basis.

2. Taking health promotion and disease prevention as the main objectives, it is committed to promoting individuals, families, groups and communities to achieve optimal health, reduce complications and disabilities, prolong life and improve the quality of life.

3. The services are comprehensive, covering health care for healthy people, disease prevention for high-risk populations and health management for patient groups. Centering on health and targeting various factors affecting health, the service provides comprehensive services for individuals, families and community groups, such as preventive health care, disease treatment, rehabilitation care, health management and community support.

4. The service is long-term and continuous, from the prenatal stage to the end of life, spanning the whole life cycle and the whole process of disease development, and it is necessary to establish a long-term and continuous service relationship with the service users.

5. Close collaboration across multiple departments and stakeholders is required, not only with health care personnel, but also with the community's various functional management

这两者并不能完全分开，只是服务的重点有所不同。

（二）社区护理的特点

1. 服务对象范围广泛，涉及个人、家庭、群体及不同健康状况、不同年龄阶段和不同社会阶层的人群。强调以社区人群为服务对象，注重以人群为单位进行健康管理。

2. 以健康促进与疾病预防为主要目标，致力于促进个体、家庭、群体和社区达到最佳健康水平，减少并发症和残障，延长寿命并提高生活质量。

3. 服务内容具有综合性，涵盖健康人群保健、高危人群疾病预防及患者群体健康管理等多个方面。以健康为中心，针对影响健康的各种因素，提供个人、家庭和社区群体的预防保健、疾病治疗、康复护理、健康管理和社区支持等综合性服务。

4. 服务具有长期性和连续性，从出生前至死亡，跨越整个生命周期及疾病发生发展的全过程，需要与服务对象建立长期且连续的服务关系。

5. 需要多部门、多主体密切合作，不仅包括卫生保健人员，还需社区各职能管理部门、社区居民或社团广泛参与及合作。

departments and community residents or associations for extensive participation and cooperation.

II. Functions and Roles of Community Nursing

i. Promoting Community, Family and Population Health

Community nursing identifies existing health problems through community assessment, assists relevant departments in community health promotion, eliminates factors that threaten the health of the community and residents, such as sources of infectious diseases, water pollution, accidents, air pollution and domestic waste disposal, etc., and ensures a safe community environment. Community nursing assesses the various health problems of families and provide personalized care, guidance, assistance and support, etc. It plays a key role in promoting the health of community residents by providing the required care services, referrals and guidance on the utilization of social resources for various groups of people according to their different ages, genders, health conditions, types of diseases, and so on.

ii. Provide Comprehensive Nursing Services to Community Residents

Unlike clinical nursing, community nursing integrates medical treatment, prevention, health care, rehabilitation, health education and family planning to provide comprehensive nursing services to community residents. In community nursing, community nurses provide a full range of nursing services to help community residents identify health problems and related influencing factors at an early stage, as well as to prevent and intervene in them. Community nurses can also integrate existing resources to provide health guidance to community residents, enhance their health literacy and further promote the healthy development of community residents.

二、社区护理的功能与作用

（一）促进社区、家庭和人群健康

社区护理通过社区评估发现存在的健康问题，协助相关部门开展社区健康促进工作，消除威胁社区和居民健康的因素，如传染病疫源、水源污染、意外事件、空气污染及生活垃圾处理不当等，确保社区环境安全。评估家庭的各种健康问题，提供个性化护理、指导、帮助及支持等。根据社区居民不同的年龄、性别、健康状况、疾病类型等，为各类人群提供所需的护理服务、转诊及社会资源利用指导，从而在促进社区居民健康方面发挥关键作用。

（二）为社区居民提供综合护理服务

与临床护理不同，社区护理将医疗、预防、保健、康复、健康教育、计划生育等融合在一起，向社区居民提供综合护理服务。在进行社区护理时，社区护士提供全方位护理服务，帮助社区居民尽早发现健康问题及相关影响因素，并加以预防和干预。社区护士还可以整合现有资源，向社区居民提供健康指导，增强他们的健康素养，进一步促进社区居民的健康发展。

III. History, Trends and Significance of Community Nursing Development

i. Brief History of Community Nursing Development

Community nursing originated in western countries, and its development process has been divided into four main stages, namely, the family nursing stage, the district nursing stage, the public health nursing stage, and the community health nursing stage, as shown in Table 1-1.

三、社区护理发展的历史、趋势与意义

(一)社区护理发展简史

社区护理起源于西方国家,其发展过程主要划分为四个阶段,即家庭护理阶段、地段护理阶段、公共卫生护理阶段和社区卫生护理阶段,见表1-1。

Table 1–1　Stages of Development of Community Nursing

Developmental stages	Periods	People engaged	Service objects	Service contents
Family nursing stage	Before the mid-19th century	Housewives	Patients	Simple, basic home living care
District nursing stage	1859–1900	Trained volunteers	Homebound indigent patients and their families	Disease care and health guidance for family members
Public health nursing stage	1900–1970	Mostly public health nurses, few volunteers	Needy community residents	Medical care and public health nursing services such as disease prevention, maternal and child health care and health education
Community health nursing stage	1970–present	Community nurses	Community	Medical care and public health nursing services

表1-1　社区护理的发展阶段

发展阶段	时期	从事人员	服务对象	服务内容
家庭护理阶段	19世纪中期以前	家庭主妇	患者	简单、基本的家庭生活照顾
地段护理阶段	1859—1900	经过培训的志愿者	居家贫困患者及家属	疾病护理及家属健康指导
公共卫生护理阶段	1900—1970	多数为公共卫生护士,少数为志愿者	有需求的社区居民	医疗护理及预防疾病、妇幼保健和健康宣教等公共卫生护理服务
社区卫生护理阶段	1970年至今	社区护士	社区	医疗护理和公共卫生护理服务

1. **Family Nursing Stage (Before the mid-19th Century)**　Due to the lack of health service resources, limitations in medical level and gaps in the nursing profession, most patients recuperated at home under the care of housewives.

1. **家庭护理阶段(19世纪中期以前)**　由于卫生服务资源匮乏、医疗水平有限及护理专业的空白,大多数患者在家中休养,由家庭主妇进行看护。由于缺乏系统的看护训练,这些看护者只能为患者提供一些简单、基本的家庭生

Due to the lack of systematic nursing training, they were only able to give the patients some simple and basic care in daily life. This laid the foundation for the birth of community nursing.

2. District Nursing Stage (1859–1900) In 1859, William Jospen, a British entrepreneur, set up a nursing school in Liverpool to train healthcare nurses to take care of homebound patients in various lots. District nursing focused on the care of the diseases of indigent patients at home and instructed the families of the patients on how to care for the patients. Most of the nurses engaged in district nursing were trained volunteers. In 1885, the district Visiting Society was established in New York, USA, which was later named "Visiting Nurses Association".

3. Public Health Nursing Stage (1900–1970) At the beginning of the 20th century, the service object of district nursing was no longer limited to poor patients, but expanded to all community residents in need. Services were also expanded from purely medical care to public health care areas such as disease prevention, maternal and child health care, and health education. The service targets expanded from individuals and families to the whole society, and district nursing has evolved into public health nursing. Among those engaged in public health nursing, most are public health nurses and a few are volunteers. At present, public health nursing is still an important element of community nursing.

4. Community Health Nursing Stage (1970–present) After the 1970s, nurses in various countries began to take the community as the scope, with health promotion and disease prevention as the goal, to provide medical care and public health nursing services, which are called community nursing, and those who are engaged in community nursing are called community nurses. In 1978, WHO required community nursing to be an "accessible, acceptable and affordable" health service for community residents. Since then, community nursing has developed rapidly around

活照顾。这为社区护理的诞生奠定了基础。

2. 地段护理阶段（1859—1900） 1859年，英国企业家威廉·若斯蓬（William Jospen）在利物浦成立了护理学校，培训保健护士（healthcare nurse），为各地段居家患者提供照护。地段护理侧重于对居家贫困患者的疾病护理，并指导患者家属如何护理患者。从事地段护理的护士大多数是经过培训的志愿者。1885年，美国纽约成立了地段访视社，后来命名为"访视护士协会"。

3. 公共卫生护理阶段（1900—1970） 20世纪初，地段护理的服务对象不再局限于贫困患者，扩大到所有有需求的社区居民。服务内容也从单纯的医疗护理扩展至预防疾病、妇幼保健和健康教育等公共卫生护理领域。服务对象从个人、家庭扩展到整个社会，地段护理演变为公共卫生护理。在从事公共卫生护理的人员中，大多数为公共卫生护士，少数为志愿者。目前，公共卫生护理仍然是社区护理的重要内容。

4. 社区卫生护理阶段（1970年至今） 20世纪70年代以后，各国护士开始以社区为范围，以健康促进、疾病防治为目标，提供医疗护理和公共卫生护理服务，称为社区护理，从事社区护理的人员称为社区护士。1978年，WHO要求社区护理成为社区居民"可接近的、可接受的、可负担得起的"卫生服务。从此，社区护理在全球迅速发展，社区护士队伍也逐步壮大。

the world, and the community nurse workforce has grown gradually.

ⅱ．Development Trend of Community Nursing

In recent years, China has deepened the reform of the medical and health system, and implemented the core concept of providing the basic medical and health system as a public product to all people. This has brought good opportunities for the development and reform of community health services and community nursing. The construction of China's community nursing talent team has been further strengthened, effectively enhancing the capacity of community nursing services and making community nursing gradually become an independent discipline in China. Although community nursing has been continuously promoted, it also faces new challenges. China's community nursing organization and management system is not yet sound, the existing supply capacity of community nursing services is insufficient, and the scope of work of community nursing services is not clear. In addition, the lack of innovation in the content and methods of nursing services to respond to social needs, the lack of high-quality community nursing personnel and other issues still constrain the development of community nursing in China, and how to incentivize community nurses also needs attention.

1. Improve the Community Nursing Quality Management System　Strengthen the leading role of the government and establish a legal system for community health services and community nursing, so that relevant policies, regulations and management standards are gradually formed and improved. Strengthen the standardized training system and personnel access system for in-service community nurses, and establish and improve the community nursing quality management and performance appraisal system, so as to ensure the efficiency, quality and rationality of resources of community

（二）社区护理发展趋势

近年来，国家深化医药卫生体制改革，秉持将基本医疗卫生制度作为公共产品向全民提供的核心理念，为社区卫生服务和社区护理的发展与改革带来了良好的机遇。我国社区护理人才队伍建设得到进一步加强，有效提升了社区护理服务能力，我国社区护理逐渐发展成为一门独立的学科。尽管社区护理得到了持续推进，但也面临新的挑战。我国的社区护理组织管理系统尚不健全，现有社区护理服务供给能力不足，社区护理服务的工作范围不明确。此外，缺乏应对社会需求的护理服务内容和方法的创新，高素质社区护理人才匮乏等问题仍然制约着我国社区护理的发展，如何激励社区护士也需要关注。

1. 完善社区护理质量管理体系　加强政府主导作用，建立社区卫生服务与社区护理法律体系，使相关政策、法规及管理标准逐步形成和完善。强化在岗社区护士的规范化培训制度和人员准入制度建设与执行，建立健全社区护理质量管理及绩效考评制度，以确保社区护理服务的高效性、优质性和资源合理性，有效约束和激励社区护理服务的发展。

nursing services, and to effectively constrain and incentivize the development of community nursing services.

2. Enrich the Mode and Content of Community Nursing Services
With the continuous expansion of the functions of community health services and the sustained increase in social demand for community health services, various studies should be conducted and diversified models of community nursing services and service functions will be developed in accordance with market demand. For example, community nursing and home care services, care for the disabled elderly, rehabilitation and health care for the disabled, psychiatric care, hospice care and other nursing services for special populations will be developed and included in the management of the community health service system.

3. Develop Community Nursing Disciplines and Build High-quality Community Nursing Teams
Colleges and universities will strengthen the education and discipline construction of community nursing, focusing on the training of community nurses at different levels that can meet the needs of the society in terms of specialization, especially strengthening the graduate education in the direction of community nursing. It is also necessary to strengthen post-graduation education, on-the-job-training and continuing education, and continuously improve the sense of professional identity of in-service community nurses and their motivation to work in community nursing services, so as to meet society's demand for community nursing manpower.

4. Enhance Interdisciplinary Penetration of Community Nursing
With the aggravation of China's population aging problem, the social demand for elderly care and chronic disease management is also on the rise. The family structure in traditional communities is also changing to smaller families, the number of elderly living alone is increasing, and the demand for nursing management of patients with chronic

2. 丰富社区护理服务模式和内容 随着社区卫生服务功能的不断拓展以及社会对社区卫生服务需求的持续增加,需根据市场需求开展各项研究并开发多元化的社区护理服务模式和服务功能。例如,开发社区养老和居家养老服务、失能老年人照料、残疾康复保健、精神护理、临终关怀等针对特殊人群的护理服务,并将其纳入社区卫生服务体系管理范围。

3. 发展社区护理学科,建设高素质社区护理队伍 各院校将加强社区护理学教育和学科建设,在专业设置上注重培养符合社会需求的不同层次社区护士,特别是加强社区护理方向的研究生教育。需继续强化毕业后教育、岗位培训与继续教育,不断提高在岗社区护士的职业认同感和社区护理服务工作的积极性,以满足社会对社区护理人力的需求。

4. 增强社区护理的跨学科渗透 随着我国人口老龄化问题的加重,社会养老需求、慢性病管理需求也呈上升趋势。传统社区内家庭结构也在不断向小型化家庭转变,独居老人不断增多,慢性病患者的护理管理需求也在不断上升。社区家庭养老以及慢性病患者管理需要护理、医疗、公共卫生、康复、生物医学工程、社会福祉等多学科的相互渗透与合作。在跨学科团队和大医学背景下,利用大数据、人工智能相关研

diseases is also rising. Community-based family care and management of patients with chronic diseases require interdisciplinary interpenetration and collaboration among nursing, medical treatment, public health, rehabilitation, biomedical engineering, and social well-being. In the context of interdisciplinary teams and advanced medicine, the research related to big data and artificial intelligence is utilized to promote and regulate the development of "Internet+Nursing Service". The emerging information dissemination and interaction methods are utilized to realize nurse-patient communication and timely feedback. This promotes the self-management of the community elders and the patients with chronic diseases, and to further realize the penetration and integration of interdisciplinary development of community nursing on a large scale, such as smart elderly care and internet remote management.

With the development of "Internet+Nursing Service", the organization and management of community nursing and quality management standards are gradually improved, and the information of community nursing management is networked through computers in order to provide timely, accurate and complete information for community services, and facilitate the timely transmission, exchange, analysis and evaluation of community health information to achieve resource sharing and rational application.

5. Realize the Form of Integrated Hospital-Community-Family Nursing Services
Professional care institutions in China have fewer links with the lower level of community health centers, making it more difficult to provide professional guidance. Most of the elderly with chronic diseases are mainly cared of at home, and the caregivers are mostly family members and carers, and there are problems such as lack of social support and guidance on care technology. To construct "Internet+" based hospital-community-family integrated extended

究,促进和规范"互联网＋护理服务"的发展。利用新兴的信息传播与互动方式实现护患沟通与及时反馈,促进社区老人、慢性病患者等的自我管理,进一步大规模实现社区护理跨学科发展渗透融合,例如智慧养老、互联网远程管理等。

随着"互联网＋护理服务"的发展,社区护理的组织管理、质量管理标准逐步完善,社区护理管理的资料通过计算机联网,以便为社区服务提供及时、准确、完整的信息,并有利于社区健康资料的及时传递、交流、分析及评价,以达到资源共享和合理应用。

5. 实现医院 - 社区 - 家庭一体化护理服务形式 我国专业照护机构与下一级社区卫生服务中心连接较少,较难提供专业性指导。多数老年慢性病患者以居家照护为主,照护员多为家属和护理员,存在社会支持及照护技术指导缺乏等问题。构建基于"互联网＋"的医院 - 社区 - 家庭一体化延续护理管理模式,以护理为主导,逐步将医院、社区、家庭联系在一起,有助于扩大护理资源,实现开放延伸、连续全程的护理服务形式,是一种上下联动、协同管理的健康管理模式。该护理服务形式有助于综合评估患者病情层级和疾病状态,并根据患者病情变化进

care management model, which advocates nursing-led approach, gradually links hospitals, communities, and families linked together, will help to expand nursing resources, realize open, extended, continuous and comprehensive forms of nursing services, and serve as a health management model with up and down linkage and collaborative management. This form of nursing service helps to comprehensively assess the patient's condition level and disease status, and carry out hierarchical medical care interventions according to changes in the patient's condition. And community doctors make referral decisions according to changes in the patient's care level, which is conducive to control medical costs.

ⅲ. Significance of Community Nursing Development

1. **Adapt to Changes in Social Demographic Structure** At this stage, China's demographic development trend has transformed from a balanced population development to an unbalanced population aging trend, with the elderly population accounting for an increasing proportion of society. It is expected that China's elderly population will reach 300 million by 2026 and exceed 400 million by 2037. Due to their physiological, psychological, social, cultural and health characteristics, the elderly are in greater need of convenient, economical, timely and high-quality care services. At the same time, changes in family structure brought about by demographic changes have weakened the function of household caregiving capatity, increased the burden on families, and put a heavy burden on social development. The development of community nursing can not only reduce the economic burden and care pressure on the family and society, but also establish and improve the social security system and old-age protection system, and promote the benign and healthy development of society.

2. **Adapt to the Increase in Demand for Chronic Disease Care** With the improvement of

行分层次医疗护理干预。社区医生根据患者护理层级变动情况制订转诊方案，有利于控制医疗成本。

（三）社区护理发展意义

1. **适应社会人口结构的变化** 当前，我国人口发展趋势已经从人口均衡化发展转向人口老龄化趋势的不均衡发展，老年人口在社会中所占比例越来越高。预计到 2026 年，我国老龄人口将达到 3 亿，2037 年将超过 4 亿。由于老年人在生理、心理、社会、文化和卫生等方面的特殊性，他们更需要方便、经济、及时且高质量的护理服务。人口结构变化带来的家庭结构变化使家庭养老功能弱化，家庭负担加重，给社会发展带来沉重的负担。发展社区护理事业不仅可以减轻家庭与社会的经济负担和照顾压力，还能建立健全社会保障体系和养老保障体系，促进社会良性健康发展。

2. **适应慢性病护理需求的增加** 随着人们生活水平的提高和疾病谱的变化，心脑血管疾

people's living standards and changes in the disease spectrum, the incidence of chronic diseases such as cardiovascular and cerebrovascular diseases, diabetes, and tumors are rising. The treatment and rehabilitation of chronic diseases is a long process, and most chronic disease patients need to maintain treatment and care in the community and at home. The large number of health needs brought by chronic diseases can hardly be accomplished by clinical nuring in hospitals alone. Community nursing provides convenient, fast, continuous, economical and comprehensive nursing services for patients with chronic diseases and their families, thus improving the patients' self-management ability and family care ability, which is of great significance to improve the quality of life of patients with chronic diseases.

3. Promote the Rational Use of Health Resources
With the improvement of social living standards, people's demand for knowledge of disease prevention and self-care is increasing while they pay attention to their physical health. Through preventive health care and health education, community nursing helps people enhance their health awareness, acquire health-related knowledge and improve their lifestyles so as to prevent diseases, promote health and improve the health level of the whole society. At the same time, community nursing can provide continuous care services and home health guidance for discharged patients, improve the turnover rate of hospital beds, reduce the number of follow-up visits for people with chronic diseases, and solve the problems of shortage of medical resources and excessive medical expenses. Using its unique functions, community nursing can well meet the service needs of community residents, promote the rational use of health resources, and gradually improve the situation of shortage of medical and health resources.

病、糖尿病、肿瘤等慢性病的发病率不断上升。慢性病的治疗和康复是一个漫长的过程，大部分慢性病患者需要在社区和家庭进行维持治疗和护理。慢性病带来的大量健康需求仅靠医院临床护理难以完成。社区护理为慢性病患者及其家庭提供方便、快捷、连续、经济、全面的护理服务，从而提高患者的自我管理能力和家庭照顾能力，对改善慢性病患者的生活质量具有重要意义。

3. 促进卫生资源的合理利用　随着社会生活水平的提高，人们在关注身体健康的同时，对疾病预防和自我保健知识的需求也在增加。社区护理通过预防保健、健康教育等途径，帮助人们增强健康意识，掌握健康相关知识，改善生活方式，从而预防疾病、促进健康，提高整个社会的健康水平。同时，社区护理能够为出院患者提供延续性护理服务和居家健康指导，提高医院床位周转率，降低慢性病患者复诊数量，缓解医疗资源紧缺、医疗费用支出过高等状况。社区护理运用其特有的功能，能够很好地满足社区居民的服务需求，促进卫生资源的合理利用，逐步改善医疗卫生资源紧缺的状况。

IV. Policies and Ethical Norms Related to Community Nursing

i. Policies Related to Community Nursing

In the more than two decades since the *Decision of the Communist Party of China Central Committee and the State Council on Health Reform and Development* in 1997, the Chinese government has issued a series of policy documents related to community health services and community nursing (Table 1-2). These policy documents have gradually standardized the community health service system, clarified service objectives and work content, and promoted the healthy development of community health services and community nursing.

四、社区护理相关政策法规和伦理规范

（一）社区护理相关政策

自 1997 年《中共中央、国务院关于卫生改革与发展的决定》发布以来的二十多年间，我国政府陆续出台了一系列与社区卫生服务及社区护理相关的政策文件（表 1-2）。这些政策文件逐步规范了社区卫生服务体系，明确了服务目标和工作内容，促进了社区卫生服务和社区护理的健康发展。

Table 1-2　Related Policies and Main Content of Community Health Services and Community Nursing

Year	Name of policy	Main content
1997	*Decision of the Communist Party of China Central Committee and the State Council on Health Reform and Development*	It proposed to reform the urban health service system, actively develop community health services, and gradually form a health service network with reasonable functions and convenient for the public
1999	*Several Opinions on the Development of Urban Community Health Services*	It standardized the definition of community health services and put forward the overall goal of developing community health services
2006	*Guiding Opinions of the State Council on the Development of Urban Community Health Services*	It improved the guiding ideology, basic principles and working objectives for the development of community health services, It emphasized strengthening the community health service workforce, improving operational mechanisms, increasing financial investment, and ensuring the effective implementation of policies through interdepartmental cooperation
2009	*National Standard for Basic Public Health Services (2009 Edition)*	It clearly put forward ten categories of standardized services: management of health records for urban and rural residents, health education, health management for children aged 0–36 months, maternal health management, elderly health management, immunization, reporting and handling of infectious diseases, health management for patients with hypertension, health management for patients with type 2 diabetes, and management of patients with severe mental disorders. Each standard specifies the target population, service content, procedures, requirements, evaluation indicators, and service record forms for the corresponding public health service items
2011	*National Standard for Basic Public Health Services (2011 Edition)*	It added health supervision and management standards, put forward 11 categories of standard services

Continued Table

Year	Name of policy	Main content
2011	*Measures for Performance Evaluation of Community Health Service Organizations (Trial Edition)*	It proposed assessment contents in five areas, namely, institutional management, public health services, basic medical services, traditional Chinese medicine services and satisfaction, and clarified the assessment index system consisting of three levels of indicators
2015	*Guiding Opinions on Promoting the Construction of a Graded Diagnosis and Treatment System*	It proposed that by 2020, a hierarchical diagnosis and treatment model of primary diagnosis, two-way referral, triage and treatment of acute and chronic diseases, and up and down linkage would be gradually formed, and a hierarchical diagnosis and treatment system in line with national conditions would be basically established. Two major work initiatives had been clarified: One was to improve the hierarchical diagnosis and treatment service system focusing on the grassroots level, and the other was to establish and improve the guarantee mechanism for hierarchical diagnosis and treatment
2015	*Guiding Opinions on Further Standardizing the Management of Community Health Services and Enhancing Service Quality*	It put forward 17 specific measures in 4 areas, including standardizing the establishment and management of community health service organizations, strengthening the capacity building of community health services, transforming the service model, and strengthening the guarantee and supervision and management of community health services
2016	*Outline of the Thirteenth Five-Year Plan for National Economic and Social Development of the People's Republic of China*	It put forward specific requirements for the construction of a healthy China in 8 areas, including comprehensively deepening the reform of the medical and healthcare system, improving the medical security system for the whole population, strengthening the prevention and treatment of major diseases and basic public healthcare services, strengthening maternal and child health care and maternity services, perfecting the medical service system, promoting the inheritance and development of traditional Chinese medicine, widely carrying out a national fitness campaign, and guaranteeing food safety
2016	*Guiding Opinions on Promoting Family Doctor Contracting Services*	It proposed to accelerate the promotion of contracted family doctor services, clarify the main body of contracted services, optimize the connotation of contracted services, improve the payment mechanism for contracted services, establish an incentive mechanism for contracted services, strengthen the performance evaluation of contracted services, strengthen the technical support for contracted services, improve the level and coverage of contracted services, promote primary diagnosis at the grassroots level and hierarchical diagnosis and treatment, and provide comprehensive, continuous and coordinated basic medical and healthcare services for the public, enhancing the people's sense of gain

Continued Table

Year	Name of policy	Main content
2017	*Guiding Opinions of the General Office of the State Council on Promoting the Construction and Development of Medical Consortia*	It proposed that according to the actual situation of the construction of the hierarchical diagnosis and treatment system in the region, various forms of medical association organization modes should be gradually formed based on local conditions and classified guidance. It required to improve the mechanism of division of labor and collaboration within the medical association. It required to establish organizational management and collaboration systems, implementing the functional positioning of medical institutions, providing demand-oriented family doctor contracting services and improve the two-way referral mechanism within the medical consortia
2017	*National Standard for Basic Public Health Services (Third Edition)*	It revised the *National Standard for Basic Public Health Services (2011 Edition)*, amended and improved the relevant contents and streamlined some of the work indicators
2018	*Guiding Opinions on Regulating the Management of Family Doctor Contracting Services*	It proposed to regulate the main providers of contracted family doctor services, clarify the contracted service targets and agreements, enrich the content of contracted services, implement the contracted service fees, optimize the technical support of contracted services, improve the two-way referral mechanism, promote the "Internet +" contracted family doctor services, strengthen the management and assessment of contracted services, and enhance the publicity and training of contracted services
2019	*Circular of the General Office of the National Health Commission on the Pilot Work of "Internet + Nursing Services"*	It proposed to standardize "Internet + Nursing Services", ensure medical quality and safety, support the implementation of the Healthy China Initiative. Beijing, Tianjin, Shanghai, Jiangsu Province, Zhejiang Province, and Guangdong Province were designated as pilot regions for "Internet + Nursing Services", focusing on exploring management systems, service models, service standards, risk prevention, and payment policies related to "Internet + Nursing Services," with the aim of pioneering and testing innovative approaches actively, summarizing and popularizing beneficial experiences
2020	*Circular on Comprehensively Promoting the Construction of Community Hospitals*	It proposed to comprehensively carry out the construction of community hospitals, and clarified the general requirements, construction principles, main construction tasks, work steps and work requirements for the construction of community hospitals
2020	*Circular of the General Office of the National Health Commission on Further Promoting the Pilot Work of "Internet + Nursing Services"*	It proposed to further expand the scope of pilot projects, and required localities to actively carry out pilot projects of "Internet + Nursing Services" in the light of the actual situation, boldly practice and innovated in the service model, management standardization, information support, risk prevention, behavioral supervision and price payment, etc., so as to form demonstration experiences and typical practices, and then take the lead to promote them step by step

Year	Name of policy	Main content
2021	*Circular on Accelerating the Construction of Community Hospitals*	It emphasized the importance of community services in improving people's livelihoods. It called for strengthening the community's functions of serving, benefiting, and ensuring the safety of citizens, while implementing the people-centered development concept and promoting grassroots governance modernization. It highlighted the need to strengthen the Party's leadership in community services, improve the participation of multiple stakeholders, and encourage collaboration between the government, market, and society to enhance service quality and efficiency. It stressed the development of key services such as community employment, elderly care, and child care, with a focus on supporting vulnerable groups and promoting the balanced allocation of community service resources between urban and rural areas. Its goal was going to further improve the community service system by 2025, enhance service supply capacity, and increase residents' sense of access, happiness, and security. Its plan also emphasized the innovation of service mechanisms, the acceleration of digital construction, and the optimization of service facility layouts to promote the high-quality development of smart communities and service systems
2021	*The 14th Five-Year Plan for the Construction of Urban and Rural Community Services Systems*	It proposed that the promotion of urban and rural community medical and health service systems would require increased efforts in five areas. These were: to promote the establishment and standardized management of primary fever clinics; to promote the construction of urban healthcare consortia and rural county healthcare communities; to strengthen the construction of human resources with talents as the core; to enrich the connotation of contracted services for family doctors, to promote integrated healthcare services, and to promote the standardization of electronic health records; and to improve the grass-roots governance system of healthcare and promote the formation of a synergy of the whole society in support of the development of grass-roots healthcare
2022	*National Nursing Development Plan (2021–2025)*	It proposed to give full play to the leading role of high-quality nursing resources of large hospitals, form urban medical consortia, county-level healthcare partnerships, and specialty alliances, improve the nursing service system with clear positioning, division of labor and cooperation between different medical institutions. It encouraged the restructuring of some primary and secondary hospitals into nursing homes or centers to increase the supply of nursing services. The document also called to innovate the nursing service model, expand the scope of "Internet + Nursing Services" pilots, support healthcare institutions in providing "Internet + Nursing Services", extended care, and home care. These services aimed to expand facility nursing care to community care and home care, offer convenient and professional medical care for discharged patients, terminally ill patients, and individuals who are immobile, elderly, frail, disabled, or cognitively impaired. Additionally, the plan supported the establishment of nursing specialty alliances and expert joint teams between secondary or higher-level medical institutions and grassroots medical institutions to enhance grassroots nursing capacity through management, training, and technical assistance

Continued Table

Year	Name of policy	Main content
2023	*Opinions on Further Improving the Healthcare Service System*	It proposed to develop healthcare workforce, increase support and training for grass-root specialties, as well as those in remote areas and in short supply, reduce the disparities in personnel distribution between urban and rural areas, regions, and specialties. It also stressed the need for standardized construction of township hospitals and community health centers, with an emphasis on enhancing their capacity for diagnosing common diseases, providing public health services, managing health, and delivering traditional Chinese medicine services. It emphasized improving the screening and prevention of infectious diseases, enhancing the management of severe chronic diseases, and providing psychological health guidance to residents. Meanwhile enhancing the capability of township health centers to perform routine surgeries classified as Grade Ⅱ or below. Besides, it proposed to improve the family doctor system, with primary medical and health institutions as the main platform, establish a family doctor contract service model with general practitioners as the main body, effective linkage of general practice and specialty, and organic integration of medical treatment and prevention, so as to provide comprehensive and continuous public health, basic medical treatment and health management services
2023	*Action Plan for Further Improving Nursing Services (2023–2025)*	It emphasized strengthening clinical nursing, implementing responsibility-based holistic nursing, improving basic nursing services, and focusing on humanistic care and communication. It aimed to enhance nursing quality, strengthen ward rounds and observations, ensure nursing safety, promote the development of traditional Chinese medicine nursing and nursing technologies. Its plan also aimed to expand the scope of nursing services by implementing continuity of care, expanding the coverage of "Internet + Nursing Services," and improving the supply of community and elderly care services. It further proposed increased support by strengthening nurse staffing, optimizing technological support, and enhancing incentive mechanisms to ensure the quality of nursing services and adequate professional compensation for nurses. It also emphasized the need for health administrative departments at all levels and medical institutions to strengthen organizational leadership, regularly assess implementation results, and continuously improve nursing services to enhance patient's sense of gain and well-being

Continued Table

Year	Name of policy	Main content
2023	*Home and Community-based Integrated Medical and Elderly Care Services Guidelines* (*Trial Edition*)	It proposed that home and community-based integrated medical and elderly care services should prioritize disabled elderly individuals (including those with dementia), with chronic diseases, old age, those in need of rehabilitation, or those in rehabilitation or end of life, and those who require medical services after hospital discharge. The scope of services included health education, health management services, medical rounds, family bed services, home medical services, traditional Chinese medicine services, psychological and mental support, and referral services
2023	*"Quality Service to the Grassroots" Initiative and the Three-Year Action Plan for Community Hospital Construction*	It proposed to standardize capacity-building efforts and community hospital construction. It focused on supporting the construction of a number of central health centers, enhancing the service capacity of village clinics, and strengthening the training and allocation of grassroots health personnel. It also aimed to improve grassroots traditional Chinese medicine services, address gaps in medical emergency response, infection disease management, and pediatrics, to expedite the construction of informatization at the grassroots level, improve patients' medical experience, strengthen the construction of work atmosphere, and ensure the bottom line of safety

表 1-2　社区卫生服务及社区护理相关政策及主要内容

年度	政策名称	主要内容
1997 年	《中共中央、国务院关于卫生改革与发展的决定》	提出改革城市卫生服务体系，积极发展社区卫生服务，逐步形成功能合理、方便群众的卫生服务网络
1999 年	《关于发展城市社区卫生服务的若干意见》	规范了社区卫生服务的定义，提出发展社区卫生服务的总体目标
2006 年	《国务院关于发展城市社区卫生服务的指导意见》	完善了发展社区卫生服务的指导思想、基本原则和工作目标，强调了加强社区卫生服务队伍建设、完善运行机制、加大经费投入以及通过跨部门合作确保各项政策的有效实施
2009 年	《国家基本公共卫生服务规范（2009 年版）》	提出了以下 10 类服务规范：城乡居民健康档案管理、健康教育、0~36 个月儿童健康管理、孕产妇健康管理、老年人健康管理、预防接种、传染病报告和处理、高血压患者健康管理、2 型糖尿病患者健康管理、重性精神疾病患者管理。在各项规范中，分别对国家基本公共卫生服务项目的服务对象、内容、流程、要求、考核指标及服务记录表单等作出了规定
2011 年	《国家基本公共卫生服务规范（2011 年版）》	增加了卫生监督管理规范，提出 11 大类卫生服务内容

续表

年度	政策名称	主要内容
2011 年	《社区卫生服务机构绩效考核办法（试行）》	提出机构管理、公共卫生服务、基本医疗服务、中医药服务、满意度 5 个方面的考核内容，并明确了由三级指标构成的考核指标体系
2015 年	《关于推进分级诊疗制度建设的指导意见》	提出到 2020 年，基层首诊、双向转诊、急慢分治、上下联动的分级诊疗模式逐步形成，基本建立符合国情的分级诊疗制度。明确了两大方面的工作举措，一是以强基层为重点完善分级诊疗服务体系；二是建立健全分级诊疗保障机制
2015 年	《关于进一步规范社区卫生服务管理和提升服务质量的指导意见》	提出规范社区卫生服务机构设置与管理、加强社区卫生服务能力建设、转变服务模式、加强社区卫生服务保障与监督管理 4 个方面 17 条具体措施
2016 年	《中华人民共和国国民经济和社会发展第十三个五年规划纲要》	从全面深化医药卫生体制改革、健全全民医疗保障体系、加强重大疾病防治和基本公共卫生服务、加强妇幼卫生保健及生育服务、完善医疗服务体系、促进中医药传承与发展、广泛开展全民健身运动、保障食品药品安全 8 个方面对健康中国建设提出了具体要求
2016 年	《关于推进家庭医生签约服务的指导意见》	提出加快推荐家庭医生签约服务，明确签约服务主体，优化签约服务内涵，健全签约服务付费机制，建立签约服务激励机制，加强签约服务绩效考核，强化签约服务技术支撑。提高签约服务水平和覆盖面，促进基层首诊、分级诊疗，为群众提供综合、连续、协同的基本医疗卫生服务，增强人民群众获得感
2017 年	《国务院办公厅关于推进医疗联合体建设和发展的指导意见》	提出各地要根据本地区分级诊疗制度建设实际情况，因地制宜、分类指导，逐步形成多种形式的医联体组织模式。要求完善医联体内部分工协作机制。完善组织管理和协作制度，落实医疗机构功能定位，以需求为导向做实家庭医生签约服务，建立医联体内转诊机制
2017 年	《国家基本公共卫生服务规范（第三版）》	修订并完善了《国家基本公共卫生服务规范（2011 年版）》有关内容，精简了部分工作指标
2018 年	《关于规范家庭医生签约服务管理的指导意见》	提出规范签约服务提供主体，明确签约服务对象及协议，丰富签约服务内容，落实签约服务费，优化签约服务技术支撑，完善双向转诊机制，推进"互联网＋"家庭医生签约服务，强化签约服务的管理与考核，加强签约服务的宣传与培训
2019 年	《国家卫生健康委办公厅关于开展"互联网＋护理服务"试点工作的通知》	提出规范"互联网＋护理服务"，保障医疗质量和安全，助力实施健康中国战略。确定北京市、天津市、上海市、江苏省、浙江省、广东省作为"互联网＋护理服务"试点省份，重点在"互联网＋护理服务"的管理制度、服务模式、服务规范、风险防控以及价格支付政策等方面积极探索，先行先试，总结推广有益经验
2020 年	《关于全面推进社区医院建设工作的通知》	提出全面开展社区医院建设，并明确社区医院建设的总体要求、建设原则、主要建设任务、工作步骤和工作要求
2020 年	《国家卫生健康委办公厅关于进一步推进"互联网＋护理服务"试点工作的通知》	提出进一步扩大试点范围，要求各地结合实际积极开展"互联网＋护理服务"试点工作，在服务模式、管理规范、信息支撑、风险防范、行为监管、价格支付等方面大胆实践、勇于创新，形成示范经验和典型做法，以点带面、逐步推广

年度	政策名称	主要内容
2021年	《关于加快推进社区医院建设的通知》	强调社区服务在民生中的重要性,要求强化社区为民、便民、安民功能,落实以人民为中心的发展思想,推动基层治理现代化。规划提出,要加强党对社区服务的领导,完善多方参与格局,推动政府、市场和社会力量共同参与,提升服务质量和效能。强调重点发展社区就业、养老、托育等服务,注重特殊困难群体的保障,推动城乡社区服务资源均衡配置。规划目标是到2025年,进一步完善社区服务体系,提升服务供给能力,增强居民的获得感、幸福感和安全感。同时,强调通过创新服务机制、加快数字化建设和优化服务设施布局,推动智慧社区和服务体系高质量发展。
2021年	《"十四五"城乡社区服务体系建设规划》	提出推动城乡社区医疗卫生服务体系需要从5个方面加大工作力度。分别是:推动基层发热诊室设置和规范管理;推进城市医联体、农村县域医共体的建设;以人才为核心,加强人才队伍建设;丰富家庭医生签约服务的内涵,推动医养结合服务,推动电子健康档案规范化;完善卫生健康基层治理体系,推动形成全社会支持基层卫生发展的合力
2022年	《全国护理事业发展规划(2021—2025年)》	提出切实发挥大型医院优质护理资源的引领带动作用,组建城市医联体、县域医共体、专科联盟等,健全完善不同医疗机构之间定位明确、分工协作的护理服务体系,将部分一级、二级医院转型为护理院、护理中心,以进一步增加护理服务供给。同时,该文件还提出要创新护理服务模式,扩大"互联网+护理服务"试点覆盖面,支持医疗机构提供"互联网+护理服务"、延续护理、上门护理等,将机构内护理服务延伸至社区和居家,为出院患者、生命终末期患者或行动不便、高龄体弱、失能失智老年人提供便捷、专业的医疗护理服务。此外,该文件还提出支持有条件的二级以上医疗机构与基层医疗卫生机构建立护理专科联盟、专家联合团队等,通过下沉或输出管理、培训、技术等方式,帮助提高基层护理服务能力
2023年	《关于进一步完善医疗卫生服务体系的意见》	提出发展壮大医疗卫生队伍,加大基层、边远地区和紧缺专业人才培养扶持力度,缩小城乡、地区、专业之间的人才配置差距。同时,加强乡镇卫生院和社区卫生服务中心规范化建设,强化常见病多发病诊治、公共卫生、健康管理和中医药服务能力,提升传染病筛查、防治水平,加强重大慢性病健康管理,开展居民心理健康指导,增强乡镇卫生院二级及以下常规手术等医疗服务能力。此外,该文件还提出要健全家庭医生制度,以基层医疗卫生机构为主要平台,建立以全科医生为主体、全科专科有效联动、医防有机融合的家庭医生签约服务模式,提供综合连续的公共卫生、基本医疗和健康管理服务

年度	政策名称	主要内容
2023 年	《进一步改善护理服务行动计划（2023—2025 年）》	强调加强临床护理，推行责任制整体护理，完善基础护理服务，注重人文关怀和沟通交流；提高护理质量，强化巡视观察和护理安全，推动中医护理和护理技术的提升；拓展护理服务领域，开展延续性护理服务，扩大"互联网＋护理服务"覆盖，提升基层和老年护理服务供给。计划还提出加大支持力度，通过加强护士人力配备、优化信息化技术支撑、强化激励机制，确保护理服务质量和护士职业待遇得到有效保障。该计划提出，各级卫生健康行政部门和医疗机构要加强组织领导，定期评估实施效果，推动护理服务不断改善，增强患者的获得感和幸福感
2023 年	《居家和社区医养结合服务指南（试行）》	提出居家和社区医养结合服务应重点关注失能（含失智，下同）、慢性病、高龄、残疾、疾病康复或终末期，出院后仍需医疗服务的老年人。服务内容包括健康教育、健康管理服务、医疗巡诊服务、家庭病床服务、居家医疗服务、中医药服务、心理精神支持服务、转诊服务等
2023 年	《"优质服务基层行"活动和社区医院建设三年行动方案》	提出规范开展能力提升和社区医院建设，重点支持建设一批中心卫生院，提升村卫生室服务能力，加强基层卫生人员配备和培训，提升基层中医药服务能力，补齐医疗应急和传染病应对及儿科等短板，加快基层信息化建设，改善群众就医体验，加强行风建设，守牢安全底线

ⅱ. Ethical Norms in Community Nursing

In community nursing, the contact between nurses and service users is closer, more direct and more frequent. To establish a good relationship between community nurses and community residents, it is necessary for community nurses to comply with the ethical norms of community nursing and improve their own professional ethics.

1. Ethical Principles of Community Nursing

Community nurses should pay attention to the construction of morality and adhere to the ethical principles in the community nursing service, and give full play to its positive role in order to facilitate the development of community nursing service.

(1) Principle of Respect and Autonomy: In community nursing service, community nurses will come into contact with different service users including healthy people, sub-healthy people and people who are sick. In order to better promote

（二）社区护理的伦理规范

在社区护理工作中，护士与服务对象之间的接触更加密切、直接且频繁。要建立社区护士与居民的良好关系，就需要社区护士遵从社区护理伦理道德规范，提升自身的职业道德修养。

1. 社区护理伦理原则　社区护士在社区护理服务中应重视道德建设，坚持伦理原则，充分发挥积极作用，以利于社区护理服务的发展。

（1）尊重与自主原则：在社区护理服务中，社区护士会接触到包括健康人群、亚健康人群及患病人群在内的不同服务对象。为了更好地促进服务对象的健康，社区护士应尊重不同服务对象的人格和尊严。同时由于社区不同于医

the health of service users, community nurses should respect the personality and dignity of different service users. At the same time, because the community is different from the specific environment of the hospital, in the community nursing service, nurses will go to the community and even the family, inevitably coming into more contact with the service users and their family privacy, community nurses should pay more attention to respecting the rights of the service users, to protect their legitimate rights and interests from being infringed upon, including the service users' right to privacy, autonomy, and the right to informed consent. When providing nursing services to individuals, families, and communities, conducting census, research, and studies, community nurses must respect the patients' right to informed consent, ensure service recipients are fully informed, and honor their autonomy to prevent harm and avoid disputes.

(2) Principle of Non-maleficence and Beneficence: When providing care to community residents, community nurses must make every effort to avoid physical and mental pain, harm, illness, or other adverse consequences, placing the health and well-being of residents at the forefront and work for their benefit earnestly.

(3) Principle of Fairness and Public Interest: Within the same community, all residents should have equal opportunities to access the same nursing services or have resources allocated according to a relatively fair system. Community nurses should treat every community resident with fairness and justice, provide equal-quality nursing services, and allocate healthcare resources fairly to ensure that all community residents receive the necessary treatment.

(4) Principle of Focus: Community nursing focuses on the community population as a whole, and should put the interests of the community first, protect people's health, and help the community health service to develop in a better direction.

院的特定环境，护士在社区护理服务中会深入到社区和家庭，不可避免会更多地接触到服务对象及其家庭隐私，社区护士应注意尊重服务对象的权利，保护其合法权益不受侵害，包括服务对象的隐私权、自主权和知情同意权等。在给个体、家庭及社区提供护理服务及进行普查、调研和研究时，应尊重其知情同意权，在服务对象知情基础上，充分尊重其自主权，预防其受到伤害并避免纠纷发生。

（2）不伤害与有利原则：社区护士对社区居民护理服务时，须帮其尽量避免肉体和精神上的痛苦、损伤、疾病或其他不良后果，并将居民健康和利益放在首位，切实为其谋利益。

（3）公平与公益原则：同一个社区中，所有居民都有均等机会获得相同的护理服务，或按照某种相对公平次序分配护理资源。社区护士应公平公正对待每一位社区居民，提供同等质量的护理服务，并且公平地分配医疗资源，确保所有社区居民都能得到必要的治疗。

（4）重点原则：社区护理重点是社区整体人群，应将社区利益放在首位，保护人民健康，帮助社区卫生服务工作向更完善的方向发展。

2. Requirements for Ethical Standardization of Community Nursing

There are significant differences between community nursing services and clinical nursing work in hospitals, their workplace, work characteristics, work content and work tasks are different, the nurse-patient relationship in community nursing practice is more likely to pose legal and ethical difficulty. For example, maintaining the right of informed consent of elderly individuals living alone, and the personal risks that community nurses may face during home visits. If these issues are not sufficiently recognized or handled properly, they will all affect the quality of community health services directly and easily lead to doctor-patient and nurse-patient disputes, and even lead medical disputes, medical malpractice, medical errors, medical accidents, non-cooperation of patients' family members, breach of contract, leakage of confidentiality, and violation of drug administration law and healthcare law.

In order to prevent ethical problems that may occur in community nursing services, at the management level, the relevant regulations on community health services should be continuously improved, legal awareness should be strengthened, legal awareness should be actively publicized and legal awareness should be enhanced, the mechanism of community health services and the construction of management systems should be improved, and the training of humanistic qualities and communication skills of community nursing staff should be strengthened. At the same time, community nurses should abide by the ethical norms of community nursing in their community nursing work, and provide a full range of nursing services to the community, families and individuals. This requires community nurses to have a high sense of professional responsibility, respect the personality and rights

2. 社区护理伦理规范要求

社区护理服务与医院临床护理工作存在显著差异,工作场所、服务特点、服务内容和任务均不同,社区护理实践中的护患关系更容易产生法律和伦理方面的争议。例如,维护空巢老年人的知情同意权,以及社区护士独自家访可能面临的人身风险等问题。如果对这些问题认识不足或处理不当,均会直接影响社区卫生服务质量,容易引发医患和护患纠纷,甚至导致医疗纠纷、医疗事故、医疗差错、医疗意外、患者家属不配合、违约、泄密、违反药品管理法或医疗保健法等问题。

为防范社区护理服务中可能发生的伦理问题,在管理层面上应不断完善社区卫生服务相关法规,增强法律意识,积极进行普法宣传和教育,完善社区卫生服务机制和管理制度建设,加强对社区护理人员人文素养和沟通技巧的培训。同时,社区护士在社区护理工作中应遵守社区护理伦理规范,为社区、家庭和个人提供全方位的护理服务。这要求社区护士在提供护理服务时,秉持高度的职业责任感,尊重服务对象的人格和权利,注重慎独,公正对待每一位服务对象,培养良好的职业素养。

of service recipients, emphasize prudence, treat every service recipient fairly, and cultivate good professionalism when providing nursing services.

Section 3   Community Nurse

I. Basic Requirements of Community Nurse

According to the document *Guidelines on Community Nursing Management* (*Trial Edition*) issued by the Ministry of Health in 2002, the definition and basic requirements of community nurses are as follows:

i. Definition of Community Nurse

Community nurse refers to nursing professionals and technicians who are engaged in community nursing in community health service organizations and other relevant medical institutions.

ii. Basic requirements of Community Nurse

1. Hold a national nursing license and be registered.

2. Pass the training for community nurses prescribed by the health administrative department above the prefecture (city) level.

3. Community nurses who are independently engaged in home-visiting nursing work shall have more than five years of clinical experience in medical institutions.

II. Work Content of Community Nurse

The work of community nurses should be centered on the maintenance of human health, with the family as the unit, the community as the scope, and the needs of community nursing as the guide, focusing on women, children, the elderly, chronically ill patients, and persons with disabilities, and providing relevant nursing services in carrying out the community's work of "prevention, healthcare, health education, family

第三节　社区护士

一、社区护士基本条件

根据卫生部 2002 年发布的《社区护理管理的指导意见（试行）》文件，社区护士的定义和基本条件如下：

（一）社区护士的定义

社区护士（community nurse）是指在社区卫生服务机构及其他有关医疗机构从事社区护理工作的护理专业技术人员。

（二）社区护士的基本条件

1. 具有国家护士执业资格并经注册。

2. 通过地（市）以上卫生行政部门规定的社区护士岗位培训。

3. 独立从事家庭访视护理工作的社区护士，应具有在医疗机构从事临床护理工作 5 年以上的工作经历。

二、社区护士的工作内容

社区护士工作内容应以维护人的健康为中心，家庭为单位，社区为范围，社区护理需求为导向，以妇女、儿童、老年人、慢性病患者、残疾人为重点，在开展社区"预防、保健、健康教育、计划生育和常见病、多发病、诊断明确的慢性病的治疗和康复"工作中，提供相关的护理服务，主要包括以下几个方面：

planning, and the treatment of common and frequent diseases, and the treatment of diagnosed chronic illnesses, as well as rehabilitation," including the following major aspects:

1. Undertake basic medical care for patients in the community, including assisting doctors to carry out diagnosis and treatment, nursing care and counseling for patients with common and frequent diseases as well as diagnosed chronic diseases.

2. Provide family medical services, undertake visits and nursing care for home-bound patients with clear diagnosis, provide basic or specialized nursing services, cooperate with doctors to provide home beds and outpatient services for mobility impaired, elderly or home-bound patients, make regular rounds home visits, offer basic nursing care such as intramuscular injection, intravenous infusion and so on, provide guidance and nursing care for the prevention of pressure ulcers and changing of wounds dressings, and provide guidance for home-based rehabilitation, etc.

3. Provide technical guidance on female health care and family planning in the community, carry out marriage health care, eugenics and genetic counseling, prenatal diagnosis, and prevention and reduction of congenital and hereditary diseases; do a good job in female health care during menstrual period, gestational period, lactation, and perimenopausal period; carry out technical guidance on family planning, and do a good job in the promotion of eugenics.

4. Implement and manage immunization of children, do a good job in the management of newborns, infants and preschool children's health care system, and provide immunization services for children aged 0–6 and other key populations within the jurisdiction.

5. Prevent and manage chronic diseases, preventing the occurrence of chronic diseases and managing patients with chronic diseases to improve the quality of life. This includes intervention for people at high risk of chronic diseases, community

1. 承担社区就诊患者的基本医疗护理工作，包括协助医生开展常见病、多发病以及确诊慢性病患者的诊疗、护理及咨询等工作。

2. 提供家庭医疗服务，承担诊断明确的居家患者的访视、护理工作，提供基础或专科的护理服务，配合医生为行动不便、老年或居家患者开展家庭病床和出诊服务，定期巡诊，提供如肌内注射、静脉输液等基础护理，以及压疮预防指导与护理、伤口换药等服务，提供家庭康复指导等。

3. 提供社区妇女保健与计划生育技术指导工作，开展婚姻保健、优生遗传咨询、产前诊断，预防和减少先天性、遗传性疾病；做好妇女经期、孕期、哺乳期、围绝经期卫生保健工作；开展计划生育技术指导，做好优生优育宣教。

4. 实施和管理儿童计划免疫工作，做好新生儿、婴幼儿、学龄前儿童保健系统的管理，为辖区内 0~6 岁儿童和其他重点人群提供免疫接种服务。

5. 防治和管理慢性病，预防慢性病的发生和管理慢性病患者，提高生活质量。包括慢性病高危人群干预，慢性病患者社区监测、咨询与转院、康复护理、居家护理及长期照护等服务。

monitoring, counseling and referral to hospitals, rehabilitation care, home care and long-term care services of patients with chronic diseases.

6. Provide physical, psychological and social health care for the elderly in the community, and provide health management services, including assessment of lifestyle and health status, physical examination, auxiliary examination and health guidance, and activity prevent common diseases among the elderly.

7. Provide rehabilitation care services to the patients with chronic diseases, the disabled and the elderly in the community to maximize the use of their residual physical functions and to improve their quality of life and comprehensive living capacity.

8. Manage major psychosis, providing rehabilitation nursing services to patients with major psychosis diagnosed and living at home in the district, helping patients to maximize the recovery of social functions and creating good conditions for their return to society.

9. Participate in community health diagnosis, be responsible for collecting, organizing and statistical analysis of community population health information, understand the health status and distribution, discover major health problems and influencing factors, and monitor adverse factors affecting the health of the population.

10. Carry out health education and consultation, behavioral intervention and screening of community populations, establish health records, and monitor and standardize the management of high-risk groups. With the community population as the target of education, carry out organized, planned and evaluated chronic disease prevention knowledge health education, improve residents' understanding of health, guide residents to develop healthy lifestyle and behavior, and improve the overall health of the community.

11. Handle emergency public health events, carry out publicity and education on relevant knowledge, skills, laws and regulations according to

6. 做好社区老年人的生理、心理、社会卫生保健，提供健康管理服务，包括评估生活方式和健康状况、体格检查、辅助检查和健康指导等，积极预防老年人常见疾病。

7. 向社区内慢性病患者、残障人士、老年人提供康复护理服务，最大限度发挥其残余身体功能，提高其生活质量和综合生活能力。

8. 重性精神病管理，为辖区确诊并居家的重性精神病患者提供康复护理服务，帮助患者最大限度地恢复社会功能，为其回归社会创造良好条件。

9. 参与社区卫生诊断工作，负责收集、整理及统计分析社区人群健康信息，了解健康状况及分布情况，发现主要健康问题和影响因素，监测影响人群健康的不良因素。

10. 开展社区人群的健康教育与咨询、行为干预和筛查，建立健康档案，监测并规范管理高危人群。以社区人群为教育对象，有组织、有计划、有评估地开展慢性病预防知识健康教育，提高居民对健康的认识，引导居民养成健康的生活方式与行为，提高社区整体健康水平。

11. 处理突发公共卫生事件，根据辖区传染病和突发公共卫生事件的性质和特点开展相关知识技能和法律法规的宣传教育；对患者、疑似

the nature and characteristics of infectious diseases and emergency public health events under the jurisdiction; carry out epidemiological investigations on patients, suspected patients and emergency public health events; give first aid to the injured and refer them to the doctor timely; do a good job of on-site control of the medical institutions, disinfection and isolation, personal protection, and treatment of medical garbage and sewage; take part in emergent inoculation, preventive medication, distribution of emergency medicines and protective equipment and provide guidance.

12. Participate in the prevention and control of infectious diseases, participate in knowledge training for the prevention of infectious diseases, and provide guidance and consultation on general disinfection, isolation techniques and other nursing techniques. Carry out prophylactic immunization, health education and guidance, home visit and management of infectious diseases, disinfection and isolation of affected areas and families, etc., to control the spread of infectious diseases such as hepatitis, pulmonary tuberculosis, sexually transmitted diseases and other infectious diseases in the community and families, and to protect the safety of people in the community.

13. Provide hospice care services for terminally ill patients and their families, reduce the physical and mental pain of patients, improve the quality of life, and ensure that their families can safely pass through the mourning period.

Ⅲ. Role and Competency Requirements of Community Nurse

i. Role of Community Nurse

1. **Primary Health Care Provider** It is the primary role of the community nurse. Community nurses use epidemiological knowledge to identify existing and potential health problems in the community and carry out nursing interventions to help people avoid harmful factors, prevent diseases, and maintain and improve people's health.

2. **Nursing Service Provider** It is the

患者和突发公共卫生事件进行流行病学调查；对伤者进行急救，及时转诊；做好医疗机构现场控制、消毒隔离、个人防护、医疗垃圾和污水的处理工作；参与应急接种、预防性服药、分发应急药品和防护用品等工作并提供指导。

12. 参与预防和控制传染病工作，参与预防传染病的知识培训，提供一般消毒、隔离等护理技术指导与咨询。开展预防接种、健康教育和指导、传染病上门访视及管理、疫区及家庭的消毒隔离等，控制肝炎、肺结核、性传播疾病等传染病在社区和家庭的传播，保护社区人群安全。

13. 为临终患者及其家属提供临终关怀服务，减轻患者身心痛苦，改善其生活质量，确保家属安全度过居丧期。

三、社区护士角色与能力要求

（一）社区护士的角色

1. **初级卫生保健提供者** 初级卫生保健提供者是社区护士的首要角色。社区护士运用流行病学知识发现社区现存和潜在的健康问题，并进行护理干预，帮助人们避免有害因素，预防疾病，维持及提高人们的健康水平。

2. **护理服务提供者** 护理服务提供者是社

basic role of community nurses. Community nurses use knowledge of medicine, nursing, psychology, sociology to provide professional nursing services to individuals, families, and communities, thereby improving the health level of the people they serve.

3. Health Educator and Counselor   It is an important role of community nurses. Community nurses are the main implementers of community health education, and should perform the function of health education and guidance, teach the necessary health knowledge and skills to the community residents clearly, accurately and unmistakably, to enhance the residents' health awareness, to enrich their health knowledge, to improve their health management skills, and to improve their bad lifestyle. At the same time, community nurses should take the initiative to answer community residents' questions about diseases and health issues, give health guidance, help individuals, families and communities to determine the best plan for disease prevention and health promotion, and guide them to effectively use health knowledge, strengthen healthy behaviors and improve health.

4. Organizer and Manager   In the multi-sectoral work and cooperation in the community, the community nurse assumes the role of organizer and manager, including community health management (such as the establishment and management of community health records, community case management, chronic disease management, etc.), the organization and management of health programs implemented by professionals (such as the division of labor and arrangement of personnel, etc.), the organization and preparation of activities in the community as well as the organization and management of training of relevant community personnel.

5. Coordinator and Collaborator   Community health service is a work that involves multi-disciplinary and multisectoral integration. Community nurses must work with community general practitioners, community administrators,

区护士的基本角色。社区护士运用医学、护理学、心理学、社会学等知识，为个人、家庭和社区提供护理专业服务，从而提高服务对象的健康水平。

3. 健康教育者与咨询者   健康教育者与咨询者是社区护士的重要角色。社区护士是社区健康教育的主要实施者，要发挥健康教育和指导的功能，清楚、准确、无误地向社区居民传授必要的健康知识及技能，增强居民健康意识，丰富健康知识，提高健康管理技能，改善不良生活方式。同时，社区护士应主动解答社区居民有关疾病与健康问题的疑惑，给予健康指导，帮助个人、家庭、社区确定预防疾病、促进健康的最佳方案，指导他们有效运用健康知识，强化健康行为，提高健康水平。

4. 组织者和管理者   在社区多部门的工作与合作中，社区护士承担组织者和管理者的角色，包括社区健康管理（如社区健康档案建立和管理、社区个案管理、慢性病管理等）、专业人员实施健康计划的组织管理（如人员的分工、安排等）、社区各项活动的组织筹备以及社区相关人员的培训等组织和管理工作。

5.协调者和合作者   社区卫生服务是多学科、多部门融合的工作，社区护士必须同社区全科医生、社区行政管理者、社区社会工作者等其他工作人员协同合作，主动联系并协调各类人员与机构之间的关系，充分运用社会资源，保证

community social workers and other staff, take the initiative to communicate and coordinate the relationship between various types of personnel and institutions, make full use of social resources, ensure the successful completion of the community health care tasks, and provide high-quality nursing care services for nursing service recipients.

6. Observer and Researcher When providing various health care services to community residents, community nurses should pay attention to timely observation, exploration and research on the health problems of community service recipients in their work practice, such as the relationship between individuals' poor life habits, the stress factors their families face, and the risk factors in the community environment, and their health, so as to maintain the health level of the community.

7. Community Resident Spokesman Community nurses need to understand the relevant health policy guidelines and laws during community work, identify issues related to the health of community residents timely, and report to the higher level authorities actively. At the same time, community residents' health care needs and suggestions and comments on health promotion policies should also be reflected to the relevant superior departments actively.

ii. Core Competencies of Community Nurse

Drawing on the core competency framework for nurses proposed by the International Council of Nurses (2003), the "core competencies" of community nurses mainly cover the following aspects:

1. Comprehensive Nursing Competence According to the concept of community nursing and the main responsibilities of community nurses, community nurses must have nursing skills in various specialties and have the integration of traditional and western medicine to meet the needs of the community population.

2. Independent Judgment and Problem-solving Competence Community nurses are

社区卫生保健工作任务的顺利完成，为护理服务对象提供高质量的护理服务。

6. 观察者和研究者 社区护士在向社区居民提供各种卫生保健服务时，应注意在工作实践中及时观察、探讨、研究社区服务对象的健康问题，如个人不良的生活习惯、家庭面临的压力因素、社区环境的危险因素等与健康的关系，以维护社区健康水平。

7. 社区居民代言者 社区护士在社区开展工作时，要了解有关卫生政策方针、法律，及时发现与社区居民健康相关的问题，积极向上级主管部门反映。同时，社区居民卫生保健方面的需求及对健康促进政策方面的建议和意见也应积极向上级有关部门反馈。

（二）社区护士的核心能力

借鉴国际护士协会于2003年提出的护士核心能力框架，社区护士的"核心能力"主要涵盖以下几方面：

1. 综合护理能力 根据社区护理的概念和社区护士的主要职责，社区护士必须具备各专科护理技能及中西医结合的护理技能，以满足社区人群的需求。

2. 独立判断、解决问题能力 社区护士在很多情况下需要独立进行各种护理操作、运用

required to independently perform various nursing operations, apply nursing process, conduct health education, and give counseling or guidance in many situations. Therefore, the spirit of prudence，along with problem-solving and adaptability skills is very important to community nurses.

3. Foresight Competence Foresight competence is mainly applied to preventive services, which are one of the main jobs of community nurses. It is the responsibility of community nurses to identify the underlying factors of a problem before it occurs so that measures can be taken in advance to avoid or minimize the problem.

4. Basic Competence to Collect and Process Information Community nurses need to have a basic knowledge of statistics, the ability to process and analyze information, and the ability to assist the community in health-related research.

5. Interpersonal and Communication Competence Community nursing requires both the support and assistance of collaborators and the understanding and cooperation of nursing clients. Community nurses need to work closely with community residents of different ages, families, cultures and social backgrounds, community managers and other health workers, and thus must have competence in sociological and psychological knowledge and interpersonal communication skills in order to carry out their work better.

6. Organizational and Management Competence Organizational and management competence is one of the necessary competencies for community nurses. Community nurses not only provide direct nursing services to community residents, but also need to mobilize positive factors in the community and organize various forms of health promotion activities. At the same time, they need to develop and lead others, promote change, foster a collaborative culture and strengthen the community nursing capacity of the nursing team.

7. Basic Competence to Cope With Common Community Emergencies Comm-

护理程序、开展健康教育、进行咨询或指导。因此，慎独精神、解决问题或应变的能力对于社区护士非常重要。

3. 预见能力 预见能力主要应用于预防性服务，这是社区护士的主要工作之一。社区护士有责任在问题发生之前，找出其潜在因素，提前采取措施，避免或减少问题的发生。

4. 收集信息和处理信息的基本能力 社区护士需要掌握基本的统计学知识，具备处理和分析资料的能力，以及协助社区进行健康相关研究的能力。

5. 人际交往和沟通能力 社区护理工作既需要合作者的支持和协助，又需要护理对象的理解和配合。社区护士需要与不同年龄、家庭、文化及社会背景的社区居民、社区管理者及其他卫生工作人员密切合作，因而必须具备社会学、心理学知识和人际沟通技巧，以便更好地开展工作。

6. 组织、管理能力 组织和管理能力是社区护士必备的能力之一。社区护士不仅需为社区居民提供直接护理服务，还需调动社区的积极因素，组织各种形式的健康促进活动。同时，社区护士需要发展和领导他人，推动变革，培养协作性文化，强化护理团队的社区护理能力。

7. 应对社区常见急症的基本能力 社区护士需具备应对常见急症的抢救和护理能力，掌

unity nurses need to have the ability to respond to common emergencies in rescue and nursing care, master the principles and methods of using all kinds of common rescue items and medicines, and cooperate with doctors in rescue efforts and transfer of critically ill patients within the community.

8. Competence to Acquire New Knowledge and Build Capacity for Their Own Development　Community nurses should continuously acquire new knowledge related to professional development, cultivate the ability to promote their own professional development, and enrich and improve the theoretical and practical abilities of community nursing, so as to enhance the level of community nursing.

9. Competence to Improve, Innovate and Research　Community nurses should have the courage to develop and deliver new technologies, try to innovate community nursing methods and processes, integrate evidence-based medicine and best pathways for practice and research, and achieve optimal health goals for target populations through nursing intervention.

10. Self-protection Competence　Community nurses' self-protection competence includes two aspects: legal self-protection and physical self-protection.

（Ni Ping）

Key Points

1. Communities can be categorized into urban, rural and town communities, which are the most common and universal division criteria.

2. The main components of a community include geographical, demographic, interactive and homogenous elements.

3. Community health refers to the health status of a specific group of community residents and the comprehensive health environment status created around the health of community residents.

4. The main factors affecting health include four major categories, namely, behavioral lifestyle

握各类常见抢救物品和药品的使用原则和方法，配合医生抢救及转诊社区急危重症患者。

8．获取新知识、培养促进自身发展的能力　社区护士应不断获取与专业发展相关的新知识，培养促进自身专业发展的能力，丰富和完善社区护理理论和实践能力，从而提升社区护理水平。

9．改善、创新和研究的能力　社区护士应勇于开发和传递新技术，尝试创新社区护理方法和流程，整合循证医学和最佳路径开展实践和研究，通过护理干预实现目标人群的最佳健康目标。

10．自我防护能力　社区护士的自我防护能力包括2个方面：法律的自我保护和人身的自我防护。

（倪　平）

内容摘要

1. 社区可以分为城市社区、农村社区和城镇社区，是最常见、最通用的划分标准。

2. 社区的主要构成要素包括地域要素、人口要素、互动要素和同质要素。

3. 社区健康是指社区居民这一特定群体的健康状况及围绕着社区居民健康所创造的综合健康环境状况。

4. 影响健康的主要因素包括四大类，即行为和生活方式因素、环境因素、生物学因素和卫

factors, environmental factors, biological factors and health service system factors.

5. Community nursing is a comprehensive application of the theories and techniques of nursing and public health, community-based, population-oriented, service-centered, integrating medical treatment, prevention, health care, rehabilitation, health education, family planning, etc. into nursing, and to promote and maintain the health of the population as the ultimate goal, to provide continuous, dynamic and comprehensive nursing services.

6. Community nursing originated in the western countries, tracing its development process，we can see that is mainly divided into four stages, namely, family nursing stage, district nursing stage, public health nursing stage and community health nursing stage.

7. Community nurse refers to nursing professionals and technicians who are engaged in community nursing work in community health service organizations and other relevant medical institutions.

生服务体系因素。

5. 社区护理是综合应用护理学和公共卫生学的理论与技术，以社区为基础、以人群为对象、以服务为中心，将医疗、预防、保健、康复、健康教育、计划生育等融于护理中，并以促进和维护人群健康为最终目的，提供连续性的、动态性的和综合性的护理服务。

6. 社区护理起源于西方国家，追溯其发展过程主要划分为 4 个阶段，即家庭护理阶段、地段护理阶段、公共卫生护理阶段和社区卫生护理阶段。

7. 社区护士（community nurse）是指在社区卫生服务机构及其他有关医疗机构从事社区护理工作的护理专业技术人员。

Exercises

1. Analyze the characteristics of community nursing and how it differs from hospital nursing.

2. Describe the role and function of community nurses with examples.

3. Briefly describe the main tasks of a community nurse.

思 考 题

1. 分析社区护理的特点及其与医院护理的不同。

2. 举例说明社区护士的角色功能。

3. 简述社区护士的主要工作内容。

Chapter 2

Community Health Service System and Models

第二章

社区卫生服务体系与模式

NURSING

02章 数字内容

Learning Objectives

Knowledge Objectives

1. Accurately recall the definitions and key points of concepts related to community health service system and models.

2. Memorize the concepts and roles of family doctor contracting services and community general practice management within the operational mechanisms of community health services.

Ability Objectives

1. Understand the basic components of community health services and the

学习目标

知识目标

1. 能够准确记忆社区卫生服务体系与模式相关概念的定义和要点。

2. 能够记忆社区卫生服务运行机制中家庭医生签约服务和社区全科医疗管理的概念和作用。

能力目标

1. 能够理解社区卫生服务的基本构成和全球健康策略的重要性。

importance of global health strategies.

2. Apply information management skills to effectively manage and utilize community resident health records, enhancing the quality and efficiency of community health services.

3. Explore the role of family doctor contracting services and community general practice management in promoting health promotion and disease prevention.

4. Integrate community health service information systems with community health management to design and implement effective community health service plans.

● Quality Objectives

1. Establish a sense of social responsibility, understand the importance of community nursing in enhancing public health and actively participate in community services.

2. Strengthen ethical awareness, recognize and address ethical issues in community nursing, and foster professional integrity of fairness and respect for patients.

3. Enhance humanistic care abilities，focus on the health needs of vulnerable groups, and improve comprehensive nursing skills.

2. 运用信息管理技巧，管理和利用社区居民健康档案，提高社区卫生服务的质量和效率。

3. 探讨家庭医生签约服务和社区全科医疗管理在推动健康促进和疾病预防方面的作用。

4. 将社区卫生服务信息系统与社区健康管理相结合，设计并实施有效的社区卫生服务计划。

● 素质目标

1. 树立社会责任意识，理解社区护理在提升公众健康中的重要性，并积极参与社区服务。

2. 强化伦理道德观念，认识和应对社区护理中的伦理问题，培养公正、尊重患者的职业操守。

3. 提升人文关怀能力，关注弱势群体健康需求，增强综合护理技能。

The community health center in a city has long been an essential institution providing basic medical care and health counseling services. Located in a diverse, multi-age community, it serves the nearby residents as well as students from nearby schools. Over the years, it has offered primary healthcare services such as diagnosis and treatment of common illnesses, prophylactic immunization, and maternity care.

However, with population growth and societal changes, the community is facing new challenges. Many residents require more comprehensive

某市的社区卫生服务中心一直以来都是提供基本医疗和健康咨询服务的重要机构。该社区卫生服务中心位于一个多元文化、多年龄段的社区，服务范围涵盖了邻近的居民和附近学校的学生。长期以来，它为社区居民提供了基本的卫生保健，例如常见疾病的诊断与治疗、预防接种、孕产妇护理等。

然而，随着人口增长和社会变迁，该社区面临着新的挑战。许多居民需要更全面和综合的健康服务，包括慢性病管理、老年护理和心理健

and integrated health services, including chronic disease management, elderly care, and mental health support. Due to the existing service model and resource constraints, the community health center is unable to meet the growing demands. Additionally, given the diverse cultural backgrounds and language differences among community residents, delivering culturally and linguistically responsive services has become an important consideration.

To address these needs, the community health center has decided to undertake a reform and transformation, to establish a more comprehensive and interdisciplinary community health service system. The goal of the reform is to provide holistic, personalized, and sustainable health services to promote the overall health and well-being of community residents. This entails investments and enhancements in human resources, equipment, and technology. Moreover, the community health center aims to strengthen collaboration with other medical institutions, social work agencies, and volunteer organizations, forming a close-knit community health network to deliver better healthcare to residents.

Questions:

1. What challenges does the community health center face in this case?

2. Why did the community health center decide to reform and transform?

The community health service system is a comprehensive service system that meets the healthcare needs of community residents, encompassing various forms of services such as prevention, treatment, and rehabilitation. Common operating models within this system include family doctor contracting services and community general practice management. With changes in population demographics and an increasing burden of chronic diseases, the healthcare needs of community residents are becoming increasingly complex. Community health services play a vital role in

康支持等方面。由于现有的服务模式和资源限制，社区卫生服务中心无法满足这些不断增长的需求。此外，由于社区居民的多元文化背景和语言差异，提供跨文化和语言适应性的服务也成为一个重要的考虑因素。

为了适应这些需求，社区卫生服务中心决定进行改革和转型，建立一个更加综合和跨学科的社区卫生服务体系。改革的目标是提供更全面、个性化和可持续的健康服务，以促进社区居民的整体健康和福祉。这意味着在人力资源、设备和技术方面需要进行投资和提升。同时，社区卫生服务中心还将加强与其他医疗机构、社会工作机构和志愿者组织的合作，形成一个紧密的社区卫生网络，共同为居民提供更好的卫生保健服务。

请思考：

1. 这个案例中的社区卫生服务中心面临了什么样的挑战？

2. 为什么该社区卫生服务中心决定进行改革和转型？

社区卫生服务体系是满足社区居民健康需求的全面服务系统，包括预防、治疗、康复等多种服务形式，其中常见的运行模式有家庭医生签约服务和社区全科医疗管理。随着人口结构变化和慢性疾病负担的增加，社区居民对健康服务的需求越来越复杂。社区护理服务在维护公共卫生、提供个性化健康服务、实现持续护理中起到了核心作用。因此，理解社区卫生服务体系与模式对于未来从事这一领域工作的护理专业人员至关重要。

maintaining public health, providing personalized healthcare services, and delivering continuous care. Therefore, understanding the system and models of community health services is crucial for nursing professionals who aspire to work in this field.

Section 1　Overview

The community health service system is an organizational structure and operational mechanism established to meet the health needs of community residents. It is based on the community and extends health services from hospitals to the daily lives of community residents. The community health service system not only focuses on individual health but also aims to promote the overall health development of the community. In the community health service system, coordinated and integrated care teams play a crucial role. In addition to the involvement of care teams, the integration and optimization of other related institutions and resources are also involved in the community health service system, forming flexible and diverse community health service models. The establishment of the community health service system and models aims to provide comprehensive, continuous, and personalized care services for community residents. By integrating resources, strengthening team collaboration, and flexibly utilizing different service models, the community health service system is committed to improving the health level and quality of life of community residents.

I. Basic Concepts of Community Health Service

1. Public Health　In 1920, Charles Winslow, the founder of public health at Yale University, proposed the classic definition of "public health". According to his definition, public health is the science and art of preventing diseases, prolonging life, promoting health, and improving efficiency

第一节　概　述

社区卫生服务体系是为满足社区居民的健康需求而建立的组织结构和运作机制。它以社区为基础，将卫生服务从医院延伸到社区居民的日常生活中。社区卫生服务体系不仅关注个体的健康，也注重促进整个社区的健康发展。在社区卫生服务体系中，协调、一体化的护理团队起着关键作用。除了护理团队的参与，社区卫生服务体系还涉及其他相关机构和资源的整合与优化，形成灵活和多样的社区卫生服务模式。社区卫生服务体系与模式的建立旨在为社区居民提供全面、连续和个性化的护理服务。通过整合资源、强化团队合作和灵活运用不同的服务模式，社区卫生服务体系致力于提高社区居民的健康水平和生活质量。

一、社区卫生服务的基本概念

1. 公共卫生　1920 年，耶鲁大学公共卫生创始人 Charles Winslow 提出了经典的"公共卫生"定义。根据他的定义，公共卫生是通过有组织的社会努力来预防疾病、延长寿命、促进健康和提高效益的科学和艺术。具体手段包括改善环境卫生、控制传染病、宣扬个人卫生教育、保

through organized social efforts. Specific measures include improving environmental hygiene, controlling infectious diseases, advocating personal hygiene education, to ensure timely diagnosis and treatment of diseases, and establishing social mechanisms to ensure that everyone can maintain a healthy standard of living. Subsequently, the definition of public health further evolved in the second half of the 20th century. In 1976, Donald Acheson, the chief medical officer of the UK, believed that public health is the science and art of preventing diseases, prolonging life, and promoting health through organized social behaviors. In 1998, the Institute of Medicine (IOM) in the United States defined public health as all collective activities conducted to ensure that the population can access the conditions and environments necessary for a healthy life. In 1999, Canadian public health scholar John Last proposed that public health is the action taken by society to protect and promote the health of the public.

In China, the definition of public health is the science and art of improving environmental hygiene conditions, preventing various diseases, promoting population health, and prolonging healthy life through organized social efforts. Public health emphasizes the mobilization of the entire society, involving the participation of all citizens, to create an environment that promotes and maintains health. Its goals are disease prevention, health promotion, and longevity. Specifically, the connotation of public health includes:

(1) Disease Prevention: Focus on preventing infectious diseases, maternal and perinatal diseases, nutritional deficiencies, as well as non-communicable diseases and injuries.

(2) Health Protection: Emphasize five major areas of hygiene, including schools, environment, occupation, food, and radiation, and address dynamic and static health issues throughout a person's life from birth to death.

(3) Health Promotion: Promote the mobili-

证疾病的及时诊断和治疗，以及建立保障每个人可以维持健康的生活标准的社会机制。随后，在 20 世纪下半叶，公共卫生的定义进一步发展。1976 年，英国首席医官 Donald Acheson 认为公共卫生就是通过有组织的社会行为预防疾病、延长寿命、促进健康的科学和艺术。1998 年，美国国家科学院医学研究所将公共卫生定义为为了保证国民能够获得健康生活的条件和环境而进行的一切群体性活动。1999 年，加拿大公共卫生学者 John Last 主张公共卫生是社会为了保护和促进民众健康而采取的行动。

我国的公共卫生定义为通过有组织的社会共同努力，改善环境卫生条件，预防各种疾病，促进人群健康，延长健康寿命的科学和艺术。公共卫生强调全社会动员，全民参与，创造促进和维护健康的环境。其目标是预防疾病、促进健康、延长寿命。具体来说，公共卫生的内涵包括：

（1）疾病预防：重点预防传染病、孕期和围生期疾病、营养缺乏性疾病，以及慢性非传染性疾病和伤害。

（2）健康保护：注重学校、环境、职业、食品、放射等五大卫生领域，关注人从出生到死亡一生的动态和静态健康问题。

（3）健康促进：推动全社会动员，全民参

zation of the entire society, involve the participation of all citizens, and create an environment that promotes and maintains health.

(4) Public Safety: Focus on injury prevention, disaster prevention, and emergency response to public health events such as emergent and emerging infectious diseases.

2. Primary Health Care　Primary health care (PHC) is an approach that involves the participation of the whole society in the field of healthcare. Its goal is to ensure the highest possible level of health and well-being, as well as equitable distribution of these benefits. To achieve this, primary health care should focus on people's needs from health promotion and disease prevention to treatment, rehabilitation, and palliative care, while being as close as possible to their daily environments. The services provided by primary health care include the following:

(1) Health Counseling and Education: Provide health counseling and education to community residents, impart health knowledge, promote improvements in health behaviors and lifestyles, and enhance individual responsibility and proactivity towards health.

(2) Diagnosis and Treatment of Common Diseases: Primary health care provides diagnosis, treatment, and management of common diseases and their symptoms such as colds, fever, respiratory tract infections, gastrointestinal problems, and other non-emergency conditions.

(3) Prophylactic Immunization: Offer vaccination services, including routine immunizations for children and vaccinations for adults, to prevent the occurrence and spread of infectious diseases and maintain individual and population immunity.

(4) Chronic Disease Management: For patients with chronic diseases such as hypertension, diabetes, and heart disease, primary health care provides regular follow-ups, medication management, lifestyle guidance, monitoring, and other services to help patients control their condition, alleviate symptoms, and improve their

与，创造一个促进和维护健康的环境。

（4）公共安全：注重伤害、灾害预防以及突发和新发传染病等公共卫生事件的应急处置。

2. 初级卫生保健　初级卫生保健是一种全社会参与卫生事业的方法，旨在确保实现最高可能水平的健康和福祉及其公平分配，为此应在从健康促进和疾病预防到治疗、康复和姑息治疗的连续过程中尽早关注人们的需求，并尽可能贴近人们的日常环境。初级卫生保健服务的内容包括以下几个方面：

（1）健康咨询和教育：提供健康咨询和教育，向社区居民传授健康知识，促进健康行为和生活方式的改善，增强个体对健康的责任意识和主动性。

（2）常见疾病的诊断和治疗：初级卫生保健提供常见疾病的诊断、治疗和管理。包括感冒、发热、呼吸道感染、胃肠道问题等非急危重症的常见病症。

（3）预防接种：提供疫苗接种服务，包括儿童常规免疫和成人疫苗接种，以预防传染病的发生和流行，维护个体和群体的免疫防护。

（4）慢性病管理：对于患有慢性疾病（如高血压、糖尿病、心脏病等）的患者，提供定期随访、药物管理、生活方式指导和监测等服务，帮助患者控制病情、减轻症状和改善生活质量。

quality of life.

(5) Maternal and Child Health Care: Provide health management for women during pre-pregnancy, pregnancy, and postpartum periods, monitor the growth and development and immunizations of children, and offer related guidance on infant feeding and early education.

(6) Mental Health Support: Primary health care also addresses mental health issues by providing psychological counseling, support, and therapy to help patients cope with stress, anxiety, depression, and other psychological distress.

(7) Emergency Medical Rescue: Primary health care institutions are also capable of providing basic first aid and emergency medical rescue services in critical situations, including simple trauma management and referral initiation.

In addition to the above, primary health care also includes other services such as health check-ups, disease screening, family planning and reproductive health, medication dispensing and management, community environmental health assessments, infectious disease surveillance and reporting, etc. It is important to note that the specific content of primary health care may vary depending on the country, region, and institution, and should be adjusted and implemented according to local health care policies and needs. These services aim to meet the basic health care needs of community residents and provide comprehensive, continuous, and accessible medical care.

The general principles for implementing primary health care are as follows:

(1) Universal Coverage: Primary health care should provide services to everyone in the community, regardless of their economic status, gender, age, or other backgrounds. Everyone has the right to access basic health care services, including health consultations, diagnosis and treatment of common diseases, prophylactic immunization, etc.

(2) Based on Evidence and Science: The implementation of primary health care should be

（5）妇幼保健：提供妇女孕前、孕期和产后的健康管理、儿童生长发育监测和免疫接种，以及相关的婴幼儿喂养指导和早期教育等服务。

（6）心理健康支持：初级卫生保健也关注心理健康问题，提供心理咨询、心理支持和心理治疗，帮助患者应对压力、焦虑、抑郁等心理困扰。

（7）紧急医疗救援：初级卫生保健机构在紧急情况下也能够提供基本的急救和紧急医疗救援服务，进行简单的创伤处理和启动转诊。

除了上述内容，初级卫生保健还包括一些其他方面的服务，如健康体检、疾病筛查、计划生育与生殖健康、药物配发和管理、社区环境卫生评估、传染病监测与报告等。需要注意的是，初级卫生保健的具体内容会因国家、地区和机构的不同而有所差异，根据当地的卫生保健政策和需求进行调整和执行。这些服务旨在满足社区居民的基本卫生保健需求，提供全面、连续且可及的医疗服务。

初级卫生保健实施的一般原则如下：

（1）全民覆盖：初级卫生保健应该为整个社区的所有人提供服务，无论其经济状况、性别、年龄或其他背景如何。每一个人都有权利享受基本的卫生保健服务，包括健康咨询、常见疾病的诊断和治疗、预防接种等。

（2）基于证据和科学：初级卫生保健的实施应基于最新的科学证据和实践准则。医疗工

based on the latest scientific evidence and practice guidelines. Health care workers need to receive ongoing professional training to stay updated on the latest medical knowledge and clinical guidelines in order to provide high-quality health care services.

(3) Emphasis on Prevention: Primary health care should focus on disease prevention and health promotion. Measures such as health education, vaccination, promotion of healthy behaviors and lifestyles, etc., should be taken to prevent the occurrence and spread of diseases and reduce the burden of illness.

(4) Individualized Care: Primary health care should provide personalized care services. Health care workers should conduct comprehensive assessments of patients' health conditions, needs, and backgrounds, and develop individualized treatment plans and health management strategies based on their specific situations.

(5) Collaborative Health care Teams: Primary health care requires the establishment of interdisciplinary health care team collaboration. Various professionals such as doctors, nurses, pharmacists, community health workers, etc., should work together to provide comprehensive health care services to patients.

(6) Community Participation and Advocacy: Primary health care should actively promote community residents' participation and advocacy. By organizing health education activities, conducting health promotion and advocacy, establishing a community environment that promotes health, etc., community residents are encouraged to actively participate in the management and improvement of their own health.

(7) Intersectoral Cooperation: Primary health care requires intersectoral cooperation and coordination. Different departments, such as the health department, education department, social welfare department, etc., should work together to establish an effective health care system and policy environment, and promote the smooth

作者需要接受持续的专业培训，了解最新的医学知识和临床指南，以提供高质量的卫生保健服务。

（3）预防为主：初级卫生保健应注重疾病的预防和健康促进。通过开展健康教育、提供疫苗接种、推广健康行为和生活方式等措施，预防疾病的发生和传播，降低疾病负担。

（4）个体化护理：初级卫生保健应该提供个性化的护理服务。医疗工作者应全面评估患者的健康状况、需求和背景，并根据其特定情况制订个性化的治疗计划和健康管理方案。

（5）医疗团队合作：初级卫生保健需要建立多学科的医疗团队合作机制。医生、护士、药师、社区健康工作者等各类专业人员应共同合作，为患者提供综合性的卫生保健服务。

（6）社区参与和倡导：初级卫生保健应积极促进社区居民的参与和倡导。通过组织健康教育活动、开展健康宣传和推广、建立健康促进的社区环境等方式，鼓励社区居民主动参与自身健康的管理和改善。

（7）跨部门合作：初级卫生保健需要跨部门的合作与协调。卫生部门、教育部门、社会福利部门等不同部门应共同努力，形成有效的卫生保健体系和政策环境，推动初级卫生保健工作的顺利开展。

implementation of primary health care work.

3. Community Health Services　Community health services are an integral part of urban health care initiatives and serve as the foundation for achieving the goal of primary health care for all. Community health service institutions provide public health services and essential medical care, which operate on a non-profit basis. The primary beneficiaries of these services are communities, households, and residents, with specific emphasis on women, children, the elderly, individuals with chronic illnesses, disabled individuals, and underprivileged residents. The core principles of community health services revolve around proactive and personalized care, including home visits, and encompass a wide range of activities such as health education, preventive measures, health promotion, rehabilitation, family planning guidance, and diagnosis and treatment of common and prevalent diseases.

II. Medical Health Service System

i. Concept of Medical Health Service System

1. Medical Health Service System The medical health service system mainly includes hospitals (public hospitals and privately-run hospitals), primary health care institutions, and specialized public health institutions. In China, the medical health service system can be divided into rural medical health service system and urban medical health service system based on regional characteristics.

(1) Rural Medical Health Service System: It is mainly composed of county hospitals as the core, with rural hospitals and village health clinics as the foundation. County hospitals are responsible for providing basic medical health services, emergency rescue for critically ill patients, as well as technical guidance and training for rural hospitals and village health clinics. Rural hospitals and village health clinics jointly provide comprehensive services

3. 社区卫生服务　社区卫生服务是城市卫生工作的重要组成部分,是实现人人享有初级卫生保健目标的基础环节。社区卫生服务机构提供公共卫生服务和基本医疗服务,具有公益性质,不以营利为目的。以社区、家庭和居民为服务对象,以妇女、儿童、老年人、慢性病患者、残疾人、贫困居民等为服务重点,以主动服务、上门服务为主,开展健康教育、预防、保健、康复、计划生育技术服务和一般常见病、多发病的诊疗服务。

二、医疗卫生服务体系

(一)医疗卫生服务体系的概念

1. 医疗卫生服务体系　医疗卫生服务体系主要包括医院(公立医院和私立医院)、基层医疗卫生机构和专业公共卫生机构。在我国按照地域医疗卫生服务体系可以划分为农村医疗卫生服务体系和城市医疗卫生服务体系。

(1)农村医疗卫生服务体系:以县级医院为主体,乡镇卫生院和村卫生室为基础。县级医院负责基本医疗卫生服务、急危重症患者的抢救,并承担对乡镇卫生院和村卫生室的业务技术指导和培训;乡镇卫生院和村卫生室共同承担农村居民的基本公共卫生服务,即常见病、多发病的综合诊疗服务。

for the diagnosis, treatment, and management of common and prevalent diseases among rural residents.

(2) Urban Medical Health Service System: It is a collaborative medical service system between community health service institutions and urban hospitals. Community health service institutions are responsible for providing basic public health services to urban residents, including primary diagnosis and treatment services for common and prevalent diseases, as well as rehabilitation services. They also serve as gatekeeper for health. Urban hospitals not only provide diagnosis and treatment for emergencies, critical illnesses, and complex medical conditions for both urban and rural residents, medical education and research, but also fulfill responsibilities in technical support, personnel training, etc., to drive the continuous optimization and development of primary health care services.

2. Public Health Service System   The public health service system is typically composed of multiple stakeholders, including the government, health departments, medical institutions, academic institutions, non-profit organizations, and others. Its goal is to provide comprehensive and sustainable public health services through effective planning, implementation and evaluation of public health programs and strategies, in order to safeguard people's health and well-being. In China, the public health service system mainly includes disease control institutions, maternal and child health care institutions, health supervision institutions, mental health specialized institutions, and more. By establishing a sound public health service system, it is possible to better prevent diseases, protect public health, and provide timely medical and health support.

ⅱ. Characteristics of the Medical Health Service System

1. Characteristics of China's Medical Health Service System

China, as a country with a large population

（2）城市医疗卫生服务体系：以社区卫生服务机构与城市医院分工协作的医疗服务体系。社区卫生服务机构负责城市居民基本公共卫生服务，包括一般常见病、多发病初级诊疗服务和康复服务，承担健康守门人的职责。城市医院除了承担城乡居民急危重症和疑难病症的诊疗、医学教育和科研等方面的职责，还需要通过技术支持、人员培训等方式，带动基层医疗卫生服务的持续优化发展。

2. 公共卫生服务体系   通常由政府、卫生部门、医疗机构、学术机构和非营利组织等多个参与者组成。其目标是通过有效的规划、实施和评估公共卫生项目与策略，提供全面、可持续的公共卫生服务，以保障人民的健康和福祉。在我国，公共卫生服务体系主要包括疾病控制机构、妇幼保健机构、卫生监督机构、精神卫生专业机构等。通过建立健全公共卫生服务体系，可以更好地预防疾病、保护公众健康，并提供及时的医疗和卫生支持。

（二）医疗卫生服务体系的特点

1. 我国医疗卫生服务体系的特点

中国作为一个拥有巨大人口数量和不同地

and varying levels of development across different regions, needs to adjust and improve its medical health service system according to actual conditions. The objectives are to improve the accessibility, equity, and quality of medical services to meet people's health needs. The main characteristics of the current medical health service system in China are as follows:

(1) Universal Medical Insurance System: China has implemented the universal medical insurance system that covers the majority of urban and rural residents. This system aims to provide basic medical security and alleviate individuals' financial burden of health care expenses.

(2) Grading Diagnosis and Treatment System: China promotes a grading diagnosis and treatment system, which encourages patients to first seek medical care at community health care institutions and then be referred to higher-level hospitals according to their needs. This helps improve the service capabilities of community health care institutions, reduce the burden on comprehensive hospitals, and ensure the rational allocation of medical resources.

(3) Health Record Management: China emphasizes health record management by setting up electronic health records for residents, which include basic information, medical history, allergies, etc. This helps health care professionals better understand patients' health conditions and provide more accurate medical services.

(4) Community Health Centers: Community health centers are the core of China's primary health care institutions, providing basic medical care, health education, prophylactic immunization, and other services. They play a crucial role in providing convenient medical services within the community. As of the end of 2023, there were 37,177 community health centers (clinics) set up in nearly 9,000 streets nationwide, achieving basic coverage in urban neighborhoods.

(5) Training Programs for Grassroots Doctors: China has implemented a series of

区发展水平差异的国家,医疗卫生服务体系需要根据实际情况进行调整和改进。目标是提高医疗服务的普及性、公平性和质量,以满足人民对健康的需求。当前我国医疗卫生服务体系的主要特点如下:

(1) 全民医保制度:中国实行全民医保制度,覆盖了绝大部分城乡居民。这种制度旨在提供基本医疗保障,减轻个人医疗费用负担。

(2) 分级诊疗制度:中国推行分级诊疗制度,鼓励患者首先到社区医疗机构就诊,根据需要再转诊至更高级别的医院。这有助于提高社区医疗机构的服务能力,减少综合医院的压力,并使医疗资源得以合理分配。

(3) 健康档案管理:中国重视健康档案管理,为居民设置电子健康档案,记录着个人的基本信息、疾病史、过敏史等。这有助于医务人员更好地了解社区居民的健康状况,提供更精准的医疗服务。

(4) 社区卫生服务中心:社区卫生服务中心是中国基层医疗机构的核心,提供基本医疗、健康教育、预防接种等服务。它们在社区内就近为居民提供便捷的医疗服务,发挥着重要作用。截至2023年底,全国共设置社区卫生服务中心(站)37 177个,基本实现了城市街道全覆盖。

(5) 基层医生培养计划:中国实施了一系列基层医生培养计划,旨在增加基层医疗机构

training programs for grassroots doctors to increase the number of medical personnel in primary health care institutions and improve their professional qualifications. This helps enhance the level and coverage of community health care services. Through various forms of training, by 2021, the number of qualified general practitioners trained nationwide reached 434,900, an increase of 26,100 from the previous year and an increase of 325,100 since 2012. The number of grassroots general practitioners has notably increased, with an additional 44,100 compared to the previous year.

2. Characteristics of Medical Health Service System in Other Countries

(1) Canada: Canada's medical health service system consists of the public and private sectors. Each province and territory is responsible for managing and providing health care services. Public hospitals and clinics provide free basic medical services to residents, while private medical insurance covers additional services and medication costs.

(2) United Kingdom: The National Health Service (NHS) in the UK provides free public health care services. Residents access medical services by registering with a general practitioner (GP). However, in recent years, the NHS has faced challenges due to resource constraints and increasing demand, including issues of long waiting times.

(3) Germany: Germany adopts a social insurance model, where all employees and self-employed individuals must participate in health insurance plans. These plans cover hospitalization, outpatient care, prescription drugs, rehabilitation, and other medical services. In recent years, the German government has strengthened support for primary health care institutions to improve the quality and accessibility of primary health care.

(4) Japan: Japan has a social insurance system where all residents must participate in the national health insurance program. Medical services are provided by public and private

的医务人员数量,并提高其专业素质。这有助于提升社区医疗服务的水平和覆盖范围。通过多种形式培养,2021 年全国培养训练合格的全科医生达到 43.49 万人,比上一年增加了 2.61 万人,比 2012 年增加了 32.51 万人,其中基层全科医生数量增幅明显,较上一年增加 4.41 万人。

2. 国外医疗卫生服务体系的特点

(1)加拿大:加拿大的医疗卫生服务体系由公共和私人部门组成。每个省份和地区负责管理和提供医疗保健服务。公立医院和诊所为居民提供免费的基本医疗服务,而私人医疗保险则用于覆盖额外的服务和药物费用。

(2)英国:英国的国家医疗服务(NHS)是免费公共医疗服务。居民通过注册在家庭医生名下来获得医疗服务。然而,近年来,由于资源限制和需求增加,NHS 面临着挑战,其中包括等待时间较长等问题。

(3)德国:德国采用社会保险模式,所有雇员和自由职业者必须参加健康保险计划。这些计划提供住院治疗、门诊就医、处方药和康复等医疗服务。近年来,德国政府加强了对基层医疗机构的支持,以提高基层医疗的质量和可及性。

(4)日本:日本实行社会保险制度,所有居民必须参加国民健康保险计划。医疗服务由公立和私立医院提供,患者可以自由选择就医。近年来,日本政府致力于推动数字化和信息技

hospitals, and patients have the freedom to choose their health care providers. In recent years, the Japanese government has been promoting the use of digitization and information technology in health care services to improve efficiency and quality of care.

(5) Australia: Australia's medical health service system follows a social insurance model. The public sector provides free or low-cost basic medical services, while the private sector offers additional medical insurance and services. The Australian government continues to invest in improving primary health care services to enhance community access to medical care.

iii. The Importance of Building a Medical Health Service System

Building a medical health service system is crucial both globally and in the context of China's national conditions. It not only concerns the well-being of people and social stability but also involves issues related to public health security and rational allocation of resources. Through continuous efforts and reforms, the quality and coverage of the medical health service system and can be continuously improved, thus contributing to the global health cause.

1. People's Well-being   Health is one of the most fundamental needs of people, and an effective medical health service system can provide timely and high-quality medical and health services to meet people's pursuit of health. Constructing a sound medical health service system can improve people's quality of life and increase their sense of happiness.

2. Social Stability and Development A healthy population is an essential factor for social stability and economic development. A robust medical health service system can prevent and control diseases, improve the overall health level of the public, reduce prevalence and disability rates, and thereby promote social stability and economic development.

3. Public Health Security   Global public

术在医疗卫生服务中的应用，以提高效率和医疗质量。

（5）澳大利亚：澳大利亚的医疗卫生服务体系遵循社会保险制度。公共部门提供免费或低收费的基本医疗服务，而私人部门则提供额外的医疗保险和服务。澳大利亚政府持续投资于基层医疗服务的改善，提高社区的医疗可及性。

（三）构建医疗卫生服务体系的重要性

构建医疗卫生服务体系在全球和中国的国情下都具有重要性。它不仅关乎人民的福祉和社会稳定，还涉及公共卫生安全和资源合理分配等方面的问题。应通过持续的努力和改革，不断提升医疗卫生服务体系的质量和覆盖范围，为全球健康事业贡献力量。

1. 人民福祉   健康是人民最基本的需求之一，而有效的医疗卫生服务体系能够提供及时、高质量的医疗和健康服务，满足人们对健康的追求。构建良好的医疗卫生服务体系可以改善人民的生活质量，增加幸福感。

2. 社会稳定与发展   健康人口是社会稳定和经济发展不可或缺的因素。一个强大的医疗卫生服务体系可以预防和控制疾病，提高公众的健康水平，减少患病率和致残率，从而促进社会稳定和经济发展。

3. 公共卫生安全   全球公共卫生面临着共

health faces common challenges such as infectious disease outbreaks and epidemic spread. Building a sound medical health service system can provide early warning, rapid response, and effective control of these public health crises, ensuring public health security at the national and global levels.

4. Allocation of Health Resources Building a medical health service system can achieve rational allocation and optimal utilization of health resources. In countries like China with a large population, developing community health care institutions and implementing grading diagnosis and treatment systems can redirect medical resources from major cities to primary health care institutions, alleviate the pressure on large hospitals, and ensure more equitable distribution of medical resources across regions and populations.

5. International Exchange and Cooperation Building a sound medical health service system facilitates international exchange and cooperation. By sharing experiences, technologies, and resources, countries can learn from and collaborate with each other to collectively address global medical challenges and improve global health levels.

III. Global Health Strategies

i. Global Health Issues and Challenges

The world is currently facing multiple global health issues and challenges, which have profound impacts on global public health.

1. Infectious Disease Epidemic There are still epidemics of various infectious diseases worldwide, including newly emerging viruses and known pathogen variations. For example, the COVID-19 pandemic has had a significant impact on global public health systems, highlighting the importance of infectious disease control and response capabilities.

2. Rising Burden of Non-communicable Diseases (NCDs) Compared to infectious diseases, non-communicable diseases

同挑战,如传染病暴发、疫情扩散等。构建健全的医疗卫生服务体系能够提前预警、迅速应对并有效控制这些公共卫生危机,保障国家和全球的公共卫生安全。

4. 健康资源分配 构建医疗卫生服务体系可以实现医疗资源的合理配置和优化利用。在中国这样人口众多的国家,通过发展社区医疗机构和推行分级诊疗制度,能够将医疗资源从大城市向基层医疗机构下沉,减轻大医院的压力,使医疗资源更加公平地分配到各个地区和群体。

5. 国际交流与合作 构建健全的医疗卫生服务体系有助于国际交流与合作。通过分享经验、技术和资源,各国可以相互借鉴和学习,共同应对全球性的医疗挑战,提高全球卫生水平。

三、全球健康策略

(一)全球卫生问题和挑战

当今世界正面临着多重全球卫生问题和挑战,这些问题和挑战对于全球公共卫生产生了深远影响。

1. 传染病流行 全球范围内仍存在着多种传染性疾病的流行,包括新出现的病毒和已知的病原体变异。例如,COVID-19疫情对全球公共卫生系统造成了巨大冲击,凸显了传染病控制和应对能力的重要性。

2. 非传染性疾病负担增加 与传染性疾病相比,非传染性疾病(如心血管疾病、脑卒中、癌症和糖尿病)在全球范围内造成的死亡数和疾

(such as cardiovascular diseases, apoplexy, cancer and diabetes) are increasingly contributing to the global burden of death and disease. These diseases are often associated with unhealthy lifestyles (such as smoking, unhealthy diets and lack of exercise) and factors like aging of populations.

3. Inequitable Distribution of Medical Resources There is an inequitable distribution of medical resources globally. People in some developing countries and impoverished areas face challenges such as inadequate medical facilities, shortages of healthcare professionals, and limited access to medical services, making it difficult for them to obtain adequate medical care.

4. Global Health Emergencies Sudden health emergencies on a global scale (such as natural disasters, epidemic outbreaks, and humanitarian crises) put tremendous pressure on public health systems. These emergencies pose significant challenges to medical resources, healthcare facilities, and personnel capacity, requiring global cooperation and coordination in response.

5. Social Determinants and Health Inequalities Socioeconomic factors play a crucial role in global health. Poverty, low educational levels, gender inequality, racial discrimination, and other social factors are closely linked to health inequalities. These factors can result in marginalized groups facing challenges in accessing health care and opportunities for good health.

ii. Contents of Global Health Strategies

A global health strategy refers to the policy framework and action plan formulated by international organizations, countries, or regions with the objective of promoting global health and enhancing the well-being of individuals worldwide. The official definitions of global health strategy may vary among different entities. WHO defines global health strategy as addressing global health issues and improving the health status of populations globally through collaboration and

病负担日益增加。这些疾病往往与不良的生活方式（如吸烟、不健康饮食和缺乏运动）以及人口老龄化等因素有关。

3. 医疗资源不平等分配 全球范围内存在医疗资源的不平等分配问题。一些发展中国家和贫困地区的人们面临着医疗设施不足、医务人员短缺和医疗服务不可及等挑战，难以获得适当的医疗保健。

4. 全球卫生紧急事件 全球范围内突发的卫生紧急事件（如自然灾害、流行病暴发和人道主义危机）对公共卫生系统造成了巨大的压力。这些紧急事件给医疗资源、卫生设施和人员能力带来了极大的挑战，需要全球合作和协调来应对。

5. 社会因素与健康不平等 社会经济因素对全球健康产生重要影响。贫困、教育水平低下、性别不平等、种族歧视等社会因素与健康不平等密切相关。这些因素可能导致弱势群体在获得医疗保健和健康机会方面面临挑战。

（二）全球健康战略的内容

全球健康战略是指国际组织、国家或地区制定的旨在促进全球卫生和改善全球居民健康水平的政策框架和行动计划。官方对全球健康战略的定义可能因不同组织而有所差异。世界卫生组织将全球健康战略定义为解决全球卫生问题，提高全球居民的健康水平，通过合作和协调采取合适的政策和措施来应对全球卫生挑战。在 2030 年可持续发展议程中，联合国将全球健康战略视为实现可持续发展目标 3 即"确保健康的生活，促进各年龄段人群的福祉"的重要组成

coordinated policies and measures. Within the 2030 Agenda for Sustainable Development, the United Nations considers global health strategy as a vital component in achieving Sustainable Development Goal 3, which entails ensuring healthy lives and promoting well-being for all age groups. The United States Agency for International Development (USAID) defines global health strategy as the provision of equitable, accessible, and high-quality health services to populations worldwide through measures such as establishing robust healthcare systems, enhancing public health capacity, promoting health service coverage, and strengthening vaccination efforts. These definitions underscore the aims of global health strategy, which encompass fostering global health equity, enhancing the capacity of health systems through international cooperation and cross-border endeavors, and safeguarding the health and well-being of individuals on a global scale. Each entity may have distinct focuses and specific action plans based on their missions and objectives.

1. Global Health Security Agenda Expand global healthcare coverage to ensure universal access to quality basic health services. Strengthen global public health emergency response capabilities and enhance the capacity for prevention, monitoring, and control of infectious diseases. Improve the prevention and treatment of non-communicable diseases, including promoting healthy diets and reducing tobacco and alcohol use. Promote the sustainable development of healthcare systems, including improving healthcare facilities and strengthening health workforce training.

2. United Nations Sustainable Development Goals (SDGs)　By 2030, reduce the global maternal mortality ratio to less than 70 per 100,000 live births（SDG 3.1）. By 2030, reduce by one third premature mortality from non-communicable diseases through prevention and treatment and promote mental health and well-being（SDG 3.4）. Achieve universal health coverage, including financial risk protection,

部分。美国国际开发署将全球健康战略定义为通过建立强大的卫生系统、改善公共卫生能力、推广健康服务覆盖并加强疫苗接种等措施，为全球居民提供平等、可及和质量优秀的卫生服务。这些定义强调了全球健康战略的目标，即通过国际合作和跨国努力，促进全球卫生公平、提高卫生系统能力，并确保全球居民的健康和福祉。每个组织根据其使命和目标，可能有不同的侧重点和具体行动计划。

1. 全球卫生议程　扩大全球医疗保健覆盖，确保人人享有可及、质量高的基本卫生服务。加强全球公共卫生应急响应能力，提升预防、监测和控制传染病的能力。提高非传染性疾病防治水平，包括促进健康饮食、减少烟草和酒的使用等。推动卫生系统的可持续发展，包括改善卫生设施、加强卫生人力资源培养等。

2. 联合国可持续发展目标（SDGs）　SDG 3.1：到2030年全球孕产妇每10万例活产的死亡率降至70人以下。SDG 3.4：到2030年，通过预防、治疗及促进身心健康，将非传染性疾病导致的过早死亡减少三分之一。SDG 3.8：实现全民健康保障，包括提供经济风险保护，人人享有优质的基本保健服务，人人获得安全、有效、优质和负担得起的基本药品和疫苗。SDG 3.D：加强各国特别是发展中国家早期预警、降低风

access to quality essential health-care services and access to safe, effective, quality and affordable essential medicines and vaccines for all（SDG 3.8）. Strengthen the capacity of all countries, in particular developing countries, for early warning, risk reduction and management of national and global health risks (SDG 3D).

3. U.S. Global Health Security Strategy Strengthen global infectious disease surveillance and early warning capabilities, and enhance the ability to detect and respond to emergency public health events. Support global vaccination programs to increase vaccine coverage and reduce the spread of infectious diseases. Establish a robust laboratory network for rapid identification and control of infectious disease threats. Provide technical assistance and training to strengthen the capacity of healthcare systems in developing countries.

4. European Union Global Health Strategy Advance global health security and improve global health monitoring and response mechanisms. Enhance the sustainability and resilience of health systems, including investment in healthcare facilities and healthcare workforce development. Promote medical innovation and research cooperation to advance medical science and technological development. Improve the accessibility and quality of health services, including ensuring universal access to basic healthcare.

5. Global Health and Medical Strategy The World Economic Forum (WEF) and L.E.K. Consulting have jointly released the *Global Health and Healthcare Strategic Outlook* aimed at uniting various stakeholders from different sectors, organizations, industries, and regions to achieve a shared vision for the health and medical industry by 2035. The strategy aims to ensure fairness in healthcare services, enhancing the resilience of healthcare systems, promoting innovation, and driving sustainable development as the 4 key pillars of future health and medical strategies.

险，以及管理国家和全球健康风险的能力。

3. 美国全球卫生安全战略 加强全球传染病监测和预警能力，提高早期检测和响应突发公共卫生事件的能力。支持全球疫苗接种计划，提高疫苗覆盖率，减少传染病的传播。建立强大的实验室网络，以便快速识别和控制传染病威胁。提供技术援助和培训，加强发展中国家的卫生系统能力。

4. 欧洲联盟全球卫生战略 促进全球卫生安全，改善全球卫生监测和应对机制。加强健康系统的可持续性和抗灾能力，包括投资卫生设施和培养卫生人力资源。推动医疗创新和研究合作，提升医学科学和技术发展水平。提高卫生服务的可及性和质量，包括保障基本医疗保健的普及。

5. 全球健康和医疗战略 世界经济论坛（WEF）与 L.E.K. 咨询联合发布了《全球健康和医疗战略展望》，旨在团结不同部门机构、行业和地区的各个相关方，以达成 2035 年健康与医疗行业的共同愿景，确保改善医疗服务公平性、增强医疗系统韧性、促进创新以及推动可持续发展这四个要素成为未来健康和医疗战略的关键支柱。该战略展望报告以四大战略支柱为基础，以公平为基本目标，描绘了 2035 年健康与医疗愿景：

Based on these four strategic pillars and with fairness as its fundamental objective, the strategy outlook report outlines the vision for health and medicine in 2035：

(1) Accessibility and Equalization of Medical Health：Equal opportunities for accessing health determinants and ensuring representative health data, enabling equal treatment outcomes for people with equal medical needs.

(2) Transformation of Healthcare Systems：Enhancing the resilience of healthcare systems to provide high-quality medical services under expected and unexpected circumstances.

(3) Technology and Innovation：Creating an environment conducive to scientific and pharmaceutical innovation, providing support for corresponding funding, applications, and implementation.

(4) Environmental Sustainability：Reducing the impact of the healthcare industry on the environment, addressing and resolving climate change issues, and ultimately improving overall health levels.

iii. Relevant Content on China's Global Health Strategy

The Chinese government released the *"Healthy China 2030" Planning Outline* in 2016 for the first time and formulated a follow-up implementation plan in 2019, aiming to provide strategic direction for addressing the major challenges faced by the Chinese healthcare system. *The 14th Five-Year Plan for National Health* released by the Chinese government serves as a guiding policy to support continuous improvements in China's health sector in the short term.

The Chinese government has been actively allocating the budget to eliminate the constraints on medical service capacity in various regions and promote the expansion of high-quality medical services. As of March 2023, more than 76 newly built national regional medical centers are under construction. Since 2016, the government has also issued multiple policy guidelines encouraging

（1）医疗健康可及性和效果均等化：均等化获取健康决定因素的机会，确保健康数据具有人口代表性，从而使有同等医疗需求的人群能够得到平等的治疗效果。

（2）医疗系统转型：增强医疗系统的韧性，使其在预期内和意料外的情况下均能够提供高质量的医疗服务。

（3）技术与创新：打造一个有利于科学和药物创新的环境，为相应的资金、应用和实施提供支持。

（4）环境可持续发展：减少医疗健康产业对环境的影响，应对和解决气候变化问题，最终改善健康水平。

（三）中国全球卫生战略的相关内容

中国政府于2016年首次发布了《"健康中国2030"规划纲要》，并于2019年制定了后续实施计划，旨在为应对中国医疗系统面临的主要挑战指引战略方向。中国政府发布的2021—2025年的五年规划文件《"十四五"国民健康规划》也作为指导方针，支持中国健康领域在短期内的不断改进。

我国政府已经着力投入预算以消除各地区医疗服务能力的限制，并推进高质量医疗服务的扩容。截至2023年3月，已有超过76个新建的国家区域医疗中心正在建设。自2016年以来，政府还发布了多项政策意见，鼓励家庭医生直接为患者提供服务，作为替代性医疗服务，以缓解医疗机构收治容量有限的问题。政府已确定了阶段性计划，该计划的目标是从2022年开

family doctors to directly provide services to patients as alternative medical services to alleviate the limited admission capacity of medical institutions. The government has established a phased plan with the goal that starting from 2022, the coverage rate of primary health care services provided by family doctors will increase by 1%~3% annually, reaching 75% of the population by 2035. In the future, the government will continue to invest in decentralizing medical services and developing alternative healthcare service models such as family medical services to help improve the accessibility of basic healthcare services globally.

In the *14th Five-Year Plan for National Health* and the *14th Five-Year Plan for the Development of the Pharmaceutical Industry*, a series of key goals have been identified, mainly focusing on improving the supply chain and designating it as a priority area for future actions. Specific goals include optimizing the research and development value chain and production capacity, and improving drug reserve systems. Increasing the supply of existing drugs and vaccines has also been explicitly recognized as a priority area. In addition, the *"Healthy China 2030" Planning Outline* proposes that China needs to streamline the drug distribution process. It also explicitly states the need to form several large-scale pharmaceutical companies to address the high industry fragmentation in the Chinese market and enhance the ability to enter the international market.

Since 2015, China has formulated a series of digital-related policies targeting the healthcare industry ecosystem with the aim of improving data collection, management, and utilization. These policies have driven a series of progress made by the healthcare system over the past decade, including the establishment of regional comprehensive health information platforms connecting over 7,000 public hospitals. By the end of 2021, this platform had covered 85% of cities and 69% of counties in China. Additionally,

始，家庭医生提供的基层医疗服务覆盖率每年增长 1%~3%，到 2035 年覆盖 75% 的人口。未来，政府将继续投资推进医疗服务的去中心化以及替代医疗服务模式（例如家庭医疗服务）的发展，以帮助改善全球基础医疗卫生服务的可及性。

在《"十四五"国民健康规划》和《"十四五"医药工业发展规划》等规划中，确定了一系列重点目标，主要集中在改善供应链，并将其认定为未来行动的优先领域。具体目标包括优化研发价值链和生产能力，改善药品储备体系。同时，增加现有药品和疫苗的供应也被明确为优先领域。此外，《"健康中国 2030"规划纲要》提出中国需要精减药品流通环节。同时，也明确指出要形成多个大型制药企业，以解决中国市场行业分散度高的问题，增强进军国际市场的能力。

自 2015 年以来，中国针对医疗健康行业生态系统制定了一系列数字化相关政策，旨在改善数据的采集、管理和利用。这些政策推动了医疗健康系统在过去十年取得的一系列进展，包括建立区域全民健康信息平台，连接了超过 7 000 家公立医院。截至 2017 年年底，该平台已覆盖中国 85% 的市和 69% 的县。此外，在新冠疫情期间，还开发了关联性的数据系统，用于监测公众疫苗接种和核酸检测状态。下一步的政策行动包括不断建设和规范国家数字医疗基础设施，扩大数字医疗在专科医疗和公共卫生领

during the COVID-19 pandemic, associated data systems were developed to monitor public vaccination and nucleic acid testing statuses. The next policy actions include continuously building and standardizing national digital medical infrastructure, expanding the application of digital healthcare in specialized medical and public health fields, as well as further formulating measures for data cleaning, governance, and security management.

域的应用,以及进一步制定数据清理、治理和安全相关的管理措施。

BOX 2-1   Learning More

Japan's *Global Health Strategy*

Since the global spread of the COVID-19 pandemic, Japan has been promoting the international initiative of "Universal Health Coverage". In addition, the Japanese government has been working on multiple levels to establish a global system for COVID-19 prevention and control. In May 2022, they released the *Global Health Strategy*. The goal of this strategy is to promote the establishment of a global health system that contributes to health security and strengthens the prevention, preparedness, and response to public health crises. Specific measures include establishing cooperation frameworks among their own finance and health institutions and relevant international organizations such as the World Health Organization and World Bank, promoting collaboration with public-private partnership funds, and sharing information. In response to public health emergencies, they are researching international financing mechanisms that strengthen both routine prevention and crisis response, allocating funds primarily to disease prevention during normal times and enhancing flexible financing systems during crises. To contribute to the response to pandemics, they engage in discussions within the framework of the World Health Organization to develop new legal documents, formulate international standards, and revise the *International Health Regulations*. This implementation is organized by the Ministry of

BOX 2-1   知识拓展

日本《全球卫生战略》

自新冠疫情全球蔓延以来,日本一直在推进“全民健康覆盖”国际性措施。此外,日本政府还在多个层面上推动建立全球新冠疫情防控体系,并于2022年5月发布了《全球卫生战略》。该战略的目标是推动建立有助于卫生安全的全球健康体系,并加强对公共卫生危机的预防和应对。具体措施包括建立本国财政、卫生机构和相关国际组织(如WHO、世界银行等)的合作框架,促进与公私合作基金的合作,共享信息;针对公共卫生危机,研究有助于加强平时预防和危机应对的国际融资机制,优先向平时疾病预防领域分配资金,强化危急时刻的机动融资制度;为应对传染病大流行作出日本贡献,如在WHO框架内讨论新的法律文件、制定国际规范、修订《国际卫生条例》等,具体由外务省和厚生劳动省组织落实;确保全民健康覆盖措施在预防与应对公共卫生危机以及构建全球卫生体系中起到重要作用。

Foreign Affairs and the Ministry of Health, Labour and Welfare. They aim to ensure that measures for universal health coverage play an important role in preventing and responding to public health crises and building a global health system.

The core goals of this strategy include the following aspects:

1. Strengthening International Cooperation and Partnerships Collaborate with other countries, international organizations, and non-governmental organizations to collectively respond to global public health challenges. This includes sharing information, providing technical support and resources, and promoting cooperation in areas such as vaccination and medical assistance.

2. Enhancing Health Security Capacity Strengthen the construction of public health systems and emergency response capabilities, and improve disease monitoring, early warning, and response capabilities. Special attention is given to the control and prevention of infectious diseases and the safety and reliability of health facilities.

3. Promoting Global Health Innovation Encourage scientific research and technological innovation, promote the development of the pharmaceutical industry, and improve the quality and accessibility of medical technology and services. Support innovation in areas such as new drug development, diagnostic tool innovation, and digital health solutions.

4. Strengthening the Training of Healthcare Workforce Promote the training and development of the global healthcare workforce, and improve the professional competence and emergency response capabilities of healthcare personnel. Facilitate international medical education and exchange of experiences to jointly promote the cultivation and mobility of healthcare talents.

Japan is actively responding to global public health challenges through international cooperation and transnational efforts, aiming to establish a safer, more stable, and sustainable global health

该战略的核心目标包括以下几个方面：

1. 加强国际合作与伙伴关系 通过与其他国家、国际组织和非政府组织合作，共同应对全球公共卫生 挑战。这包括分享信息、提供技术支持和资源，以及促进疫苗接种和医疗援助等方面的合作。

2. 提高卫生安全能力 加强公共卫生系统的建设和应急响应能力，提升疾病监测、预警和应对的能力。重点关注传染性疾病的控制和防范，提高卫生设施的安全性和可靠性。

3. 促进全球健康创新 鼓励科学研究和技术创新，推动医药产业的发展，提高医疗技术和服务的质量和可及性。支持新药研发、诊断工具创新和数字化健康解决方案等领域的创新。

4. 加强卫生人力资源培养 推动全球卫生人力资源的培训与发展，提高医务人员的专业素养和应急响应能力。促进国际医学教育和经验交流，共同推进卫生人才的培养和流动。

日本通过国际合作和跨国努力共同应对全球公共卫生挑战，建立更加安全、稳定和可持续的全球健康体系，以保障全球居民的健康和福祉。

system to ensure the health and well-being of people worldwide.

iv. The Role of Community Nursing in the Implementation of Global Health Strategies

Community nursing plays a crucial role in addressing global health challenges. With population growth, increasing burden of chronic diseases, and outbreaks of infectious diseases, community nursing has become a key strategy to improve global health and enhance health security. Its role is reflected in the following aspects.

1. Health Promotion and Disease Prevention Community nursing emphasizes health promotion and disease prevention. Through activities such as health education, behavior guidance, and promoting healthy lifestyles, it helps individuals and communities improve their health status and reduce the risk of diseases.

2. Remote Medical Services and Primary Medical Support Community nursing plays a critical role in providing medical services in areas with limited access to medical resources or in remote locations. Through regular visits and outreach programs, community nurses provide basic medical services and health consultations to residents and facilitate timely referrals to higher-level medical institutions.

3. Epidemic Control and Crisis Response Community nursing plays a key role in epidemic control and crisis response. Community nurses can conduct epidemic monitoring, early warning, and screening, provide necessary protection guidance and support to community residents, and collaborate effectively with other health departments to coordinate and manage emergencies.

4. Health Management and Chronic Disease Care Community nursing plays an important role in managing and caring for chronic diseases. Through regular follow-ups, individualized treatment plans, and nutritional guidance, community nurses help patients control disease progression, improve their quality of life,

（四）社区护理在全球健康策略实施中的作用

社区护理在应对全球卫生挑战中发挥着至关重要的作用。随着人口增长、慢性疾病负担增加以及传染病暴发等问题的日益突出，注重社区护理成为提高全球健康水平和卫生安全的关键策略之一。具体作用体现在以下方面：

1. 健康促进与疾病预防 社区护理强调健康促进和疾病预防，通过开展健康教育、提供行为指导和推广健康生活方式等活动，帮助个体和社区改善健康状况，减少疾病风险。

2. 异地医疗服务与基层医疗支持 社区护理在远离医疗资源集中地区或偏远地区的情况下起到关键作用。通过社区护理人员的巡诊和定期访问，居民得以获得基本医疗服务和健康咨询，并及时转诊至更高级别的医疗机构。

3. 疫情防控与危机应对 社区护理在疫情防控和危机应对方面发挥着关键作用。社区护理人员能够进行疫情监测、早期预警和筛查工作，为社区居民提供必要的防护指导和支持，同时与其他卫生部门合作，有效协调和管理紧急事件。

4. 健康管理与慢性病护理 社区护理在慢性病管理和护理方面起到重要作用。通过定期随访、个体化的治疗计划和营养指导，社区护理人员能够帮助患者控制疾病进展、提高生活质量，并减轻医疗系统的负担。

and alleviate the burden on the healthcare system.

5. Community Engagement and Resource Integration Community nursing emphasizes community participation and the enhancement of self-management capabilities. By establishing effective partnerships and integrating multiple resources, community nursing can better meet the health needs of community residents and achieve sustainable development.

Section 2   The Operation Mechanism of Community Health Services

I. The Concept, Target, Characteristics, Content, and Role of Community Health Services

i. The Concept and Target of Community Health Services

1. Health Services Health services encompass all activities aimed at promoting, maintaining, and restoring health. This includes both individual-based health services and population-based health services.

2. Community Health Services Community health services are grassroots-level health services that are community-oriented, comprehensive, cost-effective, convenient, and accessible. They are provided under the leadership of the government, with community participation and guidance from higher-level health institutions. Community health services are an important component of urban health work and a fundamental link in achieving the goal of universal access to primary healthcare.

3. Target of Community Health Services The targets of community health services include communities, households, and residents. This encompasses the focus on providing services to healthy individuals, sub-healthy individuals, and those who are ill.

5. 社区参与及资源整合 社区护理注重社区居民的参与和自我管理能力的提升。通过建立有效的合作伙伴关系,整合多方资源,社区护理能够更好地满足社区居民的健康需求,并实现可持续发展。

第二节　社区卫生服务运行机制

一、社区卫生服务的概念、对象、特点、内容及作用

(一)社区卫生服务的概念及对象

1. 卫生服务 卫生服务包括促进、保持和恢复健康的所有服务,既包括针对个人的卫生服务,也包括以人口为基础的卫生服务。

2. 社区卫生服务 社区卫生服务是在政府领导、社区参与、上级卫生机构指导下,以社区为基础,以社区人群的卫生服务需求为导向,综合、经济、方便、可及的基层卫生服务。社区卫生服务是城市卫生工作的重要组成部分,也是实现人人享有初级卫生保健目标的基础环节。

3. 社区卫生服务的对象 以社区、家庭和居民为服务对象,包括健康人群、亚健康人群和患病人群,以妇女、儿童、老年人、慢病患者、残疾人、贫困居民等为服务重点。

Specific emphasis is placed on providing services to women, children, the elderly, patients with chronic diseases, persons with disabilities, and impoverished residents.

ii. The Model and Institutional Structure of Community Health Service Organizations in China

1. The Organizational Models of Community Health Service Institutions   The organizational model of community health service plays a fundamental role in the structure of community health services. It can adapt to the specific needs of different regions and communities while adhering to certain principles. In the current context, the organizational models of urban community health services in China include:

(1) Established by direct extension from secondary and tertiary hospitals, with community health services or family preventive health departments. For example, in Shenzhen, each level of hospitals is responsible for operating community health centers under the mode of hospital management.

(2) Transforming primary hospitals or street clinics/health centers into community health centers or stations, is the dominant form of urban community health service institutions. Under this model, medical and health units within the jurisdiction are responsible for staffing with medical personnel and technical equipment, while the subdistrict administrations provide service venues and infrastructure. This model to some extent addresses the operational difficulties faced by grassroots medical institutions and meets the healthcare service needs of residents within their jurisdiction.

(3) Rely on enterprise health institutions combined with local health resources to form a complementary health service model. This expands the coverage of enterprise hospitals from employees to community residents. There are three approaches to forming this model: transforming enterprise hospitals into independent

（二）我国社区卫生服务组织模式及机构设置

1. 社区卫生服务机构的组织模式   社区卫生服务组织模式是社区卫生服务的结构基础，可在遵循一定原则的基础上，适应不同地区和社区的具体需求，在实施过程中具有灵活性和多样性等特点。当前，我国城市社区卫生服务的组织模式包括：

（1）由二级、三级医院直接延伸建立，设立社区卫生服务部或家庭预防保健部。例如深圳市由市各级医院作为责任单位负责运行社区健康卫生服务中心，实行院办院管的服务模式。

（2）由一级医院或街道医院、卫生院等整体转型形成社区卫生服务中心或服务站，是当前城市社区卫生服务机构的主要形成方式。该模式由辖区内医疗卫生单位负责配备医务人员和技术设备，街道办事处提供服务场地和基础设施，在一定程度上解决了基层医疗机构经营困难的问题，同时也满足了辖区内居民的卫生服务需求。

（3）依托企业卫生机构结合地方卫生资源形成互补型卫生服务模式，扩展企业医院服务群体，由企业职工扩展到企业医院覆盖地区的社区居民。该模式的形成又包含3种途径，即企业医院与企业剥离由区域管理成为独立的社区卫生服务中心，区属医院代管企业医院，区属医院和企业医院合作运行。

community health centers after separating them from enterprises and placing them under regional management; having district-owned hospitals manage enterprise hospitals; and cooperative operation between district-owned hospitals and enterprise hospitals.

(4) Expansion the home-based care of secondary and tertiary hospitals to community families in small and medium-sized cities. This model has certain advantages in terms of utilizing medical resources and implementing two-way referrals but may have limited service coverage.

(5) With the development of urbanization, social forces are allowed to competitively establish community health service institutions in newly-built communities, provided they comply with laws and regulations and can offer community health services. The government is responsible for providing related supporting facilities such as office space.

2. Establishment of Community Health Service Institutions

The *Service Capability Standards for Community Health Centers (2022 edition)* stipulates the departmental setup, facilities and equipment, and staffing requirements for community health service institutions. The specific content is as follows:

(1) Departmental Setup: Community health service institutions include: a. Clinical departments, including general practice clinics, traditional Chinese medicine clinics, rehabilitation therapists, emergency rooms, and pre-examination triage/fever surveillance points. Community health service institutions that have made continuous improvements and achieved results also include fever clinics, dental departments, rehabilitation departments, etc., with at least one specialized department and the ability to independently set up a pediatric department; b. Medical technology departments and other departments, such as pharmacies (Chinese medicine pharmacies), clinical laboratories, radiology departments, ultrasound rooms, electrocardiogram rooms, health

（4）在中小城市中将二级、三级医院的家庭病床科拓展到社区家庭中，在医疗资源使用和双向转诊的实现方面具有一定的优势，但是服务内容不全面。

（5）随着城镇化的发展，新建的社区也允许社会力量在符合法律法规并能提供社区卫生服务功能的前提下竞争性建立社区卫生服务机构，政府负责解决办公用房等相关配套设施。

2. 社区卫生服务机构设置 《社区卫生服务中心服务能力标准》（2022版）中对社区卫生服务机构的科室设置、设施设备、人员配备进行了规定。具体内容如下：

（1）科室设置：社区卫生服务机构包括：①临床科室，即全科诊室、中医诊室、康复治疗室、抢救室、预检分诊处 / 发热哨点。持续改进并取得成效的社区卫生服务机构还包括发热诊室、口腔科、康复科等，至少设立一个特色科室，可独立设置儿科。②医技及其他科室，如药房（中药房）、检验科、放射科、B超室、心电图室、健康信息管理室、消毒供应室（可依托有资质的第三方机构），持续改进的机构在承担教学任务的情况下需配置操作实训室。③公共卫生科或预防保健科，即设置听力、视力、心理和行为发育检查室，预防接种门诊，持续改进的机构可增设心理咨询室、健康小屋、预防保健特色科室。④职能科室，即党务、院务、医务、护理、财务、病案管理、信息、院感、医保结算、后勤管理等专（兼）职岗位。

information management rooms, sterilized supply rooms (which can be supported by qualified third-party institutions). Institutions that undertake teaching tasks need to have practical training rooms; c. Public health or preventive health care departments, including hearing, vision, psychological, and behavioral development examination rooms, prophylactic immunization clinics. In institutions that are making continuous improvements, additional facilities such as psychological counseling rooms, health rooms, and special preventive health care departments may be added; d. Functional departments, including party affairs, hospital affairs, medical affairs, nursing, finance, medical record management, information, nosocomial infection control, medical insurance settlement, and logistics management, etc.

(2) Facilities and Equipment: a. The building area of community health service institutions should meet the standards based on the population served, with a standard of 1,400m^2 for 30,000–50,000 people, 1,700m^2 for 50,000–70,000 people, and 2,000m^2 for 70,000–100,000 people. Community health centers that are making continuous improvements should increase the building area for beds according to relevant requirements. For 1–50 beds, the building area should be increased by at least 25m^2 per bed, and for over 50 beds, the building area should be increased by at least 30m^2 per bed. b. Based on the reasonable allocation according to the service scope and population, at least 5 observation beds or inpatient beds should be provided, with an actual capacity of 20–50 beds (inclusive). c. The equipment configuration should comply with the relevant requirements specified in the *Notice on the Issuance of Basic Standards for Urban Community Health Centers and Stations*, and necessary traditional Chinese medicine service equipment should be provided. d. Public facilities should include sanitary toilets. Barrier-free facilities should meet the relevant standards. The first floor of medical buildings should have barrier-free toilets, and if there are two floors,

（2）设施设备：①社区卫生服务机构的建筑面积按照服务人口数量业务用房面积达标标准为每3万~5万人口1 400m^2、每5万~7万人口1 700m^2、每7万~10万人口2 000m^2；继续改进的社区卫生服务中心按照相关要求增加病床建筑面积；床位在1~50张时，每增设1张床位，建筑面积至少增加25m^2，50张床位以上时，每增设1张床位，建筑面积至少增加30m^2。②根据服务范围和人口合理配置，至少设日间观察床5张或有住院床位，实际开放床位20~50张（含）。③机构设备配置参照《关于印发城市社区卫生服务中心、站基本标准的通知》要求配备相关设备，配备必要的中医药服务设备。④公共设施设置包括卫生厕所；无障碍设施符合相关标准要求，医疗用房首层应设有无障碍厕所，层数为二层时宜设电梯或无障碍坡道，三层及以上应设电梯；在门诊诊室、治疗室、多人病房等区域为服务对象提供必要的私密性保护措施；在需要警示的地方有明显的警示标识；设立服务功能适宜的独立母婴室，配备基本设施，引导标识醒目；继续改进的机构可优化相关设施，如候诊椅数量配备适宜，舒适度较好，配备使用自助查询、自助挂号、自助打印化验结果报告等设备，使用门诊叫号系统等。

elevators or barrier-free ramps should be installed. For buildings with three floors or more, elevators should be installed. Outpatient consultation rooms, treatment rooms, multi-patient wards, and other areas should provide necessary privacy protection measures for service recipients. Obvious warning signs should be placed in appropriate locations. An independent mother and baby room with suitable service functions should be established, equipped with basic facilities, and clearly marked with visible signage. Institutions that are making continuous improvements can optimize related facilities, such as ensuring an appropriate number of waiting chairs and providing better comfort, providing self-service query, self-registration, self-printing of laboratory test reports, and other equipment, as well as outpatient call systems.

(3) Staffing：The staffing of community health centers should mainly comply with the requirements specified in the *Notice on the Issuance of Basic Standards for Urban Community Health Centers and Stations*. The number of staff positions should not be less than the standards set by the province (region, city). The number of healthcare technical personnel should be no less than 80% of the total number of employees. At least one public health physician should be assigned. The number of registered general practitioners per 10,000 service population in the jurisdictional area should be no less than 2.

iii. Characteristics of Community Health Services in China

1. Public Welfare Community health services in China emphasize social welfare and public interests, playing an important role in safeguarding and improving people's health. The goal of community health services is to provide residents with high-quality, sustainable, and affordable healthcare services, rather than pursuing profits.

2. Proactivity Community health services in China actively engage with communities through regular visits, health education, home

（3）人员配备：社区卫生服务中心的人员主要按照《关于印发城市社区卫生服务中心、站基本标准的通知》要求的配备。人员编制数不少于本省（区、市）出台的编制标准。卫生技术人员数不少于单位职工总数的80%。至少配备1名公共卫生医师。辖区内每万名服务人口注册全科医师数不少于2人。

（三）我国社区卫生服务特点

1. **公益性** 中国社区卫生服务注重社会公益和公共利益，在保障和改善人民健康方面起着重要作用。社区卫生服务的目标是为居民提供高质量、可持续且廉价的医疗保健服务，而不以牟利为目的。

2. **主动性** 中国社区卫生服务积极主动地走进社区，通过定期巡诊、健康宣教、家庭访视等方式，主动发现和解决居民的健康问题。社

visits, and other methods to proactively identify and address residents' health issues. Community nurses or health workers play a crucial role in establishing close connections with residents and actively meeting their medical and health needs.

3. Comprehensiveness　Community health services in China are comprehensive, covering various fields such as prevention, treatment, rehabilitation, and health management. They provide comprehensive health services including basic medical care, health education, disease screening, planned immunization, maternal and child health care, chronic disease management, and elderly care.

4. Integration　Community health services in China emphasize integration. They not only provide medical services but also focus on public health, health education, disease prevention and control, and other aspects. Community health centers typically integrate doctors, nurses, public health experts, and other relevant professionals to provide comprehensive services.

5. Continuity　Community health services in China emphasize continuity, including ongoing monitoring, follow-up, and treatment to ensure continuous fulfillment of residents' health needs. Through regular visits, health records management, and health education activities, community health services can establish long-term cooperative relationships with residents and provide continuous medical and health support.

6. Accessibility　Community health services in China are designed to be accessible, meaning that community residents can conveniently access the necessary medical and health services. Community health centers are usually located near communities, providing close proximity medical care services, so residents do not need to travel long distances to receive basic medical services.

iv. Content of Community Health Services in China

Currently, the specific contents of community health services in our country can be summarized

区护士或社区卫生工作者在社区中扮演着关键角色，与居民建立紧密联系，主动满足他们的医疗和健康需求。

3. 全面性　社区卫生服务在中国具有全面性，涵盖了预防、治疗、康复和健康管理等多个领域。它们提供各类基本医疗服务、健康宣教、疾病筛查、计划免疫、妇幼保健、慢性病管理和老年人护理等综合性的卫生服务。

4. 综合性　中国社区卫生服务强调综合性，不仅提供医疗服务，还关注公共卫生、健康教育、疾病预防控制等多个层面。社区卫生服务中心通常整合了医生、护士、公共卫生专家和其他相关专业人员，以提供全方位服务。

5. 连续性　中国社区卫生服务强调连续性，包括持续的监测、随访和治疗，确保居民的健康需求得到持续满足。通过定期巡诊、健康档案管理和健康教育活动，社区卫生服务能够建立起与居民的长期合作关系，提供持续的医疗和健康支持。

6. 可及性　中国社区卫生服务具有可及性，意味着社区居民可以方便地获得所需的医疗和健康服务。社区卫生服务中心通常设在社区附近，提供近距离的医疗保健服务，使居民不需要长途奔波就能获得基本的医疗服务。

（四）我国社区卫生服务内容

当前，我国社区卫生服务具体的内容概括起来即"四大板块""六大功能"。"四大板块"即

as "four major components" and "six major functions." The "four major components" include basic public health services (including management of residents' health records, planned immunization, female health care, child care, health education, chronic disease management, reporting and handling of infectious diseases and emergency public health events, etc.), basic medical services (emergency treatment, general practice medicine, traditional Chinese medicine, dental care, rehabilitation medicine, pediatric care, elderly health, mental health services, etc.), special healthcare services, and assistance for urban impoverished individuals. The "six major functions" refer to prevention, medical care, health care, rehabilitation, health education, and family planning technical services, forming an integrated whole.

1. Conducting health surveys of community residents, establishing health records, and providing contractual health management services for individuals and families.

2. Performing community health diagnosis, formulating intervention plans for major health issues in the community, and carrying out standardized management of non-communicable diseases. Conducting health education and hygiene promotion. Responsible for disease prevention and control and immunization within the community. Utilizing appropriate Chinese and western medicine and technologies to diagnose and treat common and prevalent diseases. Capable of identifying and providing preliminary diagnosis for at least 50 common and prevalent diseases, as well as at least 20 traditional Chinese medicine diseases.

3. Establishing collaborative relationships with large comprehensive hospitals and specialized hospitals in the region, with at least one designated referral hospital. Signing two-way referral agreements and maintaining referral records. Receiving patients transferred from higher-level hospitals during the recovery period.

基本公共卫生服务（包括居民健康档案管理、计划免疫、妇女保健、儿童保健、健康教育、慢病管理、传染病及突发公共卫生事件报告和处理等）、基本医疗服务（急诊急救、全科医疗、中医医疗、口腔医疗、康复医疗、儿科医疗、老年人卫生、心理健康服务等）、特需服务、城市贫困人员救助。"六大功能"即预防、医疗、保健、康复、健康教育、计划生育技术服务"六位一体"。

1. 开展社区居民健康调查，建立健康档案，提供个人与家庭的合同式健康管理服务。

2. 进行社区健康诊断，制订社区主要健康问题的干预计划并开展慢性非传染性疾病的规范管理。开展健康教育和卫生科普宣传。负责社区内传染病防治及计划免疫。运用适宜的中西医药及技术，进行一般常见病、多发病诊疗。至少能够识别和初步诊断50种常见病、多发病，至少能够识别和初步诊治20种中医疾病。

3. 与所在区域内大型综合医院和专科医院建立定点协作关系，至少有1家相对固定的转诊医院，签订双向转诊协议。有转诊记录可查，建立双向转诊制度并落实。接收上级医院下转的疾病恢复期患者。

4. Providing basic medical emergency services and out-of-hospital emergency care. Capable of making preliminary diagnoses and providing emergency treatment for critically ill patients in the circulation system and respiratory system, as well as patients with renal failure, acute poisoning, shock, and other general critical conditions. Able to perform debridement, suturing, hemostasis, bandaging, and simple techniques for bone fixation (such as external splinting).

5. Providing home health services such as home visits, nursing care, and home beds. Offering hospice care services. Providing mental health services and psychological counseling.

6. Providing healthcare services for key populations such as women, children, the elderly, patients with chronic diseases, and disabled individuals.

7. Providing rehabilitation services, including making clear diagnoses and functional assessments for each rehabilitation patient and developing rehabilitation treatment plans. Capable of conducting infrared light therapy, low-frequency pulse electrical therapy, medium-frequency pulse electrical therapy, traditional Chinese medicine treatments, ultrashort wave therapy, microwave therapy, ultrasound therapy, and traction.

8. Conducting family planning counseling, promotion, and appropriate technical services. Responsible for collecting, organizing, statistical analysis, and reporting of information and data related to community health services within the jurisdiction.

9. Establishing a telemedicine collaboration network, equipped with facilities and equipment for telemedicine, and providing telemedicine services. Capable of conducting remote teaching, remote training, and other services.

v. Quality Evaluation of Community Health Services

1. Policy Related to the Quality Evaluation of Community Health Services

The evaluation of community health service

4. 提供基本医疗急诊服务和院外急救。能对循环系统、呼吸系统急危重症患者和肾功能衰竭、急性中毒、休克及一般急危重症患者作出初步诊断和急救处理。能够开展清创、缝合、止血、包扎、简易骨折固定（如夹板外固定等）等急救技术。

5. 提供出诊、护理、家庭病床等家庭卫生服务；开展临终关怀服务；提供精神卫生服务及心理健康咨询服务。

6. 提供妇女、儿童、老年人、慢病患者、残疾人等重点人群保健服务。

7. 提供康复服务，对每个康复患者有明确诊断与功能评估并制订康复治疗计划。能开展红外线治疗、低频脉冲电治疗、中频脉冲电治疗、中医药治疗、超短波治疗、微波治疗、超声波治疗、牵引等。

8. 开展计划生育咨询、宣传及适宜技术服务；负责辖区内社区卫生服务信息资料的收集、整理、统计、分析、上报。

9. 建立远程医疗协作网络，配备远程医疗的设施设备，提供远程医疗服务，能开展远程教学、远程培训等服务。

（五）社区卫生服务的质量评价

1. 社区卫生服务质量评价相关政策

社区卫生服务质量评价是对社区卫生服务

quality is a systematic assessment and monitoring process of community health service institutions, such as rural hospitals and community health centers. Its main purpose is to provide an objective, comprehensive, and scientific evaluation system to measure the quality of community health services and guide improvements and enhancements.

In China, there has been continuous development in the evaluation of community health service quality, with various policies being introduced to enhance the service capacity of primary healthcare institutions. In 2018, the National Health Commission and the National Administration of Traditional Chinese Medicine jointly launched the "quality service to the grassroots" campaign and formulated the *Service Capacity Standards for Rural Hospitals* (*2018 Edition*) and *Service Capacity Standards for Community Health Centers* (*2018 Edition*). Subsequently, in 2019, the National Health Commission further refined the content based on the service capacity standards and developed the *Guidelines for Evaluation of Service Capacity of Rural Hospitals* (*2019 Edition*) and *Guidelines for Evaluation of Service Capacity of Community Health Centers* (*2019 Edition*). In 2022, based on new circumstances and requirements, the National Health Commission revised the 2018 edition of service capacity standards and issued the *Service Capacity Standards for Rural Hospitals* (*2022 Edition*) and *Service Capacity Standards for Community Health Centers* (*2022 Edition*).

Based on this, the Department of Primary Health of the National Health Commission organized relevant industry associations, rural hospitals, community health centers, as well as experts from comprehensive hospitals and specialized hospitals to form revision working groups to revise the 2019 edition of evaluation guidelines, resulting in the *Guidelines for Evaluation of Service Capacity of Rural Hospitals* (*2023 Edition*) and *Guidelines for Evaluation of Service Capacity of Community Health Centers*

机构（如乡镇卫生院、社区卫生服务中心）进行系统性评估和监测的过程。其主要目的是提供一个客观、全面、科学的评价体系，以衡量社区卫生服务的质量水平，并指导改进和提升工作。

我国在社区卫生服务质量评价方面不断发展，相继出台各项政策，持续提升基层医疗卫生机构的服务能力。2018 年，国家卫生健康委与国家中医药局联合启动了"优质服务基层行"活动，并制定了《乡镇卫生院服务能力标准（2018版）》和《社区卫生服务中心服务能力标准（2018版）》。随后，2019 年，国家卫生健康委在服务能力标准的基础上进一步细化内容，编写了《乡镇卫生院服务能力评价指南（2019 版）》和《社区卫生服务中心服务能力评价指南（2019 版）》。2022 年，根据新形势和新要求，国家卫生健康委对 2018 版服务能力标准进行了修订，并印发了《乡镇卫生院服务能力标准（2022 版）》和《社区卫生服务中心服务能力标准（2022 版）》。

在此基础上，国家卫生健康委基层司组织相关行业协会、乡镇卫生院、社区卫生服务中心以及综合医院、专科医院的专家组成修订工作组，对 2019 版评价指南进行修订，形成了《乡镇卫生院服务能力评价指南（2023 版）》和《社区卫生服务中心服务能力评价指南（2023 版）》。这些指南进一步细化了社区卫生服务机构的服务能力标准和评价指标，为实施质量评价提供了具体的操作指导。

(*2023 Edition*). These guidelines further refine the service capacity standards and evaluation indicators of community health service institutions, providing specific operational guidance for quality evaluation.

2. The Importance of Implementing the Quality Evaluation of Community Health Service

The implementation of the quality evaluation of community health service holds significant importance, primarily in the following aspects:

Firstly, it safeguards service quality. Through regular evaluations of community health service institutions, their service quaiity can be monitored and assessed, identifying problems and shortcomings. The feedback from the evaluation results encourages institutions to take timely measures to improve service processes, strengthen personnel training, and enhance equipment and facilities, thereby raising the quality level of community health services.

Secondly, the quality evaluation of community health service can enhance resident satisfaction. Evaluation results objectively reflect residents' satisfaction with community health services. By analyzing the evaluation results, the expectations and needs of residents regarding services can be understood, enabling better fulfillment of residents' health needs through improvements and further enhancing their satisfaction.

Furthermore, the quality evaluation of community health service contributes to optimizing resource allocation. By evaluating the operation and service levels of institutions, the government and relevant departments can gain more accurate understanding of the demand and supply of community health services. Based on the evaluation results, medical resources can be allocated reasonably, providing more appropriate support and guidance to ensure that community health services meet residents' health needs and promote rational resource allocation.

Lastly, the quality evaluation of community

2. 社区卫生服务质量评价实施的重要意义

社区卫生服务质量评价的实施具有重要意义，主要体现在以下几个方面：

首先，它保障服务质量。通过对社区卫生服务机构的定期评价，可以监测和评估其服务质量，发现问题和不足之处。评价结果的反馈可以促使机构及时采取措施，改进服务流程、加强人员培训、完善设备设施等，从而提高社区卫生服务的质量水平。

其次，社区卫生服务质量评价可以提升居民满意度。评价结果能够客观地反映居民对社区卫生服务的满意程度。通过对评价结果的分析，可以了解居民对服务的期望和需求，并在改进中更好地满足居民的健康需求，进一步提高居民的满意度。

再次，社区卫生服务质量评价还有助于优化资源配置。通过评价机构的运行情况和服务水平，政府和相关部门能够更准确地了解社区卫生服务的需求与供给状况。根据评价结果，可以合理调整医疗资源的分配，提供更适宜的支持和指导，确保社区卫生服务能够满足居民的健康需求，并推动资源配置的合理化。

最后，社区卫生服务质量评价促进公平性。

health service promotes fairness. Through analysis of evaluation results, disparities in services among different regions and population groups can be identified, leading to corresponding measures being taken to promote fairness in community health services. Ensuring that everyone has access to equitable and high-quality medical and healthcare services is one of the important goals of the quality evaluation of community health services.

The formulation and implementation of policies related to the quality evaluation of community health service contribute to raising the quality level of community health services, enhancing resident satisfaction, optimizing resource allocation, and promoting fairness in community health services. This will play an active role in building a healthy China and improving the health level of the people.

II. Community Health Policy and Management

Community health policy and management refer to the guiding principles and framework for developing and implementing community health services. It plays a crucial role in safeguarding residents health, improving healthcare quality, promoting public health, and achieving comprehensive health development. Effective community health policies can ensure the rational distribution of community health resources, provide high-quality healthcare services, and promote community participation and overall well-being.

i. China's Community Health Policies

Since 1999, China has consistently promoted and developed community health policies aimed at enhancing, standardizing, and expanding access to community health services in order to meet the growing healthcare needs of the population and advance public health development. The formulation and implementation of these policies reflect the government's commitment to and prioritization of community health. In 1999, the Ministry of Health and 9 other departments

通过评价结果的分析，可以发现不同地区、不同群体之间存在的服务差异，进而采取相应的措施，促进社区卫生服务的公平性。确保每个人都能获得公平、高质量的医疗卫生服务，是社区卫生服务质量评价的重要目标之一。

社区卫生服务质量评价相关政策的制定和实施，有助于提高社区卫生服务的质量水平，增强居民满意度，优化资源配置，并促进社区卫生服务的公平性。这将为构建健康中国，提高人民群众的健康水平发挥积极的推动作用。

二、社区卫生政策与管理

社区卫生政策是制定和实施社区卫生服务的指导方针和框架。它在保障居民健康、提高医疗质量、促进公共健康和实现全面健康发展方面起着关键作用。有效的社区卫生政策能够确保社区卫生资源的合理分配、提供优质的医疗保健服务，并推动社区参与和全员健康。

（一）我国社区卫生政策

我国社区卫生政策自 1999 年以来得到了持续地推进和发展，旨在推动社区卫生服务的提升、规范和普及，以满足人民群众日益增长的健康需求，促进全民健康发展。这一系列政策的制定和实施体现了国家对社区卫生的重视和承诺。1999 年，卫生部等十个部门联合发布了《关于发展城市社区卫生服务的若干意见》，为城市社区卫生服务的发展指明了方向。随后，在 2002 年，卫生部等 11 个部门联合印发了《关于加快发展城市社区卫生服务的意见》，进一步

jointly issued the *Opinions on Developing Urban Community Health Services*, which provided guidance for the development of urban community health services. Subsequently, in 2002, the Ministry of Health and 10 other departments jointly released the *Notice on Accelerating the Development of Urban Community Health Services*, further reinforcing the construction of urban community health services. In 2006, the State Council issued the *Guiding Opinions of the State Council on Developing Urban Community Health Services* to advance urban community health services. That same year, the National Health Commission also issued the *Guiding Opinions on Strengthening the Construction of Urban Community Health Talents* to enhance the development of community health talent pools. In 2010, multiple national ministries jointly published the *Construction Plan for Primary Healthcare Workforce with a Focus on General Practitioners*, further promoting the roles and contributions of general practitioners in community health services. In 2015, the General Office of the State Council issued the *Guiding Opinions of the General Office of the State Council on Promoting the Construction of Grading Diagnosis and Treatment System* to strengthen the implementation of tiered healthcare systems and enhance the capacity of primary healthcare services. Additionally, in the same year, the National Health Commission issued the *Guiding Opinions on Further Standardizing the Management of Community Health Services and Improving Service Quality*, providing guidance and support for the regulation of community health services.From 2018, the National Health Commission has launched initiatives such as the "quality service to the grassroots" campaign and community hospital construction. They have also developed standards including the *Service Capability Standards for Community Health Centers* and *Basic Standards for Community Hospitals*. These standards encompass areas such as facility size, departmental organization,

加强城市社区卫生服务的建设。为进一步推进城市社区卫生服务，2006 年国务院发布了《国务院关于发展城市社区卫生服务的指导意见》。同年，国家卫生健康委还发布了《关于加强城市社区卫生人才队伍建设的指导意见》，以加强社区卫生人才队伍建设。2010 年，国家多个部委共同发布了《以全科医生为重点的基层医疗卫生队伍建设规划》，进一步推动全科医生在社区卫生服务中的角色和作用。2015 年，国务院办公厅发布了《国务院办公厅关于推进分级诊疗制度建设的指导意见》，以加强分级诊疗和提高基层医疗卫生服务能力。同年，国家卫生健康委颁布了《关于进一步规范社区卫生服务管理和提升服务质量的指导意见》，为规范社区卫生服务提供了指导和支持。自 2018 年起，国家卫生健康委相继启动了"优质服务基层行"活动和社区医院建设，并制定了《社区卫生服务中心服务能力标准》和《社区医院基本标准》。这些标准涵盖了社区卫生服务中心的建筑面积、科室设置、设备配置、医疗服务和基本公共卫生服务等内容，以提升社区卫生服务能力和服务质量。2019 年12 月 28 日，第十三届全国人民代表大会常务委员会第十五次会议通过了《中华人民共和国基本医疗卫生与健康促进法》，为我国基本医疗卫生和健康事业的发展提供了法律保障。

equipment allocation, medical services, and basic public health services, all aimed at improving the overall capacity and quality of community health services. On December 28, 2019, the 15th Session of the 13th National People's Congress Standing Committee passed the *Law of the People's Republic of China on Basic Medical and Health Care and the Promotion of Health*, providing legal safeguards for the development of basic healthcare and health promotion in the country.

Furthermore, the *National Basic Public Health Service Specifications* were formulated based on the *Law of the People's Republic of China on Basic Medical and Health Care and the Promotion of Health* and the *Implementation Plan for National Basic Public Health Service Projects*. These specifications aim to provide fundamental, free, and equitable public health services to both urban and rural residents. Since their implementation in 2009, the *National Basic Public Health Service Specifications* has undergone several revisions and improvements to adapt to the evolving needs of public health development in China. The latest edition was released in 2017, featuring updated and optimized service projects as well as newly added initiatives such as mental health services for children and adolescents and family doctor contracting services, thereby further enhancing the comprehensiveness of the public health service system.

The continued refinement and implementation of these policies not only improve the provision of basic healthcare services to community residents, but also enhance the quality and effectiveness of community health services, contributing to the realization of the goal of universal health coverage. The formulation and implementation of community health policies in China provide a crucial foundation for building an inclusive, efficient, and accessible public health system, thereby promoting the enhancement of health outcomes among community residents.

另外,《国家基本公共卫生服务规范》是根据《中华人民共和国基本医疗卫生与健康促进法》和《国家基本公共卫生服务项目实施方案》制定的,旨在为城乡居民提供基本、免费、均等的公共卫生服务。自 2009 年开始实施以来,《国家基本公共卫生服务规范》经过多次修订和完善,以适应我国公共卫生事业发展的需要。最新的规范于 2017 年发布,包括对现有服务项目的更新和优化,以及增加了一些新的服务项目,如儿童青少年心理健康服务、家庭医生签约服务等,进一步完善了公共卫生服务体系。

这些政策的不断完善和落实,不仅为社区居民提供了更好的基本医疗卫生服务,也推动了社区卫生服务质量和效果的提升,有助于实现全民健康目标。我国社区卫生政策的制定和实施,为构建覆盖全民、高效可及的公共卫生体系提供了重要保障,推动了社区居民健康水平的提升。

ii. Key Elements of Community Health Management

1. Planning and Organization Community health management requires systematic planning and organization, including setting goals, formulating policies, developing work plans, and establishing effective management structures. In addition, community health management needs to coordinate cooperation and communication among various departments and stakeholders. Due to the flexible and diverse organizational models of community health services in China, there exist multiple forms of management patterns, including government-managed models, hospital-managed models, enterprise-managed models, and social force-managed models.

2. Human Resources Community health management requires an adequate pool of qualified human resources. This includes general practitioners, nurses, community care workers, as well as management and support staff. Community health management should focus on personnel training, incentive mechanisms, and career development to ensure the stability of human resources and improve service quality.

3. Resource Allocation and Supervision Community health management needs to allocate and manage limited resources, including funds, equipment, and medications, in a rational manner. At the same time, supervision and evaluation are important aspects of community health management, which can ensure transparency, fairness, and effectiveness in resource utilization.

4. Data and Information Management Community health management requires the establishment of sound data and information management systems. This involves collecting and analyzing data related to community health, monitoring and evaluation, and transmitting information to policymakers, decision-makers, and implementers to support decision-making and service improvement.

（二）社区卫生管理的关键要素

1. 规划与组织 社区卫生管理需要进行系统的规划和组织，包括确定目标、制定政策、制订工作计划以及建立有效的管理结构。此外，社区卫生管理还需要协调各个部门和利益相关者之间的合作与沟通。由于我国社区卫生服务的组织模式灵活多样，对应形成了以政府管办的管理模式、医院管办模式、企事业单位管办模式以及社会力量管办模式等多种形式并存的管理格局。

2. 人力资源 社区卫生管理需要具备足够的合格人力资源。这包括全科医生、护士、社区护理人员等专业人员，以及管理人员和支持人员。社区卫生管理应关注人员培训、激励机制和职业发展，以保证人力资源的稳定性和提高服务质量。

3. 资源配置与监督 社区卫生管理需要合理配置和管理有限的资源，包括资金、设备和药物等。同时，监督和评估是社区卫生管理的重要环节，可以确保资源利用的透明度、公平性和效益性。

4. 数据与信息管理 社区卫生管理需要建立健全的数据与信息管理系统。这包括收集和分析社区卫生相关的数据，进行监测和评估，并将信息传递给政策制定者、决策者和实施者，以支持决策和改进服务。

5. Quality and Safety Management

Community health management needs to prioritize quality and safety management to ensure that the healthcare services provided conform to national standards and guidelines. This involves activities such as quality control, clinical pathway management, doctor-patient communication, adverse event reporting, and risk management.

iii. Challenges and Prospects of Community Health Policy and Management

In the process of promoting community health policy and management, there are still challenges to be overcome. These include inadequate resources, uneven service coverage, high personnel mobility, and lower community participation. To address these challenges, it is necessary to strengthen government leadership and commitment, improve the healthcare system and policy environment, and promote collaboration among multiple sectors. In the future, community health policy and management should continue to focus on achieving equitable access, improving service quality, promoting innovative technologies and models to meet evolving population needs and health challenges. Additionally, community health management should closely integrate with the development of information technology to promote digitalized, intelligent, and sustainable community health service models. It is important to enhance research and evaluation efforts. By conducting empirical research, conducting tracking evaluations, and sharing experiences, we can continuously optimize the models and effectiveness of community health services, and promote overall improvement in health levels. Through continuous improvement of community health policy and management, we can establish a healthier, fairer, and more vibrant community health system, provide residents with high-quality healthcare services, and promote the realization of national health and social well-being.

5. 质量与安全管理　社区卫生管理需要注重质量与安全管理，确保提供的医疗保健服务符合国家标准和指南。这涉及质量控制、临床路径管理、医患沟通、不良事件报告和风险管理等方面的工作。

（三）社区卫生政策与管理的挑战和展望

在推动社区卫生政策与管理的过程中，仍然存在一些挑战。这包括资源不足、服务覆盖不均衡、人员流动性高、社区参与度较低等问题。为了克服这些挑战，需要加强政府领导和承诺，改进医疗体制和政策环境，并促进多部门间的协同合作。未来，社区卫生政策与管理应继续关注公平可及、提高服务质量、推广创新技术和模式，以满足不断变化的人口需求和健康挑战。此外，社区卫生管理还应紧密结合信息技术的发展，推动数字化、智能化和可持续发展的社区卫生服务模式，加强相关研究和评估工作。通过开展实证研究、跟踪评估和经验分享，不断优化社区卫生服务的模式和效果，推动整体卫生水平的提升。通过不断完善社区卫生政策与管理，我们可以建立更健康、更公平和更有活力的社区卫生体系，为居民提供优质的医疗保健服务，促进全民健康和社会福祉的实现。

Ⅲ. Family Doctor Contracting Services

Starting in the 1970s, countries such as the UK and Denmark began gradually promoting the family doctor system as an effective health management model nationwide. Currently, more than 50 countries and regions worldwide have implemented family doctor contracting services. In the UK, family doctor contracting services are known as "general medical services contract" and are considered a crucial component of the NHS system. They provide basic, comprehensive, and continuous healthcare services to citizens and legal residents with community-based service points. The United States' "patient-centered medical home" (PCMH) focuses on patient health as the primary goal, with general practitioners leading the way and adopting a multidisciplinary collaborative approach to provide comprehensive and long-term primary healthcare services to patients, maximizing their overall health. In China, family doctor contracting services are centered around people, aiming to maintain and promote overall health, orienting towards residents' health, and targeting families and communities. It integrates various types of medical and healthcare personnel, such as community doctors, village doctors, general practitioners, and public health workers, effectively consolidating grassroots health resources. By signing mutually voluntary healthcare service agreements with residents, it provides a scientific, effective, and reasonable primary healthcare service model for basic preventive care and the diagnosis and treatment of common and prevalent diseases. Due to its fundamental attributes of focusing on residents' health, family units, and community scope, it has become an important means to support the construction of "Healthy China" and achieve comprehensive and lifelong health for the population. In 2009, with the initiation of the new healthcare reform, the family doctor system became one of the goals for the

三、家庭医生签约服务

20 世纪 70 年代开始，英国、丹麦等国家便开始将家庭医生制度作为一种有效的健康管理模式在全国进行逐步推广。目前，全球范围内已有 50 多个国家和地区开展了家庭医生签约服务。在英国，家庭医生签约服务被称为"全科医疗服务合同制"，是英国 NHS 体系中最重要的组成部分，以社区为服务点向国民和合法的常住居民提供基础、综合、持续的医疗保健服务。美国的"以患者为中心的家庭医生模式"是以患者健康为首要目标，以全科医生为主导，采用多学科协作的形式，为患者提供全面且长期的基本医疗服务，以最大限度地促进患者健康。在我国，家庭医生签约服务以人为中心，以维护和促进整体健康为方向，以居民健康为导向，面向家庭和社区，综合社区医生、乡村医生、全科医生、公卫人员等各类医疗卫生人员，有效整合基层卫生资源，通过与居民签订双向自愿的医疗卫生服务协议，为居民提供基本预防保健工作和常见病及多发病诊疗，是一种科学、有效、合理的基层医疗卫生服务模式。因其具有以居民健康为中心、以家庭为单位、以社区为范围的根本属性，成为当前助力我国"健康中国"建设，实现人群全方位全生命周期健康的重要抓手。2009 年，随着新医改拉开帷幕，家庭医生制度成为社区卫生服务发展的工作目标之一。从 2010 年将上海作为首批试点，到 2012 年发展到全国 10 个城市，全国各地陆续开展了家庭医生签约服务。为进一步完善家庭医生签约服务政策措施，推动家庭医生签约服务高质量发展，2018 年国家卫生健康委、中医药局联合印发《关于规范家庭医生签约服务管理的指导意见》，对签约服务提供主体进行了规范。

development of community health services. After Shanghai served as the first pilot city in 2010, family doctor contracting services were gradually expanded to 10 cities nationwide by 2012, and they have been implemented in various parts of the country. In order to further improve policies and measures regarding family doctor contracting services and promote their high-quality development, the National Health Commission and the National Administration of Traditional Chinese Medicine jointly issued the *Guiding Opinions on Regulating the Management of Family Doctor Contracting Services* in 2018. This document provides regulations on the main providers of contracted services.

i. Conditions for the Providers of Family Doctor Contracting Services

Family doctor contracting services are mainly provided by various primary medical and healthcare institutions. Socially-run grassroots medical institutions are encouraged to carry out appropriate contracting services based on their actual situations. According to China's national conditions, the current composition of family doctors mainly includes registered general practitioners (including assistant general practitioners and general practitioners in traditional Chinese medicine) from primary medical and healthcare institutions; qualified physicians from rural hospitals, village doctors, and physicians in traditional Chinese medicine; clinical physicians who are registered and qualified in the field of general practice or have undergone relevant training for general practitioners and choose to practice at multiple primary medical and healthcare institutions; retired clinical physicians with intermediate or higher professional titles who have passed relevant training for general practitioners. A family doctor team should be equipped with at least one family doctor and one nursing staff, and may also include public health physicians (including assistant public health physicians), specialists, pharmacists, health managers, traditional Chinese

（一）家庭医生签约服务提供主体的条件

家庭医生签约服务主要由各类基层医疗卫生机构提供，鼓励社会办基层医疗机构结合实际开展适宜的签约服务。根据我国的国情，现阶段家庭医生组成主要是基层医疗卫生机构注册全科医生（含助理全科医生和中医类别全科医生）；具备能力的乡镇卫生院医师、乡村医生和中医类别医师；执业注册为全科医学专业或经全科医生相关培训合格、选择基层医疗卫生机构开展多点执业的在岗临床医师；经全科医生相关培训合格的中级以上职称退休临床医师。而家庭医生团队至少配备 1 名家庭医生、1 名护理人员，也可根据服务对象的需求增加公共卫生医师（含助理公共卫生医师）、专科医师、药师、健康管理师、中医保健调理师、心理治疗师或心理咨询师、康复治疗师、团队助理、计生专干、社工、义工等。

medicine health therapists, psychological therapist or counselors, rehabilitation therapists, team assistants, family planning workers, social workers, volunteers, etc., according to the needs of the service recipients.

In the UK, primary healthcare mainly refers to general practitioner services, where the entire general practice clinic provides health services to residents in a team format. The team members usually include general practitioners, nurses, receptionists, clinic managers, etc., and the recruitment of these personnel needs to comply with the government's stipulated requirements for staffing. The difference between the UK's general practitioners and those in China is that the general practitioners in the UK are usually the operators of the clinics and are not affiliated with government departments. The government's health department purchases primary healthcare services from general practitioners on behalf of residents and manages the services provided by general practitioners through contracts. In Australia, general practice clinics are an important component of community health services, and in addition to general practitioners, they generally employ receptionists and a small number of nurses.

ii. Contracting Service Recipients

There is not much difference among different countries regarding the contracting services recipients. In China, the main recipients of family doctor contracting services are the permanent residents within the service area of the family doctor team's primary medical and healthcare institution. Cross-regional contracting is also possible. Currently, the key population for family doctor contracting services includes the elderly, pregnant women, children, people with disabilities, impoverished populations, special family members of family planning, as well as patients with conditions such as hypertension, diabetes, tuberculosis, and severe mental disorders.

iii. Contents of Contracting Services

The content of family doctor contracting

英国的初级卫生保健主要是指全科医师服务,整个全科诊所以团队形式为居民提供健康服务。团队成员通常包括全科医师、护士、接待员、诊所经理等,这些人员的聘用需按照政府规定的配备要求来遴选。与我国全科医生的不同之处在于英国的全科医师通常是诊所的经营者,他们不隶属政府部门。政府卫生部门从全科医师那里为居民购买初级保健服务,通过合同的形式对全科医师提供的服务进行管理。在澳大利亚,全科医疗诊所是社区卫生服务的重要组成部分之一,除了全科医生以外,一般还雇有接诊员和少量的护士。

(二)签约服务对象

各个国家签约服务对象的差异性不大,我国家庭医生签约服务对象主要为家庭医生团队所在基层医疗卫生机构服务区域内的常住人口,也可跨区域签约。现阶段,家庭医生签约服务重点人群包括:老年人、孕产妇、儿童、残疾人、贫困人口、计划生育特殊家庭成员以及高血压、糖尿病、结核病和严重精神障碍患者等。

(三)签约服务内容

我国家庭医生签约服务的内容会根据家庭

services in China is developed based on the service capabilities and healthcare resource allocation of the family doctor team, as well as the health needs of the contracted residents. Currently, the available services for contracting include：

(1) Basic medical services, such as diagnosis and treatment of common and prevalent diseases, and rational use of medications.

(2) Public health services, including national basic public health service projects and specified other public health services.

(3) Health management services, including health assessment, development and evaluation of health management plans.

(4) Health education and consultation services, providing personalized health education and consultation to the service recipients through various means.

(5) Priority appointment services, offering priority access to department appointments and regular outpatient services within the institution.

(6) Priority referral services, establishing a green referral channel to connect with secondary and higher-level medical institutions for the service recipients.

(7) Home Visits.

(8) Medicine distribution and medication guidance services.

(9) Long-term prescription services.

(10) Traditional Chinese medicine "preventive treatment of disease" services.

(11) Other tailored healthcare services according to local conditions.

In the UK's general medical services contract model, primary healthcare services mainly include health consultations, family planning, disease prevention, and rehabilitation services. In Australia, the main work of general practice clinics focuses on medical services, including disease diagnosis and management, health consultations, check-ups, prescription issuing, referrals, home visits, as well as collaborating with other healthcare institutions for specialized projects such as chronic

医生团队自身服务能力、医疗卫生资源配置情况以及签约居民的健康需求制定。当前可签约的服务包括：

（1）基本医疗服务，即常见病和多发病的诊疗、合理用药。

（2）公共卫生服务，即国家基本公共卫生服务项目和规定的其他公共卫生服务。

（3）健康管理服务，即开展健康状况的评估及健康管理计划的制订与评价。

（4）健康教育与咨询服务，即采用各种途径为服务对象提供个体化的健康教育和健康咨询。

（5）优先预约服务，即优先提供本机构科室预约、定期门诊等相关服务。

（6）优先转诊服务，即对接二级及以上医疗机构，为服务对象提供绿色转诊通道。

（7）出诊服务。
（8）药品配送与用药指导服务。

（9）长期处方服务。
（10）中医药"治未病"服务。

（11）其他因地制宜的医疗卫生服务。

英国的全科医疗合同制模式下，家庭医疗保健服务主要为健康咨询、计划生育、疾病预防和康复服务。澳大利亚的全科医疗诊所主要工作内容以医疗服务为主，包括：疾病诊断及处置、健康咨询、体检、开处方、转诊、家庭访视以及配合其他卫生机构开展专门项目，如慢性病管理、计划免疫等。美国的家庭医生式服务包括：预防保健服务、全天急诊和全年无休治疗服务、临床护理服务、全科门诊和转诊服务、特需儿童服务，同时医生具有保障患者知情权与保

disease management and planned immunization. In the United States, patient-centered medical home services include preventive healthcare services, 24/7 emergency and ongoing treatment services, clinical care services, general practice outpatient and referral services, specialized children's services, protection of patient rights to informed decision-making, and privacy protection obligations.

iv. Family Doctor Contracting Models

Since the release of the *Guiding Opinions on Promoting Family Doctor Contracting Services* in 2016, various provinces and regions in China have successively issued guiding documents or implementation plans to promote family doctor contracting services. They have also conducted a series of beneficial explorations according to local conditions. Currently, there are four categories of models and five typical models. The four categories of models are the community team service model, medical institution combined contracting model, responsibility system at the township level service model, and village doctor contracting model. The five typical models include the "1+1+1" contracting service model in Shanghai, the "basic package + personalized package" contracting service model in Dafeng District, Yancheng City, Jiangsu Province, "integration of medical care and elderly care" contracting service model in Hangzhou, Zhejiang Province, the "three-in-one" contracting service model in Xiamen, Fujian Province, and the "prepayment based on per capita amount" contracting service model in Dingyuan County and other counties in Anhui Province.

v. Management and Assessment of Family Doctor Contracting Services

Generally, the county or district-level health administrative departments are responsible for assessing the contracting services provided by grassroots medical and healthcare institutions within their jurisdiction. The core indicators for assessment include the number and composition

护患者隐私的义务。

（四）家庭医生签约模式

自 2016 年《关于推进家庭医生签约服务的指导意见》出台，我国各省（区、市）相继印发关于推进家庭医生签约服务的指导性文件或实施方案，并因地制宜地进行了一系列有益探索。目前主要形成了 4 类模式及 5 种典型模式，4 类模式分别为社区团队服务模式、医疗机构组合签约模式、片医负责制服务模式、乡村医生签约模式；而 5 种典型的模式即上海市"1+1+1"签约服务模式、江苏省盐城市大丰区"基础包＋个性包"签约服务模式、浙江省杭州市"医养护一体化"签约服务模式、福建省厦门市"三师共管"签约服务模式、安徽省定远等县"按人头总额预付"签约服务模式。

（五）家庭医生签约服务的管理与考核

一般由县区级卫生健康行政部门对辖区内基层医疗卫生机构签约服务工作实施考核。考核的核心指标包括签约对象数量与构成、服务质量、健康管理效果、签约居民基层就诊比例、居民满意度等。各个地区根据当地的情况也创新了考核的内容与方法，例如上海市浦东新区

of contracted recipients, service quality, health management effectiveness, proportion of primary care visits by contracted residents, and resident satisfaction. Different regions have also innovated in terms of the content and methods of assessment according to local conditions. For example, Tangzhen community health center in Pudong New Area, Shanghai, implements a cumulative points-based assessment and management system for community general practice teams through third-party quality control. The points are divided into three parts: management points, work points, and additional points. In Bao'an District, Shenzhen, the community health center is assessed by relevant higher-level departments once a month, with assessment indicators including medical quality, public health work, nursing quality, execution of medical insurance policies, and daily administrative management. A comprehensive assessment is conducted once a year based on service outcomes, efficiency, and health economics indicators. There are also two "five-rate assessments" conducted each year, which include family doctor contracting rate, coverage rate of contracted family services, chronic disease management rate, appointment outpatient service rate, and community resident satisfaction rate.

IV. Community General Practice Management

Community general practice management is a comprehensive, integrated, and coordinated healthcare service model that plays a significant role in promoting overall health, providing comprehensive healthcare, and coordinating medical resources. Countries and regions around the world are increasingly focusing on the development of community general practice management because it emphasizes comprehensiveness, continuity, and coordination, playing a crucial role in community care and providing residents with continuous, personalized, and high-quality medical services. Good management is a key

唐镇社区卫生服务中心采用第三方质控的方法对社区全科团队实施累加积分制考核管理，积分方法分为管理积分、工作积分、附加积分三部分；深圳市宝安区社区卫生服务中心由上级相关部门每月对家庭医生考核 1 次，考核指标包括医疗质量、公共卫生工作、护理质量、医保执行情况、日常行政管理，并以服务效果、效率及卫生经济学指标为评价量表，每年进行 1 次综合考核，进行 2 次"五率考核"，即家庭医生签约率、签约家庭服务覆盖率、慢性病管理率、预约门诊服务率、社区居民满意率。

四、社区全科医疗管理

社区全科医疗管理是一种全面、综合和协调的医疗服务模式，对促进整体健康、提供综合医疗保健服务和协调医疗资源具有重要意义。各个国家和地区越来越重视社区全科医疗管理的发展，因为它强调综合性、连续性和协调性，在社区护理中发挥着关键作用，并为居民提供持续、个性化和高质量的医疗服务。良好的管理是实现高质量和可持续服务的关键因素。近年来，我国的社区全科医疗管理在协调团队、资源管理、质量控制和教育培训等方面均有所发展。

factor in achieving high-quality and sustainable services. In recent years, China's community general practice management has made progress in team coordination, resource management, quality control, and education and training.

i. Coordinate the Team

With medical advancements and technological innovations, the diversification and interdisciplinary collaboration of healthcare teams have become increasingly important. Globally, community general practice management requires the coordination of different healthcare professionals such as nurses, pharmacists, physiotherapists, etc., to provide comprehensive medical services. Additionally, the ability to coordinate teams is particularly crucial in response to emergency public health events. In recent years, China has increased support for the construction of community general practice teams. The health authorities encourage family doctors to work in synergy with other healthcare professionals such as health managers and physiotherapists, to provide comprehensive healthcare services. The government also promotes the establishment of multidisciplinary medical consortia and the system of family doctor contracting services to integrate and rationalize the use of medical resources.

ii. Resource Management

The unequal distribution and utilization of medical resources is a common challenge faced globally. Some developing countries and impoverished regions suffer from a shortage of medical resources. In such cases, community general practice management needs to pay special attention to the fairness and sustainability of resource management in order to ensure the accessibility and availability of medical services. As the health demands of both urban and rural residents increase, China has been increasing its support for community health centers. The government provides funding and policy support to improve the conditions

（一）协调团队

随着医学进步和技术创新，医疗团队的多元化和跨领域合作变得更为重要。在全球范围内，社区全科医疗管理需要协调不同专业人员（如护士、药师、物理治疗师等）的工作，以提供综合性的医疗服务。此外，在应对突发公共卫生事件时，协调团队的能力尤为关键。中国近年来加大了对社区全科医生团队建设的支持力度。卫生部门鼓励家庭医生与其他医疗专业人员（如健康管理师、物理治疗师等）形成协同工作模式，提供全面的医疗保健服务。政府还推动建立多学科的医联体和家庭医生签约服务制度，以促进医疗资源的整合和合理使用。

（二）资源管理

医疗资源的分布和利用不均是全球范围内面临的共同挑战。一些发展中国家和贫困地区存在医疗资源短缺的问题。在这种情况下，社区全科医疗管理需要特别注重资源管理的公平性和可持续性，以确保医疗服务的普及性和可及性。随着城乡居民健康需求的增加，中国不断加大对社区卫生服务中心的支持力度。政府提供资金和政策支持，改善基层医疗设施条件，并加强医疗设备和药品的供应。同时，推行数字化健康档案和电子处方系统等信息技术手段，优化资源利用效率。自 2010 年国家多部委联合发布《以全科医生为重点的基层医疗卫生队伍建设规划》（发改社会〔2010〕561 号），提出通过多种途径培养全科医生以来，截至 2023 年，每

of primary healthcare facilities, as well as strengthen the supply of medical equipment and medicines. At the same time, digital health records and electronic prescription systems are being implemented to optimize the efficiency of resource utilization. Since the joint release of the *Construction Plan for Primary Healthcare Workforce with a Focus on General Practitioners* by multiple ministries in 2010, the density of general practitioners was 3.99 per 10,000 population, while the density of personnel in specialized public health institutions reached 7.15 per 10,000 population.

iii. Quality Control

Quality control is an essential aspect of community general practice management. Globally, countries are committed to establishing effective quality control mechanisms, such as establishing clinical guidelines, implementing medical quality assessments, and formulating standard operating procedures. Furthermore, there is a focus on leveraging information technology to improve the monitoring and feedback mechanisms for healthcare quality. In China, the health authorities actively promote the establishment of a medical quality and safety management system. Health administrative departments at all levels strengthen their supervision of community healthcare institutions, implement medical quality evaluation and auditing systems, and enhance the quality of primary healthcare services. Additionally, efforts are made to improve healthcare service quality by conducting patient satisfaction surveys and handling complaints. The National Health Commission has issued the *Guidelines for the Evaluation of Service Capacity in Community Health Centers (2019 Edition)* and the *Guidelines for the Evaluation of Service Capacity in Rural Hospitals (2019 Edition)* as blueprints for evaluating the service capacity of primary healthcare institutions. However, there is currently a lack of unified standards and methods for evaluating the clinical quality

万人口全科医生 3.99 人，每万人口专业公共卫生机构人员 7.15 人。

（三）质量控制

质量控制是社区全科医疗管理中不可或缺的一环。全球范围内，各国都致力于建立有效的质量控制机制，如制定临床指南、实施医疗质量评估和制定标准操作规程等，此外，还注重借助信息技术手段改善医疗质量监测和反馈机制。在中国，卫生部门积极推动医疗质量和安全管理体系的建立。各级卫生行政部门加强对社区医疗机构的监管，落实医疗质量评价与审核制度，提高基层医疗服务质量，此外，通过开展患者满意度调查和投诉处理等进一步改善医疗服务质量。国家卫生健康委员会印发了《社区卫生服务中心服务能力评价指南（2019 年版）》《乡镇卫生院服务能力评价指南（2019 年版）》作为基层医疗卫生机构服务能力的评价蓝本。然而，目前国内尚缺乏统一的基层医疗卫生机构全科临床质量管理评价标准和方法。2018 年上海市在全国率先开展了基层医疗卫生机构全科临床质量管理工作，成立了上海市全科医学临床质量控制中心，建立了包括 7 个一级指标（从业基本条件、全科人员配备与岗位职责、全科医疗质量管理、全科医生疾病诊疗能力、全科医生慢性病管理与处置能力、全科医生教育与培养、全科医学教学与科研）、16 个二级指标、55 个三级指标的上海市全科医学临床质量控制标准督查体系。该中心每年开展 2 轮全科临床质控督查，其中至少有 1 轮为针对全市社区卫生服务中心实施的"全覆盖式"全科临床质控督查。

management of primary healthcare institutions at the grassroots level. In 2018, Shanghai took the lead in carrying out comprehensive clinical quality management in primary healthcare institutions nationwide and established the Shanghai General Practice Clinical Quality Control Center. They developed a supervisory system for clinical quality control standards in general practice in Shanghai, which includes 7 primary indicators (such as basic employment conditions, staffing and job responsibilities of general practitioners, management of general practice medical quality, diagnostic and treatment abilities of general practitioners, chronic disease management and disposal abilities of general practitioners, education and training of general practitioners, general practice medical education and research), 16 secondary indicators, and 55 tertiary indicators. The center conducts two rounds of comprehensive clinical quality control inspections each year, with at least one round being a "full-coverage" inspection targeting community health centers across the city.

iv. Education and Training

Continuous education and training of healthcare professionals are crucial for providing high-quality medical care globally. Therefore, community general practice management needs to focus on continually updating the knowledge and skills of healthcare professionals to adapt to new developments in medical science and technology. The Chinese government attaches great importance to the continuing education and training of healthcare professionals, encouraging doctors to participate in professional certification programs and continuing education projects. At the same time, in the process of promoting the cultivation of general practitioners, efforts are made to strengthen the standardization and standardization of general practice medical education, and improve the overall quality and professional skills of general practitioners. The National Health Commission has estab-

（四）教育培训

在全球范围内，医务人员的持续教育和培训对于提供高质量的医疗护理至关重要。因此，社区全科医疗管理需要注重不断更新医务人员的知识和技能，以适应新的医疗科学和技术发展。中国政府高度重视医务人员的继续教育和培训，鼓励医生参加专业认证计划和继续教育项目。同时，在推进全科医生培养的过程中，加强对全科医学教育的规范化和标准化，提高全科医生的整体素质和专业技能。国家卫生健康委员会依据《国务院办公厅关于改革完善全科医生培养与使用激励机制的意见》构建了医学院校教育、毕业后教育、继续教育三阶段有机衔接的"5+3"为主体、"3+2"为补充的全科医学人才培养体系，通过全科专业住院医师规范化培训、助理全科医生培训、定向免费培养、转岗培训等多种途径，加大全科医生培养培训力度，大力发展互联网远程继续教育，普及全科适宜技术，实现全科医生继续医学教育全覆盖。

lished a "5+3" main body with an organic connection between medical school education, postgraduate education, and continuing education, supplemented by a "3+2" model, based on the *Opinions of the General Office of the State Council on Reforming and Improving the Mechanism for Cultivating and Using General Practitioners*. Through various approaches such as standardized training for general practice resident physicians, training for assistant general practitioners, targeted free training, and job transition training, efforts are being made to enhance the training of general practitioners. Internet-based distance continuing education has been developed extensively to promote appropriate technologies for general practice and achieve full coverage of continuing medical education for general practitioners.

Section 3　Community Health Information Management

I. Overview

Community health information management refers to the application of information technology in the management process of community nursing practice, with the aim of improving the quality, efficiency, and overall coordination of medical services. Through digitization, intelligentization, and data-driven approaches, community health information management can promote the rational allocation of medical resources, optimize medical processes, and provide more personalized and continuous care.

i. The Importance of Community Health Information Management

In the rapidly evolving digital age, the application of principles and methods of information management can bring broader development opportunities to community nursing practice and provide residents with more accurate,

第三节　社区健康信息化管理

一、概述

社区健康信息化管理是指将信息技术应用于社区护理实践中的管理过程，旨在提高医疗服务的质量、效率和整体协同性。通过数字化、智能化和数据驱动的方法，社区健康信息化管理可以促进医疗资源的合理配置，优化医疗流程，并提供更加个性化和连续的护理。

（一）社区健康信息化管理的重要性

在当前迅速发展的数字时代，充分应用信息化管理的原则和方法，可以为社区护理实践带来更广阔的发展空间，并为居民提供更加精准、便捷和个性化的医疗护理。社区健康信息化管理的重要性具体体现在以下几个方面：

convenient, and personalized medical care. The importance of community health information management is specifically reflected in the following aspects:

1. Enhancing the Quality of Medical Services

Community health information management utilizes tools such as electronic health records, remote monitoring, and medical decision support systems to improve the accuracy and timeliness of medical services. Healthcare professionals can conveniently access patients' medical history, test results, and medication information, enabling more precise diagnosis and treatment decisions.

2. Optimizing the Allocation of Medical Resources

Community health information management can help healthcare institutions achieve effective resource allocation and utilization. Through statistical analysis and predictive models, managers can understand the relationship between medical demand and resource supply and make informed decisions. This helps to avoid wastage and imbalances in resources, improving the accessibility and fairness of medical resources.

3. Strengthening the Coordination of Health Services

Community health information management promotes the coordination and integration of health services. By establishing electronic health record sharing systems and cross-institutional collaboration platforms, different medical institutions and healthcare professionals can better share patient information, exchange opinions, and work together. This contributes to improving the continuity and coordination of medical services, reducing barriers in information transfer between different institutions for patients.

4. Reinforcing Health Management and Prevention

Community health information management supports the implementation of health management and preventive interventions. By tracking and analyzing large-scale health data, managers can identify population health risks,

1. 提升医疗服务质量　社区健康信息化管理利用电子健康记录、远程监测和医疗决策支持系统等工具，有助于提升医疗服务的准确性和及时性。医务人员可以更便捷地获取患者的医疗历史、检查结果和药物信息，从而做出更精准的诊断与治疗决策。

2. 优化医疗资源配置　社区健康信息化管理可以帮助医疗机构实现资源的有效配置与利用。通过统计分析和预测模型，管理者可以了解医疗需求和资源供给之间的关系，并进行科学决策。这有助于避免资源的浪费和不平衡，提高医疗资源的可及性和公平性。

3. 加强卫生服务协同　社区健康信息化管理可以促进卫生服务的协同与整合。通过建立电子健康档案共享系统、跨机构协作平台等，不同医疗机构和卫生专业人员可以更好地共享患者信息、交流意见，并协同工作。这有助于提高医疗服务的连续性和协调性，减少患者在不同机构之间信息传递的障碍。

4. 强化健康管理和预防　社区健康信息化管理支持健康管理和预防干预的实施。通过追踪和分析大规模的健康数据，管理者可以识别人群健康风险、制订个性化的健康计划，并提供针对性的健康教育和干预措施。这有助于加强健康促进和疾病预防，提高社区居民的整体健

develop personalized health plans, and provide targeted health education and interventions. This helps strengthen health promotion and disease prevention, improving the overall health level of community residents.

II. Community Resident Health Records and Information Management

i. Definition and Purpose of Community Resident Health Records

Community resident health records are systematic documents that record information about residents' health. They serve as important tools for collecting and documenting residents' health information in community health services. Electronic health records for community residents refer to the electronic version of health records formed through basic public health service projects, which provide free basic public health services for urban and rural residents and establish corresponding databases. Community resident health records document the health status of individuals at various stages of life, as well as information related to prevention, health care, medical care, and rehabilitation. They serve as comprehensive, holistic, and continuous health data throughout individuals' lives, including personal basic information, health examination records, health management for key populations, and other health service records. The main purposes of community resident health records are as follows:

1. **Provide Comprehensive Health Information** Community resident health records collect and organize residents' personal basic information, health status assessments, clinical information, results of health assessment tools, high-risk factors and risk assessments, and nursing plans and records. They provide community nursing teams with comprehensive health information about residents, helping them better understand residents' health needs and issues.

康水平。

二、社区居民健康档案与信息化管理

（一）社区居民健康档案的定义和目的

社区居民健康档案是记录有关居民健康信息的系统化文件，它是社区卫生服务工作中收集、记录社区居民健康信息的重要工具。社区居民健康电子档案是指通过基本公共卫生服务项目，免费为城乡居民提供基本公共卫生服务并建立相应数据库而形成的健康档案的电子版。社区居民的健康档案记录了居民一生中各个阶段的健康状况以及预防、保健、医疗、康复这些相关信息，是伴随居民终生的全面、综合、连续的健康资料，包含了个人基本信息、健康体检记录、重点人群健康管理及其他卫生服务记录等内容。其主要目的在于：

1. **提供全面的健康信息** 社区居民健康档案收集并整理了居民的个人基本信息、健康状况评估、临床信息、健康评估工具结果、高危因素和风险评估、护理计划和记录等内容，为社区护理团队提供全面的居民健康信息，帮助他们更好地了解居民的健康需求和问题。

2. Personalized Care Plans and Interventions　By analyzing the data in community resident health records, community nursing teams can develop personalized care plans and take corresponding health education, behavioral interventions, and preventive measures to meet residents' specific health needs and promote health improvement and disease prevention.

3. Monitor and Evaluate Health Status　Community resident health records provide a historical record of residents' health status, which helps community nursing teams conduct ongoing clinical monitoring and evaluation. By tracking and comparing data at different time points, they can detect potential health problems, observe disease progression, and evaluate the effectiveness of interventions. This supports medical decision-making, optimizes resource allocation, and improves the efficiency and quality of medical services.

ii. Applications of Community Resident Health Records

Community resident health records have various applications in practice, and with the development of digital technology, the introduction of electronic health record systems will further enhance the availability and interoperability of health records, providing more convenient and efficient support for community residents' health management and care.

1. Health Risk Assessment and Management　Community nursing teams can identify residents' health risks based on high-risk factors and risk assessment results in community resident health records, and take corresponding interventions such as lifestyle adjustments, vaccination, and screening to reduce health risks and promote disease prevention.

2. Public Health Planning and Policy-making　Community resident health records provide important reference for public health planning and policy-making. By analyzing a large

2. 个性化护理计划和干预　通过分析社区居民健康档案中的数据，社区护理团队能够制订个性化的护理计划，并采取相应的健康教育、行为干预和预防措施，以满足居民的特定健康需求，促进健康改善和疾病预防。

3. 监测和评估健康状态　社区居民健康档案提供了对居民健康状态的历史记录，这有助于社区护理团队进行持续的临床监测和评估。通过跟踪和比较不同时间点的数据，他们可以监测潜在的健康问题、观察疾病进展和评估干预效果，从而支持医疗决策、优化资源配置、提高医疗服务效率和质量。

（二）社区居民健康档案的应用

社区居民健康档案在实际中具有多种应用，且随着数字化技术的发展，电子健康记录系统的引入将进一步提高健康档案的可用性和互通性，从而为社区居民的健康管理和护理提供更加便捷和高效的支持。

1. 健康风险评估和管理　社区护理团队可以根据社区居民健康档案中的高危因素和风险评估结果，识别居民的健康风险，并采取相应的干预措施，如生活方式调整、疫苗接种和筛查等，以降低健康风险并促进疾病预防。

2. 公共卫生规划和政策制定　社区居民健康档案为公共卫生规划和政策制定提供了重要的参考依据。通过分析大量的社区居民健康档案数据，卫生部门和政策制定者可以了

amount of data from community resident health records, health departments and policymakers can understand the health needs, disease burden, and health inequalities of community residents, thus formulating targeted public health measures and policies.

3. Epidemic Monitoring and Prevention
Community resident health records play an important role in epidemic monitoring and prevention. By analyzing the health record data of community residents, high-risk populations can be identified quickly for early intervention and tracking management to control the spread of epidemics.

4. Health Research and Academic Studies
Community resident health records are important sources of data for health research and academic studies. Medical researchers can utilize the data in community resident health records to conduct epidemiological research, health policy evaluations, and nursing practice improvements, promoting the development of community nursing and public health fields.

5. Coordinated and Continuous Care
Community resident health records provide a basis for information sharing and coordination among multiple nursing teams. Different nursing teams can achieve continuity of care and seamless transitions through the information in health records, providing more consistent, coordinated, and personalized nursing services.

Resident health records are an important manifestation of equal access to public health services for residents. They are effective tools for medical and health institutions to provide high-quality medical and health services to residents and serve as references for governments at all levels and health administrative departments to formulate health policies. In 2009, the Ministry of Health issued specific guidelines for standardizing the management of urban and rural resident health records. With the development of informatization, a national basic public health service project

解社区居民的健康需求、疾病负担和健康不平等情况，从而制定有针对性的公共卫生措施和政策。

3. 疫情监测和防控　社区居民健康档案在疫情监测和防控中起着重要作用。通过分析社区居民的健康档案数据，可以快速识别高危人群，并进行早期干预和跟踪管理，以控制疫情的传播。

4. 健康科研和学术研究　社区居民健康档案是进行健康科研和学术研究的重要数据来源。医学研究人员可以利用社区居民健康档案中的数据，开展流行病学研究、健康政策评估和护理实践改进等项目，推动社区护理和公共卫生领域的发展。

5. 协调和连续性护理　社区居民健康档案提供了多个护理团队之间的信息共享和协调基础。不同护理团队可以通过健康档案中的信息，实现连续性护理和无缝衔接，提供更一致、协调和个性化的护理服务。

居民健康档案是居民享有均等化公共卫生服务的重要体现，是医疗卫生机构为居民提供高质量医疗卫生服务的有效工具，是各级政府及卫生行政部门制定卫生政策的参考依据。我国于 2009 年由卫生部针对规范城乡居民健康档案管理印发了具体的指导意见。随着信息化的发展，我国逐步建立了国家基本公共卫生服务项目管理平台，对健康档案等 12 项国家基本公共卫生服务项目的服务规范进行了说明。

management platform has been gradually established, providing specifications for 12 national basic public health service projects, including health records.

iii. Basic Requirements for the Management of Resident Health Records

1. Rural hospitals, village health clinics, and community health centers are responsible for establishing and updating resident health records, while other medical institutions are responsible for timely updating relevant medical information in the health records. The health administrative departments are responsible for the supervision and management of health records.

2. The establishment of health records should follow the principle of voluntary participation, protect personal privacy, and ensure data security.

3. Rural hospitals, village health clinics, and community health centers should establish and update resident health records through various means. Regions with established electronic health records should achieve the aggregation of medical information.

4. A unified coding system should be used for resident health records, adopting a 17-digit coding system based on administrative divisions. Village (neighborhood) committees should be used as units, and residents' identification numbers (such as ID card numbers) should also be used as identification codes.

5. The recorded contents should be complete, accurate, and standardized. Copies of reporting documents, referral records, and consultation records should be retained. Electronic copies of laboratory and examination reports should also be provided to residents.

6. The management requirements should include necessary facilities and equipment. Designated full-time or part-time personnel should be responsible for the management of health records to ensure their integrity and security.

7. Traditional Chinese medicine methods should be applied to provide services to residents,

（三）居民健康档案管理服务的基本要求

1. 乡镇卫生院、村卫生室、社区卫生服务中心负责建立和更新居民健康档案，其他医疗机构负责将相关医疗信息及时更新至健康档案，卫生健康行政部门负责监督与管理健康档案。

2. 健康档案的建立需遵循自愿原则，保护个人隐私，并注意数据安全。

3. 乡镇卫生院、村卫生室、社区卫生服务中心应通过多种方式建立居民健康档案并及时更新信息，已建立电子健康档案的地区应实现医疗信息汇总。

4. 统一为居民健康档案编码，采用17位编码制，以行政区划编码为基础，村（居）委会为单位，同时使用身份证号作为身份识别码。

5. 记录内容应齐全、准确、规范，涉及报告单据和转诊、会诊记录时应保留副本，已电子化的化验和检查报告单据也应提供给居民。

6. 管理要求具备必要设施和设备，指定专（兼）职人员负责健康档案管理，保证档案完整、安全。

7. 应用中医药方法为居民提供服务，并在健康档案中记录相关信息。

and relevant information should be recorded in the health records.

8. Electronic health records should follow national unified data standards and specifications, be interoperable with other medical security systems, and promote the sharing of information for cross-institutional and cross-regional healthcare behaviors.

9. For residents with multiple diseases, follow-up service records can be integrated through electronic health records to avoid repetitive inquiries and data entry.

iv. The Service Targets of Resident Health Records

The service targets of resident health records include permanent residents within the jurisdiction (referring to both registered and non-registered residents who have resided for more than six months). The key focus is on population groups such as children aged 0–6, pregnant women, the elderly, patients with chronic diseases, individuals with severe mental disorders, and patients with pulmonary tuberculosis.

v. The Service Content of Resident Health Records

The community resident health record form includes the resident health record cover, personal basic information form, health examination form, key population health management record form, other medical and health service record form, and resident health information card. The content of the record may vary in different regions according to actual circumstances. The basic content of the resident health record currently includes：

1. **Personal Basic Information Form** It mainly includes demographic information such as name, gender, education level, occupation, marital status, as well as medical expense payment methods, medication allergies, exposure history, past history, family history, genetic disease history, disability status, and living environment.

2. **Health Examination Form** This form is used for annual health examinations of the

8. 电子健康档案要遵循国家统一的数据标准与规范，与其他医疗保障系统相衔接，实现数据互联互通，促进跨机构、跨地域就医行为的信息共享。

9. 对于同一居民患有多种疾病的情况，随访服务记录表可通过电子健康档案实现信息整合，避免重复询问和录入。

（四）居民健康档案服务对象

辖区内常住居民（指居住半年以上的户籍及非户籍居民），以 0~6 岁儿童、孕产妇、老年人、慢性病患者、严重精神障碍患者和肺结核患者等人群为重点。

（五）居民健康档案服务内容

社区居民健康档案表单包括居民健康档案封面、个人基本信息表、健康体检表、重点人群健康管理记录表、其他医疗卫生服务记录表和居民健康信息卡。各个地区可结合实际情况对档案内容进行适当拓展。目前基本的居民健康档案内容如下：

1. **个人基本信息表**　主要包括姓名、性别、文化程度、职业、婚姻等社会人口学资料，此外还有医疗费用支付方式、药物过敏史、暴露史、既往史、家族史、遗传病史、残疾情况以及生活环境。

2. **健康体检表**　该表用于老年人以及高血压、2 型糖尿病和严重精神障碍患者等的年度健

elderly, patients with hypertension, type 2 diabetes, severe mental disorders, etc. It can also be referred to for general residents, but it is not necessary for pulmonary tuberculosis patients, pregnant women, and children aged 0–6. The content includes symptoms, general condition (height, weight, blood pressure, waist circumference, self-assessment of elderly self-care ability, cognitive function of the elderly, emotional status of the elderly, etc.), lifestyle (physical exercise, dietary habits, smoking and alcohol consumption, occupational hazards exposure history, etc.), organ functions (oral cavity, vision, hearing, motor function), physical examination (ocular fundus, skin, sclera, lymph nodes, lungs, heart, abdomen, lower limb edema, dorsal pedis artery pulse, rectal examination, mammary gland, gynecology, etc.), auxiliary examinations (blood routine test, urine routine test, fasting blood glucose, electrocardiogram, liver and kidney function, plasma lipid, chest X-ray, B-ultrasound, cervical smear, etc.), existing major health problems, hospitalization treatment information, major medication information, non-immunization program prophylactic immunization history, health assessment, health guidance, etc.

3. Reception Record Form

This form is used when residents seek consultation or medical and health services for acute or short-term health problems. Its purpose is to truthfully reflect the entire process of residents receiving services based on their specific circumstances. The content includes subjective information of the patient such as chief complaint, consultation questions, and health service requirements; objective information of the patient such as physical examination, laboratory tests, imaging examinations, etc.; assessment, which refers to the preliminary impression, disease diagnosis, or health problem assessment based on the subjective and objective data of the patient; and disposal plan, which includes diagnosis plan, treatment plan, guidance plan, etc., formulated based on the assessment.

康检查。一般居民的健康检查可参考使用,肺结核患者、孕产妇和 0~6 岁儿童无须填写该表。内容包括症状、一般状况(身高、体重、血压、腰围、老年人自理能力自我评估、老年人认知功能、老年人情感状态等)、生活方式(体育锻炼、饮食习惯、吸烟饮酒、职业病危害因素接触史等)、脏器功能(口腔、视力、听力、运动功能)、查体(眼底、皮肤、巩膜、淋巴结、肺、心脏、腹部、下肢水肿、足背动脉搏动、肛门指诊、乳腺、妇科等)、辅助检查(血常规、尿常规、空腹血糖、心电图、肝肾功能、血脂、胸部 X 线、B 超、宫颈涂片等)、现存主要健康问题、住院治疗情况、主要用药情况、非免疫规划预防接种史、健康评价、健康指导等。

3. 接诊记录表　该表供居民在因急性或短期健康问题接受咨询或医疗卫生服务时使用,以能够如实反映居民接受服务的全过程为目的,根据居民接受服务的具体情况填写。内容包括就诊者的主观资料,如主诉、咨询问题和卫生服务要求等;就诊者的客观资料,如查体、实验室检查、影像检查等结果;评估,即根据就诊者的主、客观资料作出的初步印象、疾病诊断或健康问题评估;处置计划,即在评估基础上制订的处置计划,包括诊断计划、治疗计划、指导计划等。

4. **Consultation Record Form** This form is used when residents receive consultation services. The content includes: reasons for consultation, where the responsible doctor fills in the main situation of the patient's consultation needs; consultation opinions, where the responsible doctor fills in the main disposition and guidance opinions of the consulting doctor; consulting doctor and their affiliated medical and health institutions fill in the name of the institution and sign the name of the consulting doctor. If there are multiple consulting doctors from the same medical and health institution, the institution name can be filled once, and then the names can be signed sequentially on the same line.

5. **Two-way Referral Form** It includes the referral-out and referral-back forms. The referral-out form is used when residents need to be referred out in a two-way referral, and it is filled out by the referring doctor. The content includes preliminary impressions, the major present illness history at the time of referral, and the main past medical history. The referral-back form is used when residents need to be referred back in a two-way referral, also filled out by the referring doctor. The content includes major examination results, treatment progress, and rehabilitation suggestions.

6. **Resident Health Record Information Card** The specific content should be consistent with the corresponding items in the health record. It also includes the name of the filing institution and information related to the responsible doctor or nurse.

vi. The Establishment of Resident Health Records

The establishment of resident health records can be done through various methods, which depend on the healthcare management system and practices in different regions. The main methods include:

(1) When residents seek services at rural hospitals, village health clinics, and community health centers/stations, healthcare professionals are

4. **会诊记录表** 该表供居民在接受会诊服务时使用。内容包括：会诊原因，责任医生填写患者需会诊的主要情况；会诊意见，责任医生填写会诊医生的主要处置、指导意见；会诊医生及其所在医疗卫生机构填写其机构名称并签署会诊医生姓名，来自同一医疗卫生机构的会诊医生可以只填写一次机构名称，然后在同一行依次签署姓名。

5. **双向转诊单** 包括转出和回转。转出单供居民在双向转诊转出时使用，由转诊医生填写，内容包括：初步印象，即转诊医生根据患者病情做出的初步判断；主要现病史，即患者转诊时存在的主要临床问题；主要既往史，即患者既往存在的主要疾病史；治疗经过。回转单供居民在双向转诊回转时使用，由转诊医生填写，内容包括：主要检查结果、治疗经过和康复建议。

6. **居民健康档案信息卡** 具体内容应与健康档案对应项目的填写内容一致。此外还包括建档机构名称、责任医生或护士相关信息。

（六）居民健康档案建立方式及流程

居民健康档案的建立方式可以有多种，具体选择取决于各个地区的卫生管理制度和实践情况。主要方式包括：

（1）辖区居民到乡镇卫生院、村卫生室、社区卫生服务中心（站）接受服务时，由医务人员负责为其建立居民健康档案。

responsible for establishing resident health records for them.

(2) Through household visits/surveys, disease screenings, health check-ups, etc., healthcare professionals organized by rural hospitals, village health clinics, and community health centers/stations establish health records for residents.

(3) When residents sign up with a designated family doctor, the family doctor team from the community health service organization establishes electronic health records for residents who have not yet had one.

To keep up with the digitization of health records, many places have started to digitalize resident health records. This has enriched the methods of record establishment. For example, in Shanghai, they utilize smart health stations, Health Cloud APP and other information technology platforms that operate based on national requirements to guide residents in self-establishing records. The relevant information of electronic health records is then perfected in the management system backend.

vii. The Management and Use of Resident Health Records

When registered residents revisit rural hospitals, village health clinics, and community health centers/stations for follow-up visits, the attending doctor should update and supplement the corresponding medical records in a timely manner based on the condition of the follow-up visit. The termination reasons for resident health records include death, relocation, loss of contact, etc., and the dates should be recorded. For those who have moved out of the jurisdiction, basic information about their destination and records of transferring the health records should also be documented. Health record management should have necessary facilities and equipment for storage, and the health records should be properly preserved in accordance with requirements such as anti-theft, sun protection, high temperature resistance, fire prevention, anti-moisture, anti-dust, anti-rodent,

（2）通过入户服务（调查）、疾病筛查、健康体检等多种方式，由乡镇卫生院、村卫生室、社区卫生服务中心（站）组织医务人员为居民建立健康档案。

（3）在居民签约家庭医生时，由社区卫生服务机构家庭医生团队对尚未建档的居民建立电子健康档案。

为了紧跟健康档案信息化的脚步，各地逐步开始将居民健康档案电子化，同样，也丰富了健康档案建立的方式。例如上海地区利用智慧健康驿站、健康云 APP 等依据国家相关建档要求规范运行的信息化载体，引导居民自助建档，并在管理后台完善电子健康档案相关信息。

（七）居民健康档案的管理与使用

已建档居民在乡镇卫生院、村卫生室、社区卫生服务中心（站）复诊时，由接诊医生根据复诊情况，及时更新、补充相应记录内容。居民健康档案的终止缘由包括死亡、迁出、失访等，均需记录日期。对于迁出辖区的情况还要记录迁往地点的基本情况、档案交接记录等。健康档案管理要具有必需的档案保管设施设备，按照防盗、防晒、防高温、防火、防潮、防尘、防鼠和防虫等要求妥善保管健康档案，指定专（兼）职人员负责健康档案管理工作，保证健康档案完整、安全。电子健康档案也应有专（兼）职人员维护。

and anti-insect. Designated full-time or part-time personnel should be responsible for health record management to ensure the integrity and security of the health records. Electronic health records should also be maintained by dedicated personnel.

During the establishment, improvement, development of information systems, and the entire process of information transmission of electronic health records, national unified data standards and specifications should be followed. At the same time, the information system of electronic health records should be connected with the new rural cooperative medical system, urban basic medical insurance, and other medical security systems, gradually realizing the interoperability of health management data, medical information, and data among various medical and health institutions, thereby achieving information sharing for residents' cross-institutional and cross-regional healthcare behaviors. In addition, in terms of clarifying the content of opening electronic health records to individuals, including personal basic information, health examination information, records of key population health management, and other medical and health service records, they should be opened to individuals based on their informed consent and in accordance with laws and regulations. In order to increase the participation and trust of the public in the system, it is encouraged to integrate functions such as appointment registration, online health assessment, online query of test results, and medication guidance based on local conditions.

III. Community Health Service Information Systems and Community Health Management

Community health service information systems and community health management are important components of modern healthcare systems. With the continuous growth in health demands from community residents and the

电子健康档案在建立和完善、信息系统开发以及信息传输全过程中，应遵循国家统一的相关数据标准与规范。同时，电子健康档案信息系统应与新农合、城镇基本医疗保险等医疗保障系统相衔接，逐步实现健康管理数据、医疗信息以及各医疗卫生机构之间的数据互联互通，从而实现居民跨机构、跨地域就医行为的信息共享。此外，在明确电子健康档案向个人开放的内容方面，包括个人基本信息、健康体检信息、重点人群健康管理记录和其他医疗卫生服务记录，都应在本人或者其监护人知情同意的基础上依法依规向个人开放。为了提高群众对该系统的参与度和信任感，可以鼓励结合本地实际情况，整合预约挂号、在线健康状况评估、检验结果在线查询、用药指导等功能。

三、社区卫生服务信息系统与社区健康管理

社区卫生服务信息系统与社区健康管理是现代社会医疗保健体系中的重要组成部分。随着社区居民对健康需求的不断增长和医疗技术的不断发展，建立一个高效、全面的信息系统以及实施科学的社区健康管理变得尤为重要。

advancement of medical technology, establishing an efficient and comprehensive information system, as well as implementing scientific community health management, has become particularly important.

i. Basic Concepts

1. **Community Health Service Information System**　The community health service information system, as a product of the digital era, integrates medical resources, personal health data, and information communication technology within the community. It enables functions such as information sharing between doctors and patients, appointment registration, and electronic medical record management. It not only improves the efficiency and quality of health services but also strengthens communication and interaction between community residents and healthcare professionals. Additionally, this system facilitates comprehensive assessment and management of the health status of community residents, enabling precise medical services.

2. **Community Health Management**　Community health management focuses on disease prevention and health promotion. Through measures such as systematic health assessments, regular physical examinations, and personalized health guidance, it provides comprehensive health management services. Community health management emphasizes the overall health of community residents and aims to prevent and control diseases effectively by maintaining health records, conducting health education, and promoting healthy lifestyles. This management model can meet the diverse health needs of individuals while providing targeted allocation of medical resources for healthcare institutions.

ii. Community Health Service Information System and Community Health Management

1. **System Architecture and Basic Modules**　The architecture of the community health service information system can be divided into the front end, back end, and data

（一）基本概念

1. **社区卫生服务信息系统**　社区卫生服务信息系统作为数字化时代的产物，通过整合社区内的医疗资源、个人健康数据和信息通信技术，实现了医患间信息共享、预约挂号、电子病历管理等功能。它不仅提高了卫生服务效率和质量，也加强了社区居民与医务人员之间的沟通和互动。同时，该系统还有助于对社区居民的健康状况进行全面评估和管理，实现精准化的医疗服务。

2. **社区健康管理**　社区健康管理以疾病预防和健康促进为核心，通过系统的健康评估、定期体检和个性化健康指导等措施，提供全方位的健康管理服务。社区健康管理着眼于社区居民的整体健康，通过维护健康档案、开展健康宣教和推广健康生活方式，有效预防和控制疾病的发生。这种管理模式既能满足不同个体的健康需求，又能为卫生服务机构提供有针对性的医疗资源配置。

（二）社区卫生服务信息系统与社区健康管理

1. **系统架构和基本模块**　社区卫生服务信息系统的架构可以分为前端、后端和数据层。前端包括用户界面和移动应用程序，方便居民进行预约挂号、查询报告等操作。后端主要负

layer. The front end includes user interfaces and mobile applications that enable residents to make appointments, access reports, and perform other operations. The back end is responsible for processing user requests and providing corresponding services, including doctor-patient communication and health education. The data layer is the core of the system, encompassing personal health records, disease databases, medical institution information, and other data. The basic modules of the community health service information system in community health management generally include, but are not limited to, the following aspects:

(1) Personal Health Record Management: Records basic information, medical history, allergy history, physical examination results, etc., of community residents, supporting dynamic updates and queries.

(2) Appointment Registration System: Residents can make online appointments for doctor consultations, examinations, or surgeries, avoiding waiting times.

(3) General Practitioner Diagnosis and Treatment System: Community doctors use electronic medical record-based systems to assist in diagnosing and treating patients.

(4) Community Nurse Workstation: Manages daily nursing work and patient care information.

(5) Doctor-patient Communication Platform: Provides online consultation, doctor inquiries, medication consultations, etc., facilitating communication between residents and healthcare professionals.

(6) Electronic Medical Record Management: Stores and manages patient medical records in electronic form, making it convenient for doctors to view and diagnose.

(7) Health Education and Promotion: Provides a rich knowledge base on health education and records and evaluates the effectiveness of health education for specific individuals or groups, helping residents understand how to improve their

责处理用户请求并提供相应服务，包括医患沟通、健康教育等功能。数据层是系统的核心，涵盖个人健康档案、疾病数据库、医疗机构信息等数据。社区卫生服务信息系统在社区健康管理中的基本模块一般包括但不限于以下几个方面：

（1）个人健康档案管理：记录社区居民的基本信息、疾病史、过敏史、体检结果等，支持动态更新和查询。

（2）预约挂号系统：居民可以通过系统在线预约医生门诊、检查或手术，避免排队等待时间。

（3）全科诊疗系统：基于电子病历的社区医生工作站系统，用于辅助医生进行病情诊断和治疗。

（4）社区护士工作站：用于管理日常护理工作和患者护理信息。

（5）医患沟通平台：提供线上问诊、医生咨询、药品咨询等功能，方便居民与医务人员进行交流。

（6）电子病历管理：将患者的病历信息以电子形式存储和管理，方便医生查看和诊断。

（7）健康教育与宣传：提供一个丰富的健康教育知识库，能够对特定个体或群体进行健康教育的记录以及效果评估，帮助居民了解如何改善自己的健康状况；为居民制订健康处方，通过系统制订健康教育计划、组织、培训、宣传、督

health conditions. It includes developing health prescriptions for residents and providing content such as health education plans, organization, training, promotion, and supervision through the system to offer health knowledge, preventive measures, and promotional activities to community residents.

(8) Fee Management System: Manages the financial income and expenses of community health service institutions, including medical expenses, medication costs, etc.

(9) Two-way Referral Platform System: Facilitates information exchange between community health service institutions and higher-level hospitals, streamlining the referral process and enabling efficient and high-quality medical services for patients across different levels of healthcare institutions.

(10) Immunization Administration Information System: It includes functions such as prophylactic immunization process management, information management, risk control, queue management, and user-friendly services . It can provide functions such as recipient file query management, detailed outpatient vaccination records, outpatient vaccination statistical reports, vaccination rate statistics, appointment record management, appointment expiration queries, and queries for recipients who should have been vaccinated but haven't.

2. Data Collection and Management The community health service information system requires the collection and management of a large amount of personal health data. Data collection can be done through residents' self-reporting, doctors' input, or uploading from physical examination institutions, and other methods. At the same time, the system needs to establish a sound data management mechanism, including provisions for data privacy protection, secure storage, and appropriate use. The *Service Capacity Standards for Community Health Centers (2022 Edition)* puts forward relevant regulations

导等内容,向社区居民提供健康知识、预防措施和推广活动等内容。

(8) 收费管理系统:用于管理社区卫生服务机构的财务收支,包括医疗费用、药品费用等。

(9) 双向转诊平台系统:实现社区卫生服务机构与上级医院之间的信息互通,简化转诊流程,便于患者在不同层级医疗机构间的转诊,提高转诊效率和医疗服务质量。

(10) 免疫接种管理信息系统:包括预防接种流程管理、信息管理、风险控制、排队管理以及人性化服务等功能。能够提供受种者档案查询管理、门诊接种情况明细、门诊接种统计报表、接种率统计、预约记录管理、预约过期查询、受种者应种未种查询等功能。

2. **数据采集和管理**　社区卫生服务信息系统需要收集和管理大量的个人健康数据。数据采集可以通过居民自主填写、医生录入、体检机构上传等方式进行。同时,系统需要建立健全的数据管理机制,包括数据隐私保护、安全存储和合理使用等方面的规定。《社区卫生服务中心服务能力标准(2022 版)》中提出了保障社区卫生服务中心信息系统建设、管理和信息资源共享的相关制度。2018 年,国家卫生健康委印发《国家健康医疗大数据标准、安全和服务管理办法(试行)》,建立关键信息基础设施认定规则。2020 年,国家卫生健康委、国家中医药管理局联合制定并印发了《全国公共卫生信息化建设标

to ensure the construction, management, and sharing of information resources in community health center information systems. In 2018, the National Health Commission issued the *National Standards, Security, and Service Management Measures for Health and Medical Big Data* (*Trial Edition*), establishing rules for the recognition of key information infrastructure. In 2020, the National Health Commission and the National Administration of Traditional Chinese Medicine jointly formulated and issued the *National Standards and Specifications for Public Health Informatization Construction* (*Trial Edition*), which also includes requirements for the construction and use of electronic health records and family doctor contracting service management information systems.

BOX 2-2 Learning More

"Shanghai Health Cloud"

The "Shanghai Health Cloud" serves as a successful case of the "Internet + Health" model and an integrated chronic disease management platform under the concept of "medical and preventive integration." It has been widely promoted in various communities throughout Shanghai. This platform focuses on chronic diseases such as hypertension, diabetes, and stroke, providing targeted services including early screening, signing contracts for medical records, community primary consultations, and accurate referrals. On the one hand, advanced screening and testing equipment deployed at the grassroots level enables the identification and reporting of high-risk individuals in a timely manner. On the other hand, innovative health management models accurately match patient cases with community doctors, allowing many chronic disease patients to receive professional diagnosis and treatment advice without leaving their homes, relieving pressure on secondary and tertiary hospitals. Additionally, the backend system connects with the "Health

准与规范（试行）》，对电子健康档案和家庭医生签约服务管理信息系统的建设与使用也提出了若干要求。

BOX 2-2 知识拓展

"上海健康云"

"上海健康云"作为"互联网＋健康"模式和"医防融合"慢性病管理服务平台的成功案例，在上海全市各个社区全面推广。该平台以高血压、糖尿病、脑卒中等慢性病为重点，针对性提供早期筛查、签约建档、社区首诊、精准转诊等服务。一方面，通过布点在基层的先进筛查检测设备，在第一时间发现并上报高危人群；另一方面，创新健康管理模式，精准匹配病例和社区医生，让很多慢性病患者足不出户得到专业诊治意见，为二、三级医院构建起"减压阀"。此外，其后台的病历和就诊数据可通过上海市卫生健康委员会建成的"健康信息网"连接来自申康医联平台 38 家三甲医院 51 个院区的数据、16 个区的区域卫生信息平台和市公共卫生服务平台。截至 2020 年，其注册居民账户达 2 334 万，注册平台医护数达 78 408 人；累计上传 2 643 万人次体征电子数据、182.44 万人次异常人群信息，用于临床参考和慢性病随访依据，形成了超大单一体量及全面的医疗卫生信息平台。自 2015 年 10 月上线，截至 2020 年 8 月，通过"上海健康云"提供的糖尿病早发现和并发症筛查（包括糖网筛查）信息化服务，已查出糖尿病前

Information Network" established by the Shanghai Municipal Health Commission, incorporating data from 38 tertiary hospitals across 51 campuses through the Shanghai health link platform, as well as regional health information platforms and the municipal public health service platform from all 16 districts. As of 2020, there were 23.34 million registered resident accounts and 78,408 registered healthcare professionals on the platform. A total of 26.43 million sets of electronic health data have been uploaded, along with 1.824,4 million pieces of abnormal population information used for clinical reference and follow-up of chronic diseases. Thus, a large-scale and comprehensive medical and health information platform has been established. Since its launch in October 2015, up until August 2020, the "Shanghai Health Cloud" has provided information technology services for early detection and screening of diabetes (including retinopathy screening), resulting in the identification of 45,200 prediabetic individuals and 39,700 diagnosed diabetics. Furthermore, it has screened 159,600 individuals for complications.

iii. Advantages and Challenges of Community Health Service Information System and Community Health Management

The promotion and application prospects of the community health service information system and community health management are very broad, with potential advantages and development opportunities in the following aspects：

1. Improving Efficiency and Quality of Health Services　The application of the community health service information system can achieve rational allocation and collaborative work of medical resources, reduce residents' waiting times for medical consultations, and improve the efficiency of healthcare services. Additionally, through data collection and analysis, the system can help doctors better understand residents' health conditions, leading to more accurate diagnoses and treatments and overall improvement in healthcare quality.

期 4.52 万人、糖尿病患者 3.97 万人，筛查出并发症病变患者 15.96 万人。

（三）社区卫生服务信息系统与社区健康管理的优势与挑战

社区卫生服务信息系统与社区健康管理的推广和应用前景非常广阔，具有以下几个方面的潜在优势和发展机遇：

1. 提升卫生服务效率与质量　社区卫生服务信息系统的应用可以实现医疗资源的合理配置和协同工作，减少居民看病排队时间，提高医疗服务效率。同时，通过数据采集和分析，系统能够帮助医生更好地了解居民的健康状况，进行精确诊断和治疗，提升医疗质量。

2. Promoting Health Management and Disease Prevention Community health management is an important component of the community health service information system Through measures such as systematic health assessments, regular check-ups, and personalized health guidance, it is possible to identify and intervene in chronic disease risk factors in a timely manner, provide targeted health management services, effectively prevent and control diseases, and promote the overall health of residents.

3. Enhancing Doctor-patient Communication and Interaction The community health service information system provides a convenient platform for doctor-patient communication, making communication between doctors and patients more smooth and efficient. Patients can consult doctors online, make appointments, access reports, etc., reducing time and energy wastage. Moreover, doctors can provide personalized health education and guidance to patients through the system, enhancing trust and interaction between doctors and patients.

4. Promoting Public Health and Epidemic Prevention and Control The community health service information system plays a crucial role in public health emergencies and epidemic prevention and control. Through the system, the health status and vaccination records of community residents can be monitored in real-time, enabling prompt identification and isolation of patients to prevent disease transmission. Additionally, the system can rapidly disseminate epidemic information, health education directives, etc., improving the emergency response capabilities of community residents.

5. Strengthening Data Analysis and Scientific Research The community health service information system accumulates a wealth of personal health data and clinical data, providing a solid foundation for data analysis and scientific research. By mining and analyzing these data, risk factors, trends, and influencing factors of diseases

2. 促进健康管理与疾病预防 社区健康管理是社区卫生服务信息系统的重要组成部分。通过系统的健康评估、定期体检和个性化健康指导等措施，可以及时发现和干预慢性病风险因素，提供针对性的健康管理服务，有效预防和控制疾病的发生，促进居民的整体健康。

3. 强化医患沟通与互动 社区卫生服务信息系统提供便捷的医患沟通平台，使医生和患者之间的沟通更加流畅和高效。患者可以通过系统在线咨询医生、预约挂号、查询报告等，减少时间和精力上的浪费。同时，医生可以通过系统向患者提供个性化的健康教育和指导，增强医患之间的信任和互动。

4. 促进公共卫生与疫情防控 社区卫生服务信息系统在公共卫生事件和疫情防控中发挥重要作用。通过系统，可实时监测社区居民的健康状态、接种记录等，及时发现并隔离患者，阻止疾病传播。此外，系统还能够快速发布疫情信息、健康宣教等内容，提高社区居民的应急反应能力。

5. 强化数据分析和科学研究 社区卫生服务信息系统积累了大量的个人健康数据和临床数据，为数据分析和科学研究提供了坚实基础。通过对这些数据的挖掘和分析，可以揭示疾病的风险因素、流行趋势和影响因素，为公共卫生政策的制定和医疗资源的优化提供科学依据。

can be revealed, providing scientific evidence for the formulation of public health policies and optimization of medical resources.

However, to achieve comprehensive promotion and application of the community health service information system and community health management, some challenges need to be overcome. These challenges include data privacy protection, information technology infrastructure development, and integration of healthcare resources. To address these challenges, it is necessary to strengthen the formulation and promotion of relevant policies, improve the legal framework, and enhance technical capabilities while training healthcare professionals in information technology. This will ensure the security and feasibility of the system. By leveraging information technology, a more intelligent and more refined healthcare service system can be built, promoting the healthy development of community residents and fostering the robust growth of public health endeavors.

(Wu Fan)

然而,要实现社区卫生服务信息系统与社区健康管理的全面推广和应用,仍须克服一些挑战,包括数据隐私保护、信息技术基础设施建设、医疗资源整合等问题。因此,需要加强相关政策的制定和推动,完善法律法规体系,同时提高技术能力和培训医务人员的信息化水平,以确保系统的安全性和可行性。通过信息技术的应用,构建更加智能化、精细化的卫生服务体系,促进社区居民的健康发展,推动全民健康事业的蓬勃发展。

(吴　凡)

Key Points

1. The community health service system is a comprehensive service system that caters to the holistic needs of community residents, encompassing various forms of services such as prevention, treatment, and rehabilitation. Common operational models include family doctor contracting services and community general practice management.

2. Global health strategy refers to the policy framework and action plan developed by international organizations, countries, or regions with the objective of promoting global health and improving the health status of populations worldwide.

3. Chinese community health services possess characteristics of public welfare, proactiveness, comprehensiveness, integration, continuity, and accessibility.

内 容 摘 要

1. 社区卫生服务体系是满足社区居民健康需求的全面服务系统,包括预防、治疗、康复等多种服务形式,其中常见的运行模式有家庭医生签约服务和社区全科医疗管理。

2. 全球健康战略是指国际组织、国家或地区制定的旨在促进全球卫生和改善全球居民健康水平的政策框架和行动计划。

3. 中国社区卫生服务具有公益性、主动性、全面性、综合性、连续性、可及性等特点。

4. Community health policies serve as guiding principles and frameworks for the development and implementation of community health services, playing a critical role in safeguarding residents' health, improving medical quality, promoting public health, and achieving comprehensive health development.

5. Key elements of community health management encompass planning and organization, human resources, resource allocation and oversight, data and information management, as well as quality and safety assurance.

6. Family doctor contracting services are predominantly provided by diverse grassroots medical and health institutions, fostering the encouragement of socially-run grassroots medical institutions to undertake appropriate contract services based on their specific circumstances.

7. Community general practice management represents a comprehensive, integrated, and coordinated healthcare delivery model that holds significant significance in promoting overall health, providing comprehensive medical care, and coordinating healthcare resources.

8. Community health information management entails the application of information technology in the management processes of community nursing practice, aimed at enhancing the quality, efficiency, and overall coordination of medical services.

9. The ever-growing healthcare demands and continual advancements in medical technology have accelerated the pace of establishing an efficient and comprehensive information system, as well as implementing scientifically-driven community health management.

— Exercises —

1. Mr. Wang and his wife, Mrs. Zhang, went to the community health center to establish a family health record. Dr. Liu and Nurse Li from the community health center conducted relevant examinations and information inquiries for Mr.

4. 社区卫生政策是制定和实施社区卫生服务的指导方针和框架。它在保障居民健康、提高医疗质量、促进公共健康和实现全面健康发展方面起着关键作用。

5. 社区卫生管理的关键要素包括规划与组织、人力资源、资源配置与监督、数据与信息管理、质量与安全管理。

6. 家庭医生签约服务主要由各类基层医疗卫生机构提供，鼓励社会办基层医疗机构结合实际开展适宜的签约服务。

7. 社区全科医疗管理是一种全面、综合和协调的医疗服务模式，对促进整体健康、提供综合医疗保健和协调医疗资源具有重要意义。

8. 社区健康信息化管理是指将信息技术应用于社区护理实践中的管理过程，旨在提高医疗服务的质量、效率和整体协同性。

9. 健康需求的不断增长和医疗技术的不断发展，加速了建立一个高效、全面的信息系统以及实施科学的社区健康管理的步伐。

— 思 考 题 —

1. 王某和妻子张某到社区卫生服务中心建立家庭档案，社区卫生服务中心的刘医生和李护士对王某进行相关检查和信息询问。获取的信息为：王某，男，36 岁，小学语文教师，体温36.5℃，脉搏 90 次 /min，血压 152/98mmHg，身

Wang. The collected information is as follows: Mr. Wang, male, 36 years old, elementary school Chinese teacher; temperature 36.5℃, pulse 90 beats/min, blood pressure 152/98mmHg, height 165cm, weight 86kg, history of hypertension for 2 years, fasting blood glucose 5.2mmol/L, drinking history for 5 years, smoking history for 5 years; Mrs. Zhang, 32 years old, freelancer, temperature 36.4℃, pulse 80 beats/min, blood pressure 122/76mmHg, height 155cm, weight 50kg, pregnant for 3 months.

(1) What information needs to be filled out to establish individual health records for Mr. Wang and Mrs. Zhang?

(2) As a staff member of the community health center, how would you manage the health issues of this family?

2. Mr. Liu is a retired elderly man. Recently, the community health center in his neighborhood has actively launched family doctor contracting services. Mr. Liu is very curious about this initiative but still has some questions regarding the specific services and benefits, hoping to receive further information. After understanding the family doctor contracting service, please answer the following questions:

(1) What specific services can Mr. Liu obtain after signing the family doctor service contract? Please list at least five services and briefly explain the significance of each service.

(2) What are the advantages of signing the family doctor service contract?

高 165cm，体重 86kg，高血压史 2 年，空腹血糖 5.2mmol/L，饮酒史 5 年，吸烟史 5 年；张某，32 岁，自由职业，体温 36.4℃，脉搏 80 次 /min，血压 122/76mmHg，身高 155cm，体重 50kg，受孕 3 个月。

（1）对王某和张某建立个人健康档案，分别需要填写哪些内容？

（2）作为社区卫生服务中心的工作人员，你将如何管理该家庭成员的健康问题？

2. 刘大爷是一位退休老人，近期他居住小区的社区卫生服务中心积极开展家庭医生签约服务活动。刘大爷对此活动充满好奇，但他对具体的服务内容和优势仍存在一些疑问，希望能得到进一步的信息。在了解了家庭医生签约服务后，请回答以下问题：

（1）签约家庭医生服务后，刘大爷可以获得哪些具体的服务内容？请列举至少五项服务，并简要说明每项服务的意义。

（2）签约家庭医生服务的优势是什么？

Chapter 3

Community Health Promotion and Health Education

第三章

社区健康促进和健康教育

NURSING

03章 数字内容

2. Implement individualized health education according to the characteristics of different places.

Quality Objectives

1. In the practice of health promotion and health education, fully consider the interests of nursing objects and their families.

2. Have a holistic nursing perspective in health promotion and health education practice.

3. Establish a concept of cost-effectiveness in the practice of health promotion and health education.

A report of health diagnosis for community A in a certain city shows that the community is livable, with a well-developed environment and rich resources. The community includes kindergartens, primary schools, and secondary schools. The proportion of adolescents in the community is about 40%. However, a survey has found that the overall myopia rate among children and adolescents in this community is 52%. Therefore, the community plans to launch a special program of health education for the prevention of vision deterioration among adolescents.

Questions：

1. How to carry out community health education based on the nursing process?

2. What should be paid attention to when conducting health education for community populations?

Section 1   Overview

I. Relevant Concepts

i. Health Promotion

The World Health Organization states that the health promotion involves extensive societal and environmental interventions aimed at empowering

---

2．能根据不同场所的特点实施针对性的健康教育。

素质目标

1．在健康促进和健康教育实践中充分考虑护理对象及家属利益。

2．在健康促进和健康教育实践中具备整体护理观。

3．在健康促进和健康教育实践中树立成本经济效益理念。

某市 A 社区的卫生诊断报告显示，A 社区环境宜居、社区资源完善，辖区内覆盖了幼儿园、小学、中学等丰富的教育资源，社区居民中青少年比例约 40%。但经调查发现该社区儿童青少年总体近视率为 52%。因此，社区拟开展一项针对青少年预防视力下降的健康教育专项工作。

请思考：

1．如何基于护理程序开展社区健康教育？

2．在针对社区人群开展健康教育时应该注意什么？

第一节　概　　述

一、相关概念

（一）健康促进

WHO 指出健康促进是通过广泛的社会和环境干预措施，使人们能够增强对自身健康的控制，不仅仅是治疗和治愈疾病，还旨在通过解

individuals to take control of their own health. It is not merely about treating and curing diseases，but also aims to address health problems and prevent the emergence of their root causes，and aims at benefiting and protecting individuals' health and quality of life.

ii. Health Education

According to the definition of the World Health Organization, health education is a planned process that aims at providing learners with scientific health information, fostering a healthy concept, acquiring health - related skills, and empowering individuals with the motivation, skills, and confidence to improve their health status. It helps them make healthy decisions and effectively adopt healthy lifestyle behaviors.

iii. Health Literacy

The World Health Organization defines health literacy as a cognitive and social skill which determines an individual's ability to gain access to, understand, evaluate, and communicate information as a way of promoting and maintaining good health throughout the life course in various health contexts.

iv. Community Health Promotion

Community health promotion involves multi-sectoral cooperation and community participation to empower communities and their residents, helping them improve their ability of health management and enhancing their well-being. It focuses on addressing the root causes affecting residents' health, improving social and environmental conditions to create a healthy community living environment.

v. Community Health Education

Community health education refers to various promotional, educational, and intervention activities conducted at the community level to improve residents' health knowledge and awareness, and cultivate healthy behaviors. It covers the following aspects：

1. Health Knowledge Dissemination

Including knowledge on disease prevention,

决健康问题和预防健康问题产生的根本原因，从而保护个人健康和提升生活质量。

（二）健康教育

WHO 指出健康教育是有计划地为学习者提供科学的健康信息、树立健康观念，帮助其掌握健康技能，同时赋予个人提升健康的动机、技能和信心，帮助他们做出有益健康的决定并有效地执行健康生活方式行为的过程。

（三）健康素养

WHO 将健康素养定义为一种决定人们能够获取、理解、评价和传达信息，并在不同健康背景下促进和维护全生命周期健康的认知和社会技能。

（四）社区健康促进

社区健康促进是指通过多部门合作和社区参与，赋权社区及其居民，帮助他们提高对健康的控制能力，增进居民的健康和福祉。社区健康促进注重解决影响居民健康的根本原因，改善社会和环境条件，以创建健康的社区生活环境。

（五）社区健康教育

社区健康教育通常是指在社区层面开展的各种宣传、教育和干预活动，旨在丰富社区居民的健康知识，增强健康意识，培养健康行为。它涵盖以下几个方面：

1. **健康知识传播** 包括疾病预防、营养、心理健康、妇幼保健等方面的知识。

nutrition, mental health, maternal and child health care.

2. Promotion of Healthy Lifestyles

Promoting a balanced diet, regular exercise, smoking cessation, moderate alcohol consumption, and mental balance.

3. Disease Prevention and Management

Providing health management, consultation, and screening services for chronic and common diseases.

4. Community Engagement and Empowerment

Organizing community activities to increase residents' participation and self-management abilities.

II. Relationship of Health Promotion and Health Education

In terms of concepts, health promotion encompasses health education. Health education is a crucial strategy and method within health promotion. It is integrated into all aspects of health promotion process. Health education and health promotion cannot be separated from each other. However, there are some differences between health education and health promotion.

Health promotion encompasses broader strategies including policy-making, empowerment, and creating supportive environments to enhance overall health. It involves multi-sectoral collaboration, community participation, policy advocacy, and social mobilization. It often uses a holistic approach, emphasizing engagement, empowerment, and systemic change in the community. It often results in enhancing community capacity, reducing health disparities, and improving sustainable health through systemic changes.

Health education focuses on imparting knowledge and raising health awareness among community members. It often uses educational campaigns, lectures, and informational materials to disseminate health knowledge. It is information-centered and one-way communication. It aims

2. 健康生活方式推广　宣传平衡膳食、规律运动、戒烟限酒、心理平衡等。

3. 疾病预防与管理　针对慢性病和常见疾病提供健康管理、咨询和筛查服务。

4. 社区参与和赋权　通过组织社区活动，提高居民参与和自我管理能力。

二、健康促进和健康教育的关系

从概念上来看，健康促进包括了健康教育。健康教育是健康促进的重要策略和方法之一，融合在健康促进的各个环节之中。健康教育不能脱离健康促进，健康促进也不能离开健康教育。但两者也存在着一定的区别。

健康促进包括更广泛的策略，如政策制定、赋权和创建支持性环境，以提升整体健康水平。它涉及多部门合作、社区参与、政策倡导和社会动员。它采用整体方法，强调社区参与、赋权和系统性改变，往往能增强社区能力，减少健康差异，通过系统性改革实现可持续的健康改善。

健康教育侧重于向社区成员传授知识和增强健康意识。它经常通过教育活动、讲座和宣传材料进行健康知识的传播。它以信息为中心，通常为单向交流，旨在增加知识，往往能提高健康素养和个人决策能力。

at increasing knowledge and improving health literacy and personal decision-making.

Ⅲ. Key Elements of Health Promotion

1. Good Governance for Health

Health promotion requires policy makers across all government departments to make health as a central element of government policy. This means they must cooperate health factors into all the decisions they made, and prioritize policies that prevent people from becoming ill and protect them from injuries. These policies must be supported by regulations that match private sector incentives with public health goals. For example, by aligning tax policies on unhealthy or harmful products (e.g. ethanol, tobacco, and food products which are high in salt, sugars and fat) with measures to boost trade in other areas, and through legislation, supporting healthy urbanization by creating walkable cities, reducing air and water pollution, and enforcing the wearing of seat belts and helmets.

2. Health Literacy

People need to acquire the knowledge, skills and information to make healthy choices, such as the food they eat and healthcare services that they need. They need to have opportunities to make those choices. And they need to be assured of an environment in which people can take further actions to further improve their health.

3. Healthy City

A healthy city is the basis of a healthy country and a healthy world. Cities have a key role in promoting good health. Strong leadership and commitment at the municipal level is essential to healthy urban planning and to implement preventive measures in communities and primary health care facilities.

Ⅳ. Core Domains of Health Promotion

In 2022, WHO identifies eight core areas for an effective system of health promotion:

1. Organizational Structures: Embracing

三、健康促进的关键要素

1. 健康的良好治理 健康促进需要各政府部门的决策者将健康作为政府政策的核心内容，这意味着他们必须将健康因素纳入他们做出的所有决策，并优先考虑那些可以预防人们生病并保护他们免受伤害的政策。这些政策必须得到法规的支持，以使私营部门的激励与公共卫生目标相匹配。例如，通过将对不健康或有害产品（如乙醇、烟草和高盐、高糖、高脂肪食品）的税收政策与其他领域的贸易促进措施相结合，并通过立法，创建适宜步行的城市，减少空气和水污染，强制佩戴安全带和头盔，从而支持健康城市化的进程。

2. 健康素养 人们需要获得知识、技能和信息以作出健康选择，例如他们所吃的食物和所需的医疗保健服务。他们需要有机会作出这些选择。他们需要确保有一个环境，在这个环境中，人们可以采取进一步的正确行动，以进一步改善他们的健康状况。

3. 健康城市 健康城市是健康国家和健康世界的基础。城市在促进良好的健康方面发挥关键作用。市政一级强有力的领导和承诺对于健康城市规划和在社区、基层医疗卫生机构落实建立预防措施至关重要。

四、健康促进的核心领域

WHO（2022年）指出一个高效的健康促进系统应该具有的8个核心领域：

1. **组织结构** 包括机构的健康促进能力、

institutional capacity for health promotion, programming and service delivery structures, and emergency response systems.

2. Labor Force　Including human resources and their health-promotion competencies, training and development, and professional associations.

3. Information and Knowledge Development　Including the role of health-promotion information, monitoring (e.g. public health reporting and evaluation system), research, knowledge development infrastructure, and media in health promotion.

4. Technology and Innovation　Including digital health and social innovations, social media platforms and digital resources.

5. People-centred and Co-production of Health　Including engagement and mobilization of citizens, mobile populations and immigrants, and shared decision-making and user experiences.

6. Partnerships　Including formal and informal partnerships, joint ventures, and public-private partnerships.

7. Financial Resources　Including the generation of financial resources and resource allocation (e.g. through tax and treasury, insurance and donations).

8. Governance and Leadership　Including global governance for health, and the governance of whole government (ministry, province, city, district and county).

V. The Relationship Between Behavioral Lifestyle and Health

A healthy behavioral lifestyle refers to behaviors by individuals or groups in their daily lives that are beneficial to their own health and the health of others. The occurrence of diseases is often closely related to unhealthy behavioral lifestyles. Changing unhealthy lifestyles is an important way to prevent diseases and improve the quality of healthy life. Medicine is not the only way to deal with health threats. A healthy behavioral lifestyle

规划和提供服务结构以及应急响应系统。

2．**劳动力**　包括人力资源及其健康促进能力、培训和发展以及专业协会。

3．**信息和知识发展**　包括健康促进信息、监测（如公共卫生报告和评价系统）、研究和知识基础设施以及媒体在健康促进中的作用。

4．**技术和创新**　包括数字健康和社会创新、社交媒体平台和数字资源。

5．**以人为中心和健康的共同创造**　包括公民、流动人群和移民的参与、动员以及共享决策和用户体验。

6．**伙伴关系**　包括正式和非正式伙伴关系、合资企业和公私伙伴关系。

7．**财政资源**　包括财政资源的生成和资源分配（如通过税收和财政、保险和捐赠）。

8．**治理和领导**　包括全球健康治理、整个政府（部、省、市、区、县）的健康治理。

五、行为生活方式与健康

健康的行为生活方式指个体或群体在日常生活中表现为有利于自身和他人健康的行为。疾病的发生常与不良行为生活方式息息相关，改变不良行为生活方式是预防疾病发生和提高健康生活质量的重要途径。药物不是应对健康威胁的唯一方法，健康的行为生活方式成为应对健康威胁的有益手段。WHO建议保持健康的生活方式，应多吃水果和蔬菜，减少脂肪、糖和盐的摄入，并进行体育锻炼。人们可通过体

is a beneficial approach to counter health threats. WHO recommends keeping a healthy lifestyle by eating more fruit and vegetables, reducing the intake of fats, sugars and salts, as well as engaging in physical exercise. People can assess their health status by checking whether they are overweight by using the body mass index (BMI).

i. Impact of Unhealthy Behavioral Lifestyle on Chronic Disease

According to data from WHO in 2023, approximately 41 million people worldwide die prematurely each year due to chronic diseases. Unhealthy behavioral lifestyles, such as poor dietary habits, lack of physical activity, exposure to tobacco smoke, and excessive alcohol consumption, are major risk factors for chronic diseases among children, adults, or the elderly. These risk factors lead to metabolic risk changes such as elevated blood pressure, elevated blood glucose, elevated plasma lipids, and obesity, thereby increasing the incidence of cardiovascular diseases, which is the leading cause of premature deaths due to chronic diseases. Tobacco accounts for over 8 million deaths every year (including from the effects of exposure to second-hand smoke); 1.8 million annual deaths have been attributed to excess salt/sodium intake; more than half of the 3 million annual deaths attributable to alcohol use are from NCDs; 830,000 deaths annually can be attributed to insufficient physical activity.

ii. Impacts of Healthy Behavioral Lifestyle on Chronic Diseases

Global lifestyle changes, rapid urbanization and population aging have further exacerbated the burden of chronic diseases. Adjusting lifestyles is an effective strategy for preventing chronic diseases and improving public health, such as maintaining a balanced diet, regular exercise, adequate rest and sleep, quitting smoking, and restricting alcohol consumption. Among these strategies, exercise and diet have been demonstrated to be most closely related to the control of chronic diseases.

重指数（BMI）检查是否超重，从而评估他们的健康状况。

（一）不健康的行为生活方式对慢性病的影响

WHO 2023 年的数据显示，全球每年约有 4 100 万人因慢性病而过早死亡。不健康的行为生活方式，如不良饮食习惯、缺乏体育锻炼、接触烟草烟雾和过度饮酒，是儿童、成人或老年人患慢性病的主要风险因素。这些风险因素导致血压升高、血糖升高、血脂升高和肥胖等代谢风险变化，从而增加心血管疾病的发生，成为慢性病导致过早死亡的主要原因。每年有超过 800 万人因吸烟（包括二手烟的影响）而死亡；高盐/钠摄入每年导致约 180 万人死亡；每年因饮酒导致的 300 万死亡人数中，超过一半与非传染性疾病有关；每年因缺乏足够体育活动而死亡的人数达到 83 万。

（二）健康的行为生活方式对慢性病的影响

全球的生活方式变化、快速的城市化进程以及人口老龄化，进一步加剧了慢性病的负担。调整生活方式是预防慢性病和提高公共健康水平的有效策略，如维持合理膳食、规律运动、充足的休息与睡眠、戒烟和限酒等。其中，运动和饮食被证实与慢性病控制的相关性最密切。

1. Benefits of Regular Physical Activity

(1) Reduce Risk of Common Chronic Diseases: Physical activity can reduce the risk of cardiovascular diseases, diabetes, and osteoporosis. It is also helpful to control weight and promote mental health.

(2) Help Adolescents Avoid Risky Behaviors: Physical activities help children and adolescents build confidence and enhance skills and then help them avoid risky behaviors such as smoking and excessive drinking.

(3) Enhance Work and Learning Effectiveness: Regular physical activity can improve working efficiency, reduce rates of absenteeism and turnover among workers, and improve students' academic performance.

(4) Promote Development of Community: Participation in physical activities can strengthen social networks and cultural identity. It has a positive impact on the community by promoting social interaction and a sense of solidarity.

2. Benefits of a Balanced Diet

(1) Enhance Immunity and Healthy Development: Vitamins and minerals in the food are crucial for boosting immunity and healthy development.

(2) Prevent Common Non-communicable Diseases: A healthy diet is helpful to prevent various non-communicable diseases (e.g. obesity, diabetes, cardiovascular diseases, specific type of cancer, and bone diseases) as well as maintain a proper weight.

(3) Helpful of Emotion: Dietary diversity has a benefit for emotion.

BOX 3-1　Learning More

Suggestions of Healthy Diet

1. Eat a nutritious diet based on a variety of foods mainly from plants, rather than animals.

2. Eat bread, whole grains, pasta, rice or potatoes several times per day.

3. Eat a variety of vegetables and fruits, at least 400g per day. Preferably, choose fresh and

1. 规律身体活动的益处

（1）降低常见慢性疾病风险：身体活动可以降低心血管疾病、糖尿病和骨质疏松症的风险，有助于控制体重并促进心理健康。

（2）帮助青少年避免危险行为：身体活动帮助儿童和青少年增强自信和提高能力，从而有助于他们避免危险行为，如吸烟与酗酒等。

（3）增强工作和学习效果：定期的身体活动可以提高工作效果，降低工人的缺勤率和离职率，也能提升学生的学习成绩。

（4）促进社区发展：参与身体活动能加强社交网络和文化认同。它通过促进社会互动和团结意识，对社区产生积极影响。

2. 均衡饮食的益处

（1）增强免疫力和促进健康发育：食物中的维生素和矿物质对于增强免疫力和健康发育至关重要。

（2）预防常见非传染性疾病：健康的饮食有助于预防多种非传染性疾病，如肥胖症、糖尿病、心血管疾病、特定类型的癌症和骨骼疾病，并且有助于维持合理体重。

（3）有益于情感：饮食多样性可以带来情感上的益处。

BOX 3-1　知识拓展

健康饮食建议

1. 进食各种主要来自植物而非动物的营养食物。

2. 每天吃几次面包、全谷物、意大利面、米饭或土豆。

3. 每天吃几次多样化的、至少400g的蔬菜和水果，尤其是新鲜的和当地的。

local food.

4. Maintain body weight between the recommended limits (a BMI of 18.5–25kg/m^2) by taking moderate to vigorous levels of physical activity, preferably daily.

5. Control fat intake, not more than 30% of daily energy, and replace most saturated fats with unsaturated fats.

6. Replace fatty meat and meat products with beans, legumes, lentils, fish, poultry or lean meat.

7. Eat milk and dairy products that are low in both fat and salt.

8. Select foods that are low in sugar, and eat free sugars sparingly, limiting the frequency of sugary drinks and sweets.

9. Choose a low-salt diet. Total salt intake should not be more than 5g per day, including the salt in bread and processed, cured and preserved foods.

10. WHO does not set particular limits for alcohol consumption, but the evidence shows that the ideal solution for health is not to drink at all, therefore less is better.

11. Prepare food in safe and hygienic ways such as steaming, baking, boiling or microwaving to help reduce the amount of added fat.

12. Promote exclusive breastfeeding up at least 6 months old, and the introduction of safe and adequate dietary supplements from the age of about 6 months. Promote the continuation of breastfeeding during the first 2 years of life.

Section 2 Theories Related to Community Health Promotion and Community Health Education

I. Knowledge, Attitude, and Practice Model

i. Main Content

The knowledge, attitude, and practice (KAP)

4．通过进行中度至剧烈的身体活动，最好每天一次，保持体重在推荐的范围（BMI 为 18.5~25kg/m^2）。

5．控制脂肪摄入量，不超过每日能量的 30%，并用不饱和脂肪代替大多数饱和脂肪。

6．用豆类、扁豆、鱼、家禽或瘦肉代替肥肉和肉制品。

7．食用低脂和低盐的牛奶和乳制品。

8．选择低糖食物，少吃添加糖，限制进食含糖饮料和甜食的频率。

9．选择低盐饮食。每天盐的总摄入量不应超过 5g，包括面包和加工、熏制及腌制食品中的盐。

10．WHO 没有对饮酒量设定具体的限制量。但有证据表明，理想的有利于健康的方案是完全不喝酒，因此饮酒量越少越好。

11．以安全、卫生的方式准备食物，如蒸、烘烤、煮或微波加热，以帮助减少脂肪的添加量。

12．提倡纯母乳喂养至 6 个月，并从 6 个月时开始引入安全和充足的辅食。提倡在出生后两年继续母乳喂养。

第二节　社区健康促进及健康教育相关理论

一、知信行模式

（一）主要内容

知信行（knowledge，attitude，and practice，

model explains how personal knowledge and beliefs affect health behavior change. Essentially, it is the application of cognitive theory in health education. "K" means knowledge. It is the basis for establishment of positive and correct beliefs and attitudes, and then to change health-related behaviors. "A" means attitudes and beliefs. It's a motivator for behavior change. "P" means practice which is the goal of behavior changes. It is the process of promoting healthy behaviors and eliminating harmful behaviors.

ii. Application Status

The application of the KAP model in community nursing has achieved significant success, particularly in health education, nursing management, continuing education for the nursing staff, and nursing students. This model enhances the knowledge levels of patients and the nursing staff, strengthens health beliefs, and ultimately changes health behaviors. It has been widely applied in chronic disease management, nursing risk management, and nursing education. Studies have demonstrated that intervention measures based on KAP model can effectively improve patients' health behaviors and quality of life, while enhancing the professional standards and quality of care of nursing staff.

iii. Limitation

Transforming knowledge into behavior change is a complex process influenced by many factors. Taking smoking cessation as an example, public health departments promote knowledge about the hazards of tobacco to help the public understand the impact of smoking on health and motivate smokers to change their behaviors. However, achieving behavior change requires the establishment of beliefs and the attitude changes. In this process, many factors can lead to the failure of behavior formation or change, which highlights the limitation of the KAP model.

1. Knowledge is not a Sufficient Condition　Although knowledge is the foundation of behavior change, it alone is not

KAP）模式解释了个人知识和信念如何影响健康行为改变，其实质上是认知理论在健康教育中的应用。"知"是指知识，是建立积极正确的信念与态度，进而改变健康相关行为的基础。"信"是指信念和态度，是行为改变的动力。"行"是指行动，是行为改变的目标，是促进健康行为、消除危害健康行为的过程。

（二）应用现状

知信行模式在社区护理中的应用取得了显著成效，特别是在健康教育、护理管理、护理人员继续教育及护理学生的教学方面。该模式通过提升患者和护理人员的知识水平，增强健康信念，最终改变健康行为。目前已经广泛应用于慢性病管理、护理风险管理和护理教育等领域。研究表明，基于 KAP 模式的干预措施能够有效改善患者的健康行为和生活质量，同时提高护理人员的专业水平和护理质量。

（三）局限性

从知识转化到行为改变是一个复杂的过程，有许多因素会影响这一转变。以戒烟为例，公共卫生部门推广烟草危害的知识，帮助公众理解吸烟对健康的影响，并激发吸烟者改变行为的意愿。然而，要实现行为改变，还需经过信念的确立和态度的转变。在这一过程中，众多因素都有可能导致行为形成或改变的失败，这也就体现了知信行模式的局限性。

1. 知识并非充分条件　尽管知识是行为改变的基础，但仅有知识不足以促使行为转变。人们即使了解健康知识，也仍可能因各种原因

enough to induce behavior change. Even if people understand health knowledge, they may still fail to implement behavior changes due to various reasons.

2. Individual Differences   Each person's acceptance of knowledge and information, comprehension ability, psychological state, and cultural background varies, which affects the process of transforming knowledge into behavior.

3. Environmental Factors   Social support, economic conditions, policies, and regulations are external factors that can influence an individual's ability to change behavior. For example, smokers find it more challenging to change their smoking behavior in the absence of a smoke-free environment and support systems.

4. Effectiveness of Information Dissemination   The methods and effectiveness of information dissemination can also affect the possibility of behavior change. If the channels of information dissemination are blocked, or if the content of the information does not resonate with the audience, the effectiveness of knowledge transmission will be greatly reduced.

II. Health Belief Model

i. Main Content

The health belief model (HBM) was proposed by social scientists at United States Department of Health and Human Services in the 1950s. It was designed to understand why people failed to adopt disease prevention strategies or screening tests for early disease detection. HBM was later used to examine patients' responses to symptoms and their adherence to prescribed medical treatments. HBM indicates that one's belief in the personal threat of illness and belief in the effectiveness of recommended health behaviors or actions can predict the likelihood of their engaging in that behavior. The HBM is rooted in psychological and behavioral theory, based on two main components of health-related behavior：

(1) The desire to avoid illness, or the desire

而未能落实到行为改变上。

2. 个体差异   每个人对知识和信息的接受度、理解能力、心理状态、文化背景等都不同，这些差异会影响知识转化为行为的过程。

3. 环境因素   社会支持、经济状况、政策法规等外部环境因素也会影响个体行为改变的可能性。例如，吸烟者在缺乏禁烟环境和支持系统的情况下，更难以改变吸烟行为。

4. 信息传播的效果   信息传播的方式和效果也会影响行为改变的可能性。如果信息传播渠道不畅，或者信息内容不能引起受众共鸣，那么知识传播的效果将大打折扣。

二、健康信念模式

（一）主要内容

健康信念模型（health belief model，HBM）由美国公共卫生服务局的社会科学家于 20 世纪 50 年代提出，旨在了解人们为什么没有采用疾病预防策略或筛查来早期发现疾病。之后，HBM 用于检测患者对症状的反应和对处方药物治疗的依从性。HBM 表明，一个人对个人疾病威胁的信念，以及对推荐的健康行为或行动有效性的信念，可以用来预测他们采取该行为的可能性。HBM 以心理学和行为理论为基础，基于健康相关行为的 2 个主要部分：

（1）避免疾病的愿望，或者如果已经生病，

to get well if already ill.

(2) The belief that a specific health action will prevent or cure illness.

Ultimately, HPM model assumes that the process of an individual's actions often depends on the perception of the benefits and barriers associated with the health behavior.

The HBM comprises six constructs. The first four were developed as the original tenets of the HBM, while the last two were added as research on the HBM evolved.

1. Perceived Susceptibility　This refers to a person's subjective perception of disease risk. There is wide variation in a person's feelings of personal vulnerability to an illness or disease.

2. Perceived Severity　This refers to a personal perception of the severity of the symptoms or illness. The perception of the severity of illness varies greatly from person to person. People often considers medical consequences (e.g. death, disability) and social consequences (e.g. family life, social relationships) when evaluating the severity of a disease.

3. Perceived Benefits of Action　This refers to a person's perception of the effectiveness of various actions available to reduce the risk of disease or to cure disease. The action a person takes in preventing or curing disease relies on consideration and evaluation of both perceived susceptibility and benefit. People will accept the recommended health action if it is perceived as beneficial.

4. Perceived Barriers of Action　This refers to an individual's perception of the obstacles faced in performing recommended healthy behaviors. There is wide variation in a person's perception of these barriers, because this perception involves a trade-off between cost and benefit. The person weighs the effectiveness of the actions against the situations that they may be expensive, dangerous (e.g. side effects), unpleasant (e.g. painful), time-consuming or inconvenient.

希望康复的愿望。

（2）相信特定的健康行动将预防或治愈疾病。

归根结底，HBM 认为个人的行动过程通常取决于个人对与健康行为相关的益处和障碍的看法。

HBM 包括 6 个部分，前 4 个部分是基于 HBM 最初的原则建立，后 2 个是随着 HBM 的研究发展而增加的。

1. **感知易感性**　指个体对疾病风险的主观感知。个体对疾病易感性的感受存在较大的差异。

2. **感知严重性**　指个体对不适症状或疾病严重性的感知。不同人对疾病严重性的感知存在很大差异。人们在评估疾病的严重性时，通常会考虑医疗后果（如死亡、残疾）和社会后果（如家庭生活、社交关系）。

3. **感知益处**　指个体对采取各种措施减少疾病风险或疾病治愈有效性的感知。个体在预防或治疗疾病上所采取的行动取决于人们对易感性和感知益处的考虑和评估。如果感受到益处，人们就会接受被建议的健康行动。

4. **感知障碍**　指个体在实施推荐的健康行为时，对面临障碍的感知。因涉及成本与效益的权衡，不同人对这些障碍的感知差异很大。个人需要权衡行动的有效性，以及行动可能产生的昂贵费用、危险（如副作用）、感觉不适（如痛苦）、耗时或不便等情况。

5. Cues to Action   This is the stimulus needed to trigger the decision-making process of accepting recommended health behavior. These cues can be internal (e.g. chest pains, wheezing, etc.) or external (e.g. advice from others, illness of family members, newspaper articles, etc.).

6. Self-efficacy   This refers to an individual's level of confidence in ability to successfully perform behaviors. The application of self-efficacy in practice has two levels. One is general self-efficacy, which refers to an individual's general self-efficacy in coping with various challenges or facing new situations. The other is specific self-efficacy, which means confidence in specific health behaviors. Self-efficacy is a construct in many behavioral theories because it directly influences a person's performance of the desired behavior.

The HBM also accepts that socio-demographic factors and the individual's knowledge about diseases and health have impacts on the occurrence and maintenance of health behaviors. The socio-demographic factors include an individual's social and physiological characteristics, such as gender, age, personality traits, socioeconomic status, peer influence. The attitudes and extent to which individuals adopt healthy behaviors vary significantly based on gender, age, personality traits, and living environment. In general, people with health knowledge are more likely to adopt healthy behaviors.

ii. Application Status

The health belief model (HBM) is a theoretical framework used to explain and predict health behaviors. It is widely applied in community nursing to help design and implement effective health promotion and disease prevention programs.

1. Health Education and Behavior Change   HBM is extensively used in health education programs to raise community residents' awareness of health issues and promote behavior change.

2. Chronic Disease Management   In

5. 行为线索   这是触发接受推荐健康行为决策过程所需的刺激。这些线索可以是内部的（如胸痛、喘息等），或是外部的（如他人的建议、家庭成员的疾病、报纸文章等）。

6. 自我效能   指个体对自己有能力成功采取行为的信心水平。在实际应用中，自我效能有两个层面：一是一般自我效能，指个体在应对各种挑战或面对新事物时的普遍信心；二是特定自我效能，即针对特定健康行为的信心。自我效能是许多行为理论的组成成分，因为它直接影响一个人是否会采取期望的行为。

HBM 也认可健康行为的发生及维持受到社会人口学因素以及个体所具有的疾病与健康知识的影响。社会人口学因素包括个体的社会和生理特征，如性别、年龄、人格特点、社会经济地位、同伴影响等。不同性别、年龄、人格特征和生活环境的人，对于采纳健康行为的态度和程度有所不同。总的来说，具有健康知识的人更容易采取健康行为。

（二）应用现状

健康信念模型（HBM）是一种用于解释和预测健康行为的理论框架，被广泛应用于社区护理，以帮助设计和实施有效的健康促进和疾病预防计划。

1. 健康教育和行为改变   HBM 被广泛应用于健康教育项目中，用于提高社区居民对健康问题的认识和促进行为改变。

2. 慢性病管理   在慢性病管理中，HBM 帮

chronic disease management, HBM assists community nurses in understanding patients' perceptions of their illnesses and attitudes toward treatment. By identifying and alleviating patients' perceived barriers and enhancing their self-efficacy, nurses can improve patients' treatment adherence and quality of life.

3. Public Health Intervention　HBM has been successfully applied in public health interventions, such as controlling infectious diseases and increasing screening rates. For example, through publicity and educational activities, community nurses can reduce residents' fear and stigma associated with infectious diseases and increase participation in health screenings.

4. Mental Health Support　HBM is also used to design mental health interventions, helping residents recognize the severity and controllability of mental health issues, and encouraging them to seek professional help and support.

5. Environmental Health Promotion In community nursing, HBM is used in environmental health interventions to educate residents about the risks of environmental hazards (such as air and water pollution) and help residents take measures to reduce exposure and protect health.

iii. Limitation

The HBM has several limitations that restrict its utility. These limitations include:

(1) It does not account for individual's attitudes, beliefs, or other individual's factors determining acceptance of health behavior.

(2) It does not account for habitual behaviors, which may influence the decision-making process for accepting recommended actions (e.g. smoking).

(3) It does not take into account behaviors that are performed for non-health related reasons such as social acceptability.

(4) It does not account for environmental or economic factors that may prohibit or promote the recommended action.

(5) It does not account for the fact that

助社区护士理解患者对疾病的认知和对治疗的态度。通过识别和减轻患者的感知障碍，增强其自我效能感，护士可以提高患者的治疗依从性和生活质量。

3. 公共卫生干预　HBM 也已成功应用于公共卫生干预，如控制传染病和提高筛查率等。例如，通过宣传和教育活动，社区护士可以减少居民对传染病的恐惧和污名，提高健康筛查的参与度。

4. 心理健康支持　HBM 还被用来设计心理健康干预措施，帮助居民认识到心理健康问题的严重性和可控性，鼓励他们寻求专业帮助和支持。

5. 环境健康促进　在社区护理中，HBM 用于环境健康干预，教育居民了解环境危害（如空气污染、水污染等）的风险，并采取措施减少暴露和保护健康。

（三）局限性

HBM 的局限性限制了其应用。该模型的局限性包括：

（1）没有考虑到个人的态度、信念或其他决定接受健康行为的个人因素。

（2）没有考虑到习惯性行为，这些行为可能会影响接受推荐行动的决策过程（如吸烟）。

（3）没有考虑到因非健康相关原因而采取的行为，如社会接受性。

（4）没有考虑到可能禁止或促进所推荐行动的环境或经济因素。

（5）没有考虑到不同个体在获取疾病信息

individuals have varying abilities and opportunities to access disease information.

(6) It does not account for the possibility that cues to action are not always effective in encouraging people to act, and it ignores that "health" actions are not always the main priority in decision-making.

The HBM is more descriptive than explanatory, and does not provide a strategy for changing health-related behavior. In preventive health behaviors, early studies showed that perceived susceptibility, benefits, and barriers were consistently associated with the desired health behavior; perceived severity was less often associated with the desired health behavior. The effects of individual components depend on the health outcomes the individual interested in. It should be integrated with other models that account for the environmental context and suggest strategies for change in order to use the model more effectively.

III. The Transtheoretical Model

The transtheoretical model (TTM), also called the stages of behavior change model, was developed by Prochaska and DiClemente in the late 1970s. The model explains why some people are able to quit smoking on their own by studying the experiences of spontaneous quitters versus smokers who need further treatment. Studies have found that people quit smoking when they are ready. TTM focuses on the decision-making of the individual. It is a model regarding whether there is intentional change. The model is based on the assumption that people's behavior, especially habitual behavior change, is not rapid and decisive, but a cyclic and continuous process. The TTM is not a theory but a model. Different behavioral theories and components can be applied to various stages of the TTM model to achieve the most effective outcome.

的渠道、能力、机会等方面存在的差异。

（6）没有考虑到行为线索在鼓励人们行动方面可能并非普遍存在，忽略了"健康"行动不一定是人们决策过程中的主要目标。

HBM 更多的是描述性的而非解释性的，并未提供改变健康相关行为的策略。在预防性健康行为中，早期研究显示感知易感性、益处和障碍与期望的健康行为始终相关；而感知严重性与期望的健康行为的关联较小。个体成分的影响取决于个体感兴趣的健康结果。为了更有效地利用 HBM 模型，应将其与那些考虑环境背景并提供改变策略的模型结合使用。

三、跨理论模型

跨理论模型（transtheoretical model，TTM），又称行为转变阶段模型由 Prochaska 和 DiClemente 在 20 世纪 70 年代末提出。该模型通过研究自发戒烟者与需要进一步治疗的吸烟者的经历，解释了为什么有些人能够自己成功戒烟。研究发现，人们在准备好的情况下才会戒烟。TTM 聚焦于个体的决策，是一个关于是否有意识改变的模型。该模型基于假设人们的行为，尤其是习惯性行为的改变不是迅速、果断的，而是一个循环、持续进行的过程。跨理论模型本身不是一个理论，而是一个模型。不同的行为理论和组成成分可应用于 TTM 模型的不同阶段，以达到最有效的结果。

i. Main Content

The TTM posits that individuals move through six stages of change: pre-contemplation, contemplation, preparation, action, maintenance, and termination. Termination was not part of the original model and is less often used in the stages of change for health-related behaviors. For each stage of change, different intervention strategies are the most effective if they can help the person to the next stage of change and subsequently to the maintenance stage, the ideal stage of behavior.

1. Pre-contemplation   In this stage, people do not intend to take action in the foreseeable future (defined as within the next 6 months). People usually do not realize that their behavior is problematic or produces negative consequences. People in this stage often underestimate the pros of changing behavior and place too much emphasis on the cons of changing behavior.

2. Contemplation   In this stage, people intend to start adopting healthy behavior in the foreseeable future (defined as within the next 6 months). People recognize that their behavior may be problematic, and a more thoughtful and practical consideration of the benefits and drawbacks of changing the behavior takes place, with equal emphasis placed on both. Even with this recognition, people may still feel ambivalent towards changing their behavior.

3. Preparation   In this stage, people are ready to take action within the next 30 days. They start to take small steps toward behavior change, and believe that changing their behavior leads to a healthier life.

4. Action   In this stage, people have recently (defined as within the last 6 months) changed their behavior and intend to continue to change their behavior. People may exhibit this by modifying their problem behavior or acquiring new healthy behaviors.

5. Maintenance   In this stage, people have sustained their behavior change for a while

（一）主要内容

TTM 提出个体经历 6 个改变阶段：前意向期、意向期、准备期、行动期、维持期和终止期。终止期并非原始模型的一部分，在健康相关行为的改变阶段中较少应用。对于每一个改变阶段，能够推动个体进入下一阶段然后达到行为的理想状态——维持期的不同干预策略都是最有效的。

1. **前意向期**   在这个阶段，人们并不打算在可预见的未来（定义为在接下来的 6 个月内）采取行动。他们通常没有意识到自己的行为是有问题的，或会产生负面后果。处于这一阶段的人往往低估了改变行为的好处，并且过分强调改变行为的不利因素。

2. **意向期**   在这个阶段，人们打算在可预见的未来（定义为在接下来的 6 个月内）开始采取健康行为。他们意识到自己的行为可能存在问题，并且会更加深思熟虑地权衡改变行为的利弊，对两者给予平等的重视。即使有了这种认识，人们仍可能对改变自己行为感到矛盾和迟疑。

3. **准备期**   在这个阶段，人们准备在接下来的 30 天内采取行动。他们开始小步骤地改变行为，并且相信改变自己的行为会带来更健康的生活。

4. **行动期**   在这个阶段，人们近期（定义为在过去 6 个月内）已经改变了自己的行为，并打算继续不断改变这种行为。人们可能表现为改变他们的问题行为或者养成新的健康行为。

5. **维持期**   在这个阶段，人们已经维持一段时间（定义为超过 6 个月）的行为改变，并计

(defined as more than 6 months) and intend to maintain the behavior change. People in this stage work to prevent relapse to earlier stages.

6. Termination　In this stage, people have no desire to return to their unhealthy behaviors and are sure they will not relapse. Since this stage is rarely reached, and people tend to stay in the maintenance stage, this stage is often not considered in health promotion programs.

ii. Application Status

TTM is widely applied in community nursing to promote changes in health behaviors, particularly in the areas of lifestyle management and chronic disease management.

1. Lifestyle Management　In lifestyle management, TTM is used to promote health behavior changes through stage-matched interventions. For example, in the management of diet and physical activity, healthcare providers assess patients' stages of behavior change (such as the preparation stage, action stage, etc.) and offer personalized health education and support. TTM is also frequently used in smoking cessation interventions, where personalized counseling and feedback significantly enhance the success rate of quitting smoking.

2. Chronic Disease Management　In chronic disease management, healthcare providers use the TTM framework to assess patients' stages of self-management behaviors (such as diet control, physical activity, and blood glucose monitoring) and provide personalized education and support, including health education, goal setting, and regular follow-ups. These TTM-based interventions help patients identify and overcome barriers to behavior change, promoting sustainable healthy behavior changes.

The TTM provides suggested strategies for public health intervention to address people at various stages of the decision-making process. This can result in interventions that are tailored (i.e. a message or program is specifically created for a target population's level of knowledge and

划继续保持这种行为改变。处于这一阶段的人努力防止退回到先前阶段。

6. **终止期**　在这个阶段，人们没有回到不健康行为的欲望，并且确信他们不会退回到先前阶段。由于人们通常会停留在维持阶段，极少达到这一阶段，因此在健康促进计划中往往不考虑这一阶段。

（二）应用现状

TTM 被广泛应用到社区护理中，用于促进健康行为改变，特别是生活方式管理和慢性病管理等方面。

1. **生活方式管理**　TTM 在生活方式管理中，通过阶段匹配的干预措施促进健康行为改变。例如，在饮食和体力活动管理中，医疗保健提供者通过评估患者的行为阶段（如准备阶段、行动阶段等），提供个性化的健康教育和支持。TTM 还常被用于戒烟干预，其中个性化的咨询和反馈显著提高戒烟成功率。

2. **慢性病管理**　在慢性病管理中，医疗保健提供者以 TTM 为指导，通过评估患者在自我管理行为（如饮食控制、体力活动和血糖监测等）的阶段，提供个性化的教育和支持，包括健康教育、行为目标设定和定期随访。这些基于 TTM 的干预措施帮助患者识别和克服行为改变中的障碍，促进健康行为的持久性改变。

TTM 提供了针对各个决策过程阶段人群的公共卫生干预策略的建议，由此制订出量身定做（即针对特定目标人群的知识水平和动机而创建的信息或计划）且有效的干预措施。TTM 鼓励评估个体当前的变化阶段，并考虑到人们决策过程中的撤退情况。

motivation) and effective. The TTM encourages an assessment of an individual's current stage of change and accounts for relapse in people's decision-making process.

iii. Limitation

There are several limitations of TTM:

(1) The model ignores the social context in which change occurs, such as socioeconomic status and income.

(2) The boundaries among the stages can be arbitrary with no set criteria for determining which stage of change a person is in. The questionnaires that have been developed to identify individual stages of change are not all standardized or validated.

(3) There is no clear standard for how much time is needed for each stage, or how long a person can remain in a stage.

(4) The model assumes that individuals make coherent and logical plans in their decision-making process when this is not always the case.

IV. PRECEDE-PROCEED Model

i. Main Content

The PRECEDE-PROCEED model is a comprehensive structure for assessing health needs, and designing, implementing, and evaluating health promotion and other public health programs to meet those needs. PRECEDE provides a structure for planning a targeted and focused public health program. PROCEED also provides a framework for implementing and evaluating the public health program. The model can be divided into two stages:

1. Diagnostic Stage   It is the PRECEDE stage which means predisposing, reinforcing, and enabling constructs in educational/environmental diagnosis and evaluation.

2. Implementation Stage   It is the PROCEED stage which means policy, regulatory and organizational constructs in educational and environmental development.

（三）局限性

TTM 存在几个局限性：

（1）该模型忽略了变化发生的社会环境，如社会经济地位和收入。

（2）各阶段之间的界限可以任意划分，缺乏既定的标准来确定一个人所处的改变阶段。已经开发的用于确定个体改变阶段的问卷并非都是标准化或经过验证的。

（3）每个阶段所需的时间或一个人可以在一个阶段停留多久，没有明确的标准。

（4）该模型假设个体在决策过程中会制订连贯且合逻辑的计划，但事实并非总是如此。

四、PRECEDE-PROCEED 模型

（一）主要内容

PRECEDE-PROCEED 模型是一个综合性的架构，用于评估健康需求，并通过设计、实施、评价健康促进和其他公共卫生项目满足这些需求。PRECEDE 提供了规划有针对性、重点突出的公共卫生项目的框架。PROCEED 为实施和评估公共卫生项目提供了框架。PRECEDE-PROCEED 模型可分为 2 个阶段：

1. 诊断阶段   即 PRECEDE 阶段（predisposing, reinforcing and enabling constructs in educational/environmental diagnosis and evaluation），指在教育 / 环境诊断和评价中应用的倾向、促成及强化因素。

2. 执行阶段   即 PROCEED 阶段（policy, regulatory and organizational constructs in educational and environmental development），指执行教育 / 环境干预中应用的政策、法规和组织

According to PRECEDE-PROCEED model, the planning process is divided into 9 fundamental steps, which involve working backward from the desired outcomes to the root causes, using a deductive approach.

(1) Social Diagnosis: Begin by assessing the quality of life of the target population to evaluate their needs and health issues.

(2) Epidemiological Diagnosis: Identify specific health problems and objectives within the target population through epidemiological and related assessments.

(3) Behavioral and Environmental Diagnosis: Identify behaviors and environmental factors related to the health issues, and implement interventions to improve the environment in support of healthy behaviors. The planning process must emphasize the importance of behavior change and the influence of social forces.

(4) Educational and Organizational Diagnosis: When developing a health promotion plan, educational and organizational strategies should focus on factors influencing behavior and the environment, which can be categorized into three types: predisposing factors, enabling factors, and reinforcing factors. Predisposing factors include the knowledge, beliefs, attitudes, values, and perceptions of individuals or groups, which serve as motivations for certain behaviors. Enabling factors consist of the skills, resources, or barriers that may facilitate or hinder behavior and environmental changes during the implementation of the plan. Reinforcing factors refer to the rewards and feedback received by individuals who adopt healthy behaviors. The purpose of studying these three factors is to identify intervention priorities and allocate resources, thereby developing educational strategies.

(5) Administrative and Policy Diagnosis: Assess organizational management capacity, along with resources, policies, personnel skills, and time allocation in the implementation of the

的手段。

根据 PRECEDE-PROCEED 模型，规划设计分为 9 个基本步骤，即从最终结果回到最初原因，以演绎的方式逐步进行。

（1）社会诊断：从估测目标人群的生活质量入手，评估他们的需求和健康问题。

（2）流行病学诊断：通过流行病学和相关调查确认目标人群特定的健康问题和目标。

（3）行为与环境诊断：确认健康问题相关的行为和环境问题，通过干预改善支持健康行为的环境。计划中需重视行为改变及社会力量影响的重要性。

（4）教育与组织诊断：制定健康促进规划时，教育和组织策略应关注影响行为和环境的因素，可以归纳为 3 类：倾向因素、促成因素和强化因素。倾向因素包括个人或群体的知识、信念、态度、价值观以及感知，是产生某种行为的动机；促成因素包括在计划实施期间可能促进或阻碍行为和环境变化的技能、资源或障碍；强化因素指采取健康行为的个体获得的奖励和反馈。研究这 3 类因素旨在确定干预重点和资源分配，从而制订教育策略。

（5）管理和政策诊断：评估组织管理能力，以及在规划执行中资源、政策、人员能力和时间安排，优化社区开发与协调，确保规划顺利执行。

plan. Optimize community development and coordination to ensure the smooth execution of the plan.

(6) Implementation: Transform the intervention plan developed from earlier diagnoses into concrete actions, ensuring efficient resource allocation and coverage of the target population.

(7) Process Evaluation: Monitor the fidelity and reach of the intervention implementation, and identify any execution deviations.

(8) Impact Evaluation: Assess the intervention's effectiveness in changing behaviors, improving environments, and reducing health risks.

(9) Outcome Evaluation: Measure the long-term impact of the intervention on the target population's quality of life, verifying the ultimate value of the project.

Steps 7 through 9 involve the evaluation phase. However, evaluation is not confined to the final steps but is an integral part of the entire process.

ii. Application Status

The PRECEDE-PROCEED model is one of the most widely used and comprehensively assessed models in the health field. It is effectively applied in community health promotion and public health interventions. The model targets all populations, including both healthy individuals and patients, and has been used for various diseases such as hypertension, coronary heart disease, iron-deficiency anemia, and breast cancer. It has practical applications in multiple health fields, including disease prevention, disease management, health assessment, and health care. In terms of health assessment, the PRECEDE-PROCEED model provides a comprehensive evaluation framework that covers sociological, epidemiological, behavioral, environmental, educational, organizational, and policy management aspects, with a particular emphasis on the importance of predisposing, enabling, and reinforcing factors within educational organizations. Regarding implementation, health interventions guided by this model are typically

（6）实施：将前期诊断制定的干预方案转化为具体行动，确保资源高效配置与目标人群覆盖。

（7）过程评估：监控干预实施的保真度与覆盖率，识别执行偏差。

（8）影响评估：评估干预对行为改变、环境改善及健康风险降低的效果。

（9）结果评估：测量干预对人群生活质量的长期影响，验证项目终极价值。

步骤 7 至步骤 9 为评价阶段。但是评价不是该模型的最后步骤，是整个过程中不可分割的部分。

（二）应用现状

PRECEDE-PROCEED 模型是健康领域中使用最广泛、评估最全面的模型之一，被有效地用于社区健康促进和公共卫生干预中。该模型面向全人群，包括健康人群也包括疾病患者，已用于多种疾病，如高血压、冠心病、缺铁性贫血和乳腺癌等。它在疾病预防、疾病管理、健康评估和健康护理等多个健康领域均有实际应用。在健康评估方面，PRECEDE-PROCEED 模型提供了一个涵盖社会学、流行病学、行为、环境、教育、组织和政策管理等方面的全面评估框架，特别强调了教育组织中的倾向因素、促成因素和强化因素的重要性。实施方面，该模型指导下的健康干预通常定期进行，并采取多样化的形式，如健康教育讲座、一对一教育、电话随访。此外，PRECEDE-PROCEED 模型的有效性评价也很关键。有效测量干预结局的指标包括生物学指标、社会心理学指标以及知、信、行变化指标。

conducted regularly with various forms, such as of health education lectures, one-on-one education, and telephone follow-ups. Moreover, the evaluation of the PRECEDE-PROCEED model's effectiveness is also crucial. Indicators for effective measurement of intervention outcomes include biological indicators, social psychological indicators, and KAP change indicators.

iii. Limitation

The PRECEDE-PROCEED model also has some limitations.

(1) The model requires substantial resources and time to conduct comprehensive needs assessments and develop plans, which can be challenging for communities with limited resources.

(2) The model which involves community members may encounter low rates of participation or different opinions among stakeholders, potentially hindering project progress.

(3) The model may not be suitable for all types of projects though it is effective in various health promotion areas.

(4) Some components of the model might need to be adjusted over time, which adds complexity and uncertainty to the implementation process.

Therefore, when deciding whether to use the PRECEDE-PROCEED model for health promotion or disease prevention projects, it is crucial to carefully consider these limitations.

V. Empowerment Theory

i. Main Content

Empowerment theory's research primarily stems from two approaches: the "relational approach" and the "motivational approach". The "relational approach", also known as "managerial empowerment", emphasizes the transfer of power and originated from corporate management practices before the 1990s . The "motivational approach", also known as "psychological empowerment", focuses on individual intrinsic motivation, a result of psychological research post-1990s, emphasizing

（三）局限性

PRECEDE-PROCEED 模型也有一些局限性。

（1）该模型需要大量的资源和时间进行全面的需求评估和计划制订，这对于资源有限的社区来说可能是一个挑战。

（2）该模型涉及社区成员的参与，可能会遇到低参与率或利益相关者间意见分歧的问题，可能会妨碍项目进展。

（3）尽管该模型在多个健康促进领域中有效，但它可能并不适用于所有类型的项目。

（4）模型的一些组成部分可能需要随着时间的推移进行调整，这增加了实施过程中的复杂性和不确定性。

因此，在决定是否使用 PRECEDE-PROCEED 模型进行健康促进或疾病预防项目时，必须仔细考虑这些局限性。

五、赋能理论

（一）主要内容

赋能理论的研究主要来源于两种路径："关系路径"和"动机路径"。"关系路径"又被称为"管理授权"，源于 20 世纪 90 年代前的企业管理实践，强调权力的转移。"动机路径"又被称为"心理授权"，是 20 世纪 90 年代后心理学研究的产物，关注个体的内在动力，强调通过个人自我效能的增强驱动行为改变。

the enhancement of personal self-efficacy to drive behavior change.

ii. Application Status

As research of empowerment theory has developed, it has been widely applied in management, education, social psychology, and clinical medicine. Additionally, empowerment theory can serve as a method of health education, applied in clinical disease management and control. In 2007, the American Diabetes Association (ADA) defined empowerment health education as helping individuals discover and activate their self-management abilities to control disease. As a method of clinical health education, empowerment theory particularly emphasizes enhancing the self-management capabilities of patients and community residents. This approach has shown significant effects in managing various chronic diseases, such as diabetes, hypertension, and heart disease. Through empowerment education, patients are encouraged to engage in their own health management and improve their critical thinking skills to make autonomous and informed health decisions.

The current well-established five steps of empowerment education include:

1. Identifying the Problem　Recognize the primary health issues and needs faced by the patient through open discussions and interviews.

2. Releasing Emotions　Encourage patients to express their feelings and emotions, providing necessary emotional support to enhance self-management motivation.

3. Setting Goals　Collaborate with patients to set specific health improvement goals. Health educators provide professional advice, but the final decision-making authority belongs to the patients.

4. Confirming the Plan　Regularly communicate with patients to adjust and confirm the implementation plan, ensuring the adaptability and effectiveness of the behavior change plan.

（二）应用现状

随着赋能理论研究的发展，赋能理论被广泛应用在管理、教育、社会心理学、临床医学领域。另外，赋能理论也能作为一种健康教育的方法，应用于临床疾病管理与控制。2007年，美国糖尿病协会（American Diabetes Association，ADA）将赋能健康教育定义为帮助个体发现和激发其自我管理的能力以控制疾病。作为临床健康教育的一种方法，赋能理论特别强调激发患者及社区居民的自我管理能力。这种方法已经在处理各种慢性疾病如糖尿病、高血压、心脏病等中显示出显著效果。通过赋能教育，患者被鼓励参与到自身健康管理中，提高了批判性思考能力，从而做出自主和知情的健康决策。

目前比较成熟的赋能教育的5个步骤包括：

1. 确定问题　通过开放式讨论和访谈，识别患者面临的主要健康问题和需求。

2. 释放情感　鼓励患者表达自己的感受和情绪，提供必要的情感支持，增强自我管理的动力。

3. 设定目标　与患者协同确定改善健康的具体目标，健康教育者提供专业的建议，但最终决策权属于患者。

4. 确认计划　定期与患者沟通以调整和确认实施计划，确保行为改变计划的适应性和有效性。

5. Evaluating Behavior Evaluate the progress of health behavior changes through regular follow-ups, confirming achieved goals, and continuously motivating patients for self-management.

Empowerment education research has been widely applied domestically and internationally. These studies often use literature reviews, cross-sectional surveys, and evaluation tools to enhance patient engagement and proactive health management.

iii. Limitation

Limitations of the empowerment theory include:

1. Overemphasis on Personal Responsibility Empowerment theory may place excessive emphasis on the individual's role in problem-solving, neglecting systemic and structural issues. This focus on personal responsibility can make individuals feel isolated and unable to effectively address broader social injustices.

2. Internalized Oppression Some individuals may internalize societal unfairness and negative evaluations, perceiving problems as their own deficiencies while overlooking systemic barriers. This can exacerbate self-blame rather than promoting effective self-empowerment.

3. Complexity of Theory Implementation The practical application of empowerment theory may require a complex support system and abundant resources. For example, training and tools are necessary to help individuals enhance their self-efficacy and critical consciousness, which can be challenging for resource-limited communities.

4. Challenges of Power Dynamics The empowerment process necessitates a thorough and thoughtful handling of power dynamics. It is crucial to ensure that individuals and communities genuinely acquire substantive power rather than experiencing a nominal transfer of power.

5. 评价行为 通过定期随访，确认已达成的目标，持续激励患者自我管理，评价健康行为改变的进展。

赋能教育的研究已在国内外广泛应用。研究多采用文献回顾、横断面调查、评价工具以提升患者的参与率和促进其积极主动的健康管理。

（三）局限性

赋能理论的局限性包括：

1. 过度强调个人责任 赋能理论可能过度强调个人在解决问题中的作用，忽视了系统性和结构性问题。这种强调个人责任的方式可能会让人们感觉被孤立，无法有效地应对更广泛的社会不公的问题。

2. 内化压迫 一些个体可能内化社会中的不公平和负面评价，认为问题是自己的不足，而忽视了系统性障碍。这可能会加剧自责，而不是促进有效的自我赋能。

3. 理论实施的复杂性 赋能理论在实际操作中可能需要复杂的支持系统和丰富的资源。例如，培训和工具对帮助个体提高自我效能感和批判意识是必要的，这对于资源有限的社区来说可能具有挑战性。

4. 权力动态的挑战 赋能过程需要对权力动态进行周全地处理。至关重要的是确保个体和社区能够真正获得实质性的权力，而不是形式上的权力转移。

Section 3   Practice of Community Health Education

The practice of community health education follows the five steps of the nursing procedure, which are assessment, diagnosis, planning, implementation and evaluation of community health education.

I. Assessment of Community Health Education

Assessment of community health education refers to the process of collecting and analyzing information related to targets of health education and their environment, in order to understand the health education needs of the community.

i. The Main Contents of Data Collection

1. **Education Targets**   The health education needs of the target population should be identified at first. These needs are determined by various factors. The key data to be collected include：

(1) General Information: Include gender, age, health status, biological genetic factors, etc.

(2) Lifestyle：Include smoking, alcohol consumption, diet, sleep patterns, sexual activity patterns, physical activities, etc.

(3) Learning Ability：Include educational background, learning experiences, cognitive and learning characteristics, learning methods, learning interests, learning attitudes, psychological stress, etc.

(4) Knowledge of Health：Include understanding and knowledge of common diseases, disease prevention, emergency response to acute and severe conditions, identification of complications, medication precautions, and awareness of how unhealthy lifestyles affect diseases, etc.

第三节   社区健康教育实践

社区健康教育的实践遵循护理程序的五个步骤，分别为社区健康教育的评估、诊断、计划、实施和评价。

一、社区健康教育评估

社区健康教育评估是指通过收集健康教育对象与环境的相关信息，并对资料进行分析，了解健康教育对象的健康教育需求的过程。

（一）资料收集主要内容

1. **教育对象**   首先应明确教育对象的健康教育需求。健康教育需求由多种因素决定，应重点收集的资料有：

（1）一般资料：包括性别、年龄、健康状况、生物遗传因素等。

（2）生活方式：包括吸烟、酗酒、饮食、睡眠形态、性生活形态、身体活动等。

（3）学习能力：包括文化程度、学习经历、认知与学习特点、学习方式、学习兴趣、学习态度及心理压力等。

（4）健康知识：包括常见疾病相关知识、疾病预防、急危重症突发应对、并发症识别、用药注意事项以及对不健康生活方式影响疾病的认识等。

2. Educators This includes the abilities, educational level, and experience of the educators, as well as their enthusiasm for health education work. In the assessment of educators, it is necessary to pay attention to the barriers that educators often encounter.

(1) Cultural Differences: Cultural differences between educators and learners may lead to communication barriers, affecting the transmission and understanding of health education information.

(2) Language Barriers: Differences in language can complicate the process of health education.

(3) Low Health Literacy: Learners may have low levels of health literacy, making it difficult for them to fully understand complex health information.

(4) Limited Resources: The community's healthcare resources may be limited, potentially hindering the support needed for health education activities.

(5) Time Constraints: Both educators and learners may face time constraints, making it challenging to allocate sufficient time for comprehensive health education.

(6) Socioeconomic Factors: Socioeconomic factors such as poverty, unemployment, and low educational levels can impact the effectiveness of health education.

(7) Lack of Trust: Learners may have a lack of trust in the healthcare system or the educators themselves, which can affect their acceptance of health education information and advice.

3. Educational Environment This covers the ecological environment, learning environment, and social environment. Relevant information needed includes occupation, economic income, housing conditions, transportation means, learning conditions, etc.

4. Healthcare Services Resources This includes the number and location of healthcare institutions, access to basic healthcare services, health legislation and policies, social and

2. 教育者 包括教育者的能力、教育水平和经验以及对健康教育工作的投入热情等。在对教育者开展评估时还要关注教育者常遇到的障碍因素。

（1）文化差异：教育者和受教育者之间的文化差异可能导致沟通障碍，影响健康教育信息的传递和理解。

（2）语言障碍：语言差异可能使健康教育过程变得复杂。

（3）健康素养不足：受教育者的健康素养水平可能较低，难以完全理解复杂的健康信息。

（4）资源有限：社区的医疗卫生服务资源有限，可能无法充分支持健康教育活动。

（5）时间限制：教育者和受教育者都可能面临时间限制，难以安排足够的时间进行全面的健康教育。

（6）社会经济因素：贫困、失业、低教育水平等社会经济因素会影响健康教育的效果。

（7）缺乏信任：受教育者可能对医疗卫生系统或教育者本人的信任度不足，会影响他们接受健康教育信息和建议。

3. 教育环境 包括生态环境、学习环境和社会环境。需要收集职业、经济收入、住房状况、交通工具、学习条件等相关信息。

4. 医疗卫生服务资源 包括医疗卫生机构的数量与位置、获得基本医疗卫生服务的机会、卫生立法与政策、社会与经济背景等。

economic context, etc.

ii. Common Methods of Data Collection

1. Informant Interview Informant interview, which consists of directed talks with selected members of a community about community members or groups and events, is basic to effective data collection. It aims at accessing the process of community development, the characteristics of the community, and the common health problems and needs of the community.

When using informant interview, we should pay attention to the selection of key informants during the information collection process. Key informants are not always people who have formal titles or positions. They often have informal roles within the community, such as parents who are active and vocal about the school health curriculum.

Informant interview and participatory observation are good ways to get information about community beliefs, norms, values, power and influence structures, and problem-solving progress.

2. Participatory Observation Participatory observation is a technique of field research, used in anthropology and sociology by which an investigator (participatory observer) studies the life of a group by participating in its activities. It is important to note that: a. The recorded observations about a group of people or event are never going to be the full description; b. The researcher's worldview and personal beliefs always influence the way of data collection and interpretation; c. The impact of the "Hawthorne effect", namely, changes in the behavior of study subjects when they are aware of being observed, can affect the authenticity of the research data and the accuracy of the conclusions.

3. Windshield Survey Essentially, windshield survey is a method of systematic observation which is common in sociology. While driving a car or taking public transportation, the

（二）资料收集常用方法

1. 知情人访谈 知情人访谈是有效收集数据的基础，是指与选定的社区成员就社区成员、社区团体和社区活动进行直接交谈，旨在了解社区发展的过程、社区的特性以及社区的主要健康问题及需求。

使用这种方法时，需要关注信息收集过程中关键知情人的选择问题。关键知情人并不总是那些拥有正式头衔或职位的人。他们通常在社区中扮演非正式的角色，比如积极参与学校健康课程的家长等。

知情人访谈和参与式观察是获取有关社区信仰、规范、价值观、权力和影响结构以及问题解决进展等信息的好方法。

2. 参与式观察 参与式观察是人类学和社会学中使用的一种实地调查技术，是指调查者通过参与一个群体的活动来研究该群体的生活。需要注意的是：①对一群人或一件事的观察记录永远不会是完整的描述；②研究人员的世界观和个人信仰总是会影响数据的收集、解释方式；③"霍桑效应"的影响，即当研究对象知道自己正在被观察时，其行为会发生变化，这种变化可能会对研究数据的真实性和结论的准确性产生影响。

3. 挡风玻璃式调查 挡风玻璃式调查本质上是社会学常见的系统观察方法。在驾驶汽车或乘坐公共交通工具时，护士可以通过简短的评估更好地了解整个社区或社区的具体情况。

nurse can better understand either the community in general or a specific condition of it through a brief assessment. Nurses can observe many dimensions of community life and environment, such as common characteristics of people on the street, places where neighborhoods gather, the rhythm of community life, quality of houses, and geographic boundaries.

4. Secondary Analysis of Existing Data　Secondary analysis of existing data is one way of collecting reported data. In secondary analysis, the nurse uses previously collected data, such as public documents, health surveys, and minutes of community meetings. This type of analysis is very valuable because it saves time and effort. Much data are readily available and useful for secondary analysis.

Ⅱ. Diagnosis of Community Health Education Problems

Community health education problem is to organize and analyze the information collected from the health education assessment. Based on the common needs of health education in community groups, this stage involves identifying health education problems, making health education diagnosis, and defining priority program of health education.

ⅰ. The Specific Steps of Raising Questions

(1) Analyze the information and list current or potential health education problems.

(2) Analyze the extent to which the problems of health education pose a threat to the health of the educatees.

(3) Analyze the resources available for conducting health education.

(4) Select problems that can be improved or solved by health education.

(5) Identify behavior, environment, and facilitators of behavioral change associated with the health education problems.

护士可以观察到社区生活和环境的许多方面，如街道上人们的共同特征、社区聚会场所、社区生活的节奏、住房质量、地理边界。

4. 二次数据分析　现有数据的二次分析是收集报告数据的一种方法。护士使用以前收集的数据，如公共文件、健康调查、社区会议记录等进行二次分析。这种类型的分析非常有价值，因为它省时省力。许多数据很容易获得，对二次分析很有用。

二、社区健康教育问题诊断

社区健康教育问题是对健康教育评估收集的资料进行整理与分析，针对社区群体共同的健康教育需求，确定健康教育问题，进行健康教育诊断，并明确健康教育的优先项目。

（一）提出问题的具体步骤

（1）分析资料，列出现存的或潜在的健康教育问题。

（2）分析健康教育问题对教育对象的健康构成威胁的程度。

（3）分析开展健康教育可利用的资源。

（4）选择能够通过健康教育改善或解决的问题。

（5）识别与健康问题相关的行为、环境和促进行为改变的因素。

ii. Common Community Health Education Problems

Common problems of community health education include 3 domains of learning: cognitive learning domain, affective learning domain, and motor skills learning domain. For example, "lack of knowledge about hypertension prevention" is a problem of health education related to the cognitive learning domain; "lack of confidence in smoking cessation" is a problem of health education in the affective learning domain; "lack of skill in blood pressure self-monitoring" is a problem of health education in the motor skills learning domain.

III. Community Health Education Program

Community health education program is a teaching plan based on the diagnosis of health problems. Development of the program requires the collaboration and participation of community nurses, other healthcare professionals and educatees. Community health education programs should be clear, specific and comprehensive. A complete health education program should have expected goals, the date and location of implementation, specific content, implementation approach and evaluation methods (Table 3-1).

(二) 常见的社区健康教育问题

常见的社区健康教育问题涉及学习的 3 个领域，即认知学习领域、情感学习领域和动作技能学习领域。例如"预防高血压相关知识缺乏"是认知学习领域的健康问题；"戒烟信心缺乏"是情感学习领域的健康问题；"血压自我监测技能的缺乏"是动作技能学习领域的健康问题。

三、社区健康教育计划

社区健康教育计划指的是根据健康问题诊断制订的教学计划。计划的制订需要社区护士、其他卫生保健专业人员和教育对象的协作和共同参与。社区健康教育计划要清晰、具体、全面。一项完整的健康教育计划应该包含预期的目标、实施日期、实施地点、具体的内容、实施途径和评价方法（表 3-1）。

Table 3-1　Community Health Education Program

Item	Details
Diagnosis of health problems	Describe the main health problems and challenges that need to be addressed in the community. 　Health problem 1 　Health problem 2 　Health problem 3
Participants	Community nurses Other healthcare professionals Educatees Other related personnel
Expected goals	Short-term goals Mid-term goals Long-term goals
Implementation dates	Start date End date

Continued Table

Item	Details
Implementation location	Specific address or community venue:
Specific content	Topic 1 Topic 2 Topic 3
Implementation methods	Health lectures Interactive workshops Individual counseling Health pamphlet Multimedia promotion Other
Evaluation methods	Pre-test and post-test questionnaires Health indicator monitoring Participation rate statistics Feedback collection Other

表 3-1 社区健康教育计划

项目	详细内容
健康问题诊断	描述社区中需要解决的主要健康问题和挑战 健康问题 1 健康问题 2 健康问题 3
参与人员	社区护士 其他卫生保健专业人员 教育对象 其他相关人员
预期目标	短期目标 中期目标 长期目标
实施日期	开始日期 结束日期
实施地点	具体地址或社区场所:
具体内容	主题 1 主题 2 主题 3
实施途径	健康讲座 互动工作坊 个体咨询 健康手册 多媒体 其他
评价方法	前测与后测问卷 健康指标监测 参与率统计 反馈意见收集 其他

i. Principles of Making Goals of Community Health Education

Goals of community health education should be made according to SMART principles, that is, specific, measurable, attainable, relevant and time-bound.

1. Specific   Goals should clearly and specifically describe the expected outcomes and achievement standards. One goal can only address one health education problem.

2. Measurable   Goals of community health education should be measurable in order to quantify the level of change of the educatees. When stating the goals, the nurse should avoid using vague terms such as know, stable, acceptable, or adequate, as these words will be interpreted differently by different people, leading to bias in determining the response of the educated person.

3. Attainable   Goals of community health education programs should be attainable based on the assessment of the available resources of human, material, financial, policy and others in community. It is necessary to have a clear grasp of a range of objective information on the health problems, knowledge levels, ideological attitudes, economic conditions and customs of the target population, and to put forward a practical and feasible goal.

4. Relevant   Goals should be related to community health education and common problems in the workplace. For example, topics of health education in schools can include nutrition, hygiene habits and accidental injuries, while health education in factories focuses on occupational safety, and prevention of common and occupational diseases.

5. Time-bound   Each goal of community health education should have a time limit to help the educator determine whether the progress of educatees is being achieved at a reasonable rate.

ii. Steps for Developing a Community Health Education Program

When formulating health education programs, it is necessary to focus on the target group, define

（一）社区健康教育目标制定原则

社区健康教育的目标制定遵循 SMART 原则，即明确性（specific）、可测量性（measurable）、可实现性（attainable）、相关性（relevant）和时限性（time-bound）。

1. 明确性（specific）   目标应明确地、详细地描述预期结果和达成标准。一个目标只针对一个健康教育问题。

2. 可测量性（measurable）   社区健康教育目标应该是可测量的，以量化评价被教育者的改变程度。在陈述健康教育目标时要注意，避免使用模糊的术语，如了解、稳定、可接受或者适当等，因为不同的人对这些词会有不同的理解，导致确定被教育者的反应时产生偏差。

3. 可实现性（attainable）   制定的社区健康教育目标必须是在评估社区可利用的人力、物力、资金、政策等资源后可实现的。要清晰地掌握目标人群的健康问题、知识水平、思想观念、经济状况和风俗民情等一系列客观资料，才能提出切实、可行的目标。

4. 相关性（relevant）   目标要和社区健康教育以及工作场所中的常见问题相关。如学校的健康教育问题可以选择营养、卫生习惯和意外伤害等；工厂则以职业安全、常见病与职业病预防为重点。

5. 时限性（time-bound）   社区健康教育的每个目标都应有实现目标的时间限定，以帮助教育者确定教育对象的进步是否按照合理的速度实现。

（二）社区健康教育计划制订步骤

制订健康教育计划时，要以教育对象为中心，明确健康教育目标，确定健康教育内容，并

the goals of health education, determine the content of health education, choose appropriate methods of health information dissemination, and select effective evaluation methods and indicators of health education.

1. Problem and Policy Analysis It is necessary to assess and analyze the major health problems and needs of community members, including epidemiological data, the health status and health behaviors of community residents. It is also necessary to assess the resources available in the community, including medical facilities, professional health workers, volunteer teams, and available financial support. In addition, a review of the current policy environment is essential to ensure that the education program meets policy requirements and runs smoothly.

2. Format Analysis It is important to understand community members' preferences for receiving health information through market research, such as lectures or social media. It should take into account the cultural and socioeconomic background of the community, and respect and adapt to these factors. In addition, existing technical tools and platforms need to be evaluated to ensure effective dissemination and interaction of health education information.

3. Setting Objectives Objectives are the desired outcomes to be achieved through community health education. According to the timeliness of the goal, they can be divided into short-term and long-term goals; According to the content of health education, they can be divided into four aspects: educational goals, behavioral goals, health goals and policy environment goals, and the number of goals in each aspect depends on the actual situation.

4. Determining Educators and Educatees Health education should be implemented by health workers with specialized knowledge, including community nurses, general practitioners, other community health service workers and professional trainers. Educators should have

选择适当的健康信息传播方法，选择有效的健康教育评价方式及指标。

1. 问题和政策分析 有必要评估和分析社区成员的主要健康问题和需求，包括流行病学数据、社区居民的健康状况和健康行为。同时还需评估社区内的可用资源，包括医疗设施、专业卫生工作者、志愿者队伍以及可获得的财政支持等。此外，审查当前的政策环境以确保教育计划符合政策要求并顺利进行也是不可或缺的。

2. 形式分析 通过市场调研掌握社区成员对健康信息接收形式的偏好，如讲座或社交媒体等形式，这点很重要。同时要考虑社区的文化和社会经济背景，尊重并适应这些因素。此外，还需评估现有技术工具和平台，以确保健康教育信息的有效传播和互动。

3. 设置目标 目标是指通过社区健康教育实现的预期结果。根据目标的时效性可分为近期目标和远期目标；根据任务内容可分为教育目标、行为目标、健康目标和政策环境目标4个方面，每个方面的目标数量根据实际情况而定。

4. 明确教育者和教育对象 健康教育的实施者应是具有专业知识水平的卫生工作者，包括社区护士、全科医师、其他社区卫生服务工作者和专业培训人员等。教育者应具备全面的、科学的、与时俱进的知识和信息，具备良好的职业道德与职业形象，具有吸引力与权威性，乐于

comprehensive, scientific and up-to-date knowledge and information, good professional ethics and professional image, be attractive and authoritative, and be willing to learn educational strategies and methods. According to the special characteristics of health education targets and implementation sites, it is also possible to consider collaborating with school health educators, enterprise employees, and health maintenance workers.

5. **Determining the Content**　The content of health education should be determined according to the needs of the educatees. According to the health status of the educatees, the content of health education can generally be divided into general education, special education, education on health management regulations, etc.

6. **Selection of Education Methods**　The implementation methods of health education should be determined according to the content of education, and the cultural level, cognitive characteristics and learning ability of the education target. The scope of application of different information dissemination methods, advantages and disadvantages of the methods should be considered. We should emphasizes the combination of multiple methods and complementary advantages.

7. **Defining the Time and Place of Implementation**　The place of health education can be community health centers, schools, communities, enterprises or institutions, residents' homes, other public places, etc., according to the purpose of the health education program, the education target, education contents, and education methods.

IV. Implementation of Community Health Education

i. Forms of Community Health Education

1. **Language Education Method**　This refers to communicating through language to explain and publicize health care knowledge. The

学习教育策略和方法。根据健康教育对象和实施地点的特点,也可考虑与学校健康教育工作者、企业职工、健康维护工作者合作。

5. **确定内容**　健康教育的内容应根据教育对象的需求确定。根据教育对象的健康状态,一般可将健康教育内容划分为一般教育、特殊教育、卫生管理法规教育等。

6. **选择教育方法**　健康教育的实施方法应根据教育内容以及教育对象的文化水平、认知特点和学习能力确定。应考虑不同信息传播方法的适用范围及其优缺点。应注重多种方法联合使用,优势互补。

7. **明确实施时间和地点**　根据健康教育项目目的、教育对象、教育内容、教育方法,健康教育地点可设为社区卫生服务中心、学校、社区、企事业单位、居民家中、其他公共场所等。

四、社区健康教育实施

(一)社区健康教育的形式

1. **语言教育法**　指通过语言沟通与交流,讲解、宣传健康护理知识的方法。实施形式包括讲授、小组讨论、咨询、谈话等。该方法的特

implementation forms include lectures, group discussions, consulting, conversations, etc. This method is simpl, easy, not restrict by general objective conditions and special equipment, and can be carried out anytime and anywhere, offering great flexibility.

2. Written Education Method　This refers to a method of achieving the goal of health education by a certain text communication medium and learners' reading ability. The implementation forms include slogans, leaflets, manuals, etc. The characteristics of this method are that it is economical and convenient, not restricted by time and space, can be used for both public and individual education, and can be learned repeatedly. But it requires that the educational objects have certain reading ability. Health education prescription is a special literal education method. It is provided in the form of doctor's or nurse's orders which is issued by health care personnel when the patient visits the clinic. Health education prescriptions are often authoritative and need to be written by specially trained medical personnel according to their authority.

3. Practical Education Method　This refers to guiding learners to master certain health care skills by practice, and apply the skills in self-care or family care. For example, instructing self-monitoring of blood glucose among diabetic patients or self-monitoring of blood pressure among hypertensive patients.

4. Multimedia Education Method　It is an education method using modern sound and light equipment to transmit information to learners, such as through radio, slides, television, etc. The characteristics of multimedia education are that it is a combination of image, text, language, art, music, etc., in a novel and realistic form, which is pleasing to the learners. However, the use of multimedia education methods requires a certain material equipment and professional and technical personnel. The We media education method

点是简便易行，不受一般客观条件和特殊设备的限制，随时随地即可开展，具有较大的灵活性。

2. 文字教育法　指通过一定的文字传播媒介和学习者的阅读能力来达到健康教育目标的一种方法。实施形式如标语、传单、手册等。该法的特点是经济便捷，不受时间和空间的限制，既可针对大众宣传又可针对个体进行教育，可以反复学习，但要求教育对象有一定阅读能力。健康教育处方是一种特殊的文字教育法，是医生或护士以医嘱形式提供的健康文字材料，由医护人员在患者到诊室就诊时开具。健康教育处方往往具有权威性，需要经过特殊训练的医务人员根据权限开具。

3. 实践教育法　指通过指导学习者的实践操作，使其掌握一定健康护理技能，并应用于自我或家庭护理的一种教育方法。例如指导糖尿病患者血糖自我监测，指导高血压患者血压自我监测等。

4. 多媒体教育法　是一种应用现代化声光设备向学习者传递信息的教育方法，如使用广播、幻灯片、电视网络等。该方法的特点是将形象、文字、语言、艺术、音乐等结合起来，形式新颖、形象逼真，容易被学习者接受。但运用该方法往往需要具备一定的物资设备与专业技术人员。近些年出现的自媒体教育法是便携式网络终端普及时代背景下的一种新型健康教育形态。该方式强调健康的自我传播，是由私人化、平民化、普泛化、自主化的传播者，以现代化和电子化的手段，向非特定的大多数或者特定的个

that emerged in recent years is a new form of multimedia education method in the era of the popularity of portable network terminals. This method emphasizes the self-propagation of health. It is a general term for new media that transmits normative and non-normative information to an unspecified majority or a specific individual through means of modern and electronic means by private, civilian, generalized and autonomous communicators. Attention should be paid to the quality of information disseminated by we media education method.

5. **Experiential Education Method** Experiential education is a teaching method based on practice and experience. Providing learners with a real learning environment allows them to participate in learning activities and gain practical experience. With the development of virtual reality technology, experiential education method has been applied more and more widely. Virtual reality technology and motion sensing technology can place community residents in the "real" scene, and realize human-computer interaction through body movements and gestures to control and operate videos, pictures, games and other content, so that experience-seekers can immerse themselves in learning knowledge and skills related to disaster escape, emergency rescue and the like. However, the use of this method often requires specific equipment and is expensive, and we should pay attention to the adverse reactions such as vertigo that some learners may have when using the relevant equipment.

6. **Comprehensive Education Method** It is a health education method that appropriately combines the language, written, practical, multimedia, experience and other educational methods. This comprehensive method has a extensive publicity effects and is suitable for large-scale publicity activities, and is often applied in health education exhibitions, knowledge contests or health garden parties.

人传递规范性和非规范性信息的新媒体方法的总称。但是需要关注该方法所传播信息的质量问题。

5. **体验式教育法**　体验式教育法是一种基于实践和体验的教学方法。通过为学习者提供真实的学习环境，让他们亲自参与学习活动并获得实际经验。随着虚拟现实技术的开发，体验式教育法得到越来越广泛的应用。虚拟现实技术、体感技术能让社区居民置身于"真实的"场景，通过肢体动作和手势控制操作视频、图片、游戏等内容，通过人机交互，让体验者沉浸式地学习灾害逃生、应急救护等知识和技能。但使用该方法往往需要特定的设备，而且成本昂贵，同时要注意有些学习者在使用相关设备时可能出现眩晕等不良反应。

6. **综合教育法**　将语言、文字、实践、多媒体、体验等多种方法适当结合应用的健康教育方法。该方法具有广泛的宣传性，适合大型的宣传活动，如举办健康教育展览、知识竞赛或健康游园会等。

ii. Specific Implementation of Community Health Education

Community health education should have its characteristics in different places of implementation, such as living communities, workplaces, schools, etc.

1. Living Community Health Education

(1) Target Population: All residents including children, adolescents, women, the elderly, people with disabilities, and people with chronic diseases, etc.

(2) Main Contents

1) Dissemination of the basic knowledge and skills for health literacy promotion among residents.

2) Health education on healthy lifestyle and intervenable risk factors such as reasonable diet, weight control, proper exercise, psychological balance, improved sleep, salt restriction, tobacco control, alcohol restriction, scientific medical treatment, rational drug use, drug withdrawal, etc.

3) Health education on major non-communicable diseases (e.g. cardiovascular diseases, respiratory diseases, endocrine diseases, tumors, mental diseases) and major infectious diseases (e.g. tuberculosis, hepatitis, AIDS).

4) Health education on public health problems such as food hygiene, occupational health, radiological health, environmental hygiene, water sanitation, school health, and family planning, etc.

5) Health education on emergency response to emergency public health events, disaster prevention and reduction, and home first aid, etc.

6) Dissemination of laws, regulations, and policies related to medical and health care.

(3) Forms

1) Issuing paper or electronic materials: provide health information and behavioral guidance through the bulletin board of community health service institutions, website, mobile phones, etc.

2) Providing individualized health education:

（二）社区健康教育的具体实施

社区健康教育在不同实施场所，如生活社区、工作场所、学校等实施应各具特点。

1. 生活社区健康教育

（1）目标人群：所有居民，包括儿童青少年、妇女、老年人、失能者、慢性病患者等。

（2）主要内容

1）宣传普及提高居民健康素养的基本知识与技能。

2）开展合理膳食、控制体重、适当运动、心理平衡、改善睡眠、限盐、控烟、限酒、科学就医、合理用药、戒毒等健康生活方式和可干预危险因素的健康教育。

3）开展心血管疾病、呼吸系统疾病、内分泌疾病、肿瘤、精神疾病等主要的慢性非传染性疾病，以及结核病、肝炎、艾滋病等主要的传染性疾病的健康教育。

4）开展食品卫生、职业卫生、放射卫生、环境卫生、饮水卫生、学校卫生和计划生育等公共卫生问题的健康教育。

5）开展突发公共卫生事件应急处置、防灾减灾、家庭急救等健康教育。

6）宣传普及医疗卫生法律法规及相关政策。

（3）形式

1）发布纸质或电子类材料：通过社区卫生服务机构宣传栏、网站、手机等提供健康信息与行为指导。

2）开展个体化健康教育：社区医务人员在

Carry out targeted and individualized health knowledge and health skills education during the provision of medical services and home visits provided by community health care workers.

3) Conducting group discussion: Medical staff or "leaders" of target population bring others together to discuss health issues of concern, share information and experiences to influence others with the power of example in the target population.

4) Conducting public health consultation activities and distributing promotional materials on various health themes.

2. Workplace Health Education

(1) Target Population: Occupational population, which refers to workers engaged in professional activities in enterprises, institutions, or individual economic organizations.

(2) Main Contents

1) Strengthening the promotion of occupational health, conducting pre-job training for workers to enhance their awareness of occupational hazards, protection principles, and self-protection capabilities.

2) Promoting relevant laws and regulations of occupational health to improve the legal awareness, hazard prevention awareness, and management level of occupational health supervision and management personnel.

(3) Forms

1) Conducting health education lectures: Holding health knowledge lectures, seminars, or group discussions in the workplace to educate employees on the prevention of occupational diseases and work safety knowledge.

2) Carrying out public health consultation activities: Organize employees to participate in simulation exercises, first aid training or occupational hazard identification training, so that they can master occupational disease prevention skills through practical operations and improve their ability to cope with emergencies.

3) Health education prescriptions: Issuing health education prescriptions tailored to the

提供门诊医疗、上门访视等医疗卫生服务时，开展有针对性的个体化健康知识和健康技能的教育。

3）开展小组讨论：由医务人员或目标人群中的"领导"组织带领其他人一起，围绕大家关心的健康问题展开讨论，分享信息、介绍经验，用目标人群中榜样的力量影响其他人。

4）举办公众健康咨询活动，并派发不同健康主题的宣传资料。

2. 工作场所健康教育

（1）目标人群：职业人群，即在企事业单位或个体经济组织中从事职业活动的劳动者。

（2）主要内容

1）加强职业健康宣传，加强职工岗前培训，提高职业人群对职业有害因素、防护原则等相关知识的认知，自觉提高其自我防护能力。

2）加强职业健康相关法律法规的宣传，提高职业卫生监督管理人员的法律意识、危害防范意识和管理水平。

（3）形式

1）举办健康教育讲座：在工作场所组织讲座、座谈会或小组讨论，向员工讲解职业病的预防知识、安全生产常识等。

2）开展公众健康咨询活动：组织员工参与模拟演练、急救培训或职业危害识别训练，让他们通过实际操作掌握职业病防护技能，提高应对突发情况的能力。

3）健康教育处方：医护人员可以根据员工的职业特点和健康状况，针对性地提供健康教

occupational characteristics and health conditions of employees including providing suggestions for preventing occupational diseases and lifestyle guidance in order to enhance employee' awareness of healthcare.

4) Adopt the "Internet +" health education model: Establishing an internal health communication network platform to provide health micro-classes, health information browsing and other services, so that employees can obtain occupational disease prevention knowledge and health information anytime and anywhere.

3. School Health Education

(1) Target Population: Students, teachers and staff, parents, school administrators, etc.

(2) Main Contents

1) Sexual health education: This involves education on sexual health, sexual behavior, prevention of sexually transmitted diseases, and contraception, etc., aiming to help adolescents develop correct attitudes towards sexuality.

2) Psychological health education: This focuses on addressing psychological health issues among adolescents, including stress management, emotional regulation, self-cognition and self-care skills, etc.

3) Diet and nutrition education: This provides information on healthy eating and nutrition to educate adolescents on how to adopt healthy eating habits to prevent obesity, malnutrition, and related diseases.

4) Physical exercise education: This emphasizes the importance of physical exercise for health and teaches adolescents how to engage in safe and effective physical activities.

5) Narcotic drug and drug abuse prevention education: This educates adolescents about the dangers of narcotic drugs, raises their awareness of drug abuse, and helps them develop resistance to narcotic drugs.

6) Health promotion and disease prevention: This includes education on hygiene habits, prevention of infectious and chronic diseases,

育处方，包括预防职业病的建议和生活方式指导，以促进员工的健康保健意识。

4）采用"互联网+"的健康教育模型：建立企业内部的健康传播网络平台，提供健康微课堂、健康资讯浏览等服务，让员工随时随地获取职业病防护知识和健康信息。

3. 学校健康教育

（1）目标人群：学生、教师和教职工、家长、学校管理者等。

（2）主要内容

1）性健康教育：涉及性健康、性行为、预防性传播疾病和避孕等方面的教育，旨在帮助青少年建立正确的性观念。

2）心理健康教育：关注青少年的心理健康问题，包括压力管理、情绪调节、自我认知和自我照顾技能等方面的教育。

3）饮食与营养教育：提供关于健康饮食和营养方面的知识，教育青少年如何养成健康的饮食习惯，预防肥胖、营养不良和相关疾病。

4）运动与体育教育：强调体育锻炼对健康的重要性，教育青少年如何进行安全有效的运动锻炼。

5）预防毒品与药物滥用教育：教育青少年认识毒品的危害，提高他们对药物滥用的警觉，帮助他们培养拒绝毒品的意识和能力。

6）健康促进与疾病预防：包括卫生习惯养成、预防传染病和慢性病的教育，以及提倡健康的生活方式，预防疾病发生。

promotion of healthy lifestyles, and disease prevention.

7) Interpersonal relationships and social skills education: This assists adolescents in building positive interpersonal relationships, enhancing social skills, and acquiring effective communication and problem-solving abilities.

8) Health literacy education: This cultivates adolescents' understanding of health information and teaches them how to access, evaluate, and apply health information to avoid misinformation or harmful influences.

(3) Forms

1) Classroom education approach: This delivers health knowledge and skills to students through formal classroom teaching. The topics include nutrition, mental health, and physical exercise. This form is the core of school health education and allows for systematic delivery of health knowledge.

2) "Internet +" education approach: This utilizes internet technology to establish online health communication platforms, health "micro-classrooms," and health "micro-profiles", etc., to meet students' health needs. Utilize information technology means such as the internet and multimedia courseware to innovate forms of health education, provide diverse and convenient health education resources to meet students' learning needs.

3) Comprehensive education approach: For example, health promoting school adopts a whole-school approach, leveraging the organizational potential of schools to create conditions for school health protection and positive educational outcomes.

V. Evaluation of Community Health Education

Evaluation of community health education includes formative evaluation, process evaluation, effect evaluation, outcome evaluation and summary evaluation.

7）人际关系与社交技能教育：帮助青少年建立良好的人际关系，提高社交技能，学会如何有效沟通和解决问题。

8）健康素养教育：培养青少年对健康信息的理解能力，教育他们如何获取、评估和应用健康信息，避免受到错误或有害信息的影响。

（3）形式

1）课堂教育法：通过正式的课堂教学，向学生传授健康知识和技能，包括营养、心理健康、运动等方面的内容。这种形式是学校健康教育的核心，可以系统性地传递健康知识。

2）"互联网+"教育法：利用互联网技术，建立健康传播网络平台、开设健康"微课堂"、设立健康"微档案"等，满足学生的健康需求。利用信息技术手段，如互联网、多媒体课件等，创新健康教育形式，提供多样化、便捷化的健康教育资源，满足学生的学习需求。

3）综合教育法：如健康促进学校（health promoting school）采用全校参与法，通过开发学校的组织潜力，为保障学校健康和取得积极教育成果创造了条件。

五、社区健康教育评价

社区健康教育评价可分为形成性评价、过程评价、效应评价、结局评价以及总结评价。

i. Formative Evaluation

Formative evaluation is the process of providing information and value judgment for the design of a health education programme. It aims at making the programme plan appropriate to the actual situation of the target population, so that the programme is more scientific, complete and has the greatest chance of success. Formative evaluation mainly occurs in the beginning stage of design to the early stage of the programme implementation.

The content of formative evaluation includes: a. Basic characteristics and health problems of the target population, such as demographics and epidemiological data. b. The target population's perception of various interventions. c. The intervention strategies applicable to the target population. d. Pre-experiment of intervention. e. Perfection of health education materials. f. Delivery system of educational materials, including production, storage, distribution forms (e.g. wholesale, retail, complimentary) and distribution channels. A variety of research techniques can be used in formative evaluation, including review of literature, archives, data, survey of target population, field observation, pre-experiment, pilot study, etc. The indicators of formative evaluation are scientific nature of the plan, policy supportability, applicability of technology, and acceptability of the population.

ii. Process Evaluation

Process evaluation evaluates the quantity and quality of the health education programme during the implementation process. It aims at guaranteeing the quality of implementation of the project, and promoting the successful achievement of the project aims. Process evaluation is carried out throughout the implementation process. Data from process evaluation can provide rich information to explain the results of project implementation.

1. The Contents of Process Evaluation

a. The quality of implementers, such as the professional skills, working attitude and cooperation of the implementation personnel.

（一）形成性评价

形成性评价是为健康教育计划设计提供信息和价值判断的过程。其目的在于使项目计划适合目标人群的实际情况，让计划更科学、完善，有最大的成功机会。形成性评价主要发生在项目计划设计之初至实施早期。

形成性评价的内容包括：①目标人群的基本特征和健康问题，如人口学、流行病学资料；②目标人群对各种干预措施的看法；③适用于目标人群的干预策略；④干预预实验；⑤健康教育材料的完善性；⑥教育材料的交付体系，包括生产、贮存、发放形式（如批发、零售、赠送）及发放渠道。在形成性评价中可采用多种研究技术，包括文献、档案、资料的回顾，目标人群调查，现场观察，预实验，试点研究，等等。形成性评价的指标常采用计划的科学性、政策的可支持性、技术的适用性、人群的可接受性等。

（二）过程评价

过程评价是对健康教育计划实施过程中数量和质量的评价过程。其目的是保障项目计划实施的质量，促使项目目标成功实现。过程评价贯穿实施过程的始终。过程评价资料可为解释项目实施结果提供丰富的信息。

1. 过程评价内容

①实施人员质量，如实施人员的职业技能、工作态度和合作情况；②干预活动的实施质量，如干预是否适合目标人样且被他们接受，干预是否按计划的活动类型、时

b. The quality of intervention activities, such as whether the intervention is suitable for and accepted by the target population, and whether the intervention is implemented according to the planned type, time and frequency. c. Participation of the target population, e.g. the proportion of the target population receiving the intervention, the motivation to participate, and the reasons for non-participation. d. Use of supportive environment, such as the strength of policy implementation and other environmental support. e. Capacity of utilizing community organizations, such as the degree of participation of community organization and non-project staff. f. Significant environmental changes during project implementation and the impact on the project.

2. Methods of Process Evaluation

Establish a system of process tracking which is a monitoring and quality assessment system for implementation, aiming at providing organizational guarantee for complete and effective collection of feedback information on programme implementation. Methods of data collection for process evaluation include reviewing records files of activity, group discussions, random sample surveys, etc.

iii. Effect Evaluation

The effect evaluation of health education is to evaluate the recent effect of the project, that is, to evaluate the changes in the target population's behavior and the changes in influencing factors of behavior. Effect evaluation also includes non-behavioral changes such as support of organizations, policy and health care service.

iv. Outcome Evaluation

The outcome evaluation of health education is an evaluation of the changes in the health status and quality of life of the target population in the programme. It is also called long-term effect evaluation because changes in the health status and quality of life of the population often occur quite a long time after the behavioral change. Health status evaluation indicators, including physiological

间、频率实施;③目标人群的参与情况,如目标人群接受干预的比例、参与的动机和未参与的原因;④支持环境的利用情况,如政策贯彻和其他环境支持力度;⑤运用社区组织的能力,如社区组织和非项目工作人员的参与程度;⑥项目实施期间的重大环境变化及其对项目的影响。

2. 过程评价方法 建立过程追踪系统,即建立项目实施的监测和质量评估体系,为做到完整、有效地收集计划实施的反馈信息提供组织保证。过程评价资料收集方法包括查阅活动记录档案、小组讨论、随机抽样调查等。

(三)效应评价

健康教育的效应评价是对项目所产生的近期效果进行评价,即对目标人群的行为变化和行为影响因素的变化进行评价。效应评价的内容也包括非行为变化,包括组织、政策和卫生服务的支持变化等。

(四)结局评价

健康教育的结局评价是对项目引起的目标人群健康状况和生活质量的变化进行评价。人群健康状况和生活质量的变化往往在行为改变后相当长时间才出现,所以又称为长期效果评价。健康状况评价指标包括生理指标、疾病与死亡指标,通常通过疾病监测、现场调查来收集。生活质量常通过量表进行测量,通过调查收集相关资料。

indicators and disease and death indicators, are usually collected by disease surveillance and field surveys. Quality of life is often measured by a specific scale, and relevant data are collected through surveys.

v. Summary Evaluation

The summary evaluation of health education is a synthesis of the formative evaluation, process evaluation, effect evaluation and outcome evaluation, as well as a summary of all aspects of information. It is a comprehensive summary of health education and health promotion projects. The purpose of summary evaluation is to sum up the lessons and to provide scientific evidence for future project planning.

(Zhu Xuejiao)

Key Points

1. Community health education includes health knowledge dissemination, promotion of healthy lifestyles, disease prevention and management, community engagement and empowerment.

2. Health promotion and health education are closely related but different. Health promotion encompasses health education. Health education is a crucial strategy and method within health promotion. It is integrated into all aspects of health promotion process. However, there are some differences between health education and health promotion.

3. Key components of health promotion include good health governance, health literacy and healthy cities.

4. The occurrence of diseases is often closely related to unhealthy behavioral lifestyles. Changing unhealthy lifestyles is an important way to prevent diseases and improve the quality of healthy life.

5. Common theories related to community health education and health promotion include KAP model, health belief model, transtheoretical model, PRECEDE-PROCEED model, empowerment theory.

（五）总结评价

健康教育的总结评价是对形成性评价、过程评价、效应评价和结局评价的综合以及对各方面资料做出的总结性概况。它是对健康教育与健康促进项目的全面总结，其目的是总结经验教训，为今后计划项目提供科学依据。

（朱雪娇）

内容摘要

1. 社区健康教育涵盖健康知识传播、健康生活方式推广、疾病预防与管理、社区参与和赋权。

2. 健康促进和健康教育密切相关又有所不同。健康促进包括了健康教育，健康教育是健康促进的重要策略和方法之一，融合在健康促进的各个环节之中。但两者也存在一定的区别。

3. 健康促进的关键要素包括健康的良好治理、健康素养和健康城市。

4. 疾病发生常与不良行为生活方式息息相关，改变不良生活方式是预防疾病发生、提高健康生活质量的重要途径。

5. 社区健康教育及健康促进常见的相关理论包括：知信行（knowledge，attitude，practice，KAP）模式、健康信念模型（health belief model，HBM）、跨理论模型（又称行为转变阶段模型）、PRECEDE-PROCEED 模型、赋能理论。

6. The practice of community health education follows the five steps of the nursing procedure, which are assessment, diagnosis, planning, implementation and evaluation of community health education.

7. Assessment of community health education refers to the process of collecting and analyzing information related to health education targets and their environment, in order to understand their health education needs.

8. Common methods of community health education data collection include informant interviews, participatory observation, windshield survey, secondary analysis of existing data and questionnaire survey.

9. Common problems of community health education include 3 domains of learning: cognitive learning domain, affective learning domain, and motor skills learning domain.

10. Community health education programs should be clear, specific and comprehensive. A complete health education program should have expected goals, the date and location of implementation, specific content, implementation approach and evaluation methods.

11. Setting goals of community health education should follow SMART principles, that is, specific, measurable, attainable, relevant and time-bound.

12. When formulating health education programs, it is necessary to focus on the target group, define the goal of health education, determine the content of health education and choose appropriate methods of health information dissemination, and select effective evaluation methods and indicators of health education.

13. Common forms of community health education include language education method, literal education method, practical education method, multimedia education method, experiential education method and comprehensive education method.

14. Community health education should

6. 社区健康教育的实践遵循护理程序步骤,分别为社区健康教育的评估、诊断、计划、实施和评价。

7. 社区健康教育评估是指通过收集健康教育对象与环境的相关信息,并对资料进行分析,了解健康教育对象的健康教育需求的过程。

8. 收集社区健康教育资料的常用方法有:知情人访谈、参与式观察、挡风玻璃式调查、有数据的二次分析、问卷调查。

9. 常见的社区健康教育问题涉及三个领域:认知学习领域、情感学习领域和动作技能学习领域。

10. 社区健康教育计划要清晰、具体、全面,应该包含预期的目标、实施日期、实施地点、具体的内容、实施途径和评价方法。

11. 社区健康教育的目标制定遵循 SMART 原则:明确性(specific)、可测量性(measurable)、可实现性(attainable)、相关性(relevant)和时限性(time-bound)。

12. 制订健康教育计划时,要以教育对象为中心,明确健康教育目标,确定健康教育内容,并选择适当的健康信息传播方法,选择有效的健康教育评价方式及指标。

13. 社区健康教育常见的形式包括:语言教育法、文字教育法、实践教育法、多媒体教育法、体验式教育法、综合教育法。

14. 社区健康教育在不同实施场所,如生活

have its characteristics in different places of implementation, such as living communities, workplaces, schools, etc.

15. Evaluation of community health education includes formative evaluation, process evaluation, effect evaluation, outcome evaluation and summary evaluation.

社区、工作场所、学校等实施应各具特点。

15. 社区健康教育评价可分为形成性评价、过程评价、效应评价、结局评价以及总结评价。

Exercises

(Questions 1 to 2 share the same question stem)

Miss Wang, a community nurse, joined a newly developed community health center. Wang's team plans to conduct health education assessment for residents in the community.

1. What information should be collected during assessment process?

2. What methods can be used to collect information?

(Questions 3 to 4 share the same question stem)

In 2024, the health service for patients with chronic obstructive pulmonary disease was included in the national basic public health service project. Miss Li, a community nurse, plans to carry out a health education program aimed at improving awareness rate, early diagnosis rate and lung function screening rate of chronic obstructive pulmonary disease in the community.

3. What steps should be included in making a health education plan?

4. How to make the target plan of health education according to these steps?

思 考 题

（1~2 题共用题干）

社区王护士进入一所新建的社区卫生服务中心工作，王护士的团队拟对辖区的居民开展健康教育评估。

1. 在评估过程中，应该收集哪些资料？

2. 可以采取哪些方法收集资料？

（3~4 题共用题干）

2024 年，慢性阻塞性肺疾病患者的健康服务被纳入国家基本公共卫生服务项目，社区李护士拟开展一项健康教育项目，旨在提高辖区内慢性阻塞性肺疾病的知晓率、早诊率和肺功能筛查率。

3. 制订健康教育计划应包括哪些步骤？

4. 如何有针对性地制订该项健康教育计划？

Chapter 4

Community Family Health Management

第四章

社区家庭健康管理

04章

04章 数字内容

NURSING

Learning Objectives

Knowledge Objectives

1. Correctly describe the types of family structure, the content of family functions, the stage division of family life cycle and its development tasks, the type of family resources, the characteristics of healthy families and the necessary conditions required.

2. Correctly interpret the contents of family health care theory and the key points of family nursing assessment, diagnosis, planning, implementation and evaluation.

学习目标

知识目标

1. 正确描述家庭结构的类型、家庭功能的内容、家庭生活周期的阶段划分及其发展任务、家庭资源的类型、健康家庭的特点及应具备的条件。

2. 正确阐释家庭健康照护理论的内容，家庭护理评估、诊断、计划、实施与评价的要点。

3. Correctly describe the types, procedures, and precautions of home visit.

4. Correctly describe the purpose, object, form and content of home care.

- Ability Objectives

1. Utilize family nursing procedures to manage the health of community families.

2. Conduct home visit to the community service objects.

3. Develop personalized home care plans for homebound patients.

- Quality Objectives

1. Have a high sense of responsibility, compassion and love, and respect the privacy and rights of family members.

2. Be able to communicate effectively with family members, understand their needs and expectations, and provide personalized health services.

3. Cultivate teamwork spirit, establish good cooperative relationships with family members, other health care professionals and community institutions to jointly promote family health.

3. 正确描述家庭访视的类型、程序和注意事项。

4. 正确叙述居家护理的目的、对象、形式和内容。

- 能力目标

1. 运用家庭护理程序对社区家庭进行健康管理。

2. 对社区服务对象进行家庭访视。

3. 为居家患者制订个性化的居家护理计划。

- 素质目标

1. 具有高度的责任心、同情心和爱心，尊重家庭成员的隐私和权益。

2. 能够与家庭成员进行有效沟通，理解他们的需求和期望，提供个性化的健康服务。

3. 培养团队合作精神，与家庭成员、其他医护人员及社区机构建立良好的合作关系，共同促进家庭健康。

Mr. Zhang, 63 years old, a retired worker, suffers from chronic bronchitis and cor pulmonale, with poor cardiopulmonary function. His wife, Mrs. Li, 62 years old, a retired teacher, has had essential hypertension for many years and is being treated with oral antihypertensive medication. They have two sons who work out of town and rarely come home. One month ago, Mrs. Li was paralyzed in both lower limbs due to a stroke, and she was unable to take care of herself. After being discharged from the hospital, Mr.Zhang took care of his wife's daily life alone. Neither of the sons has returned home to take care of Mrs. Li, but they regularly provide their parents with certain living and medical expenses. During the community nurse's home visit, it was found that the couple's

张先生，63岁，退休工人，患有慢性支气管炎和肺源性心脏病，心肺功能欠佳。张先生的妻子，李女士，62岁，退休教师，患原发性高血压多年，口服降压药治疗。该夫妇有两个儿子，均在外地工作，平时很少回家。1个月前，妻子因脑卒中而导致双下肢瘫痪，生活不能自理。出院后，由张先生一个人承担妻子的日常生活照顾，两个儿子均未能回家照顾李女士，但定期给父母一定的生活费和医疗费。社区护士家庭访视时，发现夫妇二人血压控制均不稳定，喜欢吃腌制食品，指导夫妇改变饮食习惯，二人均不接受，并认为只需服用降压药控制血压即可。张先生主诉最近腰痛、入睡困难、轻微活动即胸闷气急、全身无力、疲劳。

blood pressure control was unstable and they liked to eat pickled food. When the nurse advised them to change their dietary habits, both of them refused and believed that blood pressure could be controlled solely by taking antihypertensive medication. Mr. Zhang complained of recent lumbago, difficulty falling asleep, oppression in chest and shortness of breath caused by mild activity, general weakness and fatigue.

Queations：

1. How to conduct a family nursing assessment for this family?

2. How to conduct a caregiver assessment for Mr. Zhang?

3. Please list the family's nursing diagnoses based on the nursing assessment.

4. Please make a family nursing plan for the first optimal nursing diagnosis of the family.

The family is the main environment of the individual's life and also the basic unit of the community. Individual health and family health influence each other, and community nurses should promote the health of families and their members by providing family-based health management.

Section 1   Family

I. The Concept of Family and Family Structure

i. The Concept of Family

The family is a social group characterized by permanent relationships based on blood, marriage, support, and emotional commitment, and is the most basic unit of human society. The health level of the family is closely related to the steady development of the individual's physical and mental health, and the family is an important place for the health care of family members.

ii. Family Structure

Family structure refers to the organizational

请思考：

1. 如何对该家庭进行家庭护理评估？

2. 如何对张先生进行照顾者评估？

3. 请根据护理评估列出该家庭的护理诊断。

4. 请针对该家庭的首优护理诊断制订家庭护理计划。

家庭是个体生活的主要环境，也是社区的基本单元。个体健康与家庭健康相互影响，社区护士应通过提供以家庭为单位的健康管理促进家庭及家庭成员的健康。

第一节　家　　庭

一、家庭的概念与家庭结构

（一）家庭的概念

家庭是具有血缘、婚姻、供养与情感承诺的永久关系的社会团体，是人类社会中最基本的单位。家庭的健康水平与个人生理、心理健康的稳步发展密不可分，家庭是家庭成员健康保健的重要场所。

（二）家庭结构

家庭结构是指家庭的组织结构和家庭成员

structure of the family and the relationships among family members, which is divided into the external family structure and the internal family structure.

1. External family structure　The external family structure refers to the demographic structure of the family, that is, the type of family. Here are several common types in China.

(1) Nuclear Family: A nuclear family refers to a family consisting of a couple and their biological or adopted unmarried children, including a family with only the couple. It can be further divided into the following types:

1) Standard nuclear family: It refers to a family consisting of parents and their unmarried children.

2) Couple nuclear family: It refers to a family consisting only of the couple, including DINK (dual income, no kids) families and empty-nest families in which the couples live alone due to their children leaving for work or marriage.

The nuclear family is the main family type in modern society. The nuclear family has the characteristics of small scale, simple structure, pure relationship and easy communication. There is only one power and activity center in the family, which makes it convenient to make decisions on important family events. The family structure and relationship are relatively stable and firm. However, because the family relationship is close and fragile and there are few resources available inside and outside the family,　nuclear families cannot get enough support when they encounter a crisis, which is easy to lead to family crisis or family breakdown.

(2) Lineal Family: It is also known as the stem family. It's the vertical expansion of the nuclear family. A lineal family refers to a family consisting of parents, married children, and the third generation. It can be further divided into the following types.

1) Two-generation lineal family: It refers to a family consisting of a couple and one married child.

间的相互关系，分为家庭外部结构和家庭内部结构。

1. 家庭外部结构　家庭外部结构是指家庭人口结构，即家庭的类型，我国常见的类型有以下几种。

（1）核心家庭：核心家庭是指由夫妇及其婚生或领养的未婚子女组成的家庭，包括仅有夫妇两人的家庭。具体可分为以下几种类型：

1）标准核心家庭：指由父母及其未婚子女组成的家庭。

2）夫妇核心家庭：指只由夫妇二人组成的家庭，包括丁克家庭、子女因工作或婚姻离家而父母独居的空巢家庭。

核心家庭是现代社会的主要家庭类型。核心家庭具有规模小、结构简单、关系单纯和容易沟通的特点，家庭内部只有一个权力与活动中心，便于决策家庭重要事件，其家庭结构和关系比较稳定、牢固。但由于家庭关系既亲密又脆弱且家庭内外可利用的资源少，遇到危机时，得不到足够的支持，容易导致家庭危机或家庭破裂。

（2）直系家庭：又称主干家庭，是核心家庭的纵向扩大。直系家庭是指由父母、已婚子女及第三代人组成的家庭。具体可分为以下几种类型。

1）二代直系家庭：指夫妇和一个已婚子女组成的家庭。

2) Three-generation lineal family: It refers to a family consisting of a couple, one married child, and grandchildren. A family consisting of the household head couple, their parents and their children is also considered a three-generation lineal family.

3) Four-generation lineal family: It refers to a family consisting of the household head couple, their parents, their children and grandchildren. The family has larger numbers of members, more complex structures, and a power and activity center, as well as a sub-center. However, it has more available resources and stronger abilities to cope with family crises, which is conducive to maintaining the stability of the family.

(3) Collateral Family: It is also known as the joint family or duplex family, is the horizontal expansion of the nuclear family. It can be further divided into the following types.

1) A family consisting of parents and several married children and grandchildren.

2) A family consisting of two or more married siblings. There is a power and activity center and several sub-centers in the family, or several power and activity centers coexist. The structure is relatively loose and unstable, and a variety of relationships and interests are intertwined, and the decision-making process is complex. However, there are more resources inside and outside the family, which is conducive to the family's adaptation and coping with the crisis.

(4) Others: Such as single-parent family, single family, cohabitating family, etc.

Most families in China are still based on marriage and protected by law, holding the profound traditional concepts and maintaining relatively stable family relations. However, with the development of the economy and society, the family structure has changed significantly. At present, the nuclear families have become the mainstream form, and at the same time, the number of empty-nesters and the elderly people living alone is constantly increasing, which further

2）三代直系家庭：即夫妇和一个已婚子女及孙子女组成的家庭。或者户主夫妇与父母及其子女组成的家庭也是三代直系家庭。

3）四代直系家庭：指户主夫妇与父母、子女夫妇及孙子女组成的家庭。家庭人数相对较多，结构较为复杂，往往有一个权力与活动中心和一个次中心存在，但可利用的家庭资源较多，应对家庭危机的能力较强，有利于维持家庭的稳定。

（3）旁系家庭：又称联合家庭、复式家庭，是核心家庭的横向扩大。具体可分为以下几种类型。

1）由父母同几对已婚子女及孙子女构成的家庭。

2）两对及以上已婚兄弟姐妹组成的家庭。家庭内存在一个权力与活动中心及几个次中心，或几个权力与活动中心并存。结构相对松散、不稳定，多种关系和利益交织，其决策过程复杂。但家庭内外资源较多，有利于家庭对危机的适应与处理。

（4）其他：如单亲家庭、单身家庭、同居家庭等。

我国多数家庭依然以婚姻为基础、法律为保障，秉持着深厚的传统观念，维持着相对稳定的家庭关系。然而，随着经济和社会的发展，家庭结构发生了显著变化。当前，核心家庭已成为主流形态，同时，空巢老人和独居老人的数量不断攀升，这进一步加重了社会养老的负担。此外，由于人口流动性的增强、离婚率的上升、青年晚婚现象的增加、未婚生育的频发、人类预期寿命的延长以及丧偶情况的增多，单身家庭和单亲家庭也呈现出日益增多的趋势。为了维

increases the burden of social pension. In addition, due to the increasing mobility of the population, the rising divorce rate, the increase of late marriage among young people, the frequency of unmarried births, the prolongation of human life expectancy and the increase in the number of widowed cases, single families and single-parent families also show an increasing trend. To maintain the normal functioning of their families, family members must make corresponding role adjustments to adapt to these changes. It is worth noting that such families often face higher family health risks. Therefore, community nurses, as professional health service providers, should provide necessary health guidance and support for these families with a rigorous, prudent and rational attitude, so as to promote the physical and mental health of family members and maintain the stability and harmony of the family.

2. Internal Family Structure The internal family structure refers to the interactive behaviors among family members, including four factors: family roles, family power, family communication, and family values.

(1) Family Roles: It refers to the specific status of the family members in the family. The status of family roles includes three types:

1) Role expectation: It refers to a specific role orientation formed by family members under compliance or default expectations or requirements. All family members have role expectations, such as the mother，who is expected to be gentle and loving, and whose responsibility is to raise children and do housework. Healthy role expectations are caring and encouraging for family members, which are conducive to the growth and self-realization of members, and promote family development.

2) Role learning: It means that family members need to complete corresponding role behaviors through continuous learning to achieve role expectations. This continuous learning process is called role learning. Family members learn the emotions, attitudes, powers and responsibilities

持家庭的正常功能,家庭成员必须做出相应的角色调适,以适应这些变化。值得注意的是,这类家庭往往面临着更高的家庭健康风险。因此社区护士作为专业的健康服务提供者,应以严谨、稳重、理性的态度,为这些家庭提供必要的健康指导和支持,以促进家庭成员的身心健康,维护家庭的稳定与和谐。

2. 家庭内部结构 家庭内部结构是指家庭成员间的互动行为,包括家庭角色、家庭权力、家庭沟通与家庭价值观四个因素。

（1）家庭角色:指家庭成员在家庭中的特定地位。家庭角色的状态包括3种类型:

1）角色期待:指家庭成员在遵守或默认的期望或要求下,所形成的某种特定角色定位。所有的家庭成员都存在角色期待,如母亲被期待为温柔、慈爱的形象,其职责是抚养子女、操持家务。健康的角色期待对家庭成员是关心和鞭策,有利于成员的成长和自我实现,促进家庭发展。

2）角色学习:指家庭成员需要通过不断学习来完成相应的角色行为从而实现角色期待,这个不断学习的过程称为角色学习。家庭成员要学习家庭角色的情感、态度、权力和责任。角色学习是一种综合性、无止境的学习,家庭成员需要不断适应角色的转变。如一位男士,原关

of family roles. Role learning is a kind of comprehensive and endless learning, and family members need to constantly adapt to role changes. For example, the original roles of a man are a son and a husband, and after the child is born, he must learn to be a father.

3）Role conflict：It refers to a situation where family members cannot achieve their role expectations of the family, or cannot adapt to the role changes, they will experience contradictions and conflicts, which is called role conflict. It can be caused by differences in role expectations of oneself, others, or the environment. Role conflict often leads to personal emotional and psychological function disorders. In severe cases, physical dysfunction may occur, which affects the normal function of the family, and even leads to family dysfunction, and affects the family health.

The functioning of family roles is an important factor affecting family health. Here are the criteria to determine whether the family role function is normal：a. Whether the family has the same role expectations for a certain role. b. Whether each family member can adapt to his or her own role model. c. Whether the role behavior of family members is consistent with social norms and is acceptable to society. d. Whether the role of family members can meet the psychological needs of other family members. e. Whether the family role has a certain flexibility to adapt to the role transformation and assume a variety of roles.

(2) Family Power：It refers to the influence, control, and authority of family members within the family. It can be divided into three types：

1）Traditional authoritarian type：It refers to the authority derived from tradition and derived from the social and cultural traditions in which the family is located. For example, in a male-dominated society, the father is the family authority, regardless of his social status and occupation.

2）Situational authority type：It refers to the transfer of family power due to changes in

是儿子、丈夫的角色，孩子出生后要学习做父亲的角色。

3）角色冲突：指当家庭成员不能实现家庭对其的角色期待，或不能适应角色转变时，便会产生矛盾、冲突的心理，称为角色冲突。它可由自身、他人或环境对角色期待的差异而引起。角色冲突常会导致个人情绪和心理功能紊乱，严重时会出现躯体功能障碍，影响家庭的正常功能，甚至导致家庭功能障碍，影响家庭健康。

家庭角色功能的优劣是影响家庭健康的重要因素。家庭角色功能是否正常的判断标准为：①家庭对某一角色的角色期待是否一致；②每位家庭成员是否都能适应自己的角色模式；③家庭成员的角色行为是否与社会规范一致，能否被社会所接受；④家庭成员的角色能否满足其他家庭成员的心理需求；⑤家庭角色是否具有一定弹性而适应角色转换，并承担多种角色。

（2）家庭权力：指家庭成员对家庭的影响力、控制权和支配权。可分为3种类型。

1）传统独裁型：指由传统而来，是由家庭所在的社会文化传统规定而来的权威。如男性主导的社会，父亲是为家庭权威人物，而不考虑其社会地位、职业等。

2）情况权威型：指家庭权力会因家庭情况的变化而产生权力转移，即家庭中谁负责供养

family circumstances, that is, in the family, the one who is responsible for supporting the family and controlling the family's economic power has the greatest power.

3) Sharing authority type: It refers to the situation where family members share authority and make decisions together. Each family can have multiple power structures coexisting, and there can be different types in different periods.

(3) Family Communication: It refers to the process of exchanging emotions, wishes, needs, opinions, information and values among family members, and it is an important indicator to evaluate family functioning. Effective communication can resolve family conflicts, solve family problems, and promote the formation of good relations among family members.

(4) Family Values: It refers to the thoughts, attitudes and beliefs of family members about the code of conduct of family activities and life goals. Its formation is influenced by the cultural background, religious beliefs and realistic situation of the family. The family's attitudes and beliefs toward health influence family members' perceptions of illness, health-seeking behavior, treatment compliance and health-promoting behaviors directly. Understanding family's values, especially health perspectives enable community nurses to address family's health issues more effectively.

II. Family Function and Resources

i. Family Function

Family function refers to the effective role performed by family members in family production and social life. It is mainly reflected in maintaining the integrity of the family, meeting the needs of the family and its members, and realizing the expectations of society for the family.

1. Affective Function It refers to the mutual care, support, and understanding among family members, which can meet the needs for love and to be loved, and provide family members

家庭、主宰家庭经济大权，其权力便最大。

3）分享权威型：指家庭成员分享权威，共同商量作出决定。每个家庭可以有多种权力结构并存，不同时期也可以有不同类型。

（3）家庭沟通：指家庭成员间在情感、愿望、需求、意见、信息与价值观等方面进行交换的过程，是评价家庭功能状态的重要指标。有效沟通能化解家庭矛盾、解决家庭问题，促进家庭成员间形成良好的关系。

（4）家庭价值观：指家庭成员对家庭活动的行为准则及生活目标的思想、态度和信念。它的形成受到家庭所处的文化背景、宗教信仰与现实状况的影响。家庭对健康的态度和信念直接影响家庭成员对疾病的认识、就医行为、遵医行为和健康促进行为等。社区护士了解家庭价值观，尤其是健康观，有利于解决家庭健康问题。

二、家庭功能与资源

（一）家庭功能

家庭功能是指家庭成员在家庭生产和社会生活中所发挥的有效作用。主要表现在维持家庭的完整性、满足家庭及其成员的需要、实现社会对家庭的期望等方面。

1. 情感功能 指家庭成员间彼此关爱、支持和理解，可以满足家庭成员爱与被爱的需求，使家庭成员获得归属感与安全感。

with a sense of belonging and security.

2. Economic Function   It refers to the economic resources needed to maintain family life, including material goods, space, and money, to meet the needs of family members in aspects such as clothing, food, housing, transportation, education, healthcare, and entertainment.

3. Reproductive and Nurturing Function The family has the function of reproducing and raising the next generation and supporting the elderly. It serves to perpetuate humanity and society.

4. Socialization Function   The family has the responsibility and obligation to help its young members adapt to the society, to provide them with education for social adaptation, so that they form a correct outlook on life, sound values and a healthy attitude towards health.

5. Health Care Function   Family members take care of each other, maintain each other's healths, and provide various kinds of care and support when any of them fall ill.

ii. Family Resources

Family resources refer to the material and spiritual support needed to maintain the basic functions of the family and to deal with stressful events and critical states, which can be divided into intra-family resources and extra-family resources.

1. Intra-Family Resources   The resources include economic support, maintenance support, health protection, emotional support, information education, and structural support.

(1) Economic Support: It refers to a certain economic source that ensures the basic living, educational, cultural, health care and entertainment needs of family members.

(2) Maintenance Support: It refers to supporting and maintaining the reputation, status and rights of family members.

(3) Health Protection: It refers to providing and arranging medical care for family members to maintain the health of family members.

(4) Emotional Support: It involves offering

2. **经济功能**   指维系家庭生活需要的经济资源,包括物质、空间及金钱等,以满足家庭成员的衣、食、住、行、教育、医疗、娱乐等方面的需要。

3. **生殖养育功能**   指家庭具有繁衍和养育下一代、赡养老年人的功能。它起到延续人类和社会的作用。

4. **社会化功能**   指家庭有培养其年幼成员适应社会的责任与义务,为其提供适应社会的教育,使其具有正确的人生观、价值观和健康观。

5. **健康照顾功能**   指家庭成员间相互照顾,维护家庭成员的健康,并在家庭成员患病时提供各种照顾与支持的功能。

(二)家庭资源

家庭资源是指为维持家庭基本功能及应对紧张事件和危机状态所需要的物质和精神上的支持,可分为家庭内资源和家庭外资源。

1. **家庭内资源**   包括经济支持、维护支持、健康防护、情感支持、信息教育、结构支持6个方面。

(1)经济支持:指一定的经济来源,以保证家庭成员的基本生活、教育、文化、医疗和娱乐需要。

(2)维护支持:支持维护家庭成员的名誉、地位和权利。

(3)健康防护:为家庭成员提供、安排医疗照顾,维护家庭成员的健康。

(4)情感支持:关怀、精神支持家庭成员,

care and spiritual support for family members to meet the emotional needs of family members.

(5) Information Education: It involves providing medical consulation, advice and health education for family members.

(6) Structural Support: It involves constructing or reconstructing of family residences or facilities to meet the needs of ill family members.

2．Extra-Family Resources　The resources include seven aspects: social resources, cultural resources, religious resources, economic resources, educational resources, environmental resources and health service resources.

(1) Social Resources: They refer to the care and support from relatives, friends and social groups.

(2) Cultural Resources: They refer to the support rooted in culture, tradition, customs, etc.

(3) Religious Resources: They refer to the support of religious groups and religious beliefs.

(4) Economic Resources: They refer to the sponsorship, income, welfare and insurance outside the family.

(5) Educational Resources: They refer to the educational system, educational mode and educational level.

(6) Environmental Resources: It refers to the living environment in the family, community facilities and public environment.

(7) Health service Resources: It refers to the general term of the factors of production for providing medical services, it usually includes personnel, medical expenses, medical institutions, medical beds, medical facilities and equipment, knowledge and skills, information and health care systems, etc.

Ⅲ. Family Life Cycle

1. Definition　The family life cycle is the process of the formation, development and even extinction of the family in accordance with the laws of society and nature.

满足家人的情感需求。

（5）信息教育：为家庭成员提供医疗咨询、建议及家庭内的健康教育。

（6）结构支持：建设或改建家庭住所或设施，以满足患病家庭成员的需求。

2．家庭外资源　包括社会资源、文化资源、宗教资源、经济资源、教育资源、环境资源和卫生服务资源7个方面。

（1）社会资源：指来自亲友和社会团体的关怀支持。

（2）文化资源：指文化、传统、习俗等支持。

（3）宗教资源：指宗教团体的支持及宗教信仰。

（4）经济资源：指家庭外的赞助、收入、福利与保险等。

（5）教育资源：指教育制度、教育方式和教育水平等。

（6）环境资源：指家庭内居住环境、社区设施和公共环境。

（7）卫生服务资源：指提供医疗服务的生产要素的总称，通常包括人员、医疗费用、医疗机构、医疗床位、医疗设施和装备、知识技能、信息和卫生保健制度等。

三、家庭生活周期

1．定义　家庭生活周期是家庭遵循社会与自然规律而经历的形成、发展甚至消亡的过程。

2. Stages, Tasks, and Nursing Points

In the process of family development, Duvall thought that the family life cycle is mainly divided into eight stages (Table 4-1). Families have their own family development tasks at each stage of the family life cycle. Family development tasks refer to the issues related to family health caused by normal changes in each stages of development. If the family can successfully complete family development tasks at each stage, it can form a healthy family, otherwise, there will be family problems that are not conducive to the healthy development of the family.

2. 阶段、任务及护理要点

在家庭的发展过程中，Duvall 认为家庭生活周期主要分为 8 个阶段（表 4-1）。家庭在家庭生活周期的每个阶段都有各自的家庭发展任务。家庭发展任务是指家庭在各发展阶段所面临的由正常变化所致的与家庭健康相关的课题。如果家庭能顺利完成各阶段的家庭发展任务，就能形成健康家庭，否则，就会出现家庭问题从而不利于家庭的健康发展。

Table 4-1   Duvall Family Life Cycle

No.	Stage	Definition	Developmental Tasks	Nursing Points
1	Newly married couple stage	Union of a couple	• Mutual adaptation and communication • Coordination of the sexual life • Family planning	• Premarital health check-up • Sexual life guidance • Family planning guidance
2	Childbearing and infancy stage	The oldest child is aged between 0 and 30 months	• Parental role adaptation • Economic pressure • Infant care • Maternal recovery	• Breastfeeding guidance • Establishing family-social support systems • Infant healthcare • Postpartum health care
3	Preschool-age children stage	The oldest child is aged between 30 months and 6 years old	• Physical and mental development of children • Partial separation of children from parents (kindergarten) • Prevention of accidental injuries	• Monitoring and promoting growth and development • Psychological guidance for parents and children • Accident prevention
4	School-age children stage	The oldest child is aged between 6 and 13 years old	• Physical and mental development of children • Adaptation to school • Gradual socialization	• Health care for school-stage children • Properly coping with academic pressure • Appropriate socialization
5	Adolescent stage	The oldest child is aged between 13 and 20 years old	• Education and communication for adolescents • Interactions with the opposite sex • Sex education for adolescents	• Guidance of effective communication • Education and sex education of adolescents • Prevention of early marriage and puppy love
6	Launching stage	From the oldest child leaving home to the youngest child leaving home	• Parent-child relationship • Parents gradually feel lonely • Increasing incidence of diseases	• Psychological counseling • Eliminating loneliness • Periodic physical examination

Continued Table

No.	Stage	Definition	Developmental Tasks	Nursing Points
7	Empty nest stage	From the time when all children have left home to parents' retirement	● Re-adaptation to the marital relationship ● Planning for post-retirement life ● Issues related to diseases	● Marital relationship adjustment ● Cultivating interests and hobbies ● Periodic physical examination
8	Retirement stage	From retirement to death	● Adaptation to retirement life ● High economic and living dependency ● Coping with illness and facing death	● Retirement life adjustment ● Improving self-care and social life ability ● Prevention and management of chronic diseases and hospice care

表 4-1　Duvall 家庭生活周期表

序号	阶段	定义	发展任务	护理要点
1	新婚期	男女结合	● 双方适应与沟通 ● 性生活协调 ● 计划生育	● 婚前健康检查 ● 性生活指导 ● 计划生育指导
2	婴幼儿期	最大孩子年龄为 0~30 个月	● 父母角色适应 ● 经济压力 ● 婴幼儿照顾 ● 母亲康复	● 母乳喂养指导 ● 建立家庭 - 社会支持系统 ● 婴幼儿保健 ● 产后保健
3	学龄前儿童期	最大孩子年龄为 30 个月~6 岁	● 儿童身心发育 ● 孩子与父母部分分离（上幼儿园） ● 意外伤害的预防	● 监测和促进生长发育 ● 父母和儿童的心理指导 ● 防止意外事故
4	学龄儿童期	最大孩子年龄为 6~13 岁	● 儿童的身心发展 ● 孩子适应上学 ● 逐步社会化	● 学龄期儿童保健 ● 正确应对学习压力 ● 合理社会化
5	青少年期	最大孩子年龄为 13~20 岁	● 青少年的教育与沟通 ● 青少年与异性交往 ● 青少年性教育	● 有效沟通指导 ● 青春期教育与性教育 ● 防止早婚早恋
6	孩子离家创业期	最大孩子离家至最小孩子离家	● 父母与孩子关系 ● 父母逐渐有孤独感 ● 疾病开始增多	● 心理咨询 ● 消除孤独感 ● 定期体检
7	空巢期	所有孩子离家至家长退休	● 重新适应婚姻关系 ● 开始计划退休后生活 ● 疾病问题	● 婚姻关系调适 ● 培养兴趣爱好 ● 定期体检
8	退休期	退休至死亡	● 适应退休生活 ● 经济及生活的依赖性高 ● 面临疾病及死亡的打击	● 退休生活调适 ● 提高生活自理和社会生活能力 ● 慢性病防治和临终关怀

Not every family will go through the above eight stages, and the family life cycle can start or

并非每个家庭都会一一经历上述的 8 个阶段，可在任何一阶段开始或结束，如果再婚或离

end at any stage. If there is remarriage or divorce, such families may have more family problems and need the attention of community nurses. Therefore, community nurses should predict and identify the problems that may or have occurred in the family at a specific stage according to the characteristics of the family life cycle, and take necessary preventive or intervention measures to avoid adverse consequences.

IV. Family Health Care Theory

The commonly used theories of family health care include family system theory, structural-functional theory, family stress theory, growth development theory, family resilience theory, family communication theory and family-centered care model and so on. Community nurses should flexibly apply various theories to guide nursing practice according to the actual situation.

1. Family System Theory It was proposed by American psychotherapist Murray Bowen in the late 1940s. Family system theory views the family as a system in which family members are interconnected and influence each other. In the community nursing work, community nurses should fully consider the influence of the relationship between family members and take effective measures to promote the benign operation of the family system.

2. Structural-functional Theory Also known as the harmony theory or equilibrium theory, the structural-functional theory has its main representatives are Parsons and Merton. This theory holds that society is a system with certain structure or organizational means, and all components of society are interrelated in an orderly way and play a necessary function for the society as a whole. If a part fails to play its function, there will be disharmony in the society. When the needs of the society coincide with the needs of the components, the society will remain in balance. The family is one of the social structures, and each family in the society is related to others

婚，这样的家庭可能发生更多的家庭问题，需要社区护士予以关注。因此，社区护士应根据家庭所处生活周期的特点，来预测和识别家庭在特定阶段可能或已经出现的问题，采取必要的预防或干预措施，避免出现不良后果。

四、家庭健康照护理论

家庭健康照护常用理论有家庭系统理论、结构功能理论、家庭压力理论、成长发展理论、家庭抗逆力理论、家庭沟通理论和以家庭为中心的护理模式等。社区护士在家庭护理工作中应根据实际情况灵活应用各种理论来指导护理实践。

1. 家庭系统理论 由美国心理治疗家 Murray Bowen 教授在 20 世纪 40 年代末提出。家庭系统理论认为：家庭是一个系统，家庭成员是系统的组成部分，家庭成员之间相互联系、彼此影响。社区护士在社区护理工作中，应充分考虑家庭成员间关系的影响，采取有效措施促成家庭系统良性运转。

2. 结构功能理论 又称和谐理论或均衡理论，其主要代表人物是 Parsons 和 Merton。该理论认为社会是具有一定结构或组织化手段的系统，社会的各组成部分以有序的方式相互关联，并对社会整体发挥着必要的功能。如果某一部分不能发挥其功能，社会就会出现不和谐，当社会需要与各组成部分需求一致时，社会将保持平衡。家庭是社会结构之一，社会中各家庭以有序方式相互关联，如果某家庭不能发挥其功能，社会就会出现不和谐。在社区护理工作中，社区护士应关注家庭的情感、社会化、生殖、经济、照护及卫生保健等功能是否正常，从而使家庭健康有序发展。

in an orderly way. If a family cannot play its function, the society will appear disharmonious. In the community nursing work, community nurses should pay attention to whether the family's emotional, social, reproductive, economic, care and health care functions are normal, so as to make the healthy and orderly development of the family.

3. Family Stress Theory　Hill proposed the classic ABCX family stress model. According to the ABCX model, A is the event/situation that causes stress, B is the internal and external resources possessed by the family when the stress occurs, C is the family's cognition of the stressful event, and ABC factors work together to form X, that is, the degree of stress or crisis. The model holds that families with resource advantage and positive cognition towards pressure have stronger ability to cope with family pressure. In the community nursing work, community nurses should not only understand the characteristics of the pressure faced by the family and the internal and external resources of the family, but also consider the cognitive status of the family members towards stressful events.

4. Growth Development Theory　The theory mainly studies the development of social psychology, and the representative theories include Freud's psychosexual development theory, Erikson's psychosocial development theory and Piaget's cognitive development theory. These theories divide the personality development stages from different perspectives, but they all emphasize that each development stage has its own special development tasks, and the successful completion of these development tasks is the basis for the smooth passage of the next stage. A family has the process of formation, development and termination, and it has different family development tasks in different stages. Family members in the process of family development need to properly deal with the development tasks of various stages to make the family develop healthily. If there is a conflict at a certain stage of family development and the

3．家庭压力理论　Hill 提出了经典的 ABCX 家庭压力模型。ABCX 模型认为，A 是引发压力的事件／情境，B 是在压力发生时家庭拥有的内部和外部资源，C 是家庭对压力事件的认知，ABC 因素共同作用构成了 X，即压力或危机的程度。该模型认为具有资源优势和对压力持正向认知的家庭有较强的应对家庭压力的能力。社区护士在社区护理工作中，既要了解家庭所面临的压力本身特性和家庭的内外部资源，还要考虑家庭成员对压力事件的认知状态。

4．成长发展理论　成长发展理论主要研究社会心理方面的发展，代表性理论有 Freud 的性心理发展学说、Erikson 的心理社会发展学说和 Piaget 的认知发展学说。这些理论从不同的角度划分人格发展阶段，但都强调每个发展阶段有其特殊的发展任务，成功地完成这些发展任务是顺利通过下一阶段的基础。家庭有其产生、发展和结束的过程，家庭在不同阶段有不同的家庭发展任务，家庭成员在家庭发展过程中需要妥善处理各阶段的发展任务才能使家庭健康发展。如果家庭在某发展阶段出现矛盾，不能完成家庭发展任务，则会出现家庭健康问题。社区护士在社区护理工作中，应评估家庭的发展状态，帮助处于不同阶段的家庭及家庭成员良好地完成发展任务，促进家庭健康发展。

family fails to complete the family development tasks, family health problems will occur. In the community nursing work, the community nurses should assess the development status of the family, help the family and family members to complete the development tasks well in different stages, and promote the healthy development of the family.

5. Family Resilience Theory   Since it was proposed in 1983, McCubbin and his collaborators have revised the theory many times, forming a theoretical system with a certain depth and breadth. This theory focuses on the family's ability to adapt and recover in the face of adversity, stress, or crisis. It emphasizes that as a whole, the family and the interaction and collaboration among its members have an important impact on the family's ability to cope with adversity. In the community nursing work, community nurses should help the family to overcome the adversity and achieve the growth and development of the family by mobilizing the internal potential, tapping the external resources and actively coping with the difficulties when they are faced with the challenges.

6. Family Communication Theory First proposed by American scholars McLeod and Chaffee in 1972, it is a very important theory in the field of family communication. It focuses on information flow and relationship building within the family, and divides family communication into two types: conversation orientation and conformity orientation. It mainly focuses on the influence of different family communication modes on the information processing, interaction style and social psychology of family members. In family care, the more conversation orientation leads to greater social support for caregivers and the higher perception of care quality for care recipients. In the community nursing work, community nurses should understand the status of family communication and help families to build a high conversation-oriented family communication pattern to improve the overall health of family members through an open dialogue family

5. 家庭抗逆力理论   自 1983 年提出以后，McCubbin 及其合作者对该理论进行多次修订，形成了一个具有一定深度和广度的理论体系。该理论主要关注家庭在面对逆境、压力或危机时的适应和恢复能力，强调家庭作为一个整体，其成员之间的互动和协作对家庭应对逆境的能力具有重要影响。社区护士在社区护理工作中，应帮助家庭在面对挑战时，能够通过调动内在潜能、挖掘外在资源，以及积极应对困难，来克服逆境并实现家庭的成长与发展。

6. 家庭沟通理论   最早由美国学者McLeod 和 Chaffee 在 1972 年提出，是家庭传播领域一个非常重要的理论。家庭沟通理论关注家庭内的信息流通和关系建立，将家庭沟通分为对话定向和服从定向两种类型，主要关注不同家庭沟通模式对家庭成员的信息处理、互动方式和社会心理的影响。家庭护理情境中，对话定向比例越高，照顾者获得的社会支持越多，被照顾者拥有越高的护理质量感知度。社区护士在社区护理工作中，应了解家庭沟通的状况，帮助家庭构建高对话定向的家庭沟通模式，通过开放对话的家庭环境促进提高家庭成员的总体健康。

environment.

7. Family-Centered Care Model First proposed by Fond and Luciano in 1972, the family-centered care concept has been widely accepted by both domestic and international medical systems. The model emphasizes that doctors, nurses, patients and patients' families should participate in the care of the disease, and fully mobilize the disease management ability and enthusiasm of family members, so that family members can fully participate in the patient's disease care, which can effectively promote the recovery of the patients. In the community nursing work, community nurses should encourage family members to actively participate in the patient's disease care, and provide psychological, emotional and economic support for the family.

BOX 4-1　Learning More

Family Resilience Scale

The family resilience assessment scale (FRAS) was developed by Sixbey in 2005. It includes 6 dimensions and 54 items. It uses the Likert 5-level scoring method, with total scores ranging from 54 to 216 points. A higher score indicates a higher level of family resilience. The FRAS has good applicability and is currently the most widely used and well-developed family resilience scale. However, due to cultural specificity, the scale exhibits differences across different ethnic groups and different diseases types, so it needs to be revised and adjusted when used in China.

The Chinese version of the family resilience assessment scale (C-FRAS) is an adaptation of the FRAS for assessing the resilience of families with cancer patients in China. Apart from modifications and deletions of some items, it maintains the original 6 dimensions with a total of 51 items. The scoring method is consistent with the original scale and is primarily used for studying the family resilience of lung cancer patients.

7. 以家庭为中心的护理模式 Fond 和 Luciano 于 1972 年首次提出以家庭为中心的护理理念，目前已被国内外医疗系统广泛接受。该理论强调医生、护士、患者及患者家属应共同参与疾病的护理，且充分调动家庭成员疾病管理能力及积极性，使家庭成员全面参与患者疾病护理，可有效促使患者康复。在社区护理工作中，社区护士应鼓励家庭成员积极参与患者的疾病护理，为家庭提供心理、情感和经济支持。

BOX 4-1　知识拓展

家庭抗逆力量表

家庭抗逆力评估量表（family resilience assessment scale，FRAS）由 Sixbey 于 2005 年编制，包括 6 个维度、54 个条目。采用 Likert 5 级评分法，总分 54~216 分，得分越高说明家庭抗逆力水平越高。该量表适用性良好，是目前使用最广泛、发展最成熟的家庭抗逆力量表。但由于文化特异性，量表在不同种族和不同病种之间存在差异性，因此在我国使用时需进行修订和调试。

中文版家庭韧性评估量表（C-FRAS）是基于 FRAS 发展的适用于我国癌症患者家庭的评估量表，除部分条目的修改删除外，维持了原量表的 6 个维度，共 51 个条目。计分方式与原量表保持一致，主要用于肺癌患者家庭抗逆力的研究。

Section 2　Family Health

I. Overview of Healthy Family

i. The Concept of Healthy Family

A healthy family refers to a family that can operate effectively, where every family member can feel the cohesion of the family, meet and undertake individual growth, and cope with various challenges in life.

A healthy family focuses on the overall health of the family, rather than just on the individual health of the family members. A healthy family can fully utilize its various functions and ensure the physical and mental health of each family member.

ii. Characteristics of Healthy Family

A healthy family must have the following five characteristics.

1. **Have a Good Communication Atmosphere**　Family members can share their feelings and ideals, care for and support each other, enhance mutual understanding through effective communication, and resolve family conflicts.

2. **Can Promote the Development of Family Members**　Family members have sufficient freedom and emotional support to promote their growth and enable them to adapt to changes in the family.

3. **Can Actively Face and Solve Problems**　Be responsible for the family, actively solve various family problems, and seek external assistance when necessary.

4. **Have a Healthy Living Environment and Lifestyle**　The family has a healthy living environment, and the family members have a healthy lifestyle.

5. **Maintain Contact with Society**　Do not deviate from the society, and make reasonable use of social resources to meet the needs of family members.

第二节　家庭健康

一、健康家庭的概述

（一）健康家庭的概念

健康家庭是指能有效运作、每一个家庭成员都能感受到家庭的凝聚力、能够满足并承担个体的成长、能够应对生活中各种挑战的家庭。

健康家庭注重家庭整体的健康状态，而非仅关注家庭成员的个体健康。一个健康的家庭能够充分发挥其各项功能，保障每位家庭成员的身心健康。

（二）健康家庭的特征

一个健康的家庭必须具备以下 5 个特征。

1. **有良好的交流氛围**　家庭成员能分享感受与理想，相互关心并给予支持，通过有效沟通的方式增进彼此间的了解，并能化解家庭冲突。

2. **能促进家庭成员的发展**　家庭成员有足够的自由空间和情感支持，促进家庭成员成长使其能够适应家庭的变化。

3. **能积极面对及解决问题**　对家庭负责任，积极解决各种家庭问题，必要时寻求外援帮助。

4. **有健康的居住环境及生活方式**　家庭有健康的居住环境，家庭成员具备健康的生活方式。

5. **与社会保持联系**　不脱离社会，合理利用社会资源满足家庭成员的需要。

II. The Impact of Family on Health

The influence of the family on health is profound and comprehensive, involving all aspects of life.

1. Inheritance　Biological inheritance is an important factor affecting human health, and the occurrence of some diseases is related to genetic factors, such as thalassemia, hypertension, diabetes, etc.

2. Growth and Development　Family affects children's physiological and psychological development and social maturity, which is the basic environment for children's growth and development.

3. Behavior and Lifestyle　The health beliefs of family members often influence each other, and family members have similar behaviors and lifestyles.

4. The Occurrence, Development and Spread of Diseases　The family's health beliefs, disease prevention awareness, medical care seeking behavior, and compliance with medical advice all influence the occurrence, development, and spread of diseases within the family.

5. Rehabilitation and Death　Family support has a great impact on the treatment and rehabilitation of the disease, and the degree of support will affect the rehabilitation of the sick members or the disease aggravation or even death.

BOX 4-2　Learning More

The Impact of Intergenerational Support on the Health of the Elderly Population

Intergenerational support reflects the mutual support and contribution between the parent and the child, which is a two-way relationship between the two generations. Its contribution is divided into economic support and non-economic support. Economic support is mainly for the support of goods, cash and other aspects, while non-economic

二、家庭对健康的影响

家庭对健康的影响是深远而全面的，涉及生活的各个方面。

1. 遗传　生物遗传是影响人类健康的重要因素，某些疾病的发生与遗传因素有关，如地中海贫血、高血压、糖尿病等。

2. 生长发育　家庭影响儿童的生理、心理发展和社会性成熟，是儿童生长发育的基本环境。

3. 行为与生活方式　家庭成员的健康信念往往相互影响，家庭成员有相似的行为与生活方式。

4. 疾病发生、发展与传播　家庭的健康观、防病意识、就医和遵医行为等影响疾病在家庭中的发生、发展及传播。

5. 康复与死亡　家庭支持对疾病的治疗和康复有很大的影响，支持的程度将影响患病成员的康复或疾病加重甚至死亡。

BOX 4-2　知识拓展

代际支持对老年人口健康的影响

代际支持反映了父代与子代之间的相互支持及付出，是两代人之间的双向关系。其付出分为经济支持与非经济支持，其中经济支持主要为物品、现金等方面的支持，非经济支持主要为情感互动、照料等方面的支持。

support is mainly for emotional interaction, care and other aspects.

While advocating and promoting children to provide timely intergenerational support to the elderly in the family, it is more necessary to help them support the elderly in a "correct" and "appropriate" way. Intergenerational support should pay more attention to the independent status of the elderly population in the elderly care, and support the elderly population's role in "self-supporting" rather than replacing the "self-supporting" behavior of the elderly population.

在倡导和促进子女们对家中老人提供及时的代际支持的同时，更需要帮助他们以"正确""适宜"的方式支持老人。代际支持需更多注重老年人口在养老中的自主地位，更多支持老年人口"自我养老"作用的发挥，而非替代老年人口的"自我养老"行为。

Section 3　Family Nursing Process

第三节　家庭护理程序

Family nursing procedure is the main working method of family health nursing, which is the holistic nursing model of family unit. Community nurses conduct family nursing through family nursing assessment, diagnosis, plan, implementation and evaluation to maintain normal family function and promote family health.

家庭护理程序是家庭健康护理的主要工作方法，是以家庭为单位的整体护理模式。社区护士通过家庭护理评估、诊断、计划、实施和评价进行家庭护理，以维护家庭正常功能，促进家庭健康。

I. Family Nursing Assessment

一、家庭护理评估

Family nursing assessment is the process of collecting subjective and objective information to identify family health problems.

家庭护理评估是为确定家庭健康问题而收集主、客观资料的过程。

i. Assessment Object

（一）评估对象

1. The family　It includes the assessment of the health of individual family members and the family as a whole.

1. 家庭　包括家庭成员个人和家庭整体健康的评估。

2. Family Caregiver　Family caregiver refers to the person who provides help and care for patients from the three aspects of life, emotion and economy in the home environment, and must be blood related family members who are not employed.

2. 家庭照顾者　家庭照顾者是指在居家环境下，从生活、情感、经济3个方面为患者提供帮助和照顾的人，且一定为非雇佣关系的有血缘关系的家属。

ii. Assessment Content

（二）评估内容

1. The Family　The content of the family nursing assessment is presented in Table 4-2.

1. 家庭　家庭护理评估的内容见表4-2。

Table 4-2　Content of Family Nursing Assessment

Assessment items	The specific content of assessment
General family information	1. Home address and telephone number
	2. Basic information of family members (name, gender, age, occupation, education level, marital status, etc.)
	3. Health status of family members and the form of medical insurance
	4. Living habits of family members (diet, activities, sleep, rest, etc.)
	5. Family health management status
Home environment	1. Family geographical location (distance to community health service institutions)
	2. Surrounding environment of the family (air, greening, noise, sanitation, etc.)
	3. Home environment (living area, space allocation, facilities, sanitation, potential hazards, food and water safety, etc.)
Status of the sick members in the family	1. Type and prognosis of diseases
	2. Daily living ability and impaired degree
	3. Performance of family roles
	4. Disease consumption
Family development stage and development tasks	1. The current development stage and development task of the family
	2. The implementation of development tasks by families
Family structure	1. External family structure
	2. Internal family structure (role, power, communication, value)
Family function	1. Affective function
	2. Economic function
	3. Reproductive and nurturing function
	4. Socialization function
	5. Health care function
Family resources	1. Within-family resources (economic, maintenance, medical, emotional, structural, information and educational support)
	2. External-family resources (social relations and social security measures)
Relationship between the family and the society	1. Relationship between the family and relatives, community and society
	2. The ability of the family to utilize social resources
The ability and methods of the family to cope and deal with problems	1. Family members' awareness of health problems (understanding and awareness of diseases)
	2. Emotional changes among family members (restlessness, wavering, stress reactions)
	3. The determination of the family to overcome the disease (the participation of family members in nursing care)
	4. The way of the family to deal with health problems (acceptance, avoidance, role change, etc.)
	5. Life adjustment (diet, exercise, work and rest, etc.)
	6. The financial coping capacity of the family
	7. Care capacity of the family members

表 4-2　家庭护理评估内容

评估项目	评估具体内容
家庭一般资料	1. 家庭地址、电话
	2. 家庭成员基本资料（姓名、性别、年龄、职业、文化程度、婚姻状况等）
	3. 家庭成员健康状况及医疗保险形式
	4. 家庭成员生活习惯（饮食、活动、睡眠、休息等）
	5. 家庭健康管理状况
家庭环境	1. 家庭地理位置（与社区卫生服务机构的距离）
	2. 家庭周围环境（空气、绿化、噪声、卫生等）
	3. 居家环境（居住面积、空间分配、设施、卫生、潜在危害、食物和水的安全等）
家庭中患病成员的状况	1. 疾病的种类及预后
	2. 日常生活能力及受损程度
	3. 家庭角色履行情况
	4. 疾病消费
家庭发展阶段及发展任务	1. 家庭目前所处的发展阶段与发展任务
	2. 家庭履行发展任务的情况
家庭结构	1. 家庭外部结构
	2. 家庭内部结构（角色、权力、沟通、价值观）
家庭功能	1. 情感功能
	2. 经济功能
	3. 生殖养育功能
	4. 社会化功能
	5. 健康照顾功能
家庭资源	1. 家庭内资源（经济、维护、医疗、情感、结构、信息和教育支持）
	2. 家庭外资源（社会关系和社会保障措施）
家庭与社会的关系	1. 家庭与亲属、社区、社会的关系
	2. 家庭利用社会资源的能力
家庭应对和处理问题的能力与方法	1. 家庭成员对健康问题的认识（对疾病的理解和认识）
	2. 家庭成员间情绪上的变化（不安、动摇、压力反应）
	3. 家庭战胜疾病的决心（家庭成员参与护理的情况）
	4. 家庭应对健康问题的方法（接受、逃避、角色转变等）
	5. 生活调整（饮食、运动、作息等）
	6. 家庭的经济应对能力
	7. 家庭成员的照顾能力

2. Family Caregiver　The content of the family caregiver assessment is presented in Table 4-3.

2. 家庭照顾者　家庭照顾者护理评估的内容见表 4-3。

Table 4-3　Nursing Assessment Content of Family Caregivers

Assessment items	The specific content of assessment
General information of the family caregivers	1. Home address and telephone number
	2. Basic information (name, gender, age, family member, family role, occupation, education level, marital status, religion, family income, relationship with the care recipient)
	3. Health status and the form of medical insurance
	4. Living habits (diet, activities, sleep, rest, etc.)
	5. Economic situation
	6. Length of care
	7. Willingness to care
	8. The impact of caregiving on income
Family caregiver needs	1. Health needs
	2. Supporting service needs (information support, emotional support, housekeeping service, day care, community food delivery, etc.)
Care knowledge of the family caregiver	1. Knowledge of related diseases
	2. Knowledge of the care of related diseases
Care skills of the family caregiver	1. Care ability for related diseases
	2. Disease management ability
	3. Self-management level
	4. Learning ability of knowledge and skills of taking care
	5. Ability to access social care resources
Caregiving literacy of family caregivers	1. Healthy behavior
	2. Caregiving behavior
	3. Nutritional literacy
Family caregivers' psychological status	1. Positive feelings and positive emotions
	2. Negative feelings and negative emotions
Family caregivers' social support	1. Subjective and objective support
	2. Availability of support
Family caregivers' quality of life	1. Subjective quality of life
	2. Objective quality of life
Family caregivers' care load	1. Health status
	2. Mental state
	3. Economy
	4. Social life
Family caregivers' ability feeling	1. Satisfaction with the person being cared for
	2. Satisfaction with their own caregiving behavior
	3. The impact of caring behavior on the caregivers' personal life

表4-3 家庭照顾者护理评估内容

评估项目	评估具体内容
家庭照顾者一般资料	1. 家庭地址、电话 2. 基本资料（姓名、性别、年龄、家庭成员、家庭角色、职业、文化程度、婚姻状况、宗教信仰、家庭收入、与被照顾者的关系） 3. 健康状况及医疗保险形式 4. 生活习惯（饮食、活动、睡眠、休息等） 5. 经济状况 6. 照顾时长 7. 照顾意愿 8. 照顾对收入的影响
家庭照顾者需求	1. 健康需求 2. 支持性服务需求（信息支持、情感支持、家政服务、日间照护、社区送餐等）
家庭照顾者照护知识	1. 相关疾病知识 2. 相关疾病的照护知识
家庭照顾者照护技能	1. 照顾能力 2. 疾病管理能力 3. 自我管理水平 4. 照顾知识与技能学习能力 5. 获取社会照护资源能力
家庭照顾者照顾素养	1. 健康行为 2. 照护行为 3. 营养素养
家庭照顾者心理状况	1. 积极感受与积极情绪 2. 消极感受与消极情绪
家庭照顾者社会支持	1. 主客观支持 2. 支持利用度
家庭照顾者生活质量	1. 主观生活质量 2. 客观生活质量
家庭照顾者照顾负荷	1. 健康状况 2. 精神状态 3. 经济 4. 社会生活
家庭照顾者能力感受	1. 对被照顾者的满意度 2. 对自己照顾行为的满意度 3. 照顾行为对照顾者个人生活带来的影响

iii. Common Tools of Assessment

1. Family Common tools of assessment for family nursing include the family tree, APGAR family function assessment scale and social support scale.

(1) Family Tree: It uses different symbols to display family structure and relationship, family demographic information, family life events, health

（三）评估常用工具

1. 家庭 家庭护理评估常用的评估工具有家系图、APGAR 家庭功能评估表和社会支持度。

（1）家系图：是用不同符号以家谱的形式展示家庭结构和关系、家庭人口学信息、家庭生活事件、健康问题等家庭信息。家系图可以帮助

problems and other family information in the form of family tree. Family tree can help community nurses quickly assess the basic situation of the family, judge the problems endangering the family health and the high-risk members of the family.

The requirements for drawing the family tree are as follows. a. Includes three or more generations of population. b. The elders are in the top, the younger ones are in the bottom. c. Among the same generation, the elder is on the left and the younger is on the right. d. In a couple, the man is on the left and the woman is on the right. e. Each member's symbol can be annotated with their age, birth/death dates, occupation, major health problems, etc. f. Members living in the same place are circled with dashed lines. Family tree and common symbols are shown in Figure 4-1 and Figure 4-2.

社区护士迅速评估家庭基本情况、判断危及家庭健康的问题和家庭高危人员等。

　　家系图绘制要求：①包含三代或三代以上人口；②长辈在上，晚辈在下；③同辈中，长者在左，幼者在右；④夫妻中，男在左，女在右；⑤每个成员的符号旁可标注其年龄、出生或死亡日期、职业、主要健康问题等；⑥用虚线圈出在同一处居住的成员。家系图和家系图常用符号见图4-1、图4-2。

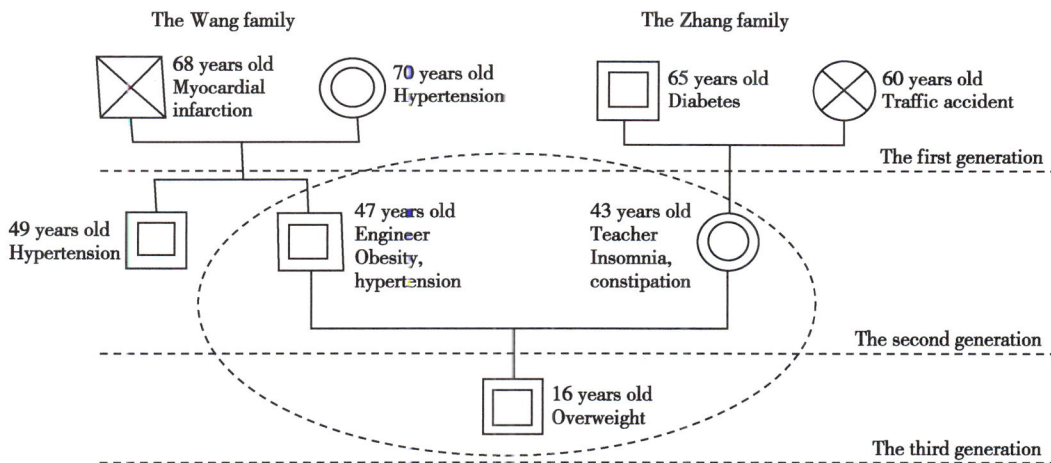

Figure 4-1　Family tree

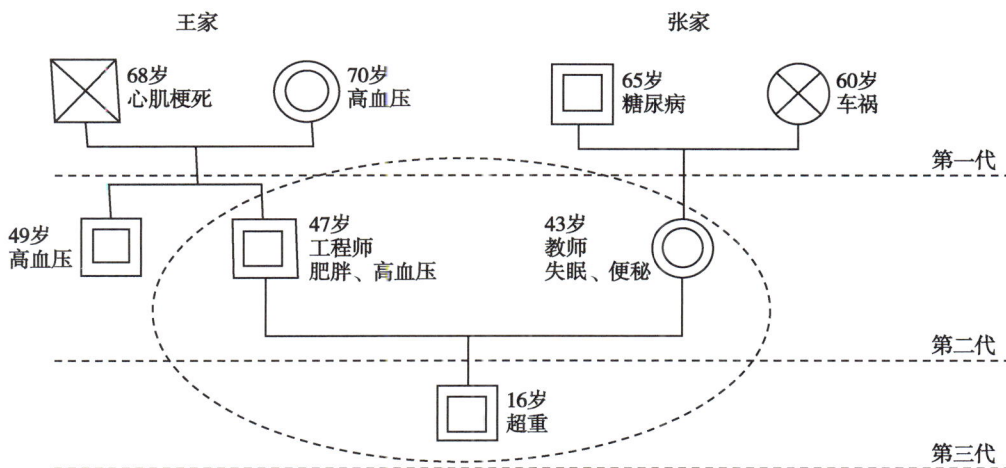

图 4-1　家系图

Male　Female　Specific object of home care　Death　Marriage(time)

Cohabitation(time)　Separation(time)　Divorce(time)　Pregnant

Dizygotic twins　Monozygotic twins　Birth order of children　Adopted child

Induced abortion　Spontaneous abortion　Stillbirth　Alienation of relationship

Very close relationship　Relationship conflict　Cold relationship　The relationship is both close and conflicting

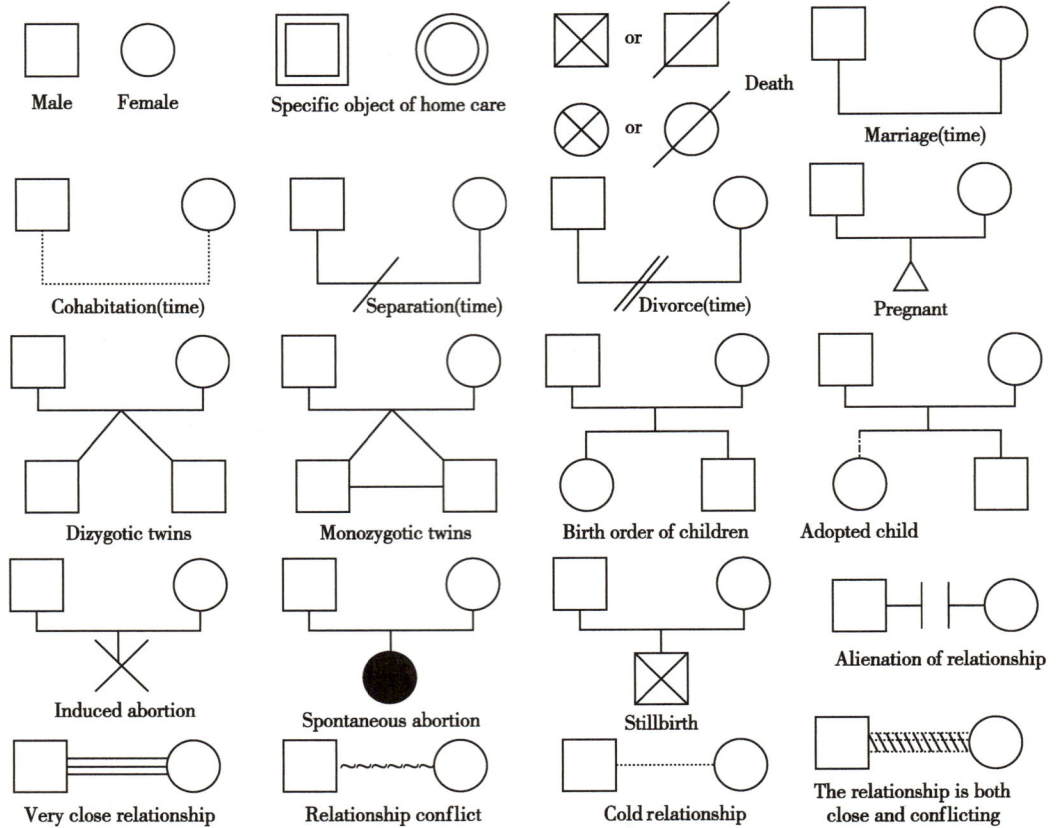

Figure 4-2　Common symbols of family tree

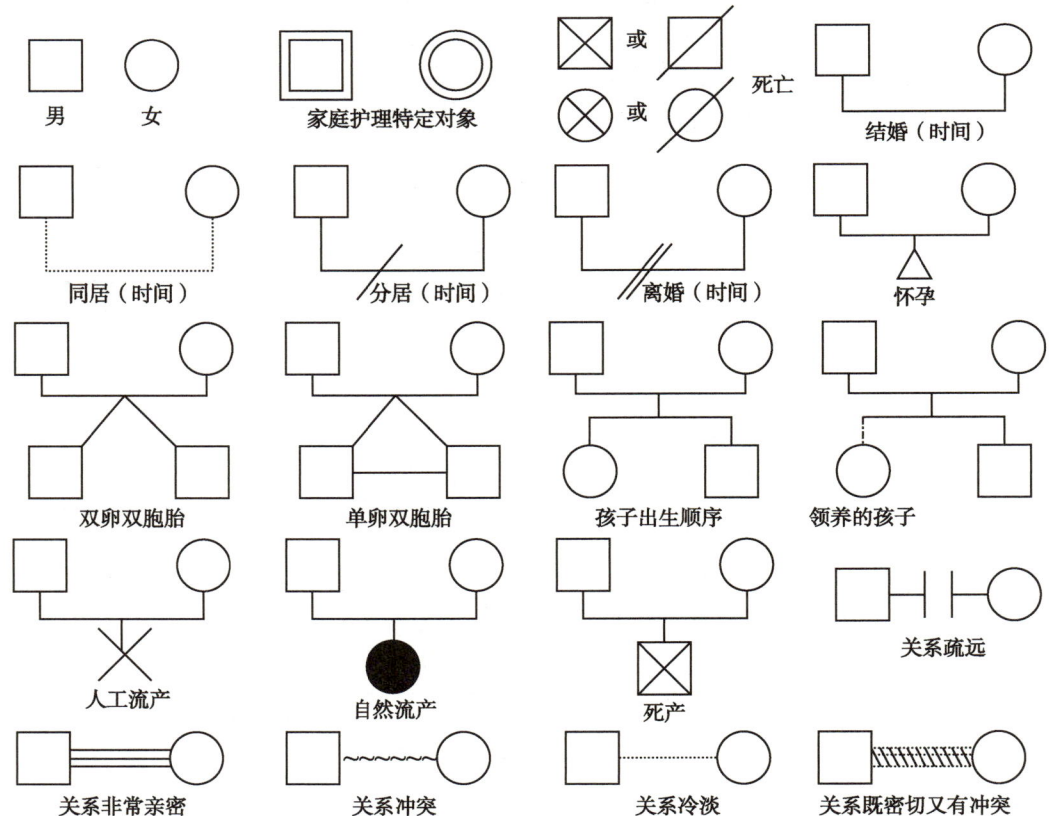

男　女　家庭护理特定对象　死亡　结婚（时间）

同居（时间）　分居（时间）　离婚（时间）　怀孕

双卵双胞胎　单卵双胞胎　孩子出生顺序　领养的孩子

人工流产　自然流产　死产　关系疏远

关系非常亲密　关系冲突　关系冷淡　关系既密切又有冲突

图 4-2　家系图常用符号

(2) APGAR Family Function Assessment Scale: It also known as the family caring index scale and is a subjective self-evaluation questionnaire designed by Smilkstein to detect family function. It mainly reflects the subjective satisfaction of individuals in the family with family function, and cannot fully reflect the functional status of the family as a whole. It includes five dimensions, namely adaptation, partnership, growth, affection and resolve, briefly referred to as APGAR family function assessment scale.

The questionnaire consists of two parts, the first part measures individual satisfaction with overall family function (Table 4-4), and the second part is used to understand the relationship between the individual and other members of the family (Table 4-5). Because the scale has few items and simple scoring, it can roughly and quickly assess the family function, which is one of the most commonly used family function assessment methods.

（2）APGAR 家庭功能评估表：又称家庭关怀度指数量表，是 Smilkstein 设计的检测家庭功能的主观自评问卷，主要反映家庭中的个体对家庭功能的主观满意程度，不能完全反映家庭作为一个整体的功能状况。包括 5 个维度，即适应度（adaptation）、合作度（partnership）、成熟度（growth）、情感度（affection）和亲密度（resolve），简称 APGAR 家庭功能评估表。

问卷包括两部分，第一部分测量个人对家庭功能整体的满意度（表 4-4），第二部分用于了解个人和家庭其他成员间的关系（表 4-5）。由于量表问题少，评分简单，可以粗略、快速地评价家庭功能，是最常用的家庭功能评估方法之一。

Table 4-4　APGAR Family Function Assessment Scale (Part Ⅰ)

Dimension	Question for assessment	Often (2 Points)	Sometimes (1 Point)	Scarcely ever (0 Point)
Adaptation	When I have problems, I can get satisfactory help from my family	☐	☐	☐
Partnership	I am very satisfied with the way my family discuss various things and shared problems with me	☐	☐	☐
Growth	When I want to engage in new activities or make new developments, my family can accept and give support	☐	☐	☐
Affection	I am very satisfied with the way my family express their feelings to me and responds to my emotions (such as anger, sadness, love)	☐	☐	☐
Resolve	I am very satisfied with the way my family spends time with me	☐	☐	☐

Note: A score of 0–3 indicates severe family dysfunction; a score of 4–6 indicates moderate family dysfunction; a score of 7–10 indicates good family function.

表 4-4　APGAR 家庭功能评估表（第一部分）

维度	评估问题	经常 （2分）	有时 （1分）	几乎从不 （0分）
适应度	当我遇到问题时，可以从家人处得到满意的帮助	☐	☐	☐
合作度	我很满意家人与我讨论各种事情以及分担问题的方式	☐	☐	☐

续表

维度	评估问题	经常 （2分）	有时 （1分）	几乎从不 （0分）
成熟度	当我希望从事新的活动或发展时，家人都能接受且给予支持	☐	☐	☐
情感度	我很满意家人对我表达感情的方式以及对我情绪（如愤怒、悲伤、爱）的反应	☐	☐	☐
亲密度	我很满意家人与我共度时光的方式	☐	☐	☐

注：0~3分家庭功能严重障碍；4~6分家庭功能中度障碍；7~10分家庭功能良好。

Table 4-5　APGAR Family Function Assessment Scale (Part II)

People who will live with you (spouse, children, friends, etc.) Sort by close degree			The relationship with these people (Spouse, children, friends, etc.)		
Relation	Age	Sex	Good	General	Bad

If you do not live with your family, the people you often ask for help (Family members, friends, colleagues, neighbors)			The relationship with these people (Family members, friends, colleagues, neighbors)		
Relation	Age	Sex	Good	General	Bad

表4-5　APGAR 家庭功能评估表（第二部分）

将与您同住的人（配偶、子女、朋友等） 按密切程度排序			与这些人相处的关系 （配偶、子女、朋友等）		
关系	年龄	性别	好	一般	不好

如果您和家人不住在一起，您经常求助的人 （家庭成员、朋友、同事、邻居）			与这些人相处的关系 （家庭成员、朋友、同事、邻居）		
关系	年龄	性别	好	一般	不好

(3) Social Support: It reflects the interaction within and outside of the family centered on the service object. A single line indicates a connection between the two, and a double line indicates a close relationship. The social support chart (Figure 4-3) can help community nurses understand the current social relationships and the available resources of the family.

（3）社会支持度：反映以服务对象为中心的家庭内、外的相互作用。单线表示两者间有联系，双线表示关系密切。社会支持度图（图4-3）可以帮助社区护士了解家庭目前的社会关系以及可利用的资源。

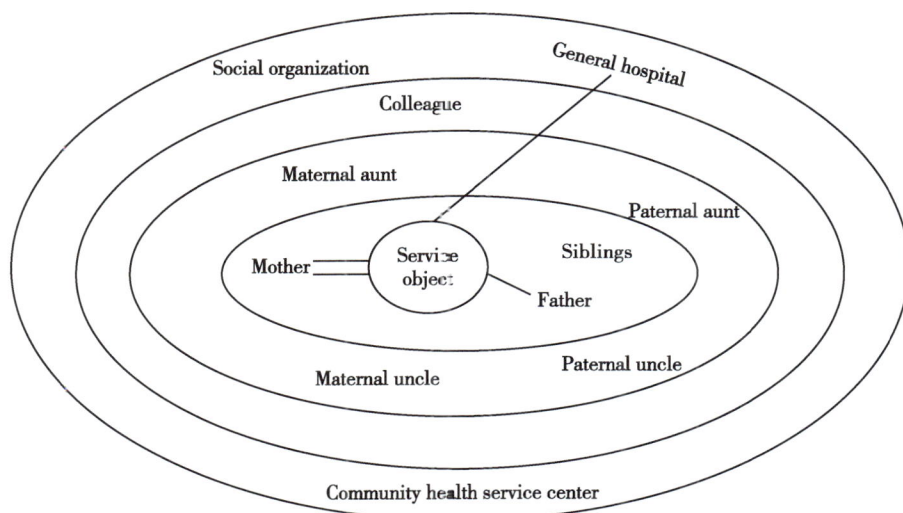

Figure 4-3　Social support chart

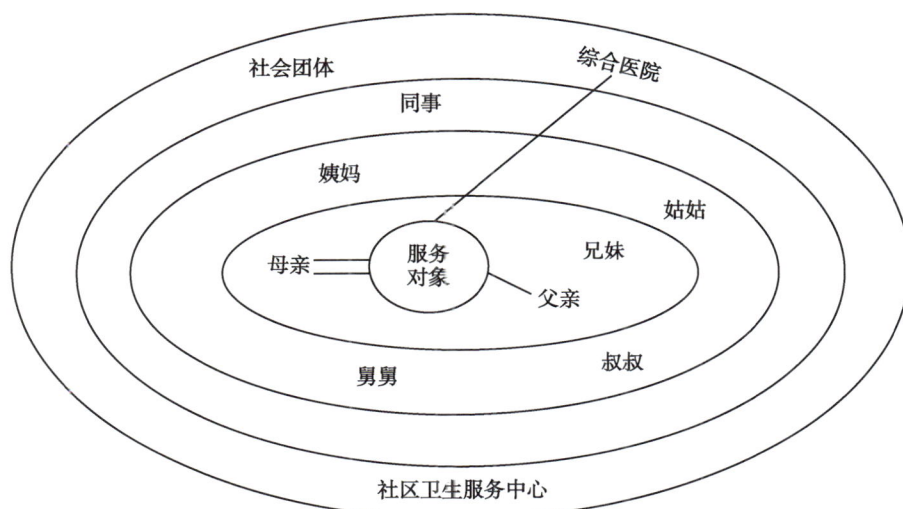

图 4-3　社会支持度图

2. Family Health Caregivers

(1) Family Caregiver Task Inventory (FCTI): This scale was developed by foreign scholars Clark and Rakowski in 1983 and is widely used in the assessment of caregivers. The scale has a total of 25 items in 5 dimensions: adapting to caregiving roles, responding to needs and providing assistance, dealing with personal emotions, assessing family and community resources, adjusting personal life and meeting caregiving needs. The score of each item is 0–2 points, and the total score is 0–50 points. The higher the score, the more difficulties the family caregivers encounter in taking care of the patient, and the lower their caregiving ability.

2. 家庭健康照顾者

（1）照顾能力测量量表：该量表由国外学者 Clark 及 Rakowski 于 1983 年编制，被广泛应用于照顾者的评估。该量表有适应照顾角色、应变需要及提供协助、处理个人情绪、评估家人及社区资源、调整个人生活及满足照顾需求 5 个维度，共 25 个条目，每个条目选项分值是 0~2 分，总分为 0~50 分，得分越高，说明家庭照顾者照顾患者时遇到的困难越多，照顾能力越低。

(2) Positive Aspects of Caregiving (PAC): This scale was developed by American scholar Tarlow in 2004 and is used to assess caregivers' positive feelings. The scale includes two dimensions: self-affirmation and life outlook, with a total of 9 items. Likert 5-level scoring method is adopted, 1 to 5 points represent "very disagree-very agree" respectively, and the total score is 9 to 45 points. The higher the score, the higher the positive feeling of the caregiver.

(3) Zarit Caregiver Burden Interview (ZBI): The scale was developed by Zarit et al. in the 1980s to comprehensively assess the physical, social, psychological, and financial burdens of caregivers. The scale has 22 items in 4 dimensions, including health condition, mental state, financial situation and social life of caregivers. The score of each question is 0–4 points, and the total score is 0–88 points. The higher the score, the heavier the burden of the caregiver. In 2006, Chinese scholars Wang Lie et al. translated the scale into Chinese version. The Chinese version of the scale has good reliability and validity, which is the most used scale by Chinese researchers at present (Table 4-6).

（2）照顾者积极感受量表：该量表由美国学者 Tarlow 于 2004 年编制，用于评价照顾者积极感受。该量表包括自我肯定和生活展望 2 个维度，共 9 个条目，采用 Likert 5 级评分法，1~5 分分别代表"非常不同意～非常同意"，总分为 9~45 分，分数越高，表示照顾者积极感受程度越高。

（3）Zarit 照顾者负担量表：该量表是 Zarit 等在 20 世纪 80 年代开发，用于全面评估照顾者的身体、社交、心理和经济负担。该量表有照顾者健康情况、精神状态、经济、社会生活 4 个维度，共 22 个条目，每道题分值是 0~4 分，总分为 0~88 分，分数越高，表示照顾者负担越重。2006 年国内学者王烈等将该量表译制为中文版，中文版量表信效度较好，是目前国内研究者使用最多的一个量表（见表 4-6）。

Table 4-6　Zarit Caregiver Burden Interview

Please select the option that best describes your situation	Never	Rarely	Sometimes	Quite frequently	Nearly always
1. Do you feel that your relative asks for more help than he/she needs?	0	1	2	3	4
2. Do you feel that because of the time you spend with your relative that you don't have enough time for yourself?	0	1	2	3	4
3. Do you feel stressed between caring for your relative and trying to meet other responsibilities for your family or work?	0	1	2	3	4
4. Do you feel embarrassed by your relative's behavior?	0	1	2	3	4
5. Do you feel annoyed when you are around your relative?	0	1	2	3	4
6. Do you feel that your relative currently affects your relationships with other family members or friends in a negative way?	0	1	2	3	4

Continued Table

Please select the option that best describes your situation	Never	Rarely	Sometimes	Quite frequently	Nearly always
7. Are you afraid what the future holds for your relative?	0	1	2	3	4
8. Do you feel your relative is dependent on you?	0	1	2	3	4
9. Do you feel strained when you are around your relative?	0	1	2	3	4
10. Do you feel your health has suffered because of your involvement with your relative?	0	1	2	3	4
11. Do you feel that you do not have as much privacy as you would like because of your relative?	0	1	2	3	4
12. Do you feel that your social life has suffered because you are caring for your relative?	0	1	2	3	4
13. Do you feel uncomfortable having friends over because of your relative?	0	1	2	3	4
14. Do you feel that your relative seems to expect you to take care of him/her as if you were the only one he/she could depend on?	0	1	2	3	4
15. Do you feel that you don't have enough money to take care of your relative in addition to the rest of your expenses?	0	1	2	3	4
16. Do you feel that you will be unable to take care of your relative much longer?	0	1	2	3	4
17. Do you feel you have lost control of your life since your relative's illness?	0	1	2	3	4
18. Do you wish you could leave the care of your relative to someone else?	0	1	2	3	4
19. Do you feel uncertain about what to do about your relative?	0	1	2	3	4
20. Do you feel you should be doing more for your relative?	0	1	2	3	4
21. Do you feel you could do a better job in caring for your relative?	0	1	2	3	4
22. Overall, how burdened do you feel in caring for your relative?	0	1	2	3	4
	No	Mild	Moderate	Severe	Very severe

表 4-6　Zarit 照顾者负担量表

请在以下问题中勾选最符合您实际情况的选项	没有	偶尔	有时	经常	总是
1. 您是否会认为,您所照料的患者会向您提出过多的照顾要求?	0	1	2	3	4
2. 您是否会认为,由于护理患者会使自己时间不够?	0	1	2	3	4
3. 您是否认为,在照顾患者和努力做好家务及工作之间,您会感到有压力?	0	1	2	3	4
4. 您是否认为,因患者的行为而感到为难?	0	1	2	3	4
5. 您是否认为,有患者在您身边而感到烦闷?	0	1	2	3	4
6. 您是否认为,您的患者已经影响到了您和您的家人与朋友间的关系?	0	1	2	3	4

续表

请在以下问题中勾选最符合您实际情况的选项	没有	偶尔	有时	经常	总是
7. 您对患者的将来感到担心吗？	0	1	2	3	4
8. 您是否认为，患者依赖于您？	0	1	2	3	4
9. 当患者在您身边时，您感到紧张吗？	0	1	2	3	4
10. 您是否认为，由于护理患者，您的健康受到影响？	0	1	2	3	4
11. 您是否认为，由于护理患者，您没有时间办自己的私事？	0	1	2	3	4
12. 您是否认为，由于护理患者，您的社交受到影响？	0	1	2	3	4
13. 您有没有由于患者在家，放弃请朋友来家的想法？	0	1	2	3	4
14. 您是否认为，患者只期盼着您的照料，您好像是他/她唯一可依赖的人？	0	1	2	3	4
15. 您是否认为，除了您的花费，您没有余钱用于护理患者？	0	1	2	3	4
16. 您是否认为，您有可能花更多的时间照护患者？	0	1	2	3	4
17. 您是否认为，开始护理以来，按照自己的意愿生活已经不可能了？	0	1	2	3	4
18. 您是否希望，能把患者留给别人来照料？	0	1	2	3	4
19. 您有对患者有不知如何是好的情形吗？	0	1	2	3	4
20. 您认为应该为患者做更多的事情是吗？	0	1	2	3	4
21. 您认为在护理患者上您能做得更好吗？	0	1	2	3	4
22. 综合看来您怎样评价自己在护理上的负担？	0	1	2	3	4
	无	轻	中	重	极重

iv. Notes of Assessment

1. Build a Trust Relationship　Only by establishing a relationship of mutual respect and trust with the family can community nurses understand the real thoughts and feelings of family members and collect valuable information.

2. Collect Data Comprehensively　Use a variety of methods to collect data, such as observation, conversation, questionnaire and so on. At the same time, community nurses should also make full use of the information collected by other personnel, such as hospital medical records, community health records, etc.

3. Recognize Diversity and Dynamics Different families have their own characteristics, and the health of the same family is also changing dynamically. Community nurses should fully realize the diversity and dynamic changes of the family, and carry out targeted family nursing assessment.

（四）评估注意事项

1. 建立信任关系　社区护士只有与家庭建立相互尊重和信任的关系，才能了解家庭成员的真实想法和感受，收集到有价值的资料。

2. 收集资料要全面　运用多种方法收集资料，如观察法、交谈法、问卷调查法等。同时还应充分利用其他人员收集的资料，如医院的病历记录、社区居民的健康档案等。

3. 认识多样性和动态变化　不同的家庭有其各自的特点，同一家庭的健康也是动态变化的，社区护士应充分认识到家庭的多样性和动态变化，有针对性地开展家庭护理评估。

BOX 4-3　Learning More

Respite Care

Respite care, also known as short-term care, originated from the deinstitutionalized movement in the United States in the 1970s and was mainly aimed at families of children with physical and mental disabilities. In the 1980s, the scope of services was extended to disabled, elderly, end-of-life patients and their family caregivers. The United States National Respite Network and Resource Center defines respite care more comprehensively as providing planned or emergency services to the caregiver of a child or adult with special needs for a period of time to make them free from caring responsibilities and then improve the health of the caregiver, the person being cared for and/or the family system significantly.

Respite care can be divided into three categories: institutional, day care and home respite care. The main form of institutional respite care is the temporary retention care in sanatoriums or hospitals, and the service items include professional nursing, leisure travel, and professional nursing skills training for family caregivers. Day care services mainly provide social, maintenance and healthcare services, and the content of services is similar to institutional respite care. Home respite care is provided by professional nursing staff to the elderly patients' homes, replacing the family caregivers to provide short-term home care. The content of services includes personal care, light housework, accompanying medical treatment, companionship, etc.

Ⅱ. Family Nursing Diagnosis

Family nursing diagnosis is the process by which community nurses judge the currently existing or underlying major health problems in the family.

i. Basic Steps

1. Determine the Family Nursing Diagnosis　Determine the nursing diagnosis and

BOX 4-3　知识拓展

喘息服务

喘息服务又称短期照顾,起源于 20 世纪 70 年代美国的去机构化运动,主要针对身心障碍儿童家庭,20 世纪 80 年代服务范围被扩展至失能、老弱和临终患者及其家庭照顾者。美国国家喘息网络和资源中心对喘息服务的定义较为全面,即为有特殊需要的儿童或成人的照顾者提供有计划的或紧急的服务,使其有一段时间不承担照顾责任,从而使照顾者、被照顾者和/或家庭系统的健康状况得到显著改善。

喘息服务大体可分机构式、日间照料式和居家式喘息服务 3 类。机构式喘息服务主要形式是疗养院或医院短暂留住照顾,服务项目有专业护理、休闲旅行、家庭照顾者专业护理技能培训等。日间照料式喘息服务主要提供社会的、维持性的和保健的服务,服务内容与机构式喘息服务相似。居家式喘息服务是由专业护理人员到老年患者家中,代替家庭照顾者提供短期的居家照顾,服务内容有个人护理、轻度家务劳动、陪同就医、陪伴等。

二、家庭护理诊断

家庭护理诊断是社区护士对家庭目前存在的或潜在的主要健康问题进行判断的过程。

(一)基本步骤

1. 确定家庭护理诊断　确定护理诊断并列出原因。要从整体上分析各种家庭健康问题,

list the reasons. It is necessary to analyze various family health problems as a whole and judge the health needs of the family.

2. Clarify the Priority of Family Nursing Diagnosis   When there are multiple family nursing diagnoses, community nurses need to prioritize family health problems and clarify the priorities of problem management.

ii. Statement of Family Nursing Diagnosis

The family nursing diagnosis is presented in the form of PES, namely problem (P), etiology (E), and symptom & sign (S). Family nursing diagnose are divided into the personal and interpersonal level and the family level, and can be proposed by using the diagnosis system of the North American Nursing Diagnosis Association International (NANDA-I) according to the actual situation of the family, even if these issues cannot be generalized by existing nursing diagnoses.

判断家庭的健康需求。

2. 明确家庭护理诊断的优先顺序   当存在多个家庭护理诊断时,社区护士需要按照家庭健康问题的轻重缓急进行排序,明确问题处置的优先次序。

(二)家庭护理诊断的陈述

家庭护理诊断采用 PES 的形式陈述,即问题(problem,P)、原因(etiology,E)和表现(symptom & sign,S)。家庭护理诊断分为个人与人际层面和家庭层面,即使这些问题不能用现有的护理诊断进行概括,也可运用北美护理诊断协会(NANDA-I)的诊断系统根据家庭实际情况提出。

BOX 4-4   Learning More

Examples of Family Nursing Diagnosis

Domain 1   Health Promotion

(1) Ineffective Family Therapeutic Regimen Management

(2) Health-seeking behaviors

(3) Ineffective health maintenance

(4) Impaired home maintenance

Domain 2   Nutrition

(1) Ineffective infant feeding pattern

(2) Impaired swallowing

Domain 3   Elimination

(1) Impaired urinary elimination

(2) Risk for constipation

Domain 4   Activity/rest

(1) Disturbed sleep pattern

(2) Diversional activity deficit

(3) Activity intolerance

Domain 5   Perception/cognition

(1) Deficient knowledge

(2) Impaired memory

BOX 4-4   知识拓展

家庭护理诊断举例

领域1   促进健康

(1)家庭执行治疗方案无效

(2)寻求健康行为

(3)保持健康无效

(4)持家能力障碍

领域2   营养

(1)无效型婴儿喂养形态

(2)吞咽障碍

领域3   排泄

(1)排尿障碍

(2)有便秘的危险

领域4   活动/休息

(1)睡眠形态紊乱

(2)缺乏娱乐活动

(3)活动无耐力

领域5   感知/认识

(1)知识缺乏

(2)记忆受损

(3) Impaired verbal communication

Domain 6　Self-perception

(1) Powerlessness

(2) Risk for loneliness

Domain 7　Role relationship

(1) Caregiver role strain

(2) Impaired parenting

(3) Interrupted family processes

(4) Parental role conflict

Domain 8　Sexuality

(1) Sexual dysfunction

(2) Ineffective sexuality patterns

Domain 9　Coping/stress tolerance

(1) Disabled family coping

(2) Compromised family coping

(3) Disorganized infant bahavior

Domain 10　Life principles

(1) Decisional conflict

(2) Noncompliance

Domain 11　Safety/protection

(1) Risk for falls

(2) Ineffective protection

Domain 12　Comfort

(1) Acute pain

(2) Social isolation

Domain 13　Growth/development

(1) Delayed growth and development

(2) Adult failure to thrive

Ⅲ. Family Nursing Plan, Implementation and Evaluation

i. Family Nursing Plan

Family nursing plan is a process of determining family nursing goals and selecting family nursing measures based on family nursing diagnosis.

1. Determine the Family Nursing Goals　Nursing goals are divided into long-term goals and short-term goals. Long-term goals are those that take a long time (such as weeks or months) to achieve, while short-term goals are those that can be achieved in a short time (such as days or hours). The establishment of goals should consider the preferences of family members, the

（3）语言沟通障碍

领域6　自我感知

（1）无能为力感

（2）有孤独的危险

领域7　角色关系

（1）照顾者角色紧张

（2）父母不称职

（3）家庭运作中断

（4）父母角色冲突

领域8　性

（1）性功能障碍

（2）无效性性生活形态

领域9　应对/应激耐受性

（1）无能性家庭应对

（2）妥协性家庭应对

（3）婴儿行为紊乱

领域10　生活准则

（1）抉择冲突

（2）不依从行为

领域11　安全/防御

（1）有摔倒的危险

（2）防护无效

领域12　舒适

（1）急性疼痛

（2）社交孤立

领域13　成长/发展

（1）成长发展迟缓

（2）成人身心衰竭

三、家庭护理计划、实施与评价

（一）家庭护理计划

家庭护理计划是以家庭护理诊断为依据，确定家庭护理目标和选择家庭护理措施的过程。

1. 确定家庭护理目标　护理目标分为长期目标和短期目标。长期目标指需要较长时间（如数周、数月）才能实现的目标，短期目标指在较短时间（如几天、几小时）能够达到的目标。目标的确立需要考虑家庭成员的意愿、家庭的特点和实际条件、社区护士自身的能力以及社区可利用的资源等。

characteristics and actual conditions of the family, the ability of community nurses and the resources available in the community.

2. Develop the Family Nursing Plan

The family nursing plan includes an implementation plan and an evaluation plan. The nursing implementation plan includes nursing measures and implementation time, and the nursing evaluation plan includes evaluation criteria and evaluation time. The family nursing plan is shown in Table 4-7.

2. 制订家庭护理计划　家庭护理计划包括护理实施计划和评价计划。护理实施计划包括护理措施和实施时间，护理评价计划包括评价标准和评价时间。家庭护理计划表见表 4-7。

Table 4-7   Family Nursing Planning Schedule

Date	Family nursing diagnosis	Goals	Implementation plan		Evaluation plan	
			Nursing measures	Implementation time	Evaluation criteria	Evaluation time

表 4-7　家庭护理计划表

日期	家庭护理诊断	目标	实施计划		评价计划	
			护理措施	实施时间	评价标准	评价时间

ii. Family Nursing Implementation

Family nursing implementation is the process of putting family nursing plan into practice.

1. **Participants**   The primary responsible persons and implementers are family members, with the participation of community nurses, other community health workers and other members of the family's social network.

2. Content of Implementation

(1) Help Families Deal with the Disease: Community nurses can help families effectively deal with the disease by introducing disease-related knowledge, teaching patients and family members the skills of disease care, and providing some specific care (such as oxygen administration, intravenous infusion, wound dressing change).

(2) Teach Families to Adapt to Developmental Changes: When families face developmental

（二）家庭护理实施

家庭护理实施是将家庭护理计划付诸实践的过程。

1. **参与人员**　主要责任者和实施者是家庭成员，另外也需要社区护士、其他社区保健人员、家庭社会关系网中的其他人员共同参与。

2. 实施内容

（1）帮助家庭应对疾病：社区护士可通过介绍疾病相关知识、教会患者及家属疾病照顾的技能、提供一些具体的护理照顾（如给氧、静脉输液、伤口换药）等帮助家庭有效地应对疾病。

（2）教会家庭适应发展性改变：当家庭面临发展性转变时，需要学习新的知识和技能去适

changes, they need to learn new knowledge and skills to adapt, and community nurses can help families prepare ahead of time to cope with the coming changes through predictive education and guidance.

(3) Help Families to Obtain the Needed Resources and Support: Community nurses can help families make full use of internal and external resources and enhance available social support.

(4) Promote Internal Change within the Family: When the original mode of operation within the family cannot adapt to the requirements of family development or changes in the environment, the community nurse can help family members make decisions and choices based on their values and ideas, and promote positive family change.

(5) Help Families to Maintain a Healthy Living Environment: Community nurses can maintain the health of the family environment by teaching family members to adjust the indoor environment and introduce environmental factors that may affect health and prevention methods.

iii. Family Nursing Evaluation

Family nursing evaluation is a comprehensive inspection and control of family nursing activities and a key measure to ensure the successful implementation of the family nursing plan, which runs through the whole process of family nursing activities.

1. Types　It includes the process evaluation and the outcome evaluation. The process evaluation is an evaluation of the different stages of family nursing, such as assessment, diagnosis, planning and implementation. The outcome evaluation is an evaluation of the effect of nursing intervention in the family, that is, whether the expected goals have been reached.

2. Content

(1) Process Evaluation

1) Assessment stage: Evaluate whether the collected data are complete.

2) Diagnosis stage: Evaluate whether the

应,社区护士可通过预见性的教育和指导,帮助家庭提前做好准备,应对即将来临的转变。

（3）帮助家庭获得所需资源和支持:社区护士能够帮助家庭充分利用内外资源和增强可获得的社会支持。

（4）促进家庭的内部改变:当家庭内部原有的运作模式不能适应家庭发展或环境改变的要求时,社区护士可帮助家庭成员依据他们的价值观和想法作出决定和选择,促成积极的家庭改变。

（5）帮助家庭维持健康的生活环境:社区护士可通过教会家庭成员调整室内环境、介绍可能影响健康的环境因素及防范的方法等方式维持家庭环境的健康。

（三）家庭护理评价

家庭护理评价是对家庭护理活动进行的全面检查与控制,是保证家庭护理计划实施成功的关键措施,贯穿于家庭护理活动的全过程。

1. 类型　包括过程评价和结果评价。过程评价是对家庭护理的评估、诊断、计划、实施等不同阶段进行的评价。结果评价是对家庭接受护理干预后效果的评价,即是否达到了预期目标。

2. 内容

（1）过程评价

1）评估阶段:评价收集的资料是否完整。

2）诊断阶段:评价护理诊断是否反映家庭

nursing diagnosis reflects the main health problems in the family.

3) Planning stage: Evaluate whether the formulation of nursing plan is reasonable.

4) Implementation stage: Evaluate whether the plan is being implemented smoothly.

(2) Outcome Evaluation

1) Evaluation of individual health in the family: Individual health status, quality of life, understanding of health problems, etc.

2) Evaluation of the interaction between family members: Mutual understanding, communication, intimacy and love, ability of judgment and decision-making, division of roles, etc.

3) Evaluation of the relationship between family and society: The use of social resources and the improvement of the family environment.

3. Results

(1) Modify the Plan: If nursing goals were not achieved, and there were unreasonable conditions in the original nursing plan, the nurse should revise the plan together with the family members.

(2) Continue to Implement the Plan: If nursing goals were not achieved, but the original nursing plan was evaluated as reasonable and feasible, the plan can continue to be implemented.

(3) Terminate the Pan: When nursing goals were achieved, the nurse could terminate the nursing activities for the family.

Section 4   Methods of Family Health Nursing

Home visit and home care are the basic methods of family nursing. Community nurses provide nursing services throughout the whole cycle of life and health through home visit and home care, and attach importance to the organic combination of prevention, treatment and health care.

主要健康问题。

3）计划阶段：评价护理计划的制订是否合理。

4）实施阶段：评价计划是否顺利执行。

（2）结果评价

1）对家庭中个体健康的评价：个体的健康状态、生活质量、对健康问题的理解程度等。

2）对家庭成员间互动的评价：家庭成员间的互相理解、交流、亲密度和爱心、判断和决策问题的能力、角色分工等。

3）对家庭与社会关系的评价：对社会资源的利用情况和改善家庭环境的情况。

3. 结果

（1）修改计划：护理目标未能达成，原定护理计划存在不合理的情况，护士应与家属一起修订计划。

（2）继续执行计划：护理目标未能达成，但原定护理计划经评价合理可行，可继续实施计划。

（3）终止计划：达成护理目标，护士可终止对该家庭的护理活动。

第四节　家庭健康护理的方法

家庭访视与居家护理是家庭护理的基本方法。社区护士通过家庭访视和居家护理为家庭服务对象提供贯穿生命健康全周期的护理服务，重视预防、治疗、康养的有机结合。

I. Home Visit

i. Concept

Home visit refers to the purposeful nursing service activities provided to the clients in their homes in order to maintain and promote their health.

Home visit is a kind of activity that goes into the family environment and provides necessary assistance and support to promote the healthy development of the family by understanding the relevant situation of the target family.

ii. Purpose

The purpose of the home visit is to fully focus on the physical and mental health of family members, prevent diseases, identify and solve health problems, and promote the overall health of the family.

1. Personalized Health Management and Guidance　Home visit is committed to gaining insight into the health status of each family member and providing customized health management programs and guidance based on their individual characteristics and needs.

2. Early Prevention and Disease Control Through the home visit, visitors can identify potential health problems or disease risks of family members in time, and take corresponding preventive measures to reduce the incidence and burden of diseases.

3. Emotional Care and Psychological Support　Home visit not only focuses on the physical health of family members, but also focus on their mental health and emotional needs, providing emotional support and comfort to family members.

4. Promoting the Integration of Family and Community Resources　Home visit is an important link between family and community resources. Through the visit, visitors can understand the needs and difficulties of family members, provide them with appropriate community resources and service information, and realize the sharing

一、家庭访视

（一）概念

家庭访视是指到服务对象家中，为了维持和促进健康而为服务对象所提供的有目的的护理服务活动。

家庭访视是一种深入家庭环境的活动，通过了解服务对象家庭的相关情况，提供必要的援助和支持，促进家庭健康发展。

（二）目的

家庭访视的目的在于全面关注家庭成员的身心健康，预防疾病、发现并解决健康问题、促进家庭整体健康。

1. 个性化健康管理与指导　家庭访视致力于深入了解每个家庭成员的健康状况，根据他们的个人特点和需求，提供定制化的健康管理方案和指导。

2. 早期预防与疾病控制　通过家庭访视，访视人员能够及时发现家庭成员潜在的健康问题或疾病风险，并采取相应的预防措施以减少疾病的发生和减轻疾病的负担。

3. 情感关怀与心理支持　家庭访视不仅关注家庭成员的身体健康，也注重他们的心理健康和情感需求，为家庭成员提供情感上的支持和安慰。

4. 促进家庭与社区资源的整合　家庭访视是连接家庭与社区资源的重要纽带。通过访视，访视人员能够了解家庭成员的需求和困难，为他们提供合适的社区资源和服务信息，实现资源的共享和优化配置。

and optimal allocation of resources.

5. Promoting Health Education and Community Development　Home visit is an important way to promote health education and health concepts. At the same time, through the development of home visit, it can also promote the improvement and development of community health services, and create a healthier and more livable living environment for community residents.

iii. Object

The subjects of home visit mainly include individuals and families with health problems, such as the elderly, patients with chronic diseases, pregnant women and newborns. The purpose of the visit is to assess their health status, provide the necessary education and support, promote healthy behavior and prevent diseases.

iv. Types

1. Preventive Home Visit　It mainly focuses on disease prevention and health care. For example, postnatal home visit and newborn home visit are designed to ensure the health of the mother and child and to provide necessary health care guidance.

2. Assessment Home Visit　It is carried out to assess the health needs and conditions of individuals and families and formulate nursing plans. It is often used to assess patients with family problems or health problems and families of the elderly, the infirm or disabled.

3. Continuous Care Home Visit It provides continuous care services for patients who need follow-up care. It is mainly used for patients with chronic diseases, patients in need of rehabilitation care, patients with mobility difficulties, terminal patients, etc.

4. Emergency Home Visit　It aims to address temporary, urgent situations or problems, such as trauma, family violence, etc.

v. Home Visit Procedure

The procedure of home visit can be divided into three stages: pre-visit preparation, work

5. 推动健康教育与社区发展　家庭访视是宣传健康教育、推广健康理念的重要途径。同时,家庭访视的开展,也能促进社区健康服务的完善和发展,为社区居民创造更加健康、宜居的生活环境。

(三)对象

家庭访视的对象主要包括有健康问题的个人和家庭,如老年人、慢性病患者、残疾人、孕妇和新生儿等。访视旨在评估其健康状况,提供必要的教育和支持,促进健康行为和预防疾病。

(四)类型

1. 预防性家庭访视　主要关注疾病预防和保健工作。例如,产后家访和新生家庭访视,旨在确保母婴的健康,并提供必要的保健指导。

2. 评估性家庭访视　评估个体和家庭的健康需求和状况,以便为制订护理计划提供依据。常用于评估有家庭问题或健康问题的患者以及年老体弱者或残疾人的家庭。

3. 连续照顾性家庭访视　为需要后续护理的患者提供连续性的护理服务。主要用于慢性病患者、需要康复护理的患者、行动不便的患者、临终患者等。

4. 急诊性家庭访视　解决临时性的、紧急的情况或问题,如外伤、家庭暴力等。

(五)家庭访视程序

家庭访视的程序可以分为访视前准备、访视中工作、访视后工作三个阶段,每一阶段都有

during the visit, and post-visit work, and each stage has corresponding work items (Table 4-8).

Table 4-8　Home Visit Procedure Worksheet

Stage	Work items	Specific contents
Pre-visit preparation	1. Select home visit objects and the priority of the visit	Priority visits are given to families with the following problems health problems that affect a large number of people, seriously impact life, are prone to disease sequelae, and diseases that can be controlled with health resources
	2. Determine the purpose of the visit	(1) Initial visit: The main purpose of the visit is to establish a relationship with the interviewed family, obtain basic information, and identify family members with major health problems (2) Continuous visit: List the specific requirements of the management objectives, and evaluate the management effect according to the objectives after a period of visit management
	3. Prepare the supplies for the visit	(1) Basic items: Include physical examination tools such as thermometers, sphygmomanometer, stethoscopes, etc.; disinfection items such as ethanol, cotton balls, gauze, etc.; isolation items such as disinfection gloves, masks, hats, etc.; commonly used drugs and injection appliances; other items such as record sheets, health education materials, etc. (2) Additional visit items: Add other necessary items according to the home visit task, such as additional weight scales for newborn visits, and additional information materials on breastfeeding during postpartum visits
	4. Contact the interviewed family	Appointments are usually made by phone. If you need to know a more real situation, you can arrange a temporary surprise visit
	5. Arrange the visit route	The community nurse arranges a one-day home visit route according to the specific situation, and leaves the purpose of the visit, departure time and scheduled return time, the address, route and contact information of the interviewed family at the visiting institution, so that in case of special circumstances, the visiting nurse can be contacted as soon as possible
Work during the visit	1. Establish a relationship	During the initial visit, the community nurse should establish a trusting, friendly and cooperative relationship with the client and the family
	2. Assessment, plan and implementation	(1) Assessment: Include preliminary individual, family, and environmental assessments (2) Plan: Develop or adjust the family nursing plan with the service clients based on the results of the assessment (3) Implementation: Conduct health education or nursing operations
	3. Briefly record the visit	During the visit, note to briefly record the subjective and objective information collected and the care provided. Be careful not to ignore the conversation with the person you visit for the sake of recording
	4. End the visit	Briefly summarize with the interviewee. If the health problem of the interviewee has been solved, the visit service can be terminated. If the health problem is not solved, make an appointment with the time and content of the next visit on the basis of the consent of the interviewee

Stage	Work items	Specific contents
Post-visit work	1. Disinfect and replenish items	After the visit, return to the community health center, organize the visit package, and carry out processes such as routine disinfection, disposal of discarded items, and replenishing the contents of the visit package
	2. Record and summarize	Organize and supplement home visit records, analyze and evaluate the effectiveness of nursing care and the achievement of nursing goals, and preferably establish a database and family health records
	3. Modify the nursing plan	The nursing plan should be revised and refined based on the collected family health information and emerging problems. If the interviewee's health problems have been resolved, the visit can be stopped
	4. Coordination and cooperation	Community nurses communicate with other relevant health workers about the situation of the interviewees and discuss solutions. If necessary, referral arrangements should be made or other community resources should be contacted

表4-8   家庭访视程序工作表

阶段	工作项目	具体内容
访视前准备	1. 选择访视对象及优先顺序	家庭中有以下问题的优先访视:健康问题影响人数多、健康问题对生命有严重影响、健康问题易产生疾病后遗症、利用卫生资源能控制的疾病
	2. 确定访视目的	(1) 初次访视:主要目的是与被访家庭建立关系,获取基本资料,确定有主要健康问题的家庭成员 (2) 连续性访视:列出管理目标的具体要求,经过一段时间的访视管理后,根据目标评价管理效果
	3. 准备访视用物	(1) 基本物品:体检工具如体温计、血压计、听诊器等;消毒物品如乙醇、棉球、纱布等;隔离用物如消毒手套、口罩、帽子等;常用药物及注射工具;其他如记录单、健康教育材料等 (2) 增设的访视物:根据家访任务增设其他必要物品,如对新生儿访视时增加体重秤,产后访视增加有关母乳喂养的宣传材料等
	4. 联络被访家庭	一般电话预约访视时间。如果需要了解更为真实的情况,可以安排临时性突击访视
	5. 安排访视路线	社区护士根据具体情况安排一天的家庭访视路线,并在访视机构留下访视目的、出发时间及预定回归时间和被访家庭的住址、路线、联络方式,以备有特殊情况时,能尽早与访视护士取得联络
访视中工作	1. 确立关系	初次访视时,社区护士要与服务对象及家庭建立信任、友好、合作的关系
	2. 评估、计划与实施	(1) 评估:包括初步的个体、家庭和环境评估 (2) 计划:根据评估结果,与服务对象共同制订或调整家庭护理计划 (3) 实施:进行健康教育或护理操作
	3. 简要记录访视情况	访视时注意简要记录收集到的主客观资料以及提供的护理服务。注意不要为了记录而忽略了与访视对象的谈话
	4. 结束访视	与访视对象一起简要总结。若访视对象的健康问题已解决,即可结束访视服务;若健康问题未解决,在访视对象同意的基础上与访视对象预约下次访视时间和内容

续表

阶段	工作项目	具体内容
访视后工作	1. 消毒及补充物品	访视结束后回到社区卫生服务中心,整理访视包,进行如常规消毒、废弃物品处理、补充访视包内的物品等处理
	2. 记录和总结	整理和补充家访记录,分析和评价护理效果和护理目标达成的情况,最好建立资料库和家庭健康档案
	3. 修改护理计划	根据收集的家庭健康资料和新出现的问题,修改并完善护理计划。如果访视对象的健康问题已解决,即可停止访视
	4. 协调合作	社区护士与其他相关的健康工作人员交流访视对象的情况,商讨解决办法。必要时,应对访视对象做出转诊安排或联系其他社区资源

vi. Precautions in Home Visit

1. Dress and Attitude　Nurses should wear professional attire, not wear expensive jewelry, and carry ID cards, work permits, communication tools and change, etc. The attitude should be stable and generous, showing concern and respect for the visited family, and keeping their privacy and secrets.

2. Visit Time　Generally within 1 hour, and it is best to avoid eating and meeting time when family members are all at home.

3. Services and Charges　Clarify the charged items and free items. Generally, the home visit personnel do not directly participate in the charging work.

4. Safety　Due to the complexity of the family's situation, community health service institutions should establish a safety system, and community nurses should ensure the safety of the visited individuals, pay attention to their own safety, property safety, traffic safety during home visits.

II. Home Care

Home care is a continuation of hospital nursing services, it is provided by community nurses in the home environment familiar to patients. The implementation of home care is conducive to the rational utilization of national health resources and the improvement of social and economic benefits.

(六)家庭访视中的注意事项

1. **着装和态度**　穿护士职业装,不佩戴贵重首饰,随身携带身份证、工作证、通信工具及零钱等。态度稳重大方,体现对访视家庭的关心和尊重,保守其秘密。

2. **访视时间**　一般在 1 小时以内,最好在家庭成员都在家的时候,同时避开吃饭和会客时间。

3. **服务项目与收费**　明确收费项目与免费项目,一般家访人员不直接参与收费。

4. **安全**　由于家庭的情况复杂,社区卫生服务机构应建立安全制度,社区护士在家访中要保证访视对象安全,注意自身人身安全、财产安全、交通安全等。

二、居家护理

居家护理是社区护士在患者熟悉的家庭环境中提供护理服务,是住院护理服务的一种延续。居家护理的开展有利于国家卫生资源的合理利用,提高社会效益和经济效益。

i. Concept

Home care refers to providing continuous, comprehensive and professional health care services for patients and their families who need continuous care in their own home environment.

ii. Purpose

1. For Patients

(1) To provide continuous treatment and care.

(2) To enhance patients' self-care awareness and ability.

(3) To shorten the length of hospital stay.

(4) To control complications and reduce the relapse rate of the disease and the re-hospitalization rate.

2. For Families

(1) To enhance families' awareness of patient care.

(2) To provide patient care related knowledge and skills.

(3) To reduce families' financial burden.

3. For the Profession

(1) To increase the utilization rate of hospital beds.

(2) To expand the field of work of the nursing profession and promote the development of the nursing profession.

iii. Objects

1. Patients with Chronic Diseases Patients with cardiovascular and cerebrovascular diseases, chronic respiratory diseases, diabetes, malignant tumors, etc.

2. Patients Discharged from Hospital to Home Convalescence Those who are in stable condition after acute attack and treatment of various chronic diseases.

3. Patients in the Rehabilitation Period Patients with spinal cord injury, motor system injury, nervous system disease, disability, etc.

4. Terminal Patients Patients with advanced tumors, aging-related frailty, irreversible organ failure.

iv. Forms

There are two main forms of home care,

（一）概念

居家护理是指对需要连续照顾的患者及其家庭，在他们自己的居家环境中，提供连续性、综合性、专业性的健康照护服务。

（二）目的

1. 患者方面

（1）提供连续性治疗与护理。

（2）增强患者自我照顾的意识与能力。

（3）缩短住院时间。

（4）控制并发症，降低疾病复发率及再住院率。

2. 家庭方面

（1）增强家庭照顾患者的意识。

（2）提供患者护理相关知识与技能。

（3）减轻家庭经济负担。

3. 专业方面

（1）增加医院病床利用率。

（2）扩展护理专业的工作领域，促进护理专业的发展。

（三）对象

1. 慢性病患者 如心脑血管疾病、慢性呼吸系统疾病、糖尿病及恶性肿瘤等患者。

2. 出院在家休养的患者 如各种慢性病急性发作治疗后病情稳定者。

3. 康复期的患者 如脊髓损伤、运动系统损伤、罹患神经系统疾病或伤残的患者。

4. 临终患者 如肿瘤晚期、衰老、不可逆的器官功能衰竭的患者。

（四）形式

居家护理主要有两种形式，即家庭病床和

namely home sickbed and the home care service center.

1. Home Sickbed It takes the family as a place for treatment and nursing, sets up a sickbed, so that patients can receive medical treatment and nursing in a familiar environment, and also meets the requirements of social medical care to the greatest extent, which is an out-of-hospital supplementary form of hospital inpatient service and an important form of community health service.

At present, the home sick-bed service not only provides traditional medical care services, but also combines modern medical technology and management concepts to innovate the service model. For example, through the introduction of internet medical care, big data analysis and other technical means, to achieve intelligent, personalized and refined management of home sick-bed services. At the same time, it can also cooperate with community medical and rehabilitation institutions to form a continuous care model of "hospital-community-family" to provide patients with more comprehensive and convenient medical care services.

2. Home Care Service Center It is an institution that provides comprehensive and personalized nursing services for the people who need to receive nursing services at home.

The home care service center greatly meets the needs of professional care for the clients who cannot take care of themselves due to illness, old age or other reasons, and also reduces the burden of care for their families.

The service content of the home care service center is very extensive, including but not limited to daily life care, medical care, rehabilitation training, psychological counseling, etc. Professional nursing staff will develop a personalized care plan based on the specific situation of the client, ensuring that they receive the most suitable care for them.

The advantage of the home care service center over traditional forms of care is its flexibility and

家庭护理服务中心。

1. 家庭病床 是以家庭作为治疗护理场所,设立病床,使患者在熟悉的环境中接受医疗和护理,也最大限度地满足社会医疗护理要求,是医院住院服务的院外补充形式,是社区卫生服务的一种重要形式。

目前,家庭病床服务不仅提供传统的医疗护理服务,还结合现代医疗技术和管理理念,进行服务模式创新。例如,通过引入互联网医疗、大数据分析等技术手段,实现家庭病床服务的智能化、个性化和精细化管理。同时,还可以与社区医疗康复机构等合作,形成"医院-社区-家庭"的连续性照护模式,为患者提供更全面、更便捷的医疗护理服务。

2. 家庭护理服务中心 是为需要在家中接受护理服务的人群提供全方位、个性化护理服务的机构。

家庭护理服务中心极大地满足了因疾病、年老或其他原因而无法自理的服务对象对专业护理的需求,同时也为服务对象家属减轻了照顾的负担。

家庭护理服务中心的服务内容非常广泛,包括但不限于日常起居照料、医疗护理、康复训练、心理疏导等。专业的护理人员会根据服务对象的具体情况,制订个性化的护理方案,确保他们得到最适合自己的护理服务。

与传统的护理方式相比,家庭护理服务中心的优势在于其灵活性和个性化。它可以根据

individuality. It can adjust the care plan at any time according to the needs of clients. In addition, since nursing services are provided at home, clients can receive care in a familiar and comfortable environment, which contributes to their recovery and mood improvment.

v. Content

Home care is a comprehensive and meticulous work, which requires professional nursing staff to provide personalized services according to the actual situation of the patient. Through home care, patients can receive a full range of care and support at home, improving their quality of life and promoting recovery.

1. **Health Status Monitoring** Patients' vital signs, such as body temperature, pulse, blood pressure, respiration, etc., are regularly monitored to assess their health status. Community nurses need to observe and record changes in patients' conditions, communicate with doctors in time and adjust nursing plans.

2. **Medical Care** It includs treatment nursing and medication nursing, treatment nursing refers to antipyretic measures, infusion, oxygen therapy and other treatment measures; medication nursing involves urging patients to take medication correctly and observing adverse drug reactions. In addition, it also includes the correct collection of laboratory specimens, nursing during various examinations, etc.

3. **Daily Life Care** Assist patients to wash, dress, make the bed, move aroud, etc. For patients with mobility difficulties, special care such as going up and down stairs and transfering is also required. In order to keep patients clean and comfortable, community nurses need to wash patients' hair, trim their fingernails and toenails, and help them to take a bath, etc., regularly.

4. **Nutrition Diet Guidance** Make a personalized diet plan according to the patients' physical conditions and nutritional needs. Provide dietary guidance to help patients match food properly, and promote nutrition absorption and

服务对象的需求，随时调整护理方案。此外，由于护理服务是在家中进行的，因此服务对象可以在熟悉和舒适的环境中接受护理，这有助于他们的康复和心情的改善。

（五）内容

居家护理是一项全面而细致的工作，需要专业的护理人员根据患者的实际情况进行个性化的服务。通过居家护理，患者可以在家中得到全方位的照护和支持，提高生活质量，促进康复。

1. **健康状况监测** 定期监测患者的生命体征，如体温、脉搏、血压、呼吸等，以评估其健康状况。社区护士需要观察并记录患者的病情变化，及时与医生沟通并调整护理计划。

2. **医疗护理** 包括治疗护理和用药护理。治疗护理指退热、输液、输氧等治疗措施；用药护理则涉及督促患者正确服药，观察药物不良反应等。此外，还包括化验标本的正确采集、各类检查时的护理等。

3. **日常生活照料** 协助患者进行洗漱、更衣、床铺整理、活动起居等。对于行动不便的患者，还需提供上下楼梯、转移等特殊照料。定期为患者洗头、修剪指（趾）甲、沐浴等，以保持其身体清洁舒适。

4. **营养饮食指导** 根据患者的身体状况和营养需求，制订个性化的饮食计划。提供饮食指导，帮助患者合理搭配食物，促进营养吸收和康复。

recovery.

5. Rehabilitation Exercise Guidance Develop appropriate rehabilitation exercise plans according to the specific conditions of patients and rehabilitation goals. Assist patients in rehabilitation exercises, including limb activities, joint movement, etc., to promote the recovery of physical function.

6. Environmental Guidance A clean and tidy home environment can maintain and promote health. Community nurses should provide corresponding guidance on the home environment of the homebound patients, ensuring that the lighting in the patient's room is suitable and soft, the temperature and humidity are suitable, and eminding patients to open windows for ventilation, so as to create a peaceful and comfortable environment for the patients.

7. Psychological Nursing Patients at home often have a variety of psychological pressures and emotional fluctuations due to the long course of the disease. Community nurses should pay attention to the patients' psychological state, provide psychological support and comfort, accompany patients through difficulties, and help them build a positive attitude and confidence in life.

BOX 4-5　Learning More

Internet + home care

"Internet + home care" provides nursing services suitable for home conditions for people with limited mobility such as rehabilitation groups after discharge, elderly groups, and maternal and infant groups, etc. It is based on the way of "mobile phone booking order, nurse door-to-door care". It avoids the pain of patients and their families running to the hospital, and effectively opens up the "last kilometer" of nursing services for the people.

At present, "Internet + home care" services have been widely carried out in China, covering people of all ages and health conditions, from

5. 康复锻炼指导　根据患者的具体情况和康复目标，制订合适的康复锻炼计划。协助患者进行康复锻炼，包括肢体活动、关节运动等，促进身体功能的恢复。

6. 环境指导　干净整洁的家庭环境能维护和促进健康。社区护士应对居家患者的家庭环境进行相应的指导，确保患者居室光线适宜柔和、温度湿度适宜，注意开窗通风，为患者创造一个安宁、舒适的环境。

7. 心理护理　居家患者由于病程较长往往会有各种心理压力和情绪波动，社区护士应关注患者的心理状态，提供心理支持和安慰，陪伴患者渡过难关，帮助他们建立积极的生活态度和信心。

BOX 4-5　知识拓展

互联网 + 居家护理

"互联网＋居家护理"是以"手机预约下单，护士上门护理"的方式，为出院后康复期群体、老年群体、母婴群体等行动不便的人群提供适合在家庭条件下进行的护理服务，免去患者和家属奔波医院之苦，切实打通护理服务群众的"最后一公里"。

目前，"互联网＋居家护理"服务已在我国广泛开展，涵盖了各个年龄段和各种健康状况的人群，包括从婴幼儿到老年人，以及慢性病患

infants to the elderly, as well as patients with chronic diseases and convalescent groups. Professional, high-quality and convenient nursing services have been extended from medical institutions to community families, and from offline to online, to meet the diverse and differentiated needs of the public.

The projects carried out under the domestic "Internet + home care" cover indwelling gastric tube/nasogastric tube, indwelling/replacement of urinary catheter, routine wound dressing change, stoma care, pressure ulcer care, PICC maintenance, implantable venous access port maintenance, newborn bathing, newborn umbilical nursing, neonatal percutaneous bilirubin measurement, postpartum breast massage, balanced cupping, ear scraping, facial scraping, auricular acupressure technology, T-tube care, drainage bags replacement, diabetic foot care, etc.

(Deng Wenfang)

者和康复者等不同群体。该服务模式将专业、优质、便捷的护理服务从医疗机构延伸至社区家庭，从线下延伸至线上，满足群众多样化、差异化的健康需求。

国内"互联网＋居家护理"开展的项目涵盖了留置胃管/鼻胃管、留置/更换导尿管、普通伤口换药、造口护理、压疮护理、PICC维护、输液港维护、新生儿沐浴、新生儿脐部护理、新生儿经皮测胆红素、产后乳房按摩、平衡火罐、耳部刮痧、面部刮痧、耳穴贴压技术、T管护理、更换引流袋、糖尿病足护理等多个方面。

（邓文芳）

Key Points

1. Family structure is categorized into external family structure and internal family structure. The external family structure refers to family types, while the internal family structure comprises four key components: family roles, family authority, family communication, and family values.

2. Duvall's Family Life Cycle Theory divides family development into eight stages: the newly married couple stage, childbearing and infancy stage, preschool-age children stage, school-age children stage, adolescent stage, launching stage, empty nest stage, and retirement stage.

3. Common tools of assessment for family nursing include the family tree, APGAR family function assessment scale and social support scale.

4. The Zarit Caregiver Burden Scale is currently the most widely used tool by researchers in China for assessing family caregivers.

5. Family nursing diagnosis is the process

内容摘要

1. 家庭结构分为家庭外部结构和家庭内部结构。家庭外部结构即家庭的类型；家庭内部结构包括家庭角色、家庭权力、家庭沟通与家庭价值观4个因素。

2. Duvall的家庭生活周期理论将家庭的发展分为8个阶段，分别是新婚期、婴幼儿期、学龄前儿童期、学龄儿童期、青少年期、孩子离家创业期、空巢期、退休期。

3. 家庭护理评估常用的评估工具有家系图、APGAR家庭功能评估表和社会支持度。

4. Zarit照顾者负担量表是目前国内研究者使用最多的一个用于评估家庭照顾者的量表。

5. 家庭护理诊断是社区护士对家庭目前存

by which community nurses judge the currently existing or underlying major health problems in the family.

6. Family nursing plan is a process of determining family nursing goals and selecting family nursing measures based on family nursing diagnosis.

7. The primary responsible persons and implementers of family nursing implementation are family members.

8. Family nursing evaluation includes the process evaluation and the outcome evaluation.

9. Home visit and home care are the basic methods of family nursing.

10. There are two main forms of home care, namely home sickbed and the home care service center.

Exercises

(Questions 1 to 2 share the same question stem)

Mr. Zhang, 32 years old, engineer; Ms. Li, 30 years old, teacher. A year after their marriage, Ms. Li gave birth to a healthy, full-term baby girl.

1. Which stage of the family life cycle is the family currently in?

2. What are the main problems at this stage?

(Questions 3 to 4 share the same question stem)

There are three generations in a family. Grandpa is 76 years old and has hypertension and diabetes. Grandma is 74 years old and has hypertension. Father is 50 years old, a taxi driver. Mother is 47 years old, a housewife. The son is 24 years old and a company employee. The daughter is 20 years old and a college student.

3. What type of family does the family belong to?

4. Please draw a family tree of the family.

(Questions 5 to 6 share the same question stem)

Ms. Wang, 70 years old, had her left leg broken from a fall half a year ago. After being

在的或潜在的主要健康问题进行判断的过程。

6. 家庭护理计划是以家庭护理诊断为依据，确定家庭护理目标和选择家庭护理措施的过程。

7. 家庭护理实施的主要责任者和实施者是家庭成员。

8. 家庭护理评价包括过程评价和结果评价。

9. 家庭访视与居家护理是家庭护理的基本方法。

10. 居家护理主要有2种形式，即家庭病床和家庭护理服务中心。

思　考　题

（1~2题共用题干）

张先生，32岁，工程师；李女士，30岁，教师。两人结婚一年后，李女士生下一健康足月女婴。

1. 目前该家庭处于家庭生活周期的哪个阶段？

2. 该阶段面临的主要问题是什么？

（3~4题共用题干）

某家庭内有3代人。爷爷76岁，患有高血压和糖尿病；奶奶74岁，患有高血压；爸爸50岁，出租车司机；妈妈47岁，家庭妇女；儿子24岁，公司职员；女儿20岁，大学生。

3. 该家庭属于哪种类型的家庭？

4. 请绘制该家庭的家系图。

（5~6题共用题干）

王女士，70岁，半年前跌倒导致左腿骨折。出院后在家休养，主要由王女士的丈夫负责照

discharged from the hospital, she recuperated at home. Ms.Wang's husband was mainly responsible for taking care of Ms.Wang. The community nurse provides Ms. Wang with rehabilitation guidance and assists with rehabilitation training through monthly home visits.

5. What type of home visit was offered to the family?

6. How to assess the family during the home visit?

顾。社区护士通过每个月的家庭访视为王女士提供康复指导，并协助进行康复训练。

5. 对该家庭提供的是哪种类型的家庭访视？

6. 家庭访视时如何对该家庭进行家庭护理评估？

Chapter 5

Community Health Care for Children and Adolescents

第五章

社区儿童和青少年保健

NURSING

05章 数字内容

Learning Objectives

Knowledge Objectives

1. Correctly describe the growth and developmental characteristics of children across different age groups.
2. Explain concepts such as prophylactic immunization and planned immunization.
3. Summarize the key points of health care guidance for children at different ages.
4. Illustrate disease prevention and injury handling methods for children at different ages.

学习目标

知识目标

1. 能正确描述儿童各年龄段生长发育特点。

2. 能解释预防接种、计划免疫等概念。

3. 能概括儿童各年龄段保健指导要点。

4. 能举例说明各年龄段儿童疾病预防及意外伤害的预防与处理。

N

Ability Objectives

1. Apply nursing procedures and health-related knowledge to conduct home visits for newborns.
2. Combine growth and development features of each stage to provide community health care guidance to children, adolescents, and their parents.
3. Utilize knowledge and skills related to prophylactic immunization for administering inoculation.

Quality Objectives

Cultivate a scientific spirit, foster a love for children, and provide health guidance for community children and adolescents.

能力目标

1. 能运用护理程序及相关保健知识与技能，开展新生儿家庭访视。

2. 能结合各年龄段生长发育特点，对儿童、青少年及其家长开展社区保健指导。

3. 能运用预防接种知识与技能进行预防接种。

素质目标

树立科学精神，培养爱幼情怀，为社区儿童和青少年提供健康指导。

Xiaohua, female, 6 months and 5 days old, visited the community health center today for vaccination. After measurement, her height was recorded as 65.1cm, and her weight was 8.0kg. She is currently on mixed feeding and has not yet started complementary feeding.

Please think about the following questions based on the case:

1. According to the national immunization program vaccination schedule for children, which vaccine should she receive during this visit?

2. How to evaluate her growth and development?

3. What are the key points for health guidance tailored to her situation?

4. What health management services should the community health center provide for her before she turns 6 years old?

Children and adolescents are the future of our nation, and their health status determines the quality of a country's future population. The physiological characteristics and health needs of children and adolescents differ from those of adults, making them a group that requires special attention from society. Consequently, implementing health management for children and adolescents is

小花，女，6月龄5天，今日来社区卫生服务中心进行疫苗接种。经测量，小花身长为65.1cm，体重为8.0kg。目前采用混合喂养，尚未添加辅食。

请根据案例情况思考以下问题：

1. 根据国家免疫规划疫苗儿童免疫程序，她此次应接种哪种疫苗？

2. 怎样评价她的生长发育情况？
3. 对小花保健指导的要点是什么？

4. 在她满6岁前，社区卫生服务中心应为其提供哪些健康管理服务？

儿童和青少年是祖国的未来，其健康状态决定一个国家未来人口的素质。儿童、青少年的生理特点、健康需求与成年人有所不同，是需要社会特殊关注的人群。因此，对儿童和青少年实施健康管理是社区卫生服务工作的重点。

a primary focus of community health services.

Section 1 Overview

I. Concept and Significance of Community Health Care for Children and Adolescents

Community care for children and adolescents refers to the systematic services provided by community health workers based on the growth and development characteristics of children and adolescents, focusing on promoting health of children and addressing health issues they face. This includes regular monitoring of growth and development, vaccination, nutritional guidance, and preventive measures and treatment for common illnesses. By conducting systematic health management for children and adolescents at every stage, community nurses can promptly identify existing issues in growth and development, implement interventions early, thereby laying the foundation for their healthy growth. Moreover, community care for children and adolescents enhances parental and community awareness of child rights, improves parenting abilities, and strengthens community support systems.

II. Techniques for Community Child and Adolescent Health Management

i. Length (Height), Weight, Head Circumference Measurement and Evaluation

1. Length (Height) Measurement For infants and toddlers two years old and under, a horizontal measuring bed shoud be placed stably on a table. Remove the infant's shoes, hat, and thick clothing, and position them to lie flat on the central line of the board. Secure the infant's head to ensure contact with the headboard, with both ears at the same level, and the upper edges of auricle and lower orbit margins aligned vertically with the board. After confirming the

第一节　概　　述

一、社区儿童和青少年保健的概念及意义

社区儿童、青少年保健是指社区卫生服务人员根据儿童、青少年的生长发育特点，以促进健康、解决健康问题为核心，为其提供的系统性服务。社区儿童和青少年保健包括定期的生长发育监测、疫苗接种、营养指导、常见疾病的预防与治疗等服务。社区护士对各阶段儿童和青少年进行系统的健康管理，可及时发现其生长发育方面存在的问题，尽早采取干预措施，为儿童的健康成长奠定基础。同时，社区儿童和青少年保健工作可以提高家长及社区成员对儿童权益的认识，提升家庭抚养能力和加强社区支持功能。

二、社区儿童和青少年健康管理技术

（一）身长（高）、体重、头围测量及评价

1. **身长（高）测量**　两岁及以下婴幼儿身长测量时，采用卧式测量床。测量床平稳放在桌面上，脱去婴幼儿的鞋帽和厚衣裤，使其仰卧于量板中线上。固定婴幼儿头部使其接触头板。此时婴幼儿面向上，两耳在同一水平上，两侧耳郭上缘与眼眶下缘的连线与量板垂直。测量者在确定幼儿平卧于量板中线后，将手置于儿童膝部，使婴幼儿两腿平行伸直，双膝并拢并固定。用另一手滑动滑板，使之紧贴婴幼儿双足跟，当两侧标尺读数一致时读数（图 5-1）。读数

infant's alignment, place a hand on the infant's knees, keeping both legs straight, knees together and securing them. With the other hand, slide the board, pressing it firmly against the infant's heels until the readings on both scales match (see Figure 5-1). Record the measurement with an accuracy of 0.1cm.

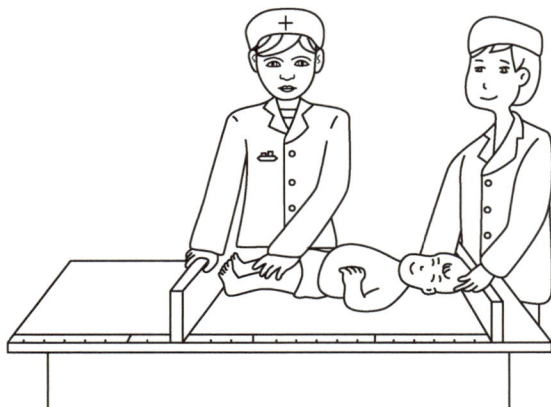

精确到0.1cm。

Figure 5-1   Length measurement of infants and toddlers

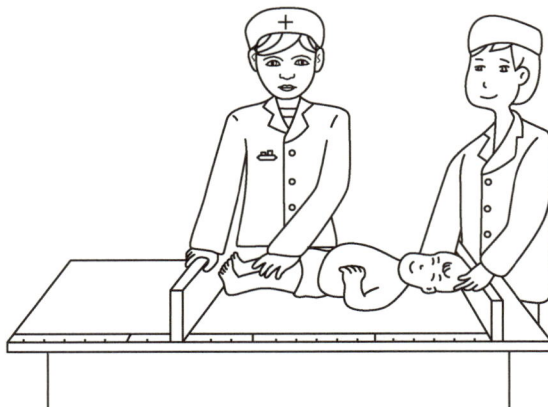

图5-1   婴幼儿身长测量

For children over two years old, height can be measured using a stadiometer. During the measurement, the child should be bareheaded, barefoot, and with hair untied. The child should take a standing position upright on the measuring board, chest out, abdomen in, arms hanging naturally, heels close together, toes spread about 60° apart, knees straightened, eyes looking straight ahead, with the lower edge of the orbit and upper edge of the auricle at the same horizontal level. Three points, the heel, buttocks, and inter-scapular, should touch the stadiometer simultaneously, with the head held upright (see Figure 5-2). The reading should be accurate to 0.1cm.

两岁以上儿童身高测量可采用立柱式身高计。测量时儿童应免冠、赤足，解开发髻。儿童取立正姿势，站在板上，挺胸收腹，两臂自然下垂，脚跟靠拢，脚尖分开约60°，双膝并拢挺直，两眼平视正前方，眼眶下缘与耳郭上缘保持在同一水平。脚跟、臀部和两肩胛间三个点同时接触立柱，头部保持正立位置（图5-2）。读数精确到0.1cm。

2. **Weight Measurement** Weight should preferably be measured in the morning, on an empty stomach, and after a bowel movement, with minimal clothing. For children two years old and under, place the infant or toddler securely on the scale, ensuring their limbs don't touch any other objects. The weight reading should be taken when the child is calm, to a precision of 0.01kg.

2. **体重测量** 测量尽量选择在清晨、空腹、排泄完毕的状态下进行，测量时尽量脱去全部衣裤。两岁及以下儿童测量体重时，将婴幼儿平稳放置于体重计上，四肢不得与其他物体相接触，待婴幼儿安静时读取体重读数，精确到0.01kg。两岁以上儿童测量体重时，儿童平静站立于体重秤踏板中央，两腿均匀负重，免冠、赤足、穿贴身内衣裤。读数精确到0.1kg。

For children over two years old, they should stand calmly on the center of the scale's platform, evenly distributing their weight, with no headwear, barefoot, and wearing only close-fitting underwear. The reading should be accurate to 0.1kg.

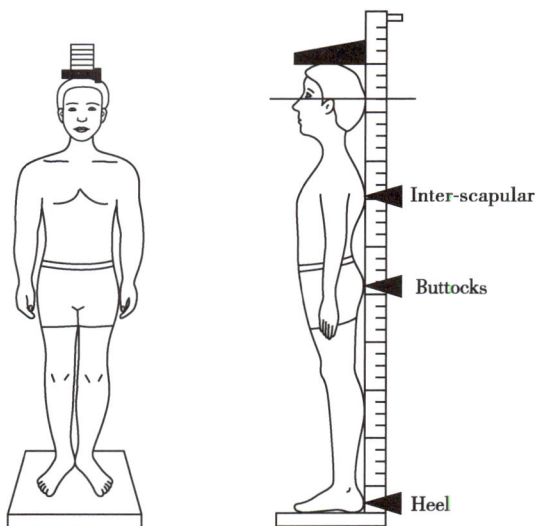

Figure 5-2　Height measurement

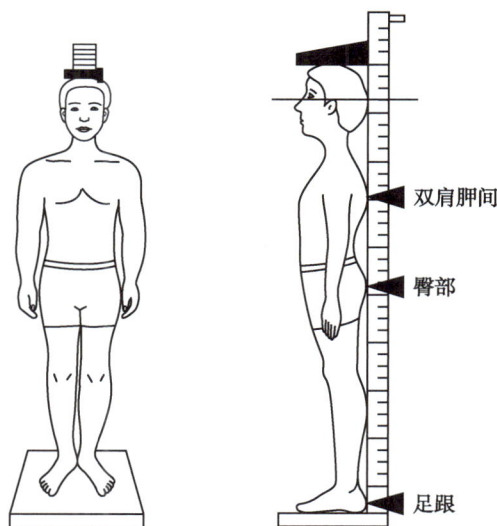

图 5-2　身高测量

3. Head Circumference Measurement

Use a flexible fiberglass tape to measure the head circumference passing through the right superciliary arch and the highest points of the occipital protuberance (see Figure 5-3). During the measurement, the tape should be snug against the skin, maintaining symmetry on both sides. The reading should be accurate to 0.1cm.

3. 头围测量 使用玻璃纤维软尺,通过右侧眉弓与枕骨隆突最高点测量平面头部周长(图 5-3)。测量时,软尺应紧贴皮肤,左右两侧保持对称。读数精确到 0.1cm。

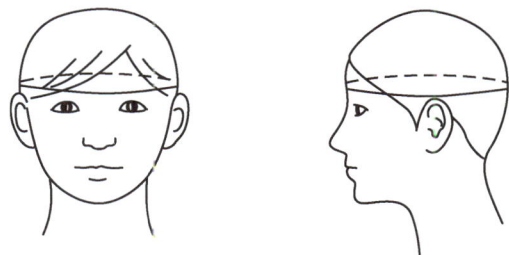

Figure 5-3　Head circumference measurement

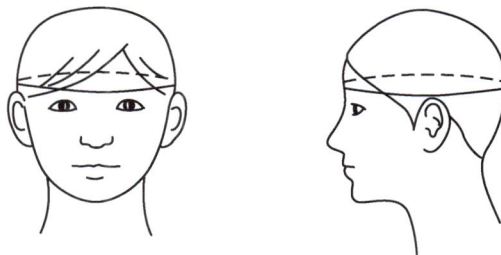

图 5-3　头围测量

4. Evaluation of Growth and Development

At each health management visit, compare the measured values with normal ranges and previous measurements to evaluate the child's growth and development. Plot the length (height) and weight on a growth curve chart. If the length (height)

4. 生长发育评价 每次健康管理时都将测量值与正常值、既往测量值进行对比,以评价儿童的生长发育情况。将身长(高)、体重记录在生长曲线图上。若身长(高)、体重曲线水平虽较低,但与平均曲线平行,可继续观察;若 3 个月曲线一直没有上升,应转诊。

and weight curve is low but parallels the average curve, continued observation is advised. If there is no upward trend in the curve for three consecutive months, referral is necessary.

ii. Prevention of Dental Caries

Inspect the child's teeth to determine the presence of dental caries. Teeth with brown or black spots, rough surfaces, or obvious structural damage are diagnosed as having dental caries. Additionally, record the number of dental caries, including both treated and untreated ones.

iii. Vision Check

Vision for children and adolescents is assessed using an international standard visual acuity chart or a logarithmic visual acuity chart, with a testing distance of 5 meters, chart illumination at 500lx, and the 1.0 line of the chart positioned at the level of the examinee's eyes. During the test, cover one eye without applying pressure to it, starting with the right eye followed by the left. The subject is guided to identify symbols from top to bottom until the line that cannot be distinguished is reached; the line before this is recorded as their visual acuity.

iv. Introduction of Complementary Feeding

Breastfeeding can be continued up to and beyond the age of two years with appropriate complementary feeding practices. At six months, introduce non-milk foods based on a milk intake of 180ml per feeding. Non-milk foods should be introduced one at a time, starting with small quantities and gradually increasing, while also transitioning from thinner to thicker textures and from finer to coarser consistencies. Foods typically start with less allergenic grains and progress to include animal-source foods (Table 5-1). If the infant experiences dyspepsia or falls ill, the introduction of new foods should be paused until the infant fully recovers.

（二）龋齿预防

检查儿童牙齿情况，判断是否有龋齿。如果牙齿出现褐色或黑褐色斑点或斑块，表面粗糙，甚至出现明显的牙体结构破坏，则判断为龋齿。此外，还要观察龋齿的数目，包括已治疗和未治疗的龋齿。

（三）视力检查

采用国际标准视力表或对数视力表检查儿童和青少年视力，检测距离为 5m，视力表照度为 500lx，视力表 1.0 行高度为受检者眼睛高度。检查时，一眼遮挡，但勿压迫眼球，按照先右后左顺序，单眼进行检查。自上而下辨认视标，直到不能辨认的一行时为止，其前一行即可记录为被检者的视力。

（四）食物转换指导

在合理食物转换的情况下，母乳喂养可坚持到孩子 2 岁以上。6 月龄的婴儿，在 180ml/ 次奶量的基础上开始添加非乳类食物。添加的非乳类食物应由一种到多种，由少量到多量，逐渐增加；食物质地由稀到稠、由细到粗，循序渐进。食物种类通常由不易导致过敏的谷类食物开始，逐渐引入动物性食物（表 5-1）。当婴儿消化不良或生病时，应暂停添加。

Table 5-1　Timing and Types of Introducing Solid Foods to Infants

Type	6months	7–9months	10–12months
Grain-based foods	Iron-fortified rice cereal	Porridge, soft noodles, biscuits, steamed bun slices, cooked potatoes	Thick porridge, soft rice, noodles, stuffed foods
Vegetables and fruits	Vegetable and fruit purees	Chopped vegetables, chopped fruits	Chopped vegetables, chopped fruits
Animal-based foods and legumes	None	Fish puree, meat puree, liver puree, tofu, egg yolk	Whole eggs, minced meat, minced fish, bean products

表 5-1　婴儿食物引入时间及种类

种类	6个月	7~9个月	10~12个月
粮食类	含铁米粉	粥、烂面、饼干、馒头片、熟土豆	稠粥、软饭、面条、带馅食品
蔬菜、水果类	菜泥、果泥	碎菜、碎果	碎菜、碎果
动物类、豆类	无	鱼泥、肉泥、肝泥、豆腐、蛋黄	全蛋、碎肉、碎鱼、豆制品

Section 2　Community Health Care for Children and Adolescents

In accordance with the characteristics of growth and development in children and adolescents, the developmental process is generally divided into five stages: neonatal period, infancy and toddlerhood, preschool stage, school stage, and adolescence. Community health service organizations should provide health guidance tailored to the growth and developmental characteristics of children and adolescents at different ages. For cases identified during health management, such as malnutrition, anemia, simple obesity, dental caries, subnormal vision or hearing abnormalities, the causes should be analyzed, guidance or referral suggestions provided, and follow-up conducted to track the outcomes post-referral.

I. Health Care during Neonatal Period

i. Characteristics of Neonatal Growth and Development

The neonatal period refers to the time from the moment of umbilical cord ligation after birth until the baby reaches 28 days old. Neonates,

第二节　社区儿童和青少年保健

根据儿童和青少年的生长发育特点，一般将生长发育过程分为新生儿期、婴幼儿期、学龄前期、学龄期和青少年期五个阶段。社区卫生服务机构应结合儿童和青少年各年龄段生长发育特点开展保健指导。对在健康管理中发现有营养不良、贫血、单纯性肥胖、龋齿、视力低常或听力异常等情况的儿童应当分析其原因，给出指导或转诊的建议，并追踪随访转诊后结果。

一、新生儿期保健

（一）新生儿生长发育特点

新生儿期是指从出生后脐带结扎时起至生后满 28 天。新生儿脱离母体开始独立生活，经历了内、外环境的巨大变化。由于新生儿各组

having separated from their mother's body, begin independent life, undergoing immense internal and external environmental changes. Due to the immaturity of their organs and systems, newborns have poor physiological regulatory functions and adaptability to external changes, making them susceptible to various diseases, which marks the stage with the highest incidence and mortality rates in childhood. The growth and development characteristics during this period include：

1. Temperature Regulation　Neonates have incomplete temperature regulation mechanisms. Exposure to a cold environment can lead to hypothermia or even scleredema neonatorum, while overheating can cause dehydration, highlighting the importance of maintaining proper warmth and ambient temperature.

2. Digestive System　Neonates possess basic feeding reflexes like rooting and swallowing. However, swallowing involves inadequate closure of the upper esophageal sphincter, lack of esophageal peristalsis, and poor closure of the lower esophageal sphincter, which can result in regurgitation. The high permeability of intestinal epithelial cells makes them prone to allergies.

3. Urinary System　Renal function of neonates is weak, with poor renal tubule phosphorus excretion. Feeding with cow's milk, which is high in protein and phosphorus, can potentially harm newborn kidneys.

4. Immune System　Both non-specific and specific immunity functions of neonates are immature, with less secretory IgA in the gut, rendering them vulnerable to respiratory tract and gastrointestinal tract infections.

5. Physical Development　A healthy full-term infant may gain 1 to 1.5kg in weight and grow 4 to 5cm in length during the first month after birth. Additionally, physiological weight loss and neonatal jaundice are common occurrences during this period.

织器官发育尚不成熟，生理调节功能和对外界变化的适应能力差，容易患各种疾病，是儿童期发病率和死亡率最高的阶段。该期生长发育特点如下：

1．体温调节　新生儿体温调节功能不完善，环境温度过低可导致体温不升甚至新生儿硬肿病，环境温度过高可导致脱水，故保温并保持合适环境温度非常重要。

2．消化系统　新生儿具有最基本的进食反射：觅食反射和吞咽反射。但吞咽时，食管上括约肌不关闭、食管不蠕动、食管下部括约肌不关闭，易发生溢奶。小肠上皮细胞渗透性高，易产生过敏。

3．泌尿系统　新生儿肾泌尿功能差，肾小管排磷功能差，选用蛋白质、矿物质磷含量高的牛乳喂养时，对新生儿肾脏有潜在损害。

4．免疫系统　新生儿非特异性和特异性免疫功能均不成熟，肠道分泌型 IgA 较少，容易发生呼吸道和消化道感染。

5．体格发育　正常足月婴儿出生后第一个月，体重增加可达 1~1.5kg，身长增长 4~5cm。此外，新生儿期可能出现生理性体重下降、新生儿黄疸等情况。

ii. Content of Health Care during Neonatal Period

Community health service personnel can provide health guidance to newborn families through home visits soon after discharge and a follow-up visit when the newborn is one month old. The neonatal home visit takes place within one week of the newborn's discharge, where medical staff visits the newborn's home. During the visit, inquiries are made about the birth details, prophylactic immunization status, newborn disease screening results, among others. Based on the specific condition of the newborn, parents are guided on feeding, development, disease prevention, injury prevention, and oral health care. At 28 to 30 days after birth, coinciding with the second dose of the hepatitis B vaccine, follow-up is conducted at rural hospitals or community health centers.

1. Nutrition and Feeding　Breastfeeding is encouraged as the optimal feeding method for infants, especially for preterm infants and low birth weight infants. Mothers should breastfeed on demand to ensure the infant receives sufficient milk. Direct breastfeeding is advocated, avoiding bottle-feeding of expressed milk unless separation necessitates it. In special circumstances requiring supplementation beyond breastmilk, medical consultation is crucial before making decisions. Partially breastfed or formula-fed infants require careful selection of formula.

2. Daily Health Care

(1) Warmth and Clothing: Room temperature should be maintained at 22–24℃ with a relative humidity of 55%–65%. Clothes and diapers should be clean, soft, highly absorbent, and light-colored. Infants' clothing should not be excessively thick, and wrapping should not restrict limb movement.

(2) Bowel Movement Care: After each bowel movement, the infant's bottom should be cleaned with warm water, and diapers changed frequently to keep the area dry. Diaper dermatitis can be prevented and treated with applications of zinc

（二）新生儿期保健内容

社区卫生服务人员可以通过新生儿家庭访视及新生儿满月访视对新生儿家庭开展保健指导。新生儿家庭访视是在新生儿出院后 1 周内，医务人员到新生儿家中进行访视。访视时询问出生时情况、预防接种情况、新生儿疾病筛查情况等。根据新生儿的具体情况，对家长进行喂养、发育、防病、预防伤害和口腔保健指导。新生儿出生后 28~30 天，结合接种乙肝疫苗第二针，在乡镇卫生院、社区卫生服务中心进行随访。

1. 营养与喂养　鼓励母乳喂养。母乳喂养是婴儿出生后的最佳喂养方式，早产儿、低体重儿更加提倡母乳喂养。母亲应当按需哺乳，确保婴儿摄入足够乳汁，应坚持让婴儿直接吸吮母乳，只要母婴不分开，就不用奶瓶喂哺人工挤出的母乳。由于特殊情况需要添加母乳之外其他食物的，应咨询医务人员后谨慎作出决定。部分母乳喂养或人工喂养婴儿则应正确选择配方奶。

2. 日常保健

（1）保暖与衣着：室温为 22~24℃，相对湿度为 55%~65%。衣着和尿布须选用清洁、柔软、吸水性好、浅颜色的布料。新生儿衣被不宜过厚，包裹不要太紧，以便新生儿四肢自由屈伸。

（2）排便护理：新生儿每次大便后宜用温水清洗臀部，勤换尿布，保持臀部干燥。必要时可使用氧化锌或 5% 鞣酸软膏涂抹局部，积极预防并及时治疗尿布皮炎。

oxide or 5% tannic acid ointment if necessary.

(3) Infant Massage: Infants should be bathed daily to maintain skin hygiene and reduce bacterial growth. Massaging after bathing promotes infant development and parent-child bonding.

(4) Umbilical Part Care: The umbilical cord usually falls off naturally between day 5 and 8 after birth. Until then, the umbilicus should be kept dry. It should be disinfected with 75% ethanol swabs 1–2 times daily. Redness, swelling, or purulent discharge around the umbilicus suggests infection and requires medical attention.

3. Disease Prevention

(1) If a newborn has a high temperature, first check if clothing is too heavy or the room is too hot. Fever requires medical guidance for medication use.

(2) Distinguish between physiological and pathological jaundice. Physiological jaundice usually resolves without intervention, but if it's pathological, prompt treatment is needed.

(3) Parents should wash hands before feeding and handling the infant. Limit visitors and avoid kissing to prevent cross-infection. Those with skin diseases, respiratory tract or digestive tract infections, or any infectious disease must not touch the newborn.

4. Prevention of Accidental Injuries

Asphyxia is a common accidental injury in newborns. Causes include incorrect breastfeeding positions obstructing breathing, overly thick or tight wrapping covering the nose and mouth, or inhaling milk during regurgitation.

Preventative measures include adopting proper breastfeeding positions, avoiding excessive wrapping, and holding the infant upright after feeds, gently patting their back until they burp before placing them on their back. If asphyxia occurs, promptly remove the cause, clear the mouth and nose, and ensure an open airway. Immediate CPR is indicated for those in respiratory and cardiac arrest.

（3）婴儿抚触：婴儿应每日沐浴，保持皮肤清洁，减少病菌繁殖。沐浴后可做婴儿抚触，以达到促进婴儿生长发育及亲子交流的目的。

（4）脐部护理：一般脐带在出生后 5~8 天自然脱落。脐带脱落前要保持脐部干燥，每天用 75% 乙醇棉签消毒脐带残端及脐周 1~2 次。如脐周皮肤红肿、有脓性分泌物，则提示感染，应及时就诊。

3. 疾病预防

（1）新生儿体温过高时，首先应检查穿戴衣物是否过多，环境温度是否过高。如确为发热，需在医生指导下服用药物。

（2）正确识别生理性黄疸和病理性黄疸，生理性黄疸一般不需处理，若为病理性黄疸，应及时救治。

（3）家长在哺乳和护理前先洗手；尽量减少亲友探视和亲吻新生儿，避免交叉感染；凡患皮肤病、呼吸道和消化道感染及其他传染病者，不能接触新生儿。

4. 意外伤害预防

窒息是新生儿常见的意外伤害。常见原因包括：哺乳姿势不适当，乳房、手臂堵塞新生儿口鼻；新生儿盖被包裹过厚、过紧，蒙住婴儿口鼻；新生儿吐奶时将奶汁或者奶块吸入气管。

窒息的预防措施为：注意哺乳姿势，避免乳房或手臂堵塞婴儿口鼻；不宜将婴儿包裹得过严、过紧、过厚；每次喂奶后要将婴儿竖立抱起，轻拍后背，待胃内空气排出后再使婴儿仰卧。当发现新生儿窒息时，应迅速解除引起窒息的原因，清除口腔和鼻腔分泌物，保持呼吸道通畅；呼吸、心搏骤停者，应立即进行心肺复苏。

II. Health Care During Infancy and Toddlerhood

Infancy refers to the period from 28 days after birth to one year of age. Toddlerhood spans from the completion of the first year to the third year. Follow-up services post the first month should ideally take place at rural hospitals or community health centers; in remote areas, village health clinics or community health stations may suffice. These visits are scheduled at 3, 6, 8, 12, 18, 24, 30, and 36 months of age, totaling 8 times. During these visits, inquiries are made about feeding practices and illnesses, physical examinations are conducted, growth and psychological-behavioral development assessments are performed, and guidance is provided on scientific feeding (balanced diet), growth and development, disease prevention, injury prevention, and oral health care.

i. Growth and Development Characteristics During Infancy and Toddlerhood

1. Infancy Growth and Development Characteristics　This period witnesses the fastest physical growth and development, with a relatively high demand for energy and nutrients (notably protein). However, their digestive systems are yet to mature, making them prone to digestive disorders and malnutrition. After six months, maternal antibodies start to fade, and their own immune system is not fully developed, increasing susceptibility to infectious and communicable diseases. Additionally, infancy marks the onset of rapid mental and behavioral development, characterized by the emergence of attachment and trust towards caregivers, and separation anxiety when apart from them.

2. Toddlerhood Growth and Development Characteristics　The growth rate slows down compared to infancy. Toddlers begin to walk and explore a wider environment, enhancing neural and psychological development, language, thinking, and adaptation to external

二、婴幼儿期保健

婴儿期是指出生 28 天后至 1 岁。幼儿期是指 1 岁到 3 岁。满月后的随访服务均应在乡镇卫生院或社区卫生服务中心进行，偏远地区可在村卫生室、社区卫生服务站进行，时间分别在 3、6、8、12、18、24、30、36 月龄时，共 8 次。随访时询问婴幼儿喂养、患病等情况，进行体格检查，做生长发育和心理行为发育评估，进行科学喂养（合理膳食）、生长发育、疾病预防、伤害预防、口腔保健等健康指导。

（一）婴幼儿期生长发育特点

1. 婴儿期生长发育特点　此期体格生长发育最为迅速，对能量和营养物质（尤其是蛋白质）的需求相对较大，但婴儿消化功能尚未成熟，易发生消化紊乱、营养不良等疾病。半年后由母体获得的抗体逐渐消失，婴儿自身免疫功能尚不完善，易发生传染病及感染性疾病。此外，婴儿期开始进入心理行为的快速发展时期，婴儿对亲人产生明显的依恋感和信任感，与亲人分开会产生分离性焦虑。

2. 幼儿期生长发育特点　幼儿期生长发育速度较婴儿期减慢。此期幼儿能够行走，活动范围渐广，接触周围事物增多，故神经、心理发育较快，语言、思维和应对外界事物的能力增强。但幼儿识别危险的能力不足，易发生意外伤害。

stimuli. However, their ability to recognize danger is limited, making them vulnerable to accidental injuries.

ii. Health Care Content During Infancy and Toddlerhood

1. Nutrition and Feeding

(1) Breastfeeding: Exclusive breastfeeding is promoted until 6 months. Mothers are guided on ways to promote lactation, primarily through frequent and thorough breastfeeding, maintaining a positive mood, adequate sleep, and balanced nutrition. Breastfeeding can continue alongside adding food supplements up to 2 years or more.

(2) Adding Food Supplements: Starting at 6 months, while continuing breastfeeding, introduce diverse nutrient-rich foods. For mixed or formula-fed infants, timely introduction of dietary supplements is also necessary at 6 months. Dietary supplements are introduced gradually, guiding infants to adapt progressively. Textures evolve from purees to lumpy and eventually solid foods: purees at 6 months, thicker consistency with small pieces by 9 months, and chunkier food by 10–12 months. By 1 year, toddlers can eat soft meals, transitioning to family diets around 2 years.

(3) Micronutrient Supplementation: Term infants commence vitamin D supplementation (400IU/d) within days under medical supervision. Iron supplementation may be considered from 4–6 months as needed. Preterm or low birth weight infants require higher initial doses of vitamin D (800–1,000IU/d), which should be reduced to 400IU/d after 3 months, and start iron supplementation 2mg/(kg·d) from 2–4 weeks of age, considering content in formulas and fortified breast milk.

(4) Regular Assessment: Visit rural hospitals, community health centers (stations), or maternal and child health hospitals periodically for health examinations to evaluate growth, development, and nutritional status. Adjust feeding practices

（二）婴幼儿期保健内容

1. 营养与喂养

（1）母乳喂养：提倡纯母乳喂养至 6 个月。指导母亲掌握促进乳汁分泌的方法：婴儿的充分吸吮是促进乳汁分泌最有效的方法；母亲心情愉悦、睡眠充足、营养均衡也是促进泌乳的重要因素。婴儿 6 个月后，在添加辅食基础上可继续母乳喂养至 2 岁及以上。

（2）辅食添加：6 个月后，应当在继续母乳喂养基础上引入其他营养丰富的食物。混合喂养及人工喂养的婴儿，满 6 个月也要及时添加辅食。添加辅食坚持由少量到多量的原则，引导婴幼儿逐步适应。辅食质地应当从泥糊状逐步过渡到团块状固体食物：婴儿 6 个月之后添加泥糊状食物；9 个月过渡到带小颗粒的稠粥、烂面、肉末、碎菜等；10~12 个月食物应当更稠，并可尝试块状食物；1 岁以后吃软烂饭；2 岁左右接近家庭日常饮食。

（3）微量营养素添加：足月儿出生后数日内开始，在医生指导下每天补充维生素 D400IU，4~6 月龄时可根据需要适当补铁。早产或低出生体重儿一般出生后数日内开始，在医生指导下，每天补充维生素 D800~1 000IU，3 个月后改为每天 400IU；出生后 2~4 周开始，按 2mg/（kg·d）补充铁元素。上述补充量包括配方奶及母乳强化剂中的含量。

（4）定期评价：定期到乡镇卫生院、社区卫生服务中心（站）或妇幼保健院接受健康检查，评价生长发育和营养状况，在医生指导下及时调整喂养行为。

promptly under the guidance of a physician based on these assessments.

2. Daily Health Care　Overall development including physical, motor, cognitive, linguistic, emotional, and social skills could be promoted through daily health care.

(1) Early Education

1) Expose infants and toddlers to a variety of items such as toys, pictures, and music to stimulate their sensory perception and cultivate their powers of observation.

2) Guide parents to follow the characteristics of their child's growth and development corresponding to each month of age, and tailor activities to the child's actual abilities. For instance, around seven to eight months, crawling exercises can be introduced to develop motor functions. Fine motor skills can be fostered through activities like drawing, picking up beans, and tearing paper.

3) Emphasize parental presence, interaction, and playtime: Caregivers should pay close attention to the infant's expressions, sounds, movements, and emotions, responding promptly and positively. This fosters self-awareness, confidence, emotional growth, and skill expansion in the child. During play, encourage the child to initiate contact with others to nurture social skills, while patiently restricting dangerous behavior to instill moral values, a sense of collectivism.

(2) Cultivating Good Habits: While ensuring safety, parents should provide infants and toddlers with opportunities for free play and encourage independent exploration. Gradually train them in developing mindful eating habits such as chewing thoroughly, eating independently, avoiding pickiness, and having a balanced diet. Additionally, instill in them good hygiene practices and establish healthy sleep routines.

(3) Physical Exercise: Physical exercise enhances physical fitness, improves adaptability to external environments, and boosts immunity

2. 日常保健　通过日常保健促进婴幼儿的体格、运动、认知、语言、情感和社会适应能力等各方面的发展。

（1）早期教育

1）使婴幼儿多接触各种事物如玩具、图片及音乐等，促进感知觉发展，培养其观察力。

2）指导家长按各月龄生长发育的特征，并结合婴儿实际能力适时训练其动作，如在七八个月左右训练爬行，发展运动功能；通过画画、拾豆、撕纸等活动发展精细动作。

3）注重亲子陪伴和交流、玩耍：应关注婴幼儿的表情、声音、动作和情绪等表现，及时给予恰当、积极的回应，使婴幼儿逐渐认识自我、建立自信、培养情感和拓展能力。在玩耍中，鼓励婴幼儿主动与他人接触，以获得社会交往能力，同时应耐心限制其危险行为，培养其道德观念、集体观念。

（2）培养良好的生活习惯：在保证安全的前提下，家长要为婴幼儿提供自由玩耍的机会，鼓励儿童自由探索。逐步训练婴幼儿细嚼慢咽、自主进食、不偏食、不挑食等，培养良好的卫生习惯及睡眠习惯。

（3）体格锻炼：体格锻炼可以增强体质，提高对外界环境的适应能力和抗病能力。婴幼儿可多做户外活动，进行空气、日光、水"三浴"锻

against diseases. Infants and toddlers should engage frequently in outdoor activities and undergo "three-bath" exercises involving fresh air, sunlight, and water exposure to prevent rickets.

(4) Regular Health Checkups: These are essential for early detection of conditions such as marasmus, overweight, obesity, growth retardation, anemia, eye disorders, hearing impairments, and dental caries. Regular checkups allow for the prompt identification of the underlying causes and implement of necessary interventions.

3. Disease Prevention

(1) Dental Caries: Teeth cleaning should start when the first deciduous tooth emerges. Depending on the child's age, options such as gauze, finger toothbrushes, or regular children's toothbrushes can be used to clean the teeth twice a day. Fluoride toothpaste is recommended, with a rice grain-sized amount. After each meal, provide plain water or clean the mouth.

Between the eruption of the first deciduous tooth and 12 months of age, the first oral examination and assessment of cavity risk should occur, followed by regular checks every 3–6 months. Infants and toddlers with moderate to low cavity risk should receive fluoride varnish application twice yearly, whereas those at high risk need it four times a year. Pits and fissures in deciduous molars can be sealed. Any change in tooth color, texture, or shape should prompt immediate medical consultation.

(2) Hearing Impairment: Families should be encouraged to actively engage in ear and hearing health care services for their children, paying attention to their children's responses to sound and language development. Avoid exposing children to loud or continuous noise, industrial or recreational noisy places, and headphones. Prevent water from entering the ears during baths or swimming. After illnesses like parotitis or meningitis, monitor their

炼,以预防佝偻病发生。

（4）定期健康检查：便于早期发现消瘦、超重、肥胖、发育迟缓、贫血、眼病、听力障碍及龋病等健康问题，查找病因，及时干预。

3. 疾病预防

（1）龋齿：婴幼儿萌出第一颗乳牙时就应开始清洁牙齿。可根据月龄选用纱布、指套牙刷、儿童常规牙刷早晚为婴幼儿清洁牙齿。建议使用儿童含氟牙膏，牙膏使用量为米粒大小。每次进食后喂白开水或清洁口腔。

第一颗乳牙萌出到 12 月龄之间，进行第一次口腔检查和患龋风险评估，之后每 3~6 个月定期检查。对患龋中、低风险的婴幼儿，每年使用含氟涂料 2 次；对高风险的婴幼儿，每年使用 4 次。乳磨牙深窝沟可行窝沟封闭。一旦发现牙齿有颜色、质地及形态改变，建议及时就诊。

（2）听力障碍：指导家庭主动接受儿童耳及听力保健服务，注意观察儿童对声音的反应和语言发育的情况。日常生活中，应远离强声或持续噪声环境，避免儿童去有强工业噪声、娱乐性噪声的场所；避免儿童使用耳机；洗澡或游泳时防止呛水和耳部进水；儿童罹患腮腺炎或脑膜炎后，应注意观察其听力变化。

children's hearing for changes.

Prompt medical evaluation is necessary if any of the following are observed: abnormalities in the ear or surrounding skin; discharge or unusual smell from the external acoustic meatus; ear-patting or scratching behavior; symptoms of ear itchiness, pain, or fullness; slow response to sound or delayed language development; frequent tilting of the head or unresponsiveness to calls.

(3) Eye Diseases: Regular eye care and vision checks should be conducted to screen for eye diseases and monitor vision and "hyperopia reserve" across all age stages. This aids early detection and treatment of blinding eye diseases like retinopathy, congenital cataracts, and retinoblastoma, preventing myopia. Adequate sleep, a balanced diet, and outdoor playtime should be ensured, minimizing prolonged near-distance viewing, and maintaining eye cleanliness.

Seek medical attention promptly if an infant or toddler exhibits any of the following symptoms: poor tracking, reduced reaction to surroundings; squinting, frowning, tilting head, or moving closer to see; white pupils, sensitivity to light, tearing, redness, or purulent discharge from the eyes.

4. Prevention of Accidental Injuries

Aspiration of foreign body in trachea is a common accidental injury among infants and toddlers. These objects include small items that can fit into the mouth, such as buttons, coins, and bottle caps, as well as foods like peanuts, melon seeds, beans, and jelly, and toy parts like detached eyes from stuffed animals. Aspiration of foreign body in trachea can potentially cause asphyxia in infants and toddlers.

To prevent foreign body aspiration, education and precautions are crucial. Avoid giving infants and toddlers small, hard, and slippery foods like peanuts, melon seeds, chewing gum, and jelly. Eating should be discouraged during active play.

如发现儿童有以下情形之一，应及时就诊，接受进一步评估：耳部及耳周皮肤异常；外耳道有分泌物或异常气味；有拍打或抓挠耳部的动作；有耳痒、耳痛、耳胀等症状；对声音反应迟钝，或有语言发育迟缓的表现；头常常往一侧歪，或对呼唤无回应。

（3）眼病：定期进行儿童眼保健和视力检查，完成各年龄阶段的眼病筛查、视力和"远视储备量"的监测，以早期发现和治疗视网膜病变、先天性白内障、视网膜母细胞瘤等致盲性眼病，预防近视的发生。日常照护中应保证婴幼儿充足睡眠、均衡膳食和充足户外活动时间，减少持续近距离用眼时间，保持婴幼儿眼部清洁卫生。

如婴幼儿出现以下症状应及时就诊：不能追视、对外界反应差；看东西时凑近、眯眼、皱眉、斜眼、歪头；瞳孔区发白、畏光、流泪、眼部发红或有脓性分泌物等。

4. 意外伤害预防　气管异物吸入是婴幼儿期常见的意外伤害。吸入的异物多是能够放入口中的小物品，包括生活用品如纽扣、硬币、瓶盖等，食品如花生米、瓜子、豆子、果冻等，玩具如脱落的绒毛动物的眼睛等。气管异物吸入可能造成婴幼儿窒息。

应加强教育和防范以预防异物吸入。避免婴幼儿进食较小、较硬而光滑的食物，如花生、瓜子、口香糖、果冻等。儿童玩耍和打闹时避免进食。选择合适玩具，玩具零部件直径不小于3.5cm，长度不小于6.0cm。将硬币、纽扣、糖果、

Toys with parts larger than 3.5cm in diameter and 6.0cm in length should be chosen. Items like coins, buttons, candies, balloons, safety pins, and can tabs should be placed out of reach to prevent accidental ingestion or inhalation.

In case of foreign body inhalation, back blows and abdominal thrusts can be used to expel the object.

1) Back blows method: Place the child face-down along the rescuer's flexed thigh, with the head lower than the trunk. Use the heel of the hand to firmly strike the back several times near the scapula, facilitating coughing and the object expulsion.

2) Abdominal thrusts method: For conscious children, the rescuer stands behind, wraps arms around the child's waist, bends the child forward, and makes the child lean the head down. One hand forms a fist with the thumb side against the child's abdomen, two finger-widths above the umbilicus and below the xiphoid process, while the other hand grasps this fist tightly. Rapid inward and upward thrusts are administered rhythmically, with the child's head lowered and mouth open to facilitate object expulsion via air flow. If the child is unconscious, lay the child in the supine position. The rescuer straddles the child's thighs, places one palm on the abdomen two finger-widths above the umbilicus, and stacks the other hand on top. Forceful, inward and upward thrusts are applied to the child's abdomen.

III. Health Care during Preschool Stage

The preschool period refers to the time from after the age of three until school entry (around 6–7 years old). Community health service providers should offer an annual health management service for preschool children. For non-institutionalized

气球、安全别针、饮料罐拉环等物品放在婴幼儿无法触及的位置，防止误食、误吸发生。

如发生异物吸入，可以采用背部叩击法和腹部冲击法清除异物。

1）背部叩击法：将患儿置于救护者屈膝的大腿上，头低于躯干，用掌根部适当用力叩击肩胛区数次使异物随咳嗽排出。

2）腹部冲击法：对于意识清醒的患儿，救护者站在患儿背后，双臂环绕患儿腰部，让患儿弯腰，头部前倾，救护者一手握空心拳，并将拇指侧顶住患儿腹部正中线脐上方两横指处，剑突下方，另一手紧握此拳，有节奏地快速向内、向上冲击，患儿低头张口，以便异物受到气流冲击而吐出。对于意识不清的患儿，将其处于仰卧位，救护者骑跨在患儿两大腿外侧，一手掌根平放其腹部正中线肚脐上方两横指处，另一手直接放在第一手上，两手掌根重叠快速向内、向上冲击患儿腹部。

三、学龄前期保健

学龄前期是指 3 岁后到入学前（6~7 岁）。社区卫生服务机构应为学龄前期儿童每年提供一次健康管理服务。散居儿童的健康管理服务应在乡镇卫生院、社区卫生服务中心进行，集居儿童可在托幼机构进行。开展健康管理时，询

children, this service is conducted at rural hospitals or community health centers, whereas for institutionalized children, it takes place within childcare settings. During these health management sessions, inquiries are made about the child's diet, illnesses, and a physical examination and psychological-behavioral development assessment are conducted, along with blood routine tests (or hemoglobin measurement) and vision screening. Guidance is given on balanced diet, growth and development, disease prevention, injury prevention, and oral health care.

i. Growth and Development Characteristics of Preschool Children

During the preschool years, children exhibit a steadily growing trend in physical development. Neurological and psychological development accelerates, with intellectual capabilities becoming more refined, language and thinking skills further developing, and their range of independent activities expanding. This is a critical period for personality formation, thus emphasis should be placed on cultivating good moral character and habits to prepare them for school entry. Preschoolers are highly curious, capable of performing more complex actions, learning to take care of themselves, and their self-care abilities and sense of independence increase. However, their awareness of danger is weak, making them susceptible to various accidental injuries.

ii. Content of Preschool Children Health Care

1. Diet and Nutrition The dietary structure of preschool children approaches that of adults, aiming for diversity, colorful presentations, and a mix of refined and whole grains to ensure ample nutrition, providing balanced nutrition for their growth and development needs.

2. Daily Health Care Emphasis is placed on fostering study habits, imagination, and thinking skills in children, cultivating a sound

问儿童膳食、患病等情况，进行体格检查、心理行为发育评估、血常规（或血红蛋白）检测和视力筛查，进行合理膳食、生长发育、疾病预防、伤害预防、口腔保健等健康指导。

（一）学龄前期儿童生长发育特点

学龄前期儿童体格发育速度呈稳步增长趋势。该时期神经精神发育迅速，智能发育更趋完善，语言和思维能力进一步发展，独立活动范围扩大，是性格形成的关键时期，因此，要注意培养儿童良好的道德品质和生活习惯，为入学做好准备。此期儿童求知欲强，对外界事物好奇，能做较复杂的动作，学会照顾自己，自理能力和独立意识逐渐增强，但危险意识淡漠，因此容易发生各种意外伤害。

（二）学龄前期儿童保健内容

1. 饮食与营养 学龄前期儿童的膳食结构接近成人，膳食安排力求多样化、颜色鲜艳、粗细搭配，保证充足营养，以提供儿童生长发育所需的均衡营养。

2. 日常保健 注意培养儿童学习习惯、想象与思维能力，使之具有良好的心理素质。在日常生活中锻炼其毅力和独立生活能力，培养

psychological foundation. Daily life is used to strengthen their perseverance and independent living skills, nurturing self-respect, self-reliance, self-improvement, and self-confidence. Physical activities and games are employed to enhance physical fitness, teaching rule adherence and social interaction through play, while simultaneously developing their ability to distinguish right from wrong.

3. Disease Prevention Developing good habits and undergoing regular health check-ups are pivotal in disease prevention. Educate children on eye hygiene during reading, writing, and watching television to prevent the development of amblyopia. Instill good oral hygiene practices, teaching the correct toothbrushing technique, and using fluoride-containing toothpaste to prevent dental caries. Annual health check-ups should be conducted, focusing on the detection and correction of common ailments such as visual impairments, dental caries, iron deficiency anemia, and parasitic infections.

4. Prevention of Accidental Injuries Preschool children are lively, but lack coordination and life experience, making them prone to accidents such as external injuries, drowning, and accidental drug ingestion. Therefore, parents and childcare settings must regularly and promptly inspect activity areas and toys, and conduct safety education in a timely manner. This includes teaching children to obey traffic rules and to stay away from rivers and ponds during play, strengthening the management of medicines and toxic substances, storing medications out of children's reach and locked away, and storing securely and using cautiously commonly used disinfectants and pesticides to prevent children's exposure. Particular attention should be paid to avoid storing toxic substances in beverage bottles or food containers, which could be mistaken for consumables by children.

自尊、自强、自立、自信的品格。通过游戏、体育活动增强其体质,在游戏中学习遵守规则和与人交往,同时培养分辨是非的能力。

3. 疾病预防 培养良好的习惯并定期健康检查以预防疾病。教育儿童在阅读、写作、看电视时注意用眼卫生,预防弱视发生。养成良好的口腔卫生习惯,学会正确的刷牙方法,使用含氟化物牙膏,预防龋齿。每年应进行健康检查,注意视力障碍、龋齿、缺铁性贫血、寄生虫感染等常见病的筛查与矫治。

4. 意外伤害预防 学龄前儿童活泼好动,但动作协调性不好,且缺乏生活经验,易发生外伤、溺水、误服药物等意外事故。因此,家长和托幼机构应定期、及时地检修活动场所、玩具等;适时进行安全教育,如要遵守交通规则、玩耍时注意远离河边与池塘边等;加强对药品、有毒物品的管理,药品放在儿童拿不到的地方,并上锁;常使用的消毒剂、杀虫剂,要妥善保管和使用,避免儿童接触,特别注意不要用饮料瓶或食具装盛有毒物品。

IV. Health Care for School-stage Children and Adolescents

School-stage refers to the period starting from primary school enrollment (around 6–7 years old) until the onset of adolescence (approximately 12 years for girls and 13 for boys). Adolescence is the transitional phase from childhood to adulthood, spanning from ages 11–12 to 17–18 for girls and 13–14 to 18–20 for boys. Community health service providers should collaborate closely with schools to offer annual health management services for children and adolescents. These services encompass physical examination, assessments of growth, development, and psychological-behavioral status. Health education is disseminated through bulletin boards, lectures, and other means, covering common health issues, disease prevention, and sexual education during adolescence.

i. Growth and Development Characteristics of School-stage Children and Adolescents

School-stage children experience steady physical growth, with organs other than the reproductive system approaching adult levels. Their cognitive, psychological, and social abilities develop rapidly, with schooling and the environment exerting significant influence. Peers become important social counterparts for children.

During adolescence, dramatic increases in weight and height occur, secondary sexual characteristics become prominent, reproductive organs rapidly mature, menstruation begins in girls, and boys experience nocturnal emission. Due to unstable neuroendocrine regulation and increased exposure to society, adolescents exhibit substantial fluctuations in psychology, behavior, and emotions. Thus, emphasis is placed on moral education and instruction regarding physiological and psychological hygiene.

四、学龄期儿童与青少年保健

学龄期是指从入小学起（6~7 岁）到青春期（女孩约 12 岁，男孩约 13 岁）。青春期又称青少年期，是指女孩从 11~12 岁开始到 17~18 岁，男孩从 13~14 岁开始到 18~20 岁，是由儿童发育到成年的一段过渡时期。社区卫生服务机构应与学校密切配合，为儿童和青少年提供每年 1 次的健康管理服务。服务内容包括：体格检查、生长发育和心理行为发育状况的评估。可以通过宣传板报、健康教育讲座等形式，普及常见健康问题、疾病防治以及青春期性教育等方面的知识。

（一）学龄期儿童与青少年生长发育特点

学龄期儿童体格稳步发育，除生殖系统外其他器官的发育已接近成人水平。学龄期儿童的认知、心理和社会能力发展非常迅速，学校和环境对其影响较大，同伴成为儿童非常重要的社交对象。

在青春期，青少年体重、身高大幅增长，第二性征逐渐明显，生殖器官迅速发育并趋向成熟，女孩出现月经，男孩发生遗精。由于神经内分泌调节不稳定，加之接触社会增多，青少年心理、行为、精神、情绪等方面的波动较大。因此加强道德品质教育及生理、心理卫生知识等教育为本期保健指导的重点。

ii. Content of Health Care for School-stage Children and Adolescents

1. Nutrition and Diet School-stage children and adolescents have heightened nutritional requirements due to rapid physical and mental development and increased physical activity. Their diets should be well-balanced and nutrient-dense, including ample staple foods, high-quality protein sources like fish, meat, eggs, beans, and generous portions of green vegetables and fresh fruits.

2. Daily Health Care Suitable learning environments are provided for school-stage children and adolescents, accompanied by strengthened quality education, safety education, and legal education. Sports and physical activities are encouraged, utilizing equipment for games, track and field events, and ball games to improve physical fitness, resilience, and a spirit of perseverance. Regular health checks are conducted, with a focus on preventing refraction errors, dental caries, iron deficiency anemia, and other common conditions.

3. Disease Prevention With the development of China's economy and society and the improvement of people's living standards, profound changes have occurred in the dietary patterns and lifestyles of children and adolescents. Coupled with heavy academic pressures and the proliferation of electronic devices, imbalanced nutrition and inadequate physical activity are widespread among this population, leading to a rapid rise in myopia, overweight, obesity, and scoliosis issues. These have become significant public health problems threatening the physical and mental health of Chinese children and adolescents.

(1) Subnormal Vision: Adolescents should undergo vision checks every six months to detect abnormalities early and enable timely correction. Schools and communities should provide health education on vision protection and myopia prevention to both children and their parents in

（二）学龄期儿童与青少年保健内容

1. 营养与饮食 学龄期儿童和青少年身心发育迅速，体力活动增加，对各种营养素需求量相对高于成人。饮食安排需营养充足、比例恰当，既要有充足的主食，也要有富含优质蛋白质的鱼、肉、蛋、豆类，以及大量的绿色蔬菜及新鲜水果。

2. 日常保健 为学龄期儿童和青少年提供适宜的学习条件，加强素质教育、安全教育和法制教育。指导体育运动，利用器械进行游戏、田径与球类锻炼，以增强体质、培养毅力和奋斗精神。定期健康检查，注意预防屈光不正、龋齿、缺铁性贫血等常见病。

3. 疾病预防 随着我国经济社会的发展和人民生活水平的提高，儿童、青少年膳食结构及生活方式发生了深刻变化，加之课业负担重、电子产品普及等因素，儿童、青少年营养不均衡、身体活动不足现象广泛存在，近视、超重、肥胖和脊柱侧弯等疾病发病率呈现快速上升趋势，已成为威胁我国儿童、青少年身心健康的重要公共卫生问题。

（1）视力低常：青少年应每半年进行一次视力检查，以便尽早发现视力异常并及时矫正。学校及社区应采取多种形式对儿童及其父母进行保护视力、预防近视的保健指导，提高对保护视力重要性的认识，加强用眼卫生。

various forms, raising awareness of the importance of eye health and promoting good eye hygiene practices.

(2) Obesity: Obesity in childhood and adolescence increases the risk of adult obesity, cardiovascular diseases, diabetes, and other chronic conditions, posing a threat to health. A comprehensive approach to addressing childhood and adolescent obesity should emphasize the roles of families, schools, and communities. Firstly, parents and caregivers should promote scientific eating habits, create a positive sports environment at home, encourage outdoor activities and physical exercise, and monitor growth and development. Secondly, schools should integrate nutrition and physical activity education into curricula, improve cafeteria offerings, enrich meal compositions, intensify physical education and extracurricular activities, ensuring at least an hour of moderate-to-vigorous daily activity and three hours of vigorous activity weekly for students. Finally, communities should implement child health management services, disseminate knowledge on balanced diets, offer individualized guidance, monitor overweight and obesity, and provide timely health education.

(3) Scoliosis: Scoliosis initially manifests as an abnormal appearance, progressing to trunk imbalance and back pain as the deformity worsens. Idiopathic scoliosis, the most common type, accounts for 70%–90%, affecting 10–16-year-olds, particularly during pubertal growth spurts.

A comprehensive approach to scoliosis prevention involves: Firstly, regular screenings for defect of vertebral column integrated into annual or new student health checks, identifying high-risk factors early for referral and prompt treatment. Secondly, promoting healthy lifestyles and behaviors that protect the vertebral column among children and adolescents is crucial. Finally, establishing a vertebral column-friendly environment entails reducing academic pressure,

（2）肥胖：儿童和青少年期肥胖会增加成年期肥胖、心血管疾病和糖尿病等慢性病过早发生的风险，对健康造成威胁。针对儿童和青少年肥胖应采取综合措施，强化家庭、学校及社区的责任。首先，应充分发挥父母及看护人的作用，帮助儿童养成科学饮食行为；营造良好的家庭体育运动氛围，积极引导孩子进行户外活动和体育锻炼；并做好儿童、青少年体重及生长发育监测。其次，学校应将膳食营养和身体活动知识融入中小学常规教育；改善学校食物供给，优化学生餐膳食结构；强化体育课和课外锻炼，保证中小学生每天在校内中等及以上强度身体活动时间达到 1 小时以上，保证每周至少 3 小时高强度身体活动。最后，社区应落实儿童健康管理服务，加强合理膳食知识普及、技能指导和个体化咨询，做好儿童和青少年超重、肥胖监测，及时进行健康教育和指导。

（3）脊柱侧弯：脊柱侧弯以外观异常为早期主要临床表现，随着畸形的进展，逐渐产生躯干失去平衡、背部疼痛等临床症状。特发性脊柱侧凸是最常见的类型，约占 70%~90%，好发于 10~16 岁的青少年，在青春期这一生长高峰期容易进展。

针对脊柱侧弯，应开展综合防控措施。首先，应定期开展脊柱弯曲异常筛查，将其纳入每学年或新生入学体检内容，早期发现影响儿童、青少年脊柱健康的高危因素，以便及时转诊与及早矫治。其次，应促进儿童和青少年建立健康的生活方式，使其培养保护脊柱的良好行为习惯。最后，应创建脊柱友好环境，家庭和学校应减轻学生学业负担；根据儿童、青少年生长情况，定期调整课桌椅高度和教室的座位位置；并强化户外活动和体育锻炼。

adjusting desk and chair heights according to growth, and encouraging outdoor activities and sports.

4. Prevention of Accidental Injuries To prevent accidents, children and adolescents should receive enhanced safety education and training in accident prevention and management. Fostering mutual love and support among peers to assist each other during emergencies is encouraged. Anti-smoking and anti-drug education should be strengthened to keep youth away from harmful behaviors. Meanwhile, school-stage children and adolescents undergo significant physical and psychological trans-formations with a rapid development of self-consciousness. It's essential to engage parents and teachers in caring for school-stage children and adolescents, enhancing positive guidance and education for their mental health.

Section 3   Prophylactic Immunization

I. Relevant Concepts

1. Vaccine   A biological product adminis-tered to humans for prophylactic immunization, designed to induce specific immunity against certain diseases, thereby preventing or controlling the occurrence and spread of diseases.

2. Prophylactic Immunization   The process of administering artificially prepared antigens or antibodies to the body through appropriate routes, enabling the body to acquire specific immunity against certain infectious diseases. This elevates the immune level of individuals or populations, serving to prevent and control the occurrence and spread of targeted infectious diseases.

3. Planned Immunization   Based on

4. 意外伤害预防   为预防意外伤害，应加强对儿童和青少年的安全教育，训练其预防和处理意外事故的能力；鼓励彼此友爱，遇到意外事故互相帮助，共同克服困难。同时，应加强对吸烟、吸毒的警示教育，使青少年远离毒品，避免不良行为发生。此外，学龄期儿童和青少年生理、心理发生巨变，自我意识迅速发展，因此需调动家长、老师共同关心青少年，增强对其心理健康的正确引导与教育。

第三节   预 防 接 种

一、相关概念

1. 疫苗   为了预防、控制疾病的发生、流行，用于人体预防接种、使机体产生对某种疾病特异性免疫的生物制品。

2. 预防接种   利用人工制备的抗原或抗体通过适宜的途径对机体进行接种，使机体获得对某种传染病的特异性免疫，以提高个体或群体的免疫水平，预防和控制针对性传染病的发生和流行。

3. 计划免疫   根据儿童的免疫特点和传染

the immune characteristics of children and the incidence of infectious diseases, a vaccination schedule is formulated to systematically and purposefully carry out primary immunization (complete primary vaccination) and subsequent booster immunizations (revaccination) at appropriate times. This ensures that children attain reliable immunity, achieving the objectives of preventing, controlling, and potentially eradicating the respective communicable diseases.

II. Types of Vaccines

1. Immunization Program Vaccines
These are free vaccines that residents are required to receive according to government regulations. They encompass vaccines specified in the national immunization program, additional vaccines incorporated by provincial, autonomous region, or municipal governments in executing the national program, as well as vaccines used in emergency vaccinations or mass prophylactic immunization organized by county-level or higher governments or their disease control authorities.

The national immunization program includes vaccines for age-appropriate children and priority groups. Currently, vaccines for age-appropriate children encompass hepatitis B vaccine, BCG (Bacillus Calmette-Guérin), poliovirus vaccine, DTP (diphtheria, tetanus, and pertussis), MMR (measles, mumps, and rubella), hepatitis A vaccine, Japanese encephalitis vaccine, and epidemic cerebrospinal meningitis vaccine, among others (Table 5-2). The vaccination time listed in the immunization schedule for each dose denotes the minimum age at which that particular dose can be administered. When a child reaches the eligible age for a specific dose, vaccination should be carried out as soon as possible.

病发生的情况制订的免疫程序,有计划和有针对性地实施基础免疫(即全程足量的初种)及随后适时的加强免疫(即复种),确保儿童获得可靠的免疫,达到预防、控制和消灭相应传染病的目的。

二、疫苗的种类

1. 免疫规划疫苗 免疫规划疫苗为免费疫苗,是指居民应当按照政府的规定接种的疫苗,包括国家免疫规划确定的疫苗,省、自治区、直辖市人民政府在执行国家免疫规划时增加的疫苗,以及县级以上人民政府或者疾控主管部门组织的应急接种或者群体性预防接种所使用的疫苗。

国家免疫规划疫苗包括适龄儿童接种疫苗和重点人群接种疫苗。目前适龄儿童接种疫苗包括乙肝疫苗、卡介苗、脊髓灰质炎疫苗、百白破疫苗、麻疹、腮腺炎和风疹联合病毒疫苗、甲肝疫苗、乙型脑炎灭活病毒疫苗等(表5-2)。免疫程序表所列各疫苗剂次的接种时间,是指可以接种该剂次疫苗的最小年龄。儿童达到相应剂次疫苗的接种年龄时,应尽早接种。

Table 5-2   National Immunization Program Vaccine Immunization Schedule for Children (2021 version)

Vaccine type	Date of inoculation														
	Day of birth	1 month	2 months	3 months	4 months	5 months	6 months	8 months	9 months	18 months	2 years	3 years	4 years	5 years	6 years
Hepatitis B vaccine	1	2					3								
Bacillus Calmette-Guérin vaccine	1														
Poliovirus inactivated vaccine			1	2											
Poliovirus attenuated live vaccine					3								4		
Pertussis diphtheria tetanus mixed vaccine				1	2	3				4					
Diphtheria and tetanus Combined vaccine															5
Measles, mumps, and rubella virus combined vaccine live								1		2					

Continued Table

Vaccine type	Day of birth	1 month	2 months	3 months	4 months	5 months	6 months	8 months	9 months	18 months	2 years	3 years	4 years	5 years	6 years
Japanese encephalitis vaccine								1			2				
Japanese encephalitis inactivated virus vaccine								1, 2			3				4
Epidemic meningitis A polysaccharide vaccine							1		?						
Epidemic meningitis A, C polysaccharide vaccine												3			4
Live hepatitis A vaccine										1					
Hepatitis A inactivated vaccine										1	2				

表5-2　国家免疫规划疫苗儿童免疫程序表（2021年版）

疫苗种类	接种年龄														
	出生时	1个月	2个月	3个月	4个月	5个月	6个月	8个月	9个月	18个月	2岁	3岁	4岁	5岁	6岁
乙肝疫苗	1	2					3								
卡介苗	1														
脊髓灰质炎灭活疫苗			1	2											
脊髓灰质炎减毒活疫苗					3								4		
百白破混合疫苗				1	2	3				4					
白喉、破伤风联合疫苗															5
麻疹、腮腺炎和风疹联合疫苗								1		2					
乙型脑炎减毒活疫苗 乙脑减毒活疫苗								1			2				
乙型脑炎灭活病毒疫苗								1、2			3				4
流脑 A 群多糖菌苗							1		2						
流脑 A、C 群多糖菌苗												3			4
甲肝减毒活疫苗										1					
甲肝灭活疫苗										1	2				

2. Non-Immunization Program Vaccines

Non-National Immunization Program Vaccines refer to other vaccines beyond the national immunization schedule that are voluntarily taken at personal expense, such as chickenpox vaccine, influenza vaccine, pneumococcal vaccine, and rotavirus vaccine. Parents can decide whether to vaccinate their children with these vaccines based on their health needs.

Ⅲ. Management and Implementation of Prophylactic Immunization

1. Management of Prophylactic Immunization　Within one month of a child's birth, the guardian should register the child at the birth hospital or the local vaccination unit responsible for prophylactic immunization services to obtain a vaccination certificate. When administering vaccines to age-appropriate children, vaccination units must verify the information on the vaccination certificate and maintain records as per regulations. When issuing the first vaccination certificate to a newborn or when a recipient comes for the first vaccination, the vaccination unit should establish a vaccination record for them.

2. Implementation

(1) Preparations Before Vaccination：Using the national immunization program's vaccine schedule and vaccination plans, potential recipients are identified through the immunization information system. Guardians are notified via verbal, written, telephone, or text messages about the vaccine type, vaccination time, location, and related requirements. Injection equipment, disinfectants, physical examination tools, and common first-aid medical supplies are prepared.

(2) During Vaccination：Prior to administration, the child's health status is inquired about, including fever, cough, diarrhea, allergies, medication history, and contraindications for vaccination. The "Three Checks, Seven Verifications, and One Confirmation" protocol is followed：The " Three Checks " involve checking the recipient's health

2. 非免疫规划疫苗　非免疫规划疫苗是指由居民自愿、自费接种的免疫规划疫苗以外的其他疫苗，如水痘疫苗、流感疫苗、肺炎球菌疫苗、轮状病毒疫苗等。家长可以根据儿童的健康需求，自主决定是否接种该类疫苗。

三、预防接种的管理与实施

1. 预防接种的管理　在儿童出生后 1 个月内，其监护人应到出生医院、儿童居住地承担预防接种工作的接种单位为其办理预防接种证。接种单位对适龄儿童实施预防接种时，应核对预防接种证信息，并按规定做好记录。接种单位在为新生儿办理预防接种证或受种者首次来接种疫苗时，应为其建立预防接种档案。

2. 实施

（1）接种前的准备：根据国家免疫规划疫苗免疫程序、接种方案等，通过免疫规划信息系统筛选受种者。采取口头、书面、电话、短信等方式，通知儿童的监护人，告知接种疫苗的品种、时间、地点和相关要求。准备注射器材、消毒用品、体检器材及常用急救药械。

（2）接种时的工作：实施接种前，首先询问儿童的健康状况，询问内容包括是否有发热、咳嗽、腹泻等患病情况及过敏史、用药史等，并核查是否存在接种禁忌证。此外，要做到"三查七对一验证"。三查包括：检查受种者健康状况、核查接种禁忌；查对预防接种证；检查疫苗、注射器的外观、批号、有效期。"七对"是指核对受

and contraindications; checking the vaccination certificate; and checking the vaccine and syringe's appearance, batch number, and expiration date. The "Seven Verifications" involve verifying the recipient's name, age, vaccine name, specification, dose, injection site, and route. "One Confirmation" requires the guardian to verify the vaccine type and expiration before vaccination. Once confirmed, vaccines are administered strictly according to the *Technical Guidelines for Immunization Practice*, considering age, injection site, route, and safe injection practices.

(3) Post-Vaccination: Prompt recording on the vaccination certificate follows, with the next vaccine type, time, and location scheduled with the guardian. Guardians are advised to observe the child in the waiting area for 30 minutes post-vaccination. In case of suspected adverse reactions, immediate measures, including medical intervention and, if necessary, hospital transfer, are taken according to established protocols.

IV. Contraindications for Prophylactic Immunization

1. **Absolute Contraindications** Absolute contraindications refer to severe allergies to any known component of the vaccine or a history of severe adverse reactions to similar vaccines in the past, such as extensive exanthem over the body, anaphylactic shock, laryngeal edema, etc. Individuals presenting with these conditions should not receive the corresponding vaccine. Monitoring data indicates that the risk of severe adverse reactions from vaccination is extremely rare, occurring approximately once in a million cases.

2. Relative Contraindications Relative contraindications refer to circumstances where the vaccine recipient is in a certain disease condition or special physiological state that temporarily precludes vaccination. Vaccination can proceed once the illness is cured or well-controlled, following assessment by both the

种者的姓名、年龄和疫苗的品名、规格、剂量、接种部位、接种途径。"一验证"是指接种前请儿童监护人验证接种疫苗的品种和有效期等。核对无误后严格按照《预防接种工作规范》规定的接种月（年）龄、接种部位、接种途径、安全注射等要求予以接种。

（3）接种后的工作：接种后及时在预防接种证上记录，与儿童监护人预约下次接种疫苗的种类、时间和地点。告知监护人，接种后应在留观室观察 30 分钟。在现场留观期间出现疑似预防接种异常反应的，应按照相关要求，及时采取救治措施，必要时转院救治。

四、预防接种禁忌证

1. **绝对禁忌证**　绝对禁忌证是指对疫苗已知任何成分严重过敏或者既往接种同类疫苗出现严重不良反应，如全身严重皮疹、过敏性休克、喉头水肿等情况，存在这种情况的受种者不可以接种相应疫苗。相关监测数据显示，接种疫苗出现严重不良反应的风险罕见，约为百万分之一。

2. **相对禁忌证**　相对禁忌证是指受种者正处于某种疾病状态或特殊生理状态暂时不能接种疫苗，如果受种者所患疾病治愈或得到良好的控制，经临床医生和接种医生评估后可以进行接种。如：体温超过 37.5℃，有腋窝淋巴结肿大；有急性传染病接触史而未过检疫期；慢性病急性发作；未控制的癫痫、脑病、进行性神经系

attending physician and the vaccinator. Examples include having a temperature over 37.5℃ with swollen axillary nodes, recent contact with a contagious disease without completing the quarantine period, acute exacerbation of chronic diseases, uncontrolled epilepsy, encephalopathy, or progressive neurological disorders.

统疾病等。

V. Suspected Adverse Event Following Immunization (AEFI)

Suspected adverse event following immunization (AEFI) is a reaction or an event that occurs after vaccination and is suspected to be associated with the vaccination process. This includes adverse reactions, vaccine quality incidents, vaccination accidents, coincidental symptoms, and psychogenic reactions. Among these, adverse reactions to vaccination are more common, which are undesirable reactions occurring after the administration of a quality vaccine in accordance with standard procedures, unrelated to the intended purpose of vaccination. These reactions can be further categorized into common reactions and abnormal reactions.

1. Classification and Concepts

(1) Common Reactions: These are transient physiological disruptions that occur after vaccination, caused inherently by the nature of the vaccine itself. They typically manifest as fever and local redness and swelling, often accompanied by general discomfort, burnout, loss of appetite, and fatigue.

(2) Abnormal Reactions: These are relatively rare and serious adverse reactions caused by the inherent properties of a qualified vaccine, administered correctly, resulting in harm to the recipient's tissues or functions. No party is at fault in such cases. These reactions can be linked to the vaccine strain, purity, manufacturing process, additives like preservatives, stabilizers, and adjuvants.

2. Handling and Reporting   If a suspected AEFI is detected, the vaccinator should handle

五、疑似预防接种异常反应

疑似预防接种异常反应（adverse event following immunization，AEFI），是指在预防接种后发生的怀疑与疫苗接种有关的反应或事件，包括不良反应、疫苗质量事故、接种事故、偶合症、心因性反应。其中较为常见的是预防接种不良反应，是指合格的疫苗在实施规范接种后，发生的与预防接种目的无关或意外的有害反应，包括一般反应和异常反应。

1. 分类及其概念

（1）一般反应：在预防接种后发生的，由疫苗本身所固有的特性引起的，对机体只会造成一过性生理功能障碍的反应，主要有发热和局部红肿，同时可能伴有全身不适、倦怠、食欲缺乏、乏力等综合症状。

（2）异常反应：合格的疫苗在实施规范接种过程中或者实施规范接种后造成受种者机体组织器官、功能损害，相关各方均无过错的药品不良反应。异常反应是由疫苗本身所固有的特性引起的相对罕见、严重的不良反应，与疫苗的毒株、纯度、生产工艺和疫苗中的附加物如防腐剂、稳定剂、佐剂等因素有关。

2. 处理及报告   如发现疑似预防接种异常反应，接种人员应按照《全国疑似预防接种异常

and report it in accordance with the requirements outlined in the *National Surveillance Plan for Suspected Adverse Events Following Immunization*.

(1) Handling: For mild reactions such as local common reactions or general systemic reactions, clinical treatment is usually not necessary and general guidance on self-care can be provided. However, in cases of severe suspected AEFIs, like acute allergic reactions occurring during the on-site observation period after vaccination, emergency rescue measures should be initiated immediately, and referral for further medical treatment should be arranged if needed.

(2) Reporting: Suspected AEFI reporting adheres to local management principles. Upon discovery, reports should promptly be made to the local county-level health and drug regulatory departments where the recipient resides. Reporting categories, based on reaction timelines, include:

1) Within 24 hours: Anaphylactic shock, anaphylaxis without shock (urticaria, maculopapule, laryngeal edema), toxic shock syndrome, hysteria, etc.

2) Within 5 days: High fever (axillary temp ＞38.6℃), angioedema, systemic purulent infections (toxemia, septicemia, pyemia), local redness/swelling and indurate at the injection site (diameter ＞2.5cm), local purulent infections (local abscess, lymphangitis, lymphadenitis, cellulitis) etc.

3) Within 15 days: Measles-like or scarlet fever-like rash, anaphylactoid purpura, local allergic necrotic reactions, epilepsy, polyneuritis, encephalopathy, encephalitis, meningitis, etc.

4) Within 6 weeks: Thrombocytopenic purpura, Guillain-Barré syndrome, vaccine-associated paralytic poliomyelitis, etc.

5) Within 3 months: Brachial plexus neuritis, sterile abscess at the injection site, etc.

6) 1–12 months after BCG vaccination: Lymphadenitis or lymphangitis, osteomyelitis, general disseminated BCG infection, etc.

7) Others: Other severe suspected AEFIs

反应监测方案》的要求进行处理和报告。

（1）处理：对局部的一般反应、全身性一般反应等较为轻微的反应，一般不需要临床治疗，可给予一般的处理指导；对接种后现场留观期间出现的急性严重过敏反应等严重疑似预防接种异常反应，应立即组织紧急抢救，必要时转诊治疗。

（2）报告：疑似预防接种异常反应报告实行属地化管理。当发现属于报告范围的疑似预防接种异常反应后应当及时向受种者所在地的县级卫生行政部门、药品监督管理部门报告。报告范围按照发生时限分为以下情形：

1）24小时内：如过敏性休克、不伴休克的过敏反应（荨麻疹、斑丘疹、喉头水肿等）、中毒性休克综合征、癔症等。

2）5天内：如发热（腋温＞38.6℃）、血管性水肿、全身化脓性感染（毒血症、败血症、脓毒血症）、接种部位发生的红肿或硬结（直径＞2.5cm）、局部化脓性感染（局部脓肿、淋巴管炎和淋巴结炎、蜂窝织炎）等。

3）15天内：如麻疹样或猩红热样皮疹、过敏性紫癜、局部过敏坏死反应、癫痫、多发性神经炎、脑病、脑炎和脑膜炎等。

4）6周内：如血小板减少性紫癜、吉兰-巴雷综合征、疫苗相关性麻痹性脊髓灰质炎等。

5）3个月内：如臂丛神经炎、接种部位发生的无菌性脓肿等。

6）接种卡介苗后1~12个月：如淋巴结炎或淋巴管炎、骨髓炎、全身播散性卡介苗感染等。

7）其他：怀疑与预防接种有关的其他严重

believed to be related to prophylactic immunization.

(Dong Yujing)

疑似预防接种异常反应。

（董玉静）

Key Points

1. The health management techniques for children and adolescents in the community include: weight, length/height and head circumference measurement and evaluation, dental caries prevention, vision tests, and guidance on complementary feeding.

2. Breastfeeding is the optimal method of feeding for infants immediately after birth, and it is particularly encouraged for preterm infants and low birth weight infants. Mothers should breast-feed on demand to ensure that their infants receive an adequate intake of breast milk.

3. Asphyxia is a common accidental injury in neonates. Common causes include inappropriate breastfeeding positions where the mother's breast or arm obstructs the neonate's mouth and nose; over bundling or excessive thickness of blankets covering the neonate, which can block the infant's airway; aspiration of milk or curdled milk into the airways during regurgitation.

4. During follow-up visits in infancy, community health care providers inquire about feeding practices and illnesses in young children, conduct physical examinations, and perform assessments of growth, development, and psychological behavior. They should also provide health guidance on scientific feeding, growth and development, disease prevention, injury prevention, and oral health care.

5. Starting from around 6 months of age, infants should begin to incorporate other nutrient-rich foods into their diet while continuing to breast-feed. The texture of dietary supplements should progress gradually from purees to lumpier, semi-solid foods, and eventually to solid chunks.

6. Aspiration of foreign body in trachea is a common accidental injury during infancy and toddlerhood. The objects most frequently inhaled

内 容 摘 要

1. 社区儿童和青少年健康管理技术包括：体重、身长（高）、头围检查及评价和龋齿预防、视力检查、食物转换指导等。

2. 母乳喂养是婴儿出生后的最佳喂养方式，早产儿、低体重儿更加提倡母乳喂养。母亲应当按需哺乳，确保婴儿摄入足够乳汁。

3. 窒息是新生儿常见的意外伤害。常见原因包括：哺乳姿势不适当，乳房、手臂堵塞新生儿口鼻；新生儿盖被包裹过厚、过紧，蒙住婴儿口鼻；新生儿吐奶时将奶汁或者奶块吸入气管。

4. 婴儿期随访时询问婴幼儿喂养、患病等情况，进行体格检查，做生长发育和心理行为发育评估，进行科学喂养、生长发育、疾病预防、伤害预防、口腔保健等健康指导。

5. 婴幼儿6个月后，应当在继续母乳喂养基础上引入其他营养丰富的食物。辅食质地应当从泥糊状逐步过渡到团块状固体食物。

6. 气管异物吸入是婴幼儿期常见的意外伤害。吸入的异物多是能够放入口中的小物品，包括生活用品如纽扣、硬币、瓶盖等，食品如花

are small items that can fit into a child's mouth, such as household items like buttons, coins, and bottle caps, food items such as peanuts, sunflower seeds, beans, jelly candies, and toy components like the eyes from plush animals that have come loose.

7. The national immunization program for children of appropriate ages includes vaccines such as the hepatitis B vaccine, Bacillus Calmette-Guérin (BCG) vaccine, poliovirus vaccine, diphtheria-tetanus-pertussis (DTP) vaccine, measles-mumps-rubella (MMR) vaccine, hepatitis A vaccine, Japanese encephalitis vaccine, and epidemic cerebrospinal meningitis vaccine. When a child reaches the age recommended for each dose of these vaccines, they should be vaccinated as soon as possible.

生米、瓜子、豆子、果冻等，玩具如脱落的绒毛动物的眼睛等。

7. 适龄儿童国家免疫规划疫苗包括乙肝疫苗、卡介苗、脊髓灰质炎疫苗、百白破疫苗、麻腮风疫苗、甲肝疫苗、乙脑疫苗、流脑疫苗等。儿童年龄达到相应剂次疫苗的接种年龄时，应尽早接种。

Exercises

(Questions 1 to 2 share the same question stem)

Xiaoqiang, male, 6 months old, breastfeeding, came to the community health center today for a health check-up.

1. What health management techniques can be applied to this child?

2. What are the focal points of health guidance concerning nutrition and feeding?

(Questions 3 to 4 share the same question stem)

Tingting, female, 18 months old. She came to the community health center for a vaccination today.

3. What type of vaccine is being administered to this child?

4. What are the precautions to be taken when implementing prophylactic immunization for this child?

思 考 题

（1~2题共用题干）

小强，男，6月龄，母乳喂养，今日来社区卫生服务中心体检。

1. 针对该儿童，可以使用哪些健康管理技术？

2. 在营养与喂养方面，保健指导的重点是什么？

（3~4题共用题干）

婷婷，女，18月龄，今天来社区卫生服务中心注射疫苗。

3. 该儿童本次注射的疫苗种类是什么？

4. 在为该儿童实施预防接种时的注意事项有哪些？

Chapter 6

Female Health Care in Community

第六章

社区女性保健

NURSING

Learning Objectives

Knowledge Objectives

1. Correctly describe the physiological characteristics of adolescent women, as well as the causes and health care of dysmenorrhea and abnormal uterine bleeding during puberty.

2. Correctly describe the key points of health care during period of pregnancy and puerperium.

3. Correctly describe the benefits of breast-feeding, the causes and nursing interventions of breast swelling and nipple

学习目标

知识目标

1. 正确描述青春期女性的生理特点，青春期痛经和异常子宫出血的病因及保健措施。

2. 正确叙述妊娠期和产褥期的保健要点。

3. 正确描述母乳喂养的优点，乳房肿胀和乳头疼痛的原因及护理要点。

pain.

4. Correctly describe common menopause related symptoms, health issues, and health care interventions of perimenopausal women.

Ability Objectives

1. Utilize knowledge and principles related to breastfeeding to develop a breastfeeding promotion plan for early postpartum women.

2. Assess the physical and mental status of puerperal women and develop a postpartum care plan for them.

3. Assess the physical and mental status of perimenopausal women and develop a health care plan for them.

Quality Objectives

1. Establish a scientific spirit, convey humanistic care, and provide health guidance for postpartum women based on scientific principles and respect for their customs and habits.

2. Enhance the sense of love and responsibility, and cultivate empathy, and provide good breastfeeding support for postpartum mothers and infants.

3. Cultivate a spirit of understanding, gratitude, and acceptance to provide health guidance for perimenopausal women.

4. 正确叙述围绝经期妇女常见的绝经相关症状、健康问题及保健要点。

能力目标

1. 运用母乳喂养相关知识与原理，为产后早期妇女制订一份促进母乳喂养计划。

2. 对产褥期妇女进行身、心状态评估，为其制订一份产后保健计划。

3. 对围绝经期妇女进行身、心状态评估，为其制订一份健康保健计划。

素质目标

1. 树立科学精神，传递人文关怀，结合科学原则和对风俗习惯的尊重为产后妇女提供健康指导。

2. 增进爱心、责任心，培养同理心，给产后母婴提供良好的母乳喂养支持。

3. 培养理解、感恩和接纳精神，为围绝经期女性提供健康保健指导。

Mrs. Zhang, 48-year-old. In the past two years, the patient's menstrual cycle has been irregular, sometimes coming 3–7 days earlier, sometimes delayed by 10–15 days, and the menstrual period has been 3–4 days. The patient had a regular menstrual cycle of about 30 days, with a period of 5–6 days before 46 years old. In the past year, the patient has felt intermittent heat waves spreading from the chest to the neck and face, accompanied by sweating. She often wakes up at night and finds it difficult to fall asleep, accompanied by

张女士，48 岁。近两年来，月经周期不规律，有时提前 3~7 天，有时后退 10~15 天，经期 3~4 天。患者既往月经规律，周期为 30 天左右，经期为 5~6 天。近 1 年来，常有自胸部至颈、面部扩散的阵发性热浪，伴有出汗。患者夜里常醒，醒来不易再入睡，伴有心慌、出汗，白天常感到烦躁，情绪容易激动，自述经常忘事。上述症状已经明显影响其生活及工作。

palpitations and sweating. The patient often feels dysphoric and gets easily agitated during the day. She reports frequently forgetting things. The above symptoms have significantly affected her life and work.

Queations：

1. What are the main health problems that the patient currently has?

2. What are the main reasons for the above problems?

3. What nursing interventions can nurses take to help patients alleviate and manage the above problems?

Female health care is an important component of the whole healthcare system. Women's health is directly related to the health of their offspring and the quality of the birth. Women's health affects the health level of families and the entire society. Women are not only important human resources for social development, but also bear responsibilities such as childbirth and breastfeeding due to their unique anatomical and physiological characteristics. During adolescence, childbearing period, perinatal period, menopause, and senility, women may experience a series of possible health problems due to changes in the physiological functions of the reproductive system. Community nurses need to understand the physiological characteristics and health issues of women at different stages of their lives, understand and meet their health needs, and promote the continuous improvement of women's physical and mental health.

请思考：

1. 患者目前主要的健康问题有哪些？

2. 出现上述问题的主要原因是什么？

3. 护士可采取哪些措施帮助患者减轻和管理上述问题？

女性保健是卫生健康体系的重要组成部分。女性健康直接关系到子代健康和出生人口素质，影响家庭和整个社会的健康水平。女性不仅是社会发展的重要人力资源，同时还因其独有的解剖和生理特点而承担着生育、哺乳等责任。女性在青春期、育龄期、围生期、绝经期和老年期，都会随着生殖系统生理功能的变化而产生一系列健康问题。社区护士要知晓女性一生不同时期的生理特点和健康问题，了解并满足女性的保健需求，促进女性身心健康水平的持续提升。

Section 1　Overview

I. Purpose and Significance of Female Health Care

i. Purpose of Female Health Care

Female Health Care provides continuous

第一节　概　　述

一、女性保健的目的和意义

（一）女性保健的目的

女性保健为女性提供生命周期各阶段连续

physiological and psychological health management for women at all stages of their life cycle, carrying out health care work that runs through various stages of women's adolescence, perimarital period, perinatal period, perimenopause, etc. The purpose of female health care is to ensure women's reproductive health, reduce the prevalence rate and disability rates, reduce maternal and perinatal mortality rates, prevent and control the occurrence of genetic diseases and other serious diseases, meet women's health needs, improve women's health level, and improve women's quality of life.

ii. Significance of Female Health Care

Female Health Care is an important component of China's healthcare work. The work of female health care is centered around women's health, adhering to the work policy of "putting health care at the center, ensuring reproductive health as the goal, combining health care with clinical practice, targeting the group, targeting the grassroots, and taking prevention as the main focus". Maintaining and promoting the physical and mental health of women, improving the overall quality of the population, and enhancing family happiness are of great significance in female health care work.

II. The Working Methods and Organizations of Female Health Care

i. The Working Methods of Female Health Care

The working methods of female health care include fully leveraging the role of various levels of maternal and child health care professional institutions and health networks, optimizing service processes according to the service population, integrating service content, combining group health care and clinical health care, combining prevention and treatment, organizing training and continuing education in a planned manner, continuously improving the knowledge and skill level of the professional team, vigorously promoting women's

的生理、心理健康管理，开展贯穿女性青春期、围婚期、围生期、围绝经期等各个阶段的保健工作。女性保健的目的是保障女性生殖健康，降低患病率和伤残率，降低孕产妇及围生儿死亡率，预防和控制遗传病和其他严重疾病的发生，满足女性健康需求，提升女性健康水平，提高女性生活质量。

（二）女性保健的意义

女性保健工作是我国卫生健康保健工作的重要组成部分。女性保健工作"以女性健康为中心"，坚持"以保健为中心，以保障生殖健康为目的，保健与临床相结合，面向群体，面向基层，预防为主"的工作方针。维护和促进女性身心健康、提高人口综合素质、增进家庭幸福是女性保健工作的重要意义。

二、女性保健的工作方法和组织机构

（一）女性保健的工作方法

充分发挥各级妇幼保健专业机构和保健网的作用，根据服务人群优化服务流程，整合服务内容，做到群体保健和临床保健相结合，防与治相结合，有计划地组织培训和继续教育，不断提高专业队伍知识和技能水平，大力开展女性保健相关科普和健康教育工作，提高妇女健康意识，提升女性健康素养和健康水平。

health related science popularization and health education, improving women's health awareness, and enhancing women's health literacy and level.

ii. Organizations of Female Health Care

1. Administrative Institutions

(1) National Level: The National Health Commission of the People's Republic of China has established the Department of Maternal and Child Health, which includes the Comprehensive Division, Women's Health Division, Children's Health Division, and Birth Defects Prevention and Control Division, leading the national maternal and child health care work.

(2) Provincial Level: The Health Commission of a province (autonomous region, municipality directly under the central government) has established a Maternal and Child Health Division.

(3) City (Prefecture) Level: The organizational setup at the city (prefecture) level is consistent with the provincial level.

(4) County (City) Level: The county (city) level Health Commission has a Maternal and Child Health Section.

2. Professional Institutions
In 2015, the National Health and Family Planning Commission of China (now the National Health Commission) issued the *Guidelines for the Establishment of Business Departments of Maternal and Child Health Service Institutions at All Levels*, which provided specific guidance and requirements for the establishment of business departments of maternal and child health service institutions.

(1) Provincial and Municipal Maternal and Child Health Service Institutions: Provincial maternal and child health service institutions are the guidance centers for maternal and child health services throughout the province. The establishment of business departments should fully reflect the characteristics of health care as the center, organic combination of health care and clinical practice, appropriate scale, and reasonable layout. It mainly includes four categories of departments:

（二）女性保健的组织机构

1. 行政机构

（1）国家级：中华人民共和国国家卫生健康委员会内设妇幼健康司，下设综合处、妇女卫生处、儿童卫生处、出生缺陷防治处，领导全国妇幼保健工作。

（2）省级：省（自治区、直辖市）卫生健康委员会内设妇幼健康处。

（3）市（地）级：与省级的设置保持一致。

（4）县（市）级：县（市）级卫生健康委员会内设妇幼健康科。

2. 专业机构
2015年中国国家卫生与计划生育委员会（现国家卫生健康委员会）发布了《各级妇幼健康服务机构业务部门设置指南》，对妇幼健康服务机构业务部门设置提出了具体指导和要求。

（1）省、市级妇幼健康服务机构：省级妇幼健康服务机构是全省妇幼保健业务指导中心，业务部门的设置应充分体现以保健为中心、保健与临床有机结合的特色，规模适宜、布局合理。主要包括4类部门：

1) Maternal health care department: Including the Maternity Group Health Section, Premarital Health Section, Prenatal Health Section, Pregnancy Health Section, Medical Genetics and Prenatal Screening Section, Obstetrics Section, Postpartum Health Section, etc.

2) Children health care department: Including Children Group Health Section, Neonatal Disease Screening Section, Neonatal Pediatrics Section, etc.

3) Female health care department: Including Female Group Health Section, Adolescent Health Section, Menopause and Senility Health Section, Gynecology Section, etc.

4) Family planning technical service department: Including Family Planning Surgery Section, Male Reproductive Health Section, etc.

(2) County and District Level Maternal and Child Health Service Institutions: County and district level maternal and child health service institutions are the foundation of three-level maternal and child health service institutions. The institutional setting should be adapted to the functions, tasks, and scale of maternal and child health service institutions at the county and district levels. They can refer to higher-level maternal and child health service institutions to set up departments, mainly including:

1) Maternity health department: Including the Maternity Health Section and Obstetrics Section.

2) Children health department: Including the Children Health Section and Pediatrics Section.

3) Female health department: Including Female Health Section and Gynecology Section.

4) Family planning technical service department: Including Family Planning Technical Service Section, Family Planning Guidance Section, etc.

1）孕产保健部：内设孕产群体保健科、婚前保健科、孕前保健科、孕期保健科、医学遗传与产前筛查科、产科、产后保健科等。

2）儿童保健部：内设儿童群体保健科、新生儿疾病筛查科、新生儿科等。

3）妇女保健部：内设妇女群体保健科、青春期保健科、更年期保健科、妇科等。

4）计划生育技术服务部：内设计划生育手术科、男性生殖健康科等。

（2）县、区级妇幼健康服务机构：县、区级妇幼健康服务机构是三级妇幼健康服务机构的基础，机构设置要与县、区级妇幼健康服务机构职能、任务和规模适应。可参照上级妇幼健康服务机构设置科室，主要包括：

1）孕产保健部：内设孕产保健科、产科。

2）儿童保健部：内设儿童保健科、儿科。

3）妇女保健部：内设妇女保健科、妇科。

4）计划生育技术服务部：内设计划生育技术服务科、计划生育指导科等。

Ⅲ. Statistical Indicators for Female Health Care

i. Indicators for Perinatal Health Care Work

1. Early Pregnancy Registration Rate Number of women who registered and underwent their first prenatal examination before 13 weeks of pregnancy/number of live birth in the same period×100%.

2. Prenatal Examination Rate Number of mothers who have undergone one or more prenatal examinations during the period/number of live births in the same period×100%.

3. Hospital Delivery Rate Number of live births during hospitalization/number of live births in the same period×100%.

4. Postpartum Visit Rate Number of postpartum women within 28 days after birth who have received one or more postpartum visits during the period/number of live births in the period×100%.

5. Newborn Visit Rate Number of newborns who have received one or more visits during the period/number of live births in the period×100%.

ii. Indicctors for Perinatal Health Care Quality

1. High-Risk Pregnancies as a Percentage of the Total Pregnancies Number of high-risk pregnant women during the period/number of pregnant women in the same period×100%.

2. Postpartum Hemorrhage Rate Number of postpartum bleeding cases during the period/number of postpartum women in the same period×100%.

3. Puerperal Infection Rate Number of puerperal infections during the period/number of postpartum women in the same period×100%.

iii. Indicators for Perinatal Health Care Outcome

1. Maternal Mortality Rate Number of

三、女性保健的统计指标

（一）围生期保健工作指标

1. 早孕建卡率　期内孕 13 周以前建卡并进行第一次产前检查人数 / 同期活产数 ×100%。

2. 产前检查率　期内接受过 1 次及以上产前检查的产妇人数 / 同期活产数 ×100%。

3. 住院分娩率　期内住院分娩的活产数 / 期内活产数 ×100%。

4. 产后访视率　期内产后 28 天内接受过 1 次及以上产后访视的产妇人数 / 期内活产数 ×100%。

5. 新生儿访视率　期内接受过 1 次及以上访视的新生儿人数 / 期内活产数 ×100%。

（二）围生期保健质量指标

1. 高危产妇占总产妇数的百分比　期内高危产妇人数 / 同期产妇数 ×100%。

2. 产后出血率　期内产后出血人数 / 同期产妇数 ×100%。

3. 产褥感染率　期内产褥感染人数 / 同期产妇数 ×100%。

（三）围生期保健效果指标

1. 孕产妇死亡率　期内孕产妇死亡数 / 同

maternal deaths during the period/total maternal number in the same period×100,000/100,000.

2. **Neonatal Mortality Rate**　Number of neonatal deaths within 28 days after birth during the period/number of live births in the same period× 1000‰.

Section 2　Common Health Problems and Health Care Guidelines for Women in Different Periods in the Community

I. Adolescent Health Care

Adolescence is a period of time that links childhood to adulthood. WHO suggests that the average age of adolescence is 10 to 19 years old. This stage is characterized by profound physical, psychological, and behavioral changes, with rapid physical development, gradual maturation of the reproductive system and development of sexual needs. Adolescent girls may face a variety of health problems, such as menstrual disorders, dysmenorrhea, unsafe sexual behavior, and unplanned pregnancy.

i. Physiological Characteristics

1. **Physical Development**　The physical growth and development during adolescence is significantly accelerated. The adolescent girl's growth spurt usually takes place between 10 and 14 years old. With the fusion of the epiphyseal plate, female growth and development usually slow down after menarche.

Adolescent women experience a significant increase in body fat content while experiencing a sudden growth spurt. Body fat content has a significant effect on both menstruation and reproductive function. Low body fat content results from anorexia nervosa or intensive athletic training can delay the onset of adolescence. Besides, too little or too much body fat content is associated

期孕产妇总数 ×10 万 /10 万。

2. **新生儿死亡率**　期内生后 28 天内新生儿死亡数 / 同期活产数 ×1000‰。

第二节　社区女性不同时期常见健康问题及保健指导

一、青春期保健

青春期是从儿童期向成年期过渡的一段时期。WHO 建议青春期的平均年龄是 10~19 岁。在这一时期，青少年身体、心理和行为方面都发生着巨大变化，他们身体发育迅速，生殖系统逐步成熟，性需求逐步发展。青春期女性面临着月经紊乱、痛经、不安全性行为及意外妊娠等一系列健康问题。

（一）生理特点

1. **身体发育**　青少年生长发育明显加速。女性青春期身高生长突增发生于 10~14 岁。月经初潮后，女性生长发育变慢。随着干骺端的融合，女性生长发育变慢。

青春期女性在生长突增的同时，体脂含量也明显增加。体脂含量对月经和生殖功能均有重要影响。青少年女性由于神经性厌食症或高强度运动训练导致体脂含量较低时，可能会出现青春期推迟。此外，过多或过少的体脂含量均可能与不孕症有关。

with infertility.

2. Sexual Development   The reproductive organs of females grow rapidly and secondary sex characteristics appear during adolescence.

(1) The ovaries develop and enlarge, with ovarian follicles in different developmental stages within the cortex. Before menarche, the ovaries have a smooth surface. After menarche, they become nodular because of ruptures of ovarian follicles at ovulation.

(2) The uterus grows during adolescence, and the ratio of the uterine body to the cervix changes from 1∶2 to 2∶1. The development of the uterus is mainly due to myometrial hyperplasia. During the mid-adolescent period, the endometrium is affected by estrogen and progestogen, undergoing periodic changes to form menstruation.

(3) The uterine tubes increase in size and cilia on the mucosa.

(4) The vagina lengthens and broadens. The epithelial layers thicken. The secretions become acidic.

(5) The mons pubis is lumped due to fat deposition. The labia majora become more prominent and develop hair. The labia minora enlarge and become more vascular.

(6) The female secondary sex characteristics consist of the growth of breast, pubic hair and axillary hair. Breast growth is the first sign of adolescence, it begins with the hyperplasia of the mammary gland tissue beneath the areola. When ovulation begins in adolescence, the increase of progestogen levels causes maturation of mammary glands. During adolescence, fat deposition and growth of fibrous tissue contribute to the increase of the mammary gland's size. The growth of breasts usually begins between 8 and 13 years old. Full development of the breasts is not achieved until after the end of the first pregnancy. Pubic hair begins to appear half to 1 year after breast budding. Axillary hair appears slightly later than pubic hair, at around 13 years old.

3. Menstrual Cycle and Menarche   As

2．性发育   青春期,生殖器官迅速发育,第二性征出现。

（1）卵巢发育增大,皮质内有不同发育程度的卵泡。初潮前,卵巢表面光滑。初潮后,随着排卵时的卵泡破裂,卵巢表面变得凹凸不平。

（2）子宫在青春期发育增大,宫体与宫颈比例由1∶2变为2∶1,子宫发育主要是肌层增生。在青春期中期,子宫内膜受到雌、孕激素的影响,发生周期性变化,形成月经。

（3）输卵管体积增大,黏膜纤毛增多。

（4）阴道变长变宽,上皮层变厚,分泌物变为酸性。

（5）阴阜因脂肪堆积而隆起,大阴唇变得突出并长出毛发,小阴唇增大,血管增多。

（6）女性第二性征主要包括乳房的发育和阴毛、腋毛的生长。乳房发育是最早出现的青春期体征,起始于乳晕下方乳腺组织的增生。卵巢开始排卵后,孕激素水平的升高可促进乳腺组织的成熟。在青春期,脂肪沉积和纤维组织的生长导致乳腺增大。乳房发育多开始于8~13岁,完全发育完成要等到第一次妊娠结束。乳房开始发育后半年到1年,阴毛开始出现。腋毛出现的时间比阴毛稍晚,大约在13岁。

3．月经周期与月经初潮   随着青春期的到

adolescence approaches, there is a progressive increase in the amplitude and frequency of pulsatile gonadotropin releasing hormone (GnRH) secreted by hypothalamus. This initially occurs only during sleep, but gradually extends to waking hours. GnRH reaches the anterior pituitary, where it stimulates increased synthesis and release of the follicle stimulating hormone (FSH) and luteinizing hormone (LH). Responding to increasing FSH, the ovarian follicles develop and produce estrogen. When a dominant follicle develops, increasing estrogen levels induce a surge of LH which triggers ovulation.

Menarche denotes the first menstruation. The age of menarche varies in different countries. Menarche occurs in most girls at between 11 and 16 years of age. Initially, periods are irregular and anovulatory. 1 or more years later, after the hypothalamic-pituitary rhythm develops, the ovary produces mature ovum and ovulates. Pregnancy can occur at any time after the onset of menses. All young adolescents would benefit from knowing that.

ii. Health Problems and Care

1. Dysmenorrhea Dysmenorrhea is differentiated as primary or secondary. Primary dysmenorrhea does not have pelvic organic lesions, while secondary dysmenorrhea is caused by pelvic organic diseases. Primary dysmenorrhea is most common in adolescents. There are no national statistical data on the incidence of dysmenorrhea in adolescent women in China. Some studies have shown that between 40%–80% of young women ages 16 to 22 years report some level of discomfort associated with menstruation.

Some degree of discomfort during menstruation is considered physiological. However, many adolescents have severe dysmenorrhea in the first 3 years after menarche, which can cause absenteeism from school. Pain is usually located in the lower abdomen and may radiate to the lower back or upper thighs. Women may describe the pain as a colicky pain or steady dull pain. It is often

来，下丘脑促性腺激素释放激素（GnRH）脉冲样分泌的幅度和频率逐渐增加。刚进入青春期时，仅在睡眠时增加，随着青春期的进展，觉醒时也有增加。GnRH 到达垂体前叶后，刺激卵泡刺激素（FSH）和黄体生成素（LH）的合成和释放。伴随着 FSH 的增加，卵泡发育并产生雌激素。当卵巢中有优势卵泡发育时，雌激素水平升高会引起 LH 峰值的出现，继而触发排卵。

第一次月经被称为月经初潮。初潮年龄在不同国家存在差异。大多数女性的初潮年龄在 11~16 岁。最初，月经常呈不规则和无排卵性。1 年或更长时间以后，随着下丘脑 - 垂体节律的建立，卵巢产生成熟卵子并开始排卵。青少年应知晓，月经开始后的任何时期均可能发生妊娠。

（二）常见健康问题及保健

1. 痛经 痛经分为原发性痛经和继发性痛经两种。原发性痛经是无盆腔器质性病变的痛经，继发性痛经是由盆腔器质性疾病引起的痛经。原发性痛经最常见于青少年。中国尚无全国性的有关痛经发生率的统计数据。一些研究显示，16~22 岁的年轻女性中，有 40%~80% 的女性报告存在月经相关的身体不适。

月经期出现一定程度的身体不适是正常现象。然而，月经初潮后 3 年内，许多青少年女性可能出现严重的痛经，影响生活和上学。疼痛常位于下腹部，常呈绞痛或持续钝痛，可放射至后背或大腿，常伴有恶心、呕吐和腹泻。疼痛多在月经来潮时最严重，一般持续不超过 2 天。

accompanied by nausea, vomiting and diarrhea. Symptoms are worst at the onset of menstruation and rarely persist beyond 2 days.

Primary dysmenorrhea is mainly associated with abnormally increased uterine activity induced by prostaglandins. Prostaglandins $F_{2\alpha}$ are secreted during the luteal phase and menstrual period. The release of most prostaglandins $F_{2\alpha}$ during menses occurs in the first 2 days. Excessive secretion of prostaglandins $F_{2\alpha}$ increases the uterine contractions and causes vasospasm of the uterine arteries, resulting in ischemia and lower abdominal pain.

Women may be worried about the impact of dysmenorrhea on reproduction. Nurses can provide reliable information about what is normal. Besides, nurses can provide some options for teenagers to decrease the pain and symptoms associated with dysmenorrhea. Heating pads minimizes cramping by increasing vasodilation and muscle relaxation. Massaging the lower back can reduce pain by increasing the pelvic blood supply and relaxing the paravertebral muscles. Pelvic rocking has been found to be helpful for dysmenorrhea by increasing vasodilation and subsequently decreasing ischemia, shunting of blood flow and less pelvic congestion. Decreased salt intake 7 to 10 days before menstruation may reduce body fluid retention. Increasing natural diuretics such as red beans, pearl barley, wax gourd, and watermelon may help reduce edema and related discomforts.

Medications used to treat primary dysmenorrhea in adolescents include prostaglandin synthesis inhibitors, primarily nonsteroidal anti-inflammatory drugs (NSAIDs), such as aspirin, ibuprofen, indometacin, acetaminophen, etc. If one NSAID is ineffective, a different one can be chosen. All NSAIDs have potential gastrointestinal side effects, including nausea, vomiting, and even bleeding. Some alternative and complementary therapies such as acupuncture and moxibustion, Chinese traditional manipulation, massage, and biofeedback are proven to be effective for dysmenorrhea.

原发性痛经主要与前列腺素引起子宫收缩异常增强有关。黄体期和月经期，前列腺素 $F_{2\alpha}$ 释放。其中，月经期前 2 天前列腺 $F_{2\alpha}$ 释放最多。前列腺素 $F_{2\alpha}$ 的过度增加引起了强烈的子宫收缩和子宫动脉痉挛，造成缺血和下腹痛。

痛经的女性可能会担心痛经对生殖功能的影响，护理人员应提供相关的可靠信息。此外，护士可以给青少年提供一些可供选择的方法，帮助其减轻疼痛及痛经相关症状。加热垫可促进血管舒张和肌肉放松，从而减轻痉挛。按摩后背下方可通过增加骨盆供血和放松椎旁肌肉减轻疼痛。骨盆摇摆可通过促进血管舒张，减少缺血，促进血液分流，减少盆腔充血，而达到缓解痛经的效果。月经前 7~10 天减少盐的摄入量可减少体液潴留。增加红豆、薏米、冬瓜和西瓜等天然利尿食物的摄入有助于减轻水肿和与痛经有关的不适。

青少年原发性痛经的治疗药物有前列腺素合成抑制剂，主要是非甾体抗炎药（NSAIDs），如阿司匹林、布洛芬、吲哚美辛、对乙酰氨基酚等。如果一种 NSAID 无效，可以选择另一种。所有非甾体抗炎药都有潜在的胃肠道副作用，包括恶心、呕吐，甚至出血。一些替代和补充疗法，如针灸、推拿、按摩和生物反馈，已被证实可有效缓解痛经。

2. Abnormal Uterine Bleeding   The most common type of abnormal uterine bleeding (AUB) during adolescence is dysfunctional uterine bleeding (DUB) which is defined as abnormal uterine bleeding with no systemic or reproductive organ organic disease cause. Dysfunctional uterine bleeding is usually divided into ovulatory and anovulatory. The anovulatory DUB is more common in adolescent women.

It takes about 4 years for adolescent women to establish a stable menstrual cycle after menarche. During the first few years after menarche, the feedback regulation of the hypothalamus-pituitary-ovarian axis is immature. The sustained low level of FSH can't facilitate the follicular maturation, and subsequently the amount of estrogen secreted by follicles cannot reach the threshold required to promote the LH surge. In addition, there is a defect in the positive feedback effect of estrogen on the central nervous system. Absence of LH surge results in anovulation. Stress and emotional disorders can also disturb the hypothalamic-pituitary-ovarian axis regulation, causing anovulation.

When ovulation does not occur, the corpus luteum will not form. Subsequently, there is not sufficient progestogen produced to support the endometrium. The endometrium will begin to proliferate and shed with the fluctuation of estrogen levels, and then irregular uterine bleeding occurs. The menstrual cycle is irregular and the duration of bleeding lasts for a few days to a few weeks, even 1–2 months. The bleeding is spotty, and it may also be heavy bleeding after the absence of menstruation for several weeks or months. Anemia is often secondary to long-term or heavy bleeding.

The therapy of AUB in adolescents is to stop bleeding and regulate the menstrual cycle. Female hormones such as estrogen, and progestogen, as well as oral contraceptives, are often used for hemostasis in the acute phase and usually last for 21 days. After that, the women are maintained on cyclic, low-dose oral contraceptive for 3 to 6

2. 异常子宫出血   青春期最常见的异常子宫出血是功能失调性子宫出血，即非全身或生殖器官器质性病变所致的异常子宫出血。功能失调性子宫出血通常分为有排卵性和无排卵性。青春期以无排卵性更为常见。

青春期女性月经初潮后大约需要 4 年时间建立起稳定的月经周期。初潮后的几年内，下丘脑 - 垂体 - 卵巢轴的反馈调节不成熟。FSH 持续低水平，导致卵泡不能发育成熟，雌激素量不能达到促使 LH 高峰释放的阈值。此外，雌激素对大脑中枢的正反馈作用存在缺陷。LH 峰值未出现导致无排卵。压力、情绪障碍也会扰乱下丘脑 - 垂体 - 卵巢轴的调节，从而引起排卵障碍。

无排卵就不会形成黄体，也就不能产生足够的孕激素支持子宫内膜。子宫内膜随着雌激素水平的波动而增生和脱落，引起不规则子宫出血。月经周期不规则，经期长短不一，持续几天至几周不等，甚至 1~2 个月。出血可为点滴或淋漓，也可在数周或数月停经后出现大出血。长时间或大量出血可导致继发性贫血。

青少年异常子宫出血的治疗主要是止血和调节月经周期。急性期止血常用药物包括雌激素、孕激素等女性激素和口服避孕药等，通常止血后还需持续用药，共 21 天。之后，需服用低剂量口服避孕药 3~6 个月，调节周期并防止功能失调性子宫出血复发。

months to regulate the menstrual cycle and prevent recurrence of dysfunctional uterine bleeding.

The adolescents may be anxious related to insufficient knowledge of the disorder. They may worry about the negative influence of the menstrual disorder on sexual and reproductive function. Nurses should provide information about the cause, physiology, pathology, and available treatment for the condition. Supporting groups are very important. Nurses can organize health education activities through community women's centers to provide learning and psychosocial support opportunities for adolescents and their parents.

3. Adolescent Pregnancy An estimated 21 million girls aged 15–19 years in developing countries and regions become pregnant every year, and approximately 12 million of them give birth. The majority of adolescent births occur in low- and middle-income countries. Within countries, adolescent pregnancies and births are more likely to occur among poor, less educated and rural populations.

Pregnancy and childbirth complications are the leading cause of death among adolescent girls. Adolescent mothers face higher risks of eclampsia, anemia, postpartum bleeding, and puerperal infection than adult women. Approximately 3.9 million adolescent women undergo unsafe abortions each year, resulting in death and health issues.

In some low- and middle-income countries, many girls marry before 18 years of age. Early marriage generally leads to early childbearing. In many places, girls choose to become pregnant because they have limited educational and employment prospects. Marriage and childbearing may be the best of the limited options they have. Some adolescents rely on chance for contraception due to gaps in their knowledge. Some adolescent women may want contraception, but they do not have easy access to it or can't use it correctly. Another cause of unwanted pregnancy is sexual violence.

青少年女性可能因月经失调知识不足而感到焦虑。她们会担心月经失调对性和生殖功能的负面影响。护士应提供有关疾病病因、生理、病理和治疗相关的信息。此外，构建支持性的组织十分重要。护士可通过社区妇女中心组织健康教育活动，为青少年及其家长提供学习和心理支持的机会。

3. 少女妊娠 据估计，发展中国家和地区每年有 2 100 万 15~19 岁的女性受孕，其中约有 1 200 万人分娩。大多数少女生育发生在低收入和中等收入国家。在国家内部，少女妊娠和生育更可能发生在贫困、受教育程度较低和农村地区人群。

妊娠和分娩相关并发症是引起青春期女性死亡的首位原因。青少年孕妇发生子痫、贫血、产后出血和产褥感染的风险均高于成年孕妇。此外，全球每年约有 390 万名青春期女性进行了不安全流产，导致死亡和健康问题。

在一些低收入和中等收入国家，许多女孩在 18 岁之前结婚。早婚通常会导致早育。在许多地方，女孩的教育和就业前景有限，婚姻和生育可能是她们有限选择中最好的选择。还有一些青少年女性因避孕知识不足而对避孕有侥幸心理。一些青春期女性有避孕需求，但可能不方便获得或不会正确使用避孕药具。此外，性暴力也是非意愿妊娠的原因。

Community healthcare providers should strengthen reproductive health education for adolescent women, helping them understand the anatomy and physiology of the female reproductive system, contraception knowledge, etc., which can help reduce the occurrence of adolescent pregnancy. In addition, more reproductive health information and contraceptive measures should be provided for left-behind girls and girls with lower education levels in economically underdeveloped areas. Protecting the privacy of adolescent pregnant girls and providing psychological counseling and guidance are important for their holistic health.

II. Perimarital Health Care

The perimarital period generally refers to the period from the determination of the marriage partner to the conception after marriage. Perimarital health care is of great significance to the health of both spouses and their offspring. The perimarital health care mainly includes premarital medical examination, premarital health consultation, and premarital health guidance.

i. Premarital Medical Examination

Premarital medical examination generally refers to the medical examination of both men and women who are preparing to enter marriage, to discover diseases that may affect marriage or childbirth. The main contents include:

1. History of Disease Evaluation To survey both men and women on the history of disease, past marriage and childbirth history, family history of close relatives in marriage, family history of genetic diseases, history of mental illness, and whether there is intellectual development disorder, the woman's menstrual history, and history of male nocturnal emission.

2. Physical Examination Both the couple need general examination, with a focus on genitalia and secondary sexual characteristics.

3. Auxiliary Examinations Including blood and urine routine tests, liver and kidney function tests, hepatitis virology tests, chest

社区卫生保健人员应加强对青少年女性的生殖健康教育，帮助其了解女性生殖系统解剖和生理知识、避孕知识等，有助于减少少女妊娠的发生。此外，还应为经济欠发达地区留守少女和受教育程度较低少女提供更多生殖健康信息和避孕措施。保护少女隐私、加强心理咨询与疏导对其整体健康十分重要。

二、围婚期保健

围婚期一般是指从确定婚配对象到结婚后受孕的一段时间。围婚期保健对夫妻双方及子代健康具有重要意义。围婚期保健主要内容包括婚前医学检查、婚前卫生咨询和婚前卫生指导等。

（一）婚前医学检查

婚前医学检查一般指对准备进入婚姻的男女双方进行的医学检查，以发现影响结婚或生育的疾病。主要内容包括：

1. **评估病史** 了解男女双方的病史、既往婚育史、家族近亲婚配史、家族遗传病史、精神病史、有无智力发育障碍，女方月经史，男方遗精史。

2. **体格检查** 夫妻双方均需进行全身检查，重点是生殖器与第二性征检查。

3. **辅助检查** 包括血、尿常规，肝、肾功能检查，肝炎病毒学检测，胸部影像学检查，女性阴道分泌物检查。必要时进行染色体检查、精

imaging examinations, and female vaginal discharge examinations. When necessary, perform examinations such as chromosome analysis, semen analysis, and sexually transmitted disease (STD) examinations, etc.

ii. Premarital Health Consultation

Premarital health counseling can help identify health issues that require both spouses to temporarily suspend marriage or avoid childbirth, reducing the number of children born with serious genetic disorders.

1. Postpone Marriage For individuals with psychosis onset, infectious disease communicable period, important organ dysfunction, reproductive developmental disorders or deformities, it is recommended to postpone marriage temporarily and receive specific therapy.

2. Unsuitable for Childbirth Individuals with severe genetic diseases and a high risk of offspring recurrence are not suitable for childbirth. These patients can use long-term contraceptive measures or undergo ligation surgery.

iii. Premarital Health Guidance

The main contents of premarital health guidance include sexual health guidance, contraceptive guidance, and fertility guidance.

1. Sexual Health Guidance Establishing healthy sexual habits, maintaining genitalia cleanliness, avoiding excessive sexual activity, prohibiting menstrual sexual activity can help reduce the occurrence of reproductive inflammatory disease.

2. Contraceptive Guidance The contraceptive method for newlyweds should be convenient to use, have good contraceptive effects, and be able to quickly restore fertility after discontinuation without affecting the health of offspring.

(1) Barrier Contraception: Men can use condoms, which are safe and convenient. When using, choose the appropriate size, check for leaks, and check for break after use. Women can also choose diaphragms, vaginal spermicides, etc.

液检查、性病检查等。

（二）婚前卫生咨询

婚前卫生咨询有助于发现暂缓结婚或不宜生育的健康问题，减少患有严重遗传性疾病子代的出生。

1. **暂缓结婚** 精神病发作期、传染病传染期、重要脏器功能不全、生殖器发育障碍或畸形的个体，建议暂缓结婚，接受专科治疗。

2. **不宜生育** 有严重遗传性疾病、子代再发风险高者，不宜生育，患者可采用长效避孕措施或行结扎手术。

（三）婚前卫生指导

婚前卫生指导的主要内容是性卫生指导、避孕指导以及生育指导。

1. **性卫生指导** 建立良好的性卫生习惯，保持生殖器清洁，避免过频性生活，禁止经期性生活，减少生殖道炎症的发生。

2. **避孕指导** 新婚避孕方法要使用方便、避孕效果好，同时在停用后能尽快恢复生育能力且不影响子代健康。

（1）屏障避孕：男性可使用阴茎套，安全、方便。使用时，要选择恰当的型号，检查有无漏孔，使用后检查有无破损。女性也可以选择阴道隔膜、阴道杀精剂等。

(2) Medicine Contraception: Commonly used contraceptives include short acting oral contraceptives, sustained release contraceptives, contraceptive patches, etc. Women should pay attention to the contraindications of contraceptives and do not miss the medication.

(3) Emergency Contraception: Emergency contraception refers to the contraceptive method adopted within hours or days after unprotected sexual activity or contraceptive failure to prevent unintended pregnancy. Common emergency contraceptive methods include placing an intrauterine device and taking emergency contraceptive pills. It is more appropriate for women who have not given birth to take emergency contraceptive pills. However, taking emergency contraceptive pills should not be used as a common contraceptive method.

3. Fertility Guidance　Only when both men and women reach a certain age and have a certain level of physiological and psychological maturity, can they take on the responsibilities of marriage and family. According to the *Civil Code of the People's Republic of China* the legal age for marriage is not earlier than 22 years old for males and not earlier than 20 years old for females. From a physiological perspective, the reproductive organs of women are generally mature after the age of 20. However, bone development usually reaches maturity around the age of 23. Therefore, the optimal reproductive age for women is 25–29 years old, and for men it is 25–35 years old.

Taking the adjustment and adaptation of both the husband and wife's body and lifestyle into account, it is generally recommended that the newlyweds become pregnant at least 3–6 months after marriage. Before pregnancy, the couple should make some preparations, for example, to balance nutrition, quit smoking and drinking, alternate work with rest, and maintain good physical and mental health. In addition, avoid the influence of harmful factors, such as high temperature, radiation, lead, mercury, pesticides,

（2）药物避孕：常用避孕药包括短效口服避孕药、缓释避孕药、避孕贴剂等。女性需注意药物使用的禁忌证，不要漏服等。

（3）紧急避孕：紧急避孕是指在无保护性生活或避孕失败后的几小时或几天内，为防止非意愿妊娠而采取的避孕方法。常用紧急避孕方法包括放置宫内节育器和服用紧急避孕药。未生育的女性服用紧急避孕药更为适宜。然而，服用紧急避孕药不可作为常用避孕方法。

3. 生育指导　男女双方达到一定年龄，具有一定的生理和心理成熟度时，才能承担起婚姻与家庭的责任。《中华人民共和国民法典》规定，男女结婚的法定年龄是男性不早于 22 周岁，女性不早于 20 周岁。从生理学角度来讲，女性 20 岁以后生殖器官基本成熟。然而，一般 23 岁左右骨骼发育才能成熟。因此，女性最佳生育年龄是 25~29 岁，男性最佳生育年龄是 25~35 岁。

考虑到夫妻双方身体和生活方式的调整与适应，一般主张新婚夫妇结婚 3~6 个月以后再受孕。受孕前，夫妻双方可进行一些准备，例如均衡营养、戒烟戒酒、劳逸结合、保持良好的身心健康状态。此外，避免有害因素的影响，如高温、放射线、铅、汞、农药、乱用药物等。避免风疹病毒和流感病毒感染，必要时接种疫苗。

and drug abuse. Avoid infection of rubella virus and influenza virus, getting vaccinated if necessary.

III. Perinatal Period Health Care

i. Prepregnancy Health Care

If a couple is planning a pregnancy, the midwife or health care provider may provide assessments of high-risk factors before pregnancy. The women should have a comprehensive physical examination, including heart and lung auscultation, measuring blood pressure, calculating body mass index (BMI), and routine gynecological examinations. Some necessary auxiliary examinations are also required, including blood routine tests, blood groups, urine routine tests, liver function, kidney function, HBsAg, HIV, and syphilis screening.

Prepregnancy health education is an important component for perinatal services. According to *Guidelines for Prepregnancy and Pregnancy Care* by Obstetrics Group of Chinese Society of Obstetrics and Gynecology of Chinese Medical Association, the main contents of prepregnancy health education may include:

1. Pregnancy should be prepared and planned, and advanced age pregnancy should be avoided as much as possible.

2. Reasonable nutrition and exercise controlling of weight gain.

3. Women should take folic acid 0.4–0.8mg/d, or folic acid-containing multivitamins. Women who have previously given birth to children with neural tube defects (NTD) need to supplement folic acid 4mg per day.

4. Women who are preparing for pregnancy with genetic diseases, chronic diseases, and infectious diseases should be assessed.

5. Avoid the use of medicine that may affect normal fetal development. Avoid exposure to toxic and harmful substances in the living and occupational environment, such as radiation, high temperature, lead, mercury, benzene, arsenic, pesticide, etc., and be cautious in contact with

三、围生期保健

（一）孕前保健

助产士或医疗保健人员可为计划妊娠的夫妇提供孕前高危因素的评估。备孕妇女应进行综合的身体评估，包括心、肺听诊，测血压，计算体重指数，常规妇科检查等。还可进行一些必要的辅助检查，包括血常规、血型、尿常规、肝功能、肾功能、乙肝表面抗原、艾滋病病毒及梅毒筛查等。

孕前健康教育是围生期保健的重要内容。根据中华医学会妇产科学分会产科学组制定的《孕前和孕期初级保健指南》，孕前健康教育的主要内容包括：

1. 有准备、有计划地妊娠，尽量避免高龄妊娠。

2. 合理营养和运动，控制体重增加。

3. 妇女应补充叶酸，每天 0.4~0.8mg，可单用叶酸制剂，也可服用含叶酸的复合维生素。既往生育过神经管缺陷（NTD）儿的妇女，每天需补充 4mg 叶酸。

4. 有遗传病、慢性疾病和传染病的备孕妇女，应给予评估。

5. 避免使用可能影响胎儿正常发育的药物；避免接触生活及职业环境中的有毒有害物质，如放射线、高温、铅、汞、苯、砷、农药等，谨慎接触宠物粪便；改变吸烟、酗酒、吸毒等不良的生活习惯；避免高强度的工作、高噪声环境和家庭暴力。

pet feces. Quit unhealthy habits such as smoking, alcohol abuse, drug abuse, etc. Avoid high-intensity work, high-noise environments, and family violence.

6. Maintain mental health and relieve mental stress.

ii. Health Care during Pregnancy

1. Health Care during Early Pregnancy Regular prenatal check-ups should be started immediately after confirming pregnancy. Evaluate the fetal health status and pay attention to whether the pregnant woman has any comorbidities. Pregnancy should be terminated in time for those who are not suitable for pregnancy. Those who can continue to carry the pregnancy should be monitored and treated reasonably. The main contents of health care during early pregnancy include：

(1) Guidance for Nutrition: During early pregnancy, the synthesis of fetal tissues places relatively few demands on maternal nutrition. When the embryo or fetus is very small in the first trimester, the nutritional needs are only slightly greater than those before pregnancy. According to the dietary recommendations for pregnant women in *The Chinese Dietary Guidelines* (*2022*) developed by the Chinese Nutrition Society, women in early pregnancy should continue to maintain a balanced diet similar to that before pregnancy and need not increase their food intake to avoid excessive weight gain. For those with mild morning sickness, it is recommended to arrange meals according to the recommended amount of food for non-pregnant women. For those with severe morning sickness, it is not necessary to overly emphasize balanced diets or force them to eat. Instead, they can choose easily digestible foods according to their personal dietary preferences and tastes, and eat small meals frequently. When morning sickness severely affects eating, in order to ensure the fetal brain's need for glucose and prevent the harm of ketoacidosis to the fetus, pregnant women must consume at least

6. 保持心理健康，解除精神压力。

（二）孕期保健

1. 孕早期保健　妇女在确定妊娠后，应即刻开始进行规律的产前检查。评估胎儿健康状况，注意孕妇有无妊娠合并症。不宜妊娠的孕妇应及时终止妊娠，可以继续妊娠者应加强监护，合理治疗。孕早期保健的主要内容包括：

（1）营养指导：孕早期胎儿生长相对缓慢，所需营养素仅稍高于孕前。根据中国营养学会制定的《中国居民膳食指南（2022）》对孕期膳食的建议，孕早期妇女应继续保持孕前平衡膳食，无须额外增加食物摄入量，以免体重增长过多。早孕反应不明显者，可根据非孕妇女食物推荐量安排膳食。早孕反应明显者，不必过分强调平衡膳食，也无须强迫进食，可根据个人饮食喜好和口味选择易消化食物，少量多餐。孕吐严重影响进食时，为保证胎儿脑组织对葡萄糖的需要，预防酮症酸中毒对胎儿的危害，孕妇每天应摄取至少 130g 碳水化合物，如米、面、薯类、根茎类蔬菜、水果等。进食困难或孕吐严重者应及时就医，可通过静脉输注葡萄糖的营养支持方式补充必要量的碳水化合物。孕妇应继续补充叶酸 0.4~0.8mg/d 至孕 3 个月。

130g of carbohydrates per day, such as rice, flour, potatoes, root vegetables, fruits, etc. People who have difficulty in eating or suffer from severe morning sickness should seek medical help in time. They can supplement necessary carbohydrates by intravenous infusion of glucose. Pregnant women should continue to supplement folic acid 0.4–0.8mg/d until the third month of pregnancy.

(2) Guidance for Weight Management: The weight change during the first trimester is not significant, and it is recommended to measure the weight once a month and avoid excessive weight gain during the first trimester.

(3) Guidance for Exercise: Nurses need to conduct a comprehensive assessment of pregnant women to rule out contraindications to physical activity during pregnancy. It is recommended that pregnant women engage in low-to-moderate-intensity physical activity during pregnancy, which has many benefits for both the mother and the baby. Pregnant women can start aerobic exercise during early pregnancy, lasting for 30–60 minutes each time, 3–4 times a week. Moderate-intensity aerobic exercise includes fast walking, swimming, stationary cycling, jogging, modified yoga, and modified Pilates. Low-intensity physical activity includes walking and daily activities. Drink water before, during, and after exercise. Warm up before exercise and relax after exercise.

(4) Guidance for Self Care:

1) Frequent and urgent urination: It is usually a result of bladder capacity reduction by compression of enlarging uterus and fetal presentation part. Pregnant women should not limit fluids to reduce the frequency of urination. Nurse should advise the women to drink at least 2L of water a day to maintain an adequate fluid intake. Pregnant women need to know that if urine looks dark, they must increase their fluid intake. When there is pain or burning sensation, be sure to report that to a nurse or other health care provider.

2) Fatigue and malaise: It may be caused by increasing levels of estrogen, progestogen,

（2）体重管理指导：孕早期体重变化不大，可每月测量 1 次体重，应避免孕早期体重增长过快。

（3）运动指导：护士需对孕妇进行全面评估，排除孕期体力活动禁忌证。推荐孕妇在孕期进行中低强度的体力活动，对母婴均有较多益处。孕妇可以在孕早期开始有氧运动，每次 30~60 分钟，每周 3~4 次。中等强度有氧运动包括快走、游泳、固定自行车、慢跑、改良瑜伽和改良普拉提等。低强度体力活动包括步行和日常生活活动。运动前、中、后均可适当喝水。运动前要热身，运动后要放松。

（4）自我护理指导：

1）尿频和尿急：尿频和尿急通常是增大的子宫和胎先露部压迫膀胱，引起膀胱容量减小所致。孕妇不应因此而限制液体的摄入。护士应建议孕妇每天至少饮水 2L，以保证足够的液体摄入。孕妇需了解，如果尿色较深，需增加饮水量。若出现尿痛或排尿烧灼感，需告知护士或医务人员。

2）疲乏和不适：可能与雌、孕激素和人绒毛膜促性腺激素水平升高，以及基础体温升高

and human chorionic gonadotropin (hCG) or by elevated basal body temperature (BBT). Women should maintain a regular lifestyle, take rest as needed and ensure adequate sleep.

3) Polysialia: It may occur 2 to 3 weeks after menelipsis. It is possibly caused by increasing levels of estrogen. Women can use astringent mouthwash, chew gum and hard candy to alleviate the symptom.

(5) Avoid Harmful Factors: Use medicine reasonably, avoiding the use of medicine that may affect normal fetal development. Avoid exposure to toxic and harmful substances, such as radiation, high temperature, lead, mercury, benzene, arsenic, pesticides, etc., and be cautious when having close contact with pet feces. Quit unhealthy habits such as smoking, alcohol abuse, drug abuse, etc. Avoid high-intensity work, high-noise environments, and family violence.

(6) Maintain mental health and relieve mental stress.

2. Health Care during Pregnant Metaphase and Late Pregnancy With the growth and development of the fetus, a series of adaptive changes will occur in women. Pregnant women should be instructed to undergo regular prenatal examinations, manage the nutrition, exercise, weight, and discomfort symptoms effectively, and pay attention to infection prevention. Besides, nurses should instruct pregnant women to count fetal movements. Breastfeeding and delivery information should also be provided in the third trimester to guide pregnant women in their preparation for delivery and feeding.

(1) Guidance for Nutrition: The growth rate of the fetus accelerates during the second and third trimester. According to the dietary recommendations for pregnant women in *The Chinese Dietary Guidelines* (*2022*) developed by the Chinese Nutrition Society, the intake of milk, fish, eggs, and lean meat needs to be increased based on the pre-pregnancy diet. Milk is a good source of calcium, and 500g of milk should be

等有关。孕妇应保持生活规律，根据身体需要休息，保持充足睡眠。

3）流涎：多发生于停经后 2~3 周，可能与雌激素升高有关。孕妇可使用收敛性的漱口水、口香糖和硬质糖果来减轻症状。

（5）避免有害因素：慎用药物，避免使用可能影响胎儿正常发育的药物；避免接触有毒有害物质，如放射线、高温、铅、汞、苯、砷、农药等，谨慎密切接触宠物粪便；改变不良的生活习惯，如吸烟、酗酒、吸毒等；避免高强度的工作、高噪声环境和家庭暴力。

（6）保持心理健康，解除精神压力。

2. 孕中晚期保健 随着胎儿的生长发育，妇女的身心状态都会发生一系列适应性的变化。护士应指导孕妇进行产前检查，并做好营养、运动、体重、不适症状管理，并注意预防感染；指导孕妇计数胎动；妊娠晚期还应提供母乳喂养和分娩相关信息，指导孕妇做好分娩和哺乳准备。

（1）营养指导：从孕中期开始，胎儿生长速度加快，根据中国营养学会制定的《中国居民膳食指南（2022）》对孕期膳食的建议，应在孕前膳食的基础上增加奶类、鱼、蛋、瘦肉的摄入。奶是钙的良好来源，孕中晚期每天可在正餐或加餐时食用 500g 奶类，包括纯牛奶、酸奶、奶粉等。体重增长较快时，可选用低脂奶。多数乳饮料含乳量不高，不能代替乳类。鱼类所含脂肪和能量明显少于畜禽肉类，当孕妇体重增长

consumed daily during meals or snacks in the second and third trimesters, including pure milk, yogurt, and milk powder. When weight gain is rapid, low-fat milk can be chosen. Most milk drinks do not contain high amounts of milk and cannot replace milk. Fish contains significantly less fat and energy than livestock and poultry meat. When pregnant women experience significant weight gain, fish can be used instead of livestock and poultry. It is best to remove the skin and fat when cooking livestock and poultry. Deep-sea fish contain more unsaturated fatty acids, which are beneficial for the development of fetal brain and retinal function. It is recommended to consume deep-sea fish 2–3 times a week.

(2) Guidance for Weight Management: The weight gain accelerates in the second and third trimesters of pregnancy, and it is recommended to measure weight once a week to avoid excessive weight gain.

(3) Guidance for Exercise: During the second and third trimesters of pregnancy, it is recommended to continue with low-to-moderate intensity exercise. It is important to gradually increase the duration and intensity of exercise. Avoid activities that involve physical contact or have a risk of falling, such as horseback riding, alpine skiing, ice hockey, gymnastics, or weightlifting. It is not recommended for pregnant women to engage in diving activities. As the fetus develops, the pressure in the pelvis increases, and the risk of pelvic floor dysfunction increases. Nurses can guide pregnant women to perform pelvic floor muscle exercises, such as Kegel exercises to strengthen the pelvic floor muscle strength. Pregnant women can lie down, sit, stand, etc., and then find the correct pelvic floor muscle groups. Slowly contract the pelvic floor muscles for 3–10 seconds and then relax for 3–10 seconds, or quickly contract for 1–2 seconds and relax for 1–2 seconds. Repeat the above actions for 10–15 times each set, 3 sets each time, 3 times a day for 3–6 weeks.

较多时，可用鱼类代替畜禽类。烹饪畜禽类时建议剔除皮和肥肉。深海鱼类含有较多不饱和脂肪酸，对胎儿大脑和视网膜功能发育有益，建议每周食用2~3次。

（2）体重管理指导：孕中晚期体重增长加快，应每周测量1次体重，避免体重增长过快。

（3）运动指导：妊娠中晚期应继续进行中低等强度的运动。运动应循序渐进，逐步增加持续时间和强度。避免进行有身体接触或有跌倒危险的活动，如骑马、高山滑雪、冰球、体操或举重。不推荐孕妇进行潜水运动。随着胎儿的发育，盆腔压力增高，可指导孕妇进行盆底肌肉锻炼，如凯格尔运动。孕妇可躺、坐、站立等，找到正确的盆底肌肉群，慢收缩盆底肌肉3~10s后放松3~10s，或快收缩1~2s后放松1~2s，重复10~15个上述动作，每次3组，每日3次，持续3~6周，有助于增强盆底肌力量。

(4) Guidance for Self Care:

1) Low back pain: The center of gravity change resulting from growth of fetus and enlargement of uterus. The lumbar, cervical and thoracic curvatures become exaggerated, and then cause low back pain. The pregnant women should maintain good posture, avoid fatigue, wear low-heeled shoes, and sleep on a firm mattress. Getting back rubs and doing pelvic tilt exercises may be helpful for low back pain.

2) Lower limb spasm: It may be related to the compression of nerves supplying lower limb by the enlarged uterus. Reduced level of serum calcium or elevation of serum phosphorus may also be associated with lower limb spasm. It can be aggravated by fatigue, increased body mass index, and poor posture. When the spasm attacks, the woman can stretch the affected muscle, straighten the leg as much as possible, and press the foot toward the direction of the body, so that the muscle tendon is straightened. Local heat can be applied if necessary. Pregnant women are advised to get plenty of rest and avoid standing for long periods of time or overexertion. Quilts over feet should be soft. Pregnant women can raise their legs after walking or while sleeping. Massage leg muscles may be helpful. Leg stretching exercise is an effective prevention and treatment measure. The specific methods include: keeping the knee extending when the foot does dorsiflexion, holding for 20 seconds for 3 consecutive times, 3 to 4 sections a day. When the attack is frequent, the pregnant woman can follow the doctor's advice to take magnesium supplements, vitamins B, and vitamin E.

3) Constipation: It usually results from slower gastrointestinal smooth muscle peristalsis caused by the increase of progestogen in pregnant women. Women can take more vegetables rich in dietary fiber and drink more water. If necessary, use lactulose as prescribed by the doctor.

4) Edema: Ankle to lower limb edema is easy to occur in the third trimester. Edema may be

（4）自我护理指导

1）腰背痛：随着胎儿的发育和子宫的增大，孕妇身体重心发生改变，腰曲、胸曲和颈曲过大，诱发腰背痛。孕妇应保持良好姿势，避免疲倦，穿低跟鞋，睡硬床垫，进行背部按摩，进行骨盆倾斜运动等，有助于缓解腰背痛。

2）下肢痉挛：孕妇下肢痉挛可能与增大的子宫压迫下肢神经有关。血清钙水平下降、血清磷水平升高等代谢紊乱也可能导致下肢痉挛。疲乏、体重指数增加、姿势不当等可使其加重。痉挛发作时，孕妇可以用力伸展受累的腿部肌肉，尽量伸直腿部，并将脚板向身体方向下压，使肌腱被拉直，必要时可采用局部热疗。建议孕妇充分休息，避免长时间站立或过度劳累，足部的被子应柔软；建议孕妇行走后或睡眠时抬高腿部；按摩腿部肌肉有助于减少痉挛发作；腿部伸展运动有助于防治痉挛，具体方法为膝关节伸直时足背屈，连续3次，每次保持20秒，每日3~4组。发作频繁时，孕妇可遵医嘱服用镁补充剂、复合维生素B、维生素E等。

3）便秘：受孕后，妇女体内孕激素水平升高，胃肠平滑肌蠕动变慢，容易导致便秘。护士可指导孕妇进食膳食纤维丰富的食物，如蔬菜，要多饮水。必要时遵医嘱使用乳果糖等。

4）水肿：妊娠晚期容易发生下肢水肿。久站、久坐、姿势不良、缺乏运动、衣服过紧等可

aggravated by prolonged standing, sitting, poor posture, lack of exercise, and constrictive clothing Pregnant women should avoid standing and sitting for long periods, and maintain moderate intensity activities. Elevating the legs at rest can help reduce edema. The pregnant women should seek help from health care provider if edema can't be relieved after rest, or generalized edema occurs.

(5) Fetal Movement Counting: Fetal movement counting is a means for pregnant women to self-monitor the fetal situation in the uterus. Community nurses should instruct pregnant women to observe fetal movement after 28 weeks of pregnancy. Under normal circumstances, pregnant women without high risk factors do not need to deliberately count fetal movement. When pregnant women perceive fetal movement is significantly reduced, it is necessary to carefully count fetal movement. Fetal movement is generally more pronounced in the afternoon and evening, and 10 or more in 2 hours is normal. When the fetal movement counting is significantly reduced, prompt medical attention should be sought.

(6) Avoid Harmful Factors: Use medicine reasonably, avoiding the use of medicine that may affect normal fetal development. Avoid exposure to toxic and harmful substances in the living and occupational environment, such as radiation, high temperature, lead, mercury, benzene, arsenic, pesticides, etc., and be cautious when having close contact with pet feces. Quit unhealthy habits such as smoking, alcohol abuse, drug abuse, etc. Avoid high-intensity work, high-noise environments, and family violence.

(7) Maintain mental health and relieve mental stress.

(8) Provision of Breastfeeding Information: During the third trimester, nurses should communicate with pregnant women and their families about newborn feeding and provide breastfeeding information, including the benefits of breastfeeding, the practice of starting breastfeeding as early as possible after childbirth.

能加重水肿。孕妇应避免久站和久坐，保持中等强度的活动。此外，休息时抬高下肢也有利于减轻水肿。孕妇如果下肢水肿休息后不能缓解，或发生全身水肿，应及时寻求卫生保健人员帮助。

（5）胎动计数：胎动计数是孕妇自我监测胎儿宫内情况的一种手段。社区护士应指导孕妇在妊娠 28 周后观察胎动。一般情况下，没有高危因素的孕妇不需要刻意计数胎动。当孕妇感知胎动明显减少时，需认真计数胎动。胎动一般在下午和晚上更明显，2 小时内出现 10 次及以上为正常。当胎动计数明显减少时，应及时就医。

（6）避免有害因素：慎用药物，避免使用可能影响胎儿正常发育的药物；避免接触有毒有害物质，如放射线、高温、铅、汞、苯、砷、农药等，谨慎密切接触宠物粪便；改变不良的生活习惯，如吸烟、酗酒、吸毒等；避免高强度的工作、高噪声环境和家庭暴力。

（7）保持心理健康，解除精神压力。

（8）母乳喂养信息提供：在孕晚期，护士应与孕妇及其家人进行新生儿喂养方式的沟通，提供有关母乳喂养的信息，包括母乳喂养的好处、产后尽早开始母乳喂养的做法、母乳喂养的技巧等相关信息，帮助其建立有关母乳喂养的科学认识和积极态度。

breastfeeding skills and other relevant information. It will be helpful for them to establish scientific understanding and positive attitudes about breastfeeding.

(9) Preparation for Delivery: Before the delivery starts, there will often be threatened labor symptoms consisting of false labor, lightening, and bloody show. Pregnant women and their families can maintain normal daily life habits and prepare for delivery in advance, including mother's clothes, postpartum perineal pads, newborn clothes, diapers, breast pumps, etc.

iii. Health Care during Delivery

Chinese experts put forward the focus of health care during delivery as "five preventions and one strengthening".

1. **Prevention of Postpartum Hemorrhage** Postpartum hemorrhage is the main cause of maternal death in China, so the prevention of postpartum hemorrhage is the focus of health care during delivery. The health care providers should assess the risk factors of postpartum hemorrhage, observe the amount of bleeding and related clinical manifestations closely, find out the cause of bleeding and actively deal with it.

2. **Prevention of Infection** Strictly implement aseptic operations during delivery, and do a good job of disinfection of the delivery room, delivery kit, maternal vulva and midwives' hands. Antibiotics should be used reasonably for the possible infections such as women suffered from premature rupture of membranes.

3. **Prevention of Prolonged Labor** Delivery powers, birth canal, fetus and maternal mental and psychological states are the main factors affecting the smooth progress of labor. The management of nutrition and weight of the mother during pregnancy helps to maintain the reasonable weight of the fetus and reduce the dystocia caused by excessively large fetus. Standard obstetric examinations can help identify conditions such as a narrow pelvis or abnormal fetal positions, including transverse and breech presentations, in a

（9）分娩准备：分娩发动前，常常会出现假临产、胎儿下降感、见红等先兆临产的症状。孕妇和家人可保持正常的日常生活习惯，并提前做好迎接分娩的准备，准备好母亲的衣物、产后会阴垫，新生儿衣物、尿布，吸奶器等物品。

（三）分娩期保健

我国专家针对分娩期保健，提出了分娩过程保健的重点为"五防、一加强"。

1. **防出血** 产后出血是我国孕产妇的主要死因，因此，预防产后出血是分娩期保健的重点。应注意评估产后出血的危险因素，密切观察出血量及相关临床表现，查找出血原因并积极处理。

2. **防感染** 接生过程中严格执行无菌操作，做好产房、产包、产妇外阴和接生者手消毒。对有胎膜早破等可能发生感染者，合理应用抗生素。

3. **防滞产** 产力、产道、胎儿和产妇的精神心理状态是影响分娩能否顺利进行的主要因素。母亲妊娠期对营养和体重的管理，有助于保持胎儿的合理体重，减少胎儿过大引起的难产。通过规范的产检，及时发现骨盆狭窄、胎位异常（如胎儿横位、臀位）等问题。分娩过程中应密切观察，及时发现和处理子宫收缩乏力、胎位异常等情况，减少因滞产导致的母婴并发症，确保母婴安全。

timely manner. Close observation should be made during delivery, timely detection and treatment of uterine contraction atony, abnormal fetal position, etc., to reduce maternal and infant complications caused by prolonged labor, and ensure maternal and infant safety.

4. Prevention of Birth Trauma   Instruct pregnant women to closely cooperate with midwives and doctors. Midwives should improve the quality of delivery technology, reduce the risk of injuries to mothers and newborns.

5. Prevention of Asphyxia   Neonatal asphyxia may have many negative effects on children's health. Delivery institutions shall have the material and technical conditions for resuscitation and rescue of neonatal asphyxia. Medical staff in delivery institutions should promptly assess and resuscitate newborns who are asphyxiated.

6. One Strengthening   Health care providers should conduct a close evaluation of the delivery process and address any problems that arise promptly and appropriately.

iv. Puerperium Health Care

In China, the puerperal period is also called "Yuezi", and women often need to "Zuo Yuezi" during the puerperal period, that is, to maintain some unique living habits. Postpartum women spend most of their lives at home, during which time they often have multiple care needs. Community nurses can assess and instruct mothers through home visits. Postpartum visits by community nurses in China generally include 3 times, within 1 week, 14 days and 28 days after delivery.

The life customs of this special stage of puerperium have multiple attributes such as humanity, geography, climate, society, economy, culture and health, and also carry many functions such as maintaining a happy mood, adapting to eating habits, and conforming to family ethics. Community nurses should not only combine scientific and evidence-based principles in their

4. 防产伤   指导孕产妇密切配合助产士和医生。助产士应提高接产技术水平,减少对产妇和新生儿损伤。

5. 防窒息   新生儿窒息可能对儿童健康造成诸多影响。分娩机构应具备新生儿窒息复苏和抢救的物质条件和技术条件。分娩机构的医护人员应及时评估并对窒息的新生儿进行复苏和抢救。

6. 一加强   医护人员应对分娩过程实施密切的评估,并及时恰当地处理出现的问题。

(四)产褥期保健

在中国,产褥期也被称为"月子",妇女在产褥期常常需要"坐月子",即保持一些特有的生活习惯。在产褥期,产妇多为居家生活,会有多种护理需求,需要社区护士给予关注。社区护士可以通过家庭访视来对产妇进行评估与指导。我国社区护士产后访视一般包括3次,分别为产后1周内、产后14天和产后28天。

产褥期这一特殊阶段的生活习俗具有人文、地理、气候、社会、经济、文化和健康等多重属性,还承载了保持心情愉悦、适应饮食习惯、符合家庭伦理等诸多功能。社区护士在工作中既要结合科学和循证原则,也要考虑不同地区的民俗文化,只要不与科学原则冲突,不会对妇女身心造成不良影响,均可依从地方、家庭或个人的生活习惯,给予恰当的指导。主要内容包括:

work, but also consider the folk culture of different regions. As long as the habits do not conflict with scientific principles and do not cause adverse effects on women's physical and mental health, they can comply with local, family or personal living habits and give appropriate guidance. The main contents include：

1. Guidance for Daily Life

(1) Environment: The room should be kept clean, air circulation, appropriate temperature and humidity. Excessive visits should be avoided.

(2) Personal Hygiene: Due to heavy sweating, women can bathe, change their clothes frequently, and keep warm. Women can clean the perineum every day and change underwear frequently to reduce the risk of perineal wound infection.

(3) Diet and Nutrition: Nutrition research results show that women in the puerperal period have no special food contraindications, and their nutritional needs and dietary principles are basically similar to those of pregnant or lactation women. According to the Chinese Nutrition Society's *Dietary Recommendations for Puerperal Women in China*, the diet of puerperal women should be based on the dietary guidelines for general population and follow the key recommendations: a. Increase animal foods and seafood rich in high-quality protein and vitamin A, and choose iodized salt. b. Food should be balanced, diverse, and not excessive. c. Keep a happy mood and sleep enough, which is conducive to promoting milk secretion. d. Adhere to breastfeeding, exercise moderately, and gradually recover the appropriate weight. e. Avoid tobacco, alcohol, strong tea and coffee.

(4) Rest and Activity: Women after spontaneous delivery can get out of bed and do light physical activity 6–12 hours after childbirth. Women who underwent cesarean section can delay the time to get out of bed and exercise, and gradually increase the amount of activity. Pregnant women without vaginal complications should start abdominal and pelvic floor muscle exercise as early

1. 日常生活指导

（1）环境：居室应保持清洁、空气流通，温、湿度适宜，避免过多探视。

（2）个人卫生：由于产妇出汗较多，妇女应在做好保暖的同时适当沐浴，勤换衣裤；注意会阴清洁，勤换内衣，减少会阴伤口感染风险。

（3）饮食与营养：现代营养学研究结果显示，产褥期妇女没有特殊的食物禁忌，其营养需要和膳食原则基本类似于孕期或一般哺乳期妇女。根据中国营养学会制定的《中国产褥期（月子）妇女膳食建议》，产褥期妇女膳食应在一般人群膳食指南基础上，遵循以下关键推荐：①增加富含优质蛋白质及维生素A的动物性食物和海产品，选用碘盐；②产褥期食物多样不过量，重视整个哺乳期营养；③愉悦心情，充足睡眠，促进乳汁分泌；④坚持哺乳，适度运动，逐步恢复适宜体重；⑤忌烟酒，避免浓茶和咖啡。

（4）休息与活动：自然分娩的产妇，产后6~12小时即可下床活动。剖宫产的产妇，可推迟下地时间，循序渐进，逐渐增加活动量。无阴道并发症的产妇，产后尽早开始腹部锻炼和盆底肌锻炼。产后前4周可进行呼吸功能训练。产后4~6周开始，产妇每周可进行4~5次、每次持续30~40分钟的中等强度有氧运动，包括体操、肌力训练、固定式自行车、普拉提、舞蹈等。

as possible after childbirth. Respiratory function training can be conducted in the first 4 weeks after childbirth. Starting from 4-6 weeks postpartum, women can engage in 4-5 times of moderate intensity aerobic exercise per week, each lasting 30-40 minutes, including gymnastics, muscle strength training, stationary cycling, Pilates, dance, etc. Starting from 8-12 weeks postpartum, women can gradually increase the intensity of exercise, engage in exercises that strengthen core muscle strength, as well as abdominal and pelvic floor exercises. Assess the pelvic floor muscles and core control ability of the parturient at 16 weeks postpartum, and resume pre pregnancy activities without any prenatal or postpartum complications.

(5) Pelvic Floor Rehabilitation: Pregnancy and delivery are risk factors for pelvic floor dysfunction. Pregnancy and delivery can damage the pelvic floor nerves, muscles and fascia, leading to pelvic floor defects. When the deformation of pelvic floor tissue and the displacement of pelvic organs exceed a certain limit, the pelvic floor dysfunction disease appears. The clinical manifestations of pelvic floor dysfunction include urinary incontinence, fecal incontinence, pelvic organ prolapse, sexual dysfunction and pelvic pain, etc.

Although the survey data in different countries and regions are various, studies have shown that the incidence of female pelvic floor dysfunction is high. It has become an important public health problem affecting the physical and mental health and quality of life of adult women. Postpartum is the key stage in the prevention and treatment process of female pelvic floor dysfunction. Postpartum pelvic floor rehabilitation is the basis of lifelong prevention and treatment of pelvic floor dysfunction.

All postpartum women should receive health guidance about pelvic floor rehabilitation, including anatomy and physiology of pelvic floor, the causes, clinical manifestations, prevention and treatment of pelvic floor dysfunction diseases.

产后 8~12 周开始可以逐步增加运动强度，进行强化核心力量的锻炼，以及腹部和盆底锻炼。产后 16 周评估产妇盆底肌肉和核心控制能力，无产前或产后并发症可恢复孕前活动。

（5）盆底康复：妊娠和分娩是盆底功能障碍的危险因素。妊娠和分娩对盆底神经、肌肉和筋膜的损伤会导致盆底缺陷，当盆底组织的变形及盆腔器官的移位超过一定限度时，即出现盆底功能障碍性疾病。盆底功能障碍的临床表现包括尿失禁、大便失禁、盆腔器官脱垂、性功能障碍及盆腔疼痛等。

尽管不同国家和地区的调查数据不同，但研究均显示，女性盆底功能障碍性疾病的发病率较高，已经成为影响成年女性身心健康和生活质量的重要公共卫生问题。产后是女性盆底功能障碍性疾病防治的关键阶段，产后盆底康复是盆底功能障碍终身防治的基础。

所有产妇均应接受盆底康复的健康指导，包括盆底生理、解剖知识和盆底功能障碍性疾病发病原因、临床表现、防治等。社区护士的健康指导有助于妇女认识到盆底疾病危害，积极主动参与盆底康复，摆脱疾病的烦恼，提高生活

Health instruction from community nurses can help women realize the harm of pelvic floor disease through, actively participate in pelvic floor rehabilitation, get rid of the trouble of disease, and improve the quality of life. In addition, community nurses also need to guide pregnant women to participate in standardized pelvic floor assessments, take systematic rehabilitation measures, learn the correct pelvic floor muscle exercise methods, and adhere to rehabilitation exercise.

(6) Family Planning Guidance：Sexual intercourse is usually restricted until the perineum and uterus have completely healed by 6 weeks after birth. Community nurses should instruct the woman and partner to choose the appropriate contraceptive methods after starting sexual activity. Condoms are useful when lactating. The breastfeeding mother should not use oral contraceptives because lactation hormones and the milk supply may be affected.

2. Psychological Assessment　The assessment of psychological status is an important part of community nursing for postpartum women. Due to the dramatic changes of hormone levels during delivery and postpartum period, abnormal delivery, poor health of newborns and other factors, some postpartum women suffered from postnatal psychological disturbances. The common postnatal psychological disturbances include postpartum blues, postpartum depression (PPD), and postpartum psychosis.

Community nurses should identify high risk factors for postpartum psychological disturbances. The risk factors usually include abnormal delivery (such as dystocia, prolonged labor, surgical delivery), poor health of newborns (such as premature delivery, stillbirth, congenital malformation or deformities, neonatal asphyxia, transferred to the neonatal intensive care unit (NICU) for treatment, neonatal death), family members' dissatisfaction with the gender of newborns，poor family relations (such as marital tension, marital breakdown, bereavement, lack of family and social support,

质量。此外,社区护士还需指导产妇进行规范的盆底评估,采取系统性的康复措施,学会正确的盆底肌锻炼方法,坚持康复锻炼。

(6)计划生育指导:产后6周内会阴及子宫伤口未愈合前禁止性生活。开始性生活后,指导妇女和伴侣选择合适的避孕措施。哺乳期妇女以工具避孕为主,不宜使用口服避孕药,以免影响乳汁的生成。

2. 心理状态评估　产后妇女的心理状态评估是社区护士产后护理工作的重要组成部分。由于分娩及产后阶段激素水平的急剧变化,以及异常分娩、新生儿健康状况不良等因素,部分产后妇女发生了产后心理障碍,包括产后沮丧、产后抑郁、产后精神病等。

社区护士应识别产后心理障碍的高危因素,包括异常分娩(如难产、滞产、手术产)、新生儿健康状况不良(如早产、死产、畸形儿、新生儿窒息、转入 NICU 治疗、新生儿死亡)、家庭成员对新生儿性别不满意、家庭关系不良(如夫妻关系紧张、婚姻破裂、丧失亲人、缺少家庭与社会支持、性暴力或家庭暴力)、家庭经济困难、文化水平低、家族精神病史、抑郁症病史、产后抑郁症病史等。

sexual or family violence), family financial difficulties, low literacy, family history of mental illness, history of depression or postpartum depression, etc.

Community nurses should assess maternal psychological and emotional state during home visits. If the mother is upset, easy to cry, unwilling to communicate with others, or has insomnia, fatigue, anxiety, discomfort in caring for the baby, and poor relationship with family members, the maternal psychological state should be screened. Commonly used screening tools include the Edinburgh postnatal depression scale (EPDS), the Beck depression inventory (BDI), and the postpartum depression screen scale (PDSS). If the screening results show that the maternal psychological condition is abnormal, the nurse should communicate with the family members and instruct them to visit the psychiatrist or psychologist.

v. Breastfeeding Health Care

Community nurses should provide knowledge and information about breastfeeding to women and their families as early as pregnancy. It is important to communicate with pregnant women and their families about breastfeeding. The grandmothers of newborns are often the important caregivers of the mother and the baby in China, so it is important to discuss breastfeeding with them.

1. Benefits of Breastfeeding It is critical that community nurses have a thorough understanding of breastfeeding benefits and discuss the benefits with mothers, fathers and other family members. Breastfeeding has many advantages for infants, for mothers and for families.

(1) Benefits for the Infant: a. Breast milk meets the nutritional needs of infants very well. Breast milk contains a proper amount of nutrients for infants. There are more unsaturated fatty acids. Proteins and fats are more easily digested, and carbohydrate content is appropriate for growth. Besides, the composition of breast milk changes over time to meet changing needs as

社区护士在家庭访视中应评估产妇心理和情绪状态，如果产妇存在情绪低落、易哭、不愿与人交流、失眠、疲乏、焦虑、护理新生儿时不愉快、与家庭成员关系紧张等情况，可进行产妇心理状况的筛查。常用的筛查工具包括爱丁堡产后抑郁量表（Edinburgh postnatal depression scale，EPDS）、Beck 抑郁量表（Beck depression inventory，BDI）、产后抑郁筛选量表（postpartum depression screening scale，PDSS）等。若筛查结果显示产妇心理状况异常，护士要与产妇家庭进行沟通，指导其去看精神心理医生。

（五）母乳喂养保健

社区护士在孕期便应提供给妇女及其家庭有关母乳喂养的知识和信息。与孕产妇及其家庭沟通母乳喂养问题非常重要。在中国，祖母或外祖母常常是产妇和婴儿的重要照顾者，因此，要重视和他们讨论母乳喂养事宜。

1. **母乳喂养的好处** 社区护士深刻理解并且与母亲、父亲和其他家庭成员讨论母乳喂养的好处十分重要。母乳喂养对婴儿、母亲和家庭都有诸多好处。

（1）母乳喂养对婴儿的好处：①母乳含有婴儿所需的适量营养，能很好地满足婴儿的营养需求。母乳中的不饱和脂肪酸更多，蛋白质和脂肪更容易被消化，碳水化合物的含量适合婴儿生长需要。此外，母乳的成分还会随着婴儿的生长发育需求而变化。②母乳包含抗体和免疫因子，有助于减少和降低中耳炎、肺炎、脊髓灰质炎、流感、胃肠道感染、泌尿系统感染、细菌

infants grow. b. Breast milk contains antibodies and immunologic factors that help decrease the incidence and severity of otitis media, pneumonia, poliomyelitis, influenza, gastrointestinal infections, urinary system infections, bacterial meningitis, etc. c. Breastfed baby has a lower risk for allergies including eczema, vomiting, diarrhea, diaper dermatitis, and asthma. d. Breastfeeding children are less likely to develop obesity and insulin-dependent diabetes. e. Breastfeeding provides a unique bonding experience between mother and child that is helpful in the development of a strong relationship between mother and infant.

(2) Benefits for Mothers: a. Nipple suction by baby stimulates the release of oxytocin from the pituitary, which causes uterus contraction, reducing the possibility of postpartum hemorrhage. b. Return of menses and ovulation is usually delayed in breastfeeding mothers, but it is not an effective method of contraception. c. Breastfeeding mothers have a lower risk of develop breast cancer and ovarian cancer. d. Breastfeeding may enhance postpartum women's weight loss.

(3) Benefits for the Family: a. Breastfeeding is convenient. It is always "on tap" and comes at the right temperature. b. It is in a clean container with a low risk of bacterial contamination. c. Breastfeeding is free. Breastfed infants have a lower incidence of illness and infection, health care costs are lower.

2. Breastfeeding Behavior Guidance

(1) Early, Frequent, Unlimited Breastfeeding: The World Health Organization (WHO) issued *Guidelines on Early Essential Newborn Care (EENC)* in 2013. WHO updated and issued the second edition of the guidelines in 2022. China issued the *Clinical Implementation Recommendations for Early Essential Newborn Care Technologies* in 2017. After three years of trial implementation, some content was updated, and in 2020, the *Expert Consensus on Early Essential Newborn Care Technologies in China* was issued. The above documents all clearly state

性脑膜炎等疾病的发生率和严重程度。③母乳喂养婴儿的过敏性疾病发生率更低，包括湿疹、呕吐、腹泻、尿布皮炎、哮喘等。④母乳喂养的孩子发生肥胖及胰岛素依赖型糖尿病的可能性更低。⑤母乳喂养提供了一种独特的母婴依恋体验，有助于母婴亲子依附关系建立。

（2）母乳喂养对母亲的好处：①婴儿吸吮乳头刺激了垂体催产素的释放，引起子宫收缩，可减少产后出血的风险；②母乳喂养的母亲排卵和月经的恢复会延迟，但不可以作为有效避孕的手段；③母乳喂养有助于减少乳腺癌和卵巢癌的患病风险；④母乳喂养有利于母亲产后体重减轻。

（3）母乳喂养对家庭的好处：①母乳喂养方便，总是保持合适的温度，并持续、随时供应；②母乳总是在乳房这一干净的环境中，细菌感染的风险低；③母乳喂养不需费用，母乳喂养的婴儿由于疾病和感染的患病率低，相应的健康支出也相对少。

2. 母乳喂养行为指导

（1）尽早、频繁、不限制地哺乳：2013 年 WHO 发布了《新生儿早期基本保健（Early Essential Newborn Care，EENC）指南》，2022 年 WHO 更新并发布了第二版指南。2017 年中国发布了《新生儿早期基本保健技术的临床实施建议》，3 年试行后更新了部分内容，并于 2020 年发布了《中国新生儿早期基本保健技术专家共识》。上述文件均明确指出，新生儿出生后 5 秒内用清洁、干燥的毛巾擦干新生儿，同时评估呼吸状况。若新生儿有呼吸或哭声，撤除湿毛巾，将新生儿置于母亲腹部或胸部，开始皮肤接触，至少 90 分钟，接触期间用干的衣服覆盖新生儿，

that start drying the baby within 5 seconds with a clean, dry cloth after birth and check breathing while drying the baby. If the baby is breathing normally or crying, remove the wet cloth and put the baby onto the mother's abdomen or chest and start skin-to-skin contact for at least 90 minutes. Cover the baby with a dry cloth and the head with a bonnet.

Healthy babies can crawl from the mother's abdomen to the breast. The baby may open the mouth, touch or lick the mother's breasts and nipples, and eventually latch on and start sucking. Babies who start skin-to-skin contact immediately after birth are able to breastfeed more effectively than babies who are separated from their mother. At the same time, early adequate skin-to-skin contact and sucking helped improve exclusive breastfeeding rates at 48 hours and 6 weeks after birth.

Although the production of large amounts of milk usually occurs two to three days after delivery, mothers should still breastfeed their babies early and frequently after delivery. There are many benefits: a. Sucking stimulates uterine contractions and reduces postpartum hemorrhage. b. The baby's sucking reflex is relatively strong in the early period after delivery, which is the best time to learn to suck. c. Babies can get the immune components of colostrum as early as possible. d. Stimulate the baby's intestinal peristalsis, which helps reduce jaundice. e. Early and frequent breastfeeding helps to reduce distending pain of breasts. f. Early and frequent breastfeeding can promote the early production of large amounts of milk and the increase of milk production through endocrine mechanisms and breast emptying.

(2) Implementation and Assessment of Breastfeeding: For new mothers, privacy is important. Non-private environments can interfere with breastfeeding. The nurse should assess the environment and ask the client to leave the nursing room, close the room door, or draw the bed curtain. Before breastfeeding, mothers should wash their

头部戴帽子。

健康的婴儿能够从母亲腹部爬行到乳房。他们通常会出现张嘴、吐舌头、舔舐等现象，最终含住乳头开始吸吮。出生后立即开始皮肤接触的婴儿，比出生后母婴分离的婴儿更能有效地吸吮母乳。同时，早期充分的皮肤接触和吸吮有助于提高出生后 48 小时和 6 周时的纯母乳喂养率。

尽管大量乳汁的生成通常出现在产后 2~3 天，然而，母亲产后仍应尽早、频繁地进行母乳喂养，这么做有许多好处，包括：①吸吮刺激子宫收缩，减少产后出血；②婴儿吸吮反射在产后短时间内比较强烈，是学习吸吮的最佳时机；③婴儿能尽早获得初乳中的免疫成分；④刺激婴儿肠道蠕动，有助于减轻黄疸；⑤尽早、频繁地哺乳有助于减轻乳房胀痛；⑥尽早、频繁地哺乳可通过内分泌机制和排空乳房，促进大量乳汁生成时间提前和泌乳量增加。

（2）母乳喂养的实施与评估：对新手妈妈而言，私密的环境很重要，非私密的环境会影响母乳喂养的进行。因此，护士应注意评估环境，请来访者离开哺乳房间，关上房间门，或者拉上床帘。哺乳前，母亲应洗净双手，去掉假指甲，因为假指甲容易增加致病菌滋生的机会，也可能伤及婴儿稚嫩的皮肤。

hands and remove fake nails, as they increase the chance of pathogens growing and may also damage the baby's tender skin.

Nurses can instruct the mother to adopt a comfortable position. The mother can lie down or sit up. The mother's back, waist, and arms should be supported with a pillow or blanket. There can be a variety of positions to hold the baby, such as cradle, football, side lying, laid-back, etc. The mother can use different positions. Unwrapping the baby so that the baby can touch the mother's body. The baby is attached to the mother's body, lying in the mother's arms, facing the mother. The back of the baby's head should not be compressed, and the head should be free to move so that the baby can move its head when the nose is blocked. The mother's hand can support the breast in the shape of the letter "C". Baby's nose should be at the level of the mother's nipples. When the baby's mouth is stimulated by touch, he will open the mouth wide and latch on due to the presence of the rooting reflex. The nurse may also instruct the mother to use her hand or forearm to quickly push the baby's shoulder toward the breast so that the baby can latch more effectively. The nurse should assess the infant's latching, because the most common cause of sore nipple is poor latching on. When the attachment is good, the baby's mouth open widely, lips turned outwards, and suck slowly and deeply with some pauses.

The timing and frequency of breastfeeding should be determined according to the needs of the baby. The nurse needs to instruct the mother to observe the cues of hunger, such as twisting the body, sucking the hand, etc. When a baby is hungry, he/she should be fed in time. Crying is often a late cue of hunger. When a baby cries, his/her mother should calm the baby first, and then feed him/her.

3. Nursing Care of Common Breast-feeding Problems

(1) Breast Engorgement: Milk usually "come in" at 36 to 96 hours postpartum. Breast

护士应协助母亲采取舒适的姿势,母亲可以躺着喂奶,也可以坐着喂奶,无论采取哪种姿势,都可以用枕头或毯子等支撑母亲的背部、腰部、胳膊等。抱婴儿的姿势可以有多种,如摇篮式、橄榄球式、侧卧式、半躺式等,母亲可以尝试不同的姿势。去掉婴儿的包被,以便婴儿可以与母亲身体贴合,躺在母亲的臂弯中,面向母亲。婴儿的头后部不能受压,头部要可以自由地活动,以便婴儿鼻堵塞时自行移动头部。母亲的手可以呈字母"C"形托住乳房,调整婴儿姿势,使婴儿鼻子位于母亲乳头水平。婴儿嘴部受到触碰刺激时,因觅食反射的存在,会张大嘴巴含住乳头。护士也可以指导母亲用手或前臂迅速把婴儿肩部推向乳房,以使婴儿能含住更多乳房组织。护士需评估婴儿的含接情况,评估母亲是否有疼痛。引起乳头疼痛最常见的原因是含接不良。含接良好时,婴儿的嘴巴张大、嘴唇外翻,吸吮深而慢,间或停顿。

哺乳的时间和频率应根据婴儿的需要来定。护士需指导母亲观察婴儿饥饿的表现,如扭动身体、吸吮手等,此时应及时喂奶。哭闹往往是饥饿的晚期信号,哭闹时应先安抚情绪,再喂奶。

3. 母乳喂养常见问题的护理

(1)乳房肿胀:产后36~96小时,泌乳量通常会急剧增加。当乳汁不能被有效排出时常引

engorgement occurs when milk is not drained effectively. Common causes of failure to empty milk include ineffective attachment, insufficiency feeding frequency and duration, and the addition of formula milk. The nurse should provide information for the woman, so that she is aware that her breasts may feel distending pain, sensitivity and stiffness when the breast milk "comes in" around 3 days after giving birth. Community nurses need to provide guidance during postpartum visits: a. Feeding frequently and on demands. Do not limit the time of feeding. b. Assess and correct the breast feeding position, and guide efficient latching on. c. If the frequency of feeding within 24 hours is less than 8 times, and the average feeding time is less than 20 minutes, the feeding time is not enough. Community nurses should assess the reasons and give guidance. If the mother cannot increase the number of feedings, it is feasible to pump milk by hand or pump. d. Emptying one breast completely per feed, and alternating which breast is offered first. e. Expressing a small amount of breast milk to soften the areola before a feed may help the baby to attach. f. Cold compress can be given between two feedings to reduce swelling, and hot compress can be given before feeding to stimulate lactation. g. A well-fitted supportive bra may give extra comfort.

(2) Nipple Pain and Rhagades: Nipple pain and rhagades are common and the most significant factors affecting breastfeeding in the early postpartum period. Nipple pain is a major cause of early weaning. Nipple pain usually occurs in the first week postpartum and peaks at 3–7 days postpartum. Most nipple pain is caused by mechanical injuries, and the pain is often accompanied by changes in nipple shapes, such as the nipple becomes wedged, pointed, and even cracked. The most common cause of mechanical injury is poor latching on. The nipple is squeezed and rubbed between the hard palate and the tongue, causing pain and injury. Therefore, community nurses should assess mothers' posture and infants'

起乳房肿胀。常见引起乳汁不能有效排空的原因包括无效含接、喂养频率不足、限制喂奶时长、添加配方奶等。护士应为产妇提供有关乳房肿胀的信息，以便让产妇意识到产后3天左右下奶时可能会出现乳房胀痛、敏感、变硬等。社区护士在产后访视时需给予指导：①按需、频繁哺乳，不要限定喂奶时间。②评估并纠正哺乳姿势，指导有效含接。③如果24小时内喂奶次数小于8次，平均喂奶时间不足20分钟，则喂奶时间不够，社区护士需评估原因，给予指导；如果母亲不能增加喂奶次数，可行手挤奶或吸奶器吸奶。④喂奶时将一个乳房完全排空，两侧交替喂养。⑤喂奶前，挤出少量的母乳软化乳晕，可以帮助婴儿吮吸。⑥两次喂奶之间可给予冷敷，减轻肿胀，喂奶前可给予热敷，刺激泌乳。⑦一件合身的支撑胸罩可能会增加舒适度。

（2）乳头疼痛和皲裂：乳头疼痛和皲裂是产后早期常见的问题，是影响母乳喂养最重要的因素，也是早期断奶的主要原因。乳头疼痛在产后第1周出现，通常在3~7天达到高峰。大多数乳头疼痛是由机械性损伤造成的，疼痛常常伴随着乳头形状的改变，如乳头变为楔形、变尖，甚至出现裂伤等。造成机械性损伤最常见的原因是含接不良，乳头在硬腭和舌头之间受到挤压和摩擦，造成疼痛和损伤。因此，社区护士需注意评估、调整哺乳姿势，指导有效含接。如果调整后乳头疼痛未能缓解，可以帮助母亲挤奶或用吸奶器吸奶，用小杯喂养。如果乳头有裂伤，可以用温水清洗，挤出乳汁涂在乳头。有研究显示，纯羊毛脂可以建立湿润的屏障，有助于伤口愈合。因证据不足，应避免使用凝胶、

latching. If nipple pain fails to relieve after adjustment, the mother can express milk by hand or pump. Baby can be fed with a small cup. If the nipple is lacerated, it can be cleaned with warm water, and the milk can be applied to the nipple. Studies have shown that pure lanolin can create a moist barrier and help trauma healing. Due to lack of evidence, avoid using gels, cooking oils, tea bags, etc.

(3) Mastitis: Mastitis is a common problem associated with breastfeeding. It usually occurs during the first few weeks after birth. Risk factors for mastitis include breast engorgement and milk stasis, fatigue and pressure, nipple pain and trauma, plugged ducts, excessive milk production, and infrequent feeding. Early mastitis is often manifested as local breast pain, swelling, and heat, often accompanied by fever, shivering, headache, fatigue and other systemic symptoms. Nurses can instruct mothers to take bed rest, continue breastfeeding, have wet hot compress, take analgesics such as acetaminophen and ibuprofen as prescribed, and take antibiotics such as penicillin or cephalosporins as prescribed. About 5%–10% of mastitis develops into breast abscess. It usually needs drainage and antibiotic treatment depending on its size and severity. Nurses or lactation consultants should provide scientific information for mothers with mastitis. Proper and timely management is significant for disease relief. At the same time, nurses or lactation consultants can discuss the risk factors with the mother to reduce recurrence.

食用油、茶包等。

（3）乳腺炎：乳腺炎常见于产后最初几周，是常见的母乳喂养相关问题。乳腺炎的危险因素包括乳房肿胀和乳汁淤积、疲劳与压力、乳头疼痛和损伤、乳导管堵塞，泌乳量过多、喂奶次数减少等。乳腺炎早期常表现为乳房局部痛、肿、热，常伴随发热、寒战、头痛、乏力等全身症状。护士应指导产妇卧床休息，继续母乳喂养，湿热敷，遵医嘱服用解热镇痛抗炎药，如对乙酰氨基酚、布洛芬等，遵医嘱服用抗生素，如青霉素或头孢菌素等。有 5%~10% 的乳腺炎患者会发展为乳房脓肿，根据大小及严重程度进行引流，并使用抗生素治疗。护士或泌乳顾问应关爱乳腺炎母亲，为其提供科学的信息，告知她们经过恰当及时的处理，病情会缓解。与此同时，可以与母亲一起分析引起乳腺炎的危险因素，减少复发。

BOX 6-1　Learning More

Ten Steps to Successful Breastfeeding(2018)

WHO and UNICEF issued the Ten Steps to Successful Breastfeeding in 1991. There is substantial evidence that implementing the Ten Steps significantly impacts early initiation of breastfeeding immediately after birth, improves

BOX 6-1　知识拓展

促进成功母乳喂养的十项措施(2018)

世界卫生组织和联合国儿童基金会于1991年发布了"促进成功母乳喂养的十项措施"。有大量证据表明，实施"十项措施"显著影响了出生后即刻母乳喂养的早期实施，提高了纯母乳喂养率和母乳喂养的总持续时间。2018 年，

exclusive breastfeeding rates and total duration of breastfeeding. In 2018, WHO revised the Ten Steps. WHO has called upon all facilities providing maternity and newborn services worldwide to implement the Ten Steps. They include:

1a. Comply fully with the *International Code of Marketing of Breast-milk Substitutes* and relevant World Health Assembly resolutions.

1b. Have a written infant feeding policy that is routinely communicated to staff and parents.

1c. Establish ongoing monitoring and data-management systems.

2. Ensure that staff have sufficient knowledge, competence and skills to support breastfeeding.

3. Discuss the importance and management of breastfeeding with pregnant women and their families.

4. Facilitate immediate and uninterrupted skin-to-skin contact and support mothers to initiate breastfeeding as soon as possible after birth.

5. Support mothers to initiate and maintain breastfeeding and manage common difficulties.

6. Do not provide breastfed newborns any food or fluids other than breast milk, unless medically indicated.

7. Enable mothers and their infants to remain together and practise rooming-in 24 hours a day.

8. Support mothers to recognize and respond to their infants' cues for feeding.

9. Counsel mothers on the use and risks of feeding bottles, teats and pacifiers.

10. Coordinate discharge so that parents and their infants have timely access to ongoing support and care.

IV. Perimenopausal Health Care

Menopause is a permanent absence of menstruation caused by the cessation of ovarian function. Perimenopause is the period of time surrounding a woman's menopause. Due to the decline in ovarian function, women will experience a series of physical and psychological symptoms caused by fluctuations or decreases

WHO 修订了"十项措施"。世界卫生组织呼吁世界各地提供孕产妇和新生儿服务的所有机构实施"十项措施",以促进全民覆盖并确保长期可持续性。具体包括:

1a. 完全遵守《国际母乳代用品销售守则》和世界卫生大会相关决议。

1b. 制定书面的婴儿喂养政策,并定期与员工及家长沟通。

1c. 建立持续的监控和数据管理系统。

2. 确保工作人员有足够的知识、能力和技能以支持母乳喂养。

3. 与孕妇及其家属讨论母乳喂养的重要性和实现方法。

4. 分娩后即刻实施不间断的肌肤接触,帮助母亲尽快开始母乳喂养。

5. 支持母亲早开奶、维持母乳喂养以及应对母乳喂养常见的困难。

6. 除非有医学指征,否则不要给母乳喂养的新生儿提供母乳以外的任何食物或液体。

7. 让母婴共处,实行24小时母婴同室。

8. 帮助母亲识别和回应婴儿需要喂奶的迹象。

9. 就奶瓶、人工奶嘴和安抚奶嘴的使用和风险向母亲提供咨询。

10. 协调出院,以便父母及其婴儿能够及时获得持续的支持和照护。

四、围绝经期保健

绝经是卵巢功能停止所致的永久性无月经状态。围绝经期是围绕妇女绝经前后的一段时间。由于卵巢功能的下降,女性在绝经前后会出现性激素波动或减少所致的一系列躯体及精神心理症状。绝经相关的症状及健康问题有月经紊乱、血管舒缩症状、自主神经功能失调症状、精神心理症状、骨质疏松、泌尿生殖道萎缩

in sex hormones before and after menopause. Symptoms and health problems associated with menopause include menstrual disorders, vasomotor symptoms, autonomic nervous dysfunction symptoms, psychological symptoms, osteoporosis, urogenital tract atrophy symptoms, cardiovascular system symptoms, etc. These symptoms and health problems plague perimenopausal women and reduce their quality of life. Good perimenopausal health care and health management can help relieve symptoms and improve quality of life. It is also the important basis for health in old age.

i. Menstrual Disorders and Health Care

Abnormal menstruation is the most common symptom during perimenopause period. Menstrual changes during perimenopause period are varied and can be manifested as changes in the menstrual cycle or menstrual volume. It is commonly believed that premenopausal menstrual changes are not completely orderly, but the most common pattern of menstrual change is from regular to irregular and then menopause.

In addition to the decline of ovarian function, the incidence of perimenopausal organic diseases of the reproductive organs (such as uterine myoma, adenomyosis, endometrial polyps, endometrial carcinoma, etc.) is also an important factor leading to abnormal bleeding. Metabolic changes resulting in weight gain, hyperlipidemia, and work and family related stress are all risk factors for menstrual abnormalities.

Community nurses should provide information and instruct women to observe menstrual abnormalities. When menorrhagia and irregular uterine bleeding occur, women must seek medical treatment in time to reduce secondary injuries. It is necessary to detect and correct anemia in time to prevent and avoid endometrial cancer.

ii. Vasomotor Symptoms and Health Care

The main manifestation of vasomotor symptoms is the repeated and brief redness, fever,

症状、心血管系统症状等。上述症状及健康问题给围绝经期妇女带来困扰，降低了她们的生活质量。良好的围绝经期保健与健康管理有助于改善症状，提升生活质量，也是老年期健康的重要基础。

（一）月经紊乱及保健

月经异常是围绝经期最常见的症状。围绝经期的月经变化多种多样，可以表现为月经周期的变化，也可有月经量的变化。普遍的观点认为，绝经前的月经变化并非完全有序，但最常见的是从规律到不规律然后绝经的月经变化模式。

除了卵巢功能衰退以外，围绝经期生殖器官器质性疾病（如子宫肌瘤、子宫腺肌病、子宫内膜息肉、子宫内膜癌等）发病率增加，也是导致异常出血的重要因素。代谢改变引起体重增加，高脂血症，工作、家庭压力大，都是月经异常的危险因素。

社区护士应为妇女提供相关信息，指导妇女观察月经异常情况，特别是当出现月经过多、不规则子宫出血时，一定要及时就诊，减少身体继发性伤害，及时发现并纠正贫血，预防和避免子宫内膜癌变。

（二）血管舒缩症状及保健

血管舒缩症状主要表现为反复出现短暂的面部、颈部及胸部皮肤发红、发热、继之出汗。

and subsequent sweating of the skin on the face, neck, and chest. It usually lasts for 1–3 minutes, with mild cases occurring several times a day and severe cases occurring more than ten times or more. It is more common at night or in a state of stress.

There are differences in the incidence and severity of vasomotor symptoms in women in different countries and regions. The incidence of vasomotor symptoms in European, American and African countries is higher, while the incidence in Asian countries is lower. The incidence of vasomotor symptoms in perimenopausal women in China is about 20%.

The pathogenesis of vasomotor symptoms is not fully understood. Current research shows that estrogen fluctuations and decrease are the basis for tidal fever. Perimenopausal sex hormone fluctuations cause neurotransmitter secretion and dysfunction, resulting in dysfunctions of the hypothalamus thermotaxic center, narrowing the range of set-point of body temperature in the thermoregulatory region, so that it is very sensitive to slight changes in central body temperature. Slightly increased body temperature can cause tidal fever, vasodilatation, sweating and other symptoms. In addition, high body mass index, smoking, and lack of exercise are risk factors of tidal fever and sweating symptoms.

A good lifestyle is an effective way to relieve vasomotor related tidal fevers. Community nurses should instruct women to quit smoking and eat a balanced diet. Regular exercise and aerobic exercise help to stabilize the thermotaxic center, promote the stability of peripheral vascular vasoconstriction and vasodilatation function, and coordinate skeletal muscle. Regular exercise is an effective way to relieve mild to moderate tidal fevers. Community nurses can also guide women to keep the living environment ventilated, cool, and promote comfort. Menopause hormone therapy is the most effective way to relieve tidal fevers and sweating. Nurses can direct women with obvious

通常持续 1~3 分钟，轻者每日发作数次，重者十几次或更多。夜间或应激状态时更多见。

不同国家和地区女性血管舒缩症状的发生率和严重程度存在差异，欧美和非洲国家的发生率较高，亚洲国家女性的发生率较低，中国围绝经期女性血管舒缩症状的发生率为 20% 左右。

血管舒缩症状的发病机制尚不完全清楚。目前研究显示，雌激素波动下降是发生潮热的基础。围绝经期性激素波动使神经递质分泌及功能失调，引起下丘脑的体温调节中枢功能失调，体温调节区的体温调定点范围变窄，以至于对中心体温的轻微变化非常敏感，略升高的体温便可引起潮热、血管扩张、出汗等症状。此外，体重指数大、吸烟、缺乏运动等也是潮热、出汗症状的危险因素。

良好的生活方式是缓解血管舒缩相关潮热的有效方法。社区护士应指导妇女戒烟，均衡饮食。规律锻炼和有氧运动，有助于稳定体温调节中枢，促进外周血管收缩、舒张功能稳定，协调骨骼肌，是缓解轻中度潮热的有效方法。社区护士还可以指导妇女保持居住环境空气流通、凉爽，提升舒适度。性激素治疗是缓解潮热出汗的最有效方法，可以指导症状明显的妇女寻求专业的妇科内分泌治疗。

symptoms to seek gynecological endocrine treatment.

iii. Neuropsychiatric Symptoms and Health Care

Neuropsychiatric symptoms are common in perimenopausal and postmenopausal women. The common psychological symptoms include emotional agitation, anxiety, depression and so on. Symptoms of autonomic nervous dysfunction include palpitations, sleep disorders, and skin paresthesia, etc.

1. Perimenopausal Depression

Depression is a common psychological symptom during perimenopause period. The incidence of perimenopausal depression varies in different countries and regions, ranging from 8% to 47%. Surveys in different regions of China show that the incidence of depression in perimenopausal women is about 20%–30%, and the incidence of co-occurrence of anxiety and depression is approximately 10%.

Factors related to perimenopausal depression include decreased estrogen levels, insufficient social support, dissatisfaction with marital status, dissatisfaction with work, negative life events of family members, women's own views on menopause, personality type, etc.

Community nurses should strengthen community health education, help community and family members understand menopause and related symptoms. Nurses should encourage family members, especially husbands, to support perimenopausal women. Women are encouraged to develop their own hobbies, express and talk to trusted social network members, and improve self emotional control abilities. In addition, avoiding overwork, learning to relieve the stress, and balancing work and rest can all help alleviate depression.

2. Perimenopausal Sleep Disorders

The common manifestations of perimenopausal sleep disorders include difficulty falling asleep, frequent waking at night, early waking in the

（三）神经精神症状及保健

围绝经期及绝经后妇女常出现神经精神症状。常见的精神心理症状有情绪激动、焦虑不安、抑郁等；自主神经功能紊乱症状包括心悸、睡眠障碍、皮肤感觉异常等。

1. 围绝经期抑郁　抑郁是围绝经期常见的精神心理症状。不同国家和地区报道的围绝经期抑郁发生率数据不同，为 8%~47%。中国不同地区的调查显示，围绝经期妇女抑郁的发生率为 20%~30%，焦虑和抑郁并存的发生率约为 10%。

围绝经期抑郁发生的相关因素包括雌激素水平下降、社会支持不足、对婚姻状况不满意、对工作不满意、家庭成员负性生活事件、自己对绝经的看法、人格类型等。

社区护士要加强社区健康教育，帮助社区及家庭成员正确认识绝经和相关症状，鼓励家庭成员特别是丈夫关心和支持围绝经期妇女。鼓励妇女发展自身的兴趣爱好，向信任的社会网络成员表达和倾诉，提高情绪控制能力。此外，避免过度劳累、学会给自己减压、劳逸结合均有助于缓解抑郁。

2. 围绝经期睡眠障碍　围绝经期睡眠障碍的常见表现包括入睡困难、夜间频繁觉醒、晨间早醒、醒后无法再入睡等。长期睡眠障碍会导致妇女身心健康受损，慢性疾病加重。

morning, and the inability to fall back asleep after waking up. Long-term sleep disorders can lead to impaired physical and mental health of women and aggravate the severity of chronic diseases.

Due to the differences in evaluation criteria and survey methods, the incidence data of sleep disorders in different countries and regions are quite different. Studies have shown that there are differences in the incidence of sleep disorders among women of different races.

Factors associated with sleep disorders include decreased estrogen levels, vasomotor symptoms, anxiety, depression, muscle pain, bone and joint pain, and genetic factors.

Community nurses should assess the timing and characteristics of sleep disorders and explore the relationship between that and perimenopause. If there is a sleep disorder before perimenopause with no recent aggravation, it is a general sleep disorder. If it does not occur until after perimenopause, it is a perimenopausal sleep disorder, and menopause hormone therapy may be considered. No matter what kind of sleep disorder, women should be guided to make lifestyle adjustments, such as reducing animal fat intake, not eating too full or too late at dinner, controlling the nap time within half an hour to 1 hour, and avoiding excessive excitement before going to bed. Regular aerobic exercise helps to promote sleep. Acupuncture and moxibustion, massage, foot bath and other traditional Chinese medicine methods helpful for sleep can also be recommended. Community nurses should also provide information on sedative-hypnotics, for patients with severe sleep disorders. It can be used short-term. Women should try to choose less dependent drugs, generally used for 1–2 weeks.

iv. Osteoporosis and Health Care

Osteoporosis is a systemic metabolic disease characterized by decreased bone mass, changes in microstructure, decreased bone strength, increased bone fragility, and easy to fracture.

According to relevant data, about 20% of

由于评价标准、调查方法等存在差异，不同国家和地区睡眠障碍的发生率数据存在较大差异。研究显示，不同种族的妇女睡眠障碍发生率存在差异。

睡眠障碍的相关因素包括雌激素水平下降、血管舒缩症状、焦虑、抑郁、肌肉疼痛、骨关节疼痛、遗传因素等。

社区护士应评估睡眠障碍的发生时间和特点，分析睡眠障碍与围绝经期的关系。如果在围绝经期之前已存在睡眠障碍，近期无加重，则属于一般睡眠障碍；如果在围绝经期后才出现，则属于围绝经期睡眠障碍，可考虑激素补充治疗。无论属于哪种睡眠障碍，护士均可指导妇女进行生活方式调整，如减少动物脂肪摄入、晚餐不宜吃得过饱过晚、午睡时间控制在半小时至 1 小时之内、睡前避免过度兴奋等。规律的有氧运动有利于促进睡眠。也可尝试使用针灸、按摩、足浴等中医药助睡眠的方法。对于睡眠障碍较严重的患者，社区护士还应提供有关镇静催眠类药物的信息，患者可以短期、适量使用，尽量选择依赖性小的药物，一般使用1~2 周。

（四）骨质疏松及保健
骨质疏松是以骨量减少、微结构改变、骨强度降低、骨脆性增加、易骨折等为特征的全身代谢性疾病。

根据有关资料显示，50 岁以上的亚洲妇女

Asian women over the age of 50 suffer from osteoporosis, and 52% suffer from decreased bone density. About 55% of Chinese women over the age of 50 suffer from osteoporosis or decreased bone density.

Decreased estrogen after menopause can accelerate osteopenia and osteoporosis. Within 5 years after menopause, estrogen decreases the fastest and osteopenia occurs the most. In addition, the occurrence of osteoporosis is also associated with race, aging, low body weight, smoking, excessive alcohol consumption, excessive intake of coffee and carbonated drinks, insufficient intake of calcium and vitamin D, and suffering from diseases affecting bone metabolism or intake of drugs that affect bone metabolism.

Community nurses should provide information related to osteoporosis, including the causes, risk factors, clinical manifestations, and hazards of osteoporosis. Nurses can guide postmenopausal women to regularly monitor bone density and receive appropriate treatment, including bone resorption inhibiting drugs such as bisphosphonates, menopause hormone therapy, and bone formation promoting drugs such as parathyroid hormone. In addition, regardless of whether osteoporosis has occurred, some basic measures should be taken in postmenopausal female health care to prevent osteoporosis or as a supplement to osteoporosis medication treatment. These basic health measures include maintaining a healthy lifestyle, eating a balanced diet rich in calcium and moderate protein. Except calcium in the diet, 500mg of elemental calcium and 400IU of vitamin D can be added daily. Women should actively engage in aerobic exercise, especially outdoor physical exercise, quit smoking and avoid alcohol.

v. Other Symptoms and Health Care

In addition to the main aspects mentioned above, due to the decrease in estrogen, perimenopausal and postmenopausal women may experience symptoms of urinary and reproductive

中约 20% 患有骨质疏松，52% 患有骨密度下降。我国 50 岁以上妇女中约 55% 患有骨质疏松或骨密度下降。

绝经后雌激素减少会加速骨量减少和骨质疏松的发生。绝经后 5 年内，雌激素下降最快，骨量减少最多。此外，骨质疏松的发生还与人种、衰老、低体重、吸烟、过度饮酒、过多咖啡和碳酸饮料摄入、钙和维生素 D 摄入不足、患有影响骨代谢的疾病或摄入影响骨代谢的药物等有关。

社区护士要提供骨质疏松相关的信息，包括骨质疏松的发病原因、危险因素、临床表现及危害，指导绝经后妇女进行骨密度监测，根据骨密度情况，及时进行恰当的治疗，包括抑制骨吸收药物治疗（如双膦酸盐类药物治疗、激素补充治疗）、促进骨形成药物治疗（如甲状旁腺激素）等。此外，无论是否发生了骨质疏松，绝经后妇女保健均应采取一些基础措施来预防骨质疏松或作为骨质疏松药物治疗的补充。这些基础保健措施包括：保持健康的生活方式；摄入富含钙和适量蛋白质的均衡饮食；除了饮食中的钙，每日可补充元素钙 500mg，维生素 D400IU；积极进行有氧运动，特别是户外体育锻炼；戒烟、避免嗜酒。

（五）其他症状及保健

除上述主要方面，围绝经期及绝经后妇女还可能出现泌尿生殖道萎缩症状、心血管系统症状等。出现盆底功能障碍症状的妇女应及时就医，评估功能障碍的程度，并进行恰当的盆底

tract atrophy. Women who experience symptoms of pelvic floor dysfunction should seek medical help promptly. They should receive professional assessment and appropriate pelvic floor rehabilitation treatment. Women with urinary tract infections should seek medical attention promptly. The symptoms of the cardiovascular system during perimenopause are mostly caused by dysfunction of the cardiovascular nervous and endocrine systems, and are usually not organic lesions. Estrogen supplementation therapy can be used according to medical advice.

(Hou Xiaoni)

康复治疗。泌尿系统感染的妇女应及时就医。围绝经期心血管系统的症状多为心血管神经和内分泌系统功能失调导致，并非器质性病变，可遵医嘱使用雌激素补充治疗。

（侯小妮）

Key Points

1. Adolescence is a period of transition from childhood to adulthood. Dysmenorrhea, menstrual disorders, and unwanted pregnancies are common health issues for adolescent women. Community nurses should strengthen reproductive health education for adolescent women, provide knowledge about dysmenorrhea and menstrual disorders, and strengthen support for adolescent women.

2. Perimarital health care is of great significance to the health of both spouses and their offspring. The Perimarital health care mainly includes premarital medical examination, premarital health consultation, and premarital health guidance.

3. Prepregnancy health guidance is an important part of perinatal health care. The main contents include: planned pregnancy, balanced nutrition and exercise, control of weight gain, supplementation of folic acid, and detailed assessment of pregnant women with genetic, chronic, and infectious diseases, avoiding harmful factors, relieving mental stress, etc.

4. The main contents of pregnancy health care guidance include: nutrition guidance, weight management guidance, exercise guidance, symptom management guidance, avoiding harmful factors, maintaining a happy mood, etc. Pay

内容摘要

1. 青春期是从儿童期向成年期过渡的一段时期。痛经、月经紊乱、非意愿妊娠等是常见的青春期女性健康问题。社区护士应加强对青少年女性的生殖健康教育，提供月经紊乱和痛经的相关保健知识，加强对青少年女性的支持。

2. 围婚期保健对夫妻双方及子代健康具有重要意义，主要内容包括婚前医学检查、婚前卫生咨询和婚前卫生指导等。

3. 孕前健康指导是围生期保健的重要内容，主要内容包括：有计划地妊娠，合理营养和运动，控制体重增加，补充叶酸，详细评估有遗传病、慢性疾病和传染病的备孕妇女，避免有害因素，解除精神压力等。

4. 妊娠保健指导的主要内容包括：营养指导、体重管理指导、运动指导、症状管理指导、避免有害因素、保持心情愉快等。注意区分妊娠早、中、晚期健康指导内容的异同。

attention to distinguishing the similarities and differences in the above health guidance content for early, middle, and late pregnancy.

5. The main contents of health care during delivery are "five preventions and one strengthening".

6. The main contents of puerperium health care include two aspects: daily life guidance and psychological state assessment. Community nurses should attach importance to assessing the psychological status of postpartum women, and nurses can use tools to screen for postpartum depression.

7. The main contents of breastfeeding health care include providing information on the benefits of breastfeeding, helping women establish early, frequent and unrestricted breastfeeding practices, guidance and assessment of breastfeeding behavior, providing information on the causes and care of common breastfeeding problems (breast engorgement, nipple pain and rhagades, mastitis) and providing care for them.

8. Due to the decline of ovarian function, women may experience a series of physical and psychological symptoms caused by fluctuations or decreases in sex hormones before and after menopause. The symptoms include menstrual disorders, vasomotor symptoms, autonomic nervous system dysfunction symptoms, psychological symptoms, osteoporosis, urogenital tract atrophy symptoms, cardiovascular system symptoms, etc., which cause distress to women and affect their quality of life. Nurses can guide women to take corresponding non-pharmacological and pharmacological measures to alleviate the symptoms, improve quality of life, and lay a good foundation for elderly health.

5. 分娩期保健的主要内容为"五防、一加强"。

6. 产褥期保健的主要内容包括日常生活指导和心理状态评估两方面。社区护士要重视对产妇心理状态的评估,可采用工具进行产后抑郁的筛查。

7. 母乳喂养保健的主要内容包括:母乳喂养优点的宣传,尽早、频繁、不限制母乳喂养理念的建立,哺乳行为的指导与评估,提供有关常用母乳喂养问题(乳房肿胀、乳头疼痛和皲裂、乳腺炎)原因与护理的信息并为产妇提供护理。

8. 由于卵巢功能的下降,女性在绝经前后会出现性激素波动或减少所致的一系列躯体及精神心理症状,包括月经紊乱、血管舒缩症状、自主神经功能失调症状、精神心理症状、骨质疏松、泌尿生殖道萎缩症状、心血管系统症状等,给妇女带来困扰,影响其生活质量。护士可指导妇女采取相应的非药物和药物措施缓解症状,提升生活质量,为老年期健康打下良好基础。

Exercises

(Questions 1 to 2 share the same question stem)

A 30-year-old primiparous woman, 3 days

思 考 题

(1~2题共用题干)

初产妇,30岁,产后3天,自述双侧乳房疼

postpartum, reported unbearable pain in both breasts. After assessment by the nurse, it was found that the mother had diffuse swelling in both breasts, shiny skin, hard breasts like stones, and cracks and clots on both nipples. The mother complained of pain and discomfort, and was unwilling to breastfeed the newborn again.

1. What breastfeeding related issues is the mother currently experiencing?

2. What nursing interventions should be taken?

(Questions 3 to 4 share the same question stem)

Ms. Li, 16 years old, sought medical attention for "vaginal bleeding for 10 days". During the past 6 months, the patient's menstrual cycle has been irregular, with a cycle of 15–40 days and a duration of 3–12 days. She had her first menstruation at the age of 13, with a previous menstrual cycle of around 35 days and a duration of 3–5 days.

3. Please assess whether the current menstrual condition of the woman is normal.

4. What nursing interventions should be taken?

(Questions 5 to 6 share the same question stem)

A primipara, 36 years old, 1 week postpartum. A community nurse found that the woman rarely engaged in activities and rarely went to the ground except for using the toilet. It was summer and the indoor temperature where the mother lived was high with poor ventilation. The family prepared a variety of nourishing foods for the mother, including pork rib soup, pig trotter soup, lamb, etc., with a large amount of meat for each meal. The mother was 160cm tall and weighed 75kg.

5. What are the main nursing diagnoses of this primipara?

6. What health guidance should nurses provide to this postpartum women and family members?

痛难忍。护士评估后发现,产妇双侧乳房弥漫性肿胀,皮肤发亮,乳房硬如石块,双侧乳头有裂纹和血痂。产妇因疼痛难受,不愿再哺乳新生儿。

1. 该产妇目前出现了哪些母乳喂养相关问题?

2. 应采取哪些护理措施?

(3~4题共用题干)

李女士,16岁,因"阴道出血10天"就诊。近6个月以来患者月经不规则,月经周期15~40天,经期3~12天。13岁月经初潮,既往月经周期为35天左右,经期为3~5天。

3. 评估该女性目前的月经情况是否正常。

4. 应采取哪些护理措施?

(5~6题共用题干)

初产妇,36岁,产后1周。社区护士发现,产妇较少下地活动,除如厕外基本不下地。时值夏日,产妇居住的房间室内温度较高,通风不良。家人为产妇准备了丰富的滋补食物,包括排骨汤、猪蹄汤、羊肉等,基本每顿都有较多肉类。产妇身高160cm,体重75kg。

5. 该产妇主要的护理诊断有哪些?

6. 护士应为该产妇及家庭成员提供哪些保健指导?

Chapter 7

Community Health Care for the Elderly

第七章

社区老年人群保健

07章 数字内容

Learning Objectives

Knowledge Objectives

1. Summarize the main content of the elderly health assessment.
2. Accurately describe the community elderly health management service content and service process.
3. Described of common physical health problems among the elderly in the community.
4. Described of common mental health problems among the elderly in the community.

学习目标

知识目标

1. 概述老年人健康评估的主要内容。

2. 准确描述社区老年人健康管理服务内容和服务流程。

3. 叙述社区老年人常见身体健康问题。

4. 叙述社区老年人常见心理健康问题。

Ability Objectives

1. Propose preventive and nursing measures for common physical health problems of the elderly.

2. Propose preventive and nursing measures for common mental health problems of the elderly.

3. Analyze the advantages and problems of different community pension models.

Quality Objectives

1. Enhance the spirit of scientific research and provide targeted health guidance for the elderly with syndrome.

2. Cultivate love, patience, and responsibility, and provide psychological support for the elderly.

能力目标

1. 能针对老年人的常见身体健康问题，提出预防及护理措施。

2. 能针对老年人的常见心理健康问题，提出预防及护理措施。

3. 分析不同社区养老模式的优势及存在的问题。

素质目标

1. 提升科学钻研精神，为老年综合征人群提供针对性的健康指导。

2. 培养爱心、耐心、责任心，为老年人提供心理支持。

Mr. Zhang, 78 years old. He has one son and one daughter, both living out of town. His wife died three months ago. At present, Mr. Zhang lives alone. Mr. Zhang suffers from hypertension and osteoporosis. Left limb movement is limited, right limb movement is okay. He can sit up on his own and can travel with crutches. Due to memory loss, he sometimes forgets to take antihypertensive drugs, calcium, etc. When he went to the bathroom two days ago, he accidentally slipped and fell, diagnosed as soft tissue contusion.

Queations：

1. What are the risk factors for falls for Mr. Zhang?

2. How to prevent Mr. Zhang from falling?

With the continuous development of economy and medical technology, as well as the improvement of people's living standards, life expectancy is increasing, the global population aging problem is becoming more and more prominent. Population aging is a common problem facing human society, which brings community both opportunities and challenges. The community is the main place for the implementation of

社区居民张先生，78 岁。育有 1 儿、1 女，均在外地。老伴 3 个月前去世。目前，张先生一个人居住。张先生患有高血压和骨质疏松症，左侧肢体活动受限，右侧肢体活动尚可，可以自行坐起，能够借助拐杖出行。由于记忆力下降，他有时会忘记服用抗高血压药、钙剂等。两天前他去卫生间时，不小心滑倒，诊断为软组织挫伤。

请思考：

1. 张先生存在哪些跌倒危险因素？

2. 如何预防张先生发生跌倒？

随着经济和医疗技术的持续发展，以及人们生活水平的提高，人均预期寿命日益延长，全球人口老龄化问题越来越突出。人口老龄化是人类社会共同面临的问题，给社区带来了机遇与挑战。社区是对老年人实施预防、保健、医疗、康复和健康教育的主要场所。做好老年人的社区健康管理，为老年人提供医疗保健服务，有利于进一步提高老年人的生活质量。

prevention, health care, medical treatment, rehabilitation and health education for the elderly. Improving community health management for the elderly and providing them with health care services is conducive to further improving their quality of life.

Section 1   Overview

I. Introduction of the Elderly

i. The Elderly

People aged 65 and above in developed countries or 60 and above in developing countries are called elderly people. WHO classified elderly people at different stages：60–74 years old are young elderly people, 75–89 years old are old elderly people, and 90-year-olds are long-lived elderly people.

ii. Population Aging

When the proportion of people aged 60 and over in a country or region exceeds 10% of the total population, or when the proportion of people aged 65 and over exceeds 7% of the total population, it is called population aging. When the population of a society reaches the standard of aging, the society is called an aging society.

iii. Coefficient of Aged Population

The coefficient of aged population refers to the proportion of the elderly population to the total population. The coefficient is an indicator of whether and to what extent the population of a society is aging. The larger the coefficient of aged population in a country or region, the deeper the degree of aging.

II. Standards for Healthy Older Adults in China

In 2022, *The Standard for Healthy Chinese Older Adults* issued by the National Health

第一节　概　　述

一、老年人群概况

（一）老年人

发达国家 65 岁及以上者，或发展中国家 60 岁及以上者，称为老年人。WHO 对不同阶段老年人做了划分：60~74 岁为年轻老年人，75~89 岁为老老年人，90 岁及以上为长寿老年人。

（二）人口老龄化

当一个国家或地区 60 岁及以上人口占总人口比重超过 10%，或 65 岁及以上人口占总人口比重超过 7%，称为人口老龄化。社会人口达到老龄化的标准，这个社会称为老龄化社会。

（三）老年人口系数

老年人口系数是指老年人口占总人口的比例。老年人口系数是判断社会人口是否老龄化和老龄化程度的指标。一个国家或地区的老年人口系数越大，老龄化程度越深。

二、中国健康老年人标准

2022 年，国家卫生健康委发布的《中国健康老年人标准》指出，"健康老年人"指 60 岁及以

Commission of the PRC pointed out that "healthy older adults" refers to the elderly who are 60 years old or above and are able to take care of themselves or basically take care of themselves. The physical, psychological and social aspects tend to be coordinated and harmonious with each other. The nine criteria for the "healthy older adults" are as follows:

(1) Living independently or taking care of oneself basically.

(2) Aging changes of vital organs do not cause obvious dysfunction.

(3) The risk factors affecting health shall be controlled within the range appropriate to the age.

(4) Good nutritional status.

(5) The cognitive function is basically normal.

(6) Optimistic and positive, and self-satisfied.

(7) Have a certain health literacy, maintain a good lifestyle.

(8) Active participation in family and social activities.

(9) Good social adaptability.

Section 2　Health Assessment and Health Management for the Elderly in the Community

I. Health Assessment for the Elderly

Health assessment for the elderly covers a wide range of topics, including general medical assessment, physical function assessment, mental and psychological assessment, social assessment, quality of life assessment, and environmental assessment. Comprehensive health assessment for the elderly can completely reflect the health status, and is an important basis for the implementation of health management.

上生活自理或基本自理的老年人，躯体、心理、社会三方面都趋于相互协调与和谐状态。"健康老年人"的9个标准，如下：

（1）生活自理或基本自理。

（2）重要脏器的增龄性改变未导致明显的功能异常。

（3）影响健康的危险因素控制在与其年龄相适应的范围内。

（4）营养状况良好。

（5）认知功能基本正常。

（6）乐观积极，自我满意。

（7）具有一定的健康素养，保持良好生活方式。

（8）积极参与家庭和社会活动。

（9）社会适应能力良好。

第二节　社区老年人健康评估与健康管理

一、老年人健康评估

老年人的健康评估内容比较广泛，主要包括一般医学评估、躯体功能评估、精神心理评估、社会评估、生活质量评估、环境评估等。对老年人进行综合健康评估，可以全面反映其健康状况，是实施健康管理的重要基础。

i. General Medical Assessment

It is a disease-centered approach to diagnosis and treatment. The purpose of the assessment is to determine what system or organ the patient is suffering from and the severity of the disease, and the method of assessment is through the process of taking a medical history, physical examination, medical imaging, laboratory tests and other special tests, and finally arriving at diagnoses.

ii. Physical Function Assessment

It includes activity of daily living (ADL) assessment, balance and gait assessment, range of motion assessment, nutritional status assessment, hearing and vision assessment, and the most commonly used assessment tool is the ADL assessment. ADL can be divided into basic activities of daily living (BADL) and instrumental activities of daily living (IADL):

1. BADL refer to the activities repeatedly performed every day to maintain the most basic survival and living needs of the human body, including two activities of self-care and functional mobility. Among them, self-care activities include eating, bathing, dressing, toileting and communication. Functional mobility activities include bed activity, sitting, standing, walking, and transferring.

2. IADL refer to the activities due to daily life that are necessary for people to maintain an independent life. They are advanced skills that people need to live independently and often need to use a variety of tools to complete, including household activities and outdoor activities. The household activities include cooking, cleaning, organizing clothes, telephone, medication, financial management, etc. Outdoor activities include shopping, socializing, transportation, and handling other personal affairs.

The common tool for evaluating BADL was the Barthel index, and the common tool for evaluating IADL was the functional activity questionnaire.

（一）一般医学评估

一般医学评估是一种以疾病为中心的诊疗方式，评估的目的在于确定患者患有什么系统或什么脏器的疾病以及疾病的严重程度，评估方法是采集病史、体格检查、医学影像学检查、实验室检查和其他特殊检查，最后得出诊断。

（二）躯体功能评估

包括日常生活活动能力（ADL）评估、平衡与步态评估、关节活动度评估、营养状况评估、听力和视力评估等，最常用的评估工具是日常生活活动能力评估。日常生活活动可分为基础性日常生活活动（BADL）和工具性日常生活活动（IADL）两种：

1. 基础性日常生活活动是指维持人体最基本的生存和生活需要的每日反复进行的活动，包括自理和功能性移动两种活动。其中自理活动包括进食、洗澡、穿衣、如厕、交流；功能性移动活动包括床上活动、坐、站、行走、转移。

2. 工具性日常生活活动是指人维持独立生活所必须进行的与日常生活相关联的活动，是人们独立生活所需的高级技能，常需要使用各种工具才能完成，包括家务活动和外出活动两种。其中家务活动包括做饭、打扫卫生、整理衣服、打电话、服药、管理财务等；外出活动包括购物、社交、交通、处理其他个人事务等。

评定基础性日常生活活动的常用工具为Barthel指数，评定工具性日常生活活动的常用工具为功能活动问卷。

iii. Mental and Psychological Assessment

It is mainly to evaluate the cognitive function and emotional state of the elderly. Commonly used assessment tools for cognitive function include Montreal cognitive assessment, mini-mental state screening scale, and clock-drawing test. In the assessment of cognitive impairment and delirium, the assessment of cognitive function is a very important and very effective method. The assessment of emotional state mainly includes anxiety and depression, etc.

iv. Social Assessment

Social assessment is an assessment for the elderly of the social adaptation, social support or relationships, use of social services, economic situation, special needs, roles and cultural background. Community medical staff should play an important role in social assessment and pay attention to the personal values, spiritual sustenance and religious beliefs of the elderly.

v. Environmental Assessment

Environmental assessment is an assessment of the physical, social, spiritual, and cultural environment in which the elderly live. In the assessment of physical environment, the home safety assessment of the elderly is the most important, which is of great significance to preventing the occurrence of falls and other accidents of the elderly.

vi. Quality of Life Assessment

The quality of life assessment is a comprehensive assessment of the quality of life of the elderly, and is of great significance for measuring the happiness of the elderly. There are many quality of life rating scales in the world, and the commonly used ones are the MOS item short from health survey (SF-36) and the World Health Organization quality of life (WHOQOL).

（三）精神心理评估

主要是对老年人的认知功能和情绪状态等的评估。认知功能的常用评估工具包括蒙特利尔认知评估量表、简易智能状态筛查量表、画钟试验等。在认知障碍和谵妄的评估中，进行认知功能评估是一种非常重要且十分有效的方法。情绪状态的评估主要包括焦虑、抑郁评估等。

（四）社会评估

社会评估是对老年人的社会适应能力、社会支持或社会关系、社会服务的利用、经济状况、特殊需求、角色和文化背景等方面的评估。在社会评估中，社区医护人员应发挥重要的作用，重视老年人的个人价值观、精神寄托和宗教信仰等。

（五）环境评估

环境评估是对老年人生活的物理环境、社会环境、精神环境和文化环境等的评估。在对物理环境的评估中，老年人的居家安全评估是最主要的，对预防老年人跌倒和其他意外事件的发生具有重要意义。

（六）生活质量评估

生活质量评估是对老年人生活质量的综合评估，对衡量老年人的幸福度具有重要意义。国际上有许多生活质量评定量表，常用的生活质量评定量表有健康调查简表（SF-36）、世界卫生组织生存质量测定量表（WHOQOL）等。

II. Health Management Services for the Elderly

i. The Content of Health Management Services for the Elderly

Health management services, including lifestyle and health status assessment, physical examination, auxiliary examination and health guidance, are provided to the elderly aged 65 and above once a year by community health centers.

1. **Lifestyle and Health Status Assessment**　The basic health conditions, physical exercise, diet, smoking, drinking, common symptoms of chronic diseases, previous diseases, treatments, current medication and self-care ability in daily life of the elderly are understood through inquiry and self-assessment of health status of the elderly.

2. **Physical Examination**　It includes routine physical examinations such as body temperature, pulse, respiration, blood pressure, height, weight, waist circumference, skin, superficial lymph nodes, lungs, heart, and abdomen, and makes a rough judgment on oral cavity, vision, hearing, and motor function.

3. **Auxiliary Examination**　It includes blood routine test, urine routine test, liver function (serum glutamic-oxaloacetic transaminase, serum alanine aminotransferase and total bilirubin), renal function (serum creatinine and blood urea nitrogen), fasting blood glucose, plasma lipids (total cholesterol, triglyceride, LDL cholesterol, HDL cholesterol), electrocardiogram, and ultrasound examination of the abdomen (liver, gallbladder, pancreas and spleen).

4. **Health Guidance**　Inform the assessment results and the corresponding health guidance.

(1) Chronic disease health management should be carried out simultaneously for patients diagnosed with confirmed essential hypertension

二、老年人健康管理服务

（一）老年人健康管理服务内容

社区卫生服务中心每年为 65 岁及以上老年人提供 1 次健康管理服务，包括生活方式和健康状况评估、体格检查、辅助检查和健康指导。

1. **生活方式和健康状况评估**　通过问诊及老年人健康状态自评了解其基本健康状况、体育锻炼、饮食、吸烟、饮酒、慢性疾病常见症状、既往所患疾病、治疗及目前用药和生活自理能力等情况。

2. **体格检查**　包括体温、脉搏、呼吸、血压、身高、体重、腰围、皮肤、浅表淋巴结、肺部、心脏、腹部等常规体格检查，以及对口腔、视力、听力和运动功能等进行的粗测判断。

3. **辅助检查**　包括血常规、尿常规、肝功能（血清谷草转氨酶、血清谷丙转氨酶和总胆红素）、肾功能（血清肌酐和血尿素氮）、空腹血糖、血脂（总胆固醇、甘油三酯、低密度脂蛋白胆固醇、高密度脂蛋白胆固醇）、心电图和腹部 B 超（肝、胆、胰、脾）检查。

4. **健康指导**　告知评估结果并进行相应健康指导。

（1）对已确诊原发性高血压和 2 型糖尿病等的患者同时开展相应的慢性病健康管理。

and type 2 diabetes.

(2) For the elderly with other diseases (excluding hypertension or diabetes), timely treatment or referral should be provided.

(3) Elderly persons found to have abnormalities are advised to undergo regular reviews or are referred to higher-level medical institutions.

(4) Provide health guidance such as healthy lifestyle, vaccination, osteoporosis prevention, fall prevention measures, accidental injury prevention and self-help, cognition and emotion, etc.

(5) Inform or reserve the time for the next health management service.

ii. The Requirement of Health Management Services for the Elderly

1. Rural hospitals and community health centers that carry out health management services for the elderly should have the basic equipment and conditions required for the content of the services.

2. Strengthen contact with village (neighborhood) committees, local police stations, and other relevant departments to grasp changes in information on the elderly population under their jurisdiction. Strengthening publicity to inform about the services so that more elderly people are willing to receive them.

3. Timely record relevant information into health records after each health examination. For details, please refer to the health and physical examination form in the *Service Specifications for Management of Residents' Health Records*. For the elderly who have been included in the corresponding chronic disease health management, this health management service can be used as a follow-up service.

4. Actively applying traditional Chinese medicine methods to provide health guidance to the elderly on health care and disease prevention and treatment.

iii. The Process of Health Management Services for the Elderly

The health management of the community's elderly population should be based on health

（2）对患有其他疾病（非高血压或糖尿病）的老年人，应及时治疗或转诊。

（3）对发现有异常的老年人建议定期复查或向上级医疗机构转诊。

（4）进行健康生活方式、疫苗接种、骨质疏松预防、防跌倒措施、意外伤害预防和自救、认知和情感等方面的健康指导。

（5）告知或预约下一次健康管理服务的时间。

（二）老年人健康管理服务要求

1. 开展老年人健康管理服务的乡镇卫生院和社区卫生服务中心应当具备服务内容所需的基本设备和条件。

2. 加强与村（居）委会、派出所等相关部门的联系，掌握辖区内老年人口信息变化。加强宣传，告知服务内容，使更多的老年人愿意接受服务。

3. 每次健康检查后及时将相关信息记入健康档案。具体内容详见《居民健康档案管理服务规范》中的健康体检表。对于已纳入相应慢性病健康管理的老年人，一次健康管理服务可作为一次随访服务。

4. 积极应用中医药方法为老年人提供养生保健、疾病防治等健康指导。

（三）老年人健康管理服务流程

社区老年人群健康管理应在健康评估的基础上，按照健康状况进行归类管理，针对当前威

assessment, categorized according to health status, and prioritized for intervention and management of important factors that currently threaten health, as shown in the specific flowchart 7-1.

胁健康的重要因素优先干预及管理，具体见流程图 7-1。

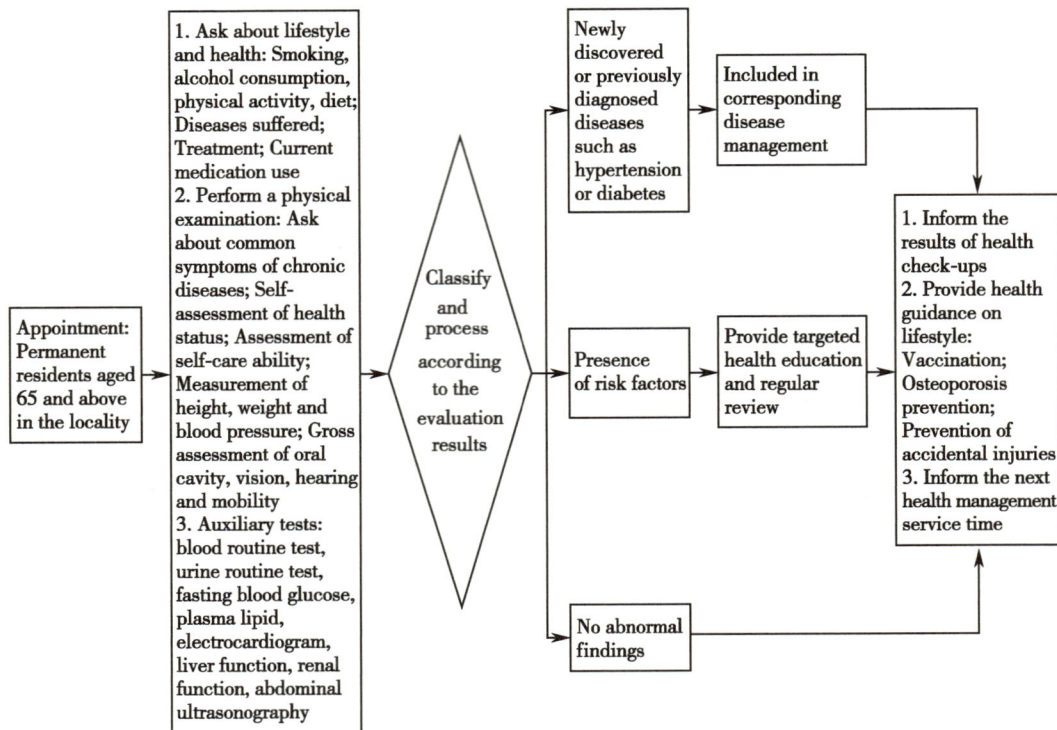

Figure 7-1 Service process

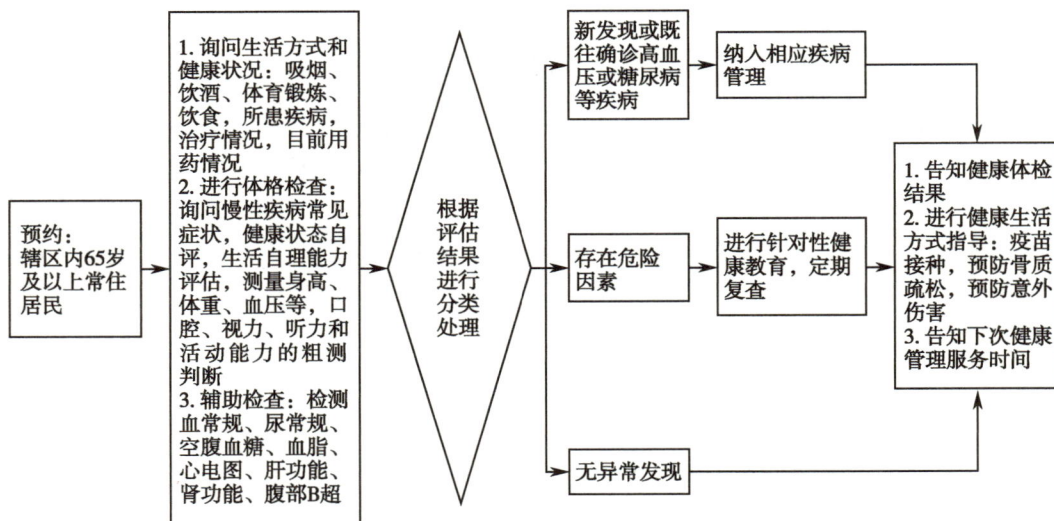

图 7-1 服务流程

community health service systems, and in 2019, the implementation manual for people-centered assessment and care pathways based on primary health care systems was further supplemented. The integrated care for older people (ICOPE) is an evidence-based service model network that guides community health care providers to take the elderly as the center, monitor the intrinsic capacity of the elderly through comprehensive assessment, set nursing goals, formulate nursing plans, take intervention measures to prevent and slow down the decline of the intrinsic capacity of the elderly, and provide support for caregivers. The core point of this model is that different service providers such as medical institutions, social care agencies, family caregivers, etc., need to share the same comprehensive assessment and care plan for older people, adopt common care and treatment goals, and cooperate to provide care for older people in a coordinated manner.

初级保健系统以人为中心的评估和照护路径实施手册。老年人整合照护模式（ICOPE）具体是以证据为基础，指导社区医疗服务人员以老年人为中心，通过综合评估监测老年人的内在能力，设定护理目标，制订护理计划，采取干预措施预防和减缓老年人内在能力的下降，同时为照顾者提供支持的一种服务模式网。该模式的核心要点在于不同的服务提供方如医疗机构、社会照护机构、家庭照护者等需要共享同一份老年人的综合评估和照护计划，采纳共同的照护和治疗目标，相互合作，以一种协调的方式为老年人提供照护。

Section 3　Common Physical Health Problems and Care for the Elderly in the Community

第三节　社区老年人常见身体健康问题及护理

I. Frailty

Frailty refers to a non-specific state in which the steady-state network system composed of multiple systems (the nervous system, the metabolic - endocrine system, and immune system, etc.) characterized by sarcopenia in the elderly leads to a decrease in physiological reserve, a decrease in anti-strike ability, and a decrease in recovery ability after stress. It is the most clinically significant geriatric syndrome. Frailty is an early reversible process. Preventing reversible factors, early identification and active intervention can delay the development of frailty and disability in healthy and pre-frailty elderly people.

一、衰弱

衰弱是指老年人以肌少症为基本特征的由全身多系统（神经、代谢内分泌及免疫等）构成的稳态网体系受损，导致生理储备下降、抗打击能力减退及应激后恢复能力下降的非特异性状态，是最具临床意义的老年综合征。衰弱是一个早期可逆的过程，预防可逆性因素、早期识别和积极干预可以延缓健康、衰弱前期老年人走向衰弱和失能状态。

i. Assessment of Frailty

Currently, there is no unified gold standard for the evaluation of frailty. The Fried diagnostic criteria for frailty, the FRAIL scale, and the Tilburg frailty assessment scale are often used in clinical assessment and research.

1. The Fried Diagnostic Criteria for Frailty　It is also known as the Fried frailty phenotype. Frailty is defined when three or more of the following five criteria are met: a. Unexplained weight loss. b. Fatigue. c. Loss of grip strength. d. Loss of walking speed. e. Reduction in physical activity. People with one or two of these conditions are considered to be in the pre-frailty stage, while those without any of the above five conditions are considered to be able-bodied elderly people without frailty.

2. FRAIL Scale　The International Association of Nutrition and Aging proposed that the FRAIL scale also includes five items: a. Fatigue. b. Sense of resistance: difficulty in climbing the next stair. c. Decline of free activity: the patient could not walk a disatance of one block. d. Coexistence of multiple diseases: ≥5. e. Body weight loss: body weight loss >5.0% within one year. Frailty is judged in the same way as Fried's.

3. Tilburg Frailty Assessment Scale (TFAS)　This scale is a self-assessment scale that measures the physical and mental conditions of the elderly in three dimensions: Physical frailty includes 8 entries on physical health, and natural weight loss, difficulty in walking, balance, hearing problems, vision problems, grip strength, and fatigue; psychological frailty includes 4 entries on memory, depression, anxiety, and coping ability; Social frailty includes 3 entries on living alone, social relationships, and social support. The scale consists of 15 entries and a score ranging from 0 to 15 points, with higher scores indicating a greater degree of frailty.

ii. Prevention and Care of Frailty

Early identification of older people in the pre-frail stage and effective intervention can prevent

（一）衰弱的评估

目前衰弱的评估缺少统一的金标准，在临床评估和研究中通常采用 Fried 衰弱诊断标准、FRAIL 量表、Tilburg 衰弱评估量表等。

1. Fried 衰弱诊断标准　也称 Fried 衰弱表型，满足以下 5 条中 3 条或以上则评定为衰弱：①不明原因体重下降；②疲乏；③握力下降；④行走速度下降；⑤躯体活动降低（体力活动下降）。满足 1 条或 2 条为衰弱前期，而无以上 5 条的人群为无衰弱的健壮老年人。

2. FRAIL 量表　国际老年营养学会提出 FRAIL 量表，该量表包括 5 项：①疲劳感；②阻力感：上一层楼梯即感困难；③自由活动下降：不能行走 1 个街区；④多种疾病共存：≥ 5 个；⑤体重减轻：1 年内体重下降 > 5.0%。判断衰弱的方法与 Fried 标准相同。

3. Tilburg 衰弱评估量表（TFAS）　该量表是一个自我评估量表，从身体、心理、社会 3 个维度测评老年人的身心状况。其中生理衰弱维度包括身体健康、自然的体重下降、行走困难、平衡、听力问题、视力问题、握力、疲劳感 8 个条目；心理衰弱维度包括记忆力、抑郁、焦虑、应对能力 4 个条目；社会衰弱维度包括独居、社会关系、社会支持 3 个条目。量表共计 15 个条目，分值范围为 0~15 分，得分越高代表其衰弱程度越重。

（二）衰弱的预防与护理

尽早识别衰弱前期老年人并进行有效干预，可以预防或延缓不良结局发生。运动锻炼是预

or delay adverse outcomes. Exercise is the most effective intervention to prevent and delay frailty. Other interventions such as nutritional support, multimorbidity and polypharmacy management, and social support, can be combined with exercise interventions to develop a comprehensive intervention program.

1. Exercise Exercise is considered to be the preferred scheme for the prevention and treatment of frailty at present. It can improve physical function, improve the ability of the elderly to take care of themselves, quality of life, mental health, and resistance to injuries and falls, and can effectively prevent the occurrence of frailty. A multi-component exercise program that combines resistance, strength, and balance training is recommended, such as a combination of aerobic exercise, stretch or flexibility exercise, balance training, and resistance training, in accordance with the principles of personalization, staging, and gradual increase. Traditional Chinese fitness activities also offer unique advantages, our national traditional fitness movement has a long history, and a wide range, including taijiquan, wuqinxi, baduanjin, etc., has a positive effect on maintaining body function, and it is recommended that the elderly practice that for a long time.

2. Individualized Nutrition Intervention Nutrition plays a crucial role in the onset and development of frailty. Nutrition-related risk factors for frailty include poor dietary habits, excessive alcohol consumption, and dietary nutrient deficiencies. Nutritional recommendations for frail older persons include adjusting dietary structure, supplementing protein, using appropriate nutritional supplements and correcting poor eating habits.

(1) Protein Supplementation: Protein supplementation can effectively ensure positive nitrogen balance and effectively promote muscle

防和延缓衰弱最有效的干预措施。其他干预方式如营养支持、多病共存和多重用药管理、社会支持等，可以与运动干预结合开展，形成综合性的干预方案。

1. 运动锻炼 运动锻炼被认为是目前预防和治疗衰弱的首选方案，可以改善躯体功能，提高老年人生活自理能力、生活质量、心理健康以及对受伤和跌倒等事件的抵抗力，可以有效预防衰弱的发生。推荐实施将抗阻、力量及平衡训练联合的多组分运动计划，如将有氧运动、伸展或柔韧性运动、平衡训练、抗阻训练等相结合，并遵循个性化、分期和逐步增加的原则。还可以采用传统健身方式，我国民族传统健身运动有着悠久的历史，种类繁多，包括太极拳、五禽戏、八段锦等，均对维持身体机能有积极的作用，建议老年人群长期练习。

2. 个性化的营养干预 营养在衰弱的发生和发展中起着至关重要的作用。与营养相关的衰弱危险因素包括不良的饮食习惯、过量饮酒、膳食营养素缺乏等。针对衰弱老年人的营养建议包括调整膳食结构、补充蛋白质、增加营养补充剂、纠正不良的饮食习惯等。

（1）补充蛋白质：补充蛋白质可以有效地确保正氮平衡，并且有效促进肌肉合成，最大限度地提高衰弱老年人肌肉蛋白质合成效率。建

synthesis, maximizing muscle protein synthesis in the frail elderly. It is recommended that the total protein intake of the elderly be increased to 1.2–1.5g/(kg·d), with high quality protein (common foods include fish, lean meat, milk, eggs, beans, and legumes) accounting for more than 50%.

(2) Micronutrient Supplementation: It mainly includes long-chain fatty acids, vitamin D, and other multivitamins. Fatty acids can effectively improve frailty through antioxidant and anti-inflammatory effects；vitamin D supplementation can effectively improve the activity of the elderly to reduce the risk of fracture, and it is recommended to supplement 700–1,000IU of vitamin D every day. The elderly are encouraged to stay in the sun for 15–20min once a day to help vitamin D production and calcium absorption.

(3) Adjustment of Diet Structure: The effect of a diet pattern rich in a variety of nutrients on the improvement of frailty was better than that of a single nutrient intake, which was beneficial to the recovery of body function and had a positive effect in delaying the decline of cognitive function. For example, the Mediterranean diet structure can delay the process of frailty.

3. Management of Multimorbidity and Polypharmacy

(1) Multimorbidity is a potential risk factor for frailty. It is necessary to pay attention to the continuity of health status and quality of life in chronic disease management for the elderly, give full play to the comprehensive coordination role of community health centers, and make full use of the "Internet + chronic disease" management platform to carry out the continuous management such as education, treatment, and follow-up for the elderly with chronic disease. Outpatient physicians can use the Beers criteria and the STOPP/START criteria for potentially inappropriate prescriptions for the elderly for medication assessment, and regularly review commonly used medications to avoid increasing the risk of drug interactions.

议老年人总蛋白摄入量增加到 1.2~1.5g/（kg·d），要求优质蛋白（常见食物有：鱼、瘦肉、牛奶、蛋类、豆类及豆制品）占 50% 以上。

（2）补充微量营养素：主要包括长链脂肪酸、维生素 D 及其他复合维生素。脂肪酸可以通过抗氧化和抗炎症作用来有效地改善衰弱；补充维生素 D 可以有效改善老年人活动能力以降低骨折发生风险，建议每天补充维生素 D 700~1 000IU。此外，鼓励老年人多晒太阳，每日前臂暴露太阳光 15~20 分钟，促进维生素 D 生成和钙的吸收。

（3）调整饮食结构：富含多种营养元素的饮食模式对衰弱的改善效果优于摄入单一营养元素，并且有利于机体功能恢复，延缓认知功能衰退，例如，地中海饮食结构可以延缓衰弱的进程。

3. 多病共存和多重用药的管理

（1）多病共存是衰弱的潜在危险因素。在老年人慢性病管理中需要关注连续性的健康状况与生活质量，充分发挥以社区卫生服务中心为主的综合协调作用，充分利用"互联网 + 慢性病"管理平台，对慢性病患者进行宣教、治疗、随访等连续性管理。门诊医师可使用老年人潜在不恰当处方 Beers 标准和 STOPP/START 标准进行药物评估，定期检查常用药物，避免增加药物相互作用风险。

(2) Follow the principle of polypharmacy, combine drugs in a "small but precise" way, reduce the use of over-the-counter drugs, avoid prescription waterfalls, pay attention to individualized dosage, use drugs with multiple indications, and improve drug compliance.

4. Improve the level of Social Support Good social support is an important measure for preventing the occurrence and development of frailty in the elderly, and social support includes objective support and subjective support. Objective support generally refers to direct material and economic assistance, as well as stable marriages and children's concerns; subjective support refers to the degree of emotional satisfaction of the elderly in terms of respect, understanding, and support. Social support also includes older persons' use of social support and the extent to which they make use of the support and assistance of others.

II. Fall

Fall refers to a sudden, involuntary, unintentional change in body position that causes any part of the body (excluding the feet) to fall to the ground or a lower plane than the initial position. Falls are a common adverse event in older adults. Falls and related injuries are a serious impediment to healthy ageing, while imposing a heavy economic burden on families, society, and the state.

i. Assessment of Fall

Prospective identification of fall risk factors in older adults is a prerequisite for the effective implementation of fall prevention and intervention measures, so the selection of fall risk assessment tools is extremely important. Depending on the purpose of the assessment, fall risk assessment can be classified into the following four categories: comprehensive assessment, physical function assessment, psychological assessment, and environmental assessment.

1. Comprehensive Assessment Comprehensive assessment is often used for rapid

（2）遵循多重用药的原则，联合用药应"少而精"，减少非处方药的使用，避免处方瀑布，注意剂量个体化，使用一药多用的药物，提高药物依从性。

4. 提高社会支持水平 良好社会支持是预防老年人衰弱发生和发展的重要措施。社会支持包括客观支持和主观支持。客观支持泛指物质上、经济上的直接援助以及稳定的婚姻、子女的关心等；主观支持指老年人受尊重、被理解和支持，在情感上的满意程度。社会支持还包括老年人对社会支持利用的情况，以及利用他人支持和帮助的程度。

二、跌倒

跌倒是指突发的、不自主的、非故意的导致身体任何部位（不包括双脚）的体位改变，倒在地面或比初始位置更低的平面上。跌倒是老年人常见不良事件。跌倒及相关伤害严重阻碍健康老龄化进程，同时给家庭、社会和国家带来沉重的经济负担。

（一）跌倒的评估

前瞻性识别老年人跌倒风险因素是有效实施跌倒预防和干预措施的前提，因此，选择跌倒风险评估工具极为重要。根据不同的评估目的，跌倒风险评估可分为以下4类：综合评估、躯体功能评估、心理评估及环境评估。

1. 综合评估 综合评估常用于跌倒风险的快速筛查，通过评估生物学、行为、环境及经济

screening of fall risk to quickly determine the fall risk of the elderly through assessment of biological, behavioral, environmental, economic, and social risk factors. Common comprehensive fall risk assessment tools include Morse fall risk assessment scale, Thomas fall risk assessment tool, and fall risk assessment scale for the elderly.

2. Psychological Assessment   Fall risk assessment should cover psychological problems related to falls, with fear of falling as the dominant factor. At present, there are two main assessment methods for fear of falling. One is through a single-item question for assessment："Are you afraid/worried about falling?", the other is measured by using scales. The commonly used scales include the international version of the fall efficacy scale, the image version of the fall efficacy scale, and the specific activity balance confidence scale, all of which showed good psychometric characteristics in the elderly.

3. Assessment of Body Function   Fall is closely related to the body function of the elderly. Muscle strength, gait and balance function are important aspects of body function, and their testing is an important part of fall risk assessment. The muscle strength test mainly includes upper limb muscle strength and lower limb muscle strength test. The upper limb muscle strength is represented by the grip strength, which can be measured with a grip strength meter. Lower extremity strength can be assessed by the 5-times sit-to-stand tests. Gait and balance functions are measured using the timed standing-up walk test, the Berg balance scale, and the Tinetti gait and balance scale.

4. Environmental Assessment   Falls occur as a result of a combination of internal and external risk factors, with the environment being the main external factor. It has been reported that 30% to 50% of falls are caused by environmental factors, and environmental factors such as slippery and uneven surfaces, obstacles, stairs, and uneven lighting increase the risk of falls in older persons.

社会危险因素，对老年人跌倒风险进行快速判定。常用的跌倒风险综合评估工具包括 Morse 跌倒风险评估量表、托马斯跌倒风险评估工具及老年人跌倒风险评估量表等。

2. 心理评估   跌倒风险评估应涵盖跌倒相关心理问题，以跌倒恐惧为主。目前跌倒恐惧的评估主要有两种方法：一种是通过单条目问题，即"您害怕／担心跌倒吗？"评估；另一种是通过量表测量，常用量表有国际版跌倒效能量表、图像版跌倒效能量表、特异性活动平衡信心量表，均在老年人群中表现出良好的心理测量特性。

3. 躯体功能评估   跌倒与老年人躯体功能状况密切相关。肌力、步态和平衡功能是躯体功能的重要方面，其测试是跌倒风险评估的重要组成部分。肌力测试主要包括上肢肌力测试和下肢肌力测试两方面内容，上肢肌力以握力为代表，可使用握力器测量；下肢肌力可通过 5 次起坐测试评估。步态和平衡功能可通过计时起立步行测验、Berg 平衡量表、Tinetti 步态和平衡量表测量。

4. 环境评估   跌倒的发生是内、外风险因素共同作用的结果，环境是主要的外在因素。据报道，30%~50% 的跌倒由环境因素导致，湿滑、不平坦的路面和障碍物、楼梯、照明不均等环境因素会增加老年人跌倒风险。常采用居家危险因素评价工具（HFHA）对老年人居住内外环境中的地面、照明、卫生间等 9 个方面进行评估。

The home fall hazards assessment (HFHA) is often used to assess nine aspects of flooring, lighting toilet, etc., in the internal and external environments of older people's homes.

ii. Prevention and Care of Fall

The prevention of falls in the elderly is mainly targeted at risk factors, with the intervention objectives of improving function, increasing awareness, and reducing risk. It can be achieved through disease and medication management, health education, exercise training, and environmental transformation.

1. **Health Education**　Health education is an essential component of fall interventions. Health education for medical staff and older people can reduce the incidence of falls and can be used to change older people's perception of falls and reduce the risk of falls through lectures, videos, pamphlets, and group common problem-solving. With the development of information technology, health education based on smart devices is increasing, and the research on the form of health education mediated by information technology means such as APP is gradually becoming a hot spot. In the process of health education, not only the danger of falls should be emphasized, but also the preventability of falls should be pointed out. At the same time, according to the preferences of the elderly, we should choose appropriate educational methods to help the elderly to establish good exercise habits, so as to reduce the risk of falls in the elderly.

2. **Disease and Medication Management** There is a positive linear relationship between the number of diseases and drugs and the risk of falling in the elderly. Diseases and complications such as arthritis, postural hypotension, hypoglycemia, and diabetic peripheral neuropathy can increase the risk of falling. The type, number of drugs and medication compliance are all related to the occurrence of falls. High-risk drug factors for falls include benzodiazepine sedative-hypnotics, digitalis and loop diuretics, and

（二）跌倒的预防与护理

老年人跌倒的预防主要针对风险因素开展，以改善功能、增强意识和降低风险为干预目标，可通过疾病及用药管理、健康教育、运动训练和环境改造实现。

1. **健康教育**　健康教育是跌倒干预的基本组成部分，针对医护人员和老年人的健康教育可减少跌倒发生。可通过讲座、视频、宣传手册、小组共同解决问题等方法，改变老年人对跌倒的认知，降低跌倒风险。随着信息技术的发展，基于智能设备的健康教育越来越多，对以 APP 等信息化手段为媒介的健康教育形式的研究逐渐成为热点。在健康教育的过程中，不仅应强调跌倒的危害性，还应指出跌倒的可预防性，同时根据老年人喜好，选择适宜的教育方式，帮助老年人建立良好的锻炼习惯，从而降低老年人跌倒风险。

2. **用药管理**　老年人患病及用药数量与跌倒风险呈正向线性关系。疾病及其并发症，如关节炎、体位性低血压、低血糖及糖尿病周围神经病变等均可增加跌倒风险。药物种类、数量及用药依从性均与跌倒发生有关，跌倒高风险药物相关因素包括苯二氮䓬类镇静催眠药物，洋地黄类药物，袢利尿剂类药物，多重用药等。观察老年人是否有眩晕、困倦，若眩晕发生频繁，应去医院调整药物。对老年人用药方案进行调整，并加强宣教和用药指导。帮助老年人总结和归类日常服用的药物，最好制成随身携

polypharmacy. Observe whether there are vertigo and drowsiness. If vertigo occurs frequently, go to the hospital to adjust the medication. Adjust medication plans for the elderly, and strengthen education and medication guidance. Help the elderly summarize and classify the medications they take on a daily basis, it is best to prepare cards for them to carry around so that medical staff can identify the medication situation in time.

3. Exercise　The fall prevention training mainly includes strength training, balance and gait training, flexibility training, endurance training, comprehensive training, etc. The amount of exercise should be appropriate. If the elderly feel tired, they could use crutches, walkers, and other aids. Appropriate and effective exercise plans should be made according to the specific situation of the elderly.

4. Environmental Transformation Environmental transformation includes both indoor and outdoor environments, with the following main considerations: a. Floors should be non-slip, water should be removed in a timely manner, uneven floor coverings should be removed, and non-slip mats and non-slip strips should be used reasonably; b. Obstacles to the main access routes should be removed, and unstable furniture should be secured; c. Lighting should be even and should not be too dark or overly glaring, and night-lights should be installed; d. Cabinets, beds, chairs, and toilet bowls should be at the appropriate heights; e. Installation of handrails in shower stalls, toilets, and stairwells should be carried out; f. Avoid installing door thresholds or steps indoors, and there should be conspicuous markings when necessary.

5. Management after Falling

(1) Immediately assess the circumstances of the fall and immediately moved the elderly to a safe environment.

(2) Observe the condition after the fall: a. Observe the relevant signs after the fall. If the

带的卡片，便于医护人员能够及时明确其服药情况。

3. 运动锻炼　预防跌倒的运动训练方式主要包括力量训练、平衡和步态训练、灵活性训练、耐力训练、综合性训练等。锻炼的量要适宜，若老年人感觉走路很疲劳，可以使用拐杖、助行器等辅助器具。应根据老年人具体情况制订合适、有效的锻炼计划。

4. 环境改造　环境改造包括对室内环境和室外环境的改造，主要从以下方面考虑：①地面应防滑，及时清除积水，去除不平整的地板覆盖物，合理使用防滑垫和防滑条；②移除主要通道的障碍物，固定不稳定的家具；③照明均匀，不宜过暗或过于炫目，配备夜灯；④使用高度适宜的柜子、床、椅子、马桶；⑤淋浴间、卫生间、楼梯间安装扶手；⑥避免安装门槛或在室内设置台阶，必要时应有醒目标识。

5. 发生跌倒后的处理

（1）立即评估跌倒环境，并立即转移老年人到安全环境。

（2）观察跌倒后状况：①观察跌倒后的表现。如老年人意识不清，立即拨打急救电话；若

elderly person is unconscious, call the emergency phone number immediately; If there is trauma or bleeding, stop bleeding and bandage immediately; if there is vomiting, tilt the head to one side and clean up the vomit in the mouth and nasal cavity to keep the airway open; if there are convulsions, move the elderly person to a flat and soft ground or cushion the body with soft objects underneath, to prevent injuries, and to prevent tongue bites if necessary; For sudden respiratory and cardiac arrest, immediately implement cardiopulmonary resuscitation on the spot. b. Observe for headache, dizziness, palpitations, chest pain, shortness of breath, unfavorable speech, weakness of arms and legs, etc. If necessary, send them to the hospital immediately and inform the health care personnel. c. Observe whether the elderly person can stand up independently or with support after a fall.

(3) The elderly who suffer from falls should be accompanied by their family members to hospitals for diagnosis and treatment, to find out the risk factors for falls, to assess the risk of falls, and to formulate measures and programs for the prevention of falls.

III. Osteoporosis

Osteoporosis is a systemic bone disease characterized by osteopenia, damage to the microstructure of bone tissue, increased bone fragility and susceptibility to fracture. Osteoporosis is a bone disease associated with aging, with a higher prevalence with age, and is most common in postmenopausal women and older men.

i. Assessment of Osteoporosis

As the simplest and easiest means of assessment, scale screening can be used for initial screening to understand the bone health status of people with no obvious clinical symptoms, poor mobility and limited mobility, as well as for those who are to be screened by community health centers and those who are unwilling to cooperate with Bone Mineral Density BMD testing. However, the results of the initial screening cannot be used

出现外伤、出血，应立即包扎、止血；若有呕吐，将老年人的头偏向一侧，并清理其口、鼻腔呕吐物，保持呼吸道通畅；若有抽搐，将其移至平整软地或在其身体下垫软物，防止损伤，必要时防止其舌咬伤；对呼吸和心搏骤停者，立即就地实施心肺复苏。②观察有无头痛、头晕、心悸、胸痛、呼吸急迫、言语不利、手脚无力等，必要时立即送医院，并告知医护人员。③观察老年人跌倒后是否能独立或扶助站起。

（3）老年人发生跌倒均应在家属陪同下到医院诊治，查找跌倒危险因素，评估跌倒风险，制订预防跌倒措施及方案。

三、骨质疏松症

骨质疏松症是一种以骨量减少、骨组织微结构损坏、骨脆性增加、易发生骨折为特征的全身性骨病。骨质疏松症与增龄相关，随着年龄增长其发病率增高，多见于绝经后女性和老年男性。

（一）骨质疏松症的评估

量表筛查是最简单易行的评估手段。对于没有明显临床症状、活动能力差、行动不便的人群，以及社区卫生服务中心拟进行大规模普查的人群和不愿配合进行骨密度检测的老年人群，可以采用量表评估的方法进行初筛，了解他们的骨质健康状况。但是，量表筛查的结果不能用于诊断，量表筛出的疑似骨质疏松症的老年人可进行下一步的评估。目前国际上通用的量表包括以下两种：

for diagnosis, and those suspected of having osteoporosis by the scale can be evaluated in the next step. At present, the international general scales include the following two:

1. International Osteoporosis Foundation (IOF) Osteoporosis Risk One-minute Test　The test consists of 19 questions, which only require subjects to judge yes or no, simple, fast, and easy to understand. As long as one of the questions is answered 'yes', it suggests that there is a risk of osteoporosis, which needs to be prevented through lifestyle changes, and it is recommended to go to the hospital for further examination.

2. Osteoporosis Self-assessment Tool for Asians (OSTA)　The tool is mainly used by the tester to make a quick check and assessment based on the distribution of age and weight on the chart. OSTA index = [weight (kg) − age (years)] × 0.2, and risk stratification of osteoporosis is made according to the obtained OSTA index: OSTA index < −4 is high risk; −4 ≤ OSTA index ≤ −1 is moderate risk; OSTA index > −1 is low risk. Currently, it is mainly applied to elderly women, but there are also cases of applying this assessment tool to men, and the reliability of its results needs to be further confirmed.

ii. Prevention and Care of Osteoporosis

For patients with osteoporosis, prevention is crucial and mainly involves calcium and vitamin D supplementation, exercise interventions, a balanced diet, and the prevention of falls.

1. Calcium and Vitamin D Supplementation　Combined supplementation with calcium and vitamin D can increase bone density in the lumbar vertebrae and femoral neck, and modestly reduce the risk of hip fracture. The total daily intake of elemental calcium for elderly patients with osteoporosis is 1,000 to 1,200mg, with a tolerable upper intake level of 2,000mg. In addition to dietary supplementation, supplementation with elemental calcium of 500

1. 国际骨质疏松基金会（IOF）骨质疏松风险一分钟测试题　该套测试题包括 19 个题目，仅需要受试者判断是或否，简单快速，通俗易懂，只要有 1 题回答为"是"，则提示存在患骨质疏松症的风险，需要从生活方式上预防骨质疏松，并建议到医院做进一步检查。

2. 亚洲人骨质疏松自我筛查工具　该工具主要由测试者根据图表上年龄和体重的分布情况进行快速查对评估。OSTA 指数 =［体重（kg）-年龄（岁）］×0.2，根据所得 OSTA 指数进行骨质疏松的风险分层。OSTA 指数 < -4 为高度风险；-4 ≤ OSTA 指数 ≤ -1 为中度风险；OSTA 指数 > -1 为低度风险。目前主要应用于老年女性，但也有将该评估工具应用于男性的案例，其研究结果的可靠性有待进一步证实。

（二）骨质疏松症的预防与护理

对于骨质疏松症，预防是关键，主要包括补充钙和维生素 D、运动干预、平衡膳食等方式，并且要预防跌倒的发生。

1. 补充钙和维生素 D　联合补充钙和维生素 D 可以增加腰椎和股骨颈的骨密度，小幅降低髋骨骨折风险。老年骨质疏松症患者每日摄入元素钙的总量为 1 000~1 200mg，可耐受最高摄入量为 2 000mg，除饮食补充外，每日尚需补充元素钙 500~600mg。钙剂选择需要考虑元素钙含量、安全性、有效性和依从性。另外，建议老年人多晒太阳，促进皮肤内源性维生素 D 的形成，促进肠道内的钙吸收，进而促进钙盐在骨骼中的沉积，提升骨密度，改善骨质疏松，但是

to 600mg per day is needed, and the choice of calcium supplements needs to take into account the content, safety, efficacy, and compliance of elemental calcium. In addition, it is recommended that the elderly should sunbathe more often to promote the formation of endogenous vitamin D in the skin and the absorption of calcium in the intestinal tract, which in turn promotes the deposition of calcium salts in the bones, enhances the bone density, and alleviate the condition of osteoporosis, but it is necessary to prevent the skin from being burned by strong sunlight.

2. Exercise Intervention Elderly patients with osteoporosis should follow the principles of individualization, capacity building, and gradual progression, and regularly perform some diversified exercises (aerobic exercise, muscle strengthening, balance training, etc.) of medium and low intensity, with the aim of maintaining the existing functions. When the physical condition of the elderly permits, they should perform some weight-bearing exercises regularly to enhance muscle strength and prevent falls. Most elderly osteoporosis patients are accompanied by osteoarthritis of the lower limbs. Exercises such as squatting, stair climbing, mountain climbing, etc. are not recommended, so as to avoid excessive movements such as bending and twisting, or injuries brought about by inappropriate exercises.

3. Nutritional Intervention Patients with osteoporosis need a balanced diet consisting of calcium-rich foods, low-salt (5g/d) diet and moderate protein intake (daily protein intake of 1.0–1.2g/kg, or 1.2–1.5g/kg for older adults undergoing resistance training). The daily intake of animal food is 120–150g, and the daily intake of milk is 300–500ml or dairy products with equivalent protein content. Quit smoking and limit alcohol consumption, and avoid excessive consumption of coffee, strong tea, and carbonated

需要防止强烈阳光照射灼伤皮肤。

2. **运动干预** 老年骨质疏松症患者应遵循个体化、量力而行、循序渐进的原则,有规律地进行一些中、低强度的多元化运动(有氧运动、肌肉强化、平衡训练等),以维持现有功能为目的。老年人在身体条件允许的情况下,定期进行一些负重运动来增强肌肉强度和预防跌倒。老年骨质疏松症患者多合并下肢骨关节炎,不建议进行下蹲、登楼梯、爬山等运动,避免弯腰、扭腰等过度动作带来的损伤。

3. **营养干预** 骨质疏松症患者需要均衡膳食,包括富钙、低盐(5g/d)和适量蛋白质(每日蛋白质摄入量为1.0~1.2g/kg,进行抗阻训练的老年人为1.2~1.5g/kg)。动物性食物每日摄入120~150g,每日摄入牛奶300~500ml或同等蛋白质的奶制品。戒烟限酒,避免过量饮用咖啡、浓茶及碳酸饮料,以降低骨质疏松症的风险。

drinks to reduce the risk of osteoporosis.

4. Traditional Chinese Medicine and Rehabilitation Interventions   For elderly patients with osteoporosis can be carried out with low-intensity exercises to increase muscle strength and prevent falls, such as taijiquan, baduanjin, wuqinxi, and other forms of exercise. In addition, physiotherapies such as electrotherapy and magnetotherapy can be used to reduce pain, improve body movement function, and promote bone calcium deposition.

5. Health Education and Psychological Intervention   Through systematic and regular health education ,we can raise the patients' awareness of the disease, including informing patients of the risk factors, hazards and prevention of osteoporosis, underscoring the importance of improving lifestyle, and imparting general knowledge of medication and monitoring, etc., to improve compliance with the intervention. Through communication and psychological interventions, we can help patients alleviate negative mindsets such as anxiety and depression, overcome their fear of falls and fractures, and improve their quality of life. The common methods of psychological intervention include cognitive therapy, horticultural therapy, music therapy, aromatherapy, forest therapy and so on.

6. Fall Prevention   Measures to prevent falls in elderly patients with osteoporosis include regular exercise, selection of appropriate clothing and shoes, scientific selection and use of age-appropriate assistive devices, age-appropriate modifications to the home environment, and regular fall prevention assessments. Interventions that improve balance and/or include a comprehensive exercise program should be offered to patients at risk.

IV. Urinary Incontinence

Urinary incontinence refers to the loss of automatic urination control ability due to the damage of the urinary sphincters or

4. 中医及康复干预　老年骨质疏松症患者可以进行低强度运动以增加肌肉强度和预防跌倒，比如太极拳、八段锦、五禽戏等运动方式。另外可以通过电疗、磁疗等理疗方式减轻患者疼痛，改善躯体运动功能，促进骨钙沉积。

5. 健康教育及心理干预　通过系统性、经常性健康宣教，增加老年人对疾病的认识，包括告知骨质疏松症的危险因素、危害及防范，改善生活方式的重要性，用药常识与监测等，提高干预依从性。通过沟通及心理干预，帮助患者缓解焦虑、抑郁等消极心态，克服对跌倒和骨折的恐惧，改善生活质量。常用的心理干预方法包括认知疗法、园艺疗法、音乐疗法、芳香疗法、森林疗法等。

6. 预防跌倒　老年骨质疏松症患者预防跌倒的措施包括：规律锻炼、选择合适的服装和鞋子、科学选择和使用适老辅助器具、进行家居环境适老化改造、定期进行防跌倒评估。对有风险的患者应提供改善平衡和/或包含综合运动方案的干预措施。

四、尿失禁

尿失禁是指由于尿道括约肌损伤或神经功能障碍而丧失排尿自控能力，使尿液不自主地流出。根据国际尿控协会制定的标准，尿失禁

neurological dysfunction, making the urine flow out involuntarily. According to the standards established by the International Continence Society, urinary incontinence is divided into true urinary incontinence, stress incontinence, urge incontinence, mixed urinary incontinence, overflow incontinence , reflex incontinence, unstable urinary incontinence and incompetent urethral closure dysfunction.

分为：真性尿失禁、压力性尿失禁、急迫性尿失禁、混合性尿失禁、充溢性尿失禁、反射性尿失禁、不稳定性尿失禁、完全性尿道关闭功能不全。

i. Assessment of Urinary Incontinence

1. Clinical Symptoms were Subjectively Graded It uses the Ingelman-Sundberg scale. Mild: incontinence occurs when coughing, sneezing, without the need to use a pad; moderate: incontinence occurs during daily activities such as running, jumping and walking at a fast pace, requiring the use of a pad; severe: incontinence occurs during light activities and when the lying position changes.

（一）尿失禁的评估

1. 临床症状主观分度 采用 Ingelman-Sundberg 分度法。轻度：尿失禁发生在咳嗽、喷嚏时，不需使用尿垫；中度：尿失禁发生在跑、跳、快步行走等日常活动时，需要使用尿垫；重度：轻微活动、平卧体位改变时发生尿失禁。

2. The 1-hour Urine Pad Test It should be performed with a full bladder for 1h. The elderly should not urinate from the start of the test. A weighed urine pad (e.g., sanitary towel) is pre-positioned. Let the elderly drink 500ml of plain water within 15min from the start of the test; for the next 30min, the elderly walk, go up and down 1 flight of steps. For the last 15min, the elderly should sit up 10 times, cough 10 times, run in place for 1 minute, pick up objects on the ground 5 times, and wash their hands with running water for 1 minute. At the end of the test, the pads will be weighed, the elderly will be required to urinate and the urine output will be weighted. Urine leakage ≥2g was considered positive. Mild: 2g≤urine leakage ＜5g; moderate: 5g ≤ urine leakage ＜10g; severe: 10g≤urine leakage ＜50g; very severe: urine leakage≥50g.

2. 1 小时尿垫试验 试验时膀胱要充盈，持续 1 小时，从试验开始老年人不再排尿。预先放置经称重的尿垫（如卫生巾）。试验开始 15 分钟内老年人喝 500ml 白开水；之后的 30 分钟，老年人行走，上下 1 层楼的台阶；最后 15 分钟，老年人应坐立 10 次，用力咳嗽 10 次，原地跑步 1 分钟，拾起地面物体 5 次，再用流动的自来水洗手 1 分钟。试验结束时，称重尿垫，要求老年人排尿并测量尿量。漏尿量≥2g 为阳性。轻度：2g≤漏尿量＜5g；中度：5g≤漏尿量＜10g；重度：10g≤漏尿量＜50g；极重度：漏尿量≥50g。

3. The ICI Urinary Incontinence Questionnaire Short Form It is applied to the screening and evaluation of urinary incontinence. The questionnaire include six items: age, gender, symptoms of urinary incontinence (times and amount of urine leakage), influence on the daily

3. ICI 尿失禁问卷简表 应用于尿失禁的筛查和评估。该问卷共 6 项内容：年龄、性别、尿失禁症状（漏尿次数及漏尿量）、对日常生活影响程度以及尿失禁类型。该问卷按总分将尿失禁严重程度分为 3 级：轻度，总分≤7 分；中度，7 分＜总分＜14 分；重度，14 分≤总分≤21

life, and type of urinary incontinence. According to the total score of this questionnaire, the severity of urinary incontinence is classified into 3 levels: Mild, total score ≤ 7; moderate, 7 < total score < 14; severe, 14 ≤ total score ≤ 21. The short-form score not only reflects the degree of impact of urinary incontinence on the elderly's quality of life but also allows for a more accurate classification of urinary incontinence and an assessment of the severity of urinary incontinence.

ii. Prevention and Care of Urinary Incontinence

For urinary incontinence in older adults, a comprehensive intervention approach is used to relieve symptoms and improve quality of life.

1. Lifestyle Interventions　It includes reducing weight, especially for those with a body mass index (BMI) > 30kg/m², quitting smoking, reducing consumption of caffeinated beverages, and avoiding or reducing activities that increase abdominal pressure.

2. Pelvic Floor Muscle Training　Pelvic floor muscle training should reach a considerable amount of training to be effective. Specific methods can be as follows: Continuous contract the pelvic floor muscles (that is, the anal contraction exercise) for no less than 3s, relax and rest 2–6s, perform this continuously for 15–30min, and repeat it 3 times a day; or perform the anal contraction movement 150 to 200 times a day. Continue for 3 months or longer. Outpatient follow-up should be conducted after 3 months of training for subjective and objective evaluation of the treatment effects.

3. Regular Urination Training

(1) Keep a Diary of Urination: Assist the older person to record the time of each urination, the volume of each urination, the time of each water intake, the volume of each water intake, the symptoms accompanying each urination, and the time of urinary incontinence.

(2) Selecte Urination Intervals: Select an

分。评分不仅反映尿失禁对老年人生命质量的影响程度,而且可较准确地对尿失禁进行分类,并对尿失禁严重程度作出评估。

(二)尿失禁的预防与护理

针对老年人的尿失禁,主要采用综合干预方法,改善症状,提高生活质量。

1. 生活方式干预　减轻体重,尤其是体重指数(BMI) > 30kg/m² 者;戒烟;减少饮用含咖啡因的饮料;避免或减少腹压增加的活动。

2. 盆底肌训练　盆底肌训练应达到相当的训练量,才可能有效。具体方法如下:持续收缩盆底肌(即缩肛运动)不少于 3 秒,松弛休息 2~6 秒,连续做 15~30 分钟,每天重复 3 遍;或每天做 150~200 次缩肛运动。持续 3 个月或更长时间。应在训练 3 个月后门诊随访,进行主、客观治疗效果的评价。

3. 定时排尿训练

(1)做好排尿日记:协助老年人记录每次排尿时间、每次排尿量、每次饮水时间、每次饮水量、每次排尿的伴随症状、尿失禁时间等。

(2)选定排尿间隔时间:根据排尿日记选定

appropriate interval between urinations based on the urination diary. For example, 1 hour, i.e., urinate first thing in the morning and then empty the bladder every 1 hour thereafter. There is no need to urinate every 1 hour at night.

(3) Gradually Extend the Interval between Urinations: After getting used to the original 1 hour interval between urination, extend it by 15 minutes on the original basis, and adhere to it for 1 week. Then extend it again, and so on to gradually reach the final goal, that is, urinate every 2 to 4 hours, each time the volume of urine is greater than 300ml, and no occurrence of incontinence.

4. Keep Perineal Skin Clean and Dry Change clothes and trousers promptly, wash the perineum regularly and use urinary pads if necessary. Also strengthen the support system, assist with nursing care and prepare adequate clothing and drying facilities.

5. Psychological Care Elderly people with urinary incontinence often have low self-esteem due to clothing and covers often being wet and emitting a foul odour by urine. At the same time , nurses should help change the concept of the elderly, urinary incontinence is a pathological phenomenon accompanied by the physiological aging of the body organs, and is not difficult to talk about shameful things. This approach can relieve the psychological pressure of the elderly.

Section 4　Common Mental Health Problems and Care for the Elderly

I. Anxiety

Anxiety is the feeling of an inner disturbance or unfounded fear that lacks an obvious objective cause, and it is an emotional response that occurs when older persons encounter some difficulties, challenges or dangers. There are individual

适当的两次排尿间隔时间。如 1 小时，即晨起后先排尿，以后每间隔 1 小时排空膀胱。夜间无须每 1 小时排尿一次。

（3）逐步延长排尿间隔时间：习惯 1 小时排尿间隔时间后，将其在原有基础上延长 15 分钟，坚持 1 周。再延长，以此类推逐步达到最终目标，即每 2~4 小时排尿 1 次，每次排尿量大于 300ml，且无尿失禁。

4. 保持会阴部皮肤清洁干燥　及时更换衣裤，勤洗会阴部，必要时使用尿垫。同时加强支持系统的作用，协助生活护理，准备足够的衣被和烘干设施。

5. 心理护理　尿失禁老年人因衣被常尿湿而有臭味，自卑心理较为突出。护士应尊重和理解老年人，维护老年人尊严。同时，应转变老年人的观念，使他们认识到尿失禁是伴随机体器官生理性老化的病理现象，不是难以启齿和令人羞愧的事，减轻老年人的心理压力。

第四节　老年人常见心理健康问题及护理

一、焦虑

焦虑是个体一种缺乏明显客观原因的内心不安或无根据的恐惧，是老年人遇到一些困难、挑战或危险时出现的一种情绪反应。焦虑反应强度存在个体差异，有的老年人只有认知反应，无生理或行为表现，而有的老年人表现为强烈

differences in the intensity of anxiety responses, ranging from cognitive responses with no physical or behavioral manifestations to strong physical and psychological responses.

i. Anxiety Assessment

1. Hamilton Anxiety Scale　In the 1950s, Hamilton developed the Hamilton anxiety scale, which is widely used as an examiner-rating scale to assess the severity of anxiety. The scale consists of 14 entries and is divided into two categories: psychogenic and somatic. The scale is based on a 5-point scale from 0 to 4, ranging from asymptomatic, mild, moderate, severe to very severe. The results of the assessment can be analyzed by total scores. A total score > 29 suggests severe anxiety; 22–29 suggests significant anxiety; 15–21 suggests definite anxiety; 7–14 suggests possible anxiety; < 7 suggests no anxiety.

2. State-Trait Anxiety Inventory　The State-Trait anxiety inventory, developed by Spielberger et al., is a self-assessment questionnaire that can intuitively reflect the subjective feelings of the subjects. The questionnaire consists of 40 items, of which 1 to 20 items rate state anxiety and 21 to 40 items rate trait anxiety. A scale of 1 to 4 was used, ranging from almost never, some, moderate to very marked. The total score range for state anxiety and trait anxiety is 20 to 80 points each. The former is a cumulative score of items 1 to 20, reflecting the degree of state anxiety, and the latter is a cumulative score of items 21 to 40, reflecting the degree of trait anxiety. Higher scores indicate greater anxiety.

ii. Anxiety Prevention and Care

1. Dealing with Factors that Cause Anxiety　Instruct and help the elderly and their families to analyze the causes and manifestations of anxiety, to correctly deal with problems such as retirement, and to adapt to a new life and new roles as soon as possible; actively treat the original disease, and avoid using or use with caution medicines that may cause anxiety symptoms as far

的身心反应。

（一）焦虑的评估

1. 汉密尔顿焦虑量表　20 世纪 50 年代，Hamilton 编制的汉密尔顿焦虑量表，是广泛用于评定焦虑严重程度的他评量表。量表包括 14 个条目，分为精神性和躯体性两大类。评分标准采用 0~4 分的 5 级评分法，从无症状、轻度、中度、重度到极重度。测评结果按总分进行分析。总分 > 29 分，提示有严重焦虑；22~29 分，提示有明显焦虑；总分 15~21 分，提示有肯定的焦虑；总分 7~14 分，则提示可能有焦虑；总分 < 7 分，则提示没有焦虑。

2. 状态 - 特质焦虑问卷　由 Spielberger 等人编制的状态 - 特质焦虑问卷，是自我评价问卷，能够直观地反映受试者的主观感受。该问卷包括 40 个条目，其中 1~20 个条目评定状态焦虑，21~40 个条目评定特质焦虑。采用 1~4 级评分法，从几乎没有、有些、中等程度至非常明显。状态焦虑和特质焦虑的总分范围各为 20~80 分。前者为被试者 1~20 项的累加分，反映状态焦虑的程度；后者为 21~40 项的累加分，反映特质焦虑的程度。分数越高，说明焦虑程度越严重。

（二）焦虑的预防与护理

1. 处理导致焦虑的因素　指导和帮助老年人及其家属分析焦虑的原因和表现，正确对待引起焦虑的问题，如离退休等，尽快适应新生活、新角色；积极治疗原发病，尽量避免使用或慎用可能引起焦虑症状的药物。

as possible.

2. Learning Relaxation Techniques

By instructing the elderly to learn to channel and relax themselves and to take the initiative to seek help can help relieve anxiety. Try relaxation methods such as deep breathing and meditation. In addition, listening to music and reading can also help them relax.

3. Professional Psychological Counselling

When anxiety persists and affects the normal life of the elderly, the help of professional psychologists can be sought. Through psychological counseling, cognitive behavioral therapy, and other methods, we can help the elderly adjust their mental state and alleviate their anxiety.

4. Seeking a Social Support Network

Establishing a good social support network can help reduce anxiety. Elderly people should keep close contact with family and friends and share each other's thoughts and confusion. At the same time, actively participate in social activities to expand interpersonal relationships and enhance their sense of belonging.

5. Providing Good Medication Guidance

Patients with severe anxiety should follow the doctor's orders to take anti-anxiety drugs to relieve anxiety symptoms. However, the drugs should be taken under the guidance of the doctor, and the patients should pay close attention to the drug effect and side effects.

II. Depression

Depression is a common mental and psychological problem in the elderly, which is mainly characterized by low spirits, pessimism, talking and moving less, and slow thinking. The level of self-consciousness and self-control of the elderly is low. If the depression lasts for a long time, it can cause the decline of psychological functions and the damage to social functions.

i. Depression Assessment

1. Hamilton Depression Scale (HAMD)

It was developed by Hamilton in 1960 and is the

2. 学会放松技巧 指导老年人学会自我疏导、自我放松，主动寻求帮助，有助于缓解焦虑情绪。可以尝试深呼吸、冥想等放松方法。此外，听音乐、阅读等也有助于放松心情。

3. 进行专业心理疏导 当焦虑情绪持续存在且影响老年人正常生活时，可寻求专业心理医生的帮助。通过心理疏导、认知行为疗法等方法，帮助老年人调整心态，缓解焦虑情绪。

4. 寻求社会支持网络 建立良好的社会支持网络有助于减轻焦虑情绪。与家人、朋友保持密切联系，分享彼此的心声和困惑。同时，积极参加社交活动，拓宽人际关系，增强归属感。

5. 做好用药指导 重度焦虑患者应遵医嘱，适当使用抗焦虑药物来缓解焦虑症状。但是需要在医生的指导下使用，并密切关注药物效果和副作用。

二、抑郁

抑郁是以情绪低落、悲观消极、少言少动、思维迟缓等为主要特征的一种老年人常见的精神心理问题。老年人自我意识和自我控制水平较低，如果抑郁持续的时间较长，可以导致心理功能下降和社会功能受损。

（一）抑郁的评估

1. 汉密尔顿抑郁量表（HAMD） 1960 年由 Hamilton 研制，是临床上评定抑郁程度时

most commonly used scale for assessing the degree of depression in clinical practice. The scale belongs to examiner-rating scale. There are 24 entries reflecting the subject's situation in recent days or the recent 1 week. Most of the HAMD entries use a 5-point scale from 0 to 4 points. The scale for each level is 0=none, 1=mild, 2=moderate, 3=severe, and 4=very severe. The higher the total score，the more severe the depression. According to Davis JM's classification criteria, a total score of > 35 is likely to be severely depressed；21–35 indicates definite depression；8–20 suggests possible depression；< 8 indicates no depression.

2. Geriatric Depression Scale (GDS)
It was developed in 1982 by Brink et al. and is a depression screening scale specific designed for the elderly. The scale consists of 30 items, which are assessed by choosing a "yes" or "no" about the subject's feelings over the last week. A "yes" is scored as 1 point and a "no" is scored as 0 points, with entries marked with an * being reverse scored. For general screening, the suggested criteria are：normal, 0–10 points；mild depression, 11–20 points；moderate to severe depression, 21–30 points.

ii. Depression Prevention and Care

1. Identify the Causes and Give Targeted Interventions   Nursing staff should explore the causative factors in depth, such as disease, drug use, emotional status in later life, family relationships, etc., and formulate an intervention program based on a comprehensive consideration of the causes, contributing factors, and characteristics of morbidity in the elderly.

2. Timely Psychological Counseling   Nurses need to guide the elderly to treat themselves correctly, correctly understand the disease, establish a correct outlook on life, correctly deal with various unfavorable factors, and avoid unnecessary mental stimulation.

3. Strictly Prevent Suicide   Community medical staff should take the initiative to

应用最普遍的量表。该量表属于他评量表，有 24 个条目，反映被试者近几天或近 1 周的情况。HAMD 大部分条目采用 0~4 分的 5 级评分法。各级评分标准为：0= 无、1= 轻度、2= 中度、3= 重度、4= 极重度。总分越高抑郁程度越重。按照 Davis JM 的划分标准，总分＞ 35 分，有严重抑郁症；总分 21~35 分，肯定有抑郁症；总分 8~20 分，可能有抑郁症；总分＜ 8 分，则为无抑郁症。

2. 老年抑郁量表（GDS）   1982 年由 Brink 等人研制，是老年人专用抑郁筛查量表。该量表共有 30 个条目。评定时被试者结合最近 1 周以来的感受选择回答"是"或"否"。"是"计 1 分，"否"计 0 分，其中标有 * 号者为反向计分条目。用于一般筛查时，建议标准为：正常，0~10 分；轻度抑郁，11~20 分；中重度抑郁，21~30 分。

（二）抑郁的预防与护理

1. 找出原因，给予针对性干预   护理人员应该深入探讨致病因素，如疾病、药物使用、晚年感情状况、家庭关系等，针对老年人的发病原因、促发因素、发病特征等综合考虑，从而制订干预方案。

2. 及时进行心理疏导   护理人员需要劝导老年人正确对待自己，正确认识疾病，树立正确的人生观，正确对待和处理各种不利因素，避免不必要的精神刺激。

3. 严防自杀   社区医护人员应该主动与老年人沟通交流，及时发现其自杀企图，从而进行

communicate with the elderly, and discover their suicide attempts in time, so as to carry out effective interventions and prevent suicidal accidents from occurring. Cognitive psychotherapy and medication can be used when necessary.

4. Strengthen Family and Social Support Relatives need to contact the elderly frequently, have emotional exchanges with them, and encourage them to express their inner negative emotions. Give full play to the role of the social support system, give care and attention to the elderly, provide support, and build a social support network for the elderly, such as activity centers for the elderly and universities for the aged.

III. Mild Cognitive Impairment

Mild cognitive impairment (MCI) is an intermediate stage between normal aging and dementia, in which patients have memory or cognitive impairments that do not yet affect their ability to perform daily activities and do not meet the diagnostic criteria for dementia. Early identification of mild cognitive impairment and early intervention are very important to avoid or delay the decline of cognitive function or the occurrence and development of dementia.

i. Assessment of Mild Cognitive Impairment

1. Overall Cognitive Function Screening The Montreal Cognitive Assessment (MoCA) covers a wide range of cognitive domains, including attention and concentration, executive functioning, memory, language, visuospatial construction ability, abstract thinking, computation, and orientation, and it is specifically designed for screening mild cognitive impairment. Moreover, it has a high degree of sensitivity and specificity in identifying mild cognitive impairment.

2. Memory Assessment Examines The examination of episodic memory is mainly through learning and delayed recall tests, including various versions of the auditory word learning test, and the logical memory subtest of the Wechsler

有效干预,防止意外事件的发生。必要时可采用认知心理治疗、药物治疗等。

4. 加强家庭及社会支持 亲属需要经常与老年人联系,与老年人进行情感交流,鼓励老年人宣泄内心的负面情绪。充分发挥社会支持系统的作用,给予老年人关心、关爱,提供支持,为老年人搭建社会支持网络,如老年人活动中心、老年大学等。

三、轻度认知障碍

轻度认知障碍(MCI)是介于正常衰老与痴呆之间的中间阶段,此阶段患者虽然具有记忆或认知损害,但尚未影响到其日常生活能力,且没有达到痴呆的诊断标准。轻度认知障碍的旦期识别及尽早干预非常重要,可以有效避免或延缓认知功能的下降或向痴呆的发生发展。

(一)轻度认知障碍的评估

1. 总体认知功能筛查 蒙特利尔认知评估量表(MoCA)涵盖的认知领域较广,包括注意力与集中、执行功能、记忆、语言、视空间结构能力、抽象思维、计算和定向力,是专门为筛查轻度认知障碍而设计的,在识别轻度认知障碍时有较高的灵敏度和特异度。

2. 记忆力评估 对情景记忆的检查主要通过学习和延迟回忆测验,包括各种版本的听觉词语学习测验、韦氏记忆量表逻辑记忆分测验等。需要注意的是,在轻度认知障碍的诊断过程中,对于高文化程度的个体,纵向随访对比

memory scale. It should be noted that in the diagnostic process of mild cognitive impairment, longitudinal follow-up comparisons are very important for individuals with a high educational background; if the subject's assessment results show a significant decrease compared previously, the results should be regarded as abnormal even if the examination results are within the normal range.

3. Assessment of Executive Function
Executive function refers to the ability to effectively initiate and complete purposeful activities. It is a complex cognitive process involving planning, initiation, sequencing, operation, feedback, decision-making and judgment, and its core components include abstract thinking, working memory, set shifting, and response inhibition. Commonly used tests of executive function include the Trail Making test, the Stroop test, the phonological fluency test, and the semantic fluency test.

4. Assessment of Language Ability
Due to the different locations of the lesion, aphasia can be classified into various types with diverse manifestations, and the patient's abilities, such as the ability to express, comprehend, repeat, name, read and write, may be impaired. Commonly used tests include the Boston naming test, the word fluency test, and the aphasia battery in Chinese.

5. Assessment of Visuospatial Structural Ability   Tests of visuospatial structural ability include two main categories, one is copying or drawing shapes, and the other is assembling three-dimensional patterns. Commonly used tests for assessing visuospatial ability include the Balloon Cancellation Test, Clock Cancellation test, Benton Face Recognition Test, Rey-Osterricth Complex Figures Test, the Clock Drawing Test, and the Building Blocks Test.

ii. The Prevention and Care of Mild Cognitive Impairment

1. Non-pharmacological Therapies
It mainly includes moderate exercise interventions

非常重要；如果受试者评估结果较之前有明显下降，即使检查结果在正常范围之内，也应视为异常。

3. 执行功能评估　执行功能指有效启动并完成有目的活动的能力，是一项复杂的认知过程，涉及计划、启动、顺序、运行、反馈、决策和判断，主要包括抽象思维、工作记忆、定势转移和反应抑制等。常用的执行功能测验包括连线测验、Stroop 测验、语音流畅性测验、语义流畅性测验等。

4. 语言能力评估　由于病变部位不同，失语可分为多种类型，表现多样，患者的表达、理解、复述、命名、阅读和书写能力都可能受损。常用的测验包括 Boston 命名测验、词语流畅性测验、汉语失语成套测验等。

5. 视空间结构能力评估　视空间结构能力的测验包括两大类，一类为图形的临摹或自画，另一类为三维图案的拼接。常用的视空间能力评估测验包括气球划消测验、钟划消测验、Benton 面孔再认测验、Rey-Osterrieth 复杂图形测验、画钟测验、积木测验等。

（二）轻度认知障碍的预防与护理

1. 非药物疗法　主要包括适度的运动锻炼和认知功能的训练。建议每周进行 150 分钟（每

and cognitive training. It is recommended that 150 minutes of moderate-intensity aerobic exercise per week (about 30 minutes a day, 5 days a week) can effectively alleviate cognitive decline. Adopting a healthy lifestyle, such as quitting smoking, stop drinking, and eating a healthy diet, can control the risk factors for mild cognitive impairment and help to slow down the decline of cognitive function. Cognitive training and participation in intellectual activities can improve cognitive functions such as memory and executive ability.

2. Strengthening Psychological and Social Support　The elderly with mild cognitive impairment are likely to suffer from inferiority, anxiety, depression, and other negative emotions due to the decline of cognitive function. Community medical staff should inform the elderly and their families about the methods to delay cognitive function decline so as to strengthen patients' confidence in treatment.

3. Strengthening Caregiver Support It is very important to provide support for caregivers of the elderly with mild cognitive impairment. Caregivers should be trained in their daily caregiving duties and caregiving skills, so as to improve their caregiving level and reduce their caregiving burden. In addition, peer exchange activities can be organized and caregivers can be instructed in relaxation training, so as to reduce caregivers' stress and prevent the occurrence of adverse events.

4. Regular Testing of Cognitive Function　Instruct the elderly to go to the memory clinic to test the changes in cognitive function and detect mild cognitive impairment as early as possible to achieve early treatment and slow down the further decline of cognitive function.

5. Guidance on Healthy Lifestyles Guide older people to choose moderate activities according to their age and physical strength, and

天 30 分钟左右，每周 5 天)的中等强度有氧运动，能有效缓解认知功能的下降。采取健康的生活方式，如戒烟、戒酒及健康饮食等，可以控制轻度认知障碍的危险因素，有助于延缓认知功能的下降。认知功能训练及多参加益智活动可训练老年人记忆力、执行能力等认知功能。

2. 加强心理及社会支持　轻度认知障碍老年人由于认知功能下降，容易产生自卑、焦虑、抑郁等负面情绪。社区医护人员应让老年人及其家属了解到延缓认知功能下降的方法，从而坚定患者的治疗信心。

3. 加强照顾者支持　对轻度认知障碍患者照顾者的支持非常重要，应对照顾者的日常照料职责和照顾技能进行培训，提升其照料水平，减轻照料负担。另外可组织同伴交流活动，指导照顾者进行放松训练，减少照顾者的压力和预防不良事件的发生。

4. 定期检测认知功能　指导老年人去记忆门诊检测认知功能的变化，尽早发现轻度认知障碍，早期治疗，延缓认知功能的进一步下降。

5. 指导健康的生活方式　根据老年人的年龄和体力，指导老年人选择合适的活动项目，以及采用地中海饮食结构，即以蔬菜、水果、鱼类、

guide them to adopt the Mediterranean diet, a style of eating that focuses on vegetables, fruits, fish, cereals, pulses and healthy fats and oils, Which helps reduce the risk of memory loss.

Section 5　Community Elderly Care Model

At present, China is endeavoring to explore a model for providing long-term, continuous care for the elderly that involves the participation of several parties, including the government, communities, social organizations, and families. The main models include the home care model, the community-based home care model, and the community-based integrated medical and care model.

I. Home Care Model

The home care model refers to the socialized elderly care services provided by the government and social forces, relying on the community, for the elderly who live at home, providing them with services in the areas of life care, home economics, rehabilitation, and spiritual comfort, with the main focus on solving the difficulties of daily life. The mainstay of home care services is the socialized elderly care system established in the community, which enables the elderly to live in their familiar environment and at the same time receive appropriate living and spiritual care. Generally speaking, there is no need to carry out other infrastructure construction, thus maximizing the saving of limited social resources. The operability of this model of elderly care is highly operable, and is currently the main model of elderly care in China. However, the development of home care inevitably faces problems such as a single type of service, shortage of human resources and uneven service quality.

五谷杂粮、豆类和健康油脂为主，有助于降低记忆力减退的风险。

第五节　社区养老模式

目前，我国正在努力探索由政府、社区、社会组织、家庭等多方主体参与的，为老年人提供长期、持续照护的模式。主要包括居家养老模式、社区居家养老模式、社区医养结合养老模式。

一、居家养老模式

居家养老模式是指政府和社会力量依托社区，为居家的老年人提供生活照料、家政服务、康复护理和精神慰藉等方面服务，以解决日常生活困难为主要内容的社会化养老服务。居家养老服务提供的主体是依托社区建立起来的社会化的养老服务体系，使得老年人既能生活在自己熟悉的环境中，又能获得适当的生活及精神照护。一般来说，无须进行其他基础设施建设，能够最大限度地节约有限的社会资源。这种养老模式的可操作性较强，是我国目前最主要的养老模式。但是，在居家养老服务发展中不可避免地面临服务种类单一、人力资源短缺、服务质量参差不齐等问题。

Ⅱ. Community-based Home Care Model

The community-based home care model relies on community services, making use of and integrating the existing environment, facilities, and other resources available in the community for the elderly, and, through the establishment of community day-care centers and the like, providing the elderly at home with services that focuses on life care, medical care, spiritual comfort, culture and recreation, and so on. The core of the community-based home care model is a model that integrates the strengths of all parties in society, with "family care as the mainstay" and "community institutions as a supplement". It is characterized by the fact that the elderly still live in their own homes, without having to leave their families, and that they can enjoy the home-based services or care services provided by the relevant community-based elderly care service agencies or personnel specifically for the elderly. The advantage of community-based home care, unlike family-based care, is that under this mode of aging, older persons choosing the service do not need to leave the familiar living environment of their own community, or even change their daily habits. In addition, the participation and provision of services by community professionals can also alleviate the care burden on family members.

Ⅲ. Community-based Integrated Medical and Care Model

The integrated medical and care refers to a new old-age service model that integrates life care, spiritual comfort, cultural entertainment, and other old-age services, as well as medical care services with a certain professional level such as health examination, medical care, disease diagnosis and treatment, and hospice care for the elderly.

The community-based integrated medical and careis a combination of medical care and support services carried out within the community, which

二、社区居家养老模式

社区居家养老模式以社区服务为依托，利用和整合社区现有的可利用的环境、设施等养老资源，通过建立社区日间照料中心等，向居家老人提供以生活照料、医疗保健、精神慰藉、文化娱乐等为主要内容的服务。社区居家养老模式的核心是"以家庭养老为主，以社区机构养老为辅"的整合社会各方力量的养老模式。其特点在于老年人仍然住在自己家里，既不用离开家人，又可以享受由社区相关养老服务机构或人员专门为老年人提供的上门服务或托老服务。社区居家养老不同于家庭养老，其优势在于在这种养老模式下，选择服务的老年人不需要离开自己熟悉的社区居住环境，甚至不需要改变日常生活习惯；此外，由社区专业人员参与和提供服务，也会减轻家属的照料负担。

三、社区医养结合养老模式

医养结合是指面向老年人，提供集生活照料、精神慰藉、文化娱乐等养老服务，以及具备一定专业水平的健康检查、医疗保健、疾病诊治、临终关怀等医疗照护服务为一体的新型养老服务模式。

社区医养结合是在社区范围内开展的医养结合服务，其将社区卫生服务中心的医疗资源、养老资源和生活服务中心的设施资源有机结合，

organically combines the medical resources of the community health center, the endowment resources, and the facilities resources of the life service center, and maximizes the utilization of the endowment resources in advance. Special care areas for the elderly have been established in community health centers with multiple functional areas, including disease treatment areas, rehabilitation care areas, health education areas, cultural and leisure areas, and living service areas. To strengthen institutional interaction, medical institutions in the community provide professional medical services for pension institutions, such as the use of community health center doctors home visits service. Doctors regularly patrol pension institutions, and once there is a disease of the elderly, on call, timely treatment. Community health service institutions provide daily care, chronic disease management, rehabilitation, health education and traditional Chinese medicine health care, and other services for the elderly. Community-based integrated medical and care model is conducive to meeting the increasing needs of community elderly medical care, while improving the service level, is conducive to the health management of the elderly in the community.

(Yang Lili)

实现养老资源利用效益最大化。在社区卫生服务中心建立老年人特护区，设置多个功能区域，包括疾病治疗区、康复护理区、健康宣教区、文化休闲区、生活服务区等。强化机构互动，由社区内医疗机构为养老机构提供专业医疗服务，如采取社区卫生服务中心医生上门问诊的服务方式，医生定期巡视养老机构，一旦有老年人患病，随叫随到，及时治疗。社区卫生服务机构为老年人提供日常护理、慢性病管理、康复、健康教育和咨询、中医养生保健等服务。社区医养结合养老模式有利于满足社区老年人日益增加的医疗护理需求，提升服务水平，以及社区老年人的健康管理。

（杨莉莉）

Key Points

1. Health assessment for the elderly covers a wide range of topics, including general medical assessment, physical function assessment, mental and psychological assessment, quality of life assessment, and environmental assessment. Comprehensive health assessment for the elderly can comprehensively reflect their health status, and is an important basis for the implementation of health management.

2. Health management services, including lifestyle and health status assessment, physical examination, auxiliary examination and health

内容摘要

1. 老年人的健康评估内容比较广泛，主要包括一般医学评估、躯体功能评估、精神心理评估、社会评估、生活质量评估、环境评估等。对老年人进行综合健康评估，可以全面反映其健康状况，是实施健康管理的重要基础。

2. 社区卫生服务中心每年为65岁及以上老年人提供1次健康管理服务，包括生活方式和健康状况评估、体格检查、辅助检查和健康指导。

guidance, are provided to elderly people aged 65 and above once a year by community health centers.

3. Common physical health problems among elderly people in the community include frailty, falls, osteoporosis, urinary incontinence, etc. Key assessments should be conducted to provide prevention and health guidance, and targeted nursing measures should be provided.

4. Common mental health problems among the elderly include anxiety, depression, mild cognitive impairment, etc. It is necessary to promptly identify the mental health problems of the elderly, provide prevention and health guidance, and offer targeted psychological support.

5. At present, China is endeavoring to explore a model for providing long-term, continuous care for the elderly that involves the participation of several parties, including the government, communities, social organizations, and families. The main models include the home care model, the community-based home care model, and community-based integrated medical and care model.

3. 社区老年人常见身体健康问题包括衰弱、跌倒、骨质疏松症、尿失禁等，要进行重点评估，给与预防和保健指导，提供针对性的护理措施。

4. 老年人常见心理健康问题包括焦虑、抑郁、轻度认知障碍等，要及时发现老年人存在的心理健康问题，给与预防和保健指导，提供针对性的心理支持。

5. 目前，我国正在努力探索由政府、社区、社会组织、家庭等多方主体参与的，为老年人提供长期、持续照护的模式。主要包括居家养老模式、社区居家养老模式、社区医养结合养老模式。

Exercises

(Questions 1 to 2 share the same question stem)

Mr. Wang, male, 86 years old. Due to his advanced age, he cannot take care of himself completely. During the day, when his son and daughter-in-law go to work, a domestic helper comes to his home to take care of the elderly, helping with cooking, assisting with meals, and so on.

1. Please think about what kind of pension model is this?

2. What are the advantages of the pension model?

(Questions 3 to 4 share the same question stem)

Mrs. Li, female, 74 years old, widowed,

思 考 题

（1~2题共用题干）

社区居民王某，男，86岁。由于高龄，生活不能完全自理。白天儿子、儿媳上班，由家政人员上门照顾王某，帮助做饭、协助进餐等。

1. 请思考这属于什么养老模式？

2. 该养老模式的优势是什么？

（3~4题共用题干）

社区居民李某，女，74岁，丧偶，独居，小学

living alone, primary school education. She has a son and a daughter, all of whom have married and are working and living in other places. For more than half a year, Mrs. Li has been feeling tired, inactive and slow in response. She is always alone, doesn't like to communicate with people, has poor sleep quality with frequent dreams, and   shows no interest in anything. She has felt that she is in poor health.

3. What is the most likely health problem that Mrs. Li may have?

4. What intervention measures can community nurses take?

(Questions 5 to 6 share the same question stem)

Mr. Zhang, male, 85 years old. Diagnosis: history of cerebral infarction for half a year. Now he is recovering at home, taken care of by his daughter. Through family visit, the community nurse assessed Mr. Zhang's weak activity ability and gave him a score of 7 on the falling risk assessnent, which made him a high-risk group for falling. She advised Mr. Zhang to seek assistance when being active, and explained the precautions and health education to him and his daughter.

5. From what aspects should we evaluate Mr. Zhang's home environment?

6. How to prevent Mr. Zhang from falling?

文化。育有一子一女，均已成家，在外地工作、生活。李某最近半年多以来常感觉疲乏，不爱活动，反应迟钝，独来独往，不爱与人交流，睡眠较差、多梦，对任何事情提不起兴趣。她自觉身体健康状况很差。

3. 李某最可能存在的健康问题是什么？

4. 社区护士可以采取哪些干预措施？

（5~6题共用题干）

社区居民张某，男，85岁。诊断：脑梗死，病史半年。现居家康复，由女儿照顾。社区护士通过家庭访视评估发现张某活动能力弱，跌倒危险评分7分，属于跌倒高危人群，因此嘱张某活动时需他人协助，并向张某及其女儿交代注意事项和进行健康教育指导。

5. 请问可以从哪些方面对张某居家环境进行评估？

6. 如何预防张某跌倒？

Chapter 8

Management of Chronic Disease Patients in Community

第八章

社区慢性病患者的管理

NURSING

08章

08章　数字内容

Learning Objectives

Knowledge Objectives

1. Correctly describe the definition, characteristics and risk factors of chronic diseases.

2. Correctly describe the management principles and self-management promotion strategies of chronic diseases, key management points of patients with hypertension, diabetes, mental disease and pulmonary tuberculosis.

Ability Objectives

1. Manage hypertension and diabetes

学习目标

知识目标

1. 正确描述慢性病的定义、特点和危险因素。

2. 正确描述慢性病的管理原则、自我管理的促进策略，高血压、糖尿病、精神疾病及肺结核等疾病患者管理要点。

能力目标

1. 能够管理社区中的高血压和糖尿病患者。

patients in the community.

2. Guide patients with chronic diseases in self-management.

● Quality Objectives

1. Cultivate new-era nursing professionals capable of shouldering the great mission of advancing Healthy China initiatives and addressing the challenges of aging development.

2. Establish a professional attitude of wholeheartedly dedicating oneself to the service of human health, and provide health management guidance for chronic disease patients in the community.

2. 能够指导慢性病患者自我管理。

● 素质目标

1. 培养能够担当推进健康中国建设和应对老龄化发展大任的新时代护理人。

2. 培养全心全意为人类健康事业服务的奉献精神和职业态度，为社区慢性病患者提供健康管理指导。

Mrs. Zhang, 45 years old, has a chief complaint of shortness of breath on fatigue. She reports that she exhibited similar symptoms at her primary care physician's office six months ago. At that time, she was diagnosed with acute bronchitis and treated with bronchodilators, empiric antibiotics, and a short course of oral steroid taper. However, this management did not relieve her symptoms, and the condition has gradually worsened over the past six months. She reports a 9kg intentional weight loss over the past year. She denies camping, spelunking, or hunting activities. Physical examination was negative for fever, night sweats, palpitations, chest pain, nausea, vomiting, diarrhea, constipation, abdominal pain, sensory function changes, and increased bruising or bleeding. She reports a cough, and shortness of breath. Her tobacco use is 33 packs per year; however, she quit smoking shortly after the onset of symptoms six months ago. She denies history of alconol consumption and drug abuse.

Questions:

1. What is the nursing diagnosis for the client at present and potentially?

2. What measures can the nurse take to help the client release breathing difficulties?

张阿姨，45 岁。主诉劳累时呼吸急促。6 个月前，她在初级保健医生办公室就诊时曾出现类似症状，当时被诊断为急性支气管炎，并接受支气管扩张剂、抗生素和短期口服类固醇逐渐减量治疗。但是，当时的治疗并没有改善症状，6 个月来病情逐渐恶化。此外，去年她主动减重了 9kg。否认露营、洞穴探险或狩猎活动。查体显示：发热、盗汗、心悸、胸痛、恶心、呕吐、腹泻、便秘、腹痛、感觉功能变化。声称伴有咳嗽、气短的症状。平时有吸烟习惯，烟草使用量为 33 包 / 年，但 6 个月前已经戒烟。否认饮酒史和药物滥用史。

请思考：

1. 该患者目前及潜在的护理诊断是什么？

2. 护士可以采取哪些措施帮助患者缓解呼吸困难？

Section 1　Overview of Chronic Disease Management

Chronic non-communicable diseases are referred to as chronic diseases. Common chronic diseases include malignant tumors, hypertension, type 2 diabetes, coronary atherosclerotic heart disease, stroke, chronic obstructive pulmonary disease, overweight, obesity, osteoporosis, and oral diseases. Chronic diseases are defined broadly as conditions that last for 1 year or more and require ongoing medical attention or limit activities of daily living. Many chronic diseases are caused by unhealthy behaviors, such as tobacco use and exposure to secondhand smoke, poor nutrition, low in fruits and vegetables, high in sodium and saturated fats, lack of physical activity and excessive alcohol use.

I. Chronic Disease

Chronic diseases tend to occur among older adults and can usually be controlled but not cured. The most common types of chronic disease include cancer, heart disease, stroke, diabetes, and arthritis, depression, chronic obstructive pulmonary disease (COPD) and so on. Chronic diseases are prolonged conditions that generally cannot be prevented by vaccines or cured completely. Many chronic diseases develop slowly over time sometimes because of unhealthy behaviors such as smoking or inactivity. Chronic diseases can be associated with reduced quality of life and/or functional disability and can have a profound effect on the physical, emotional and mental well-being of those afflicted, often making it difficult to maintain daily routines and personal relationships. Many chronic conditions may be controllable and deterioration in health can be minimized by maintaining a healthy lifestyle and accessing sufficient social support.

第一节　慢性病管理概述

慢性非传染性疾病，简称慢性病。常见慢性病有恶性肿瘤、高血压、2 型糖尿病、冠状动脉粥样硬化性心脏病、脑卒中、慢性阻塞性肺疾病以及超重、肥胖、骨质疏松和口腔疾病等。慢性病被广泛定义为持续 1 年或 1 年以上的疾病，需要持续的医疗护理或限制日常生活活动。许多慢性病是由一系列不健康行为引起的，如吸烟和接触二手烟、营养不良、水果和蔬菜摄入少、钠和饱和脂肪摄入多、缺乏身体运动、过度饮酒等。

一、慢性病

慢性病往往发生在老年人群，通常可以控制但无法治愈。最常见的慢性疾病是癌症、心脏病、脑卒中、糖尿病、关节炎、抑郁症、慢性阻塞性肺疾病等。慢性病是指无法通过疫苗预防或完全治愈的长期疾病，许多慢性疾病随着时间的推移呈现发展趋势，有时是吸烟或不运动等不健康行为导致。慢性病会导致个体生活质量下降和 / 或功能残疾，并可能对患者的身体、情绪和精神健康产生深远影响，往往使患者难以维持日常生活和人际关系。然而，多数慢性病是可控的，坚持健康的生活方式和获取足够的社会支持，可帮助个体维持良好健康状态，避免疾病发展或恶化。

II. Chronic Disease Prevention and Management

Chronic disease prevention and management is a common approach to health care that emphasizes helping individuals maintain independence and stay as healthy as possible through prevention, early detection, and management of chronic conditions. The most effective method of preventing and/or managing chronic disease is　providing continuous health education and supervision. Such prevention strategies are directed at minimizing or eliminating future chronic illnesses with initiatives like smoking cessation, healthy diet and physical activity programs to actual health care delivery where patients are encouraged to take an active role in their own care, health care service providers should be supported with the necessary resources and expertise to better assist their patients in managing their illness.

i. Quit Smoking

Smoking leads to disease and disability and harms nearly every organ of the body. Smoking causes cancer, heart disease, stroke, diabetes, chronic obstructive pulmonary disease, and chronic bronchitis, etc. Smoking also increases the risk of pulmonary tuberculosis, certain eye diseases (cataracts, macular degeneration, dry eye disease, etc.), and problems of the immune system.　Secondhand smoke causes stroke, lung cancer, and coronary heart disease in adults. Children who are exposed to secondhand smoke are at increased risk of sudden infant death syndrome (SIDS), acute respiratory infections, severe asthma, other respiratory symptoms, and pulmonary hypoplasia.

ii. Regular Physical Activity

Regular physical activity helps improve overall health, fitness, and quality of life. It also helps reduce individual's risk of chronic conditions like obesity, type 2 diabetes, heart disease, stroke, cancer, depression and anxiety, and dementia.

二、慢性病的预防与管理

慢性病的预防和管理是一种常见的卫生保健方法，强调通过预防、早期发现和管理慢性病来帮助个人保持独立性并尽可能保持健康。预防和管理慢性病最有效的方式是提供持续的健康教育和监督，旨在减少或避免慢性病的发生，例如通过制订戒烟、健康饮食和体育活动计划，鼓励患者在自我护理中发挥积极作用，即做好自我管理。此外，医疗卫生保健服务提供者也需要获得必要的资源和专业知识支持，以更好地帮助患者管理疾病。

（一）戒烟

吸烟会导致疾病和残疾，并几乎损害身体的每个器官。吸烟会导致癌症、心脏病、脑卒中、糖尿病、慢性阻塞性肺疾病和慢性支气管炎等。吸烟还会增加肺结核、眼疾和免疫系统问题（包括类风湿性关节炎）的风险。二手烟还会导致成人脑卒中、肺癌和冠心病。对于接触二手烟的儿童，其患婴儿猝死综合征、急性呼吸道感染、严重的哮喘、其他呼吸道症状和肺发育不良的风险会增加。

（二）规律的体育活动

规律的运动一般有助于改善个体整体健康、体能和生活质量。还有助于降低个体患慢性疾病的风险，如肥胖、2型糖尿病、心脏病、中风、癌症、抑郁、焦虑和痴呆。

iii. Reduce Ethanol Intake

The Chinese Dietary Guidelines (*2022*) suggest that residents should not be encouraged to drink alcohol. If alcohol must be consumed, it should be in limited quantities and spirits should be avoided. Additionally, the guidelines advise against drinking on an empty stomach. It is recommended to consume some carbohydrate-rich foods (staple foods) before drinking. Drinking on an empty stomach increases the irritation of ethanol on the gastrointestinal tract and allows for faster absorption of ethanol, leading to intoxication more easily.

iv. Healthy Diet

Adults who eat a healthy diet live longer and have a lower risk of obesity, heart disease, type 2 diabetes, and certain cancers. In addition, healthy eating can help people with chronic diseases control the symptoms and avoid complications.

v. Control Weight

Maintaining a healthy weight is a critical factor in preventing chronic diseases and promoting overall health. Overweight or obesity elevates the risk of cardiovascular diseases, type 2 diabetes, hypertension, and certain cancers, while underweight may lead to malnutrition, compromised immunity, and osteoporosis. A balanced diet, regular physical activity, and healthy lifestyle habits play a vital role in sustaining an ideal body weight.

vi. Control Blood Pressure

The advantage of the chronic disease management model is that it realizes the infrastructure and support issues required for high quality care. The role of the patient, primary care team, system, and community are all represented in this model. Experience suggests that the application of chronic disease management principles to hypertension can result in significant benefits to all concerned, such as reducing workload, improving efficiency, and increasing disease control rates.

vii. Control Cholesterol Levels

High cholesterol can cause some serious problems to start (like coronary artery disease). But

（三）减少乙醇摄入

《中国居民膳食指南（2022）》建议，不提倡居民饮酒，如果必须饮酒，则应该限制饮酒量，且不宜饮用烈性酒；此外，也建议不应该空腹饮酒，饮酒前应吃一些碳水类的食品（主食）。空腹饮酒加大乙醇对胃肠道的刺激，并使乙醇吸收更快，更容易醉酒。

（四）饮食健康

饮食健康的个体寿命更长，患肥胖症、心脏病、2型糖尿病和特定癌症的风险也会更低。此外，健康的饮食还可以帮助慢性病患者控制症状并避免并发症。

（五）控制体重

保持健康的体重是预防慢性疾病和促进整体健康的关键因素。超重或肥胖会增加心血管疾病、2型糖尿病、高血压和某些癌症的患病风险；而体重过轻则可能导致营养不良，免疫力下降和骨质疏松。均衡饮食、规律运动和良好的生活习惯有助于维持理想体重。

（六）控制血压

慢性病管理模式的优势在于提供了高质量护理所需的基础设施和支持资源。患者、初级保健团队、系统和社区的角色作用都在这个模式中得到了很好的体现。既往经验表明，将慢性病管理模式应用于高血压，可为所有相关人员带来显著的益处，如减轻工作负担、提高效率及疾病控制率等。

（七）控制胆固醇水平

高胆固醇会导致一些严重的疾病（如冠状动脉疾病），但它也可能是其他疾病的结果，尤

it can also be the result of other diseases, especially ones that trigger inflammation in your body (like systemic lupus erythematosus). In addition, people with high cholesterol often have a high risk of developing hypertension as well.

其是那些会引发自身炎症反应的疾病（如系统性红斑狼疮）。此外，高胆固醇个体患高血压的概率也非常高。

Section 2   Technologies for Promoting Chronic Disease's Self-management

Self-management refers to "strategies to change behavior using the individual's internal strength, and the ability to manage the symptoms, treatment, physical and social consequences, and lifestyle changes inherent in living with a chronic condition". One of the goals of community health professionals working with patients to achieve self-management is to empower them to manage their health by emphasizing their central role in their health care. "Empowerment" is not a technique or strategy, but rather a vision that guides each encounter with our patients and requires that both professionals and patients adopt new roles. There is a difference between traditional patient education and self-management education. The goal of self-management education and training is to enable patients to take the information that they learn about their illness, then solve problems that are meaningful to them, and enhance a greater sense of confidence and self-efficacy with respect to their disease self-management.

第二节   慢性病自我管理促进技术

自我管理指的是"利用个人内在的力量来改变行为的策略，以及管理慢性病症状、治疗、身体与社会结局和改变固有生活方式的能力"。社区医护人员与患者合作实现自我管理的目标之一，是通过强调患者在医疗保健中的核心作用，促使他们管理自己的健康。其中"赋权"不是一种技术或策略，而是一种愿景，它指导工作人员与患者的每次会面，并要求专业人员和患者都扮演新的角色。传统的患者教育和自我管理教育是有区别的。自我管理教育和培训的目标是使患者能够获得有关他们自身疾病的信息，然后解决对他们有意义的问题，让患者对自身疾病管理有更大的信心和自我效能感。

I. Motivational Interviewing

To offer appropriate opportunities for behavior change to patients with chronic illness, the patient's willingness to change needs to be assessed first. Assessing confidence and importance perceptions is one of several strategies employed in motivational interviewing. Motivational interviewing has its roots in addiction medicine and is now used in other settings to achieve many different behavior

一、动机访谈

为了给慢性病患者提供适当的行为改变机会，首先需要评估患者的改变意愿。此外，评估信心和重要性认知也是动机访谈中采用的几种策略之一。动机访谈起源于成瘾医学，现在被用于其他场合，以改变许多不同的行为和生活方式，是"一种以人为中心的指导性沟通方法，通过帮助一个人解决改变的矛盾心理来增强改变的内在动机"。

and lifestyle changes. Motivational interviewing is "a person-centered, directive method of communication used for enhancing intrinsic motivation to change by helping a person resolve her or his ambivalence to change".

Motivational interviewing is one patient-centered strategy to empower patients to engage in self-care. The spirit of motivational interviewing recognizes that the patients are the experts on their illness experience, and that it is the patients who should decide what behavior, if any, should be the focus. Achieving a small change may give patients enough confidence to try other changes. By honoring the autonomy of the patients and their choices, there is more likely to be an interaction that can be mutually beneficial. The four techniques of motivational interviewing are the following:

1. Express Empathy Expression of empathy is critical to motivational interviewing. Once we are able to express an understanding of patients' experiences, they may consider to change. When receiving an empathetic response, their psychological or physical defenses will decrease. Questions such as "What is the hardest thing about diabetes for you" can play an important role in starting a dialogue with the patient.

2. Develop Discrepancy Motivation to change occurs when people perceive a discrepancy between where they are and where they want to be. The partial responsibility of community health workers is to facilitate patients' understanding of the long-term effects of a behavior. By empowering patients to understand that the behavior may not be leading them to "achieve their goals", they may become more likely to consider changing the behavior. This intervention needs to be gentle and gradual and to enable the patient to recognize the long-term effects of the behavior.

3. Accept Resistance Opposing a patient's reflexive resistance to change usually leads the patient to act defensively. The healthcare professionals can help the patient explore

动机访谈是一种以患者为中心的策略，可以让患者参与自我护理。动机访谈的核心理念是：患者是他们疾病经历的专家，应该由患者决定什么行为（如果有的话）应该成为焦点。实现一个小的改变就可能会让患者有足够的信心尝试其他改变。通过尊重患者的自主性和选择，更有可能产生互利的互动。动机访谈的 4 种技巧如下：

1. 表达同理心 表达同理心对动机访谈至关重要。一旦能够表达对患者经历的理解，他们可能会考虑改变。当患者感受到同理心时，他们的心理或者躯体防御意识会下降。诸如"对你来说，管理糖尿病最难的事情是什么？"之类的问题可以在与患者建立对话时发挥重要作用。

2. 呈现差异 当人们意识到自己所在的位置和想要的位置之间存在差异时，就会产生改变的动机。社区医护人员的部分职责是促进患者对行为长期影响的理解。让患者了解一种行为可能不会引导他们"去他们想去的地方"，他们可能会考虑改变这种行为。这种干预需要温和、循序渐进，使患者能够认识到行为的长期影响。

3. 接纳抵抗 反对患者对改变的反射性抵抗通常会导致他们采取防御行动。医疗保健专家可以帮助患者自由地探索其他行为或行动，将其抵抗力作为寻找可能性的能量。

alternative behaviors or actions freely, using his or her resistance as energy for possibilities.

　　4. Increase Self-efficacy　When patients feel efficacious with a change, there is a greater likelihood that they will continue to attempt more changes. The role of the health professionals is to help identify patients' successes. This has the potential to be a very powerful technique in motivating the patient to continue behavior change. When one change is not successful, consider assisting the patient to identify an alternative plan.

Ⅱ. Agenda Setting

　　Agenda setting is a tool that can be used to help with motivational interviewing. It needs to be very specific; for example, if the long-term goal is to lose weight, the patient needs to narrow it down to specific short-term behaviors, perhaps beginning with walking. One way to set the agenda is to use a decision-making wheel. It is a structured, visual tool designed to guide individuals or groups through a systematic process of evaluating options and making informed choices. It typically breaks down complex decisions into manageable steps, integrating criteria such as priorities, risks, benefits, and constraints to facilitate clarity and objectivity.

Ⅲ. Typical Day Strategy

　　The spirit of this strategy is to encourage the patient to verbally paint a picture of a typical day for themselves as the support physician or educator to appreciate the context of what change may involve. The patient describes a typical day for the purposes of establishing rapport and helping the evaluator understand the barriers that may exist for the patient. The conversation can start like: "I appreciate that change can be tough. Can you take me through your typical day so I can get a picture of what day-to-day life is like for you?" The strategy is most effective if the healthcare

　　4. 提高自我效能　当患者对要采取的改变有信心时，他们更有可能继续尝试更多的改变。专业技术人员的职责是帮助患者识别成功。这有可能成为一种非常强大的技术，激励患者继续改变行为。当一个改变不成功时，应考虑帮助患者确定替代计划。

二、设置日程

　　设置日程是一种可以用来辅助进行动机访谈的工具。设置日程需要非常具体，例如，如果长期目标是减肥，患者需要将其缩小到特定的短期行为，也许从走路开始。设置日程有一种方法是使用决策轮。决策轮是一个结构化的、可视化的工具，旨在指导个人或团队通过一个系统的流程来评估选项并做出明智的选择。它通常将复杂的决策分解为可管理的步骤，并结合优先级、风险、收益和限制等标准，以增强决策的清晰度和客观性。

三、典型的一天

　　该策略的核心是鼓励患者口头描绘典型的一天，以便支持医生或教育工作者能够理解可能涉及的变化的背景。患者描述了一个典型的一天，目的是建立融洽关系并帮助评估者了解患者可能存在的障碍。交流可以这样开始："我知道改变可能很艰难。你能带我了解你典型的一天吗？这样我就能更清楚你的日常生活。"专业人员应尊重患者的陈述同时避免审问或形成意见，这时策略才最为有效。因为这是患者自己表述的经验。作为日常讨论对话的伙伴，专业人员的回应仅应该反映患者所描述的困难或他们认识到的障碍。

professionals respect the patients' narrative but avoid interrogation or forming opinions. This is the patient's experience as the patient sees it. As a partner in the dialogue of a typical day discussion, the professionals' responses simply mirror the difficulties or recognize the barriers that the patient is describing.

IV. Exploring Pros and Cons of Changing or Not Changing

This strategy encourages the patient to weigh the "pros and cons" of a behavior change. An alternative strategy is to ask the patient to weigh the "pros and cons" of not making a behavior change. The healthcare professionals' role as the provider is to describe a structure in which the pros or the cons can happen and to support the patient in the process. Table 8-1 provides a simple example of exploring the pros and cons of quitting smoking.

四、探索改变与不改变的利弊

该策略主要是鼓励患者权衡行为改变的"利弊"。同时也让患者权衡不改变行为的"利弊"。医疗保健专业人员的角色是描述一个有利或不利的结构，并在这个过程中支持患者。表 8-1 提供了一个探索利弊的简单示例。

Table 8-1 Discussing the Pros and Cons of Behavior Change: Quit Smoking

Pros	Cons
Improved health	Possible sense of failure
Money saved	Possible weight gain
Better sense of smell	Possible increased nervousness
Possibly making new friends	Possible loss of smoking friends

表 8-1 讨论戒烟行为的损失和获益

获益	损失
促进健康	可能引发失败感
省钱	可能导致体重上升
嗅觉改善	可能增加紧张情绪
可能结交新朋友	可能损失烟友

V. Appropriate Information Exchange

Before giving instructions, it is important to determine the patient's knowledge of their illnesses. Before patients consider changing

五、适当的信息交流

给患者指导前，一定要确定患者对其疾病的了解。例如，在患者考虑改变饮食行为之前，他们可能需要获得营养信息，以便确定对其日

diatery behavior, for example, they may need to receive nutrition information so they can determine the impacts on their typical day. Before giving information, ask patients about their interest in receiving information. If a patient verbalizes a disinterest in a topic of information or a negative opinion about learning more about an issue, clearly it will not be time well spent to do so. In fact, it may undermine the rapport with the patient for future meetings. By simply asking about the patients' interest levels, providers can gain insight into their motivations.

In addition, along the way when delivering information, it is a good idea to check in with patients in a nonjudgmental way. Questions such as "Have you heard this information before?" or "Some people find this difficult to do. How does it sound to you?" may help elicit feedback. Offering a self-management class to a patient is an option, but not necessarily a "magic bullet." Unless the patient elects to participate in the class, it is unlikely that the class will be an effective option. Certainly, making the intervention available to the patient is an appropriate step by the provider, but the patient's willingness is important for the training session to be effective.

Overall, it is important to recognize that chronic illness is largely self-managed by the healthcare providers. There are many different strategies and tools that can support self-management. The patient's perception of importance and confidence are extremely important and often overlooked. More advanced techniques involving motivational interviewing can help patients who are interested in a behavior change. The most effective and positive changes are those arrived at mutually by the patient and the provider. These create a trust-filled launching pad toward more successful action plans and a cascade of successes.

常生活的影响。提供信息之前，应评估患者对接收信息的兴趣。如果患者口头表示对某个信息主题不感兴趣，或对了解更多有关某个问题的信息持负面看法，那么这显然不是一个很好的沟通和交流时刻。事实上，这还可能会破坏与患者在未来沟通中的融洽关系。通过简单地询问患者的兴趣水平，专业人员还可以更深入地了解他们的动机。

另外，在传递信息的过程中，最好以非评判的方式与患者交流。采取诸如"你以前听过这些信息吗？"或"有些人觉得很难做到这一点，你觉得这听起来怎么样？"之类的问题，可能有助于获得反馈。为患者提供自我管理课程是一种选择，但不一定是"灵丹妙药"。除非患者愿意选择参加该课程，否则该课程不太可能是一种有效的选择。当然，向患者提供干预是专业人员的一个标准的步骤，但为了使培训课程有效，对患者个人意愿的评估是很重要的。

总之，专业人员应该充分意识到，慢性病在很大程度上需要自我管理，而且有许多不同的策略和工具可以支持自我管理。尽管患者对重要性和自信的感知是极其重要的，但是这常常被忽视。更高级的技术，如动机访谈，可以帮助那些对行为改变感兴趣的患者。最有效和积极的改变是患者和专业人员提供者共同达成的。这些行为可以创造一个充满信任的起点，朝着行动计划和后续系列的成功前进。

Section 3　Community Management of Hypertension

I. Concept of Hypertension

Hypertension is defined as a clinic blood pressure of ≥ 140/90mmHg or a home blood pressure of ≥ 135/85mmHg when not using antihypertensive medications; or a 24-hour ambulatory blood pressure of ≥ 130/80mmHg, a daytime blood pressure of ≥ 135/85mmHg, or a nighttime blood pressure of ≥ 120/70mmHg.

II. Epidemiology of Hypertension

In 2023, the World Health Organization released the *Global report on hypertension*. It is stated that the global prevalence of hypertension in adults aged 30–79 is about 33%, with the prevalence of hypertension slightly higher in men than in women (34% vs. 32%). In 2018, the prevalence rate of hypertension in China is on the rise, and the prevalence rate of hypertension in adults over 18 years old is 27.5%. In addition to the increase in the prevalence rate of hypertension in elderly people, the prevalence rate of hypertension in middle-aged and young people in China is also on the rise in recent years, and most of them are diastolic hypertension. The prevalence of hypertension increased from south to north. The prevalence rate of hypertension increased faster in rural areas than in urban areas. In addition, the awareness rate, treatment rate and control rate of hypertension patients in our country have achieved good results, but overall are still at a low level, up to 51.6%, 45.8%, and 16.8%, respectively.

III. Risk Factors of Hypertension

i. A High-sodium, Low-potassium Diet

Excessive sodium intake can raise blood pressure. Of all deaths from cardiovascular causes

第三节　高血压的社区管理

一、高血压的概念

高血压被定义为在未使用抗高血压药的情况下，诊室血压≥140/90mmHg，或家庭血压≥135/85mmHg；或24h动态血压≥130/80mmHg，白天血压≥135/85mmHg，夜间血压≥120/70mmHg。

二、高血压的流行病学

世界卫生组织于2023年发布了《全球高血压报告》，报告中指出，全球30~79岁成人高血压患病率约为33%，其中男性高血压患病率略高于女性（34% vs. 32%）。2018年，中国高血压调查数据显示，我国高血压患病率总体呈上升趋势，18岁以上成人高血压患病率为27.5%；近年来，除老年高血压患病率升高外，我国中青年高血压的患病率也呈明显上升趋势，且多表现为舒张压增高；从南方到北方，高血压患病率递增；农村地区高血压患病率增长速度快于城市地区。此外，我国高血压患者的知晓率、治疗率和控制率已取得较好成绩，但总体仍处于较低的水平，分别为51.6%、45.8%和16.8%。

三、高血压的危险因素

（一）高钠低钾饮食

过量摄入钠会升高血压。在2019年发生的所有心血管原因导致的死亡中，近200万人是

that occurred in 2019, nearly 2 million were due to excessive sodium intake resulting in 24-hour urinary sodium excretion above the reference level of 1–5g per day, more than any other dietary factor. The global average sodium intake is estimated at 4,310mg/d (10.78g/d for salt), far exceeding physiological requirements and more than double the WHO recommendation (an adult sodium intake of <2,000mg/d, equivalent to <5g salt). In many high-income countries, and increasingly in low- and middle-income countries, a significant portion of sodium in the diet comes from processed foods such as breads, cereals, processed meats, and dairy products. Moderate reductions in sodium intake and increases in potassium intake can significantly lower blood pressure and could prevent millions of premature deaths. Using potassium-rich salt substitutes are an affordable strategy for simultaneously reducing sodium and increasing potassium intake and have been shown to be beneficial for lowering blood pressure and preventing cardiovascular events.

ii. Excessive Drinking

In 2023, the World Health Organization has released *Global report on hypertension*, in which it is pointed out that excessive alcohol consumption ranked eighth in the global risk of death in 2019. Excessive drinking includes hazardous drinking (41–60g for men, 21–40g for women of alcohol intake per occasion) and harmful drinking (more than 60g for men, more than 40g for women). There are a large number of drinkers in China, and the harmful drinking rate among residents over 18 years old is 9.3%. Ethanol restriction was significantly associated with lower blood pressure, with an average 67% reduction in alcohol intake, 3.31mmHg in SBP, and 2.04mmHg in DBP. Studies have shown that even for light drinkers, reducing ethanol intake can improve cardiovascular health and reduce the risk of cardiovascular disease. Due to the lack of clinical trials demonstrating the beneficial effects of

由于钠摄入过量导致 24 小时尿钠排泄量高于每天 1~5g 的参考水平，这一数字超过了其他饮食因素造成的死亡数。全球平均钠摄入量为 4 310mg/d（盐 10.78g/d），远远超过生理需求，是世界卫生组织建议摄入量（成人钠摄入量<2 000mg/d，相当于<5g 盐）的两倍之多。在许多高收入国家，以及越来越多的中低收入国家，饮食中很大一部分钠来自加工食品，如面包、谷物、加工肉类和乳制品。适度减少钠摄入量和增加钾摄入量可以显著降低血压，并可以防止数百万人过早死亡。使用富含钾的盐替代品是一种同时减少钠和增加钾摄入量的经济实惠的策略，已被证明对降低血压和预防心血管事件有益。

（二）过量饮酒

2023 年，世界卫生组织发布《全球高血压报告》，报告指出 2019 年过量饮酒在全球死亡风险中排名第八。过量饮酒包括危险饮酒（单次饮酒量：男性 41~60g，女性 21~40g）和有害饮酒（单次饮酒量：男性 60g 以上，女性 40g 以上）。我国饮酒人数众多，18 岁以上居民饮酒者中有害饮酒率为 9.3%。限制饮酒与血压下降显著相关，乙醇摄入量平均减少 67%，SBP 下降 3.31mmHg，DBP 下降 2.04mmHg。相关研究表明，即使对少量饮酒的人而言，减少乙醇摄入量也能够改善心血管健康，降低心血管疾病的发病风险。由于缺乏临床试验证明乙醇对主要心血管事件的有益影响，并且考虑到高血压和其他疾病的风险，因此，不支持通过饮酒来预防心血管疾病。

ethanol on major cardiovascular events, and given the risk of hypertension and other diseases, alcohol intake is not supported to promote cardiovascular disease prevention.

iii. Smoking

Tobacco was responsible for 8.7 million deaths globally in 2019, including 3.2 million from cardiovascular disease. The relationship between smoking and blood pressure is complex. While the scientific evidence on the chronic effects of tobacco use on hypertension levels is inconclusive, smoking and exposure to second-hand smoke have an indirect and sustained effect on hypertension, primarily by stimulating the sympathetic nervous system. At the same time, studies have shown that smokeless tobacco use may dramatically raise blood pressure as well. Smoking not only reduces life expectancy for individuals and those exposed to second-hand smoke but also adversely affects quality of life.

iv. Overweight and Obesity

Overweight and obesity significantly increase the risk of all-cause death worldwide and are important risk factors for hypertension. According to the *Report on the Nutrition and Chronic Diseases Status of Chinese Residents (2020)*, the proportion of overweight and obesity in our population has increased significantly, the overweight rate of middle-aged people aged 35–64 is 34.3%, and the obesity rate is 16.4%, among which women are higher than men, urban people are higher than rural people, and northern residents are higher than southern residents. A follow-up study on the relationship between overweight and obesity and hypertension in Chinese adults found that with the increase of body mass index, the risk of hypertension in the overweight and obesity group was 1.16–1.45 times that of the normal weight group. Visceral obesity is closely related to hypertension, and the risk of hypertension increases with the increase of visceral fat index. In addition, visceral obesity is closely related to

（三）吸烟

2019 年烟草在全球造成 870 万人死亡，其中 320 万人死于心血管疾病。吸烟和血压之间的关系是复杂的。尽管烟草使用是否直接导致血压水平升高以及具体的影响机制等方面，还没有确凿的、一致性的科学结论，但吸烟和接触二手烟可以通过刺激交感神经系统，对高血压产生间接且持续的影响。同时研究表明，无烟烟草的使用也可能会显著升高血压。吸烟不仅会缩短个人和二手烟接触者的预期寿命，还会对生活质量产生不利影响。

（四）超重和肥胖

超重和肥胖显著增加全球人群全因死亡的风险，同时也是高血压患病的重要危险因素。《中国居民营养与慢性病状况报告（2020 年）》显示我国人群中超重和肥胖的比例明显增加，35~64 岁中年人的超重率为 34.3%，肥胖率为 16.4%，其中女性高于男性，城市人群高于农村，北方居民高于南方。一项关于中国成年人超重和肥胖与高血压发病关系的随访研究发现，随着体重指数的增加，超重肥胖组的高血压发病风险是体重正常组的 1.16~1.45 倍。内脏型肥胖与高血压的关系较为密切，高血压患病风险随着内脏脂肪指数的增加而增加。此外，内脏型肥胖与代谢综合征密切相关，可导致糖代谢、脂代谢异常。

metabolic syndrome, which can lead to abnormal glucose and lipid metabolism.

v. Chronic Stress

Long-term mental stress is a risk factor for hypertension. Mental stress can activate the sympathetic plexuses and increase blood pressure. The *Chinese Hypertension Prevention and Treatment Guidelines 2024* emphasizes the importance of understanding individuals' psychological and mental states, including the presence of anxiety, depression, insomnia, etc. The report points out that a meta-analysis including 59 cross-sectional and prospective studies found that the risk of developing hypertension for individuals with anxiety disorders is 1.37 and 1.40 times that of normal people, respectively.

vi. Lack of Exercise

Physical activity is associated with hypertension control. There is evidence that increasing physical activity can improve physical function in people with high blood pressure and reduce the progression of cardiovascular disease and the risk of death. For example, people with high blood pressure who exercise can lower their systolic blood pressure by about 12mmHg and their diastolic blood pressure by about 6mmHg compared to people who don't exercise; in addition, people with high blood pressure who are physically active can significantly improve their health-related quality of life. For adults with high blood pressure, there is evidence to support that aerobic exercise, muscle-strengthening activities and the combination of both can improve the progression of cardiovascular disease. On the other hand, prolonged sedentary behavior is associated with higher rates of all-cause mortality, cardiovascular mortality, and cardiovascular disease incidence.

vii. Air Pollution

Air pollution is one of the major risk factors for non-communicable diseases. Globally, 99% of

（五）慢性压力

长期精神压力是高血压患病的危险因素，精神压力可激活交感神经丛而使血压升高。《中国高血压防治指南 2024》强调应该了解个体的精神心理状态，包括是否存在焦虑、抑郁、失眠等。报告指出，一项包括 59 项横断面研究和前瞻性研究的荟萃分析发现，焦虑障碍患者发生高血压的风险分别是正常人的 1.37 和 1.40 倍。

（六）运动缺乏

体力活动与高血压控制相关。有证据表明，增加体力活动可以改善高血压患者的身体功能，延缓心血管疾病的进展和降低死亡风险。例如，与不运动者相比，积极运动的高血压患者可以将收缩压降低约 12mmHg，舒张压降低约 6mmHg；此外，积极运动的高血压患者与健康相关的生活质量也会得到改善。对于患有高血压的成年人，有证据支持有氧运动和肌肉强化活动以及两者结合可预防心血管疾病的进展。此外，长时间的久坐行为与更高的全因死亡率、心血管死亡率和心血管疾病发病率有关。

（七）空气污染

空气污染是非传染性疾病的主要危险因素之一。在全球范围内，99% 的人口暴露在不符

the population is exposed to air quality that does not meet the levels recommended by the WHO *Air Quality Guidelines*. In 2021, 2.3 billion people worldwide rely primarily on polluting fuels and cooking equipment, exposing them to dangerous levels of air pollutants, especially in low- and middle-income countries where access to clean energy remains challenging. Particulate matter 2.5 (PM2.5), the best indicator for assessing the health effects of air pollution, ranked fourth in the global risk of death in 2019. Cardiovascular diseases such as ischemic heart disease and stroke are the main diseases attributable to air pollution exposure, and high blood pressure is a more common cause of these diseases. In addition, comprehensive evidence suggests that long-term exposure to PM2.5 increases the risk of hypertension in adults for every $10\mu g/m^3$ increase in PM2.5.

viii. Other Risk Factors

In addition to the above risk factors for hypertension, other risk factors include increased age, family history of hypertension, high altitude, anti-tumor therapy, and low education level.

IV. Chinese Community Management Model

The prevention and treatment of hypertension in the community should adopt the comprehensive prevention and treatment strategy of the whole population, the high risk population and patients with hypertension, and the integrated intervention measures of primary prevention, secondary prevention, and tertiary prevention.

1. Population Strategy

The population strategy mainly adopts health promotion theories, emphasizing the following aspects:

(1) Policy Development and Environmental Support: Promoting healthy lifestyles, especially reducing salt intake and weight control, promoting

合世界卫生组织《全球空气质量指南》建议水平的空气中。2021年全球有23亿人依赖污染性燃料和烹饪设备，这使他们暴露在危险水平的空气污染物中，特别是在不易获得清洁能源的中低收入国家。细颗粒物（PM2.5）是评估空气污染对健康影响的最佳指标，在2019年全球死亡风险中排名第四。缺血性心脏病和脑卒中等心血管疾病是空气污染暴露引起的主要疾病，而高血压是这些疾病较为普遍的病因。此外，综合证据表明，长期暴露于PM2.5中，PM2.5每增加$10\mu g/m^3$，成年人患高血压的风险就会增加。

（八）其他危险因素

除以上高血压发病的危险因素外，其他危险因素还包括年龄增加、家族史、高海拔、抗肿瘤治疗以及低文化水平等。

四、我国社区管理模式

社区高血压防治应采取面对全人群、高血压易患（高危）人群和高血压患者的综合防治策略，采取一级预防、二级预防与三级预防相结合的综合一体化的干预措施。

1. 全人群策略

全人群策略主要采用健康促进相关理论，强调以下几方面：

（1）政策制定与环境支持：提倡健康生活方式，特别是强调减少食盐的摄入和控制体重，促进政策制定，为高血压的早期发现和治疗创造

the development of policies, and creating a supportive environment for the early detection and treatment of hypertension.

(2) Health Education: Community health care service providers should strive for the support and cooperation of the local government, and carry out various forms of hypertension prevention and control publicity and education for the whole population in the community.

(3) Community Participation: Based on the existing health care network, multi-sectoral collaboration and mobilization of the whole community to participate in the prevention and treatment of hypertension.

(4) Place Intervention: Health promotion places are divided into five categories: city proper, hospitals, residential communities, workplaces, and schools. According to the characteristics of different places to develop and implement hypertension intervention plan.

2. High-risk Groups Strategy (Susceptible to Hypertension)

The intervention of community high risk groups mainly emphasizes early detection of risk factors that may lead to hypertension and effective intervention to prevent the occurrence of hypertension.

(1) Screening of at High Risk of Hypertension: Hypertension risk factors mainly include high normal blood pressure, overweight and obesity, alcoholism and a high salt diet.

(2) Prevention and Treatment Strategies for People Prone to Hypertension: Health examination. Health examination should include general inquiry, height, weight, blood pressure, urine routine test, blood glucose, plasma lipid, kidney function, electrocardiogram, etc.

(3) Level of Control of Risk Factors: As with the population strategy, follow-up management and lifestyle guidance are given to individuals at high risk of physical examination.

支持性环境。

（2）健康教育：社区卫生保健服务提供者应争取当地政府的支持和配合，对社区全人群开展多种形式的关于高血压防治的宣传和教育。

（3）社区参与：以现有的卫生保健网为基础，多部门协作，动员全社区参与高血压防治工作。

（4）场所干预：健康促进的场所分为五类：市区、医院、社区、工作场所、学校。根据不同场所的特点制订和实施相应的高血压干预计划。

2. 高血压高危（易患）人群策略

社区高危人群的干预主要强调早期发现可能导致高血压的危险因素并加以有效干预，预防高血压的发生。

（1）高血压易患人群的筛选：高血压危险因素主要包括正常高值血压、超重和肥胖、酗酒以及高盐饮食。

（2）高血压易患人群的防治策略：健康体检。健康体检应包括一般询问，测量身高、体重、血压，尿常规，测定血糖、血脂、肾功能，心电图等。

（3）风险因素的控制水平：与全人群策略相同，对体检高危人群进行随访管理和生活方式指导。

V. International Typical Hypertension Management Project

i. India Hypertension Control Initiative (IHCI)

IHCI is a collaborative initiative of the Ministry of Health and Family Welfare, the Government of India, State Governments, the Indian Council of Medical Research, WHO India, and Resolve to Save Lives as technical partners. Launched in 2018, the initiative aims to improve community hypertension control using the WHO HEARTS strategy of evidence-based treatment programmers, uninterrupted drug supply, patient-centered care, task sharing and digital information systems. IHCI was launched in selected districts in five states and has expanded to 155 districts in 27 states as of June 2023, enrolling a total of 5.8 million hypertensive patients.

ii. Hypertension Management Program (HMP)

HMP is a team-based, patient-centered, integrated care model made up of 10 key program components to address challenges in hypertension management. The program is modeled on the hypertension management program of Kaiser Permanente (KPCO) in Colorado and packaged by the U.S. Centers for Disease Control and Prevention. The goal is to improve the quality of care for people with hypertension and reduce the number of people with uncontrolled hypertension, thereby improving the overall health and well-being of each patient.

BOX 8-1　Learning More

World Hypertension Day

In 2005, the World Hypertension League (WHL) first initiated the World Hypertension Day campaign decided to designate May 17 as the "World Hypertension Day" each year to draw attention to the prevention and treatment of hypertension.May 17, 2025 marks the 21st World

五、国际典型高血压管理项目

（一）印度高血压控制计划

印度高血压控制计划（India Hypertension Control Initiative，IHCI）是由印度卫生和家庭福利部、印度政府、各联邦政府、印度医学研究委员会、世界卫生组织印度办事处和"拯救生命决心"作为技术合作伙伴的一项合作倡议。该倡议于 2018 年启动，旨在利用世界卫生组织 HEARTS 战略，即循证治疗方案、不间断药物供应、以患者为中心的护理、任务共享和数字信息系统，改善社区高血压控制。IHCI 在 5 个州的选定地区启动，截至 2023 年 6 月，已扩大到 27 个州的 155 个地区，共招募了 580 万高血压患者。

（二）美国高血压管理计划

美国高血压管理计划（Hypertension Management Program，HMP）是一种以团队为基础、以患者为中心的综合护理模式，由 10 个关键项目组成，以应对高血压管理方面的挑战。该计划以美国科罗拉多州 Kaiser Permanente（KPCO）的高血压管理计划为蓝本，由美国疾病控制和预防中心（U.S. Centers for Disease Control and Prevention）整理，其目标是提高高血压患者护理质量，减少高血压管理失败患者的数量，从而改善每位患者的整体健康。

BOX 8-1　知识拓展

世界高血压日

2005 年，世界高血压联盟首次发起世界高血压日活动，决定将每年的 5 月 17 日定为"世界高血压日"，旨在引起人们对防治高血压的重视。2025 年 5 月 17 日是第 21 个世界高血压日，主题为"精准测量，有效控制，健康长寿"。

Hypertension Day, with the theme "Measure Your Blood Pressure Accurately, Control It, Live Longer".

Section 4   Community Management of Diabetes

I. Concept of Diabetes

Diabetes is a series of metabolic disorders of sugar, protein, fat, water, and electrolytes caused by genetic factors, endocrine disorders and other pathogenic factors, resulting in pancreas islet dysfunction and insulin resistance. Clinically, hyperglycemia is the main feature. The typical symptoms of diabetes are three more and one less, that is, excessive drinking, excessive eating, excessive urine and weight loss. Based on etiological evidence, in 2019, the World Health Organization updated the classification of diabetes into six types, namely type 1 diabetes, type 2 diabetes, mixed diabetes, other specific types of diabetes, unclassified diabetes, and gestational diabetes. Type 2 diabetes mellitus (T2DM) is predominant in China.

II. Epidemiology of Diabetes

The International Diabetes Federation (IDF)'s Diabetes Atlas (10th edition) released in 2021 points out that there are 537 million people with diabetes globally . It is estimated that there are 485 million diabetic patients in the population aged 20–79 years. There are 43 countries or regions in the world with an age-standardized prevalence of diabetes of more than 10%. In recent 30 years, the prevalence rate of diabetes in China has increased significantly. According to data from the International Diabetes Federation (IDF), as of 2021, the number of people with diabetes in the 20–79 age group in China has reached 141 million. The outbreak is mainly concentrated in people with

第四节   糖尿病的社区管理

一、糖尿病的概念

糖尿病是由遗传因素、内分泌功能紊乱等多种致病因素引发的糖、蛋白质、脂肪、水和电解质等一系列代谢紊乱，导致胰岛功能减退和胰岛素抵抗。临床上以高血糖为主要特点。糖尿病的典型症状是三多一少，即多饮、多食、多尿和体重减少。根据病因学证据，2019 年世界卫生组织将糖尿病分类更新为 6 种类型，即 1 型糖尿病、2 型糖尿病、混合型糖尿病、其他特殊类型糖尿病、未分类糖尿病和妊娠糖尿病。我国以 2 型糖尿病（T2DM）为主。

二、糖尿病的流行病学

国际糖尿病联盟（IDF）2021 年发布的《全球糖尿病地图》（第 10 版）指出全球共有 5.37 亿糖尿病患者。据估计，20~79 岁人群中有 4.85 亿糖尿病患者。全球有 43 个国家或地区的糖尿病年龄标准化患病率超过 10%。近 30 多年来，我国糖尿病患病率显著上升。根据国际糖尿病联盟（IDF）的数据，截至 2021 年，中国 20~79 岁人群中，糖尿病的患病人数达到了 1.41 亿，主要集中在低学历人群、低家庭收入者、超重肥胖人群、有糖尿病家族史人群；城乡患病率几乎没有差异；汉族患病率高于少数民族；随着年龄的增加，患病风险也随之增加，50 岁以后增长更快。

low education, low family income, overweight and obese people, and people with a family history of diabetes. There is almost no difference in urban and rural prevalence, and the prevalence rate of Han people is higher than that of ethnic minorities. The risk of disease also increases with age and increases more rapidly after the age of 50.

III. Risk Factors of Diabetes

i. Urbanization and Aging

With economic development, China's urbanization process has accelerated significantly, and the proportion of urban population in the national population has risen from 36.2 percent in 2000 to 65.2 percent in 2023. Urbanization has changed people's lifestyles, the pace of life has significantly accelerated and physical activity has significantly decreased, which are all risk factors for promoting diabetes. In addition, diabetes is also an aging disease, with the increasing degree of aging in China, the prevalence of diabetes is also rising rapidly.

ii. Overweight and Obesity

Overweight and obesity can seriously affect a person's health, quality of life, and life expectancy. Obesity is a risk factor and pathological basis for chronic noninfectious diseases such as hypertension, diabetes, cardio-cerebrovascular disease and, tumors. Obesity, especially central obesity (waist circumference ≥ 90cm in men and ≥ 85cm in women), is a major risk factor for type 2 diabetes mellitus and its cardiovascular and cerebrovascular complications. In recent years, the population of overweight and obesity has increased rapidly in our country. *The Dietary Guidelines for Chinese Residents* (*2022*) states that the overweight and obesity prevalence among China's adult population exceeds 50%, the overweight or obesity rate of children and adolescents aged 6 to 17 years old is 19%, and the overweight or obesity rate of children under 6 years old is 10.4%. According

三、糖尿病的危险因素

（一）城市化、老龄化

随着经济发展，我国的城市化进程明显加快，城镇人口占全国人口比例从 2000 年的 36.2% 上升到 2023 年的 66.2%。城市化改变了人们的生活方式，生活节奏明显加快、身体活动显著下降，这些都是促进糖尿病发生的危险因素。此外，糖尿病亦是一种老龄化疾病，随着我国老龄化程度的不断加深，糖尿病患病率也快速上升。

（二）超重和肥胖

超重和肥胖会严重影响人的健康、生活质量和期望寿命。肥胖是引起高血压、糖尿病、心脑血管疾病、肿瘤等慢性非传染性疾病的危险因素和病理基础。肥胖，尤其是中心型肥胖（男性腰围 ≥ 90cm，女性腰围 ≥ 85cm），是 2 型糖尿病及其心脑血管并发症发生的主要危险因素。近年来，我国超重及肥胖人群比例快速上升。《中国居民膳食指南（2022）》指出，根据中国的超重与肥胖标准，我国成年人超重或肥胖率已超过 50%，6~17 岁儿童和青少年的超重或肥胖率为 19%，6 岁以下儿童的超重或肥胖率为 10.4%。按照中国标准［体重指数（BMI）≥28kg/m^2］，中国的肥胖症数量位居全球第一，肥胖已成为我国严重的公共卫生问题之一。我国糖尿病患者中超重和肥胖的比例分别为 41% 和 24.3%，即约有 2/3 的糖尿病患者处于超重或肥胖状态，其中中心型肥胖患者占比高达 45.4%。减轻体重可以改善胰岛素抵抗、降低血糖并改善

to the Chinese standard [body mass index (BMI) ≥ 28kg/m²], China ranks first in the world in the number of obesity. Obesity has become one of the serious public health problems in our country. The proportion of overweight and obesity among diabetic patients in China is 41% and 24.3% respectively, that is, about 2/3 of diabetic patients are overweight or obese, of which 45.4% are central type obese patients. Weight loss can improve insulin resistance, lower blood glucose, and improve risk factors for cardiovascular disease. In overweight and obese patients with type 2 diabetes, a 3% to 5% weight loss can significantly reduce HbA1c, triglyceride, and blood pressure levels, and improve quality of life.

iii. Unhealthy Diet

Unhealthy diets high in salt, sugar, and fat are risk factors for diabetes and other metabolic diseases. According to a survey in 2018, the daily intake of cooking salt per capita of Chinese residents was 6.3g (recommended value by the World Health Organization is 5g), and the daily intake of edible oil per capita of Chinese households was 43.2g (recommended standard of *the Chinese Dietary Guidelines* (*2022*) is 25–30g per day). The proportion of energy provided by dietary fat reached 32.9% (the upper limit of the recommended value in *the Chinese Dietary Guidelines* is 30%). At present, China's per capita daily intake of added sugar (mainly sucrose, that is, white granulated sugar, brown sugar, etc.) is about 30g, of which the intake of children and adolescents deserves great attention. A proper diet is the basis for the treatment of all types of diabetes and is an indispensable measure for prevention and control at any stage of the natural course of diabetes. A reasonable diet is helpful to control blood glucose, maintain ideal weight and prevent malnutrition, which is an important part of the prevention and treatment of diabetes and its complications. The diet of diabetic patients should

心血管疾病的危险因素。超重和肥胖的 2 型糖尿病患者减重 3%~5%，即能使糖化血红蛋白（HbA1c）、甘油三酯及血压水平显著降低，并提高生活质量。

（三）不健康饮食

高盐、高糖、高脂等不健康饮食是引起糖尿病及其他代谢性疾病的危险因素。2018 调查显示，我国居民人均每日烹调盐摄入量为 6.3g（世界卫生组织推荐值为 5g）；居民家庭人均每日食用油摄入量为 43.2g（《中国居民膳食指南（2022）》推荐标准为每天 25~30g）；居民膳食脂肪提供能量比例达到 32.9%（《中国居民膳食指南（2022）》推荐值上限为 30%）。目前我国人均每日添加糖（主要为蔗糖，即白砂糖、红糖等）的摄入量为 30g，其中儿童和青少年的摄入量问题值得高度关注。合理膳食是所有类型糖尿病治疗的基础，也是糖尿病自然病程中任何阶段预防和控制不可或缺的措施。合理膳食有利于控制血糖，有助于维持理想体重并预防营养不良的发生，是糖尿病及其并发症的预防和治疗的重要内容。糖尿病患者的饮食要遵循平衡膳食的原则，在控制总能量的前提下调整饮食结构，满足机体对各种营养素的需求，达到平稳控糖、减少血糖波动、预防糖尿病并发症的目的。

follow the principle of a balanced diet, adjust the diet structure under the premise of controlling the total energy, meet the needs of the body for various nutrients, and achieve the purpose of stable sugar control, reducing blood glucose fluctuations, and preventing diabetes complications.

iv. Lack of Exercise

The General Administration of Sport of China 2020 national fitness activity survey results show that: China's urban and rural residents regularly participate in physical exercise proportion of 37.2%. Among them, the regular exercise rate for adults is 30.3%, which is considered low. Lack of physical activity is an important reason for a variety of chronic diseases. Exercise is essential for the prevention of diabetes and plays an important role in the comprehensive management of people with type 2 diabetes. Regular exercise helps to control blood glucose, reduce cardiovascular risk factors, lose weight, and improve well-being. Epidemiological study results show that regular exercise for more than 8 weeks can reduce the HbA1c of type 2 diabetes patients by 0.66%, and the mortality of diabetes patients who insist on regular exercise for 12 to 14 years is significantly reduced.

v. Smoking

Smoking is harmful to health. There are more than 300 million smokers in China, and more than 1 million people die every year from smoking-related diseases, and more than 100,000 people die from second-hand smoke exposure. Smoking is associated with an increased risk of tumors, diabetes, diabetic macroangiopathy, diabetic microangiopathy, and premature death. Studies have shown that quitting smoking in people with type 2 diabetes can help improve metabolic indicators, lower blood pressure, and improve proteinuria. Every diabetic who smokes should be advised to stop smoking or tobacco products, reduce passive smoking, assess the patient's

（四）运动缺乏

国家体育总局 2020 年全民健身活动状况调查结果显示：我国城乡居民经常参加体育锻炼的比例为 37.2%，其中成年人经常锻炼率为 30.3%，处于较低水平。缺乏身体活动是多种慢性病发生的重要原因。运动锻炼对预防糖尿病至关重要，同时在 2 型糖尿病患者的综合管理中也占有重要地位。规律运动有助于控制血糖、减少心血管危险因素、减轻体重、提升幸福感。研究表明，规律运动 8 周以上可使 2 型糖尿病患者的 HbA1c 含量降低 0.66%，坚持规律运动 12~14 年的糖尿病患者病死率显著降低。

（五）吸烟

吸烟有害健康。我国现有吸烟者逾 3 亿，每年因吸烟相关疾病所致的死亡人数超过 100 万，二手烟暴露导致的死亡人数超过 10 万。吸烟与肿瘤、糖尿病、糖尿病大血管病变、糖尿病微血管病变、过早死亡的风险增加有关。研究表明 2 型糖尿病患者戒烟有助于改善代谢指标、降低血压、改善蛋白尿情况。应劝告每一位吸烟的糖尿病患者停止吸烟或停用烟草类制品，并减少被动吸烟，对患者吸烟状况和尼古丁依赖程度进行评估，提供戒烟咨询、戒烟热线，必要时使用药物等帮助患者戒烟。

smoking status and nicotine dependence, and provide counseling, a smoking cessation hotline, and medication if necessary to help the patient quit smoking.

vi. Mental and Psychological Stress

The occurrence and development of diabetes mellitus are closely related to mental and psychological factors, especially to individual psychological characteristics, emotional states, life events, or stress. For example, social and psychological adverse stimuli such as long-term excessive tension in work and study, disharmony in interpersonal relations, sudden unfortunate events in life, etc., will cause different degrees of emotional disorders, make people appear angry, anxiety, tension, depression, etc. cause blood glucose to rise, induce or aggravate diabetes. Mental and psychological factors may increase the risk and control difficulty of diabetes through behavioral mechanisms. Bad social and psychological states such as depression, anxiety and stress may lead to a series of unhealthy lifestyle behaviors, including smoking and drinking.

IV. Chinese Community Management Model

i. Service Target

Patients with type 2 diabetes among permanent residents aged 35 years and older in the community.

ii. Service Content

1. Screening

Targeted health education should be carried out for people at high risk of type 2 diabetes, and fasting blood glucose should be measured at least once a year, and health guidance should be received from medical staff.

2. Follow-up Evaluation

Patients with confirmed type 2 diabetes are offered free fasting blood glucose testing four times a year and at least four face-to-face follow-up visits.

（六）精神心理压力

糖尿病的发生和发展与精神心理因素密切相关，特别是在个人心理特征、情绪状态、生活事件或应激等方面。如工作学习长期过度紧张、人际关系不协调、生活中的突发不幸事件等社会、心理上的不良刺激等，都会造成不同程度的情绪障碍，使人出现愤怒、焦虑、紧张、抑郁等，引起血糖升高，诱发或加重糖尿病。精神和心理因素可能通过行为机制增加糖尿病的发病风险与控制难度。处于抑郁、焦虑、压力等不良社会心理状态可引发一系列不利于身体健康的生活方式行为习惯，包括吸烟、饮酒等。

四、我国社区管理模式

（一）服务对象

辖区内 35 岁及以上常住居民中的 2 型糖尿病患者。

（二）服务内容

1. 筛查

对工作中发现的 2 型糖尿病高危人群进行有针对性的健康教育，建议其每年至少测量 1 次空腹血糖，并接受医务人员的健康指导。

2. 随访评估

对确诊的 2 型糖尿病患者，每年提供 4 次免费空腹血糖检测，至少进行 4 次面对面随访。

3. Classified Intervention

(1) Patients who are satisfied with blood glucose control (fasting blood glucose <7.0mmol/L), have no adverse drug reactions, no new complications or no aggravation of the original complications will be scheduled for the next follow-up visit.

(2) Patients with unsatisfactory blood glucose control (fasting blood glucose ≥ 7.0mmol/L) or adverse drug reactions for the first time are guided according to their medication compliance, and existing drug dosages are increased if necessary, hypoglycemic drugs of different kinds are replaced or added, and follow-up is conducted at 2 weeks.

(3) Patients with unsatisfactory fasting blood glucose control or adverse drug reactions for two consecutive times, as well as new complications or aggravation of original complications, are recommended for referral to a superior hospital, and the referral situation is actively followed up within 2 weeks.

(4) Conduct targeted health education for all patients, work with patients to set lifestyle improvement goals and assess progress at the next follow-up visit. Inform patients which abnormal symptoms require immediate medical attention.

4. Physical Examination

For patients diagnosed with type 2 diabetes, a more comprehensive health examination should be conducted once a year, which can be combined with follow-up. The contents include body temperature, pulse, respiration, blood pressure, fasting blood glucose, height, weight, waist circumference, skin, superficial lymph nodes, heart, lungs, abdomen and other routine physical examinations, and oral, visual, hearing, and motor function judgment.

V. International Typical Diabetes Management Project

i. Global Diabetes Compact

The World Health Organization launched the *Global Diabetes Compact* on April 14, 2021,

3. 分类干预

（1）对血糖控制满意（空腹血糖＜7.0mmol/L）、无药物不良反应、无新发并发症或原有并发症无加重的患者，预约下一次随访。

（2）对首次出现空腹血糖控制不满意（空腹血糖值≥7.0mmol/L）或药物不良反应的患者，结合其服药依从情况进行指导，必要时增加现有药物剂量、更换或增加不同类的降糖药物，2周时随访。

（3）对连续两次出现空腹血糖控制不满意或药物不良反应难以控制以及出现新的并发症或原有并发症加重的患者，建议其转诊到上级医院，并在2周内主动随访转诊情况。

（4）对所有的患者进行针对性的健康教育，与患者一起制定生活方式改进目标，并在下一次随访时评估疾病进展。告诉患者出现哪些异常时应立即就诊。

4. 健康体检

对确诊的2型糖尿病患者，每年进行1次较全面的健康体检，体检可与随访相结合。内容包括体温、脉搏、呼吸、血压、空腹血糖、身高、体重、腰围、皮肤、浅表淋巴结、心脏、肺部、腹部等常规体格检查，并对口腔、视力、听力和运动功能等进行判断。

五、国际典型糖尿病管理项目

（一）全球糖尿病契约

世界卫生组织于2021年4月14日启动了《全球糖尿病契约》，该契约旨在联合全球合作

which aims to unite global partners to increase access to treatment and improve health outcomes for type 1 and type 2 diabetes, ensuring that everyone has access to comprehensive, affordable, and quality care in primary care settings. The eight key components of the *Global Diabetes Compact*：

1. UNITE   Collaboratively unite stakeholders, including people living with diabetes, around a common agenda.

2. INTEGRATE   Integrate diabetes prevention and management in primary health care and universal health coverage.

3. INNOVATE   Close research and normative gaps while spurring innovation.

4. TREAT   Improve access to diabetes diagnostics, medicines and health products, particularly insulin, in low-and middle income countries.

5. TRACK   Develop global coverage targets for diabetes care,accompanied by a "global price tag".

6. FUND   Improve diabetes care for those living through humanitarian emergencies.

7. EDUCATE   Improve understanding of diabetes.

8. POWER AHEAD   Build back better based on experiences from the COVID-19 pandemic.

ii. Finnish Diabetes Prevention Study (FDPS)

The FDPS is a four-year multicenter study (5 central cities) that began in 1993 and is the world's first controlled, individualized randomized trial to examine the possibility of preventing type 2 diabetes through lifestyle interventions. A total of 522 middle-aged, overweight subjects at high risk of type 2 diabetes were recruited and randomly divided into lifestyle intensive intervention group

伙伴,增加 1 型和 2 型糖尿病患者获得治疗的机会,并改善其健康结局,确保每个人都能够在基础医疗机构中获得全面、负担得起的优质护理。《全球糖尿病契约》的 8 个组成部分如下:

1. **团结**   围绕一个共同议程,以一致的方式团结利益相关者,包括糖尿病患者。

2. **整合**   将糖尿病的预防和管理纳入初级卫生保健体系和全民健康覆盖范围。

3. **创新**   在促进创新的同时,缩小研究和规范差距。

4. **治疗**   在低收入和中等收入国家 / 地区增加获取糖尿病诊断、药物和保健产品(尤其是胰岛素)的途径。

5. **追踪**   制定全球覆盖目标,并附上全球价格标签,以量化缩小能够获得糖尿病服务的人与无法获得糖尿病服务的人之间的成本差距。

6. **资助**   通过人道主义紧急救助,改善糖尿病幸存者的护理。

7. **教育**   提高健康素养以及对糖尿病预防和管理的了解。

8. **变强**   在新型冠状病毒感染疫情管理经验的基础上重建更完善的体系。

(二)芬兰糖尿病预防研究

芬兰糖尿病预防研究(Finnish Diabetes Prevention Study,FDPS)是 1993 年开始的一项为期 4 年的多中心研究(5 个中心城市),是世界上第一个试图通过生活方式干预预防 2 型糖尿病的对照、个体化随机试验。研究共招募了 522 名中年、超重的 2 型糖尿病高危对象,将其随机分为生活方式强化干预组和对照组,主体研究平均随访 3 年,主体研究后继续对未诊断为 2 型

and control group. The main study was followed up for an average of 3 years. After the main study, subjects who were not diagnosed with type 2 diabetes continued to be followed up, and the follow-up phase continued to continue their lifestyle as that during the study.

The results of the study showed that the intervention group improved any of the intervention goals better than the control group, especially in terms of weight, over time. After 1 year and 3 years of follow-up, the weight of the intensive intervention group decreased by 4.5kg and 3.5kg, respectively, while that of the control group decreased by 1.0kg and 0.9kg, respectively. The improvement of blood glucose and plasma lipids in the intensive intervention group was also significantly better than that of the control group. At 3 years of follow-up, the proportion of the intensive intervention group progressing to type 2 diabetes was 9%, which was significantly better than 20% in the control group. In the follow-up study (from randomization to the end of the study, the average follow-up time was 9 years), the risk of diabetes in the original intensive lifestyle intervention group was only 61% of that in the control group, and their body weight and blood glucose remained lower than that in the control group.

iii. National Diabetes Prevention Program (NDPP)

The NDPP was implemented on a large scale by the Centers for Disease Control and Prevention of the US in 2010. The program lasted for 1 year, involving diet, exercise and stress management, to support the implementation of evidence-based lifestyle change programs to help prevent or delay type 2 diabetes. The program has been shown to reduce the risk of developing type 2 diabetes by 58 percent in people with prediabetes (71 percent in people 60 years and older).

糖尿病的受试者进行随访观察,随访阶段受试者继续各自研究期间的生活方式。

研究结果显示,随着时间的推移,干预组在任何干预目标上的改善均优于对照组,特别是在体重方面,在随访 1 年和 3 年后,强化干预组体重分别下降了 4.5kg 和 3.5kg,对照组分别下降了 1.0kg 和 0.9kg。强化干预组在血糖和血脂方面的改善也明显优于对照组,随访 3 年时,强化干预组进展为 2 型糖尿病的比例是 9%,明显低于对照组的 20%。后续随访研究(从随机分组到研究结束,平均随访时间 9 年)中,原强化生活方式干预组糖尿病的发生风险仅是对照组的 61%,并且其体重、血糖也保持低于对照组的水平。

(三)美国国家糖尿病预防计划

美国国家糖尿病预防计划(National Diabetes Prevention Program,NDPP)由美国疾病控制和预防中心于 2010 年开始大规模实施。该计划为期 1 年,涉及饮食、运动、压力管理等方面,旨在支持循证生活方式改变计划的实施,以帮助预防或延缓 2 型糖尿病的发生发展。该项目已被证明可将糖尿病前期患者罹患 2 型糖尿病的风险降低 58%(60 岁及以上人群降低 71%)。

Section 5 Community Management of Mental Disorders

I. Concept of Mental Disorders

Mental disorders refer to a group of diseases under the influence of various biological, psychological and social environmental factors, brain dysfunction or disorder, resulting in cognitive, emotional, volitional, behavioral, and other mental activities with different degrees of disorders as clinical manifestations.

II. Epidemiology of Mental Disorders

There are many kinds of mental disorders, and the 10th edition of the *International Classification of Diseases* divides it into 10 categories and about more than 100 kinds of mental diseases. Domestic public and academic consensus: mood disorders, anxiety disorders, alcohol use disorders, and dementia are on the rise and need targeted interventions. On february 18, 2019, professor Huang Yueqin et al. from Peking University Sixth Hospital published a research article online in *The Lancet Psychiatry*, reporting the prevalence data of the Chinese Mental Health Survey (CMHS). CMHS is a cross-sectional epidemiological survey that examines the prevalence of seven categories of mental disorders (mood disorders, anxiety

第五节　精神疾病的社区管理

一、精神疾病的概念

精神疾病是指在各种生物学、心理学以及社会环境因素影响下,大脑功能失调或紊乱,导致认知、情感、意志和行为等精神活动出现不同程度的障碍。

二、精神疾病的流行病学

精神疾病的种类很多,《国际疾病分类》第 10 版把其分为 10 大类,100 余种精神疾病。国内公共领域及学术界已达成共识:情绪障碍、焦虑症、酒精使用障碍及痴呆症的患病率正在升高,需要针对性的干预措施。2019 年 2 月 18 日,北京大学第六医院黄悦勤教授等在《柳叶刀 - 精神病学》在线发表研究文章,报告了中国精神卫生调查(China Mental Health Survey,CMHS)的患病率数据。CMHS 为一项横断面流行病学调查,调查了七大类精神疾病(情绪障碍、焦虑症、酒精 / 药物使用障碍、精神分裂症及其他精神病性障碍、进食障碍、冲动控制障碍以及痴呆症)的患病率。研究发现焦虑障碍是终生患病率最高的精神障碍(7.6%),其次为情绪障碍(7.4%)、物质滥用障碍(4.7%)、冲动控制障碍

disorders, alcohol/drug use disorders, schizophrenia and other psychiatric disorders, eating disorders, impulse control disorders, and dementia). Anxiety disorders were found to have the highest lifetime prevalence of mental disorders (7.6%), followed by mood disorders (7.4%), substance use disorders (4.7%), impulse control disorders (1.5%), schizophrenia and other psychotic disorders (0.7%), and eating disorders (0.1%).

Nowadays, the prevalence of some common mental diseases is increasing, and the course of the disease is prolonged, easy to relapse, and poor prognosis. In addition, the awareness rate of mental disorders, identification rate, consultation rate, and treatment rate are low, and about 90% of depressed patients do not know that they are ill and do not seek medical attention in time. According to estimates by the World Health Organization, in 2020, the burden of mental disorders in China accounted for approximately 25% of the total disease burden in the country. In China and some high-income countries, the disease burden caused by mental diseases has ranked first, more than the disease burden caused by tumors, cardiovascular and cerebrovascular diseases. As a serious disease that endangers human health, mental disorders have become one of the greater security risks in the community.

Ⅲ. Risk Factors of Mental Disorders

Physiological characteristics, early childhood trauma, and behavioral tendency all have an impact on mental health, but existing studies know little about the regulatory process among these factors, and generally divide the influencing factors of mental disorder into three categories: biological factors, psychological factors, and social factors. Studies show that the three-factor model can predict 90% of the onset of mental disorders.

i. Biological Factors

A person with a mental disorder may have a

（1.5%）、精神分裂症和其他精神病性障碍（0.7%）及进食障碍（0.1%）。

目前，一些常见精神疾病的患病率呈升高趋势，并且疾病的病程迁延，易反复发作且预后差。此外，精神疾病的知晓率、识别率、就诊率和治疗率皆较低，约90%的抑郁症患者不知自己患病而未及时就医。精神疾病给人类社会带来的疾病负担较重，据世界卫生组织推算，2020年我国精神疾病负担约占我国总疾病负担的25%。在我国和其他一些高收入国家，精神障碍所致的疾病负担已居首位，超过了肿瘤、心脑血管疾病等所致的疾病负担。精神疾病作为严重危害人类健康的疾病，已成为社区较大的安全隐患之一。

三、精神疾病的危险因素

生理特征、早期童年创伤以及行为倾向等都对精神健康产生影响，但是现有研究对各因素间的调节过程知之甚少。一般将精神疾病的影响因素分为生物学因素、心理因素和社会因素三类。有研究显示，包含以上3个方面因素的模型能预测90%的精神疾病发作。

（一）生物学因素

精神疾病患者可能有不同的脑部结构或功

different brain structure or function or may have a different neurochemical response, whether caused by genetic or environmental damage (such as fetal alcohol syndrome). For example, many patients diagnosed with schizophrenia have been shown to have enlarged ventricles and atrophied gray matter in the brain. In addition, some studies show that an imbalance of neurotransmitters can also cause mental disorders, and brain dopamine levels are linked to cognitive deficits and susceptibility to depression. Many genetic and twin studies have confirmed that mental disorders such as bipolar disorder and schizophrenia are inherited.

ii. Psychological Factors

Psychologists believe that adolescent external performance characteristics such as conflict, crisis, tension, and impulsivity may increase the risk of mental disorders, especially in a person who is psychologically vulnerable. Individual temperament and personality reveal the development track of a variety of mental diseases, including substance use disorders, and different personality characteristics are usually the important psychological factors that cause the difference in mental disorders.

iii. Social Factors

Childhood trauma is considered a typical cross-diagnostic risk factor. Early life adversity, such as physical or emotional abuse or neglect, sexual abuse, or other forms of trauma in childhood, increases the probability of developing mental disorders in adolescence and adulthood. Individuals who are more resilient to past trauma will have more variable coping skills, which will greatly reduce the probability of disease.

Knowing these traits in themselves with the help of a professional may help patients better understand the risk factors in their mental health development. Individuals who have experienced childhood trauma and have overt behavioral problems should be evaluated for mental disorders

能，或者是有不同的神经化学反应，这是由基因或环境伤害（如胎儿酒精综合征）引起的。例如，许多被诊断有精神分裂症的患者被证实在大脑中有肿大的脑室和萎缩的灰质。另外，有些研究认为神经递质不平衡也会导致精神疾病，大脑多巴胺水平与认知缺陷和抑郁的易感性有关。许多遗传学和双胞胎研究都证实，双相障碍、精神分裂症等精神疾病可遗传。

（二）心理因素

心理学家认为，青少年的外部表现特征，如矛盾、危机、紧张和冲动，可能增加其罹患精神疾病的风险，特别是在心理脆弱的个体中。个体的气质性格揭示了物质使用障碍等多种精神疾病的发展轨迹，不同的性格特征通常是造成精神疾病患病差异的重要心理因素。

（三）社会因素

儿童期创伤被认为是典型的交叉诊断风险因素。早期生活的逆境，如身体或情感上的虐待或忽视、性虐待或童年时期其他形式的创伤，增加了青少年期和成年期罹患精神疾病的概率。而过往创伤抗逆力较强的个体，则会拥有可变性较强的应对技能，从而使患病概率大大降低。

在专业人士的帮助下了解儿童创伤有关的特点，可能会帮助者更好地理解自身心理健康发展中存在的风险因素。经历过童年创伤并且有外显行为问题的个体，应该尽快接受精神疾病的评估，并学习相关的应对技能。早期干预治疗可以减少精神疾病对患者日常生活的影

and learn coping skills as soon as possible. Early intervention treatment can reduce the impact of mental disorders on patients' daily lives, shorten the course of illness, and even prevent the onset of mental disorders.

响，缩短病程甚至预防精神疾病的发作。

Ⅳ. Chinese Community Management Model

ⅰ. Community Basic Management Model

In accordance with the *National Standard for Basic Public Health Services*, management of patients with severe mental disorders shall be implemented for permanent residents who have been clearly diagnosed with severe mental disorders in the community. Service contents are as follows：

1. Patient Information Management Patients with severe mental disorders will be included in the management, and a comprehensive assessment will be conducted for the patients to establish resident health records for them.

2. Follow-up Assessment Patients with severe mental disorders under corresponding management should be followed up at least 4 times a year, and risk assessment should be carried out for each follow-up. Examine the patient's mental state, including sensation, perception, thinking, emotion and volitional behavior, self-knowledge, etc. Inquire and evaluate the patient's physical disease, social function, medication, and laboratory test results.

3. Classified Intervention Classified intervention is performed on patients according to their risk assessment, social function status, mental symptom assessment, self-knowledge judgment, and whether they have adverse drug reactions or physical diseases.

4. Physical Examination A physical examination is conducted once a year, which can be combined with follow-up. The contents include general physical examination, blood pressure,

四、我国社区管理

（一）社区基础管理模式

按照《国家基本公共卫生服务规范》，对辖区内明确诊断为严重精神障碍的常住居民实施规范管理。服务内容如下：

1. **患者信息管理**　将严重精神障碍患者纳入管理，同时对患者进行 1 次全面评估，为其建立居民健康档案。

2. **随访评估**　对接受相应管理的严重精神障碍患者，每年至少随访 4 次，每次随访应对患者进行危险性评估；检查患者的精神状况，包括感觉、知觉、思维、情感和意志行为、自知力等；询问和评估患者的躯体疾病、社会功能情况、用药情况及各项实验室检查结果等。

3. **分类干预**　根据患者的危险性评估、社会功能状况、精神症状评估、自知力判断，以及患者是否存在药物不良反应或躯体疾病情况对患者进行分类干预。

4. **健康体检**　每年进行 1 次健康检查，可与随访相结合。内容包括一般体格检查、血压、体重、血常规、转氨酶、血糖、心电图等。

weight, blood routine test, transaminase, blood glucose, and electrocardiogram.

ii. Severe Mental Disorders Management and Treatment Project—Project 686

Since 2004, Project 686, subsidized by the central government, has been implemented nationwide.

1. Project Objectives To explore the establishment of a hospital-community integrated mental health service model, improve the accessibility and equity of mental health services, early detection of patients, early treatment, and reduction of violence.

2. Implementation Team Train psychiatrists at provincial, city, and county levels, and set up a grass-roots comprehensive prevention and treatment team, including doctors and nurses from grass-roots medical and health institutions, residents' committees, disabled persons' federations and civil affairs officers, police and family members, who will form a care and support team to provide follow-up management services for patients.

3. Service Content Patients suspected of severe mental disorders are screened by primary medical and health personnel in the community, diagnosed by psychiatrists, and registered with informed consent of patients/family members. Follow-up services include providing medication and rehabilitation guidance for patients, psychological support and health education for family members, and free drug treatment and hospitalization services for poor patients; a two-way referral mechanism has been established between professional mental health institutions and primary medical and health institutions, with psychiatrists providing technical guidance for follow-up visits to community doctors and providing emergency medical treatment for patients with dangerous and violent behavior.

（二）重性精神疾病管理治疗项目——686项目

2004 年起，"中央补助地方严重精神障碍管理治疗项目"（简称 686 项目）开始在全国范围内实施。

1. 项目目标 探索建立医院 - 社区一体化的精神卫生服务模式，提高精神卫生服务的可及性和公平性，早期发现患者，及早治疗，减少暴力行为。

2. 实施团队 培训省、市、县各级精神科医生，组建基层综合防治队伍，包括基层医疗卫生机构的医生和护士、居委会人员、残联及民政干事、民警和家属等，由他们组成关爱帮扶小组为患者提供随访管理服务。

3. 服务内容 由基层医疗卫生人员在社区筛查发现疑似重性精神疾病患者，由精神科医生进行诊断，获得患者 / 家属的知情同意后进行登记及社区随访服务。随访服务包括为患者提供服药和康复指导、为家属提供心理支持和健康教育等，对贫困患者提供免费药物治疗和住院服务；建立精神卫生专业机构和基层医疗卫生机构之间的双向转诊机制，由精神科医生为社区医生提供随访技术指导，对有危险暴力行为的患者提供应急医疗处置。

V. International Typical Mental Disorders Management Project

i. Australia's Model of Integration Aimed at Rehabilitation

Mental health services in Australia use the integrated recovery-oriented model (IRM), which is run by a tripartite agreement and includes acute/emergency mental health care, professional clinical rehabilitation, and community management/ non-governmental organizations providing integrated community services to provide rehabilitation-oriented services in an integrated and seamless manner. Each core service may also operate in conjunction with a range of other specialty services (e.g. subacute inpatient care, substance abuse, neuropsychiatry), as well as community-based institutional services (e.g. general practice services, residential services, vocational services, educational provision, relief, community engagement, recreational services), reflecting specialty hospital-community integration.

ii. Japan's Social Welfare Cooperative Organization Model

This model is based on the Growth Society of Mitaka City, Japan, which was established in 1992 as a community-based practice run by a non-profit organization to promote the discharge of mental patients. At the beginning, the Growth Society only established some basic living facilities to meet the patient's daily living and work and also enabled them to receive corresponding support from other patients and service staff. Since then, the Growth Society has gradually expanded in size. The Growth Society attaches great importance to vocational training and housing support to ensure that rehabilitated persons have viable living conditions in the community, which is precisely what they need to have a high quality of life in the community. Relevant data show that this service of the Growth Society is a boon to patients. If continuous 24-hour support services and stable housing can be guaranteed, many mental patients

五、国际典型精神疾病管理项目

（一）澳大利亚以康复为目标的整合模式

澳大利亚的精神卫生服务采用以康复为目标的整合模式，由三方协议运行，包括急性／紧急精神卫生保健、专业的临床康复和提供社区综合服务的社区管理／非政府组织，以综合、无缝的方式提供以康复为主的服务。每一个核心服务也可能与其他专科服务（如针对亚急性住院、物质滥用、神经精神病学问题的专业服务），以及以社区为基础的机构服务（如全科医学、住宿、职业、教育提供、救助、社区参与及娱乐服务）相结合，体现了专科医院-社区一体化。

（二）日本以社会福利合作组织为主的模式

该模式来源于日本三鹰市的成长协会。该成长协会成立于1992年，是一个以社区为基础，由非营利组织运行，旨在促进精神病患者出院的社会组织。成长协会初期只是建立一些基本生活设施，满足患者的起居、工作要求，还能使其从病友、服务人员处得到相应的支持。随后，成长协会逐渐扩大了规模。成长协会高度重视职业培训和住房支持，以确保康复者们有切实可行的社区居住条件，而这恰恰是他们在社区拥有较高生活质量所必需的。数据表明，成长协会的这项服务对患者来说是有利因素，如果能够保证持久的24小时支持服务、稳定的住所，许多精神病患者可以在出院后回到社区，在社区中有比较好的生活质量。

can return to the community after discharge and have a better quality of life in the community.

Section 6　Community Management of Pulmonary Tuberculosis

I. Concept of Pulmonary Tuberculosis

Pulmonary tuberculosis refers to tuberculosis of the lung tissue, trachea, bronchus, and pleura. It is a chronic infectious disease caused by mycobacterium tuberculosis (Mtb) infection. The bacteria may invade all organs of the body, but the lungs are most obvious and spread mainly through the respiratory tract. Pulmonary tuberculosis including lung parenchyma, tracheobronchial tuberculosis, and tuberculous pleurisy account for 80%–90% of the total number of tuberculosis in various organs.

II. Epidemiology of Pulmonary Tuberculosis

According to the World Health Organization (WHO)'s Global Tuberculosis Report 2023, there were about 10.6 million new cases of TB globally in 2022, with an incidence rate of 133 per 100,000, tuberculosis of the lung accounted for 83%.

According to the number of new TB patients registered in China's TB information monitoring system and the TB death data from the monitoring points of China's cause of death monitoring system, WHO and the expert group of the National Center for Tuberculosis Control and Prevention of China CDC jointly calculated and analyzed: The number of cases of tuberculosis in China decreased from 1.182 million in 1990 to 718,000 in 2019, and the trend is decreasing year by year. It is estimated that the number of new cases of tuberculosis in China in 2022 will be about 748,000, and the incidence of tuberculosis will be about 52/100,000 (55/100,000

第六节　肺结核的社区管理

一、肺结核的概念

肺结核是指发生在肺组织、气管、支气管和胸膜的结核,是由结核分枝杆菌(mycobacterium tuberculosis,Mtb)感染引起的慢性传染性疾病;该病菌可能会侵入全身各器官,但以肺部最为明显,主要通过呼吸道传播。肺结核包含肺实质的结核、气管支气管结核和结核性胸膜炎,占各器官结核病总数的80%~90%。

二、肺结核的流行病学

根据世界卫生组织(WHO)发布的《2023年全球结核病报告》,2022年全球新发结核病患者约为1 060万例,发病率为133/10万,肺结核占83%。

WHO根据我国结核病信息监测系统的结核病新患者登记数,以及我国死因监测系统监测点的结核病死亡数据等,与中国疾控中心结核病预防控制中心的专家组共同测算分析而得:我国结核病发病人数从1990年的118.2万例降低至2019年的71.8万例,且呈逐年下降的趋势;2022年我国的结核病新发病例数约为74.8万例,结核病的发病率约为52/10万(2021年为55/10万);在全球30个结核病高负担国家中,我国的结核病发病数排名第3位,占全球发病数的7.1%,仅次于印度(27%)和印度尼西亚(10%)。中国结核病信息管理系统2015—2021年全国老年肺结核患者的登记情况,发现≥65岁老年人

in 2021). Among the 30 countries with a high burden of TB in the world, China ranks third in the number of TB cases, accounting for 7.1% of the global incidence, second only to India (27%) and Indonesia (10%). The registration situation of elderly pulmonary tuberculosis patients nationwide from 2015 to 2021 in the Chinese Tuberculosis Information Management System revealed that the reported incidence rate of pulmonary tuberculosis in individuals aged ≥ 65 years showed a downward trend. However, the proportion of elderly patients among all pulmonary tuberculosis patients increased year by year, suggesting that the elderly remain a key population in China's tuberculosis prevention and control efforts.

III. Risk Factors of Pulmonary Tuberculosis

i. Basic Demographic Characteristics

The incidence of TB is related to basic demographic characteristics, such as age, sex, occupation, living environment, educational level, economic level, and family history.

ii. Lifestyle

Smoking and alcoholism are risk factors for tuberculosis. Tobacco contains a variety of harmful substances including nicotine, and long-term smoking, harmful substances will continue to attack human lung tissue, resulting in lung resistance to mycobaterium tuberculosis decline. Chronic drinkers are at increased risk of developing tuberculosis, ethanol impairs the immune system and increases susceptibility to MTB infection, and ethanol also affects the ability of alveolar macrophages to respond to foreign pathogens.

The onset of TB is also associated with lack of sleep. Lack of sleep can lead to impaired lymphocyte mitotic proliferation, decreased HLA-DR expression, upregulation of $CD14^+$, and mutation of $CD4^+$ and $CD8^+$ T lymphocytes, weakening the body's immunity and increasing the organism's susceptibility to infection.

肺结核报告发病率呈下降趋势，但在总体肺结核患者中的占比却逐年上升，提示老年人仍是中国肺结核防控工作中的重点人群。

三、肺结核的危险因素

（一）基本人口特征

结核病是否发病与人口学基本特征有关，如年龄、性别、职业、居住环境、文化程度、经济水平和家族史等。

（二）生活方式

吸烟和酗酒是发生肺结核的危险因素。烟草中含有尼古丁等多种有害物质，如果长期吸烟，有害物质会不断攻击人体肺组织，导致肺部对结核分枝杆菌的抵御能力下降；长期饮酒者罹患肺结核的风险增加，乙醇会损害免疫系统并增加对结核分枝杆菌感染的易感性，同时，乙醇还会影响肺泡巨噬细胞对外来病原体的反应能力。

结核病发病还与睡眠不足有关。睡眠不足会导致淋巴细胞有丝分裂增殖受损、HLA-DR表达降低、$CD14^+$上调以及$CD4^+$和$CD8^+$T淋巴细胞变异，削弱了机体的免疫力，增加生物体对感染的易感性。

iii. Nutritional Status

The relationship between TB and malnutrition runs in both directions: Malnutrition is a risk factor for TB, and simultaneous malnutrition in TB patients can lead to reduced treatment effectiveness and poor prognosis.

iv. Vaccination

BCG vaccine is the only tuberculosis vaccine available in the world, and it is also one of the vaccines that must be vaccinated in the planned immunization of newborns in China. BCG vaccination has been included in the WHO Expanded Programme on Immunization (EPI) since 1974. The BCG vaccine is protective against tuberculosis, reducing the risk of developing the disease by a third, and people who receive the vaccine are less likely to have occupationally acquired pulmonary tuberculosis than those who are not vaccinated. The simplest and most convenient approach to the primary immunization booster strategy is a second BCG vaccination; however, the protection of BCG revaccination against mycobacterium tuberculosis infection in the population remains to be further studied.

v. Air Pollution

The inhalation of large doses of air pollutants by the body leads to functional damage to the respiratory system, cardiovascular system and other systems, especially patients with abnormal cardiopulmonary function, children and the elderly. For indoor air pollution, long-term exposure to indoor air pollutants is associated with increasing incidence of tuberculosis, mainly in two aspects, one is biomass fuel smoke, and the other is tobacco smoke. Inhalation of inhalable particles and chemicals in biomass fuel fumes can induce inflammation and impair the normal clearance function of mucosal surface secretions of the trachea and bronchus, which may allow Mtb to break through the first line of host defense and enter the alveoli. For outdoor air pollution, long-term exposure to particulate pollutants may increase the risk of Mtb infection and continued

（三）营养状况

结核病和营养不良之间的关系是双向的，营养不良是引发结核病的一个危险因素，而结核病患者如果同时有营养不良，会导致治疗效果降低和预后不良。

（四）疫苗接种

卡介苗是目前世界上唯一可用的结核疫苗，也是我国新生儿计划免疫中必须接种的疫苗之一。自 1974 年，卡介苗疫苗接种已被纳入 WHO 扩大免疫规划。卡介苗对结核病具有保护作用，可将发病风险降低三分之一，并且接种卡介苗的人比未接种疫苗的人患职业获得性肺结核的可能性更小。初级免疫加强策略的最简单和最方便的方法是二次接种卡介苗，然而，卡介苗再接种对人群结核分枝杆菌感染的保护性仍有待进一步研究。

（五）空气污染

身体吸入较大剂量的空气污染物会导致呼吸系统、心血管系统以及其他系统的功能损害，尤其是心肺功能异常的患者、儿童和老年人。对于室内空气污染，长期暴露于室内空气污染物与结核病的发病率升高有关，主要表现为 2 个方面：一是生物质燃料烟雾，二是烟草烟雾。生物质燃料烟雾中可吸入颗粒物和化学物质的吸入能诱发炎症反应，并损伤气管、支气管黏膜表面分泌物的正常清除功能，这可能允许 Mtb 突破宿主防御的第一防线而进入肺泡。对于室外空气污染，颗粒污染物的长期接触可能会增加 Mtb 感染和结核病继续发展的风险，大多数空气污染物（PM2.5，SO_2，O_3 和 CO）与结核病的发病风险增加显著相关。

development of TB, and most air pollutants (PM2.5, SO_2, O_3, and CO) are significantly associated with an increased risk of developing TB.

vi. Economic Factors

According to the WHO, economic factors are strongly associated with TB incidence and also influence access to TB diagnosis and treatment. Studies have shown that TB patients mostly belong to low-income groups, and the disease will further increase the family's economic burden, and will increase the risk of death from TB. The influence of economic factors on tuberculosis is multifaceted. At present, it is still necessary to further improve the basic medical security system, rationally allocate health resources, strengthen tuberculosis screening work, standardize diagnosis and treatment behavior, and achieve multiple measures.

vii. Floating Population

From the perspective of the impact on tuberculosis, the floating population is mainly divided into two aspects: social and economic population flow and cross-regional mobile medical treatment. The delay rate of seeking treatment for TB in the migrant population was higher than that in the local population. Due to the long treatment cycle of tuberculosis, population flow is not conducive to the standardized treatment of the whole process, which will also lead to poor treatment efficacy of tuberculosis patients and a high relapse rate.

viii. Co-infection with Other Diseases

HIV infection or AIDS patients with MTB infection have a great degree of disease progression and harm to the body. Patients infected with HIV have immune system defects, which will greatly increase the risk of tuberculosis, and MTB infection will also promote the process of AIDS.

In addition, tuberculosis and diabetes are common and frequent chronic diseases at present, they can co-exist and affect each other. The increase of blood glucose can promote the growth and reproduction of mycobacterium tuberculosis,

（六）经济因素

WHO 指出，经济因素与结核病发病率密切相关，同时也会影响结核病诊断和治疗可及性。研究表明，结核病患者多属于低收入人群，而且这种疾病会进一步增加家庭经济负担，从而增加患者死于结核病的风险。经济因素对结核病的影响是多方面的，目前仍需要进一步完善基本医疗保障制度，合理分配卫生资源，加强结核病筛查工作以及规范诊疗行为，做到多措并举。

（七）流动人口

从对结核病的影响来看，流动人口主要分为社会经济人口流动和跨地区流动就诊两方面。流动人口结核病的就诊延迟率高于本地人口；结核病的治疗周期较长，并且人口流动不利于全程规范治疗，这也会导致结核病患者疗效差，复发率高。

（八）与其他疾病合并感染

HIV 感染或 AIDS 患者合并 MTB 感染对疾病的进展程度和对机体的危害程度影响均很大，感染了 HIV 的患者其免疫系统缺损，将大大增加患结核病的风险，而感染 MTB 同时也会促进 AIDS 的进程。

此外，结核病与糖尿病是目前常见和多发的慢性疾病，两者可共同存在并相互影响。血糖升高可促进结核分枝杆菌生长和繁殖，抑制巨噬细胞吞噬功能，改变淋巴细胞亚群。免疫细胞因子变化、Th1/Th2 比例失衡、白细胞功能

reduce the phagocytosis function of macrophages, and change the lymphocyte subpopulation. The changes of immune cytokines, the imbalance of Th1/Th2 ratio, and the decrease of white blood cell function are all important reasons for tuberculosis complicated with diabetes.

减弱等均是结核病合并糖尿病的重要原因。

IV. Chinese Community Management Model

i. Service Target

Confirmed resident pulmonary tuberculosis patients in the community.

ii. Service Content

1. Screening and Referral

For residents or patients in the jurisdiction who come to see a doctor, if they are found to have a chronic cough, expectoration for ≥ 2 weeks, hemoptysis, bloody sputum, fever, night sweating, chest pain or unexplained marasmus, and other suspicious symptoms of pulmonary tuberculosis, fill in the "two-way referral form" on the basis of differential diagnosis and recommend them to tuberculosis-designated medical institutions for tuberculosis examination. Telephone follow-up within 1 week, to know whether to go to the doctor, urge them to seek medical treatment in time.

2. The First Home Follow-up Visit

Rural hospitals, village health clinics, and community health centers (stations) after receiving the notification of the management of pulmonary tuberculosis patients by higher professional institutions, to visit patients within 72 hours, the specific content is as follows:

(1) Determine the supervisor, priority for medical personnel, but also for the patient's family. According to the chemotherapy protocol, inform the supervisor of the filling method of the patient's "treatment record card for pulmonary tuberculosis patients" or "medication card for multi-drug resistant pulmonary tuberculosis patients", the time and place of taking medicine, and remind the patient to take medicine on time and return visit.

(2) Evaluate the living environment of the

四、我国社区管理模式

（一）服务对象

辖区内确诊的常住肺结核患者。

（二）服务内容

1. 筛查及转诊

对辖区内前来就诊的居民或患者，如发现有慢性咳嗽、咳痰 ≥ 2 周，咯血、血痰，或发热、盗汗、胸痛或不明原因消瘦等肺结核可疑症状者，在鉴别诊断的基础上，填写"双向转诊单"，推荐其到结核病定点医疗机构进行结核病检查。1 周内进行电话随访，了解患者是否前去就诊，督促其及时就医。

2. 第一次入户随访

乡镇卫生院、村卫生室、社区卫生服务中心（站）接到上级专业机构管理肺结核患者的通知单后，要在 72 小时内访视患者，具体内容如下：

（1）确定监护人员，优先安排医务人员，也可安排患者家属。按照化疗方案，告知监护人员患者的"肺结核患者治疗记录卡"或"耐多药肺结核患者服药卡"的填写方法、取药的时间和地点，提醒患者按时取药和复诊。

（2）对患者的居住环境进行评估，告诉患者

patient, and tell the patient and his family to take proper precautions to prevent infection.

(3) Educate the patients and their families about tuberculosis prevention and control.

(4) Tell the patient to see a doctor in time when there are abnormal conditions such as aggravation, serious adverse reactions, complications, etc. If the patient is not seen during two visits within 72 hours, the results of the visit will be reported to the superior professional authority.

3. Supervising Medication and Follow-up Management

(1) Supervision of drug administration.

(2) Follow-up Evaluation: For patients supervised by medical staff, medical staff should record the follow-up evaluation results of patients at least once a month; for patients supervised by family members, primary healthcare institutions should follow up once every 10 days during the intensive or injection period and once every 1 month during the continuation or non-injection period.

(3) Classified Intervention: For patients who can take medicine on time and have no adverse reactions, continue to supervise the taking of medicine and make an appointment for the next follow-up time. The patient does not take medicine according to the doctor's order of the designated medical institution, and the reason should be found out. If it is caused by adverse reactions, then referral; if there are other reasons, health education should be strengthened for patients. If the patient misses the medication for more than 1 week, it should be reported to the superior professional institution in time. Patients with adverse drug reactions, complications, or comorbidities should be referred immediately and followed up within 2 weeks, and remind and urge the patient to return to the designated medical institution on time.

4. Case Closing Evaluation

When patients stop anti-tuberculosis therapy, they should conduct a case closing evaluation,

及家属做好防护工作，防止传染。

（3）对患者及家属进行结核病防治知识宣传教育。

（4）当患者出现病情加重、严重不良反应、并发症等异常情况时，告知患者要及时就诊。若 72 小时内 2 次访视均未见到患者，则将访视结果向上级专业机构报告。

3. 监督服药和随访管理

（1）监督服药。

（2）随访评估：对于由医务人员监护的患者，医务人员至少每月记录 1 次对患者的随访评估结果；由家庭成员监护的患者，基层医疗卫生机构要在患者的强化期或注射期内每 10 天随访 1 次，继续期或非注射期内每 1 个月随访 1 次。

（3）分类干预：对于能够按时服药且无不良反应的患者，继续督导服药，并预约下一次随访时间。如果患者未按定点医疗机构的医嘱服药，应查明原因，若是不良反应引起的，则转诊；若是其他原因，则要对患者强化健康教育。若患者漏服药次数超过 1 周，要及时向上级专业机构报告。对于出现药物不良反应、并发症或合并症的患者应立即转诊，并在 2 周内随访，提醒并督促患者按时到定点医疗机构进行复诊。

4. 结案评估

当患者停止抗结核治疗后，要对其进行结案评估，包括：记录患者停止治疗的时间及原

including recording the time and reason for the patient to stop treatment; to evaluate the whole process of medication management; collecting and reporting the patient's "treatment record card for pulmonary tuberculosis patients" or "medication card for multi-drug resistant pulmonary tuberculosis patients". At the same time, patients were referred to designated TB medical institutions for treatment outcome assessment, and telephone follow-up was conducted within 2 weeks to know whether to go to the doctor and the diagnosis result.

V. International Typical Pulmonary Tuberculosis Management Project

The Stop TB Partnership is a global alliance established in 2001 to coordinate international efforts to end tuberculosis (TB). Its founding members include the American Lung Association (ALA), the American Thoracic Society (ATS), the International Union Against Tuberculosis and Lung Disease (IUATLD), KNCV Tuberculosis Foundation (KNCV), the U.S. Centers for Disease Control and Prevention (CDC), and the World Health Organization (WHO). The Stop TB Partnership has since grown. The Stop TB Partnership now has more than 2,000 partners from more than 100 countries, including government organizations, donors, the private sector, and people and organizations affected by TB (civil society organizations, patient organizations, etc.).

The Stop TB Partner's vision is to create a world free of TB, where all people have equal access to the TB diagnosis, treatment, and care they need. In particular, its actions and policy development are focused on the following five key objectives:

(1) To ensure that everyone with TB has access to effective diagnosis and treatment.

(2) Stop the spread of tuberculosis.

(3) Reduce the inequities and social and economic losses caused by TB.

(4) Develop and promote products and

因；对其全程服药管理情况进行评估；收集和上报患者的"肺结核患者治疗记录卡"或"耐多药肺结核患者服药卡"。同时将患者转诊至结核病定点医疗机构进行治疗结果评估，并在2周内进行电话随访，了解是否前来就诊及诊断结果。

五、国际典型肺结核管理项目

遏制结核病合作伙伴组织是一个全球联盟，成立于2001年，旨在协调国际力量终结结核病。创始成员包括美国肺脏协会（ALA）、美国胸腔协会（ATS）、国际结核病联盟（IUATLD）、荷兰结核病基金会（KNCV）、美国疾控中心（CDC）和世界卫生组织（WHO）。在当下遏制结核病合作伙伴组织已有2 000多个来自100多个国家的合作伙伴，有政府组织、捐助者、私人部门，也有受到结核病影响的个人和其他组织（民间社会组织、患者组织等）。

遏制结核病合作伙伴组织的愿景是创造一个没有结核病的世界，向所有人平等地提供其所需的结核病诊断、治疗和护理服务。具体而言，其行动以及政策制定主要围绕以下5个关键目标展开：

（1）确保每个结核病患者都能获得有效的诊断和治疗。

（2）阻止结核病的传播。

（3）减少结核病造成的不公平及社会和经济损失。

（4）研发和推广产品、制定战略以预防和诊

strategies to prevent, treat and treat tuberculosis.

(5) Amplify the voices of people living with and affected by TB and ensure effective change through strategic advocacy and communication.

Under the five core key goals, Stop TB Partner comes up with specific action plans for the coming years every few years, and in this year's latest edition of *The Global Plan to End TB* (2023–2030), TB prevention and control work is divided into three aspects: first, promote the development of vaccines to protect susceptible populations; second, popularize modern diagnosis and treatment methods, and promote the family-and society-based TB prevention and control model; the third is to reduce the negative economic and social impact of TB.

BOX 8-3　Learning More

World Tuberculosis Day

24 March is World Tuberculosis Day. To commemorate the discovery of Mycobacterium tuberculosis by Robert Koch on 24 March 1882, and to raise awareness, and awareness of tuberculosis, At the end of 1995, the World Health Organization designated March 24 as World Tuberculosis Day. The theme for the 29th World TB Day in 2024 is "Yes! We can end TB: Commit, Invest, Deliver".

(Lin Beilei)

Key Points

1. Preventing chronic diseases involves strategies such as quitting smoking, engaging in regular physical activity, reducing ethanol intake, monitoring diet, maintaining a healthy weight, controlling blood pressure, regulating blood glucose levels, and keeping cholesterol levels within a normal range.

2. Strategies to promote self-management of chronic diseases include motivational interviews, agenda setting, typical day strategy, exploring pros and cons of changing or not changing, and

治结核病。

（5）扩大结核病患者和受结核病影响者的声音，并通过战略性宣传和沟通确保实现有效变革。

在五个核心关键目标下，遏制结核病合作伙伴组织每几年就会提出关于未来几年的具体行动计划，最新版本的《全球终结结核病计划》（2023—2030年）中，结核病防治工作分为3个方面：一是促进疫苗开发，保护易感人群；二是普及现代诊疗方法，推动以家庭和社会为单位的结核病防治模式；三是消减结核病对经济与社会带来的负面影响。

BOX 8-3　知识拓展

世界防治结核病日

3月24日是世界防治结核病日。为了纪念1882年3月24日罗伯特·科赫（Robert Koch）对结核分枝杆菌的发现，也为了强化社会对结核病的关注，提高民众对结核病的认识，1995年底世界卫生组织将每年3月24日作为世界防治结核病日（World Tuberculosis Day）。2025年是第29个世界防治结核病日，主题是"我们能战胜结核病：承诺、投入、实现"。

（林蓓蕾）

内 容 摘 要

1. 预防慢性病的措施包括戒烟、规律体育运动、减少乙醇摄入、合理饮食、保持健康体重、维持血压、维持血糖以及保持正常的胆固醇水平。

2. 常见慢性病自我管理促进策略包括动机访谈、设置日程、典型的一天、探索改变或不改变利弊、适当的信息交流。

appropriate information exchange.

3. Community patients with hypertension, diabetes, mental disorders, and pulmonary tuberculosis belong to the key management groups and should be managed according to the *National Standard for Basic Public Health Services*.

3. 社区高血压、糖尿病、精神疾病及肺结核患者属于重点管理人群，应该根据《国家基本公共卫生服务规范》进行管理。

— Exercises —

(Questions 1 to 2 share the same question stem)

A male patient of 50 years old. He has had type 2 diabetes for 10 years. Oral medications have been used to control blood glucose and blood glucose changes have not been monitored. There was no obvious cause of the right plantar skin rupture 2 years ago, and at first, the scope was small, so it wasn't given attention. After the progression of the disease, the scope of necrosis increased, pus secretion increased, and the bottom of the big toe of the right foot appeared to be ulcerated. He attempted to disinfect the foot at home, but the outcome was unsatisfactory. Consequently, he came to the hospital for further treatment.

1. What are the possible causes of diabetic foot in this patient?

2. Please design nursing care program for this patient to manage his diabetic foot.

(Questions 3 to 4 share the same question stem)

A male patient of 70 years old He has had hypertension for 20 years and diabetes for 15 years. He was a former smoker, smoking 1–3 cigarettes a day and has quit smoking for 2 years. He drinks alcohol but not more than 20ml per day on average. Blood pressure is usually controlled between 160–170/100–105mmHg.

3. What is the risk level of this patient?

4. What are the main points of the patient's health education?

— 思　考　题 —

（1~2题共用题干）

患者，男，50岁。患2型糖尿病10年。一直使用口服药物控制血糖，未监测血糖变化。2年前无明显诱因出现右足底皮肤破溃，起初范围较小，未给予重视。病情进展后，坏死范围扩大加重，脓性分泌物增多，右足踇趾底部位出现溃烂，自行在家消毒换药，效果欠佳，来院治疗。

1. 该患者糖尿病足发生的可能原因有哪些？

2. 请为该患者制订糖尿病足的护理措施。

（3~4题共用题干）

患者，男，70岁。高血压病史20年，糖尿病病史15年。既往吸烟，每天1~3支，目前已经戒烟2年；饮酒但平均每日不超过20ml；平时血压范围，收缩压为160~170mmHg，舒张压为100~105mmHg。

3. 该患者的高血压风险分层属于什么？
4. 该患者健康教育的要点是什么？

Chapter 9

Rehabilitation Nursing of Disabled Patients in Community

第九章

社区伤残患者的康复护理

NURSING

09章 数字内容

第九章

社区伤残患者的康复护理

Learning Objectives

Knowledge Objectives

1. Correctly describe the concept of community-based rehabilitation.

2. Correctly describe the service targets and contents of community-based rehabilitation.

3. Correctly describe the modern community-based rehabilitation nursing techniques and methods of patients with common injuries, disabilities and mental disorders.

学习目标

知识目标

1. 能准确描述社区康复的概念。

2. 能正确描述社区康复的服务对象和内容。

3. 能正确描述常见伤、残、精神障碍患者的现代康复护理技术与方法。

Ability Objectives

1. By rehabilitation assessment methods, conduct community-based rehabilitation assessments on patients with common injuries, disabilities and mental disorders.
2. Use rehabilitation assessment results to develop community-based rehabilitation nursing measures and provide community-based rehabilitation nursing guidance.

Quality Objectives

1. Enhance students' love, patience, and social responsibility, encourage them to participate in community-based rehabilitation as volunteers, serve patients with injuries, disabilities and mental disorders, and increase social warmth.
2. Through collaborative participation in rehabilitation activities, cultivate students' teamwork spirit and improve rehabilitation outcomes.
3. Enhance students' humanistic care for patients with injuries, disabilities and mental disorders, advocate for social respect for every individual, pay attention to their psychological needs, and create an inclusive and harmonious community environment.

能力目标

1. 能运用康复评定方法对常见伤、残、精神障碍患者开展社区康复评定。
2. 能运用康复评定结果制订社区康复护理措施并进行社区康复护理指导。

素质目标

1. 提升学生爱心、耐心和社会责任感,鼓励其作为志愿者参与社区康复,服务于伤、残、精神障碍患者,增加社会温暖。
2. 通过协作参与康复活动,培养学生团队合作精神,提升康复效果。
3. 提升学生对伤残患者和精神障碍患者的人文关怀,倡导社会尊重每一个生命个体,关注他们的心理需求,营造包容和谐的社区环境。

Patient Mr. Chen, 48 years old, is a worker. Recently, while working, he was accidentally hit on his back by a steel plate from a construction site, causing pain in his back and abdomen, as well as weakness and decreased sensation in both lower limbs. He was taken to a nearby hospital for treatment. After surgical treatment, he experienced decreased sensation in both lower limbs and was unable to move on the ground. He was diagnosed with "spinal cord injury". Currently, his upper limbs are functioning normally. He was discharged from the hospital and returned home.

患者,陈先生,48岁,工人。近日在工作时不慎被工地钢板砸到背部,出现后背部及腹部疼痛,双下肢乏力及感觉减退,被送往附近医院就诊。经手术治疗后,出现双下肢感觉减退,不能下地活动,被诊断为"脊髓损伤"。目前患者双上肢功能正常,今日出院回家,社区护士开展家访。陈先生的妻子今年46岁,目前已辞职,可参与陈先生的后期康复护理。

The community nurse will conduct a home visit today. Mr. Chen's wife is 46 years old and has resigned. She can participate in Mr. Chen's later rehabilitation care.

Questions：

1. As a community nurse, how do you assess the patient's current level of dysfunction?

2. What rehabilitation nursing services can community nurses provide for the patient?

On August 16, 2021, the China Disabled Persons' Federation, the Ministry of Education of the People's Republic of China, the Ministry of Civil Affairs of the People's Republic of China, the Ministry of Human Resources and Social Security of the People's Republic of China, the National Health Commission of the People's Republic of China, and the National Healthcare Security Administration issued the *Implementation Plan of Rehabilitation Services for Persons with Disabilities during the 14th Five-Year Plan Period*. The main measures mentioned the need to deepen community-based rehabilitation for persons with disabilities, based on community resources and conditions, improve rehabilitation facilities and teams, and carry out suitable rehabilitation services such as day care, occupational therapy, entertainment therapy, rental of rehabilitation auxiliary equipment and so on. Developing community-based rehabilitation is the only way for rehabilitation demanders to achieve comprehensive rehabilitation and ideal and lasting rehabilitation outcomes.

Section 1 Community-based Rehabilitation

Ⅰ. Relevant Concepts of Community-based Rehabilitation

With the continuous deepening of people's

请思考：

1. 作为一名社区护士，如何评定该患者目前的功能障碍程度？

2. 社区护士可以为该患者提供哪些康复护理服务？

2021 年 8 月 16 日，中国残联、教育部、民政部、人力资源和社会保障部、国家卫生健康委、国家医疗保障局印发了《"十四五"残疾人康复服务实施方案》，在主要措施中提到，要深化残疾人社区康复，立足社区资源、条件，完善康复设施、队伍，开展日间照料、工疗、娱疗、康复辅助器具租赁等适宜康复服务。发展社区康复，是康复需求者实现全面康复和理想、持久康复效果的必由之路。

第一节　社 区 康 复

一、社区康复的相关概念

随着人们对社区康复（community-based

understanding of community-based rehabilitation (CBR) and the dynamic development of CBR, its definition is gradually being updated and improved. Different countries and organizations have different understandings of the definitions and contents of CBR.

i. The Definition of Community-based Rehabilitation in the Three Major United Nations Organizations

In 2004, the World Health Organization, the United Nations Educational, Scientific and Cultural Organization, and the International Labour Organization updated the *CBR Joint Position Paper* from 1994 to accommodate the Helsinki recommendations. It redefines CBR as a strategy within general community development for the rehabilitation, poverty reduction, equalization of opportunities and social inclusion of all people with disabilities and promotes the implementation of CBR programmers through the combined efforts of people with disabilities themselves, their families, organizations and communities, and the relevant governmental and non-governmental health, education, vocational, social and other services institutions.

ii. The Definition of Community-based Rehabilitation in China

At present, the definition of CBR in China is: Community-based rehabilitation is an important part of community construction, which refers to a process in which, under the leadership of the government, with the close cooperation of relevant departments, the extensive support from social forces, and the active participation of persons with disabilities and their relatives and friends, the comprehensive rehabilitation services are provided to people with disabilities through a socialized approach. The goal is to achieve equal opportunities and full participation in social life.

rehabilitation，CBR）认识的不断深入，以及社区康复的动态发展，其定义也在逐渐更新和完善，各个国家和组织机构对社区康复的定义和内容有着不同的理解。

（一）联合国三大组织对社区康复的定义

2004 年，世界卫生组织、联合国教科文组织、国际劳工组织按照赫尔辛基会议意见，对 1994 年的《社区康复的联合意见书》进行了更新。意见书重新将社区康复定义为残疾人康复、机会均等、减少贫困和社会包容提供的一种社区发展战略，需要通过残疾人自己，他们的家庭、组织和社区，以及相关的政府和非政府卫生、教育、职业、社会和其他服务机构的共同努力，促进社区康复项目的完成。

（二）我国对社区康复的定义

目前我国对社区康复的定义为社区康复是社区建设的重要组成部分，是指在政府领导下，相关部门密切配合，社会力量广泛支持，残疾人及其亲友积极参与，采取社会化方式，使广大残疾人得到全面康复服务，以实现机会均等、充分参与社会生活的目标。

Ⅱ. Content of Community-based Rehabilitation

i. Service Targets of Community-based Rehabilitation

In China, the service targets of community-based rehabilitation mainly include three categories: people with disabilities, patients with chronic diseases, and the elderly.

1. People with Disabilities

The definition of people with disabilities in China is: Those who have lost or have an abnormal function of some tissue or organ in psychology, physiology, or human body structure, and have lost or partially lost the ability to engage in certain activities in a normal way. According to the data from the second national sample survey of people with disabilities, the total number of people with various types of disabilities in China is about 82.96 million.

2. Patients with Chronic Diseases

Chronic diseases in China refer to chronic non-communicable diseases, which mainly include:

(1) Cardiovascular and cerebrovascular diseases.

(2) Malignant tumors.

(3) Metabolic disorders.

(4) Mental abnormalities and psychosis.

(5) Genetic diseases.

(6) Chronic occupational diseases.

(7) Chronic bronchitis and emphysema.

(8) Others, such as obesity, etc.

3. The Elderly

According to the *Law of the People's Republic of China on the Protection of the Rights and Interests of the Elderly*, the elderly in China are defined as people over 60 years old. According to the data from the National Bureau of Statistics, as of the end of 2023, the population aged 60 and over in China is 296.97 million, accounting for 21.1% of the total population; the population aged 65 and over is 216.76 million, accounting for 15.4% of the

二、社区康复的内容

（一）社区康复的对象

在我国，社区康复的对象主要包括三类人群：残疾人、慢性病患者和老年人。

1. 残疾人

我国对残疾人的定义是在心理、生理、人体结构上，某种组织、功能丧失或者不正常，全部或者部分丧失以正常方式从事某种活动能力的人。根据第二次全国残疾人抽样调查数据推算，全国各类残疾人的总数约为 8 296 万人。

2. 慢性病患者

我国慢性病指慢性非传染性疾病，主要包括：

（1）心脑血管疾病。

（2）恶性肿瘤。

（3）代谢异常。

（4）精神异常和精神病。

（5）遗传病。

（6）慢性职业病。

（7）慢性支气管炎和肺气肿。

（8）其他，如肥胖症等。

3. 老年人

根据《中华人民共和国老年人权益保障法》，我国对老年人的定义为 60 岁以上的人群。根据国家统计局数据，截至 2023 年末，我国 60 岁及以上人口为 29 697 万人，占总人口的 21.1%；65 岁及以上人口 21 676 万人，占总人口的 15.4%。

total population.

ii. Matrix of Community-based Rehabilitation

The World Health Organization, the United Nations Educational, Scientific and Cultural Organization, the International Labour Organization, and the International Disability and Development Consortium have worked closely together to develop the *Community-based Rehabilitation Guidelines* in 2010. The guidelines bring together all that is currently known about CBR from around the world and provide a new framework for action as well as practical suggestions for implementation.

In light of the evolution of CBR into a broader multisectoral development strategy, a matrix was developed in 2004 to provide a common framework for CBR programmes, as shown in Figure 9-1. The matrix consists of five key components—the health, education, livelihood, social and empowerment components. Within each component there are five elements. The first four components relate to key development sectors, reflecting the multisectoral focus of CBR. The final component relates to the empowerment of people with disabilities, their families and communities, which is fundamental for ensuring access to each development sector, improving the quality of life and enjoyment of human rights for people with disabilities.

（二）社区康复结构图

世界卫生组织、联合国教科文组织、国际劳工组织和国际残疾与发展联盟于 2010 年共同出版了《社区康复指南》，该指南综合了现阶段来自世界各地的有关 CBR 的全部知识，并提供了新的行动框架以及完成 CBR 的实用建议。

按照社区康复广泛多层面发展的策略，相关组织 2004 年创建了社区康复结构图，为社区康复项目提供了共同框架（图 9-1）。结构图由健康、教育、谋生、社会和赋能 5 个关键部分组成。每一部分中又有 5 个要素。前 4 个部分与关键性发展层面相关，反映了社区康复多层面的重点；最后一部分是关于残疾人及其家庭和社区的赋权增能，它是保证残疾人无障碍地参与发展的各个层面、提高生活质量、分享人权的基础。

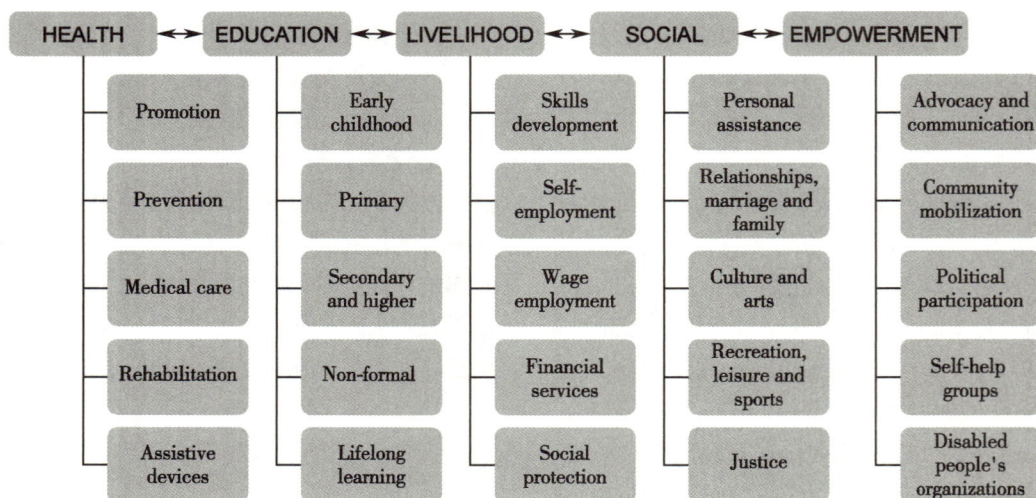

HEALTH	EDUCATION	LIVELIHOOD	SOCIAL	EMPOWERMENT
Promotion	Early childhood	Skills development	Personal assistance	Advocacy and communication
Prevention	Primary	Self-employment	Relationships, marriage and family	Community mobilization
Medical care	Secondary and higher	Wage employment	Culture and arts	Political participation
Rehabilitation	Non-formal	Financial services	Recreation, leisure and sports	Self-help groups
Assistive devices	Lifelong learning	Social protection	Justice	Disabled people's organizations

Figure 9-1   CBR matrix

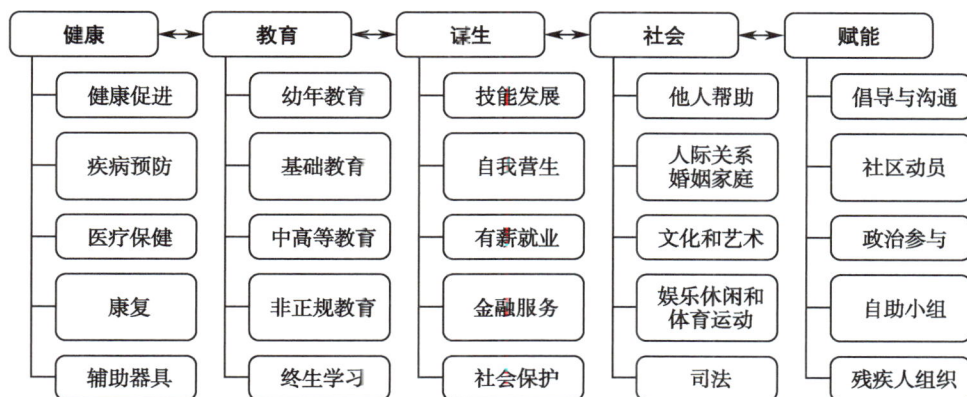

图 9-1　社区康复结构图

CBR programmes are not expected to implement every component and element of the CBR matrix. Instead, the matrix has been designed to allow communities to select options which best meet their local needs, priorities and resources. In addition to implementing specific activities for people with disabilities, CBR programmers will need to develop partnerships and alliances with other sectors not covered by CBR programmes to ensure that people with disabilities and their family members are able to access the benefits of these sectors.

iii. Principles of Community-based Rehabilitation

The principles of CBR are based on the principles of the *Convention on the Rights of Persons with Disabilities*, with the addition of two additional principles, including "Empowerment, including self-advocacy" and "Sustainability", for a total of 10 principles. These principles should be used to guide all aspects of CBR work:

1. Respect for inherent dignity, individual autonomy including the freedom to make one's own choices, and independence of persons.

2. Non-discrimination.

3. Full and effective participation and inclusion in society.

4. Respect for difference and acceptance of persons with disabilities as part of human diversity and humanity.

5. Equality of opportunity.

社区康复项目并不要求实施结构图中的每一个组成部分和要素。相反，这个结构图的设计旨在让社区能够根据其当地需求、重要事项和资源情况来选择最适合的康复项目。另外，为了残疾人能够完成特殊活动，社区康复相关人员将需要与未包含在社区康复中的其他层面人员建立伙伴关系和联盟关系，以保证残疾人和他们的家庭能从这些层面中受益。

（三）社区康复工作的原则

社区康复工作的原则以《残疾人权利公约》的原则为基础，增加另外 2 个原则，包括自我倡导在内的赋权和维持，共 10 个原则。这些原则应该用于指导社区康复工作的所有方面：

1. 尊重固有的尊严和个人自主权，包括自由做出自己的选择，以及个人自立。

2. 不歧视。
3. 充分和有效地参与社会并融入社会。

4. 尊重差异，接受残疾人是人的多样性的其中一个部分，也是人类一份子。

5. 机会均等。

6. Accessibility.

7. Equality between men and women.

8. Respect for the evolving capacities of children with disabilities and respect for the right of children with disabilities to preserve their identities.

9. Empowerment, including self-advocacy.

10. Sustainability.

iv. Service Contents of Community-based Rehabilitation

The service contents of CBR mainly include disability screening, medical rehabilitation, rehabilitation training guidance, day care and maintenance, work (agriculture) and recreational therapy, vocational rehabilitation, psychological support, knowledge promotion and popularization and so on.

1. **Disability Screening**　Conduct a disability clue investigation meeting within the community to jointly record the situations of suspected persons with disabilities by community residents (village) committee cadres, CBR personnel, CBR coordinators, and other professionals, and report to the local community health center (station), rural hospitals, and the disabled persons' federation. The county-level disabled person rehabilitation expert technical guidance group (composed of medical, rehabilitation, education, assistive device fitting, vocational rehabilitation, and other professionals) comprehensively evaluates the screened disabled persons, establishes a file in the community, and incorporates them into the existing rehabilitation service network to provide timely and effective services.

2. **Medical Rehabilitation**　According to the disfunction situation, rehabilitation needs, and family economic conditions of the disabled, relying on urban community health centers (stations) and rural hospitals, village health clinics, and other medical rehabilitation institutions with conditions, provide services such as diagnosis, functional assessment, rehabilitation nursing, and referral for

6. 无障碍。

7. 男女平等。

8. 尊重残疾儿童逐步发展的能力，并尊重残疾儿童保留其身份特性的权利。

9. 包括自我倡导在内的赋权。

10. 维持。

（四）社区康复服务内容

社区康复服务主要包括残疾筛查、医疗康复、康复训练指导、日间照料与养护、工（农）与娱乐治疗、职业康复、心理支持、知识宣传普及等多方面内容。

1. **残疾筛查**　以社区为单位召开残疾人线索调查会议，由社区居（村）委会干部、社区康复员、社区康复协调员和其他专业人员共同对疑似残疾人情况进行记录，并向当地社区卫生服务中心（站）、乡镇卫生院和残疾人联合会报告。县级残疾人康复专家技术指导组（由医疗、康复、教育、辅助器具适配、职业康复等专业人员组成）对筛查出的残疾人进行综合评定，在社区建档立卡，纳入已有的康复服务网络，以便及时提供有效服务。

2. **医疗康复**　根据残疾人的功能障碍情况、康复需求及家庭经济条件，依托城市社区卫生服务中心（站）和有条件的农村乡镇卫生院、村卫生室及其他医疗康复机构，采取直接服务、家庭病床和入户指导等形式，为残疾人提供诊断、功能评定、康复护理和转诊等服务。

the disabled in the form of direct services, family beds, home guidance and so on.

3. Rehabilitation Training Guidance

Under the guidance of expert technical guidance groups and professional personnel from community health centers (stations), rural hospitals, and other institutions, provide rehabilitation training guidance services for disabled persons of all types in the community and at home. For example, guide physically disabled persons to carry out various functional trainings, carry out rehabilitation for low vision patients and orientation walking training for the blind, etc.

4. Day Care and Maintenance

Relying on existing community resources, such as day care centers and nursing homes, provide daytime care and maintenance services for severely mentally, intellectually, and physically disabled persons who have lost the ability to take care of themselves, enhance their ability to participate in social life, and enable the mentally, intellectually and physically disabled persons in the community to receive rehabilitation services nearby.

5. Work (Agriculture) and Recreational Therapy

Utilize existing community facilities and personnel, such as recreational therapy stations and agricultural therapy stations, to arrange mild intellectually disabled persons and mentally disabled patients with stable conditions, as well as physically disabled persons with certain mobility, to engage in recreational games, simple production labor, handicraft production, and other rehabilitation activities, to carry out social adaptation ability training and various recreational and sports activities.

6. Vocational Rehabilitation

According to the relevant information from the labor employment department and the needs of the disabled in vocational training and employment, based on the evaluation of the individual abilities of the disabled, rely on the community to carry out targeted vocational rehabilitation activities, and provide vocational skills training to help the

3. **康复训练指导** 在专家技术指导组和社区卫生服务中心（站）、乡镇卫生院等机构的专业人员指导下，在社区和家中为各类残疾人提供康复训练指导服务。如指导肢体残疾人开展各项功能训练，开展低视力患者康复和盲人定向行走训练等。

4. **日间照料与养护** 依托社区现有资源，如日间照料中心、养老院等，为丧失生活自理能力的重度精神疾病患者或智力残疾人、肢体残疾人等，提供日间照料和养护服务，增强其参与社会生活的能力，使社区中的精神、智力与肢体残疾人能得到就近康复服务。

5. **工（农）与娱乐治疗** 利用社区现有设施和人员，如娱乐治疗站、农业治疗站，安排轻度智力残疾人和病情稳定的精神疾病患者以及有一定活动能力的肢体残疾人，进行娱乐游戏、简单生产劳动、手工制作等康复活动，开展社会适应能力训练和各种文体娱乐活动。

6. **职业康复** 根据劳动就业部门的相关信息以及残疾人在职业培训、劳动就业等方面的需求，通过对残疾人个体能力的评定，依托社区开展针对性的职业康复活动，并提供职业技能培训，助力残疾人参与职业生活。

disabled participate in professional life.

7. Psychological Support　Organize the establishment of relatives' associations and mutual aid organizations for the disabled, to carry out psychological counseling and psychological therapy activities in various ways such as individual interviews and group exchanges, to encourage the disabled and their relatives and friends to face disability correctly and establish confidence in rehabilitation.

8. Knowledge Promotion and Popularization　Organize professional and technical personnel in health, education, psychology, and other fields to publicize national rehabilitation policies, hold knowledge lectures, carry out rehabilitation counseling activities, distribute rehabilitation science popularization reading materials and so on for disabled persons and their relatives and friends in the community.

Ⅲ. Management of Community-based Rehabilitation

ⅰ. Organizational Network of Community-based Rehabilitation Management

The implementation of CBR relies on a sound network structure. According to the experience of some urban and rural community rehabilitation work pilot projects in China, the current effective CBR management system can be summarized as a three-level CBR network, which includes a three-level CBR management network involving government departments, a three-level medical and health rehabilitation network involving health departments, and a three-level social welfare security network involving civil affairs departments. The three levels refer to the district (county), street (township), and residents (village) committee, that is, led by the district (county), based on the street (township), and with the residents (village) committee as the foundation, coordinating departments such as education, the disabled persons' federation, finance, labor, and publicity, to provide comprehensive rehabilitation

7. 心理支持　组织成立残疾人亲友会和残疾人互助组织等，以个别访谈和小组交流等多种方式开展心理咨询和心理治疗活动，鼓励残疾人及其亲友正确面对残疾，树立康复信心。

8. 知识宣传普及　组织卫生、教育、心理等专业技术人员，为社区内残疾人及其亲友宣传国家康复政策、举办知识讲座、开展康复咨询活动、发放康复科普读物等。

三、社区康复的管理

（一）社区康复管理的组织网络

社区康复的开展依赖于健全的网络化结构。根据我国部分城乡社区康复工作试点经验，目前行之有效的社区康复管理体制可概括为三级社区康复网络，包括政府部门参与的三级社区康复管理网、卫生部门参与的三级医疗保健康复网和民政部门参与的三级社会福利保障网。三级是指区（县）、街道（乡镇）、居（村）委会，即以区（县）为主导，以街道（乡镇）为基地，以居（村）委会为基础，协调教育、残疾人联合会、财政、劳动、宣传等部门，在社区为残疾人提供全面康复服务。

services to the disabled in the community.

ii. Construction and Management of the Community-based Rehabilitation Work Team

Establishing a CBR project requires different personnel from the higher level to the grassroots to take on different roles and responsibilities. Therefore, to provide comprehensive rehabilitation services for the disabled, patients with chronic diseases, and the elderly, it is necessary for the management personnel, rehabilitation guidance personnel, grassroots rehabilitation personnel, community members, volunteers, the disabled, patients with chronic diseases, the elderly, and their relatives and friends to work closely together.

1. Management Personnel   Mainly include members of the CBR work leading group, technical guidance center and rehabilitation training service institution personnel, street and township CBR work management personnel, and residents committee and village committee directors.

2. Rehabilitation Guidance Personnel   They are an important human resource to ensure that CBR training and service work is carried out scientifically and effectively. Mainly include members of the technical guidance group, medical personnel from institutions undertaking training and service tasks, teachers, and trained business personnel from relevant departments.

3. Grassroots Rehabilitation Personnel   Mainly refers to medical personnel from street, township, and village health centers, school teachers, and grassroots workers from the civil affairs, education, family planning, women's federation, and other systems.

4. Community-based Rehabilitation Social Workers   Refer to community members, volunteers, rehabilitation service targets themselves and their relatives and friends. We should fully mobilize social forces, organize enthusiastic service volunteers, rehabilitation service targets themselves and their relatives and

（二）社区康复工作团队的建设与管理

建设社区康复项目，需要从上级到基层的不同人员担任不同角色、承担不同责任。因此，为残疾人、慢性病患者和老年人提供健全康复服务，需要管理人员、康复指导人员、基层康复人员、社区成员、志愿工作者、残疾人、慢性病患者和老年人及其亲友等各方密切配合。

1. 管理人员   主要有社区康复工作领导小组成员，技术指导中心和康复训练服务机构负责人员，街道、乡镇、社区康复工作管理人员，社区居委会和村委会主任等。

2. 康复指导人员   他们是使社区康复训练与服务工作科学、有效进行的重要人力资源，主要有技术指导组成员、承担训练和服务任务机构的医务人员、教师以及经培训的相关部门业务人员。

3. 基层康复人员   主要指街道、乡镇、社区和村卫生中心站的医务人员，学校教师，民政、教育、计生、妇联等系统的基层工作人员。

4. 社区康复社会工作人员   指社区成员、志愿者、康复服务对象本人及其亲友。要充分动员社会力量，组织热心服务的志愿者、康复服务对象本人及其亲友积极参与社区康复，帮助康复服务对象及其亲友预防和解决部分经济问题或生活问题，提高他们的社会福利水平和生活质量。

friends to actively participate in community-based rehabilitation, to help rehabilitation service targets and their relatives and friends prevent and solve some economic or living problems, and improve their social welfare level and quality of life.

iii. The Socialized Work System of Community-based Rehabilitation

The implementation of CBR relies on a socialized work system, which is composed of organizational management network, technical guidance network, and training service network.

1. Organizational Management Network

(1) Strengthen government leadership and improve the rehabilitation work offices for the disabled at the provincial, city, and county (district) levels. Incorporate the goal of "everyone has access to rehabilitation services" for the disabled into the social and economic development plan, include it in the work assessment targets of the government and related departments, formulate measures to ensure rehabilitation, and organize the development and implementation of CBR plans.

(2) The disabled persons' federations at the street and township levels coordinate with relevant units to consider the rehabilitation needs and resources of the disabled in an appropriate manner and carry out CBR work accordingly.

(3) The residents committees and village committees of communities are equipped with full-time or part-time CBR workers to provide convenient rehabilitation services for the disabled.

2. Technical Guidance Network

(1) Adjust and enrich the CBR technical guidance teams at all levels to play a role in formulating technical standards for common rehabilitation diseases, promoting practical and suitable rehabilitation technologies, training personnel, and evaluating rehabilitation effects.

(2) Establish and improve the rehabilitation centers for the disabled at the provincial and municipal (city) levels, strengthen standardized management, continuously expand rehabilitation services, broaden the service areas, and play a role

（三）社区康复社会化工作体系

社区康复的实施依靠社会化的工作体系，该体系由组织管理网络、技术指导网络和训练服务网络组成。

1. 组织管理网络

（1）加强政府领导，完善省、市、县（区）残疾人康复工作办公室。将残疾人"人人享有康复服务"的目标纳入社会经济发展规划，列入政府及相关部门工作考核指标，制订康复保障措施，组织制订并实施社区康复计划。

（2）街道、乡镇残疾人联合会协调有关单位，统筹考虑残疾人的康复需求和康复资源，因地制宜开展残疾人社区康复工作。

（3）社区居委会、村委会配备专职或兼职的社区康复员，为残疾人提供就近方便的康复服务。

2. 技术指导网络

（1）调整和充实各级社区康复技术指导组，在制定常见康复疾病的技术标准、推广实用适宜康复技术、培训人员和评估康复效果方面发挥作用。

（2）建立和完善省级、地（市）级残疾人康复中心，加强规范化管理，不断扩展康复业务，扩大服务领域，发挥技术示范和指导作用。

in technical demonstration and guidance.

(3) Integrate local rehabilitation resources, and establish rehabilitation technical guidance centers and supply service stations for assistive devices for the disabled at the county (district) level to provide services for the disabled, and play a role in popularizing knowledge, training personnel, guiding family in community, providing consultation and referral services and so on.

3. Training Service Network

Based on the community and relying on the family, fully utilize the role of existing institutions, facilities, and personnel such as community health centers (stations), rural hospitals, schools, welfare enterprises and institutions, and venues for the disabled, share resources, and form a CBR training network to provide convenient, timely, and effective rehabilitation training and services for the disabled.

IV. Models of Community-based Rehabilitation

i. Social Medical Cooperation Model

The social medical cooperation model is led by various government departments (such as health, disabled persons' federations, welfare, and social security, etc.), with a team composed of rehabilitation experts, rehabilitation physicians, rehabilitation therapists, and rehabilitation nurses providing technical support.

1. Advantages

(1) Policy Support: The development of this model is strongly supported by national health departments and public welfare units for the disabled.

(2) Technical Support: Under the leadership of government departments, the expert team actively works to provide technical support on improving the CBR structure and cultivating professional rehabilitation personnel for the community.

(3) Financial Support: The state provides financial support for the development of the

（3）整合当地康复资源，建立县（区）康复技术指导中心和残疾人辅助器具供应服务站，为残疾人提供服务，并发挥普及知识、人员培训、社区家庭指导、咨询转诊等服务作用。

3. 训练服务网络

以社区为基础、家庭为依托，充分发挥社区卫生服务中心（站）、乡镇卫生院、学校、福利性企业事业单位、残疾人活动场所等现有机构、设施、人员的作用，资源共享，形成社区康复训练网络，为残疾人提供就近方便、及时有效的康复训练与服务。

四、社区康复的模式

（一）社会医疗合作模式

社会医疗合作模式由政府各部门（如卫生、残疾人联合会、福利和社会保障等）领导，康复专家、康复医师、康复治疗师、康复护士组成团队提供技术支持。

1. 优势

（1）政策支持：该模式的发展得到国家卫生部门及残疾人公共卫生福利性事业单位的大力扶持。

（2）技术支持：在政府部门领导下，专家团队积极提供技术支持，致力于社区康复结构的完善及社区专业康复人员的培养。

（3）资金支持：国家对残疾人事业发展给予资金支持，将经费列入各级财政预算。

disability cause, and funds are included in the financial budgets at all levels.

2. Problems

(1) Insufficient Funds: China has a large number of disabled people, and the funds allocated by the government and health departments are relatively insufficient, with a low per capita value.

(2) Lack of Experts and Rehabilitation Teams: Due to the relatively slow development of rehabilitation medicine in China, there is a shortage of more than 300,000 rehabilitation therapists nationwide.

(3) Low Coverage Rate in Relatively Remote and Backward Areas: Due to poor basic medical facilities and weak awareness of rehabilitation in some areas, less effort is put into the field of rehabilitation, resulting in policies not being fully implemented.

ii. Hospital Affiliated Model

The hospital affiliated model refers to a CBR institution being directly affiliated with or attached to a regional large comprehensive hospital. In this model, the general hospital provides technical support and talent training, while the workforce at the CBR institution is expanded through social recruitment.

1. Advantages

(1) The hospital directly leads the community to carry out CBR, providing rich medical resources and professional guidance for rehabilitation patients.

(2) The hospital's rehabilitation center provides technical training and talent cultivation, strengthening the exchange between the hospital and the community through a rotation system.

(3) The extension of hospital patient treatment is met, and the four major medical systems of health care, prevention, treatment, and rehabilitation are fully completed.

2. Problems

(1) Due to issues such as institutional crossover, unclear finances, and unclear affiliation of staff, the feasibility of hospital rehabilitation

2. 问题

（1）经费不足：中国残疾人基数大，政府、卫生部门支出经费相对不足，人均值较低。

（2）专家及康复团队缺乏：由于我国康复医学事业发展相对迟缓，全国康复治疗师缺口为30余万人。

（3）相对偏远落后地区覆盖率低：部分地区基础医疗措施较差、康复意识不强，在康复领域投入精力较少，导致政策不能完全执行。

（二）医院附属模式

医院附属模式是指社区康复机构作为区域性大型综合医院直属或附属单位，由综合医院提供技术支持及人才培养，同时通过社会招聘的形式扩充基层社区康复人员的模式。

1. 优势

（1）医院直接领导社区开展社区康复，提供丰富的医疗资源，对需要康复的患者提供专业指导。

（2）医院康复中心提供技术培训及人才培养，通过轮转方式加强了医院与社区间的康复交流。

（3）医院患者的延伸治疗得以满足，全方位完成保健、预防、治疗、康复四大医学体系。

2. 问题

（1）因机构交叉、财务不清、工作人员所属机构不明等各种人事及制度问题，医院康复医师及治疗师延伸到社区服务的可行性受到限制。

physicians and therapists extending their services to the community is limited.

(2) The two-way referral system is not well-established. The exchange of patient medical record information is insufficient, and the timing of referral is unclear.

(3) There is a significant gap in the level of rehabilitation medical services between community and large comprehensive hospitals, and patients have low trust in CBR.

iii. Community Health Center Integrated Model

The community health center integrated model is the main form of CBR in China. Community health centers set up rehabilitation treatment rooms at service stations, equipped with basic evaluation facilities and rehabilitation training equipment. They regularly provide functional assessment and rehabilitation treatment for the disabled within the community's jurisdiction. At the same time, they also open family rehabilitation beds and regularly send rehabilitation workers to the homes of the disabled for rehabilitation treatment. Rehabilitation centers in each district and county should have rehabilitation doctors regularly visit the surrounding community health centers to provide technical guidance, rehabilitation knowledge lectures and so on for rehabilitation workers in the community, such as holding targeted CBR technology training classes, or conducting remote education through the internet.

1. Advantages

(1) This is currently the most important form of integration of rehabilitation medicine and the community, with a broad base of regional institutions.

(2) As a basic medical and health department of the country, community health centers have a wide coverage and a relatively balanced distribution.

(3) It has mature community health center management institutions, and the basic clinical facilities and personnel are relatively complete.

（2）双向转诊体制不完善,患者病历信息交流不充分,转诊时机不明确。

（3）社区与大型综合医院的康复医疗水平差距较大,患者对社区康复的信任度较低。

（三）社区卫生服务中心一体化模式

社区卫生服务中心一体化模式是中国社区康复的主要形式。社区卫生服务中心在服务站设置康复治疗室,并配有基础的评定设施和康复训练器材,定期对社区所辖范围内的残疾人进行功能评定和康复治疗,同时开设家庭康复病床,定期派康复工作者到残疾人家中进行康复治疗。各区县所在康复中心,应有康复医生定期到周围的社区卫生服务中心对社区康复工作者进行技术指导和康复知识讲座等,例如有针对性地开设一些社区康复技术培训班,或通过互联网进行远程教育。

1. 优势

（1）这是目前康复医学与社区结合的最主要形式,具有广泛的区域机构基础。

（2）社区卫生服务中心作为国家基础医疗卫生部门,其覆盖范围广,城镇分布相对较平衡。

（3）具有成熟的社区卫生服务中心管理机构,基础类临床设施及人员配备较齐全。

(4) The construction cost is low. On the basis of mature community health centers, the introduction or expansion of rehabilitation medical facilities enriches the medical field, with flexible management and relatively easy resolution of personnel establishment issues.

(5) This makes it convenient for people with rehabilitation needs to seek medical treatment, reducing rehabilitation costs and saving social resources.

(6) Grassroots propaganda of rehabilitation knowledge can improve the rehabilitation awareness of residents and improve the quality of life for residents.

2. Problems

(1) The service content is relatively single, mostly involving traditional Chinese medicine physiotherapy massage, and modern rehabilitation concepts have not yet been popularized.

(2) There is a shortage of professional rehabilitation therapists.

(3) Rehabilitation facilities are relatively incomplete.

(4) Limited community funding, and insufficient talent introduction.

(5) Limited cooperation with large hospitals, and an imperfect referral system.

iv. Social Forces Independently Founded Community-based Rehabilitation Hospital Model

Also known as individual CBR, with a unique private business model, aiming to serve the rehabilitation population and reasonably obtain benefits.

1. Advantages

(1) Adequate funding, equipped with advanced rehabilitation equipment, attracting advanced professionals, and providing professional services.

(2) Flexible system, streamlined personnel, and high efficiency.

(3) Rich service content is conducive to extending to family rehabilitation directions.

（4）建设成本低，在成熟的社区卫生服务中心基础上引进或增加康复医疗设施，扩大了医疗范围，管理灵活，人事编制问题较容易解决。

（5）使有康复需求的人群就医方便，降低了康复成本，节约了社会资源。

（6）基层宣传康复知识，可提高居民康复意识，改善居民生存质量。

2. 问题

（1）服务内容较单一，大多只涉及中医理疗按摩类，现代康复理念尚未普及。

（2）专业康复治疗师不足。

（3）康复设施相对不齐全。

（4）社区经费有限，人才引进不足。

（5）与大型医院合作有限，转诊体制不完善。

（四）社会力量独立创办社区康复医院模式

简称个体社区康复，拥有独特的私人经营模式，以服务康复人群为目的，合理获得利益。

1. 优势

（1）经费充足，可配备先进的康复器材，吸引高级专业人才，提供专业服务。

（2）体制灵活，人员精简，效率高。

（3）服务内容丰富，有利于延伸至家庭康复方向。

(4) Can draw on the operation model of private hospitals, with clear rules to follow.

2. Problems

(1) Although the national medical insurance has a certain coverage of rehabilitation equipment treatment, it has not yet achieved full coverage. Advanced rehabilitation equipment in individual CBR has led to treatment limitations for some insured groups.

(2) Due to the instability of profit income and operation, the sustainability of CBR is affected, leading to hesitation or loss of rehabilitation-needing groups.

(3) There is a contradiction between the profit model of individual CBR and the welfare nature of community.

Section 2 Modern Rehabilitation and Traditional Chinese Medicine Rehabilitation Nursing Techniques and Methods for Patients with Common Injuries, Disabilities and Mental Disorders in the Community

I. Community-based Rehabilitation of Patients with Stroke

i. Overview

1. Definition Stroke refers to a group of syndromes characterized by acute onset of neurological deficits due to local cerebral blood circulation disorders in the brain, divided into two types: ischemic stroke and hemorrhagic stroke.

2. Main Dysfunctions Main dysfunctions include motor dysfunction, sensory dysfunction, speech dysfunction, swallowing dysfunction, cognitive dysfunction, etc., which can lead to a decline in daily activities, thereby affecting the

（4）可借鉴私人医院运作模式,有章可循。

2. 问题

（1）虽然国家医保对康复器械类治疗有一定的覆盖,但尚未实现全覆盖,个体社区康复中先进的康复设备等导致部分医保人群治疗受限。

（2）因其利润收入及运作的不稳定性,影响社区康复的可持续性,导致康复需求人群犹豫或流失。

（3）盈利模式与社区福利性质有所矛盾。

第二节 社区常见伤、残、精神障碍患者的现代康复和中医康复护理技术与方法

一、脑卒中患者的社区康复

（一）概述

1. 定义 脑卒中指急性起病,由脑局部血液循环障碍所致的神经功能缺损的一组综合征,分为缺血性脑卒中和出血性脑卒中两种类型。

2. 主要功能障碍 包括运动功能障碍、感觉功能障碍、言语功能障碍、吞咽功能障碍、认知功能障碍等,可导致日常活动能力下降,从而影响患者生活。

patient's life.

3. **The Goals of CBR**　The rehabilitation goals for patients with stroke at different stages are different. For patients who have not completed medical rehabilitation, the goal is to further improve functional status, enhance self-care ability, and strive to return to the family and society as soon as possible. For patients who have completed medical rehabilitation, the main goal is to make full use of community resources, transform the home and community environment to facilitate barrier-free living for patients, improve their independent living ability, and at the same time, according to the patient's wishes, promote their development in education, occupation, social functions and so on.

ii. Rehabilitation Assessment

1. **Assessment of Motor Function**

(1) Assessment of Limb Motor Function：The Brunnstrom 6 stages assessment method can be used, which is a widely applied limb motor function assessment method.

(2) Assessment of Muscle Tone：The modified Ashworth scale (MAS) can be used, which is a commonly used, simple, and easy-to-master muscle tone assessment scale.

2. **Assessment of Balance**　The three-level balance assessment and the Berg balance scale (BBS) can be used.

3. **Assessment of Swallowing Function** The Kubota water swallow test and Saito seven-grade evaluation method can be utilized.

4. **Assessment of Activities of Daily Living**　This evaluates a patient's ability to live independently and the level of disability, commonly assessed using the Barthel index.

5. **Assessment of Quality of Life** Commonly used assessment scales include the World Health Organization quality of life-100 (WHOQOL-100), the 36-item short-form health survey (SF-36), the quality of well-being scale (QWB) and so on.

6. **Assessment of Other Dysfunctions** Including assessments of sensory function,

3. **社区康复目标**　不同时期的脑卒中患者，其康复目标不同。对于未完成医学康复的患者，其康复目标是进一步改善功能状况，提高生活自理能力，争取早日重返家庭和社会；对于已完成医学康复的患者，主要目标是充分利用社区资源，改造家庭和社区环境，以促进患者无障碍生活，提高其独立生活能力，同时根据患者意愿，促进其在教育、职业和社会功能等方面的发展。

（二）康复评定

1. **运动功能评定**

（1）肢体运动功能评定：可采用 Brunnstrom 六期评估法，这是目前应用较为普遍的肢体运动功能评定方法。

（2）肌张力评定：可采用修订的 Ashworth 痉挛评定量表，这是目前常用的较简单、易于掌握的肌张力评定量表。

2. **平衡评定**　可采用三级平衡评定和 Berg 平衡评定量表。

3. **吞咽功能评定**　可采用洼田饮水试验和才藤氏七级评价指导法评估。

4. **日常生活活动能力评定**　是对患者独立生活能力及残损状况进行测定，常用 Barthel 指数评定。

5. **生存质量评定**　常用的评定量表包括世界卫生组织生存质量评定量表（WHOQOL-100）、健康状况 SF-36（36-item short-form）及健康生存质量表（quality of well-being scale，QWB）等。

6. **其他功能障碍评定**　包括感觉功能评定、认知功能评定、失语症评定、构音障碍评定

cognitive function, aphasia, dysarthria, and psychology, which can refer to relevant books.

iii. Modern Rehabilitation Nursing Techniques and Methods

1. The Position of Patients with Hemiplegia

(1) Correct Supine Position: Patients should alternate between the supine position and other positions. When the patient is supine, the head should be placed on a pillow and the thoracic vertebrae should not be bent, and on the affected side, a pillow is needed to be placed under the scapula, with the shoulders extended forward, elbows extended, wrist back extended, and fingers extended. Meanwhile, the rehabilitation worker should extend the patient's affected lower limb and place a pillow under the affected buttocks and thighs to prevent external rotation of the affected lower limb, as shown in Figure 9-2.

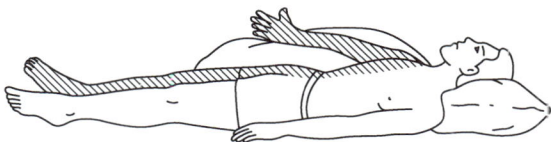

Figure 9-2　Correct supine position for patients with hemiplegia

When positioning patients, attention should be paid to the following things: a. The bed should be flat, and the head of the bed should not be raised. b. There should be nothing in patients' hands. c. Nothing should be placed under the soles of the feet and a bed frame can be used to support the bedding or an ankle-foot orthosis can be worn to prevent foot drop deformity.

(2) Correct Affected Side Lateral Position: Lying on the affected side can increase stimulation and stretch the affected side, thereby reducing spasms. At the same time, the healthy hand can move freely. The correct affected side lateral position for the patient is as follows: the head slightly flexed forward, the trunk slightly reclined backward, the back firmly supported by a pillow, the affected upper limb extended forward at an angle of not less than 90° from the trunk, palm

和心理评定等,可参考康复功能评定相关书籍。

（三）现代康复护理技术与方法

1. 偏瘫患者的体位摆放

（1）正确的仰卧位:患者需仰卧位与其他体位交替。患者仰卧时,头部枕在枕头上,不要使胸椎屈曲;患侧肩胛骨下方放置一个枕头,使肩前伸,肘部伸展,腕背伸,手指伸开;患侧下肢置于伸展位,在患侧臀部及大腿下面放置一个枕头,防止患侧下肢外旋(图9-2)。

图 9-2　偏瘫患者正确的仰卧位

体位摆放时,应注意:①床放平,床头不得抬高;②患者手中不应有任何东西;③不在足底放东西,可选择用床架支撑被褥或佩戴踝足矫形器的方式,避免发生足下垂畸形。

（2）正确的患侧卧位:患侧卧位可以增加对患侧的刺激,并拉长患侧,从而减少痉挛,同时健侧手可以自由活动。正确的患侧卧位是:头部稍前屈,躯干稍向后倾,后背用枕头稳固支持,患侧上肢前伸,与躯干的角度不小于90°,手心向上,手腕被动背伸;患侧下肢伸展,膝关节稍屈曲。护士可将一只手放在患者肩后,使肩胛骨前伸。如果前伸不够充分,患者常主诉肩痛或不舒适,见图9-3。

up, and the wrist passively extended backward; the affected lower limb extended, with the knee slightly flexed. The nurse can place one hand behind the patient's shoulder to facilitate forward extension of the scapula. If the forward extension of the scapula is not sufficient, such patients often complain of shoulder pain or discomfort, as shown in Figure 9-3.

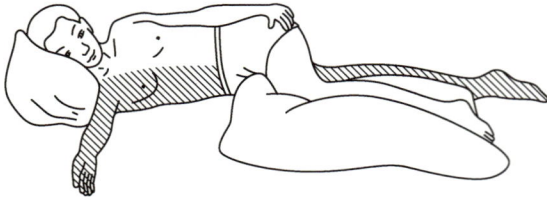

Figure 9-3　Correct affected side lateral position for patients with hemiplegia

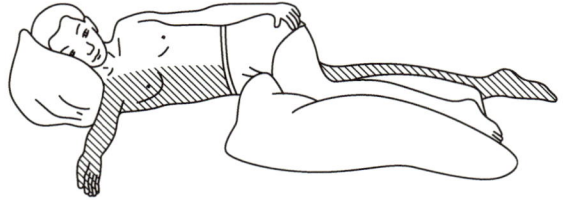

图 9-3　偏瘫患者正确的患侧卧位

(3) Correct Healthy Side Lateral Position: The healthy side lateral position is beneficial for blood circulation on the affected side, can reduce spasms in the affected limb, and prevent edema in the patient. When the patient is in the healthy side lateral position, the head is still supported by a pillow to ensure the patient's comfort. At the same time, the healthy side of the patient is below, the affected side is above, the trunk is at a right angle to the bed surface and does not lie forward in a semi recumbent position; the affected upper limb is supported by a pillow in front and raised about 100° upwards; the affected lower limb should be bent forward with the hip and knee flexed, and completely supported by a pillow. The foot should not be suspended at the edge of the pillow, but should also be placed completely on the pillow; place the healthy limb on the bed in a comfortable position, gently stuff the back with a pillow and let the patient rest against it, as shown in Figure 9-4.

（3）正确的健侧卧位：健侧卧位有利于患侧的血液循环，可减轻患侧肢体的痉挛，预防患者水肿。健侧卧位时，头仍由枕头支撑，以确保患者舒适。同时健侧在下，患侧在上，躯干与床面保持直角，不要向前呈半卧位；患侧上肢由枕头在前面垫起，上举约 100°；患侧下肢向前屈髋、屈膝，并完全由枕头垫起，足不能悬在枕头边缘，也应完全放于枕头上；健侧肢体放在床上，取舒适位置，背部可用枕头轻塞靠住，见图 9-4。

Figure 9-4　Correct healthy side lateral position for patients with hemiplegia

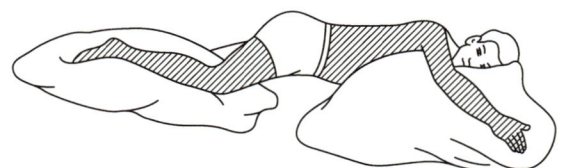

图 9-4　偏瘫患者正确的健侧卧位

2. The Positioning Changes of Patients with Hemiplegia

Patients with hemiplegia have no voluntary movement on the affected side of their body, which makes it difficult to turn over. If they are fixed in one position on the bed for a long time, pressure ulcers may occur, and it is also not conducive to expectoration. Prolonged immobility may leads to lung infections. Therefore, it is necessary to turn them over every two hours to prevent the above-mentioned complications. Bed turning mainly includes two methods: active turning training and passive turning training.

(1) Actively Turning Towards the Healthy Side: The patient lies on their back with their hands crossed, and the thumb of the affected hand is pressed above the thumb of the healthy hand (Bobath handshake); bend the shoulder joint 90° and straighten the elbow joint; and insert the healthy lower limb into the lower part of the affected lower limb; turn the head to the healthy side, and the healthy upper limb and trunk drive the affected upper limb to swing towards the affected side, then swing in the opposite direction towards the healthy side, using the inertia of swing to rotate the body towards the healthy side. At the same time, bend the knee joint back on the healthy side, hook the affected leg, and under the drive of the healthy lower limb, turn the pelvis and affected lower limb towards the healthy side.

(2) Actively Turning Towards the Affected Side: The patient lies on their back with their hands crossed, and the thumb of the affected hand is pressed above the thumb of the healthy hand (Bobath handshake); bend the shoulder joint 90° and straighten the elbow joint; turn the head to the affected side, step on the bed with the healthy feet, and bend the knees; the healthy upper limb drives the hemiplegic upper limb to swing towards the healthy side, then drives it in the opposite direction towards the affected side. At the same time, the healthy foot pedals on the bed surface, exerting force towards the affected side, and with

2. 偏瘫患者的体位变换

偏瘫患者患侧肢体无自主活动，翻身很困难。如果在床上固定于一种姿势，容易出现压疮，也不利于咳痰，久之可能造成肺部感染，所以要每两小时翻身一次，防止上述并发症。床上翻身主要包括主动翻身训练和被动翻身训练两种方式。

（1）主动向健侧翻身：患者仰卧位，双手十指交叉，患手拇指压在健手拇指上方（即 Bobath 式握手）；屈曲肩关节 90°，伸直肘关节，用健侧下肢插入患侧下肢下方；头转向健侧，健侧上肢、躯干带动偏瘫侧上肢摆向患侧，再反向摆向健侧，利用摆动惯性向健侧旋转身体，同时健侧膝关节背屈，勾住患侧小腿，在健侧下肢的带动下使骨盆和患侧下肢转向健侧。

（2）主动向患侧翻身：患者仰卧，双手十指交叉，患手拇指压在健手拇指上方（即 Bobath 式握手）；屈曲肩关节 90°，伸直肘关节；头转向患侧，健足踩在床面上，屈膝；健侧上肢带动偏瘫侧上肢摆向健侧，再反向摆向患侧，同时健侧足蹬踏床面，向患侧用力，在躯干和上肢手的配合下向患侧翻身，见图 9-5。

the cooperation of the trunk and upper limb hands, flipping towards the affected side, as shown in Figure 9-5.

Figure 9-5   Actively turning towards the affected side

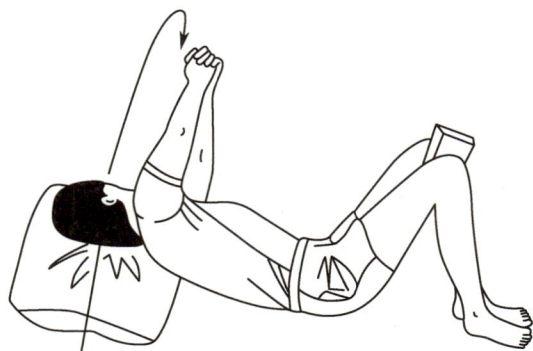

图 9-5   主动向患侧翻身

(3) Passively Turning Towards the Healthy Side: Rotate the upper trunk first, then rotate the lower trunk. The nurse places one hand under the patient's neck and the other hand around the affected scapula, turning the patient's head and upper trunk into a healthy lateral position. Next, the nurse places one hand in the affected pelvis to turn it forward, and the other hand behind the affected knee joint to rotate and place the affected lower limb in a natural semi flexion position, as shown in Figure 9-6.

（3）被动向健侧翻身：先旋转上半部躯干，再旋转下半部躯干。护士一手置于患者颈部下方，一手置于患侧肩胛骨周围，将患者头部及上半部躯干转为健侧卧位；接下来护士再将一手置于患侧骨盆将其转向前方，另一手置于患侧膝关节后方，将患侧下肢旋转并摆放于自然半屈位（图 9-6）。

Figure 9-6   Passively turning towards the healthy side

图 9-6   被动向健侧翻身

(4) Passively Turning Towards the Affected Side: Nurses assist patients in placing the affected upper limb in a 90° position for abduction; the patient turns their body to the affected side on their

（4）被动向患侧翻身：护士帮助患者将患侧上肢外展置于 90°体位；患者自行将身体转向患侧。若患者完成有困难，护士可采用"被动向健侧翻身"的方法，帮助患者完成动作。

own. If the patient has difficulty completing the task, the nurse can use the method of "passively turning towards the healthy side" to help the patient complete the movement.

3. The Transfer Methods of Patients with Hemiplegia

(1) Assisting the Patient in Transferring from Bed to Chair:

1) The patient sits at the edge of the bed with both feet flat on the ground. The nurse faces the patient, pressing his/her own knees against the patient's knees, placing the patient's forearms on nurse's shoulders, and nurse's hands on the patient's scapula, gripping the inner edge of the scapula, making patient lean forward, shifting the patient's center of gravity onto their feet until the patient's buttocks lift off the bed. Using the patient's healthy foot as the axis, align the patient's buttocks with the chair surface and assist the patient in slowly sitting on the chair.

2) If the patient has some active movement, a stool can be placed in front of the patient. The patient can place his clasped hands on the stool, with enough distance between the stool and the patient so that patient's head can extend beyond feet when placed on the stool. The nurse assists the patient's buttocks by lifting them up from the bed and then rotating patient to sit on the chair.

(2) Self-transferring from Bed to Chair by the Patient: When the patient can transfer with the assistance of the stool in front of him/her, the patient can learn to do it independently. The patient first extends clasped hands forward and downward. When the center of gravity is on both feet, patient lifts the buttocks, stands up with the trunk, shifts the center of gravity onto the healthy lower limb, rotates, aligns the buttocks with the chair seat, and slowly sits down.

(3) Sitting from Bed to Wheelchair: Place the wheelchair on the patient's healthy side, with the wheelchair and bed forming a 30° to 45° angle, and lock the brakes. Depending on the patients' capabilities, they can transfer with full assistance

3. 偏瘫患者的转移方法

（1）帮助患者从床上转移到椅子上的方法：

1）患者坐于床边，双足平放地上。护士面对患者，以自己双膝抵住患者双膝，将患者前臂放在自己的肩上，把自己的手放在患者的肩胛骨上，抓住肩胛骨的内侧缘，使患者向前，将其重心前移至其足上，直到患者臀部离开床面。以患者健侧足为轴，使其臀部对准椅面，协助患者缓慢坐在椅子上。

2）如果患者有一些主动运动，可在患者的前面放一个凳子，患者可以在上面放置叉握的双手。凳子与患者之间应有足够的距离，使患者的手放在上面时，其头部前伸能超过足。护士扶住患者的臀部，协助其从床上抬起臀部站起，然后旋转坐到椅子上。

（2）患者自己从床上转移到椅子上的方法：当患者能借助于前面的凳子进行转移时，就可以学习自己独立完成这种动作了。先将叉握的双手主动向前向下伸，当重心置于双足上时，抬起臀部，躯干顺势站起，重心落于健侧下肢上，转身，使臀部对准椅面慢慢坐下。

（3）从床上坐到轮椅上的方法：把轮椅置于患者健侧，轮椅与床呈30°~45°夹角，关好刹车。患者完全依靠护士，或部分借助于护士，或完全独立地转移（同前述"患者自己从床上转移到椅子上的方法"）。从轮椅回到床上与从床上

from the nurse, partial assistance, or independently (following the previous transfer method "self-transfer from bed to chair by the patient"). Returning from the wheelchair to the bed follows the same method as from bed to wheelchair.

(4) Transferring from Wheelchair to Toilet Seat: The method of transferring from the wheelchair to the toilet seat is the same as transferring between the wheelchair and the bed. If conditions allow, handrails can be installed on the wall next to the toilet seat to assist the patient during the transfer.

(5) Assisting the Patient in Standing Up: When the patient's lower limbs can bear weight relatively well, they should practice standing up in a normal movement pattern. The patient sits with both feet flat on the ground, clasps their hands on the stool in front of them. The position of the stool should allow the patient's elbows to extend straight when their hands are placed on it, and their head to extend forward beyond their feet. The nurse stands on the affected side of the patient, pulling the knee of the affected side forward with one hand, placing the other hand on the opposite side of the patient's hip to help lift the buttocks. To prevent the patient's trunk from leaning backward, the nurse can use their shoulder to support the patient's scapula. Finally, the patient straightens their body into a standing position.

(6) The Patient Stands Up Independently: When the patient can transition from sitting to standing with the assistance of the nurse, they should practice completing this action independently. The patient's hands are placed separately on the stool, shifting the center of gravity forward onto both feet, lifting the buttocks. Finally, the patient can stand up without using the stool, extending both hands forward or slightly swinging both upper limbs forward, practicing the transition from sitting to standing. Maintain a straight trunk while performing this action.

4. Training for Activities of Daily Living

Activities of daily living (ADL) refer to a

到轮椅上的方法相同。

（4）从轮椅上转移到坐式马桶上的方法：从轮椅到坐式马桶的方法和轮椅与床之间的转移方法相同。有条件时，可在坐式马桶旁的墙壁上加装扶手，以利于患者转移时扶持。

（5）帮助患者站起来的方法：当患者双下肢负重比较好时，就应该练习以正常的运动模式起立。患者坐位，双足平放地上，叉握的双手放在前面的凳子上，凳子所放的位置应使患者的手放在上面时两肘能伸直，头向前能超过足。护士站在患者患侧，一手将患侧膝部向前拉，另一手放在患者对侧胯部帮助患者抬起臀部。为防止患者躯干向后倒，护士可用肩抵住患者的肩胛骨。最后，患者直起身体成站立位。

（6）患者自己站起来的方法：当患者能在护士帮助下从坐到站时，就应该练习独立完成这一动作。患者的手分开平放在凳子上，重心前移至双足上，抬起臀部。最后患者可以不用凳子，双手向前伸直，或两上肢稍向前摆动，练习由坐到站。做这个动作时，保持躯干伸直。

4. 日常生活活动能力的训练

日常生活活动（activities of daily living，

series of basic activities necessary for individuals to care for themselves in their daily lives, including clothing, food, housing, transportation, maintaining personal hygiene, and engaging in independent social activities. These activities are essential for survival and adaptation to the environment, and individuals must repeatedly perform them daily. ADL training aims to help individuals with disabilities minimize dependence on others or partially depend on others to complete various functional activities at home and in society.

(1) Dressing Training: Once the patient can maintain sitting balance, they can be guided to practice dressing and undressing, including putting on and taking off clothes, shoes, and socks. For patients wearing prosthetics, attention should be paid to coordinating the wearing of the prosthetic. Most patients can use one hand to dress and undress, for example, hemiplegic patients putting on the affected limb first when dressing and removing the healthy limb first when undressing. Paraplegic patients who can sit steadily may dress and undress themselves from the upper body independently. When putting on pants, the patient can first sit down to put lower limbs into the pants, then stand up or switch to a lying position to lift the hips and pull up and fasten the pants. If the patient's joint mobility is limited and putting on regular clothes is difficult, specially designed clothes should be considered, such as loose-fitting front-opening garments. For patients with poor finger coordination who cannot tie or untie belts or buttons, alternatives such as snaps, zippers, or hook-and-loop fasteners can be used.

(2) Eating Training: Select appropriate utensils based on the patient's functional status and guide eating training. For example, eating in a sitting position on the bed can be broken down into changing positions, grasping utensils, bringing food to the mouth, chewing, and swallowing actions.

1) Eating position training: It is advisable to choose a sitting or semi-sitting position for eating.

ADL）是指人们在日常生活中为了照顾自己的衣、食、住、行、保持个人卫生整洁和独立的社会活动所必需的一系列基本活动，是人们为了维持生存和适应生存环境而每天必须反复进行的、最基本的、最有共性的活动。ADL 训练是为了使残疾者在家庭和社会中尽量不依赖或部分依赖他人而完成各项功能活动。

（1）更衣训练：患者能够保持坐位平衡后，可指导其进行穿脱衣服、鞋袜等训练。对穿戴假肢的患者注意配合假肢的穿戴。大部分患者可用单手完成穿脱衣服的动作，如偏瘫患者穿衣时先穿患肢，脱衣时先脱健肢；截瘫患者若可坐稳，可自行穿脱上衣。穿裤子时，可先取坐位将下肢穿进裤子，再站起或转换成卧位抬高臀部，将裤子提上、穿好。如患者关节活动范围受限，穿脱普通衣服困难，应设计特制衣服，如宽大的前开襟衣服；如患者手指协调性差，不能系、解衣带或钮扣，可使用按扣、拉链、搭扣等。

（2）饮食训练：根据患者的功能状态选择适当的餐具，进行进餐姿势的训练。如床上坐位进餐过程中涉及体位改变、抓握餐具、送食物入口、咀嚼和吞咽等动作，需分别进行训练。

1）进餐体位训练：进餐时宜选择坐位或半坐位，因此最基础的训练为指导患者从仰卧位

Therefore, the most basic training is to guide the patients to change from a supine position to the corresponding position and maintain balance. If the patients cannot sit up, they should be guided to adopt a lateral lying position with the healthy side down.

2) Utensil grasping training: Initially, the patients can be trained to grasp wooden sticks or rubber bands, and once proficient, they can use utensils such as spoons. Patients who have lost grip strength, have poor coordination, or have limited joint mobility often cannot use regular utensils. In such cases, utensils should be modified, such as special bowls, plates, utensils with horizontal or extended handles, etc., and necessary fixation should be provided according to the situation.

3) Eating action training: Train hand movements before training eating movements. For example, place utensils and food in positions accessible to the patient, instruct the patients to use their healthy hands to place food into their affected hands, and then use the affected hand to put the food into their mouths, training the transition of function between both hands.

4) Chewing training: After ensuring that the patients have no risk of aspiration and can drink water smoothly, they can try eating independently. Start with consuming liquid food first, such as thick soup, pureed food and thin congee, then gradually transition to semi-solid and solid foods, progressing from a small amount of food to a regular diet. Encourage the patients to chew more with the affected side during eating.

5) Swallowing function training

a. Lip closure training: Hemiplegic patients often have a slightly open mouth or lips tightly pressed against the teeth, and may frequently drool. The following methods can be used to improve lip closure function: Rub with ice cubes or stimulate the lips with the back of an electric toothbrush, and the movement direction should be from the outer to the middle; Finger sucking training is also a simple and effective method, in which the

改变为相应体位，并维持平衡；若患者无法坐起，应指导患者采取健侧在下的侧卧位。

2）抓握餐具训练：开始可训练患者抓握木条或橡皮，待其熟练后可使用汤匙等餐具。丧失抓握能力、协调性差或关节活动范围受限的患者常无法使用普通餐具，应将餐具进行改良，如特制碗、碟，特制横把或长把匙、刀、叉等，并根据情况进行必要的固定。

3）进食动作训练：先训练手部动作再训练进食动作。如将餐具及食物放在便于患者使用的位置，指导患者用健手把食物放在患手中，再由患手将食物放入口中，以训练两侧手功能的转换。

4）咀嚼训练：在确定患者无误吞危险并能顺利喝水后，可试行让患者自己进食。可先试进食浓汤、糊状食物、稀粥等流质食物，逐步过渡到半流质再到普食，从少量饮食过渡到正常饮食。在进食时，应多鼓励患者用患侧咀嚼。

5）吞咽功能训练

① 口唇闭合训练：偏瘫患者往往表现为嘴微张或唇紧贴于齿外，且经常流涎，可采取以下方法改善嘴唇的闭合功能：用冰块快速摩擦，或用电动牙刷背面刺激口唇部，运动方向从外侧向中间移动；吸指训练也是一种简便易行的方法，患者自己将示指放入嘴里，嘴唇闭合行吸吮动作。

patient places the index finger into the mouth and performs a sucking motion to close the lips.

b. Tongue muscle exercise training: Before starting tongue muscle exercise training, the nurses can place their hands under the patient's jaw, at the soft tissue area of the mouth floor, and perform a semi-circular motion, using fingers to push and press the soft tissue upwards and forwards to improve tongue muscle tension and stimulate forward movement. If the patient's tongue cannot move, the nurse can wrap a clean damp gauze around the tongue and use fingers to hold the tongue, then perform movements in different directions. If the patient's tongue has some movement ability, the nurse can guide the patient to press the tongue against the back of the cheek. The nurse points to the area and the patient tries to push the cheek with the tongue to strengthen the tongue muscle. Alternatively, the patient can extend the tongue outside the mouth, and the nurse can stimulate the tip of the tongue with a straw or tongue depressor, encouraging movement both inside and outside the mouth.

c. Soft palate activity training: The nurse presses down the patient's tongue with a tongue depressor while quickly rubbing the soft palate with a frozen cotton swab, and stimulating upwards and outwards. After the ice stimulation, the patient is instructed to make the "ah" sound to lift the soft palate. The patient blows air into a cup of water using a straw, attempting to maintain a uniform airflow to stimulate soft palate activity.

d. Larynx movement training: Instruct the patient to produce sounds such as "oh-ah" or "yi-oh," varying the pitch to induce active movement of the larynx. The patient sits upright, and the nurse's thumb and index finger gently guide the patient's larynx upwards and forwards, then the patient is instructed to perform the swallowing motion.

(3) Mobility Training: Mobility training assists patients in learning various movements required for independent completion of daily

② 舌肌运动训练：开始进行舌肌的运动训练之前，护士可把手放在患者颌下、口腔底部软组织区，以半圆形运动，用手指向上、向前推压软组织以改善舌肌的张力，刺激其向前运动。如果患者的舌不能活动，护士可用干净的湿纱布裹住其舌头，并用手指把住舌，再做不同方向的运动。如果患者的舌有一定的运动能力，护士可指导患者将舌抵向颊后部，护士用手指指点地方，患者试着用舌推颊，以增强舌肌的力量；也可让患者将舌伸于口腔外，护士用吸管或压舌板刺激其舌尖部，并使其在口腔内、外运动。

③ 软腭活动训练：护士一手用压舌板压住患者的舌头，另一手用冰冻的棉棒快速擦软腭，刺激的方向为向上向外，冰刺激后嘱患者发"啊"音，使软腭上抬。患者用吸管向一杯水里吹气泡，尽量保持气流量的均匀，可刺激软腭活动。

④ 喉部运动训练：嘱患者发"哦-啊"或"咿-哦"的音，通过音调变化使喉部主动运动；患者取坐位，护士的拇指和示指用适当的力量引导患者的喉部，做向上向前方向的运动，完成后嘱患者做咽下动作。

（3）移动训练：是帮助患者学会移动时所需的各种动作，以独立完成日常生活活动。当患者能平稳站立时，应进行立位移动训练，起立动

activities. When a patient can stand steadily, upright mobility training should commence, with the action of standing up and walking initiated almost simultaneously. Before walking training, the affected leg of the patient should have sufficient weight-bearing capacity and good standing balance. Indoor walking requires achieving a balance level of 2, while outdoor walking requires a balance level of 3.

1) Preparatory steps for walking: With assistance, patients are able to complete the decomposition movements of walking, including weight shifting exercises, weight-bearing exercises for the affected limb, cross step to the side, forward and backward steps, strengthening exercises for knee and hip control and so on.

2) Walking with parallel bars or support training: Parallel bars are the primary tools for practicing standing and walking. Patients can utilize parallel bars to practice alternating weight-bearing between the healthy and affected limbs, correct the gait, and improve walking posture. In the initial stages of walking training, to ensure patient safety, it is recommended to practice walking forward, backward, turning, sideways walking, etc. within the parallel bars. For hemiplegic patients who require assistance, the nurse stands on the affected side, with one hand placed under the patient's armpit, supporting the scapula upwards and passing through from under the armpit to the chest, while the other hand holds the patient's affected hand to maintain wrist and elbow extension, with the thumb on top and palm facing forward, slowly walking forward together with the patient.

3) Walking training: Walking training can be conducted for patients when assistance is not required for walking. Initially, short-distance walking on flat indoor surfaces is recommended. Patients with unrecoverable lower limb function can use assistive devices such as walkers, canes, or crutches for training.

4) Cane walking training: Cane walking

作与行走动作几乎同时开始。步行训练前，患者患腿要有足够的负重能力，同时有良好的站位平衡力，室内步行需达到 2 级平衡，室外步行需达到 3 级平衡。

1）步行前准备：患者在帮助下能完成步行的分解动作，包括重心转移练习，患肢负重练习，交叉侧方迈步，前后迈步，加强膝、髋控制能力的练习等。

2）平衡杠或扶持行走训练：平衡杠是练习站立和行走的主要工具，患者可以借助平衡杠练习健肢与患肢交替支持体重，矫正步态，改善行走姿势。步行训练初期，为保证患者安全，可先在平衡杠内练习向前、向后倒走、转身、侧方行走等；偏瘫患者需要扶持时，护士站在患侧，一手放在患侧腋下，支持肩胛带向上，并从患侧腋下穿出置于胸前，另一手握住患侧手，保持腕肘伸展位，拇指在上，掌心向前，与患者一起缓慢向前行走。

3）行走训练：患者不需要扶持可以行走时可进行行走训练，开始时先在室内平坦的地面上短距离行走，如下肢功能不能恢复的患者可借助助行器、拐杖、手杖等辅助用具进行训练。

4）拐杖行走训练：拐杖行走训练是使用

training is an important exercise method for restoring walking ability in patients with prosthetics or hemiplegia. Before starting cane walking training, muscle strength in both upper arms, waist, back, and abdomen should be developed, and sitting up and standing balance should be trained. After completing the aforementioned training, the cane's armpit pad should be positioned near the armpit rib cage, with the angle between the upper arm abduction and the body axis line being 30°, ensuring cane firm contact with the ground.

5) Up-down stair activity training

a. Up stair activity training: The patient uses their healthy hand to hold onto the handrail and shifts their weight onto the affected lower limb. Then, the healthy foot steps onto the step while the nurse assists the patient's affected lower limb to move forward. When the patient shifts their weight onto the healthy foot in front, the nurse's hand can move to the front of the patient's affected lower leg to assist the affected foot onto the second step. As the patient's function improves, assistance can gradually be reduced.

b. Down stair activity training: The patients use healthy hands to hold onto the handrail and shifts their weight onto the affected lower limb. They first use the healthy lower limb to descend the stairs, while the nurse ensures control of the affected lower limb's knee, guiding it forward and shifting the weight onto the healthy lower limb. When the patient uses the affected lower limb to descend the stairs, the nurse uses their hand to prevent the affected lower limb from crossing inward.

(4) Personal Hygiene Training: This includes activities such as moving to the washbasin, turning on/off the tap, washing face and hands, and brushing teeth. Toiletry items should be placed in accessible positions for the patient. When wringing a towel, the patient can be guided to wrap the towel around the faucet or the forearm of the affected limb, and then use the healthy hand to wring it dry. Depending on the patient's actual situation,

假肢或偏瘫的患者恢复行走能力的重要锻炼方法。进行拐杖行走训练前应先锻炼双侧上臂、腰背部及腹部的肌力，并训练坐起和立位平衡。完成上述训练后，将拐杖的腋垫贴于腋下胸壁肋骨处，上臂外展与人体中轴线之间的角度为30°，并确保拐杖紧实接触地面。

5）上下楼梯训练

①上楼梯训练：患者用健侧手扶持扶手，并将重心转移到患侧下肢上，然后健侧足迈上台阶，此时护士帮助患者患侧下肢向前；当患者将重心前移至前面的健侧足上时，护士的手可移至患者患侧小腿前面，帮助患侧足放在第二个台阶上。随着功能的好转，可逐渐减少帮助。

②下楼梯训练：患者用健侧手扶持扶手，重心转移至患侧下肢上，先用健侧下肢下楼梯，护士注意控制患者患侧下肢膝部，使其向前，重心转移至健侧下肢上；当患者用患侧下肢下楼梯时，护士用手防止其患侧下肢内收。

（4）个人卫生训练：引导患者移动到洗漱处，并进行开关水龙头、洗脸、洗手、刷牙等训练。洗漱用品应放在便于患者取用的位置；患者拧毛巾时可指导其将毛巾绕在水龙头上或患肢前臂，再用健手将其拧干；根据患者实际情况，可设计辅助器具，如加粗牙刷的手柄直径，以方便抓握。

auxiliary aids can be designed, such as increasing the diameter of the toothbrush handle for easier gripping.

iv. Traditional Chinese Medicine Rehabilitation Nursing Techniques and Methods

1. Acupuncture and Moxibustion Therapy Acupuncture and moxibustion rehabilitation can be used in all stages of hemiplegia, and there are many acupoint selection and acupuncture techniques such as body acupuncture, scalp acupuncture, ear acupuncture, and point injection.

For patients undergoing CBR, mainly for hemiplegia spasticity pattern, select the yang meridian acupoints in the affected side of the upper limb, such as Jianyu, Shousanli, Waiguan, Hegu, Yuji. Select the yin meridian acupoints in the affected side of the lower limb, such as Sanyinjiao, Yinlingquan, or located in the Taiyang bladder meridian of foot, such as Weizhong, Chengshan. Electroacupuncture should not be strongly stimulated. In addition, with the moxibustion, warm stimulation can relieve spasm. Acupuncture yangming meridians in hand and foot during sequelae stage, supplementing the healthy side, diarrhea the affected side. It can be used together with moxibustion, hydro-acupuncture, scalp acupuncture and electric acupuncture.

2. Massage Treatment Massage treatment has the effect of dredging meridians, adjusting qi and blood, and easing spasm in the treatment of hemiplegia.

(1) Point Selection：Yangming meridian points are the main points in the upper and lower limbs. The back mainly uses the back-shu point, and the head and face take Yintang, Shenting, Jingming, Taiyang, Fengchi, Fengfu, Yamen and other points.

(2) Common Techniques：More gentle methods such as the rolling manipulation, pressing manipulation, grasping manipulation, kneading manipulation, rotating and shaking manipulation and rubbing manipulation are used. The treatment

（四）中医康复护理技术与方法

1. 针灸治疗 针灸康复可以在偏瘫的各个阶段使用,选穴方法、针刺手法很多,如体针、头针、耳针、穴位注射等。

对于社区康复的患者,主要针对偏瘫痉挛者,上肢取患侧阳经腧穴,如肩髃、手三里、外关、合谷、鱼际;下肢取患侧阴经腧穴,如三阴交、阴陵泉,或足太阳膀胱经腧穴,如委中、承山。电针不宜用强刺激。此外,可配合灸法,温热的刺激可以缓解痉挛。后遗症期针刺手足阳明经穴,补健侧,泻患侧。可以和灸法、水针、头针、电针等配合运用。

2. 推拿治疗 推拿疗法治疗偏瘫具有疏通经络、调节气血、缓解痉挛的作用。

（1）取穴:上、下肢以阳明经穴为主。背部主要用背俞穴,头面部取印堂、神庭、睛明、太阳、风池、风府、哑门等穴。

（2）常用手法:多采用较缓和的手法如滚法、按法、拿法、揉法、摇法、擦法等。治疗时间宜长,每次持续 20~30 分钟,根据患者的耐受能力和实际情况进行调整,以使痉挛肌群松弛。上肢操作以伸肌侧为主,可从近端向远端进行,

time should be long, lasting 20–30 minutes each time, and be adjusted according to the patient's tolerance and actual situation to relax the spastic muscle group. The upper limb operation is mainly on the extensor side, which can be carried out from the proximal end to the distal end. The light manipulation such as grasping, pinching kneading and rubbing should be used for a long time to improve the extensor tension and reduce the spasticity flexor. The points of the three yang meridian points of the joint, such as Jianyu, Quchi, Shaohai, Waiguan, Hegu, and so on, heavier methods can be used and can often immediately reduce muscle tension. For lower limbs ,there is mainly extensor spasm. The patients are in prone position, and the urinary bladder meridian of the affected limb is applied with the method of grasping manipulation and rolling manipulation. The technique should be heavy to press the acupoints such as Huantiao, Chengfu, Weizhong and Chengshan. The patients take the supine position and use the palm root meridian to push the three yin meridians along the inside of the inner side of foot to the femoral root, and then push the three yang meridians of foot along the lateral dorsum of foot to the femoral root. The movement should be consistent, slow and strong, and the patient was performed more than 10 times.

II. Community-based Rehabilitation for Patients with Spinal Cord Injury

i. Overview

1. Concept　Spinal cord injury (SCI) refers to the impairment of neural structures (including the spinal cord and nerve roots) and functions within the vertebral canal caused by various reasons, which leads to dysfunction of spinal cord functions (motor, sensory, reflex, etc.) at or below the level of injury, ultimately affecting the patient's physical and mental health as well as their social

采用拿、捏、揉、摩等轻手法，时间宜长，以提高伸肌张力，降低屈肌痉挛。关节部位三阳经穴位行点按重手法，如肩髃、曲池、少海、外关、合谷等，往往可立即降低肌张力。下肢主要针对伸肌痉挛，患者取俯卧位，用拿、滚法施行于患肢膀胱经，点按环跳、承扶、委中、承山等穴位，手法要重；患者取仰卧位，用掌根循经先顺三阴经由足内侧推至股根部，再顺足三阳经推至足背外侧，动作连贯，徐缓有力，行10余次。

二、脊髓损伤患者的社区康复

（一）概述

1. **概念**　脊髓损伤（spinal cord injury，SCI）是由各种原因导致椎管内神经结构（包括脊髓和神经根）及其功能的损害，出现损伤水平及以下脊髓功能（运动、感觉、反射等）障碍，最终影响患者的身体、心理健康以及社会参与能力。颈脊髓损伤引起四肢运动感觉功能障碍，称为四肢瘫。胸段以下脊髓损伤造成躯干及双下肢瘫痪而未累及上肢时，称为截瘫。

participation abilities. Cervical spinal cord injury causes motor and sensory dysfunction in all four limbs, known as tetraplegia. When spinal cord injury occurs below the thoracic segment, causing paralysis of the trunk and both lower limbs without affecting the upper limbs, it is called paraplegia.

2. **Main Dysfunctions**　The main dysfunctions include motor dysfunction, sensory dysfunction, respiratory dysfunction, circulatory dysfunction, sphincter dysfunction, and autonomic nerve dysfunction.

3. **Goals of Community-based Rehabilitation**　Utilizing the existing community resources, based on the patient's wishes and thorough assessment, comprehensive rehabilitation measures are adopted to ensure that the patient and their family members' needs in health promotion, prevention, medical care, rehabilitation, and assistive devices are met to achieve the patient's maximum functional status commensurate with the degree of injury, improve the patient's quality of life, improve the family and community environment to facilitate the patient's barrier-free living. At the same time, based on the patient's wishes, promote their development in education, skills, cultural life, and other aspects, aiming to achieve self-care and social integration as much as possible.

ii. Rehabilitation Assessment
1. Assessment of Neurological Function

(1) Level of Injury: The planes of movement and sensory impairment are determined by conducting strength assessments of 10 key muscle groups on both sides of the body and sensory examinations of 28 pairs of key points. The functional recovery of patients with spinal cord injury is typically based on the planes of movement.

(2) Severity of Injury: According to the American Spinal Injury Association (ASIA), the severity of injury is graded based on the presence or absence of residual function in the lowest sacral

2．**主要功能障碍**　包括运动功能障碍、感觉功能障碍、呼吸功能障碍、循环功能障碍、括约肌功能障碍、自主神经功能障碍等。

3．**社区康复目标**　利用现有的社区资源，根据患者的意愿，在充分评定的基础上，采用全面康复的有效措施，以确保患者及其家属在健康促进、预防、医疗保健、康复和辅助器具方面的需求得到满足，达到与其损伤程度相适应的最大功能状态，提高患者的生存质量，改善家庭和社区环境，以利于患者无障碍地生活；同时，根据患者的意愿，促进其在教育、技能、文化生活等方面的发展，尽可能达到生活自理、回归社会的目标。

（二）康复评定
1. 神经功能评定

（1）损伤平面：通过身体两侧 10 组关键肌肌力检查和 28 对关键点的感觉检查确定运动损伤平面和感觉损伤平面。脊髓损伤患者的功能恢复通常以运动平面为依据。

（2）损伤程度：美国脊髓损伤协会（American Spinal Injury Association，ASIA）对损伤程度是以最低骶节（$S_4 \sim S_5$）有无残留功能进行分级，骶部感觉功能包括刺激肛门皮肤黏膜交界的感觉

segments (S₄–S₅). The sacral sensory function includes the sensation of stimulating the skin and mucosal junction of the anus and the deep sensation of the anus, while the motor function refers to the autonomous contraction of the anal sphincter during digital rectal examination.

2. Assessment of Motor Function　Determine the key muscles in each of the 10 muscle segments on both sides of the human body according to ASIA standards and use manual muscle testing (MMT) to assess muscle strength from top to bottom. The Ashworth scale is used to evaluate muscle spasm.

3. Assessment of Sensory Function ASIA's sensory index score is utilized for assessment.

4. Assessment of ADL　Tools such as the Barthel index (BI) and functional independence measure (FIM) are employed for assessment.

5. Assessment of Psychosocial Status Including personal life satisfaction, mental state, psychological activities, and resilience　Mental status can be evaluated using the Hamilton anxiety scale and Hamilton depression scale.

iii. Modern Rehabilitation Nursing Techniques and Methods

1. Positioning　Correct positioning is crucial for maintaining the normal alignment of fracture, preventing pressure injuries and joint contractures, and inhibiting spasms.

(1) Correct Supine Position: When the patient is in the supine position, the nurse should ensure that the patient's head, back, shoulders, buttocks, and knee joints are in a straight line without any body distortion. The shoulders are adducted in a neutral or adducted position, avoiding retraction. The elbows are extended, wrists are dorsiflexed at approximately 45°, and fingers are slightly flexed with the thumb in opposition. Both upper limbs are placed on pillows on either side of the body, with a sufficiently high pillow under the shoulders to prevent shoulder retraction. Alternatively, pillows can be placed under the forearm or hand

及肛门深感觉，运动功能是指直肠指检时肛门处括约肌的自主收缩。

2. 运动功能评定　按照 ASIA 标准，确定人体两侧各自 10 个肌节中的关键肌，采用徒手肌力测定（manual muscle testing，MMT）法从上到下检查，进行肌力评定；采用 Ashworth 痉挛评定量表进行痉挛评定。

3. 感觉功能评定　采用 ASIA 的感觉指数评分进行评定。

4. ADL 评定　可采用 Barthel 量表（Barthel index，BI）和功能独立性评定量表（functional independence measure，FIM）进行评定。

5. 心理社会状况评定　包括个人生活满意度、精神状态、心理活动和承受力等。其中精神状态可采用汉密尔顿焦虑量表和汉密尔顿抑郁量表进行评定。

（三）现代康复护理技术与方法

1. 体位摆放　正确的体位摆放有利于保持骨折部位的正常排列，且是预防压力性损伤和关节挛缩及抑制痉挛的重要措施。

（1）正确的仰卧位：患者仰卧位时，保证其头、背、肩、臀和膝关节成直线，无身体扭曲。肩关节内收，呈中立位或内收，勿后缩；肘关节伸展，腕背伸约 45°，手指轻度屈曲，拇指对掌。患者双上肢放在身体两侧的枕头上，肩下垫的枕头要足够高，以确保两肩不后缩，也可将枕头垫在前臂或手下，使手的位置高于肩部，可预防重力性肿胀；髋关节伸展并轻度外展，膝伸展但不能过伸，踝关节背屈，脚趾伸展。在两下肢之间可放一枕头，以保持髋关节轻度外展（图 9-7）。

to elevate the hand above the shoulder, preventing gravitational swelling. The hips are extended with slight abduction, knees are extended but not hyperextended, ankles are dorsiflexed, and toes are extended. A pillow may be placed between the legs to maintain slight hip abduction, as shown in Figure 9-7.

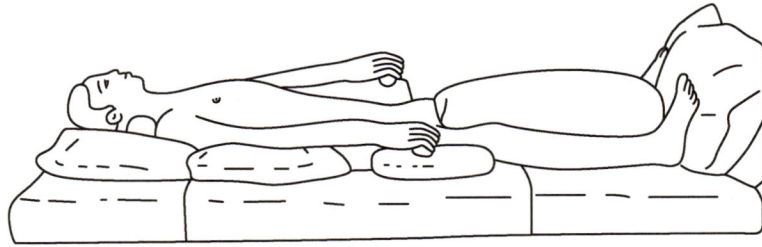

Figure 9-7　Correct supine position for patients with spinal cord injury

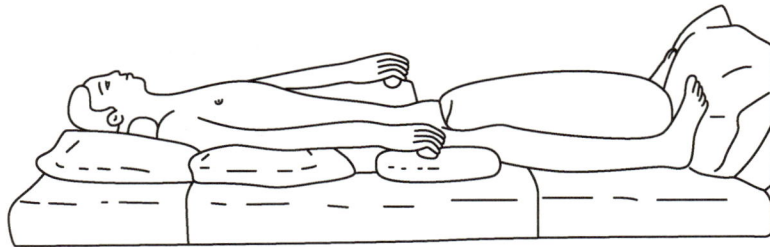

图 9-7　脊髓损伤患者正确的仰卧位

(2) Correct Lateral Position: The patient lies on the side of the bed, with the hip and knees flexed, facing the same side; the lower shoulder is flexed, and the lower upper limb is placed between two pillows placed under the head and chest, reducing pressure on the shoulder. The elbow is extended, and the forearm is supinated. The upper arm is also in a supinated position, with a pillow placed between the chest wall and the upper limb. The hips and knees are flexed, and double pillows are placed between the legs, with the upper leg gently pressing on the pillow beneath. Ankles are dorsiflexed, and toes are extended.

2. Positioning Changes　Positioning changes are the effective methods to prevent pressure injuries and limb contractures. During the changes, attention should be paid to maintaining spinal stability while avoiding the patient from being dragged on the bed to prevent skin damage.

（2）正确的侧卧位：患者侧身卧床，屈髋屈膝，面向同侧；下面的肩呈屈曲位，下方上肢放于垫在头下和胸背部的两个枕头之间，以减少肩受压，肘关节伸展，前臂旋后，上面的上肢也呈旋后位，胸壁和上肢之间垫一枕头。髋、膝关节屈曲，两下肢之间垫上双枕，使上面的下肢轻压在下面的枕头上，踝关节背屈，脚趾伸展。

2. 体位变换　体位变换是防止压力性损伤和肢体挛缩的有效方法，变换时应注意维持脊柱的稳定性，同时避免在床上拖动，以免损伤皮肤。

(1) Turning Over:

1) Independent turning over: For patients with the necessary conditions, the elbow extension swinging method can be adopted. The patient vigorously swings their upper limbs on both sides towards the body, turns their head towards the side they want to turn, and simultaneously uses their upper limbs to swing and rotate the trunk to complete the turning. Extend the upper limb forward with force to complete the turning movement.

2) Using a belt for turning: A belt is tied to the bedrail or bed frame, and the wrists are hooked into the belt. By flexing the elbows vigorously, the body is rotated. Meanwhile, the upper limb on the other side is swung towards the turning side. The belt is then released, and the upper arm on the turning side is extended forward to complete the turning.

(2) Transition from Lying to Sitting: Flexibility of the trunk and extension function of at least one upper limb is the basic conditions for independent sitting. Patients with injuries at or below C_7 can sit up directly from a supine position, while patients with C_6 injuries need to turn to a side or prone position before sitting up.

1) Sitting up for patients with quadriplegia: a. Place both elbows slightly away from the body and press down, bending the head and shoulders forward. b. Move the elbows closer to the body, raise the upper trunk, and support the head and shoulders forward. c. Lean the body towards the left elbow and maintain balance. d. Place the right upper limb behind the body and straighten it. Lean towards the extended right upper limb and maintain balance. e. Place the left upper limb behind the body and straighten it. f. Bend the head and shoulders forward to straighten the body and sit up.

2) Sitting up from a lateral position for patients with quadriplegia: a. Place the right hand on the left, head to the left, and turn to the left. b. Cross the body with the right hand, place both

（1）翻身：

1）患者独立翻身：有条件的患者，可采用伸肘摆动法翻身。患者双上肢向身体两侧用力摆动，头转向翻身侧，同时双上肢用力甩向翻身侧，带动躯干旋转而翻身，位于上方的上肢用力前伸，完成翻身动作。

2）利用布带翻身：布带系于床栏或床架上，腕部勾住带子，用力屈肘带动身体旋转，同时将另一侧上肢摆向翻身侧，松开带子，位于上方的上肢前伸，完成翻身。

（2）从卧位到坐位：躯干具备柔软性和至少一侧上肢具备伸展功能是完成独立坐起的基本条件。C_7及以下水平损伤的患者可以从仰卧位直接坐起，C_6损伤的患者需要翻身至侧卧或俯卧位后再坐起。

1）四肢瘫患者从仰卧位坐起：①将双肘放在离身体稍远的两侧并向下压，向前屈头和肩；②将肘移近身体，抬高上半身，支持头和肩向前；③身体靠向左肘并保持平衡；④将右上肢放到身后并伸直，身体靠向伸直的右臂并保持平衡；⑤将左臂放在身后并伸直；⑥将头和肩向前屈使身体向前挺直坐起。

2）四肢瘫患者从侧卧位坐起：①右手放在左边，头向左，并向左翻身；②右手横跨过身体两肘都放在床面上，用双肘向下肢的方向移动，直到躯干与下肢成一个正确的角度；③用右前

elbows on the bed surface, and use both elbows to move towards the lower limbs until the trunk is at the correct angle with the lower limbs. c. Hook the back of the right lower limb with the right forearm. d. Use the right upper limb to pull while pushing with the left upper limb to sit up.

3) Sitting up for patients with paraplegia: a. Swing both upper limbs simultaneously towards one side, turning the trunk towards that side. b. Use one hand and the opposite elbow to support the bed surface, extend the elbow joint, and move to a sitting position supported by the hand.

4) Using assistive devices for sitting up: Tie a rope ladder to the end of the bed and lift the upper body by pulling the rope ladder and bending the elbow joints. Alternatively, tie multiple suspension straps above the bed to help the patients sit up.

3. Transfer Methods   They are crucial for patients' self-care, assisting patients in transferring from wheelchairs to different locations.

(1) Anterior Transfer Method: It is suitable for patients with quadriplegia and upper thoracic spinal cord injuries. a. The patient moves the wheelchair to a position where the lower limbs can be lifted and placed on the bed. b. Apply the brakes, remove shoes, and place both lower limbs on the bed. c. Push the wheelchair forward closer to the bed. d. Use both hands to support and move the body onto the bed.

(2) Lateral Transfer Method: It is a commonly used method. The patient positions the wheelchair laterally next to the bed, places both lower limbs on the bed, and uses supporting movements to shift their hips onto the bed.

(3) Diagonal Transfer Method: The patient positions the wheelchair diagonally about 30° next to the bed, applies the brakes, places both feet flat on the ground, and then uses supporting movements to shift their hips onto the bed. Patients with quadriplegia can use a transfer board to shift their hips onto the board and then onto the bed.

臂钩住右下肢后面；④用右上肢拉的同时用左上肢推，使自身坐起。

3）截瘫患者坐起：①双上肢同时用力向一侧摆动，躯干转向一侧；②一只手和对侧肘支撑床面，伸展肘关节，由手支撑移动至坐位。

4）借助辅助用具坐起：可在床尾系上绳梯，通过拉绳梯和弯曲肘关节抬起上半身；或在床上方系多个悬吊带，帮助患者坐起。

3．转移方法   是患者生活自理的关键动作，可帮助患者从轮椅转移到不同的地方。

（1）前方转移法：适用于四肢瘫和上位胸髓损伤的患者。①患者将轮椅移至下肢能抬起放至床上的位置。②刹闸，脱下鞋子，将双下肢放于床上。③将轮椅再推向前靠近床。④双手支撑将身体移至床上。

（2）侧方转移法：较常用的方法。患者将轮椅侧方靠近床旁，将双下肢放于床上，利用支撑动作将臀部移至床上。

（3）斜向转移法：患者将轮椅斜向30°左右靠近床，刹闸后并将双脚平放于地面上，而后利用支撑动作将臀部移至床上；四肢瘫患者可利用移乘板，将臀部移至板上后再移至床上。

4. Training for Activities of Daily Living

(1) Dressing Training: Patients with complete quadriplegia need assistance in dressing and undressing; those with paralysis of both lower limbs but who are able to turn over can dress and undress their upper clothes independently after training, and can also tie various buttons using their hands.

1) Wearing and taking off a pullover: When putting on a pullover, the patient inserts both hands into the sleeves one by one, starting with the same side, pulls up the opposite sleeve with the hand to extend the wrist out of the cuff, raises both hands, inserts the head through the neckline, and adjusts the shirt to make it flat. To take off the pullover, the patient leans forward, first removes the head, pulls up the pullover from the back of the neckline with both hands, and then withdraws both arms separately.

2) Wearing and taking off clothes with buttons in front: When wearing clothes, the patient use the right hand to grasp the collar, the left hand is inserted into the sleeve, and the sleeve is pulled up onto the arm while the collar is draped over the back of the neck. The right hand reaches behind to find the right sleeve. The right hand is raised to the side, allowing the sleeve to slide onto the right upper arm. Buttons are fastened, and if necessary, a buttonhook can be used to button and unbutton.

Patients using this method must be able to lean forward and sit steadily without support. Clothing can be taken off by reversing these actions.

3) Wearing and taking off pants: If paraplegic patients can sit up, they should be trained to wear and take off pants independently. After putting one leg into a pant leg, the patient uses hand or wrist to slightly flex the knee and pull the pants up to the upper thigh. The same method is used for the other side. The patient then lies on the right side, using the left elbow to support the body and lift the right pants leg. The patient then turn to the left side, using the right elbow to support the body and lift

4. 日常生活活动能力的训练

（1）更衣训练：四肢完全瘫痪的患者，需依赖他人穿脱衣物；双下肢瘫痪能翻身者，在训练后可自行穿脱上衣，还可用手系各种扣子。

1）穿脱套头衫：患者穿套头衫时，双手分别插入同侧衣袖，用手将对侧衣袖上拉使手腕伸出袖口，上举双手，头部从领口套入后伸出，将上衣整理平整。脱套头衫时，躯干前倾，先褪头部，用双手从领口后部将套头衫上拉，然后分别褪出双臂。

2）穿脱有前扣的衣服：穿衣服时，用右手抓住衣领，把左手伸到袖子里面，把袖子向上拉到手臂上，并使衣领搭在颈后；右手后伸到背后找右边的袖子；右手向侧边举起，使袖子滑到右上臂；扣上纽扣，必要时可以用纽扣钩来扣纽扣、解纽扣。

使用这种方法的患者，身体必须能够前倾，且不需支撑就可坐稳。按相反动作可将衣服脱下。

3）穿脱裤子：截瘫患者如能坐起，则应训练独立穿脱裤子。患者先将一条裤腿套在脚上后，用手或腕部使膝部呈稍屈曲状，向上拉裤子至大腿上部，再用相同的方法穿好对侧；取右上侧卧位，用左侧肘部支撑身体将右侧裤子提起，再转身呈左上侧卧位，用右侧肘部支撑身体，将左侧裤子提起，交替反复，将裤子提到腰部。脱裤子动作与穿裤子相反。

the left pants leg. This is repeated alternately until the pants are pulled up to the waist. The actions for taking off pants are the reverse of putting them on.

(2) Eating Training: For patients with spinal cord injuries, injuries at C_4 and above will affect the patients' independent feeding ability and they will need assistance. Patients with injuries at C_5 and below can eat independently using assistive devices. Patients with C_6 and C_7 injuries can eat independently after training. Paraplegic patients with normal upper limb function can eat independently.

(3) Mobility Training

1) Training for walking with crutches：

a. Dragging step training: Place both axillary crutches in front of the body；lean the trunk forward, supported by the crutches；drag both feet forward simultaneously in a small step.

b. Swing-through step training: Place both axillary crutches in front of the body；lean the trunk forward, supported by the crutches；swing both feet forward simultaneously in a small step, landing at the position of the crutches.

c. Swing-to step training: Place both axillary crutches in front of the body；lean the trunk forward, supported by the crutches；swing both feet forward simultaneously in a large step, with the feet exceeding the crutches and landing in front of them.

d. Four-point walking training: Walk in the following sequence：one crutch, opposite lower limb, other crutch, other lower limb.

2) Training for ascending and descending stairs with crutches：

a. Ascending stairs training: Stand balanced with the toes at the step edge ；place both crutches on the step；raise both feet onto the step by extending the elbows and depressing the shoulder blades, relying on the crutches；push the pelvis forward by swinging the head backward and contracting the shoulder blades.

b. Descending stairs training: Stand balanced with the crutches placed at the platform edge；

（2）进食训练：对于脊髓损伤患者来说，C_4及以上水平的损伤造成的双上肢瘫痪会影响患者独立进食，这类患者只能依靠他人才能进食；C_5及以下水平损伤的患者，可自行使用辅助器具进食；C_6、C_7水平损伤的患者，经训练可独立进食；下肢截瘫患者上肢功能正常，可独立进食。

（3）移动训练

1）使用双拐行走训练：

①蹭步训练：将双腋拐放至身体前方；躯干前倾，由腋拐支撑体重；将双足同时向前拖动一小步。

②摆至步训练：将双腋拐同时放至身体前方；躯干前倾，由腋拐支撑体重；将双足同时向前摆出一小步，双脚落至腋拐处。

③摆过步训练：将双腋拐同时放至身体前方；躯干前倾，由腋拐支撑体重；将双足同时向前摆出一大步，双脚超过腋拐，落于腋拐前方。

④四点步行训练：按照一侧拐、对侧下肢、另一侧拐、另一侧下肢的顺序行走。

2）使用双拐上下台阶：

①上台阶训练：脚尖位于台阶边缘平衡站位；双拐置于台阶上；通过伸肘、压低肩胛骨，依靠拐杖把双脚提到台阶上；通过向后摆头和收缩肩胛骨来推动骨盆向前。

②下台阶训练：双拐置于平台边缘平衡站立；摆过步；通过向后摆头和收缩肩胛骨来推动

perform a swing-to step; push the pelvis forward by swinging the head backward and contracting the shoulder blades.

3) Training for using a walker

a. Stepping walking: Move one side of the walker forward, then step out with the opposite lower limb. Move the other side of the walker forward, and then step out with the other lower limb.

b. Swing walking: Lift the walker and place it about a step in front of the body. Use a supporting movement to lift the body, then swing both lower limbs forward in a small step and land firmly.

c. Standing up with a walker: First stabilize the walker, grasp the handles firmly with both hands, lean the trunk forward, and use the upper limbs to push up the body while extending the trunk. The feet support the body weight to stand up.

(4) Personal Hygiene Training: Patients with spinal cord injuries, if they have good function in both upper limbs, may be able to complete daily hygiene activities independently with proper training. However, modifications to the bathroom may be necessary. To simplify the activities, self-care aids can be used, such as combs and toothbrushes with thicker or longer handles and fixed straps, brushes with suction cups to attach to the sink for handwashing, and nail clippers with fixed plates.

iv. Traditional Chinese Medicine Rehabilitation Nursing Techniques and Methods

1. Acupuncture and Moxibustion Therapy　Acupuncture and moxibustion has a good promoting effect on restoring weakness and relaxation of the affected limbs.

(1) Point Selection: Jianyu, Quchi, Shousanli, Hegu, Waiguan, Jingjiaji, Xiongjiaji, Biguan, Futu, Zusanli, Fenglong, Fengshi, Yanglingquan, Sanyinjiao, and Yaojiaji. Electroacupuncture

骨盆。

3）使用助行器的训练

①迈步行走：将助行器的一侧向前，然后迈出对侧下肢，再将助行器的另一侧向前，然后迈出另一侧下肢。

②摆步行走：将助行器抬起，放至身体前方左右一步处，用支撑动作将身体撑起，然后将双下肢向前摆出一小步，双足落地站稳。

③使用助行器站起：首先将助行器稳定住，双手紧握扶手，躯干前倾，而后双上肢用力撑起身体，同时躯干伸展，双足支撑体重站起。

（4）个人卫生训练：脊髓损伤患者若双上肢功能良好，经过训练有可能自己完成洗漱活动，但需要对洗澡间加以改造。为了简化活动难度，可加用自助器具，如使用手柄加粗、加长或加装固定带的梳子、牙刷，使用带有吸盘固定在水池边的刷子刷手，使用带有固定板的指甲刀等。

（四）中医康复护理技术与方法

1. 针灸治疗　针灸对于恢复患肢软弱无力、筋脉弛缓有较好的促进作用。

（1）取穴：肩髃、曲池、手三里、合谷、外关、颈夹脊、胸夹脊、髀关、伏兔、足三里、丰隆、风市、阳陵泉、三阴交、腰夹脊。选用电针断续波中强度刺激，以患者出现规律性收缩为佳，每次

with intermittent waves and moderate intensity stimulation is used, aiming for regular contractions in the patient. Each session lasts 20–30 minutes.

2. Massage Treatment   Massage treatment can stimulate the corresponding neural segments of the body, promoting the recovery of damaged nerves.

(1) Body Parts and Point Selection: The urinary bladder meridian on both sides of the spinal cord injury site, governor channel, lumbarsacral region, paralyzed muscle groups of the lower limbs, abdomen; Jiaji on both sides of the spinal cord injury site, Huantiao, Weizhong, Chengfu, Chengshan, Zusanli, Yanglingquan, Yinlingquan, Futu, Sanyinjiao, Xiyan, Jiexi. Additional acupoints can include Zhongwan, Tianshu, Qihai, and Guanyuan.

(2) Supine Position Technique: The patient lies in a supine position and the therapist massages the paralyzed limbs 3–5 times. Along the direction of lymphatic return, push and rub the inner side of the paralyzed limb 3–5 times. Massage the taiyin spleen meridian of foot and the yangming stomach meridian of foot until a sensation of soreness and distension is achieved. For upper limb paralysis, massage the three yang meridians of hand and pluck the axillary nerve, sulcus for ulnar nerve, and radial nerve to relieve spasms. Finally, knead the body surface of the four limbs and perform passive joint movements. If the patient has bowel or bladder dysfunction, gently massage the abdomen clockwise for 3–5 minutes and press Zhongwan, Tianshu, Qihai, and Guanyuan, spending 1 minute on each point.

(3) Prone Position Technique: The patient lies in a prone position and the therapist massages both lower limbs to the waist and back, then performs spinal manipulation from Changqiang to Dazhui 5–10 times. Use both thumbs to press Jiaji and the acupoints of the urinary bladder meridian 3–5 times. Pluck and rub the acupoints such as Huantiao, Chengfu, Weizhong, and Chengshan.

20~30 分钟。

2. 推拿治疗   推拿可以刺激机体相应的神经节段，促进受损的神经恢复。

（1）部位与取穴：脊柱损伤部位两侧膀胱经、督脉、腰骶部、下肢瘫痪肌群、腹部；脊柱损伤部位两侧夹脊、环跳、委中、承扶、承山、足三里、阳陵泉、阴陵泉、伏兔、三阴交、膝眼、解溪等穴。还可以选择中脘、天枢、气海、关元等穴。

（2）仰卧位操作方法：患者仰卧位，治疗师按揉瘫痪肢体 3~5 遍。沿淋巴回流方向在瘫痪侧肢体内侧推揉 3~5 遍。按揉足太阴脾经和足阳明胃经，以酸胀为度。上肢瘫痪按揉手三阳经，并弹拨腋神经、尺神经沟、桡神经，以缓解痉挛，最后拿揉四肢体表，并做关节被动运动。若有大小便障碍的患者，在腹部顺时针摩腹 3~5 分钟，并点按中脘、天枢、气海、关元，每穴 1 分钟。

（3）俯卧位操作方法：患者俯卧位，治疗师按揉双下肢至腰背部，然后用捏脊法自长强至大椎 5~10 遍。用双手拇指点按夹脊穴和膀胱经腧穴 3~5 遍。拨揉环跳、承扶、委中、承山等穴。用拿揉法作用于背部及双下肢 3~5 遍，再作腰骶、髋、膝、踝的被动运动。最后轻叩腰背部及下肢，结束治疗。

Use kneading techniques on the back and both lower limbs 3–5 times, followed by passive movements of the waist, hips, knees, and ankles. Finally, lightly tap the back and lower limbs to end the treatment.

Ⅲ. Community-based Rehabilitation for Patients with Schizophrenia

i. Overview

1. **Concept**　Schizophrenia is a chronic, severe and disabling brain disease. It is characterized by the disintegration of thought processes and emotional responses, most commonly manifested as auditory hallucinations, paranoid ideation, exotic delusions, or language and thinking disorders, accompanied by significant social or occupational dysfunction, often with typical symptoms appearing in early adulthood. The important factors influencing its occurrence are heredity, early growth environment, neurobiology, psychological and social influences.

2. **Goals of Community-based Rehabilitation**

(1) Prevention of Mental Disorders：Early detection, early treatment and comprehensive rehabilitation to prevent the occurrence of mental disorders and the further development into mental disabilities.

(2) Reducing the Degree of Mental Disorders As Much As Possible：Mental deterioration should be prevented as much as possible and the ability to take care of oneself should be gradually improved.

(3) Improvement of the Social Adaptability of People with Mental Disorders：The original social functions of patients with mental disorders should be improved or restored.

(4) Restoration of Labor Capacity：Various rehabilitation measures and training means should be used to equip persons with mental disorders with compensatory living and working skills and to give full play to their retained abilities.

三、精神分裂症患者的社区康复

（一）概述

1. **概念**　精神分裂症是一种慢性、严重性、致残性脑病。它以思维过程和情感反应的解体为特征，最常见的表现为幻听、偏执、奇特的妄想或语言和思维紊乱，伴随明显的社会或职业功能障碍，通常典型症状出现在成年早期。遗传、早年成长环境、神经生物学、心理和社会影响，都是其发生的重要影响因素。

2. 社区康复目标

（1）预防精神障碍的发生：早期发现、早期治疗和全面康复，防止精神障碍的发生以及进一步发展成为精神残疾。

（2）尽可能减轻精神障碍程度：尽可能防止精神障碍患者出现精神衰退，逐步提高其生活自理能力。

（3）提高精神障碍患者的社会适应能力：提高或恢复精神障碍患者原有的社会功能。

（4）恢复劳动能力：通过各种康复措施和训练手段，使精神障碍患者具有代偿性生活和工作技能，充分发挥其保留的各项能力。

ii. Rehabilitation Assessment

The ultimate goal of the CBR Assessment is to promote community mental health services, to provide a reliable basis for further scientific research, and to promote the vertical development of the whole cause of mental rehabilitation.

The assessment of chronic schizophrenic patients can be refined as follows:

(1) Symptom Assessment: What the positive or negative symptoms are.

(2) Abnormal Behavior Assessment: What are the abnormal behaviors, especially those socially unacceptable behaviors, such as obscene language or impulsive behaviors.

(3) Daily Life Activities Assessment.

(4) Employability Assessment: Assess the individual's occupational functioning as well as his or her attitudes and expectations.

(5) Family and Social Environment Assessment.

For the specific contents and methods of the above functional assessment, please refer to the relevant contents of rehabilitation evaluation and assessment.

iii. Modern Rehabilitation Nursing Techniques and Methods

1. Training for Activities of Daily Living
This includes training the patient's personal ability in clothing, food, housing, transportation and basic personal hygiene, so that he or she can take care of basic living matters on his or her own. The vast majority of mental ill patients do not have obvious intellectual disabilities, but the decline in social and learning skills leads to a decline in intellectual activity. Most scholars have adopted social skills training measures, including training, behavioral shaping, role playing, skill reinforcement and corrective feedback. During the training process, the patient is allowed to play a certain role, and the therapist repeatedly asks the patient some questions; the therapist constantly corrects and guides, and then repeatedly reinforces the correct part, and in the

（二）康复评定

社区康复评定的最终目的，是促进社区精神卫生服务工作，为进一步科学研究提供可靠的依据，推动整个精神康复事业向纵深发展。

对慢性精神分裂症患者评定的内容，可细化为：

（1）症状评定：有哪些阳性或阴性的症状。

（2）异常行为评定：有哪些异常行为，特别是那些社会不接受的行为，譬如秽言或冲动性行为。

（3）日常生活活动能力评定。

（4）就业能力评定：评定个体的职业功能及其态度和期望。

（5）家庭和社会环境评定。

以上功能评定的具体内容和方法，可参考康复功能评定学相关内容。

（三）现代康复护理技术与方法

1. 个人生活活动能力训练　包括训练患者个人的衣食住行及个人基本卫生等方面能力，使其能够自行料理基本生活事务。绝大多数精神疾病患者没有明显智力障碍，但由于社交、学习技能减弱，导致智力活动下降。多数学者采用了社会技能训练措施，包括训练、行为塑造、角色扮演、技能强化和矫正反馈等几个阶段。训练过程中，让患者扮演某一角色，反复向患者提出一些问题；治疗师不断地予以纠正和引导，对正确的部分再反复进行强化，在解决问题的过程中给患者设置某些障碍，鼓励患者主动采取有效的方法进行克服。

process of solving the problem, certain obstacles are set for the patient, and the patient is encouraged to take the initiative to adopt effective methods to overcome.

2. Training for Disease and Drug Self-management Skills This includes patients' knowledge and understanding of their own illnesses and symptoms, basic knowledge of mental illnesses and psychopharmacology, and learning to recognize their own symptoms, common adverse drug reactions, and master simple self-management. They should learn to seek help and support from doctors, family members and the society when necessary, and improve their adherence to medication and treatment.

3. Psychotherapy Psychotherapy for this disease is mainly supportive psychotherapy. It focuses on helping patients to establish confidence and improve their psychological situation, and it should run through the whole rehabilitation process. As most of the chronic schizophrenic patients show poor initiative, lack of will and reduced ability to live, at present, the token economy therapy in behavioral therapy is more often used to achieve incentive and conditioned reinforcement, while correcting those maladaptive behaviors.

4. Vocational Rehabilitation This is an important component and objective of rehabilitation for mental disability, and a difficult task that must be accomplished to the best of one's ability. Vocational rehabilitation in the community mainly adopts work therapy. According to the conditions of the community, some work therapy facilities should be created as far as possible, such as mechanical processing workshop, carpentry workshop, handicraft manufacturing, gardening and farming, etc.; and as far as possible, occupational therapists should give guidance and help to the patients. The purpose of these trainings is mainly to improve the patients' occupational functioning and their ability to socialize with other people, to adjust the patients' mental state and to

2. 疾病及药物自我管理技能培训 培训内容包括患者对自身疾病病情、症状的认识和理解,基本的精神疾病知识及精神药理知识,使患者学会识别自身症状、常见的药物不良反应,并能进行简单的自我处理,学会必要时寻求医生、家属以及社会的帮助和支持,提高自身的服药依从性及治疗依从性。

3. 心理治疗 对本病的心理治疗,主要是支持性心理治疗。其重点是帮助患者树立信心,改善其心理处境等,并应贯穿整个康复过程。由于慢性精神分裂症患者大部分呈现主动性差、意志要求缺乏及生活能力减退,目前,较多采用行为疗法中的标记奖励疗法(或称代币法),以进行激励和条件性强化,矫正那些适应不良性行为。

4. 职业康复 这是精神残疾康复的一个重要内容和目标,也是一项艰巨而又必须尽力完成的任务。社区的职业康复,主要是采用工作疗法。要根据社区的条件,尽可能地创造一些工疗设施,如机械加工车间、木工车间、工艺品制造、园艺劳动及养殖等;并尽可能由职业治疗师对患者进行指导和帮助。这些训练的目的,主要是提高患者的职业能力和社交能力,调整患者心态,为其重新就业做好准备。

prepare them for re-employment.

5. Regular Follow-up　Community healthcare workers should make regular visits to patients, especially those with chronic conditions. At the same time, patients should also have regular consultation to get medication, and the psychiatrists will also provide targeted rehabilitation guidance according to the specific conditions and environments of the patients.

iv. Traditional Chinese Medicine Rehabilitation Nursing Techniques and Methods

Mental disorders are called "manic depressive psychosis" "hysteria" "lily disease" and so on in traditional Chinese medicine. Traditional Chinese medicine treatment is based on the principle of adjusting yin-yang, and uses traditional Chinese medicine that has the effects of releasing depression and resolving phlegm, reducing fire and removing blood stasis, and calming the mind. Acupuncture and moxibustion therapy is based on the principles of clearing the heart and refreshing the brain, sweeping phlegm and diffusing the lung, suppressing the sthenic yang and purging fire, and mainly focuses on the conception and governor vessels, shaoyin heart meridian of hand and jueyin pericardium meridian of hand.

5. 定期随访　社区医务工作者应对患者定期随访，尤其是慢性病患者。同时患者也要定期复诊，除了取药外，还需要精神科医生根据其病情变化及其所处环境等提供针对性的康复指导。

（四）中医康复护理技术与方法

精神障碍在中医中有"癫狂""脏躁""百合病"等称谓。中药治疗以调理阴阳为原则，使用具有解郁化痰、降火化瘀、宁心安神作用的中药。针灸治疗则以清心醒脑、豁痰宣肺、潜阳泻火为治疗原则，以任督二脉、手少阴心经及手厥阴心包经穴位为主。

BOX 9-1　Learning More

International Day of Persons with Disabilities

Due to physical, legal and social barriers, persons with disabilities are often unable to enjoy political, economic, social and cultural rights on an equal basis with persons without disabilities. This phenomenon has not been paid enough attention by the society for a long time. In 1976, to raise awareness of the disabled, the General Assembly of the United Nations proclaimed 1981 as the International Year of Persons with Disabilities and established the theme of "full participation and equality". On 12 and 13 October 1992, the 47th session of the General Assembly of the United

BOX 9-1　知识拓展

国际残疾人日

由于生理、法律和社会方面的障碍，残疾人往往不能和正常人一样平等地享受政治、经济、社会和文化等权利。这种现象长期以来一直未能受到社会的足够重视。1976 年，为唤起社会对残疾人的关注，联合国大会宣布 1981 年为"国际残疾人年"，并确定了"全面参与和平等"的主题。1992 年 10 月 12 日至 13 日，第 47 届联合国大会举行了自联合国成立以来首次关于残疾人问题的特别会议。大会通过决议，将每年的 12 月 3 日定为"国际残疾人日"（International Day of Persons with Disabilities）。2024 年国际残疾人日的主题

Nations held its first special session on the issue of persons with disabilities since the founding of the United Nations. The General Assembly of the United Nations adopted a resolution designating December 3 of each year as the International Day of Persons with Disabilities. The theme of the 2024 International Day of Persons with Disabilities is "Amplifying the leadership of persons with disabilities for an inclusive and sustainable future".

(Zhang Xiaonan)

为"增强残疾人领导力，共创包容且可持续的未来"。

（张晓楠）

Key Points

1. Community-based rehabilitation is an important part of community construction, which refers to a process in which, under the leadership of the government，with the close cooperation of relevant departments, the extensive support from social forces, and the active participation of persons with disabilities and their relatives and friends, the comprehensive rehabilitation services are provided to people with disabilities through a socialized approach. The goal is to achieve equal opportunities and full participation in social life.

2. In China, the service targets of community-based rehabilitation mainly include three categories of people：people with disabilities, patients with chronic diseases, and the elderly.

3. The service contents of CBR mainly include disability screening, medical rehabilitation, rehabilitation training guidance, day care and maintenance, work (agriculture) and recreational therapy, vocational rehabilitation, psychological support, knowledge promotion and popularization and so on.

4. Modern rehabilitation nursing techniques and methods for patients with stroke or spinal cord injury include positioning, positioning changes, transfer, training for activities of daily living and so on.

5. For patients with schizophrenia, modern rehabilitation nursing needs to consider the

内容摘要

1. 社区康复是社区建设的重要组成部分，是指在政府领导下，相关部门密切配合，社会力量广泛支持，残疾人及其亲友积极参与，采取社会化方式，使广大残疾人得到全面康复服务，以实现机会均等、充分参与社会生活的目标。

2. 在我国，社区康复的对象主要包括三类人群：残疾人、慢性病患者和老年人。

3. 社区康复服务主要包括残疾筛查、医疗康复、康复训练指导、日间照料与养护、工（农）与娱乐治疗、职业康复、心理支持、知识宣传普及等多方面内容。

4. 脑卒中患者和脊髓损伤患者的现代康复护理技术与方法包括体位摆放、体位变换、转移、日常生活活动能力的训练等。

5. 对精神分裂症患者的现代康复护理需要考虑以下几方面：个人生活活动能力训练、疾病

following aspects: training for activities of daily living and disease and drug self-management skills, psychotherapy, vocational rehabilitation and regular follow-up.

及药物自我管理技能培训、心理治疗、职业康复和定期随访。

Exercises

(Questions 1 to 2 share the same question stem)

The patient, a 50-year-old female, was diagnosed with large-area cerebral infarction in the right hemisphere at a hospital due to consciousness disorders. After admission for treatment, her condition stabilized and she was discharged. The patient has a course of more than 3 months, with clear consciousness, poor mental state, limited mobility of the right limb, unclear speech expression, and reliable wheelchair mobility. Community nurses are conducting follow-up on her.

1. What rehabilitation activities can the patient engage in herself?

2. What health education can be provided to caregivers? What situations do we need to pay attention to for caregivers at the same time?

(Questions 3 to 4 share the same question stem)

The patient, male, 40 years old, is a company employee. Due to high work pressure and difficulty falling asleep, he has recently repeatedly complained that someone was secretly monitoring and wanted to harm him, He often talked to himself and laughed without reason, and has been diagnosed with schizophrenia. After hospitalization, his condition stabilized and took medication home. He was included in the management scope of severe mental illness by the community health center. Community nurses are now conducting follow-up on him.

3. What are the rehabilitation goals of the patient?

4. What rehabilitation activities can be carried out for the patient?

思 考 题

（1~2 题共用题干）

患者，女，50 岁，因意识障碍就诊于某医院，诊断为右侧大脑半球大面积脑梗死，入院治疗后，病情稳定出院。现患者病程 3 个多月，神志清楚，精神差，右侧肢体活动不灵，言语表达不清楚，可靠轮椅移动，社区护士对其开展随访。

1. 患者自身可进行哪些康复活动？

2. 可对照顾者开展哪些健康教育？同时需要关注照顾者的哪些情况？

（3~4 题共用题干）

患者，男，40 岁，公司职员。因工作压力大难以入睡，近期反复诉说有人暗中监视他、要害他，经常自言自语、无故发笑，被诊断为精神分裂症。住院治疗后，患者病情稳定，带药回家，被社区卫生服务中心纳入重性精神疾病管理范围。现社区护士对其开展随访。

3. 患者的康复目标是什么？

4. 可以对患者开展哪些康复活动？

NURSING

10章
10章 数字内容

Knowledge Objectives

1. Correctly describe the concept and connotation of hospice care.
2. Correctly describe the key points of common symptom control and care in community hospice care.
3. Correctly describe the concept, meaning, and contents of death education.

Ability Objectives

1. Utilize symptom control and care to conduct hospice care for terminal patients.

知识目标

1. 正确叙述安宁疗护的概念及内涵。

2. 正确描述社区安宁疗护中常见的症状控制和护理要点。

3. 正确叙述死亡教育的概念、意义和内容。

能力目标

1. 运用症状控制和护理要点，为终末期患者实施安宁疗护。

2. Assess the physical and mental status of community terminal patients and develop a community hospice care plan for them.

Quality Objectives

1. Establish a scientific spirit, convey humanistic care, and provide hospice care for terminal patients based on scientific principles and respect for their customs and habits.

2. Cultivate a spirit of understanding, gratitude, and acceptance to provide death education for terminal patients and their families.

Li, male, 72 years old. Diagnosis: advanced colon cancer. The expected survival period was less than 2 months. He received hospice care at home. During the community home visit, the patient was conscious but mentally fatigued, and complained of general discomfort and unbearable pain. The patient had obvious emotional fluctuation. The patient and his wife lived on the fifth floor of the residence, without an elevator, and received the minimum living allowance of residents.

Questions：

1. How to control and care for the patient's symptoms?

2. How to provide psychological support and humanistic care for the patient?

Section 1　Overview

I. The Origin and Development of Hospice Care

i. The Origin of Hospice Care

Hospice care originated from the English word "hospice", originally meaning "poor house", or "almshouse", it was an early charitable service organization for the injured or homeless people to stay for a while, later developed into a service

2. 对社区终末期患者进行身心状态评估，为其制订一份社区安宁疗护计划。

素质目标

1. 树立科学精神，传递人文关怀，遵循科学原则，尊重风俗习惯，为终末期患者提供安宁疗护。

2. 培养理解、感恩和接纳精神，为终末期患者及家属提供死亡教育。

李某，男，72 岁。诊断：结肠癌晚期，预计生存期不足 2 个月，接受居家安宁疗护。社区护士家访时发现：患者意识清、疲乏无力，主诉全身不适和疼痛难忍，且情绪波动明显。患者和妻子居住在某老旧小区的 5 楼，无电梯，享受居民最低生活保障。

请思考：

1. 如何做好患者的症状控制和护理？

2. 如何做好患者的心理支持和人文护理？

第一节　概　　述

一、安宁疗护的起源和发展

（一）安宁疗护的起源

安宁疗护，起源于英文"hospice"，原意是"济贫院""救济院"，最初是为受伤者、无家可归者提供短暂居所的慈善服务机构，在 20 世纪发展成为针对终末期患者提供护理和治疗的服务体系。1967 年，桑德斯（Cicely Sanders）在英国

system for the terminal patients to provide care and treatment in the 20th century. In 1967, Cicely Sanders founded St.Christopher's Hospice in the United Kingdom, which has since become a model for modern hospice care.

ii. The Development of Hospice Care

1. The Development of Hospice Care Abroad　Some European countries commonly use the term palliative care or hospice to refer to hospice care. In 1982, the World Health Organization promoted the use of hospice care globally in its cancer control program. At present, some European countries have developed a relatively complete and comprehensive palliative service system. The U.S. enacted the *Patient Self Determination Act* in 1991 and *Medicare Patient Access to Hospice Act* in 2018. On January 8th, 2016, the South Korea's congress enacted *Act on Decisions on Life-sustaining Treatment for Patients in Hospice and Palliative Care or at the End of Life*, which came into effect on August 4th, 2017.

2. The Development of Hospice care in China　China attaches great importance to the development of hospice care, it is regarded as an important way to improve the quality of life for terminal patients and actively cope with the aging population. In 1988, Hospice Research Center of Tianjin Medical College was established. Hospice care has been included in the key work of the national health system. Since the issue of the *Basic Standards for Medical Institutions (Trial)* in 1994, China has continuously expanded service supply and improved service capabilities in the setting of relevant diagnosis, treatment subjects and the protection of health rights and interests. Chinese Taiwan enacted the *Hospice-Palliative Act* and *Patient Autonomy Act* in 2000 and 2016 separately. In 2006, The Law Reform Commission of Hongkong, China issued *Substitute Decision-making and Advance Directives in Relation to Medical Treatment*. And the Hospital Authority of Hong Kong, China issued the *Palliative Care Services Strategy* and *Guidelines of Advance*

创建 St.Christopher's Hospice 机构，并发展为现代安宁疗护的典范。

（二）安宁疗护的发展

1. **国外安宁疗护的发展**　一些欧洲国家通常使用临终关怀、舒缓医疗指代安宁疗护。1982 年世界卫生组织在癌症控制项目中向全球推广使用安宁疗护。目前部分国家已发展了较为完善和全面的安宁疗护服务体系。美国 1991 年颁布了《患者自决法》，2018 年颁布了《老年医疗保险患者获得安宁疗护法》。2016 年 1 月 8 日，韩国国会颁布了《关于临终关怀·缓和医疗及临终期患者的延命医疗决定的法案》，该法于 2017 年 8 月 4 日正式实施。

2. **国内安宁疗护的发展**　我国高度重视安宁疗护事业的发展，将其作为提高终末期患者生活质量、积极应对人口老龄化的重要途径。1988 年，天津医学院临终关怀研究中心成立。我国安宁疗护已经纳入国家医疗卫生系统的重点工作中。从 1994 年出台《医疗机构基本标准（试行）》至今，我国在相关诊疗科目设置、健康权益保障等方面不断扩大服务供给、提升服务能力。台湾省分别在 2000 年和 2016 年发布了《安宁缓和医疗条例》和《病人自主权利法》。2006 年，香港发布了《医疗上的代作决定及预设医疗指示》；2017 年及 2019 年，香港医院管理局分别发布了《纾缓治疗服务策略》及《预设照护计划指引》。2024 年，香港特别行政区立法会通过《维持生命治疗的预作决定条例草案》。2009 年，中国老龄事业发展基金会发布了《关于开展安宁疗护工作的意见》。2016 年 4 月，在全国"推进安宁疗护发展"专题调研的基础上，全国政协第 49 次双周协商座谈会提出要明确安宁疗护的内涵与功能定位。同年，《"健康中国 2030"规划纲要》提出加强安宁疗护等接续性医疗机构的建设，加强健康人才培养培训，推动医养结

Care Planning in 2017 and 2019 separately. In November 2024, the Legislative Council of the Hong Kong Special Administrative Region of China passed the *Advance Decision on Life-Sustaining Treatment Bill*. In 2009, the China Aging Development Foundation issued the *Opinions on the Development of Hospice Care Work*. In April 2016, on the basis of the national research on "Promoting the development of hospice care", the 49th Bi-weekly Consultative Forums of the National Committee of the Chinese People's Political Consultative Conference proposed to clarify the functional positioning and connotation of hospice care. In the same year, the *"Healthy China 2030" Planning Outline* proposed to strengthen the construction of continuous medical institutions such as hospice care, strengthen the training of health personnel, promote the combination of medical and nursing, and provide health and old-age services integrating hospitalization during treatment, nursing during rehabilitation, stable life care and hospice care for the elderly.In February 2017, the National Health and Family Planning Commission successively issued three documents: *Basic Standards for Hospice Care Centers* (*Trial*), *Management Norms for Hospice Care Centers* (*Trial*), and *Guidelines for Hospice Care Practice* (*Trial*). The definition, beds, department settings, building requirements, equipment configuration and management norms and practices of hospice care centers are clearly stipulated and required, and guiding suggestions are given on the management, nursing, comfort care, psychological support, and humanistic care of terminal patients with pain and other symptoms. In 2017, China launched the first batch of hospice care pilots in Beijing, Changchun, Shanghai, and other places; in 2019, the second batch of hospice care pilots were carried out nationwide, and the hospice care service system which accords with our national conditions is gradually improving. With the rapid development of hospice care, policy documents kept emerging, and regional hospice care service

合，为老年人提供治疗期住院、康复期护理、稳定期生活照料、安宁疗护一体化的健康和养老服务。2017 年 2 月，国家卫生和计划生育委员会连续颁布《安宁疗护中心基本标准（试行）》《安宁疗护中心管理规范（试行）》和《安宁疗护实践指南（试行）》3 个文件，对安宁疗护中心的定义、床位、科室设置、建筑要求、设备配置与管理规范和实践提出明确规定和要求，并对终末期患者疼痛及其他症状的治疗、护理、舒适照护、心理支持和人文关怀等给出了指导性建议。2017 年，我国首批安宁疗护试点于北京、长春、上海等地启动，2019 年，全国更多范围内开展了第二批安宁疗护试点，符合我国国情的安宁疗护服务体系正逐步完善。随后，以国家级安宁疗护试点为主要形式的安宁疗护服务体系快速发展，安宁疗护政策文件不断涌现，区域安宁疗护服务体系逐步建立和完善。2019 年 12 月，"安宁疗护"作为法律语言在我国《基本医疗卫生与健康促进法》中出现。2022 年，国家卫生健康委等 15 部门联合印发《"十四五"健康老龄化规划》，提出稳步扩大全国安宁疗护试点，支持有条件的省市全面开展安宁疗护工作。2022 年 6 月，《深圳经济特区医疗条例》规定，医疗机构在给生命末期患者实施医疗措施时，应尊重患者生前预嘱的意愿，该条例自 2023 年 1 月 1 日起开始实行。2023 年 7 月，第三批安宁疗护试点工作启动。目前，3 批国家级安宁疗护试点已覆盖全国 185 个市（区）。2024 年 7 月，国家卫生健康委员会发布《老年安宁疗护病区设置标准》，对人员配置、工作内容及要求进行详细规定。2024 年 11 月 12 日，国家医疗保障局首次将"安宁疗护"纳入《综合诊查类医疗服务价格项目立项指南（试行）》，要求安宁疗护按日收费，所定价格涵盖患者病情评估、诊查、分级护理、各类评估工具使用、心理及精神疏导、情绪安抚、沟通陪伴、临终关怀、个性化支持等所需的人力资源和基本物质资源消耗。

systems were gradually established and improved. In December 2019, "hospice care" appeared as a legal language in *Law of the People's Republic of China on Basic Medical and Health Care and the Promotion of Health*. In 2022, 15 departments including the National Health Commission jointly issued the *"14th Five-Year Plan" for Healthy Aging*, proposing to steadily expand the hospice care pilot nationwide, and supporting qualified provinces and cities to carry out hospice care work in an all-round way. In June 2022, *Shenzhen Special Economic Zone Medical Regulations* stipulated that medical institutions should respect the patients' advance directives when implementing medical measures, which came into effect on January 1st, 2023. In July 2023, the third batch of hospice care pilot work was launched. At present, three batches of national hospice care pilots have covered 185 cities (districts) across China. In July 2024, the National Health Commission issued the *Setting Standards for Elderly Hospice Care Wards* which detailed regulations on staffing, work content and requirements. On November 12th, 2024, the National Healthcare Security Administration (NHSA) included "hospice care" in the *Guidelines for the Establishment of Comprehensive Diagnostic Tests and Medical Service Price Projects* (*Trial*) for the first time, which required that hospice care be charged on a daily basis, and the price should cover the consumption of human resources and basic material resources required for patients' condition assessment, diagnosis, graded care, use of various assessment tools, psychological and spiritual counseling, emotional comfort, communication and companionship, hospice care, personalized support, etc.

II. The Concept and Connotation of Hospice Care

i. Relevant Concepts of Hospice Care

In 2002, the WHO revised the definition of hospice care to supportive care that prevents and relieves patients' physical and mental suffering through early identification and management of

二、安宁疗护的概念与内涵

（一）安宁疗护的相关概念

2002 年 WHO 将安宁疗护的定义修订为：通过早期识别、控制疼痛和缓解其他躯体、社会心理症状，预防和缓解患者身心痛苦，改善面临威胁生命疾病的患者及其家庭生活质量的支持

pain and relieves other physical and psychosocial symptoms, and improves the quality of life of patients with life-threatening illnesses and their families. In 2017, the *Guidelines for Hospice Care Practice* (*Trial*) issued by the National Health and Family Planning Commission clearly defined hospice care is a practice centered on terminal patients and their families and conducted in a multidisciplinary collaboration model. The main contents include pain and other symptoms control, comfort care, psychological, spiritual, and social support.

The related concepts of hospice care involve living wills, enduring power of attorney for healthcare, advance directives, proxy decision maker, and advance care planning.

Living wills (LW) are the predecessor of advance directives, which were first proposed by a lawyer in the United States in 1969, the lawyer argued that individuals have the right to make plans and arrangements in advance whether to receive certain medical measures, and this kind of "will" is formulated before the individual's death, so it is called "living will".

An Enduring Power of Attorney for Healthcare is a concept derived from the legal system. When the patient is conscious, a power of attorney that entrusts another person to make medical decisions on behalf of the patient when he or she is incapacitated is a health care enduring power of attorney, and the person who is appointed to make decisions on behalf of the patient is the proxy decision maker.

Advance directives (AD) are formal legal statement documents. When an individual is conscious and has the ability to make decisions, he/she states his/her preferred medical treatments he/she wishes to accept or refuse when he/she loses his/her decision-making capacity, personal values, beliefs, and designated healthcare proxy decision maker in the form of document in advance.

Advance care planning (ACP) is the process of supporting adults of any age or health level to understand and share their personal values, life goals, and medical care preferences. Advance care planning

性照护。2017 年，国家卫生计生委办公厅颁布的《安宁疗护实践指南（试行）》中规定，安宁疗护是以终末期患者和家属为中心，以多学科协作模式进行的实践，主要内容包括疼痛及其他症状的控制，舒适照护，心理、精神及社会支持等。

安宁疗护的相关概念涉及生前预嘱、医疗保健持久授权委托书、预立医疗指示、决策代理人及预立医疗照护计划等。

生前预嘱是预立医疗指示的前身，最初由美国一名律师 1969 年提出，认为个人有权利提前对是否接受某种医疗措施做出计划和安排。这种"嘱托"是在个人生前制定，所以称为"生前预嘱"。

医疗保健持久授权委托书是法律制度下衍生出的概念。患者意识清醒时，委托他人在自己没有行为能力时代替自己做出医疗决定的委托书即医疗保健持久授权委托书，被指定代替自己做决定的人为决策代理人。

预立医疗指示，是正式的法律声明文件，指个人在意识清醒并具备决策能力的情况下，预先以文件形式陈述其将来失去决策能力时希望接受或拒绝的医学治疗，个人价值观、信仰，和 / 或个人指定的医疗决策代理人。

预立医疗照护计划是指支持任何年龄或健康阶段的成年人理解和分享他们的个人价值观、生活目标和未来医疗照护偏好的过程。预立医疗照护计划涉及患者、家属或其他决策者以及

involves communication between patients, family members or other decision-makers, and health care providers, patients' interpersonal and cultural background should be considered, to ensure that patients receive care that aligns with their goals and values, which can be recorded in AD.

ii. The Idea of Hospice Care

1. Respect for Life and Dignity Hospice care emphasizes respect for the life of every terminal patient, believing that life is important. It respects the dignity of patients and helps patients achieve a life state without physical pain, psychological fear, worries about family affairs and spiritual disturbance.

2. Provide Comprehensive Care Hospice care aims to help patients and their families, and it focuses not only on the patient's physical pain, but also on the patient's inner feelings , so that the patient can complete the final journey of life with dignity.

3. Managing Pain and Discomfort By controlling pain and other discomfort symptoms, hospice care improves the quality of life and helps patients die comfortably, peacefully, and with dignity.

4. Accept the Natural Process of Dying The core philosophy of hospice care is to accept death as a natural process that neither accelerates nor delays death, but provides clinical care that relieves pain and other painful symptoms, as well as integrates psychological and spiritual care to help patients live as positively as possible to the end of their lives.

iii. The Goal of Hospice Care

The goal of hospice care is to improve the quality of life for patients with life-threatening illnesses and their family members, alleviate patients' physical, psychological, social and spiritual suffering while preserving their dignity and autonomy, ultimately helping patients to die peacefully and reduce the burden of the bereaved.

iv. The Principle of Hospice Care

1. The Humanitarian Principle It means that in the practice of hospice care, people should be cared for and respected, and taking

医护人员之间的沟通交流，需要考虑患者的人际关系和文化背景，确保患者得到符合其目标和价值观的医疗护理服务，可记录于预立医疗指示中。

（二）安宁疗护的理念

1. **尊重生命与尊严** 安宁疗护强调尊重每一个终末期患者的生命，认为生命都是重要的。它尊重患者的尊严，帮助患者实现生理上无痛苦、心理上无恐惧、家庭事务上无牵挂、精神上无困扰的生命状态。

2. **提供全面的照护** 安宁疗护旨在为患者及其家庭提供帮助，不仅关注患者的身体疼痛，更注重患者的内心感受，让患者有尊严地走完人生最后一段旅程。

3. **控制痛苦和不适** 安宁疗护通过控制痛苦和不适症状，提高生命质量，帮助患者舒适、安详、有尊严地离世。

4. **接受死亡的自然过程** 安宁疗护的核心理念是接受死亡是一个自然的过程，既不刻意加速，也不拖延死亡，而是提供缓解疼痛及其他痛苦症状的临床医疗服务，关怀患者，帮助患者尽可能以积极的态度走完生命的最后历程。

（三）安宁疗护的目标

安宁疗护的目标是提高面临威胁生命疾病的患者及其家庭成员的生活质量，减轻患者身体、心理、社会和精神的痛苦，同时维护他们的尊严和自主选择权，最终帮助患者平静离世，减轻丧亲者的负担。

（四）安宁疗护的原则

1. **人道主义原则** 指在安宁疗护实践中，应以关怀人、尊重人、以人为中心作为观察问题、处理问题的准则，要有敬畏并尊重生命的意

people-oriented as the criteria for observing and dealing with problems. We should show reverence and respect for life, respect each terminal patient, respect the quality and value of life of the patients, and respect the legitimate wishes of the terminal patients. Provide patients with physical, psychological, social and spiritual care and grief counseling for family members.

2. The Principle of Care-first　It means that in the practice of hospice care, death should be regarded as a normal process of life, and meaningless examination and treatment should no longer be given to terminal patients with ineffective anti-tumor treatment. Instead, appropriate technologies and methods should be used to provide positive holistic care to alleviate pain, manage symptoms and provide comfortable care, and keep patients in a peaceful state, enabling them to die comfortably, peacefully, with dignity and without pain.

3. The Principle of Multidisciplinary Integration　It means the establishment of multidisciplinary integrated medical care teams in hospice care practice, the formulation of personalized plans for patients, and the provision of whole-person, whole-body, whole-process, comprehensive, systematic, continuous and accessible integrated care services for patients and their families.

v. The Hospice Care Team

The hospice care service team includes doctors, nurses, volunteers, social workers, pharmacists, nutritionists, physiotherapists, psychologists and so on.

vi. The Service Recipients of Hospice Care

In general, hospice care services are available to patients of all ages who suffer significant health-related distress as a result of serious illnesses, especially those near the end of life. Specifically, patients with serious or terminal diseases, such as terminal cancer, end-stage Alzheimer's disease, etc.; patients with chronic progressive diseases, such as chronic kidney disease, progressive heart or lung disease, malignant tumors, peripheral vascular diseases, etc.; children and adults with congenital conditions or who are dependent on others for life support or long-term care for daily activities; patients with acute, serious life-threatening diseases, such as leukemia, severe trauma, etc.

识，尊重每一名终末期患者，尊重患者的生命质量与生命价值，尊重终末期患者的正当愿望，给患者提供身体、心理、社会、精神等全方位的照顾，并对家属提供哀伤辅导。

2. 照护为主原则　指在安宁疗护实践中，应将死亡视为生命正常过程，对抗肿瘤治疗无效的终末期患者，不再给予无意义的检查和治疗，而是使用适宜的技术和方法提供积极的整体关怀来缓解痛苦，做好症状管理和舒适照护，使之处于安静祥和状态，舒适、平和、有尊严、无痛苦地离世。

3. 多学科整合原则　指在安宁疗护实践中，应组建多学科整合医学照护团队，为患者制订个性化方案，为患者及其家属提供全人、全身、全程、全息的全面、系统、连续、可及的整合照护服务。

（五）安宁疗护的服务团队

安宁疗护的服务团队包括医生、护士、志愿者、社工、药师、营养师、理疗师及心理师等。

（六）安宁疗护的服务对象

一般而言，因严重疾病而遭受健康相关重大痛苦的所有年龄段患者，尤其是接近生命末期的患者，均可获得安宁疗护服务。具体而言，即严重疾病或绝症患者，如癌症晚期、终末期阿尔茨海默病等；患有慢性进行性疾病者，如慢性肾病、进展性心脏病或肺疾病、恶性肿瘤、周围性血管性疾病等；有先天性疾病或日常活动需要依赖他人提供生命支持或需要长期照护的儿童和成年人；患有急性和严重危及生命疾病的患者，如白血病、严重创伤等。

BOX 10-1 Learning More

Specific Contents of Hospice Care Principles in Different Periods

The specific contents of hospice care principles in different periods are presented in Table 10-1.

Table 10-1 Specific Contents of Hospice Care Principles in Different Periods

Issuing Organizations and Years	The Worldwide Hospice Palliative Care Alliance (2011)	World Health Organization (2018)	World Health Organization (2022)
Specific contents of hospice care principles	1. Relieve pain and other discomfort 2. Affirm life and accept death as a normal process. 3. Neither accelerate nor unduly delay death 4. Integrate the psychological and spiritual aspects of care for patients according to the needs and expectation of patients and families 5. Provide support systems that enable patients to access and adhere to optimal clinical care, address social and legal issues, and in particular reduce the impact of poverty on patients and their family members (including children). Help patients live as actively as possible until death 6. Provide support systems to help families cope with the patient's illness and their own bereavement 7. If needed, use a team approach to fully meet the needs of the patient and family, including bereavement counseling 8. Improve the quality of life of patients and their families, and may also have a positive effect on the disease process 9. Applicable to the disease in early stage, combined with other therapies (e.g., chemotherapy or radiotherapy of cancer patients, and antiretroviral therapy of AIDS patients) aimed at prolonging life, and includes better understanding, assessing, and managing clinical complications	1. Early detection of problems and comprehensive assessment and management 2. Improve the quality of life and promote dignity and comfort, and may also have a positive impact on the disease process 3. Support patients and their families throughout the disease process 4. Considered with serious or life-limiting diseases, and combined with prevention, early diagnosis and treatment 5. Applicable to the disease in the early stage, combined with other therapies aimed at prolonging life 6. Provide alternatives for alleviation and life-sustaining treatments of diseases with questionable value at the end of life, and facilitate decisions about optimal use of life-sustaining treatments 7. Applicable to patients with serious or life-threatening diseases and long-term physical, psychological, social or spiritual suffering 8. If needed, provide bereavement support to family members after the patient's death 9. Aim at reducing the impact of poverty caused by illness on patients and families and avoiding financial difficulties caused by illness 10. Not to hasten death, but to provide the necessary treatment and to provide adequate comfort according to the patient's needs and values 11. It should be provided by health care workers at all levels of the health service system, including primary health providers, general practitioners and specialists. Provide hospice care skills training at different levels (basic, intermediate and professional) 12. Encourage active participation of communities and citizens 13. Provide outpatient, inpatient and home-based care at all levels of the health service system 14. Strengthen health delivery systems by providing continuous services	1. Relieve pain and other discomfort 2. Affirm life and accept death as a normal process 3. Neither accelerate nor delay death 4. Integrate the psychological and spiritual aspects of care for patients 5. Provide support systems to help patients live as actively as possible until death 6. Provide support systems to help families cope with the patient's illness and their own bereavement 7. If needed, use a team approach to meet the needs of the patient and family, including bereavement counseling 8. Improve the quality of life, and may also have a positive effect on the disease process 9. Applicable to the disease in early stage, combined with other therapies aimed at prolonging life, and to better understand, assess, and manage clinical complications

BOX 10-1 知识拓展

不同时期安宁疗护原则的具体内容

不同时期安宁疗护原则的具体内容见表 10-1。

表 10-1 不同时期安宁疗护原则的具体内容

发布组织与年份	世界安宁缓和医疗联盟（2011 年）	世界卫生组织（2018 年）	世界卫生组织（2022 年）
安宁疗护原则的具体内容	1. 缓解疼痛和其他痛苦症状 2. 肯定生命并将死亡视为正常过程 3. 既不加速也不过度地推迟死亡 4. 根据患者和家属的需要和期望，整合患者护理的心理和精神方面 5. 提供支持系统，使患者能够获得并遵循最佳临床照护，解决社会和法律问题，特别是减少贫困对患者及其家庭成员（包括儿童）的影响。帮助患者尽可能积极地生活直至死亡 6. 提供支持系统，帮助家属应对患者疾病和自己的丧亲之痛 7. 如果有需要，采用团队方法来全面满足患者及其家属的需求，包括丧亲辅导 8. 提高患者及其家属的生活质量，也可能对疾病过程产生积极影响 9. 适用于疾病早期，与其他旨在延长生命的疗法（如癌症患者的化学疗法或放射疗法、艾滋病患者的抗逆转录病毒疗法）相结合，并包括更好地了解、评估和管理临床并发症	1. 早期发现问题并全面评估和处理 2. 提高生活质量，促进尊严和舒适，也可能对疾病进程产生积极影响 3. 在整个疾病过程中为患者及其家人提供支持 4. 与严重或限制生命的疾病问题结合考虑，并加以预防、早期诊断和治疗 5. 适用于疾病早期，与其他旨在延长生命的治疗共同使用 6. 为临终时价值存疑的疾病缓解和生命维持治疗提供替代方案，并协助关于生命维持治疗的优化利用决策 7. 适用于患有严重或危及生命疾病并长期遭受身体、心理、社会或精神痛苦的患者 8. 如果需要，在患者去世后为家庭成员提供丧亲支持 9. 旨在减轻因病致贫对患者和家庭的影响，避免因疾病导致经济困难 10. 不是加速死亡，而是提供必要的治疗，根据患者的需求和价值观为其提供足够的舒适度 11. 应由各级卫生服务系统的医护人员提供，包括初级卫生服务提供者，全科医生和专科医生。提供不同层次（基础、中等、专业）的安宁疗护技能培训 12. 鼓励社区和民众积极参与 13. 在各级卫生服务系统提供门诊、住院和居家照护 14. 提供连续性服务，从而强化卫生服务系统	1. 缓解疼痛和其他痛苦症状 2. 肯定生命并将死亡视为正常过程 3. 既不加速也不推迟死亡 4. 整合患者护理的心理和精神方面 5. 提供支持系统，帮助患者尽可能积极地生活直至死亡 6. 提供支持系统，帮助家庭应对患者疾病和自己的丧亲之痛 7. 如果有需要，采用团队方法来满足患者及其家属的需求，包括丧亲辅导 8. 提高生活质量，也可能对疾病过程产生积极影响 9. 适用于疾病早期，与其他旨在延长生命的疗法相结合，并更好地了解、评估和管理临床并发症

III. The Practice Form of Hospice Care

The development of hospice care in China implements the values and policy orientation of the development of China's medical security system, and meets the people's needs for universality, fairness, adaptability and diversity of medical resources. According to the *Statistical Bulletins of the Development of China's Health Undertakings in 2020*, there were more than 510 hospitals with

三、安宁疗护的实践形式

我国安宁疗护的发展贯彻了我国医疗保障制度发展的价值理念和政策取向，满足了人民对医疗资源实现普遍性、公正性、适应性及多样性的需求。据《2020 年我国卫生健康事业发展统计公报》统计，2020 年我国设有安宁疗护科的医院有 510 多家，包含了市、县、社区，形成了涵盖医院、社区、居家 3 种模式的服务体系。

hospice care departments in China, covering cities, counties and communities, and forming a service system that combines three modes: hospital-based, community-based, home-based.

i. Hospital-based Hospice Care

Hospital-based hospice care refers to setting hospice care departments, hospice care areas, independent hospice care centers, or hospice care beds in hospitals. The facilities utilize existing medical staff and other professionals to provide comprehensive care to terminal patients and their families. With the development of technology, some medical institutions provide "unaccompanied" hospice care center services by accelerating the construction of intelligent infrastructure, including the installation of intelligent monitoring equipment, human behavior sensors, etc., to reduce the families' care burden, while ensuring that patients receive high-quality care services. Hospital-based hospice care is conducive to promoting the construction of hospice care team, and supporting the construction of hospice care three-level referral network, and optimizing the allocation of medical resources.

ii. Community-based Hospice Care

The community-based hospice care model refers to the situation where a community-based hospice care team　provides hospice care to terminal patients and their caregivers in their community area. Hospice care services are usually provided by a health care facility near the dying patient's home, such as a nursing home, nursing facilities, hospice care facility, or community health center.

iii. Home-based Hospice Care

The home-based hospice care model refers to the care of patients at home by their families, and the hospital, community and other multidisciplinary service teams visit the home for assessment and care once or twice or even more frequently per week, providing patients and their families with services such as symptom control, comfort care, psychological support and humanistic care. Home-

（一）医院安宁疗护模式

医院安宁疗护模式是指在医院开设安宁疗护科、安宁疗护病区、独立的安宁疗护中心或安宁疗护病床，利用现有的医护人员及其他专业人员，为终末期患者及其家属提供全方位的照护。随着技术的发展，一些医疗机构通过加快智能化基础设施建设，提供"无陪护"安宁疗护中心服务，包括安装智能监测设备、人体行为感知仪等，以减轻家属的照护压力，同时确保患者得到高质量的照护服务。医院安宁疗护模式有利于推动安宁疗护团队的建设、支撑安宁疗护三级转诊网络的建设、优化医疗资源配置。

（二）社区安宁疗护模式

社区安宁疗护模式是指以社区为基础的安宁疗护团队为本区域内的终末期患者及其照护者提供安宁疗护。通常由临终患者家庭附近的医养结合机构，如养老院、护理院、安宁疗护机构或社区卫生服务中心就近提供安宁疗护服务。

（三）居家安宁疗护模式

居家安宁疗护模式是指患者在家中由家属照顾，医院、社区等多学科服务团队每周一到两次或多次上门评估与照顾，为患者及家属提供症状控制、舒适照顾、心理支持和人文关怀等服务。居家安宁疗护以家庭病床为载体开展，通过入户提供帮助，确保患者在生命的最后阶段能够在熟悉的环境中得到关怀和支持。

based hospice care is carried out in a home-based hospital bed. Through providing assistance at home, patients can receive care and support in a familiar environment during the final stages of life.

In 2021, the *14th Five-Year Plan for the Development of National Aging Undertakings and Pension Service System* issued by the State Council pointed out that it is necessary to develop geriatric medical care, rehabilitation care and hospice care services, support the development of community and home hospice care services, establish a hospice care service mechanism that connects institutions, communities and homes, and form a scientific hospice care "two-way referral and upper and lower linkage" mechanism. The integrated hospice care service of institution-community-home linkage can provide patients with continuous care services, and is conducive to integrating community medical resources and saving medical expenses effectively.

2021 年,国务院印发的《"十四五"国家老龄事业发展和养老服务体系规划》中指出,发展老年医疗、康复护理和安宁疗护服务,支持社区和居家安宁疗护服务发展,建立机构、社区和居家相衔接的安宁疗护服务机制,形成科学的安宁疗护"双向转诊、上下联动"机制。机构 - 社区 - 居家上下联动的安宁疗护整合服务能为患者提供连续性的照护服务,有利于整合社区医疗资源、节省医疗费用开支。

Section 2   The Service Content of Community Hospice Care

第二节　社区安宁疗护的服务内容

I. Symptom Control and Care

一、症状控制和护理

Symptom control and care are the core components of hospice care. Common symptoms in terminal patients include pain, edema, fever, dyspnea, nausea, vomiting, sleep disorder and so on, bringing great pain to patients. Hospice care services such as rational drug use, symptomatic treatment and nursing can relieve and control symptoms, relieve pain, and improve the quality of life of patients to the fullest extent.

症状控制和护理是安宁疗护的核心内容。终末期患者常见的症状包括疼痛、水肿、发热、呼吸困难、恶心呕吐、睡眠障碍等,给患者带来极大的痛苦。通过合理用药、对症治疗和护理等安宁疗护服务,可缓解和控制症状、减轻痛苦,最大程度地提高患者的生活质量。

i. Pain

(一)疼痛

Pain in cancer patients is an unpleasant feeling and emotional experience related to tumor invasion or potential damage, and is one of the main symptoms of advanced cancer patients. It is characterized by all-round, multi-type, co-

癌症患者的疼痛是与肿瘤侵犯或潜在损伤相关的一种不愉快的感觉和情感体验,是终末期癌症患者主要症状之一,具有全方位、多类型、疼痛与痛苦并存、伴有心理学异常等特点。据统计,约有 25% 的早期癌症患者及 60%~80%

existence of pain and suffering, and psychological abnormalities. According to statistics, about 25% of cancer patients are accompanied by pain in the early stage, and as high as 60% to 80% in the late stage. Cancer patients have poor long-term analgesia, refractory cancer pain, or cancer outbreak pain, and may be accompanied by anxiety, depression, and other mental symptoms.

1. Assessment Proactive pain screening is an important measure to effectively improve the quality of life of advanced cancer patients. It should follow the principles of routine, quantitative, comprehensive, and dynamic communication with patients and their families in a timely and effective manner. If patients cannot communicate verbally, attention should be paid to non-verbal ways, including expressions and groans. The cause and pathophysiological mechanism of pain are evaluated by medical history, physical examination, laboratory and imaging. The evaluation of pain includes four major factors: location (including scope), intensity, nature, and time of occurrence. The evaluation should also take into account the duration of the pain, aggravating and/or mitigating factors, previous pain history, and the presence or absence of concurrent emotional problems.

Pain can be assessed by using self-assessment and other-assessment tools (Table 10-2). Self-assessment tools include: numeric rating scale (NRS), visual analogue scale (VAS) and verbal rating scale (VRS), faces pain scale-revised (FRS-R), verbal descriptors scale (VDS) and other single-dimensional assessment tools; short-form of McGill pain questionnaire (SF-MPQ), global pain scale (GPS), brief pain inventory (BPI) and other multi-dimensional self-assessment tools. Children's finger span scale (FSS) and other assessment tools are for special populations. The adult pain behavioral scale (APBS) is an assessment tool for adults who cannot report pain.

的晚期癌症患者伴有疼痛。癌症患者长期镇痛效果不佳、出现难治性癌痛或癌性爆发痛，有可能并发焦虑、抑郁等精神症状。

1. 评估 积极主动的疼痛筛查是有效改善终末期癌症患者生存质量的重要措施。应遵循常规、量化、全面、动态原则，与患者和家属及时有效沟通。如患者不能语言交流，需关注非语言方式，包括表情、呻吟等。通过病史、体检、实验室及影像学检查评估疼痛原因及病理生理机制。疼痛的评估内容包括四大要素：疼痛的部位（包括范围）、强度、性质、发生时间。评估时也要注意疼痛的持续时间、加重和/或缓解疼痛的因素、既往疼痛史和有无并发情绪问题等。

可用自评和他评工具评估疼痛（见表 10-2）。自评工具包括：疼痛数字评分量表（numeric rating scale，NRS）、视觉模拟评分量表（visual analogue scale，VAS）、词语分级量表（verbal rating scale，VRS）、改良面部表情疼痛评估量表（faces pain scale-revised，FRS-R）、疼痛文字描述评分量表（verbal descriptors scale，VDS）等单维度评估工具；简明版 McGill 疼痛问卷（short-form of McGill pain questionnaire，SF-MPQ）、整体疼痛评估量表（global pain scale，GPS）、简明疼痛评估量表（brief pain inventory，BPI）等多维度自评工具。针对特殊人群的评估工具：儿童指距评分法（finger span scale，FSS）。他评工具：成人疼痛行为评估量表（adult pain behavioral scale，APBS），适用于不能主诉疼痛的成人患者。

Table 10-2   The Differences Between Several Pain Assessment Tools

	Visual Analogue Scale (VAS)	Faces Pain Scale (FPS)	Numerical Rating Scale (NRS)	Verbal Rating Scale (VRS)
Score interval	The value ranges from 0 to 100	Integer score from 0 to 10	Integer score from 0 to 10	Integer score from 0 to 5
Time duration	<1min	<1min	<1min	<1min
Recommended group	Adults	Designed for patients older than 3 years, especially for the elderly	Aged 10 years and above with a certain degree of education	Aged 10 years and above with a certain degree of education
Strengths	Continuous variables are beneficial for statistical analysis	Visualized and vivid	The classification is clear for patient assessment and can be used for telephone assessment	Convenient and quick
Shortcomings	Patients should have a certain ability of abstract think	The evaluator needs to look at the face carefully, and the pain intensity represented by the face may be interpreted differently by different patients. The ability to detect small differences in pain is not as good as the visual analogue scale	The evaluator is required to have language comprehension and abstract mathematical concepts, which are easy to confuse in understanding and have poor measurement repeatability, so it is not recommended to use in follow-up studies. The ability to detect small differences in pain is not as good as the visual analogue scale	The evaluator is required to have some conceptual language understanding, and the assessment may be influenced by culture and dialect. The ability to detect small differences in pain is not as good as the visual analogue scale. And when the assessment classification is less than 7, non-parametric test should be used, and the statistical efficacy is lower than other scales

表 10-2   几种疼痛评估量表的区别

	视觉模拟评分量表	面部表情疼痛评估量表	疼痛数字评分量表	词语分级量表
评分区间	0~100 连续数值	0~10 整数评分	0~10 整数评分	常用 0~5 整数评分
测试时间	<1 分钟	<1 分钟	<1 分钟	<1 分钟
推荐使用群体	成年人	3 岁以上患者均可,老年患者首选	10 岁以上有一定文化程度	10 岁以上有一定文化程度
优点	连续变量利于统计分析	直观形象	分类明确,有助于患者进行评估,可以用于电话评估	方便、快速
缺点	患者要具有一定的抽象思维能力	需要评估者仔细观察患者面孔,且不同患者对面孔代表的疼痛强度理解可能不同。体现疼痛微小变化差异的能力不如视觉模拟评分量表	需要评估者有语言理解能力和抽象数学概念。容易在理解上产生混淆,测量重复性差,不建议在追踪研究中使用。体现疼痛微小变化差异的能力不如视觉模拟评分量表	需要评估者有一定的概念化语言理解能力,评估可能会受到文化和方言的影响。体现疼痛微小变化差异的能力不如视觉模拟评分量表。且当评估分类小于 7 种时,要用非参数检验,统计效能低于其他量表

2. Treatment Based on the comprehensive evaluation of patients, and combined with multidisciplinary approaches, adopt comprehensive treatment principles including pharmacological treatment to give patients personalized intervention.

(1) Pharmacological Treatment: Follow the three-step analgesic treatment guidelines for cancer pain is the principle of clinical analgesic drug selection. When the pain control effect is not good, pay attention to combined drug use and multi-mode analgesia. Common combined analgesia drugs include opioids, nonsteroidal anti-inflammatory agents and adjuvant drugs.

(2) Non-pharmacological Treatment: Non-pharmacological treatment of end-stage cancer pain refers to palliative interventional surgery, palliative radiotherapy and other treatment methods for advanced cancer patients. For example, for patients with severe pain of tumor bone metastasis, according to the status of bone destruction, supplemented by appropriate local radiotherapy Nerve destruction, percutaneous vertebroplasty, radioactive particle implantation and implantation of intrathecal drug delivery system are commonly used.

3. Nursing

(1) Observation: Observe the location, nature, degree, occurrence and duration of the patient's pain, inducible factors of pain, accompanying symptoms, psychological reactions of the patient, the impact on daily life and laboratory test results. The evaluation process should follow the principles of "routine, quantitative, comprehensive and dynamic" under the premise of minimizing interference and without increasing pain, and should be active, timely and accurate in evaluating as much as possible. The first assessment should be completed within 8 hours of the patient's admission and should be done as early as possible. Different assessment tools are selected for different patients. The same assessment tool should be used for the same patient, except when the patient's condition changes. It is necessary to conduct a

2. 治疗 应在全面评估患者的基础上，联合多学科，采用药物治疗等综合治疗原则，给予患者个性化的干预。

（1）药物治疗：遵循癌痛三阶梯止痛治疗指南是临床镇痛药选择的原则，当疼痛控制效果欠佳时，注意联合用药和多模式镇痛。常用的联合镇痛包括阿片类药物、非甾体抗炎药、辅助药物等。

（2）非药物治疗：终末期癌痛非药物治疗是指针对终末期癌症患者进行的姑息性介入手术治疗、姑息性放疗等治疗方法，例如对于肿瘤骨转移患者的剧烈疼痛，根据骨破坏状况，采用适合的局部放疗。比较常用的有神经损毁术、经皮椎体成形术、放射性粒子植入术和鞘内药物输注系统植入术等。

3. 护理

（1）病情观察：观察患者疼痛的部位、性质、程度、发生及持续的时间、疼痛的诱发因素、伴随症状、患者的心理反应、对日常生活的影响以及实验室检查结果等。评估过程应在尽量减少干扰、不增加痛苦的前提下，遵循"常规、量化、全面、动态"的原则，尽可能做到主动、及时、准确评估。首次评估应在患者入院后 8 小时内完成，且应尽早进行。针对不同患者选择合适的评估工具；同一位患者应使用同一种评估工具，患者病情发生变化时除外。需要对肿瘤患者疼痛情况和相关病情进行全面评估，综合了解患者状况。应当对患者的疼痛症状及其变化进行持续、动态的评估及评价。动态评估时机为疼痛时、给药时、给药后、剂量滴定过程中、爆发痛处理后。

comprehensive assessment of the pain and related conditions of tumor patients to comprehensively understand the status of patients. The patient's pain symptoms and their changes should be continuously and dynamically assessed and evaluated. The timing of dynamic assessment is at the time of pain, at the time of administration, after administration, during the course of dose-titration, and after the outbreak of pain.

(2) Drug Care: Oral sustained-release drugs should be swallowed as a whole and can't be taken after broken or crushed. Long-term use of large doses of nonsteroidal anti-inflammatory drugs may lead to upper gastrointestinal hemorrhage, platelet dysfunction, cardiohepatic and renal toxicity, so patients should be closely observed for signs of bleeding and status of cardiohepatic and renal functions. When opioid analgesia is applied, the patient's defecation, nausea, vomiting symptoms and sedation effect should be assessed, especially attention should be paid to nervous system changes, such as consciousness disorder or respiratory depression, timely detection of abnormal conditions, use naloxone rescue treatment if necessary.

(3) Health Education: It should be emphasized to patients and their families that analgesic treatment should be carried out under the guidance of medical staff, regular medication should be used, and it is not appropriate to adjust the dose and program by themselves; guide how to relieve pain through relaxation techniques such as music therapy, distraction, and self suggestion; assist the patient to take a comfortable position according to the location of the pain.

(4) Follow-up: Attention should be paid to the patient's pain relief and analgesic medication adherence, which should be recorded.

ii. Edema

Edema, as one of the common symptoms of advanced cancer patients, can lead to swelling, pain, dysfunction, as well as pleural, abdominal, pericardial effusion, etc., which seriously reduces

（2）药物护理：口服缓释药物应整片吞服，不能掰开、碾碎服用。长期大剂量服用非甾体抗炎药存在消化道出血、血小板功能障碍、心肝肾毒性的危险，应密切观察患者有无出血征象、心肝肾功能状态等。使用阿片类药物镇痛时，须评估患者的排便情况，恶心、呕吐症状以及镇静效果等，尤其应该注意神经系统变化，如意识障碍或呼吸抑制等，及时发现异常情况，必要时使用纳洛酮解救处理。

（3）健康教育：向患者和家属强调应在医务人员指导下进行镇痛治疗，规律用药，不宜自行调整剂量和方案。指导患者通过音乐疗法、注意力分散法、自我暗示法等放松技巧来缓解疼痛。根据疼痛的部位，协助患者采取舒适的体位。

（4）随访：应重点关注患者的疼痛缓解情况、对所服用镇痛药的依从性情况等，做好记录。

（二）水肿

水肿（edema）作为终末期癌症患者常见的症状之一，会导致肿胀、疼痛、功能障碍，以及胸腔、腹腔、心包积液等，严重降低患者的生存质量，有时甚至可导致系统脏器功能障碍甚至

the quality of life of patients, and can lead to systemic organ dysfunction or even death.

1. Assessment　It requires a detailed understanding of the diagnosis and treatment history of surgery, radiotherapy and chemotherapy. It also needs an understanding of edema due to disease or treatment, and the results of relevant tests for targeted edema management. The specific method should be selected according to age, site of edema and cause of formation. For general peripheral edema, choose circumference measurement or weight monitoring; bioimpedance analysis (BIA), volume measurement and ultrasound were used for lymphedema. To evaluate the site, type and degree of edema, and the change of edema with position and time; evaluate the impact of edema on joint flexibility, skin condition, daily activities, and quality of life.

2. Treatment　The biggest difference in intervention measures between patients with advanced cancer and other patients with edema is that patients with advanced cancer need to choose appropriate and reasonable intervention methods to alleviate the discomfort caused by edema. If only the etiological treatment is targeted, the patient's body burden will be too heavy to bear. In the face of edema that cannot be eliminated, if the patient has no obvious discomfort, it can be left untreated.

(1) Pharmacological Treatment：The main pharmacological treatment is diuretics, loop diuretics such as furosemide and tolasemide are preferred. If loop diuretic is normally used, the initial dose should be equal to or more than the long-term daily dose. Patients with peripheral edema or ascites can be treated with thiazide diuretics. If edema worsens or weight gain is greater than 2kg within 3 days, it is recommended to increase the dose. Diuretics can cause a variety of adverse reactions, and most of the drugs used for hospice care can cause peripheral edema. It is advisable to pay attention to the occurrence and degree of edema after medication. Serum electrolyte and acid-base balance should be monitored during medication.

死亡。

1. 评估　需详细了解手术、放疗、化疗等诊疗史；了解因疾病或治疗引起的水肿；了解相关检查结果，从而进行针对性的水肿管理。根据年龄、水肿部位和形成原因选择具体方法。普通周围水肿选择周径测量法或体重监测；淋巴水肿采用生物阻抗分析（bioimpedence analysis，BIA）、体积测量、超声检查等。评估水肿部位、类型、程度及水肿随体位和时间推移的变化；评估水肿对关节灵活性、皮肤状态、日常活动、生活质量的影响。

2. 治疗　终末期癌症患者水肿和其他水肿患者在干预措施上最大的区别是：终末期癌症患者需要选择恰当、合理的干预方法缓解水肿所导致的不适，若仅针对病因治疗，会导致患者身体负担过重而无法承受。面对无法消除的水肿时，若患者无明显不适感受，可暂不处理。

（1）药物治疗：药物治疗主要为利尿剂，首选袢利尿剂如呋塞米、托拉塞米。若平时使用袢利尿剂治疗，最初剂量应等于或大于长期用药的每日剂量；对周围性水肿或腹水者可联合噻嗪类利尿药治疗；如水肿加重或3天内体重增加大于2kg，建议增加药物剂量。利尿剂可引起多种不良反应，且大多数用于安宁疗护的药物会引起周围性水肿，宜在用药后关注是否有水肿并评估水肿程度。用药期间应监测血清电解质和酸碱平衡情况。

(2) Non-pharmacological Treatment

1) Manipulation：Manual lymph drainage (MLD)：MLD is a massage technique that promotes the return of lymph and tissue fluid. The direction of drainage should follow the direction of lymphatic return, and each drainage and relaxation should be adapted to the pulsation rhythm of lymphatic vessels, first the trunk and then the limbs, first the healthy side and then the affected side, first the proximal end and then the distal end.

2) Pressure treatment：Pressure treatment is to promote lymph fluid circulation by producing a certain pressure gradient, reducing lymph fluid accumulation in the tissue, so as to effectively reduce the affected limb edema. Wearable pressure garment, graded pressure elastic bandages can be used combined with foam padding, as well as intermittent inflation and compression therapy.

3) Exercise therapy：Exercise therapy refers to the use of body muscle contraction exercise training to eliminate edema. In principle, light aerobic exercise is the first choice, and then increased the amount of exercise gradually, yoga, taijiquan, walking and doing exercises are suggested, accompanying with yawning, stretching and abdominal breathing, etc., in order to change the chest pressure and try to drain the fluid retention in the chest and abdominal cavity.

3. Nursing

(1) Observation：Observe the site, range, degree, speed of development, skin blood supply, tension changes, the relationship between edema and diet, posture and activity. Observe the vital signs, body weight, jugular vein engorgement degree, nutritional status, relevant examination, the presence or absence of hydrothorax signs, ascites signs and other accompanying symptoms. Accurately record the 24-hour fluid intake and output；closely monitor the changes in urine volume, color and character of urine；regularly measure body weight and abdominal circumference, which should be measured daily if

（2）非药物治疗

1）手法治疗：手法淋巴引流（manual lymph drainage，MLD）是一种按摩技术，可促进淋巴液与组织液回流。引流方向应顺淋巴回流方向，每一次引流与放松要与淋巴管的脉动节律相适应，先躯干后肢体、先健侧后患侧、先近心端后远心端。

2）压力治疗：压力治疗是通过产生一定压力梯度促进淋巴液循环，减少淋巴液在组织中聚集，从而有效减轻患肢水肿。可使用可穿戴压力衣、分级加压弹力绷带并结合泡沫衬垫，也可使用间歇充气加压疗法。

3）运动治疗：运动治疗是指通过肌肉收缩运动训练来消除水肿。原则上先选择较轻的有氧运动，再逐渐增加运动量，一般可选择瑜伽、太极拳、行走和做操等，锻炼时配合打哈欠、伸懒腰和腹式呼吸等，以改变胸腔压力，尽量排出胸腔和腹腔潴留液体。

3. 护理

（1）病情观察：观察水肿的部位、范围、程度、发展速度以及皮肤血供、张力变化等，及其与饮食、体位和活动的关系。观察患者生命体征、体重、颈静脉充盈程度、营养状况、相关检查及有无胸水征、腹水征等伴随症状；准确记录24小时液体出入量，密切监测患者尿量、尿液的颜色和性状等变化；定期监测体重，若患者存在腹水，应同时每天测量腹围。

the patient has ascites.

(2) Skin Care: Patients with more severe edema should wear loose and soft clothes, use an air mattress or soft cushion to support the pressure part if necessary, and regularly assist them in changing their position for those who have been bedridden for a long time. When large blisters appear, sterile gauze should be bandaged after sucking the seepage, and the damaged skin should be treated in time to prevent infection. Avoid hot compress, puncture, injection, infusion and monitoring of blood pressure and body temperature at the site of edema.

(3) Dietary Care: Give a low-salt diet, limit sodium intake to 2–3g per day. Provide personalized nutritional support with high calories, appropriate protein and high vitamins according to the needs of the disease and dietary preferences, maintain a balanced nutrition, guide to eat frequent small meals, and supplement enough calories, various trace elements and vitamins.

(4) Postural Care: Use anti-embolism (elastic) stockings, and take good care of bony protrusions and pressure points. In case of dyspnea or increased pleural effusion or ascites, the patient may be in the high-pillow or semi-decumbent position. For the patients with scrotal edema, the gauze should be placed under the scrotum after cleaning, and the scrotum should be elevated to relieve the edema discomfort of the patient.

(5) Drug Care: Understand the effects and adverse reactions of related drugs, and pay attention to drug incompatibility. Do a good job of medication guidance, introduce the name, usage, dosage, effects and adverse reactions of the relevant drugs to the patients in detail, and require the patients not to increase or decrease the amount of medication without authorization, and not to stop the drug without authorization, so as to improve medication compliance.

(6) Exercise Care: According to the comprehensive physical conditions of advanced cancer patients, guide appropriate physical activity or exercise training, adhere to the combination of

（2）皮肤护理：水肿程度较重者应穿宽松、柔软衣物，必要时使用气垫床或软垫支撑受压部位，对卧床时间较长者，应定时协助其变换体位。出现大水疱时，应抽吸渗液后予以无菌纱布包扎，及时处理破损皮肤，防止感染。避免在水肿部位进行热敷、穿刺、注射和输液及监测血压、体温等操作。

（3）饮食护理：给予低盐饮食，限制钠盐摄入，每天以 2~3g 为宜。根据病情需要、饮食偏好提供高热量、适量蛋白、高维生素的个性化营养支持，保持营养均衡，指导少量多次进食，补充足够热量、各种微量元素和维生素。

（4）体位护理：使用抗栓塞（弹力）袜，做好骨凸处及受压部位护理；出现呼吸困难或胸腔积液、腹水加重时，可予以高枕卧位或半卧位；阴囊水肿者，需清洁后将纱布垫于阴囊下，并抬高阴囊，缓解患者的水肿不适。

（5）药物护理：了解相关药物的作用与不良反应，注意药物配伍禁忌。做好服药相关指导，向患者详细介绍相关药物的名称、用法、剂量、作用和不良反应，并告诉患者不可擅自增减药量，不可擅自停药，提高服药依从性。

（6）运动护理：根据终末期癌症患者身体综合情况，指导适量体力活动或运动训练，坚持动静结合，循序渐进增加活动量，适当进行肿胀肢体的功能锻炼，严重水肿患者取适宜体位卧

dynamic and static, gradually increase the amount of activity, appropriate functional exercise of swollen limbs. Patients with severe edema should take appropriate posture in bed rest.

iii. Fever

Fever in advanced cancer patients can lead to symptoms such as fatigue, weakness, and sleep disorders. The metabolic demands associated with frequent fever can lead to tumor cachexia.

1. Assessment Infectious fever should be investigated in detail by medical history, result of physical examination, time and type of the last chemotherapy, whether there is infection in the past 3 months, recent antibiotic use, epidemiological history, laboratory and imaging results, etc., so as to determine the potential site and pathogen of infection, and to assess the risk of infection-related complications. Diagnostic criteria for non-infectious fever include: body temperature is higher than 37.8°C; the fever lasts for more than 2 weeks; lack of evidence of infection; no allergic mechanism; no response to at least 7-day adequate empirical antibiotic therapy; and complete relief of fever symptoms after the naproxen test.

2. Treatment

(1) Pharmacological Treatment

1) Antipyretic drugs: Nonsteroidal anti-inflammatory drugs and steroids are effective antipyretic drugs, such as acetaminophen, ibuprofen and indomethacin for first-line treatment, dexamethasone for second-line treatment.

2) Antibacterial drugs: When controlling infection can improve the quality of life of patients, it is recommended to select appropriate antibacterial drugs according to the type of pathogen and the results of drug susceptible test.

(2) Non-pharmacological Treatment

1) Physical cooling: Warm water baths, ice blanket, ice pack and fan can also be used to relieve discomfort. To cool down with an ice pack, wrap the pack in a towel and place it on

床休息。

（三）发热

终末期癌症患者发热（fever）可以导致疲劳、乏力、虚弱、睡眠障碍等症状，与频繁发热相关的代谢需求可导致肿瘤恶病质。

1. 评估　感染性发热应详细询问病史、体格检查结果、末次化疗时间和类型、过去 3 个月内有无感染、近期抗生素使用情况、流行病学史、实验室及影像学检查结果等，确定感染潜在部位和病原体，并评估发生感染相关并发症的风险。非感染性发热的诊断标准包括：体温大于 37.8℃；发热持续时间大于 2 周；缺乏感染证据；无过敏机制；对至少 7 天足量的经验性抗生素治疗无反应；经萘普生试验，发热症状完全缓解。

2. 治疗

（1）药物治疗

1）退热药：非甾体抗炎药和类固醇等药物是有效的退热药，例如对乙酰氨基酚、布洛芬及吲哚美辛为一线治疗用药，地塞米松为二线治疗用药。

2）抗菌药：当控制感染可改善患者生存质量时，建议根据病原体类型和药敏试验结果选择适宜的抗菌药物。

（2）非药物治疗

1）物理降温：温水拭浴，也可用冰毯、冰袋、风扇等缓解不适。用冰袋降温时，用毛巾包裹冰袋放在额部、腋窝、腹股沟及颈动脉处。

the forehead, axillary fossa, groin and carotid arteries.

2) Infection control: Anti-infection prevention and infection control measures, such as hand hygiene can be taken.

3. Nursing

(1) Observation: Observe the heating time, degree and trend; evaluate concomitant symptoms, presence of signs of infection, medication history, tumor progression, and relevant test results to determine the type of fever; and assess changes in state of consciousness and vital signs.

(2) Skin Care: Choose the appropriate cooling method, pay attention to the reaction after cooling, dry the skin when sweating during the cooling process timely, change clothes at any time, keep the skin and sheets clean and dry, assist the patient to move or turn over, and prevent skin stress damage.

(3) Nutrition Care: Choose a diet with high nutritional content and easy to digest during fever. When the body temperature drops and the condition improves, it can be changed to a semi-liquid diet with high protein and high calories. Those who sweat more or are unable to eat can follow the doctor's advice to accept intravenous fluids to prevent electrolyte disorders, maintain fluid balance, and avoid collapse.

(4) Infection Prevention: Actively search for the source of infection through bacterial culture and drug susceptible test. When catheter-associated infection occurs, extubation and symptomatic treatment are recommended. When surgical wound infection or ulcerative wound infection occurs, the infected lesion should be treated in time. Take good oral care and keep mouth clean.

(5) Pharmacological Care: Follow the doctor's advice to use cooling drugs, observe and record the patient's temperature changes, gastrointestinal discomfort, sweating, granulocytopenia and other adverse reactions after medication.

2）感染控制：抗感染预防以及感染控制措施，如手卫生等。

3. 护理

（1）病情观察：观察发热时间、程度、变化趋势；评估伴随症状、是否存在感染迹象、药物治疗史、肿瘤进展情况，了解相关检查结果，以确定发热类型；评估意识状态、生命体征变化。

（2）皮肤护理：选择合适的降温方法，注意观察降温后的反应；降温过程中出汗时及时擦干皮肤，随时更换衣物，保持皮肤和床单清洁、干燥；协助患者活动或翻身，预防皮肤压力性损伤。

（3）营养护理：发热期间选用高营养且易消化的饮食；体温下降、病情好转时可改为高蛋白、高热量的半流质膳食；出汗较多或无法进食者可遵医嘱给予静脉补液，预防电解质紊乱，保持体液平衡，避免虚脱。

（4）感染预防：通过细菌培养和药敏试验等积极查找感染源；出现导管相关性感染时，建议拔管并对症处理；出现手术伤口感染或破溃伤口感染时，及时处理感染病灶；做好口腔护理，保持口腔清洁。

（5）药物护理：遵医嘱使用降温药物，观察记录用药后患者体温变化及有无胃肠道不适、大汗淋漓、粒细胞减少等不良反应。

iv. Fatigue

Cancer-related fatigue (CRF) is the most common concomitant symptom in advanced cancer patients, characterized by severe severity, long duration, and cannot be relieved by rest or sleep.

1. Assessment　According to dimension, fatigue assessment tools can be divided into:

(1) Single-dimensional Assessment: The brief fatigue inventory (BFI), fatigue severity scale (FSS), visual analogue fatigue scale (VAFS).

(2) Multi-dimensional Assessment: The revised piper fatigue scale (PFS-R), cancer fatigue scale (CFS), function assessment of cancer therapy-fatigue (FACT-F).

2. Treatment

(1) Pharmacological Treatment: Stimulants (e.g. methylphenidate), antidepressants and sedatives (e.g. paroxetine), corticosteroids (e.g. prednisone, dexamethasone) may be used.

(2) Non-Pharmacological Treatment

1) Psychosocial support: Behavioral cognitive therapy, psychoeducational therapy, mindfulness-based stress reduction training can reduce cancer-related fatigue.

2) Nutritional treatment: Targeted and individualized nutrition management plan has a positive effect on the improvement of fatigue symptoms.

3) Sleep management: Relaxation therapy, stimulus control therapy, sleep restriction therapy can improve sleep disorders.

4) Other supportive therapies: Exercise therapy, music therapy, bright white light therapy, taijiquan, etc.

3. Nursing

(1) Observation: Assess the degree of cancer-related fatigue dynamically, and identify the risk factors of fatigue in patients timely. Observe whether pain, anorexia, sleep disorders and other factors affecting fatigue exist.

（四）疲乏

癌因性疲乏（cancer-related fatigue，CRF）具有程度重、持续时间长、不能通过休息或睡眠缓解等特点，是终末期癌症患者最为常见的伴随症状。

1. 评估　疲乏评估工具根据维度分为：

（1）单维度测评：简明疲乏量表（the brief fatigue inventory，BFI）、疲乏等级量表（fatigue severity scale，FSS）、疲乏视觉模拟评分法（visual analogue fatigue scale，VAFS）。

（2）多维度测评：piper 疲乏修订量表（the revised piper fatigue scale，PFS-R）、癌因性疲乏量表（cancer fatigue scale，CFS）、癌症治疗功能评估疲乏量表（function assessment of cancer therapy-fatigue，FACT-F）。

2. 治疗

（1）药物治疗：可使用中枢兴奋剂（如哌甲酯）、抗抑郁和镇静药物（如帕罗西汀）、类固醇皮质激素（如强的松、地塞米松）。

（2）非药物治疗

1）心理社会支持：行为认知疗法、心理教育疗法、正念减压训练等可以减轻癌因性疲乏。

2）营养治疗：针对性、个体化的营养管理计划，对患者疲乏症状的改善有积极作用。

3）睡眠管理：松弛疗法、刺激控制疗法、睡眠限制疗法等可改善睡眠障碍。

4）其他支持疗法：运动疗法、音乐疗法、亮白光疗法、太极拳等。

3. 护理

（1）病情观察：动态评估癌因性疲乏的程度，及时识别患者发生疲乏的危险因素。观察有无疼痛、食欲减退、睡眠障碍等影响疲乏的因素。

(2) Pharmacological Care: Observe closely the adverse reactions of patients after taking drugs, and pay attention to observe the fatigue of patients taking drugs such as antiepileptics and sedatives.

(3) Environmental Care: Music can be played according to the preferences of patients to create a comfortable, quiet, dark and good sleep environment.

(4) Nutrition Care: Do a good job in nutrition counseling, enteral or parenteral nutrition support, correct anemia, improve nutritional status.

(5) Exercise Care: The exercise plan should be gradually and timely adjusted so as not to cause discomfort. Exercise methods such as yoga, baduanjin, taijiquan and qigong can be used. Encourage patients to take care of themselves and record a fatigue diary.

(6) Psychosocial Support: Life-and-death education for patients with excessive fear of death. For patients with little social activities, group support and family members are encouraged to accompany them. For patients with insufficient social support, try to link social resources.

v. Frailty

The clinical manifestations of frailty in advanced cancer patients are mainly weight loss, fatigue, disturbance of consciousness, gait or balance.

1. Assessment　Based on the *Guidelines for Screening and Management of Frailty in Primary Health Care*, assessment tools for frailty in advanced cancer patients include: FRAIL scale, integrated care for older people (ICOPE), the vulnerability elders survey-13 (VES-13).

2. Treatment

(1) Pharmacological Treatment

1) Anorexia: Use appetite improving drugs.

2) Sleep disorders: Use sedative-hypnotic drug.

3) Pain: Use analgesic drugs.

4) Severe nausea and vomiting: Use antiemetic drugs, pay attention to correct water and electrolyte balance disorders.

（2）药物护理：密切观察患者服药后的不良反应，注意观察服用抗癫痫药、镇静药等药物患者的疲乏情况。

（3）环境护理：可根据患者喜好播放音乐，创造舒适、安静、光线暗的良好的睡眠环境。

（4）营养护理：做好营养咨询、肠内或肠外营养支持，纠正贫血，改善营养状态。

（5）运动护理：运动计划应循序渐进、适时调整，以不出现不适为宜。可选用瑜伽、八段锦、太极拳、气功等运动方式，鼓励患者自我照护并记录疲乏日记。

（6）心理社会支持：对于过分恐惧死亡的患者，给予生死教育；对于社交活动少的患者，给予团体支持，鼓励家属陪伴；对于社会支持不足的患者，争取联系社会资源。

（五）衰弱

终末期癌症患者衰弱的临床表现，以体重减轻、疲劳、意识障碍、步态或平衡障碍等为主。

1. 评估　参照《初级卫生保健中衰弱的筛查和管理指南》，终末期癌症患者衰弱的评估工具包括：衰弱（FRAIL）量表、老年人综合照护（integrated care for older people，ICOPE）、脆弱老年人调查问卷-13（the vulnerability elders survey-13，VES-13）。

2. 治疗

（1）药物治疗

1）食欲减退：应用改善食欲药物。

2）睡眠障碍：应用镇静催眠药。

3）疼痛：应用镇痛药物。

4）严重恶心呕吐：应用止吐药物，注意纠正水电解质平衡紊乱。

5) Depression: Timely antidepressant treatment.

6) Anemia: Correct anemia.

7) Leukocyte reduction: Use leukocyte drugs.

(2) Non-Pharmacological Treatment: Including exercise, nutrition intervention, cognitive therapy, etc. It is recommended that advanced cancer patients should carry out multidimensional interventions to improve the frailty state.

3. Nursing

(1) Observation: Observe whether the patient has weight loss, fatigue, consciousness disturbance, etc., and timely identify the risk factors of the patient's frailty.

(2) Pharmacological Care: Evaluate the reasonableness of drug use in patients with frailty, correct inappropriate drug use in time, and pay attention to the adverse reactions caused by the simultaneous action of multiple drugs.

(3) Exercise Care: Under the premise of safety risk assessment and patient protection, exercise intensity, frequency, mode and time should be selected according to patients' personal interests, training conditions and purposes, carry out a gradual and individualized exercise plan for the patients.

(4) Nutrition Care: Adequate daily protein intake is recommended. Amino acid especially leucine has a positive effect on muscle protein synthesis, and leucine intake is at least 3g/d, or 0.8–1.2g/d of high-quality protein per kilogram of body weight. If the patient is deficient in vitamin D, he/she can be supplemented with vitamin D, the dose is 800–1,000IU per day.

vi. Nausea and Vomiting

Nausea is a subjective feeling of wanting to vomit, and/or unpleasant vomiting, and usually includes autonomic symptoms such as salivation, cold sweats, tachycardia, and sometimes diarrhea. Vomiting involves a complex reflex that coordinates the gastrointestinal tract, abdominal muscles, and diaphragm to expel stomach contents

5）抑郁症：及时行抗抑郁治疗。

6）贫血：纠正贫血。

7）白细胞降低：应用升白细胞药物。

（2）非药物治疗：包括运动、营养干预、认知疗法等，建议终末期癌症患者通过多维度干预方式改善衰弱状态。

3. 护理

（1）病情观察：观察患者是否体重减轻、疲劳、意识障碍等，及时识别患者发生衰弱的危险因素。

（2）药物护理：评估衰弱患者用药合理性并及时纠正不恰当用药，注意多种药物同时使用带来的不良反应。

（3）运动护理：在做好安全风险评估和保护患者的前提下，根据患者个人兴趣、训练条件和目的选择运动强度、频率、方式和时间，实施循序渐进的个体化的锻炼计划。

（4）营养护理：建议每日摄入足够的蛋白质。氨基酸尤其是亮氨酸对肌肉蛋白质合成具有积极作用，亮氨酸摄入至少 3g/d，或每天每千克体重摄入 0.8~1.2g 高质量蛋白质；若患者维生素 D 缺乏，可补充维生素 D，每天剂量为 800~1 000IU。

（六）恶心、呕吐

恶心（nausea）是一种想要呕吐或呕吐不愉快的主观感觉，通常包括自主神经症状，如流涎、冷汗、心动过速，有时还会出现腹泻。呕吐（vomiting）是一种复杂的协调反射动作，通过协调胃肠道、腹肌和膈肌经过口腔排出胃内容物。超过 46% 的终末期癌症患者会出现恶心呕吐。可引起厌食、体重减轻、疲劳及其他并发症，导

through the mouth. Nausea and vomiting are present in more than 46% of advanced cancer patients, which can cause anorexia, weight loss, fatigue and other complications, resulting in a decline in quality of life.

1. Assessment　Assessment can be made using the visual analogue scale (VAS), combined with medical and medication history.

2. Treatment

(1) Pharmacological Treatment: Metoclopramide is the first choice, haloperidol and levomepromazine could be used as alternatives. When dopamine antagonists are contraindicated or ineffective, 5-hydroxytryptamine 3 (5-HT3) receptor antagonists may be selected for treatment. For patients with persistent nausea and vomiting, titrating dopamine receptor antagonists to the maximum beneficial and tolerated dose, corticosteroids may also be considered.

(2) Non-pharmacological Treatment: Psychological therapy, behavioral therapy and other methods can be adopted to relieve symptoms.

3. Nursing

(1) Observation: Identify the causes and inducement of nausea and vomiting, evaluate the time and frequency of nausea and vomiting, and observe the color, nature, amount and odor of the vomit.

(2) Dietary Care: According to the preferences of patients, provide warm and cool food, appropriate light, avoid too sweet, greasy and spicy food with strong odor. If vomiting is frequent, monitor electrolyte changes and replenish fluids and electrolytes if necessary.

(3) Environmental Care: Keep the room quiet, clean, well-ventilated, no odor, and with appropriate temperature and humidity. Eliminate visual, auditory and olfactory discomfort caused by external stimuli. Maintain a relaxed mood.

(4) Drug Care: Comprehensive evaluation is required before medication. It requires medical staff, patients, and family members to participate in dose titration, observe the effects and adverse

致生活质量的下降。

1．评估　可采用视觉模拟量表（visual analogue scale，VAS），并结合病史和用药史进行评估。

2．治疗

（1）药物治疗：甲氧氯普胺为首选，氟哌啶醇、左美丙嗪可作为替代方案；多巴胺拮抗剂禁止使用或无效时，可选择 5- 羟色胺 3（5-HT$_3$）受体拮抗剂治疗。对持续性恶心、呕吐的患者，选用滴定多巴胺受体拮抗剂至最大获益、耐受剂量，也可考虑皮质类固醇。

（2）非药物治疗：可采用心理疗法、行为疗法等缓解症状。

3．护理

（1）病情观察：识别恶心及呕吐的原因及诱因，评估患者恶心及呕吐发生的时间、频率，观察呕吐物的颜色、性质、量及气味等。

（2）饮食护理：根据患者喜好，提供温凉食物，适当清淡，避免过甜、油腻、辛辣及带有强烈气味的食物。呕吐频繁时，监测电解质变化，必要时补充水分与电解质。

（3）环境护理：保持房间安静、整洁、通风良好、无异味、温湿度适宜。消除引起视觉、听觉及嗅觉等不适的外在刺激，保持心情放松。

（4）药物护理：用药前需全面评估，需要医护人员、患者、家属共同参与剂量滴定，观察效果和不良反应，并做好记录。

reactions, and make records.

vii. Cachexia

Cachexia is a multifactorial syndrome characterized by loss of appetite, weight loss, and skeletal muscle loss, accompanied by fatigue, dysfunction, increased treatment-related toxicity, poor quality of life, and reduced survival. About 80% of patients with malignant tumors will have cachexia before death, and about 30% of patients with malignant tumors will have cachexia as the direct cause of death.

1. Assessment Cachexia in advanced cancer patients is a continuous process, which can be divided into pre-cachexia, cachexia stage and refractory cachexia stage. Common assessment tools include: Anderson symptom assessment scale, visual analogue scale of appetite, anorexia/cachexia status subscale, memory symptom assessment scale, Edmonton symptom assessment scale, Beck self-rating depression scale, hospital anxiety and depression scale.

2. Treatment

(1) Pharmacological Treatment: Progesterone (such as megestrol acetate tablets, megestrol acetate suspension, medroxyprogesterone acetate tablets), cortisol (such as methylprednisolone, prednisone, dexamethasone), gastrointestinal motonics, psychiatric drugs (such as olanzapine, mirtazapine) can be used to improve symptoms.

(2) Non-pharmacological treatment: Including nutritional therapy, psychosocial intervention, exercise and traditional Chinese medicine therapy.

3. Nursing

(1) Observation: Observe the changes of weight loss, metabolic status, mental status, self-care ability and anorexia degree of the patients.

(2) Nutrition Care: For patients who can eat orally by themselves, oral eating should be encouraged. The infusion temperature and speed of nutrient solution should be controlled in enteral nutrition, and the nutrition tube should be properly cared. The parenteral nutrient solution should be

(七)恶病质

恶病质(cachexia)是一种多因素综合征,特征是食欲缺乏、体重下降和骨骼肌丧失,伴有疲劳、功能障碍、治疗相关毒性增加、生活质量差和生存率降低。约80%的恶性肿瘤患者死亡前会出现恶病质,约30%的恶性肿瘤患者死亡的直接原因为恶病质。

1. 评估 终末期癌症患者的恶病质是一个连续过程,可分为恶病质前期、恶病质期、难治性恶病质期。常用的评估工具包括:安德森症状评估量表、食欲视觉模拟量表、厌食/恶病质状况亚表、记忆症状评估量表、Edmonton症状评估量表、贝克抑郁自评量表、医院焦虑抑郁量表。

2. 治疗

(1) 药物治疗:可选用孕酮类药物(如醋酸甲地孕酮片、醋酸甲地孕酮混悬液、醋酸甲羟孕酮片)、皮质醇类药物(如甲泼尼龙、泼尼松、地塞米松)、胃肠动力药、精神科药物(如奥氮平、米氮平)等改善症状。

(2) 非药物治疗:营养治疗、心理社会干预、运动与中医疗法等。

3. 护理

(1) 病情观察:观察患者体重下降、代谢状态、精神状态、自理能力及厌食程度的变化情况。

(2) 营养护理:对可自行经口进食的患者,应鼓励经口进食;肠内营养应控制营养液输注温度和速度,妥善护理营养管;肠外营养液应现配现用,室温状态下24小时内应输注完毕。

prepared and used immediately, and the infusion should be completed within 24 hours at room temperature.

(3) Skin Care: Keep the patient's skin, sheets and clothes clean and dry, develop a targeted and individualized turnaround plan to avoid long-term pressure on local skin.

(4) Exercise Care: Develop individualized exercise prescription, combine passive and active exercise, resistance exercise 2–3 times per week and appropriate aerobic exercise and endurance training.

(5) Psychological Care: Provide patients with emotional support and care, encourage patients to participate in social activities.

viii. Intestinal Obstruction

Intestinal obstruction is a common digestive system symptom in advanced cancer patients, especially in patients with abdominal tumors. The incidence of advanced tumors combined with malignant intestinal obstruction is 5% to 43%, especially small intestinal obstruction is more common.

1. Assessment Abdominal examination of patients with malignant intestinal obstruction shows abdominal distension, intestinal pattern, peristaltic wave or asymmetric uplift, increased and hyperactive bowel sounds, and gas-over-water or high pitched metallic sounds can be heard. Imaging examination is a common and accurate way to evaluate the location and degree of intestinal obstruction, and determine the clinical stage initially by upright abdominal plain film or abdominal CT scan.

2. Treatment

(1) Pharmacological Treatment: Intestinal obstruction may be relieved by antisecretory drugs (e.g. scopolamine, octreotide), corticosteroids, opioids, antiemetics (e.g. metoclopramide, haloperidol), laxatives, or palliative chemotherapy.

(2) Non-pharmacological Treatment: Palliative intervention such as stent implantation can be used for patients with survival longer

（3）皮肤护理：保持患者皮肤、床单和衣服的整洁、干燥，制订针对性、个体化的翻身计划，避免局部皮肤长期受压。

（4）运动护理：制订个体化运动处方，被动和主动运动相结合，每周 2~3 次抗阻运动以及适当的有氧运动和耐力训练。

（5）心理护理：充分给予患者情感上的支持与照顾，鼓励患者参与社交活动。

（八）肠梗阻

肠梗阻（intestinal obstruction）是终末期癌症患者常见的消化系统症状，尤其是腹部肿瘤患者。晚期肿瘤合并恶性肠梗阻的发生率为 5%~43%，尤其以小肠梗阻更常见。

1. 评估 恶性肠梗阻患者腹部查体可见腹胀、肠型、蠕动波或非对称性隆起，肠鸣音增多、亢进，可听到气过水声或高调金属音。影像学检查是较为常见且准确的评估方式，一般采取腹部立位平片或腹部 CT 扫描评估肠梗阻部位及程度，初步确定临床分期。

2. 治疗

（1）药物治疗：可采用抗分泌药物（如东莨菪碱、奥曲肽）、皮质类固醇、阿片类药物、止吐药（如甲氧氯普胺、氟哌啶醇）、泻药或姑息性化疗方式缓解肠梗阻。

（2）非药物治疗：生存期大于 2 个月者可采用支架植入等姑息性介入手段；也可根据梗阻位置、并发症、预后等情况决定是否行造瘘手

than 2 months. Fistula surgery can also be decided according to the location of obstruction, complications, prognosis, etc., in order to relieve symptoms and restore intestinal function as soon as possible. After multidisciplinary discussion, parenteral nutrition intervention can be initiated for terminal patients with intestinal obstruction fasting, but parenteral nutrition is not recommended for patients in agonal stage.

3. Nursing

(1) Observation: Observe and record the degree, duration and accompanying symptoms of obstruction, and pay attention to the recovery of electrolyte and gastrointestinal function, as well as the effects and adverse reactions after medication.

(2) Dietary Care: Patients with malignant intestinal obstruction should abstain from eating and drinking, when the symptoms are relieved, they can resume eating slowly.

(3) Oral Care: During gastrointestinal decompression, patients have dry mouth and thirst symptoms, which can be alleviated by gargling cooling liquid and other measures. Pay attention to maintaining oral cleanliness.

(4) Exercise Guidance: Patients are encouraged to exercise appropriately to promote intestinal peristalsis when the condition permits.

(5) Gastrointestinal Decompression: Gastrointestinal decompression is feasible for patients with malignant intestinal obstruction, and the gastrointestinal decompression device is properly fixed to prevent the aggravation of pharyngeal stimulation during the change of position. Prevent the gastric tube from being compressed, protruding, blocking, etc., and maintain effective decompression.

(6) Abdominal Massage: Abdominal massage can effectively relieve intestinal obstruction and abdominal distension, but it is prohibited for patients with abdominal tumors. The specific method is to lie flat, overlap the roots of the palms of the patients, apply moisturizer on the abdomen to massage clockwise for 5 minutes,

术,以缓解症状并尽快恢复肠道功能;对禁食的肠梗阻终末期患者,经多学科讨论后可启动肠外营养干预,但濒死期患者不推荐使用肠外营养干预。

3. 护理

(1)病情观察:观察并记录梗阻程度、持续时间、伴随症状,关注患者电解质及胃肠功能恢复情况以及用药后的效果与不良反应。

(2)饮食护理:出现恶性肠梗阻应禁食禁饮,当症状缓解时,可缓慢分级地恢复进食。

(3)口腔护理:胃肠减压期间患者有口干、口渴症状,通过含漱清凉液等措施可减轻,注意保持口腔清洁。

(4)运动指导:鼓励患者在病情许可的情况下适量运动,促进肠道蠕动。

(5)胃肠减压术:恶性肠梗阻患者可行胃肠减压术,妥善固定胃肠减压装置,防止变换体位时加重对咽部的刺激,防止胃管受压、脱出、阻塞等,保持有效减压。

(6)腹部按摩:行腹部按摩能有效缓解肠梗阻及腹胀情况,但有腹腔肿瘤者禁止按摩。具体方法为:患者平卧,双手掌根处相互叠加,在腹部涂抹润肤霜后进行顺时针按摩,持续5分钟,每日3~4次。

3 to 4 times a day.

ix. Dyspnea

Dyspnea is a subjective feeling of insufficient inspiration and labored breathing, which is objectively manifested by changes in breathing rate, rhythm, and depth. The incidence of dyspnea increased significantly among advanced cancer patients.

1. Assessment Patient self-reports are the gold standard for assessing the severity of dyspnea. Other tools include: numerical rating scale (NRS), visual analogue scale (VAS), modified Borg scale (MBS), the modified British medical research council (mBMRC), etc.

2. Treatment

(1) Pharmacological Treatment: Common drugs are bronchodilators and opioids. When the patient's condition permits and there is no respiratory depression, the use of opioids, including morphine, cocaine, fentanyl, can significantly reduce the respiratory center sensitivity of patients, reduce oxygen consumption, and effectively improve the symptoms of dyspnea. Anxiolytics can be targeted used for dyspneic patients with severe anxiety.

(2) Non-Pharmacological Treatment: Including increased air flow, oxygen therapy, non-invasive ventilation, etc., other measures can also be taken, such as breathing relaxation training, relaxation therapy, meditation, music therapy, etc.

3. Nursing

(1) Observation: Observe the frequency, depth, and rhythm of the patient's breathing, as well as whether the patient has symptoms such as hypoxia, painful facial expressions, and flaring of alaenasi.

(2) Environmental Care: Keep the room quiet, clean, well ventilated, no odor, and with appropriate temperature and humidity. Maintaining indoor air circulation and avoiding smoke and other irritants.

(3) Drug Care: Follow the doctor's advice to administer the drug. Bronchodilators such as

（九）呼吸困难

呼吸困难（dyspnea）是患者主观上感觉吸气不足、呼吸费力，客观上表现为呼吸频率、节律和深度的改变。终末期癌症患者呼吸困难发生率明显增加。

1. 评估 患者的自我报告是评估呼吸困难严重程度的金标准。其他工具包括：呼吸困难数字分级法（numerical rating scale，NRS）、呼吸困难视觉模拟法（visual analogue scale，VAS）、改良 Borg 量表（modified Borg scale，MBS）、改良版英国医学研究会呼吸困难量表（modified British medical research council，mBMRC）等。

2. 治疗

（1）药物治疗：常见的药物有支气管扩张剂和阿片类药物。在患者病情允许、不存在呼吸抑制的情况下，使用阿片类药物包括吗啡、可卡因、芬太尼，可明显降低患者的呼吸中枢敏感性、减少耗氧量，有效改善呼吸困难的症状。针对严重焦虑的呼吸困难患者，可针对性地使用抗焦虑药。

（2）非药物治疗：包括增加空气流动、氧疗、无创通气等，也可采取其他措施，如呼吸放松训练、放松疗法、冥想、音乐疗法等。

3. 护理

（1）病情观察：观察患者呼吸的频率、深度和节律，以及患者是否有缺氧、痛苦表情和鼻翼扇动等症状。

（2）环境护理：保持房间安静、整洁、通风良好、无异味、温湿度适宜。保持室内空气流通，避免烟雾和其他刺激物。

（3）药物护理：遵医嘱给药，可使用沙丁胺醇、异丙托溴铵等支气管扩张剂雾化吸入。这

salbutamol and ipratropium bromide can be used for aerosol inhalation. These drugs relax smooth muscle, dilate bronchus, open airways and relieve dyspnea.

(4) Position Care: Patients should take a semireclining position or sitting position to reduce the returned blood volume. This method reduces the burden on the heart and relieves dyspnea by changing the position of the body.

(5) Nutrition Management: Eat a high-protein, high-nutrition, light and easy to digest diet, eat frequent small meals to avoid constipation.

(6) Respiratory Management: High-flow oxygen inhalation is administered using an oxygen mask or nasal cannula. Increasing the amount of oxygen in the blood can improve the hypoxic state of the tissues, thus easing dyspnea. Breathing training techniques, including pursed-lip breathing, and abdominal breathing (diaphragmatic breathing) can be provided to improve expiratory flow, reduce the use of auxiliary muscles, and normalize breathing rate.

x. Sleep Disorder

Sleep disorder refers to abnormal sleep amounts, changes in sleep quality, or abnormal behaviors during sleep due to various factors. The incidence of sleep disorder in advanced cancer patients is about 24% to 59%, and can even reach 95%. Insomnia is one of the most common symptoms associated with advanced cancer and can affect the quality of life of 50% to 75% of patients.

1. Assessment　Evaluation of sleep disorder includes: sleep quality, insomnia and severity, daytime sleepiness, etc. Assessment tools include: Pittsburgh sleep quality index (PSQI), insomnia severity index (ISI), Epworth sleeping scale (ESS), polysomnography (PSG), etc.

2. Treatment

(1) Pharmacological Treatment: For patients with severe sleep disorder, drugs with different mechanisms should be used in combination,

些药物能够松弛平滑肌,扩张支气管,使呼吸道通畅,缓解呼吸困难。

(4)体位护理:患者应采取半卧位或坐位,以减少回心血量。此方法通过改变身体姿势来减轻心脏负担,缓解呼吸困难。

(5)营养管理:进食高蛋白、高营养、清淡易消化饮食,少食多餐,避免便秘。

(6)呼吸管理:使用氧气面罩或鼻导管给予高流量氧气吸入。增加血液中的氧气含量可以改善组织缺氧状态,从而缓解呼吸困难。同时提供呼吸训练技巧,包括缩唇呼吸、腹式呼吸(膈式呼吸),改善呼气流量,减少辅助肌肉的使用,使呼吸频率正常化。

(十)睡眠障碍

睡眠障碍(sleep disorder)指由于各种因素影响而出现睡眠量不正常、睡眠质量改变,或是睡眠过程中出现异常行为的表现。终末期癌症患者睡眠障碍发生率约为24%~59%,甚至可达95%。失眠(insomnia)是终末期癌症患者最常伴随的症状之一,可能影响50%~75%患者的生活质量。

1. 评估　睡眠障碍的评估内容包括:睡眠质量、失眠及严重程度、白天嗜睡情况等。评估工具包括:匹兹堡睡眠质量指数量表(Pittsburgh sleep quality index,PSQI)、失眠严重程度指数(insomnia severity index,ISI)、Epworth嗜睡量表(epworth sleepness scale,ESS)、多导睡眠监测(polysomnography,PSG)等。

2. 治疗

(1)药物治疗:对严重睡眠障碍患者,不同机理药物可联合使用,如合并疼痛者给予镇痛药物,合并抑郁者联用抗抑郁药,合并精神障碍

such as analgesic drugs for patients with pain, antidepressants for patients with depression, and antipsychotic drugs for patients with mental disorders.

(2) Non-Pharmacological Treatment: Including cognitive behavioral therapy, psychotherapy, music therapy, etc.

3. Nursing

(1) Observation: Observe the patients' sleep quality, insomnia and severity, daytime sleepiness, etc., as well as the effects and adverse reactions after medication.

(2) Drug Care: Regular use of sleep promoting drugs as prescribed by the doctor, the application of interval drug therapy, usually 2 to 4 times per week. For short-term administration, it is generally no more than 3 to 4 weeks. It should be noted that when stopping the drug, it is necessary to stop the drug gradually and pay attention to the withdrawal reaction to avoid withdrawal syndrome.

(3) Environmental Management: Create a comfortable sleep environment, control sleep environmental stimulation, mainly including daytime control and sleep time control. Daytime control emphasizes getting up at a fixed time in the morning regardless of the length of sleep at night, being fully exposed to bright environments during the day (unless necessary), and reducing the number of naps during the day. Control of sleep time emphasizes the establishment and maintenance of good sleep behavior habits, limiting bed time, reducing non-sleep time in bed, such as do not use electronic products and watch TV for a long time in bed, and controling the indoor temperature during sleep, reducing the stimulation of light and noise at night.

(4) Exercise Management: Arrange appropriate recreational activities and exercise according to the patient's physical strength and condition. Moderate increases in daytime activity and regular exercise can improve the quality of sleep at night, but avoid strenuous exercise.

(5) Diet Care: Avoid eating irritating food

时合用抗精神病药。

（2）非药物治疗：包括认知行为疗法、心理疗法、音乐疗法等。

3. 护理

（1）病情观察：观察患者睡眠质量、失眠及严重程度、白天嗜睡情况等，以及用药后的作用及不良反应。

（2）药物护理：遵医嘱有规律地使用促进睡眠的药物，应用间隔给药方法进行药物治疗，通常为每周 2~4 次；而短期给药时，一般不超过 3~4 周。要注意在停药时需逐渐停药，关注停药反应，避免出现戒断综合征。

（3）环境管理：营造舒适的睡眠环境，控制睡眠环境刺激，主要包括日间控制和睡眠时间的控制。日间控制强调不管夜间睡眠时间长短都要做到清晨固定时间起床、日间充分暴露在明亮环境中（除非必需时）、减少日间小憩次数等。睡眠时间的控制强调建立并保持良好睡眠行为习惯，限制卧床时间，减少卧床的非睡眠时间，如不要在床上长时间使用电子产品、观看电视等，并控制睡眠时室内的温度，减少夜间强光及噪声的刺激。

（4）运动管理：根据患者的体力与病情安排适当的娱乐活动和运动锻炼。适当增加日间活动时间和有规律的锻炼能提高夜间的睡眠质量，但要避免进行剧烈的运动。

（5）饮食护理：避免进食刺激性的食物或药

or drugs, such as coffee, strong tea, eat a small amount of snacks and hot drinks before going to bed, but not too full, in order to promote sleep.

II. Psychological Support

Terminal cancer patients are prone to psychological crisis due to diagnosis, treatment, economic pressure, anxiety, depression, poor prognosis and other comprehensive factors. If it can't be controlled timely and alleviated effectively, it will cause individual emotional, cognitive, behavioral dysfunction of different degrees, and even suicide. The purposes of psychological support for terminal cancer patients include: helping patients and their families actively cope with illness and death, reducing the negative emotions caused by illness, improving their mental health level, to let the patients die comfortably, peacefully and with dignity.

i. Psychological Assessment

1. Assessment Tools   Include: triage assessment form (TAF), self-rating depression scale (SDS), self-rating anxiety scale (SAS), connor davidson resilience scale (CD-RISC), Herth hope index (HHI), patient health questionnaire-9 (PHQ-9), Beck scale for suicide ideation (BSS), etc.

2. Assessment Contents

(1) The assessment of the severity of psychological crisis includes three dimensions: emotion, cognition and behavior.

(2) The content of suicide risk assessment includes the risk factors of suicide, the protective factors of suicide and the assessment of suicide aura. The risk factors of suicide include demographic factors, physical disease factors, mental disease factors, sociological factors, family factors, suicidal attempt history, environmental safety factors, etc. Protective factors for suicide include coping capacity, family social support, mental health service resources, and limited access

物，如咖啡、浓茶，睡前可进食少量的点心和热饮，但不宜过饱，以促进睡眠。

二、心理支持

终末期癌症患者因诊断、治疗、经济压力、焦虑、抑郁、预后不良等综合因素，易出现心理危机（psychological crisis），若不能及时控制和有效缓解，会对个体情感、认知、行为造成不同程度的功能障碍，甚至出现自杀行为。对终末期癌症患者进行心理支持的目的包括：帮助患者和家属积极应对病情和死亡，减少病痛带来的负面情绪，提高其心理健康水平，让患者舒适、安详、有尊严地离世。

（一）心理评估

1. 评估工具   包括：三维危机评估量表（triage assessment form，TAF）、自评抑郁量表（self-rating depression scale，SDS）、自评焦虑量表（self-rating anxiety scale，SAS）、心理弹性量表（connor davidson resilience scale，CD-RISC）、Herth 希望量表（Herth hope index，HHI）、患者健康问卷（patient health questionnaire-9，PHQ-9）、贝克自杀意念量表（Beck scale for suicide ideation，BSS）等。

2. 评估内容

（1）心理危机严重程度评估包括情感、认知、行为 3 个维度。

（2）自杀风险评估内容包括自杀的危险因素、自杀的保护因素和自杀先兆评估。其中自杀的危险因素包括人口学因素、躯体疾病因素、精神疾病因素、社会学因素、家庭因素、自杀未遂史、环境安全因素等；自杀的保护因素包括应对能力、家庭社会支持、心理卫生服务资源、限制高致命性自杀方式的可及性等；自杀先兆评估包括言语和行为两种征兆，前者如直接表达"不想活了"或间接诉说"生活毫无意义"等，后者包括突然出现明显的行为改变，如"突然与朋

to highly lethal suicide methods. The assessment of suicide aura includes two signs of speech and behavior, the former one directly express "don't want to live" or indirectly telling "life is meaningless", the latter one includes sudden obvious behavior changes, such as "suddenly say goodbye to friends or family", "cutting wrists" and other suicide preparation, self-injurious behaviors.

ii. Psychological Intervention

A psychological crisis intervention team composed of multidisciplinary team members like psychological crisis intervention experts, doctors, nurses and other members, to jointly formulate and implement the psychological crisis intervention program for patients according to the evaluation results.

1. Identify the Problem Adopt the method of adapting frequency and face-to-face communication, use core listening skills such as sincerity, compassion, understanding and acceptance to understand the existing psychological crisis of patients, and understand their inner problems from the perspective of patients. Encourage patients to speak out their true feelings and help patients face reality correctly.

2. Safety Guarantee In the process of psychological crisis intervention, the primary goal of crisis intervention is to ensure safety, so as to minimize the physiological and psychological risks of patients to themselves and others. To ensure the safety of the environment, conduct regular safety checks on the environment, such as regularly checking the management of windows, knives, ropes, etc., limiting the opening size of windows, and properly keeping dangerous materials. For patients at risk of suicide, keep them in the line of sight of medical staff and family members, so as to facilitate timely observation, evaluation and emergency treatment. In the process of communicating with patients, avoid using irritating language to ensure the emotional stability of patients.

3. Psychological Counseling Implement

友或家人道别""割腕"等自杀准备、自伤行为。

（二）心理干预

成立由心理危机干预专家、医生、护士等多学科团队成员组成的心理危机干预团队，根据评估结果共同拟定并实施患者心理危机干预方案。

1. 明确问题 采取适宜频次、面对面沟通的方式，使用真诚、同情、理解和接纳等核心倾听技巧了解患者现存的心理危机，从患者角度理解其内心问题。鼓励患者说出内心的真实感受，帮助患者正确面对现实。

2. 保证安全 在心理危机干预过程中，将保证安全作为危机干预的首要目标，把患者对自我和他人的生理、心理危险性降到最低。确保环境安全，定时对环境进行安全检查，如定期检查窗户、刀具、绳索等管理情况，限制窗户开启的大小，妥善保管危险物品。对存在自杀风险的患者，使之处于医护人员及家属的视线之内，便于及时观察、评估和紧急处理。与患者沟通过程中，避免使用刺激性的语言，保证患者情绪稳定。

3. 心理疏导 针对不同心理状态的患者，

individualized care for patients with different psychological states. Listen to patients' demands, provide vent opportunities, and use language, body and other ways to soothe patients, so as to alleviate their fear of disease progression and death. Using cognitive behavior therapy, meaning therapy and other methods to give psychological support to help them step out of psychological difficulties.

4. **Plan** Make a plan according to the actual ability of the patient to make a practical plan to help them solve the problem, restore the patient's control and autonomy, and correct the emotional imbalance. In the planning process, help patient develop short-term plans to step out of the current crisis, but also to develop long-term plans to develop the patient's ability to actively respond to the crisis.

5. **Family Support** Strengthen the education for family members, encourage family members to deal with the disease correctly, do not let patients feel that they are a burden to the family, to provide patients with a steady stream of support, hope and confidence, reduce their self-felt burden, so as to help patients restore a stable psychological state.

6. **Follow-up and Feedback** Medical staff should regularly track and follow-up, timely understand the follow-up psychological treatment and rehabilitation of patients, and adjust the intervention plan according to different situations, so that patients can get timely and effective continuation of services.

iii. Psychological Evaluation

After the implementation of psychological crisis intervention, the corresponding scale is used to measure whether the psychological crisis level and suicide risk of patients have changed compared with that before the intervention. Meanwhile, the strategies used by people to promote health (SUPPH) and self-perceived burden scale (SPBS) could be used before and after the intervention to assess patients' self-efficacy and self-perceived burden, to evaluate the effect of psychological crisis intervention.

实施个体化护理。倾听患者诉求,提供宣泄机会,同时采用语言、肢体等方式予以抚慰,缓解患者对病情进展及死亡的恐惧感。运用认知行为疗法、意义疗法等方法给予心理支持,帮助他们走出心理困境。

4. **制订计划** 根据患者实际能力制订切实可行的计划,帮助其解决问题,恢复患者控制性及自主性,纠正情绪失衡状态。在制订计划的过程中,既要帮助患者制订短期计划,以协助其走出当前危机,还要拟定长期计划,培养患者积极应对危机的能力。

5. **家庭支持** 加强对家属的教育,鼓励家属正确看待疾病,不能让患者觉得自己是家属的累赘,要给患者提供源源不断的支持、希望和信心,降低其自我感受负担,从而帮助患者恢复稳定的心理状态。

6. **随访反馈** 医护人员应定期追踪、随访,及时了解患者后续心理治疗和康复情况,并根据不同的情况调整干预方案,使患者得到及时有效的延续服务。

(三)心理评价

心理危机干预实施后,使用相应量表测量患者心理危机水平和自杀风险较干预前有无改变,同时可在干预前后使用肿瘤自我效能感量表(strategies used by people to promote health,SUPPH)、自我感受负担量表(self-perceived burden scale,SPBS)评估患者的自我效能感及自我感受负担,以评价心理危机干预的效果。

III. Death Education

Death education is to provide patients with overall psychological, social and spiritual care, help them establish a scientific and positive view of life and death, respect the natural law of death inevitability, plan the final journey of life with an optimistic and positive attitude, alleviate death anxiety and fear, and improve the quality of life. At the same time, help family members rationally face the progression of the patient's disease, provide powerful psychological support, spiritual comfort and caring companionship for patients, and alleviate the bereavement grief.

i. The Meaning of Death Education

1. Let the educated understand the limitation of life and accept death as a part of life. This helps to create a sense of urgency in life, arrange life reasonably, and avoid wasting life. At the same time, it can also eliminate the fear of death, calmly face the death of oneself and others, and cherish life and love life more.

2. Develop a human spirit that respects life. To respect life is to protect life, love life, and do not abandon and harm life at will.

3. Comfort the relatives of the deceased, give them comfort and care, soothe grief, and alleviate a series of problems caused by the death.

4. It is beneficial to the palliative treatment of terminal patients and improve the quality of life.

5. Deepen people's deep understanding of death. This understanding can be transformed into a strong driving force to cherish life and health, and then improve their life and quality of life.

ii. The Content of Death Education

1. **Assessment** Assess the patient's illness, physical and mental status, cognitive ability, cooperation degree, life-and-death values, and educational level; assess patients' understanding of disease information, disease progression and

三、死亡教育

死亡教育（death education）是通过为患者提供心理、社会和精神层面的整体照护，帮助其树立科学正向的生死观，尊重死亡必然性的自然规律，以乐观、积极的态度规划生命的最后里程，缓解死亡焦虑和恐惧，进而提高生存质量。同时协助家属理性面对患者的疾病进展过程，为患者提供有力的心理支持、精神慰藉和关爱陪伴，减轻丧亲哀伤。

（一）死亡教育的意义

1. 让受教育者理解生命的有限性，接纳死亡为生命的一部分。这有助于使其产生生命的紧迫感，合理安排自己的人生，避免虚掷生命。同时，也能消除其对死亡的恐惧，坦然面对自己和他人的死亡，更加珍惜生命和热爱生活。

2. 培养尊重生命的人文精神。尊重生命就是要保护生命，热爱生命，不随意抛弃和伤害生命。

3. 安慰死者亲属，给予家属慰藉和关怀，疏导悲痛，减轻因死亡引起的一系列问题。

4. 有利于临终患者的舒缓治疗，提高生命质量。

5. 加深人们对死亡的深刻认识，这种认识能转化为珍惜生命、珍爱健康的强大动力，进而提高自己的生命和生活质量。

（二）死亡教育的内容

1. **评估** 评估患者的病情、身心状况、认知能力、配合程度、生死观、教育水平；评估患者对病情信息、疾病进展和预后的了解，以及对相关话题的交流意愿和态度；评估患者家属对患者预期病程的理解、预后的担忧和沟通需求。

prognosis, willingness and attitude to communicate on relevant topics; assess family concerns and communication needs regarding the patient's expected course of disease and prognosis.

2. Implementation   Centered on patients and their families, according to the different psychological stages of patients, choose the appropriate time and use the appropriate way to provide appropriate education and support, master communication skills and pay attention to the role of non-verbal communication.

(1) Education Environment: Provide patients with a relaxed atmosphere and privacy, and invite family members to participate and accompany.

(2) Education Content: Guide patients to correctly understand their own disease, treatment measures and current physical conditions; establish a correct view of life and death; affirm the meaning of life; correctly face and think about death-related issues; relieve death anxiety and fear; encourage family companionship and emotional support to maximize the quality of patient survival; guide family members to understand the patient's expected course of disease, rationally face the patient's prognosis, and alleviate bereavement reaction.

(3) Education Methods

1) Patient education: Start with open questions or questions that patients are interested in, carry out personalized communication, encourage patients to express their true thoughts, actively listen to patients' feelings, and truly understand and appreciate their situation. Inspire patients' values and preferences related to quality of life, affirm the value of life, enhance the dignity of life and the ability to cope and deal with death events. Patients are encouraged to make appropriate plans for their post-illness life within the limited survival period, express their expectations and wishes for family members, and encourage patients to communicate more emotionally with family members and friends, cherish the time spent together, and make

2. 实施　以患者和家属为中心，根据患者不同的心理阶段，选择适当时机、利用适当方式，提供相应的教育和支持，掌握沟通技巧并注重非语言沟通的作用。

（1）教育环境：为患者提供轻松氛围和隐私环境，邀请家属参与和陪伴。

（2）教育内容：指导患者正确认识自己的疾病、治疗措施和目前的身体状况，树立正确的生死观，肯定生命的意义，正确面对和思考死亡相关问题，缓解死亡焦虑和恐惧；鼓励家属陪伴和情感支持，最大可能提高患者生存期质量；指导家属对患者预期病程的理解，理性面对患者的预后，减轻丧亲反应。

（3）教育方法

1）患者教育：可以从开放式问题或患者感兴趣的问题开始，开展个性化交流，鼓励患者表达自己内心的真实想法，积极倾听患者的感受，真正理解和体会其处境；激发患者与生活质量相关的价值观和偏好，肯定生命价值，增强其生命的尊严和对死亡事件应对和处置的能力；鼓励患者在有限的生存期内对得病后的生活进行适当规划，表达对家庭成员的期待与愿望，鼓励患者与家属、朋友情感上多交流，珍惜共处时光，与过往和解。

peace with the past.

2) Patients' family education: Encourage family members to accompany, listen and continue to take care of their loved ones, express love for their loved ones, give emotional support, respect the patient's way of doing things, and allow them space for silence and solitude. Guide family members to discuss diseases, medical decisions, choice of treatment preferences, thoughts and wishes for later treatment, encourage patients and family members to participate in the development of advanced care planning according to their conditions, values, culture and preferences, and make rational choices and dynamic adjustments. Encourage family members and patients to discuss the future, including the choice of death location, funeral arrangements, responsibility sharing, etc., so that patients can still have a "sense of control" over their lives and achieve a peaceful death.

(4) Education Forms: Common forms of death education include death education courses in schools, death education campaigns by civil society groups, death education campaigns by academic organizations, widespread promotion of death education in the mass media, and death education by national government agencies. Flexible use of life review therapy, dignity therapy, narrative therapy, etc.; and lectures, written materials, film and media, art and music and other ways can be used together to gradually enter the topic, or by discussing other people's stories, slowly lead patients to express their own views and feelings about life and death.

Life review therapy (LRT) refers to the psychological intervention that re-analyzes and reorganizes the life course by reviewing and evaluating a person's life, and discovers the meaning of life in life review, so as to improve the level of hope. LRT was initially applied to the elderly population and has gradually been applied to cancer patients.

Dignity therapy (DT) is a patient-centered intervention. Through in-depth discussions with

2）患者家庭教育：鼓励家属陪伴、倾听和持续照顾，表达对患者的关爱，给予情感支持，尊重患者的处事方式，允许其有沉默和独处的空间；引导家人之间讨论疾病、医疗决策、治疗偏好的选择、后期治疗的想法和意愿，鼓励患者和家属根据病情、价值观、文化及偏好共同参与制订预立医疗照护计划，做出理性选择并进行动态调整；鼓励家属和患者对后事准备进行讨论，包括离世地点的选择、丧礼安排、职责分担等，让患者对自己的生活仍旧有一份"控制感"，达到平静离世。

（4）教育形式：死亡教育常使用的形式包括学校开设死亡教育课程、民间社会团体开展死亡教育活动、学术组织开展死亡教育活动、大众媒体广泛宣传死亡教育，以及国家政府机构开展死亡教育。可灵活运用人生回顾疗法、尊严疗法、叙事疗法等；也可通过讲座、书面材料、影视和媒体、艺术和音乐等方式渐入话题，或从讨论他人的故事入手，慢慢带动患者表达自己对生死的看法和感受。

人生回顾疗法（life review therapy，LRT）指通过回顾、评价人的一生来重新剖析与整理人生历程，在人生回顾中发现生命的意义，从而起到改善希望水平的心理干预作用。LRT 最初应用于老年人群，后逐渐应用于癌症患者。

尊严疗法（dignity therapy，DT）指以患者为中心，通过医护人员与患者及家属的深入沟通，

healthcare providers, patients, and their families, to respect patients' preferences and choices, and then to create individualized care plans that not only emphasize disease management but also alleviate the existential distress among terminal patients, minimize patients' suffering and discomfort, improve patients' sense of meaning in life, often used in hospice care for dying patients. DT is often conducted in the form of interviews by healthcare professionals or counselors who have been trained in systemic DT or psychological training. The interviews will be recorded, transcribed and shared with patients, providing them with an opportunity to express themselves, look back on their own life at the end of life, and feel the love and support of their families and society, thereby to alleviate psychological distress, strengthen the personal sense of value and meaning, and spend the last days of their lives with dignity.

Narrative Therapy (NT) involves encouraging patients and their families to share personal stories, helping them to express their feelings and emotions. In hospice care, NT can not only help patients and their families to pour out their pain, fear, and grief, release their repression, but also help them better face the reality of terminal illness, and find inner peace and tranquility.

IV. Social Support

Social support refers to the sum of the behaviors of a certain social network using certain material and spiritual means to provide free help to socially disadvantaged groups, and generally encompasses all external support.

1. **Assessment**　The content of social support assessment includes emotion, information, material support and social participation support. The interview schedule for social interaction (ISSI) and social support rating scale (SSRS) can be used to evaluate the social support.

2. **Implementation**　The physical, psychological, social and spiritual needs of patients and their families can be comprehensively assessed

尊重患者的意愿和选择，制订个性化的治疗计划，不仅关注疾病的控制，更注重缓解生命终末期患者对生存的困扰，减轻其痛苦和不适，提高患者的生命意义感，主要用于临终患者的姑息治疗。尊严疗法多采用访谈形式，由受过系统尊严疗法培训或心理培训的医护人员、心理咨询师实施，干预最终访谈录音将被转录成文本并反馈给被访者，为疾病终末期患者提供表达自我的机会，让患者在最后的时光回顾自己的一生，感受来自家庭和社会的关爱和支持，从而减轻患者心理痛苦，提高个人价值感和意义感，使其有尊严地度过人生的最后时光。

叙事疗法（narrative therapy，NT）指通过让患者和家属讲述自己的故事，帮助他们表达内心的感受和情绪。在安宁疗护服务中，叙事疗法不仅能帮助患者和家属倾诉内心的痛苦、恐惧和悲伤，释放内心的压抑情绪，还能帮助其更好地面对终末期疾病的现实，寻找到内心的平静和安宁。

四、社会支持

社会支持（social support）是指一定社会网络运用一定的物质和精神手段对社会弱势群体进行的无偿帮助行为的总和，一般是指来自个人之外的各种支持的总称。

1. **评估**　社会支持评估的内容包括情感、信息、物质上的支持以及社会参与支持等。可用社会交往调查表（interview schedule for social interaction，ISSI）、社会支持评估量表（social support rating scale，SSRS）进行评估。

2. **实施**　通过问卷调查、定性访谈、家庭访谈等方式全面评估患者和家属的生理、心理、社会和精神上的需求，了解其可获得的社会资

through questionnaires, qualitative interviews and family interviews, so as to understand the social resources available to them and the amount and stability of social connections, thus providing a variety of social supports. Respect and care the patients and their families, listen to their needs; provide information about the disease, palliative institutions, policy welfare and others; encourage families participate in the patient stuff to provide psychological support and emotional support.

Section 3　Hospice Services

I. Grief Counseling

Grief is the mental state and emotional response to loss. Grief resulting from bereavement can cause serious effects on health. Carers who do not receive timely and effective psychological counseling and help during bereavement will show various degrees of sadness or depression, and may develop emotional disorders or even prolonged grief disorders. Grief counseling (GC) refers to professionals who help the bereaved to adjust to the loss of a loved one and gradually return to normal life, providing counseling to prevent abnormal sadness from evolving into abnormal grief.

1. Assessment　Medical staff trained in grief counseling intervene with caregivers in need prior to the patient's death. The grief evaluation measure (GEM) and the revised grief experience inventory (R-GEI) are commonly used as assessment screening and guidance intervention tools.

2. Implementation

(1) Implementation Methods: Individual counseling, group grief counseling, behavioral therapy, mindfulness therapy, psychosocial supportive cooperation intervention, etc.

(2) Implementation Process

1) Accept the fact of death: Help caregivers accept the fact that their loved ones are about to

源、社会联系的数量和稳定性，从而提供多种多样的社会支持。如尊重、关怀患者及家属，耐心倾听其需求；提供有关疾病信息、临终机构、政策福利等信息；鼓励家属参与患者事务，提供心理支持和情感支持。

第三节　善 终 服 务

一、哀伤辅导

哀伤（grief）是由于丧失引起的心理和情绪反应。丧亲引起的哀伤会对健康造成严重影响。照顾者在丧亲时若得不到及时有效的心理辅导和帮助，会表现出不同程度的悲伤或抑郁状态，可能发展为情绪障碍甚至延长哀伤障碍。哀伤辅导（grief counseling，GC）是指专业人员协助丧亲者适应失去亲人，并逐渐恢复正常生活，对非正常的悲伤给予辅导以阻止其向非正常的哀伤演变。

1. 评估　经过哀伤辅导培训的医护人员在患者离世前对有需求的照顾者进行哀伤辅导。通常使用悲伤评估量表（grief evaluation measure，GEM）和修订版悲伤体验量表（revised grief experience inventory，R-GEI）作为评估筛查和指导干预工具。

2. 实施

（1）实施方法：个人心理辅导、团体哀伤辅导、行为疗法、正念疗法、心理社会支持性协作干预等。

（2）实施过程

1）接纳死亡事实：帮助照顾者接纳亲人即将离去的事实，鼓励当事人向逝者告别。提供

leave, and encourage the parties to bid farewell to the deceased. Provide counselling to guide caregivers to understand the facts of survival, dying, death and grief, think about life, and positively face life.

2) Encourage the release of emotions: Listen to and understand the concerns of the bereaved with empathy without interruption, and pay attention to eye contact during the process, which can be supplemented by music therapy, aromatherapy, color therapy and relieve mental pressure of the bereaved to improve the grief mood.

3) Help establish a social support network: After the death of the patient, take the initiative to contact relatives or friends of the bereaved, guide relatives and friends to comfort each other, so that the bereaved can adapt to the life after the death, know how to cope with the change of role in the future, and enter the new life as soon as possible, provide contact information such as grief support groups and psychological counseling public welfare organizations.

4) Guide life back to the right track: Guide the bereaved to give the meaning of death to the deceased and promote rapid growth after trauma.

II. Corpse Care

Corpse care refers to a series of nursing procedures after the death of the patient, involving the deceased, family, hospital, psychology, sociology and other issues. Corpse care is an important factor to improve the quality of hospice care, and it is a necessary link of hospice care for advanced cancer patients. Good corpse care is not only sympathy and respect for the deceased, but also support and psychological comfort for the family.

1. Assessment　The care team assesses the family's wishes and needs for corpse care to determine if the deceased had the need of body donation. Assess the general condition of the body (appearance, cleanliness, whether has wounds and

善别辅导，引导照顾者认识生存、临终、死亡和哀伤等事实，思考生命，积极面对人生。

2）鼓励释放情绪：以同理心聆听和了解丧亲者的担忧，中间不打断，过程中应注意眼神接触和目光交流，可辅以音乐疗法、香薰疗法、色彩疗法等缓解丧亲者精神压力，改善哀伤情绪。

3）帮助建立社会支持网络：患者离世后，主动联系丧亲者亲戚或朋友，指导亲友间相互安慰诉说，使丧亲者适应逝者离去后的生活，知晓如何应对日后角色的转变，尽快投入新生活，提供哀伤互助小组和心理咨询公益组织的联系方式。

4）引导生活重回正轨：引导丧亲者赋予逝者死亡的意义，促进创伤后的快速成长。

二、遗体护理

遗体护理是指患者死亡后，对其遗体进行一系列的护理程序，涉及逝者、家庭、医院以及心理学、社会学等多方面的问题。遗体护理是提高安宁疗护质量的重要因素，是终末期癌症患者安宁疗护的必要环节。良好的遗体护理既是对离世者的同情和尊重，也是对家属的支持和心理慰藉。

1. 评估　护理团队评估家属对遗体护理的意愿及需求，明确逝者是否有遗体捐献需求。评估遗体的一般情况（面容，清洁程度，有无伤口、引流管等）、诊断、治疗、抢救过程、死亡时间、死亡原因以及逝者是否有传染病。评估家

drainage tubes, etc.), diagnosis, treatment, rescue process, time of death, cause of death, and whether the deceased had infectious diseases. Assess the mood and level of cooperation of family members, and understand the cultural background of the deceased and their families.

2. Implementation   After the death of the patient, the corpse is cared for after a thorough evaluation.

(1) Preparations Before Implementation

1) The implementer should dress neatly, manicure nails, wash hands, wear a mask and gloves, and prepare isolation gowns, medical round hats and disinfectant if necessary. It requires a serious manner and solemn expression.

2) Prepare vascular forceps, scissors, cotton swabs, turpentine, bandages, non-absorbent cotton balls, kidney dishs, combs, corpse bags or sheets, scrubbing tools, screens, identification cards, etc.

3) The environment is quiet and solemn, close the doors and windows, and use screens if necessary.

4) Politely address and sincerely greet the family members of the deceased, and take the initiative to introduce yourself.

(2) Implementation Process

1) Tube care: If there are no special circumstances, after obtaining the consent of the family, remove all kinds of medical instruments, oxygen tubes, infusion tubes, drainage tubes, gastric tubes, urethral catheters and other therapeutic materials.

2) Caulk the cavity: Use the vascular clamp to caulk the cotton ball in the nasal cavity, mouth, ear canal, anus, vagina and other cavity openings, so as to avoid the outflow of liquid from the cavity, pay attention that the cotton ball is not exposed.

3) Corpse cleaning: Put the head of the bed flat, make the corpse lie on the back, cushion the pillow under the head, prevent facial congestion and discoloration. Clean the face, comb the hair of the deceased. Close the mouth and eyes to maintain the appearance of the corpse and avoid facial deformation. Cover with a screen, remove the

属情绪及合作程度,了解逝者及其家属的文化背景。

2. 实施   患者死亡后,进行全面评估后开展遗体护理。

(1)实施前准备

1)实施者应衣帽整洁,修剪指甲、洗手、戴口罩、戴手套,必要时备隔离衣、医用圆帽及消毒剂等。态度严肃认真、表情庄重。

2)准备血管钳、剪刀、棉签、松节油、绷带、不脱脂棉球、弯盘、梳子、尸袋或尸单、擦洗用具、屏风、尸体鉴别卡等。

3)环境安静、肃穆,关好门窗,必要时使用屏风遮挡。

4)礼貌称呼并真诚问候离世者家属,主动进行自我介绍。

(2)实施过程

1)管道护理:若无特殊情况,征得家属同意后,撤去各种医疗仪器,包括吸氧管、输液管、引流管、胃管、导尿管等治疗用物。

2)填塞腔道:用血管钳将棉球填塞于鼻腔、口腔、耳道、肛门、阴道等腔道口,以免腔道流出液体,注意棉球不外露。

3)遗体清洁:放平床头,使遗体仰卧,头下垫软枕,防止面部淤血、变色。清洁面部,为逝者梳理头发。闭合口、眼,维持遗体外观,避免面部变形。用屏风遮挡,脱去逝者衣裤,擦净全身,用松节油或乙醇擦净胶布痕迹。按逝者生前遗愿或家属要求穿好衣物。双臂置于遗体两侧,用大单遮盖遗体。

deceased's clothes, wipe the corpse, and wipe away any tape traces with turpentine or ethanol. Dress in accordance with the wishes of the deceased or at the request of the family. Keep the arms at the sides of the corpse and cover the corpse with a large sheet.

4) Corpse identification: The first identification card is tied to the right wrist of the corpse, the corpse is put into a corpse bag or wrapped with a corpse sheet, and the chest, waist, and ankle are firmly fixed with bandages. The second ID card is attached to the chest of the corpse bag or to the corpse sheet.

(Ni Ping)

4）遗体辨识：第一张识别卡系在遗体右手腕部，把遗体放进尸袋里或用尸单包裹，需用绷带在胸部、腰部、踝部牢牢固定。第二张识别卡缚在尸袋胸前或尸单上。

（倪　平）

Key Points

1. Hospice care is a supportive therapy for patients with advanced cancer. It is called hospice care when the disease is managed from clinical treatment to symptom control.

2. Hospice care is not giving up treatment, but the goal of treatment is shifted from the disease to the symptoms.

3. Hospice care can control patients' painful symptoms and relieve their physical, mental and spiritual distress, with the ultimate goal of making the dying die well, the bereaved separate well, the living live well, and live with more dignity.

4. Hospice care can only be provided to patients who have been professionally determined by two physicians, be suffering from an incurable disease and whose survival is not more than six months.

5. Hospice care service connotation is mainly reflected in five aspects, namely, "whole person, whole family, whole process, whole team, whole community".

6. While hospice care is important, it still faces some problems in its development, such as lack of funding and resources, insufficient professional staff and low public awareness.

7. Symptom control and care are core

内容摘要

1. 安宁疗护是针对终末期癌症患者的一种支持性疗法，当疾病处理从临床治疗走向症状控制的时候，就可以称为安宁疗护。

2. 安宁疗护并不是放弃治疗，而是治疗的目标从疾病转向症状。

3. 安宁疗护可以控制患者的痛苦症状，缓解他们的身体、心理和精神困扰，而最终目的是让临终者善终、失亲者善别、在世者善生，让生命更有尊严。

4. 须由两位专业医师认定，罹患的是无法治愈的疾病，其生存期大概不超过 6 个月的患者，才可以接受安宁疗护。

5. 安宁疗护的服务内涵主要体现在 5 个方面，即"全人、全家、全程、全队、全社区"。

6. 安宁疗护虽具有重要意义，但在发展过程中仍面临着一些问题，例如资金和资源的短缺、专业人员的不足以及公众认知度低等问题。

7. 症状控制和护理是安宁疗护的核心内

components of hospice care. Common symptoms of terminal patients include pain, edema, fever, dyspnea, nausea and vomiting, and sleep disorder, which bring great pain to patients. Through hospice care services such as rational medication, symptomatic treatment, and nursing care, symptoms can be relieved and controlled, pain can be alleviated, and the quality of life of patients can be improved to the greatest extent.

8. The purposes of psychological support for terminal patients include: appropriately applying communication skills to establish a trusting relationship with the patient, guiding the patient to face and accept the disease situation, helping the patient to cope with emotional reactions, respecting the patient's will to make decisions, and allowing the patient to maintain an optimistic and adaptive attitude through the end of life, so as to pass away comfortably, peacefully and with dignity.

9. Death education aims to provide patients with overall psychological, social and spiritual care, help them establish a scientific and positive outlook on life and death, respect the natural law of death inevitability, plan the final journey of life with an optimistic and positive attitude, alleviate death anxiety and fear, and improve the quality of life. At the same time, help family members rationally face the progression of the patient's disease, provide powerful psychological support, spiritual comfort and caring companionship for patients, and alleviate the bereavement grief.

10. Grief counseling refers to professionals assisting the bereaved to adapt to the loss of their loved ones and gradually return to a normal life, providing counseling for abnormal sadness to prevent it from evolving into abnormal grief.

11. Corpse care refers to a series of nursing procedures for the body after the death of the patient, involving the deceased, the family, the hospital, as well as psychological, sociological and other issues.

容。终末期患者常见的症状包括疼痛、水肿、发热、呼吸困难、恶心呕吐、睡眠障碍等，给患者带来极大的痛苦。通过合理用药、对症治疗和护理等安宁疗护服务，可缓解和控制症状、减轻痛苦，最大程度地提高患者的生活质量。

8. 对终末期患者进行心理支持的目的包括：恰当地应用沟通技巧与患者建立信任关系，引导患者面对和接受疾病状况，帮助患者应对情绪反应，尊重患者作出决策的意愿，让其保持乐观顺应的态度度过生命末期，从而舒适、安详、有尊严地离世。

9. 死亡教育是通过为患者提供心理、社会和精神层面的整体照护，帮助其树立科学正向的生死观，尊重死亡必然性的自然规律，以乐观、积极的态度规划生命的最后里程，缓解死亡焦虑和恐惧，进而提高生存质量。同时协助家属理性面对患者的疾病进展过程，为患者提供有力的心理支持、精神慰藉和关爱陪伴，减轻丧亲哀伤。

10. 哀伤辅导是指专业人员协助丧亲者适应失去亲人，并逐渐恢复正常生活，对非正常的悲伤给予辅导以阻止其向非正常的哀伤演变。

11. 遗体护理是指患者死亡后，对其遗体进行一系列的护理程序，涉及逝者、家庭、医院以及心理学、社会学等多方面的问题。

Exercises

(Questions 1 to 2 share the same question stem)

Li, a 61-year-old female, was diagnosed with stage Ⅳ colon cancer three months after undergoing palliative surgery and colostomy, with multiple metastases in both lungs, abdomen, mediastinal lymph nodes and liver. After palliative surgery, the patient received three rounds of chemotherapy, but the response was poor. After the third round, the patient experienced nausea and vomiting, as well as persistent pain in the lower left abdomen and intermittent pain in the left leg (pain score NRS 4–5), with two to three episodes of breakthrough pain during the night (NRS 6–7). The patient lived with her daughter, who is married and has two daughters. When healthy, the patient was primarily responsible for taking care of her two granddaughters, but since falling ill, her daughter became the primary caregiver. Upon admission, the patient presented with a low mood. Due to her husband and daughter concealing part of her diagnosis, the patient could not understand why her condition had not improved after treatment. The patient reported poor sleep at night, difficulty falling asleep, and difficulty waking up in the morning. Physical examination showed that the patient was emaciated with a mildly distended abdomen. B-ultrasound revealed a small amount of ascites, with healthy mucosa around the stoma and normal bowel motility. The patient's serum albumin level was low (29g/L), with a nutritional score of 4. The Depression Screening Scale (PHQ-9) score was 15, indicating moderate to severe depression. The patient's condition is complex and in the terminal stage, and the hospital implements palliative care with the consent of the patient and their family.

1. How can we help to alleviate the patient's physical and psychological suffering based on her condition? Please analyze this using pain management and psychological interventions for

思　考　题

（1~2 题共用题干）

李某，女，61 岁，姑息手术和结肠造口术后 3 个月被诊断为Ⅳ期结肠癌，双肺、腹部、纵隔淋巴结肝脏等多处有转移。患者在姑息性手术后接受了 3 轮化疗，但反应不佳，在第三轮化疗后出现恶心呕吐，且表现出左下腹持续性疼痛和左腿间歇性疼痛（疼痛评分为 NRS 4~5 分），夜间伴有 2 至 3 次突发性疼痛（NRS 6~7 分）。患者与女儿同住，女儿已婚并有 2 个女儿。患者健康时主要负责照顾 2 个外孙女，但患病后，女儿成为患者的主要照顾者。患者入院时情绪低落。由于患者丈夫与女儿隐瞒部分病情，患者未能理解病情为何经持续治疗后仍未好转。患者报告夜间睡眠差、入睡困难，早晨醒来困难。体格检查结果显示患者体形消瘦，腹部轻度膨隆。B 超提示少量腹水，造口周围黏膜红润，肠道蠕动良好。患者血清白蛋白水平较低（29g/L），营养评分 4 分，抑郁筛查量表（PHQ-9）15 分，提示中度至重度抑郁。患者病情复杂且处于终末期，医院在患者及其家属同意下实施安宁疗护。

1. 针对患者病情，如何帮助缓解其身体和心理痛苦？请结合本案例中的疼痛管理和抑郁症心理干预进行分析。

depression in the context of this case.

2. During the end-of-life phase, family members often face immense psychological pressure and emotional distress. Please analyze how psychological support can assist family members in coping with the emotional challenges of end-of-life care.

(Questions 3 to 4 share the same question stem)

Zhao, a 28-year-old female, presented with pain in her buttocks and legs, bowel and bladder discomfort, gait disturbances, and a large mass in her sacrum. After the mass was surgically removed, the lesion was diagnosed as alveolar soft part sarcoma (ASPS). Post-surgery, the patient experienced improvements in pain and mobility, but she refused adjuvant therapy and chose hospice care, and passed away two years later. After her death, her husband was deeply distressed and unable to accept her departure. He often sits alone by the window where his wife used to sit, crying uncontrollably, unwilling to communicate with others, and exhibiting noticeable feelings of loss and helplessness in daily life.

3. Please analyze the potential psychological distress that caregivers may experience during the grieving process.

4. After the patient's death, her husband faces immense grief and psychological pressure. Discuss how bereavement counseling can be provided to the caregiver to alleviate their suffering.

2. 在患者生命末期,家庭成员常面临巨大心理压力与情感困扰。请分析如何通过心理支持帮助患者家庭成员缓解临终护理中的情感困境。

(3~4 题共用题干)

赵某,女,28 岁,因臀腿部疼痛,肠道、膀胱不适,步态障碍以及骶部大肿块就诊。肿块经手术切除后,经病理检查确诊为肺泡软组织肉瘤。手术后,患者疼痛和行走能力有所改善,但患者拒绝辅助治疗选择安宁疗护,术后 2 年去世。患者去世后,其丈夫深感痛苦,无法接受妻子的离世,常独自坐在妻子生前常坐的窗前,泪流满面,不愿与外界沟通,甚至在日常生活中表现出明显的失落和无助感。

3. 请分析照顾者在丧亲过程中可能遇到的心理困扰。

4. 患者丈夫在患者去世后,面临巨大的哀伤和心理压力。请讨论如何对照顾者进行丧亲辅导以减轻其痛苦。

Chapter 11

The Management and Nursing of Community Emergency Public Health Events

11章 数字内容

第十一章

社区突发公共卫生事件的管理和护理

NURSING

Learning Objectives

Knowledge Objectives

1. Can state the concepts of emergency public health events, emergency management for public health, and disasters.

2. Can briefly describe the characteristics and grading of emergency public health events; key points for prevention, monitoring, early warning, and reporting of emergency public health events in communities.

学习目标

知识目标

1. 能陈述突发公共卫生事件、突发公共卫生应急管理、灾害的概念。

2. 能简述突发公共卫生事件的特点、分级；社区突发公共卫生事件预防、监测、预警和报告要点。

3. Can briefly describe the key points of reporting and classification management for infectious diseases.

4. Can explain the psychological stress response of the population after disasters.

5. Can explain the theoretical content of the 4R in crisis response.

- Ability Objectives

1. Can accurately and quickly assess emergency public health events, establish community contingency plans, and manage key patients.

2. Can properly apply relevant knowledge to provide on-site rescue for disaster victims.

3. Can properly apply relevant knowledge to conduct psychological assessment and care for post disaster populations.

- Quality Objectives

1. Enhance the sense of responsibility of "healthy China, medical care first", establish the professional ideal of wholeheartedly serving the people's health, and adopt a social prevention view of prevention-first and combining prevention and treatment.

2. Cultivate the spirit of humanity, universal love, dedication, and possess the qualities of preventing, responding quickly, and providing assistance to emergency public health events.

3. Establish a correct view of disasters, cultivate crisis awareness and a sense of responsibility.

In a certain winter, a community with approximately 25,000 residents experienced a sudden influenza outbreak. The first case was identified in an elementary school, with over 200 febrile cases reported within 72 hours. Daily patient volume at community clinics surged to five times the normal capacity. Panic-buying of medications

3. 能简述传染病的报告与分类管理要点。

4. 能阐述灾害后人群心理应激反应。

5. 能阐述危机应对的4R理论内容。

- 能力目标

1. 能正确、快速评估突发公共卫生事件,建立社区预案并对重点患者进行管理。

2. 能运用相关的知识对灾害伤病员进行现场救护。

3. 能运用相关知识对灾后人群进行心理评估和心理护理。

- 素质目标

1. 提升"健康中国,医护先行"的责任感,树立全心全意为人民健康服务的职业理想和预防为主、防治结合的社会预防观。

2. 培养人道、博爱、奉献精神,具备突发公共卫生事件预防、快速反应及救助的素质。

3. 树立正确的灾难观,培养危机意识和担当精神。

某年冬季,一个常住人口约2.5万的社区突然暴发流感疫情。首例病例出现在社区小学,三天内累计报告发热病例超过200例,社区医疗机构单日接诊量突破日常5倍。居民中出现恐慌性囤药、社交媒体谣言传播等现象,部分老年人因基础疾病加重需要转诊上级医院。请结合突发公共卫生事件管理原则分析:

and misinformation spreading on social media were observed, while some elderly patients with chronic conditions required emergency referrals. Based on public health emergency management principles, discuss:

Queations:

1. What are the procedures and methods for reporting infectious diseases and emergency public health events, and how are the reporting deadlines defined?

2. What measures should be taken to handle infectious diseases and emergency public health events?

Since the 20th century, China has continuously faced the challenges of emergency public health events due to accelerated urbanization, environmental changes, climate change, pathogen variation, and other factors. Emergency public health events have a wide range of impacts, causing significant harm and far-reaching consequences. They not only cause harm to the health of community residents and endanger their lives, but also pose a serious threat to the social economy, ecological environment, and national stability. The community, as the lowest-level organization for emergency management, bears important responsibilities in emergency management. It assumes the responsibility of monitoring, reporting, preventing the occurrence and controlling their development in various kinds of emergency public health events and infectious disease control.

Section 1　Overview

I. Concept of Emergency Public Health Events

Emergency public health events refer to major infectious disease outbreaks, group diseases of unknown causes, major food and occupational poisoning, and other events that suddenly occur

请思考：

1. 传染病和突发公共卫生事件的报告程序和方式是怎样的？报告时限是如何规定的？

2. 传染病和突发公共卫生事件的处理措施有哪些？

20世纪以来，由于城市化进程加快、环境改变、气候变化、病原微生物变异等多种因素的共同影响，我国面临着各类突发公共卫生事件的挑战。突发公共卫生事件波及面广、危害较大、影响深远，不仅对社区居民造成健康伤害，甚至危及生命，同时也对社会经济、生态环境和国家稳定造成严重威胁。社区作为应急管理最基层的组织，承担着应急管理重要任务，在各类突发公共卫生事件及传染病防控中承担监测、报告、预防和控制的责任。

第一节　概　　述

一、突发公共卫生事件的概念

突发公共卫生事件是指突然发生，造成或者可能造成社会公众健康严重损害的重大传染病疫情、群体性不明原因的疾病、重大食物和职业中毒以及其他严重影响公众健康的事件。亦

and cause or may cause serious damage to public health. It also refers to sudden, unpredictable public health-related emergencies with a certain degree of harmful impact.

Community emergency public health events must:

1. Affect beyond a single community.

2. Result in significant casualties, economic losses, or threat to residents' lives and property.

3. Escalate and result in more severe consequences if without timely control measures.

4. Require government coordination of multiple departments and social resources.

5. Mobilize community for joint assessment, prevention, and control.

6. Activate an emergency plan.

II. Classification, Grading, and Characteristics of Emergency Public Health Events

i. Classification of Emergency Public Health Events

Classification methods for emergency public health events vary by cause. Types include:

1. Plague, cholera, viral hepatitis, dysentery, epidemic hemorrhagic fever, anthrax, and other significant outbreaks caused by epidemics.

2. Bacterial and chemical food contamination, poisoning, and toxic animal and plant poisoning causing large numbers of poisoned individuals or critically ill patients.

3. Tap water factory water, pipe network water, water supply system, simple tap water pollution, etc.

4. Radioactive contamination due to the use of radioactive isotopes, intense radiation exposure, reactor operation failures, or accidental emissions.

5. Mass acute chemical poisoning resulting from asphyxiating gases, irritating gases, anesthetic toxins, neurotoxins, and other substances.

6. Events that endanger the lives and health of groups, such as earthquakes, floods, wind damages, fires, mud avalanche, landslides, various

指突然发生的、不可预测的、有公共卫生属性，并且其危害影响达到一定程度的突发事件。

符合以下几个特征，可界定为社区突发公共卫生事件。

1. 波及范围超过一个社区。

2. 伤亡人数较多、经济损失较大，或者可能危及居民生命、导致财产损失。

3. 如不及时采取有效控制措施，将进一步扩大并引发更严重后果。

4. 需要政府协调多部门参与，统一调配社会资源。

5. 需要社区总动员，共同评估、预防和控制。

6. 需要启动应急预案。

二、突发公共卫生事件的分类、分级及特点

（一）突发公共卫生事件的分类

突发公共卫生事件的分类方法有多种，从发生原因上来分，常见的突发公共卫生事件如下：

1. 鼠疫、霍乱、病毒性肝炎、痢疾、流行性出血热、炭疽等暴发、流行引发的重大疫情。

2. 中毒人数多或导致大量危重患者的细菌性、化学性食品污染、中毒，有毒动植物中毒。

3. 自来水出厂水及管网水污染、供水系统污染、简易自来水污染等。

4. 使用放射性同位素及强辐射照射、反应堆运转故障或事故排放引起的放射性污染。

5. 因窒息性气体、刺激性气体、麻醉性毒物、神经性毒物等引起的群体性急性化学物质中毒等。

6. 地震、水灾、风灾、火灾、泥石流、山体滑坡、各类交通事故、非人为因素爆炸、建筑物倒塌、煤井坑道坍塌及生产事故，以及恐怖事件、

traffic accidents, non-human factor explosions, building collapses, coal mine tunnel collapses and production accidents, as well as explosions, poisoning, arson, and other incidents caused by terrorist events and other reasons.

ii. Grading of Emergency Public Health Events

Under the *National Public Health Emergency Response Plan*, public health emergencies are classified into four levels based on their nature, severity of harm, and geographical scope: extremely severe (Level Ⅰ), severe (Level Ⅱ), relatively severe (Level Ⅲ), general (Level Ⅳ). Extremely severe emergency public health events mainly include:

1. Occurrence of pulmonary plague or pulmonary anthrax in large/medium cities with spreading trends, or such epidemics spreading across two or more provinces with continued expansion;

2. Emergence of Severe Acute Respiratory Syndrome (SARS) or highly pathogenic avian influenza cases with transmission risks;

3. Clustering of unexplained diseases across multiple provinces with a spreading trend;

4. Outbreak or introduction of novel infectious diseases previously unidentified in China showing transmission potential, or resurgence of eradicated infectious diseases;

5. Loss incidents involving highly virulent bacterial strains, viral strains, or pathogenic agents;

6. Importation of severe infectious disease cases from neighboring countries/regions or those with flight connections to China, seriously endangering national public health security;

7. Other particularly significant public health emergencies as determined by the health administrative department under the State Council.

iii. Characteristics

1. Uncertainty of Event Occurrence

From a macro perspective, emergency public health

其他原因引发的爆炸、投毒、纵火等危及群体生命健康安全的事件。

（二）突发公共卫生事件的分级

根据《国家突发公共卫生事件应急预案》，按照突发公共卫生事件性质、危害程度、涉及范围，突发公共卫生事件可划分为特别重大（Ⅰ级）、重大（Ⅱ级）、较大（Ⅲ级）和一般（Ⅳ级）四级。其中，特别重大突发公共卫生事件主要包括：

1. 肺鼠疫、肺炭疽在大、中城市发生并有扩散趋势，或肺鼠疫、肺炭疽疫情波及2个以上的省份，并有进一步扩散趋势。

2. 发生传染性非典型肺炎、人感染高致病性禽流感病例，并有扩散趋势。

3. 涉及多个省份的群体性不明原因疾病，并有扩散趋势。

4. 发生新传染病或我国尚未发现的传染病发生或传入，并有扩散趋势，或发现我国已消灭的传染病重新流行。

5. 发生烈性病菌株、毒株、致病因子等丢失事件。

6. 周边以及与我国通航的国家和地区发生特大传染病疫情，并出现输入性病例，严重危及我国公共卫生安全的事件。

7. 国务院卫生行政部门认定的其他特别重大突发公共卫生事件。

（三）突发公共卫生事件的特点

1. 发生的不确定性　从宏观上讲，突发公共卫生事件的发生有其内在的规律，但是，就目

events follow certain inherent regularity, but at the current level of human understanding, it is still difficult to fully comprehend these regularity. In recent years, emergency public health events have occurred very suddenly, and neither professional technical institutions nor relevant professionals can predict the specific location and timing of their occurrence.

2. Uncertainty of Event Development First of all, emergency public health events are inherently uncertain, and their emergence, development and evolution trajectory are influenced and driven by multiple factors. Secondly, the uncertainty of information itself and the lack of information will increase the uncertainty of decision-making. On the other hand, the high intensity of information demand will also give rise to excessive information, which will make chaotic and complicated information flooded in various information carriers. In the absence of effective information filtering means, it will lead to decision-makers at a loss, thus increasing the difficulty of decision-making. Finally, an emergency may evolve into a crisis due to the amplification effect of the media, the urgent demands and pressures of the public, and the limitations of managers' experience and ability.

3. Group and Publicity Both outbreaks of infectious diseases and food safety incidents pose a threat to public life and health safety. The group and publicity of emergency public health events are manifested through the group harm, group behavior, group events, and group social pressure they cause. The media and public attention caused by the event will further push it onto the agenda of the government and the public, making it a major public issue of concern for the entire society.

4. Urgency and Difficulty Emergency public health events are often unpredictable and sudden, threatening the lives and health of the people and the normal life of the society as soon as they appear. Emergency public health events are characterized by uncertainty and dynamic evolution in their occurrence and development,

前人类的认识水平来看，还很难把握其内在的规律。近年来发生的突发公共卫生事件，发生都非常突然，无论是专业技术机构，还是相关的专业技术人员，都无法预测其发生的具体地点和时间。

2. 发展的不确定性 首先，突发公共卫生事件本身具有不确定性，其产生、发展、演变轨迹受多重因素的影响和驱动。其次，信息本身的不确定性和信息缺乏会加大决策的不确定性，另一方面，高强度的信息需求则会导致信息过量，使混乱而繁杂的信息充斥于各种信息载体，在缺乏有效信息过滤手段的情况下，会导致决策者无所适从，从而加大决策难度。最后，有可能因为媒体的放大效应、公众迫切的诉求和压力、管理者经验和能力的限制，突发事件演变成危机。

3. 群体性和公共性 无论是传染病疫情暴发，还是食品安全事件的发生都会给公众的生命和健康安全带来威胁。突发公共卫生事件的群体性和公共性通过其造成的群体性危害、群体行为、群体社会压力等方式表现出来。事件所引发的媒体和公众的关注，又会进一步将其推向政府和公众的议事日程，使之成为整个社会关注的重大公共问题。

4. 紧迫性和艰巨性 突发公共卫生事件往往不易预测，具有突发性，一出现就威胁到群众的生命健康和社会的正常生活。突发公共卫生事件发生、发展变化的不确定性和动态演变的特点，迫切要求应对处置的及时性。此外，紧迫性还体现在应对者所面临的时间和心理的巨大压力：首先是快速决策的压力，事发突然、情况

which urgently requires timely response and handling. In addition, the urgency is reflected in the tremendous time and psychological pressures faced by the responders: first, the pressure to make quick decisions. The incident is sudden, the situation is urgent, the harm is serious, the information is limited, and the correct decision must be made quickly in a short time. If the decision is not made timely, it is likely to miss the opportunity and cause endless problems. Secondly, the pressure to quickly mobilize human, financial, material and information resources in a very short period of time to achieve effective coordination and integration of various resources.

Section 2　Emergency Management for Community Emergency Public Health Events

Emergency management for public health refers to the various activities that take corresponding measures such as monitoring, early warning, material reserve, and on-site disposal after the occurrence or occurrence of emergency public health events, in order to timely prevent potential factors that may cause emergency public health events, control the occurrence of emergency public health events, and reduce its harm to society, politics, economy, people's health, and life safety.

I. Relevant Theories of Emergency Management

Emergency management refers to the process of effectively responding, controlling, and handling emergencies based on scientific analysis of their causes, processes, and consequences, utilizing various resources, methods to reduce their harm. The most representative emergency management theory among them is the crisis management theory of Robert Heath, an American crisis management expert. This theory divides crisis management

紧急、危害严重、信息有限，还要在有限的时间内快速作出正确的决策，如果不及时作出决策，很可能错失良机，贻患无穷。其次，需要应对者在极短的时间内迅速调动人、财、物、信息资源，实现对各种资源有效的协调与整合。

第二节　社区突发公共卫生事件应急管理

突发公共卫生应急管理指在突发公共卫生事件发生或发生后，采取相应的监测、预警、物资储备等应急准备，以及现场处置等措施，及时预防引起公共卫生事件的潜在因素，控制已发生的突发公共卫生事件，以减轻其对社会、政治、经济、人民健康与生命安全危害的各项活动。

一、应急管理相关理论

应急管理是指为了降低突发事件的危害，基于对突发事件的原因、过程以及后果的科学分析，有效利用各方面资源，运用各种手段与方法对突发事件进行有效的应对、控制和处理的过程。其中最有代表性的应急管理理论是美国危机管理专家 Robert Heath 的危机管理理论。该理论将危机管理分为 4 个阶段，即危机管理的 4R 模式，包括缩减力、预备力、反应力、恢复力。该理论指出：管理者要主动进行突发事件的风

into four stages, namely the 4R model of crisis management, including reduction, readiness, response, and recovery. This theory points out that managers should proactively conduct risk assessments for emergencies, reduce the severity of the events, prepare for emergency response, resume production work as soon as possible, and minimize the impact of emergencies. The basic process of crisis management is illustrated in Figure 11-1.

险评估，做好处理突发事件的准备工作，尽快恢复生产工作，减少突发事件带来的影响。危机管理的基本过程见图11-1。

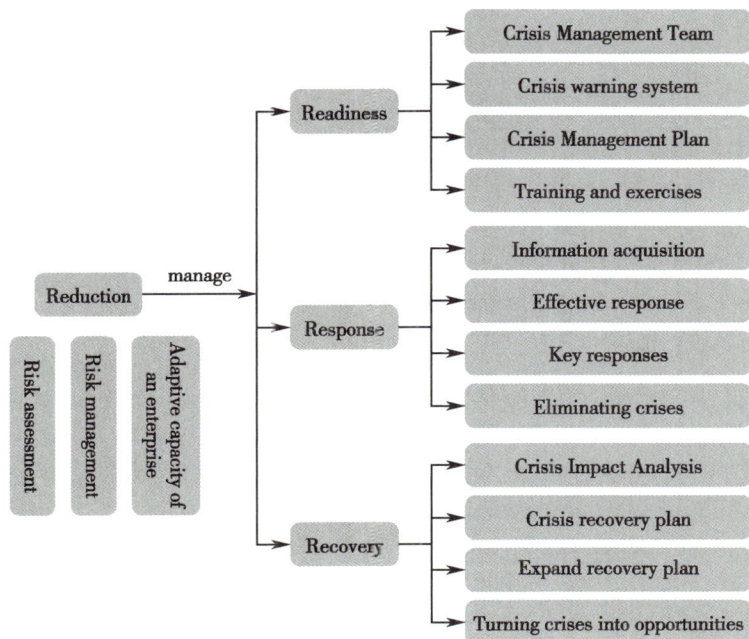

Figure 11-1　The basic process of crisis management

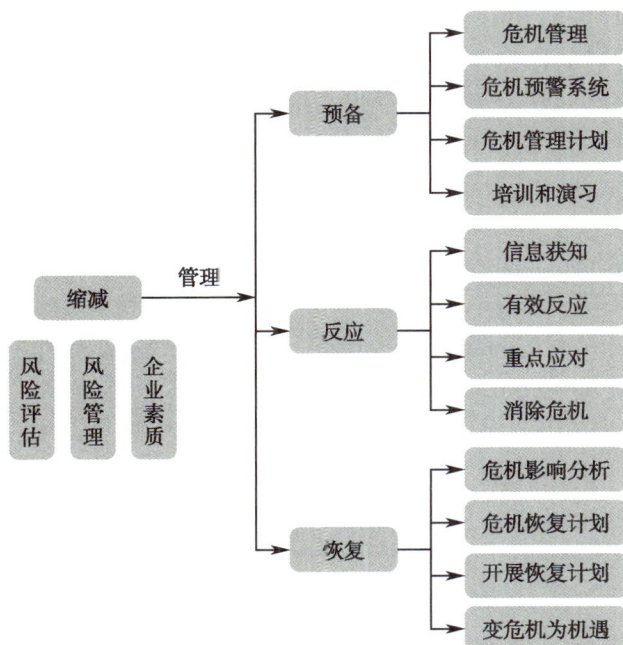

图 11-1　危机管理的基本过程

i. Reduction

Crisis reduction management is the core content of crisis management. Effective resource management can greatly reduce the occurrence and impact of crises by reducing risks and avoiding wasting time. In the reduction stage, crises are relatively easy to control and the cost of investment is also the lowest. The reduction of crisis management strategies mainly focuses on the environment, structure, system, and personnel. The main task of this stage is to prevent the occurrence of crises and reduce the impact of crises after they occur. The core of effective crisis management is to reduce impact. Therefore, in the reduction stage, it is necessary to pay more attention to various small changes in the event, prevent them from happening gradually, and do a good job in normalized emergency plan management.

ii. Readiness

This stage is mainly for the early warning and prevention of emergency management. A crisis preparedness management team composed of experts from multiple aspects should develop a crisis management plan and carry out normal crisis management work. At the same time, a complete and effective crisis warning management system should be established, and training and exercises should be conducted to ensure that each participant are familiar with warning signs and response methods, so that they can calmly respond to emergencies.

iii. Response

During an emergency, the organization should respond quickly and solve problems strategically. Crisis communication, media management, decision-making, and communication with stakeholders all fall within the scope of crisis response management. Use a variety of resources, human resources, and management methods to solve the incident crisis timely, in the shortest possible time to curb the development of the incident harm momentum, to prevent the further deterioration of the situation. This stage is the

（一）缩减阶段

危机缩减管理是危机管理的核心内容。因为降低风险，避免浪费时间，有效的资源管理，可以大大缩减危机的发生及冲击力，并且在缩减阶段，危机相对比较容易控制，投入的成本也最低。缩减危机管理策略主要从环境、结构、系统和人员着手。该阶段主要任务是预防危机的发生和减少危机发生后的冲击程度。有效危机管理的核心是缩减影响。因此，在缩减阶段，必须对事件的各种细小变化多加注意，防微杜渐，做好常态化的应急预案管理。

（二）预备阶段

主要是进行突发事件管理的预警与防范工作。由多方面专家组成突发事件预备管理团队，制订危机管理计划，进行常态下的危机管理工作，同时要建立一套完整而有效的危机预警管理体系，进行训练和演习，使每个参与者都掌握一定的预警和处理方法，使其在面对突发事件时可以从容应对。

（三）反应阶段

在突发事件来临时，组织应该迅速作出反应，并策略性地解决问题。危机的沟通、媒体管理、决策的制定、与利益相关者进行沟通等，都属于危机反应管理的范畴。运用各种资源、人力和管理方法，及时出击，解决事件危机，在尽可能短的时间内遏制事件危害发展的势头，防止事态进一步恶化。反应阶段是突发事件应急管理中最关键的步骤，包括：信息获知、有效反应与重点应对、消除影响。

most critical step in the emergency management of sudden events, including information acquisition, effective response and focused coping, and eliminating impacts.

1. Information Acquisition This is the first step in emergency management. Timely and accurate acquisition of effective information on the occurrence of emergencies is an important part of emergency management. Emergency measures and response plans can be determined based on the source, content, and characteristics of the information.

2. Effective Response and Focused Coping This is the most important step in emergency management. Verify and quickly analyze the obtained information through multiple channels, and complete various preparations for crisis management in a short period of time, especially focusing on key areas and populations affected by emergencies to prevent further evolution of the event and the occurrence of secondary disasters.

3. Eliminating Impacts In the process of emergency management, reducing and eliminating the adverse effects of events can effectively help the injured population maintain life and meet their needs, providing a solid foundation for subsequent comprehensive recovery.

iv. Recovery

Usually, after experiencing emergencies, people and objects will be impacted to varying degrees. Once the incident situation is under control, recovery work should be carried out simultaneously as soon as possible. Any issues identified during the emergency response should be promptly addressed, management practices should be enhanced, and management plans should be revised.

Effective crisis management is the integration of all aspects of the 4R model, in which reduction management runs through the entire crisis management process. In the readiness stage, the risk assessment method of reduction management

1. 信息获知 这是应急管理的第一步。突发事件发生时，及时、准确地获知突发事件发生的有效信息是进行应急管理的重要部分，可以通过信息的来源、内容及特征，决定应急对策和启动应对方案。

2. 有效反应与重点应对 这是应急管理最重要的步骤。对获取的信息进行多渠道验证和快速重点分析，并在短时间内完成危机处理的各种准备，尤其是对突发事件影响的重点区域和人群实施重点应对，以防事件进一步演化和次生灾害发生。

3. 消除影响 在突发事件管理过程中，减少和消除事件不良影响可以有效帮助受伤害人群维持生命和满足生活需要，为进一步全面恢复提供良好保证。

（四）恢复阶段

通常在经历过突发事件之后，人和物都会受到不同程度的冲击和影响。事件情境一旦得到控制，就应尽快开展恢复工作，并对突发事件处理过程中反映出来的问题及时改进，完善管理工作、优化管理计划。

有效的危机管理是对 4R 模式所有方面的整合，其中，缩减管理贯穿整个危机管理的过程。在预备阶段，运用缩减管理的风险评估法可以确定哪些预警系统可能会失效，就可以及时地予以修正或加强。在反应阶段，缩减管理

can be used to determine which warning systems may fail, and can be corrected or strengthened timely. In the response stage, reducing management can help managers identify the root causes of crises and find methods that are conducive to responding to them. In the recovery stage, reducing management can assess the potential risks that may arise during the execution of the recovery plan, thereby enabling the recovery work to have a greater rebound effect.

Emergency management for public health is a dynamic and interactive process. The crisis management 4R model theory proposes that emergency management for public health must be comprehensively integrated. Managers should carry out emergency management for public health from the perspective of overall strategy.

II. Emergency Management System of Community Emergency Public Health Events

i. Emergency Management Principles

According to the *Emergency Response Law of the People's Republic of China* and *Regulation on the Urgent Handling of Emergency Public Health Events*, emergency management must be strengthened to prevent, control and eliminate hazards of public emergencies to ensure health, safety, stability and development. The content includes 5 aspects:

1. **Prevention-Oriented** Establish emergency plans for various types of emergency public health events, strengthen monitoring and prevention of emergencies, and promptly identify and eliminate hidden dangers. Regularly conduct response drills and provide health education to residents.

2. **Quick Response** Timely identify and report potential hidden dangers of emergency public health events, establish a fast channel for information dissemination, and activate early warning mechanisms in the shortest possible time. After receiving the reported information,

可以帮助管理者识别危机的根源,找到有利于应对危机的方法。在恢复阶段,缩减管理可以评估执行恢复计划时可能产生的风险,从而使恢复工作产生更大的反弹效果。

突发公共卫生应急管理是一个动态的、交互的过程。危机管理 4R 模型理论提出了突发公共卫生应急管理必须是全局的和全面整合的,管理者应从总体战略的高度进行突发公共卫生应急管理。

二、社区突发公共卫生事件应急管理体系

(一) 应急管理原则

根据《中华人民共和国突发事件应对法》《突发公共卫生事件应急条例》,切实加强应急管理,能及时有效预防、控制和消除突发公共卫生事件的危害,保障人民身体健康和生命安全,维护社会安定和发展。内容包括 5 个方面:

1. **预防为主** 建立各类突发公共卫生事件应急预案,加强对突发事件的监测和防范,及时发现并排除隐患;经常进行应对演练,对居民进行健康教育。

2. **快速反应** 及时发现并上报可能存在的突发公共卫生事件隐患,建立信息通报快速通道,在最短时间内启动预警机制;接收到上报信息后及时核实、判断、上报,做好应急准备;建立预警预防机制,明确职责和责任,事件发生时,能快速做出反应。

verify, judge, report timely, and make emergency preparations. Establish a warning and prevention mechanism, clarify responsibilities and duties, and be able to respond quickly when an event occurs.

3. Classification Guidance　According to the types of emergency public health events that seriously affect public health and safety caused by major infectious diseases, mass diseases of unknown cause, major food poisoning, natural and artificial disasters should be handled differently to achieve the best effect.

4. Timely Handling　When emergency public health events happened, community medical institutions shall not refuse to diagnose or treat patients for any reason. Community medical staff should implement appropriate treatment measures for patients in an efficient and timely manner.

5. Territorial Management　When emergency public health events occur in the community, the community leadership agency has the right to deploy all kinds of response resources within its jurisdiction. Community health service institutions should obey the arrangement and assume the responsibility of protecting the health of residents.

ii. Organizational System

The architecture of China's health emergency system is composed of numerous departments and organizations, including the emergency command and management organization system, disease prevention and control system, health supervision institution system, medical rescue organization system, non-governmental organizations, etc., forming a complex response system with multiple subjects, departments, and roles involved. Different organizations and institutions have different roles and responsibilities in the management practice of health emergencies. By constructing a series of systems, rules, and norms among organizations, the responsibilities and division of labor of different organizations are clarified, ensuring that numerous participants perform their respective duties, cooperate organically to ensure effective response

3．分类指导　根据突发公共卫生事件的类型，对重大传染病疫情、群体性不明原因疾病、重大食物中毒、自然和人为灾害引发的严重影响公众健康和安全的事件区别处理，以求达到最佳效果。

4．及时处理　在发生突发公共卫生事件时，社区医疗机构不得以任何理由拒诊、拒收伤病员。社区医护人员应对伤病员采取相应救治措施，做到及时、快速、高效。

5．属地管理　社区发生突发公共卫生事件时，社区领导机构有权对辖区内的各种应对资源进行统一调配。社区卫生服务机构应服从安排，担负起保卫居民健康的责任。

（二）组织体系

我国卫生应急体系的架构是由应急指挥管理组织系统、疾病预防控制系统、卫生监督机构体系、医疗救援组织体系、非政府组织等众多部门和组织机构组成，形成多主体、多部门、多角色参与的复杂应对系统。不同的组织和机构在卫生应急的管理实践活动中拥有不同的角色和职责。各组织之间通过构建一系列的制度、规则、规范，明确不同组织的责任和分工，确保众多的参与者各司其职、有机合作、密切配合，以保证有效应对突发公共卫生事件。

to emergency public health events.

The community health center takes on the following roles in the emergency command center:

1. Formulate technical plans for emergency public health events.

2. Establish and train a medical emergency team composed of professional technical personnel.

3. Investigate infectious disease patients, observe contacts, and conduct lab tests.

4. Implement hygiene measures at the scene of the incident, suggest control and supervision measures for emergency public health events.

5. Provide health education, protect susceptible populations, and curb the epidemic spread.

6. Coordinate emergency responses across government, departments, and communities.

iii. Guarantee System

1. **Establish an Emergency Guarantee System** The establishment of an emergency guarantee system is an important condition for dealing with emergencies correctly, reducing and avoiding losses, and ensuring the normal operation of emergency rescue. Including:

(1) Provide staff with training in prevention and control of emergency public health events.

(2) Create an emergency technical reserve team, participate in professional training and clarify roles of various emergency professionals.

(3) Establish an epidemic reporting management team to ensure resources and network connectivity.

(4) Establish on-site hygiene disposal teams, such as disinfection teams, comprehensive prevention and support teams, and other emergency organizations to participate in event investigation, on-site hygiene disposal, and preparation of medical supplies.

(5) Create a reward and punishment system. Commendation and rewards shall be given to personnel involved in emergencies. Hold accountable those who fail to fulfill reporting responsibilities, lie about emergencies and disobey commands.

2. **Establish A High-quality Professional Team** Establishing a high-quality professional

根据应急指挥中心的安排,社区卫生服务中心承担以下职责:

1. 负责制订预防和控制突发公共卫生事件的各项技术方案。

2. 组建、培训由专业技术人员组成的医疗急救队伍。

3. 做好传染病患者的流行病学调查、密切接触者的医学观察及实验室检测工作。

4. 对事件现场进行卫生处置,提出突发公共卫生事件的控制和监督措施。

5. 开展健康教育,保护易感人群,防止疫情扩散。

6. 协调政府及各相关部门、社区协同开展应急处置。

(三)保障体系

1. **建立应急保障体系** 应急保障体系的建立是正确应对突发事件、减少和避免损失、保证应急救援工作正常进行的重要条件。包括:

(1)对医护人员进行相应突发公共卫生事件防治知识和技术培训。

(2)成立应急技术预备队,参加业务培训,明确各应急专业人员职责。

(3)成立疫情报告管理组,保证所需资源及网络畅通。

(4)成立现场卫生处置小组,如消毒组、综合预防保障组等应急组织,参加事件调查、现场卫生处置、救治物品准备等工作。

(5)建立奖惩制度,对在应对突发事件中作出贡献的人员,给予表彰和奖励;对未按规定履行报告职责,隐瞒、缓报、谎报突发事件以及不服从指挥者,追究责任。

2. **建立高素质的专业队伍** 建立高素质的专业队伍是突发公共卫生事件应急管理的重要

team is an important guarantee for emergency management, such as introducing urgently needed professional talents; establishing a public health training and emergency drill base for emergencies; carrying out training for all staff centered on capacity-building, with a focus on enhancing abilities in epidemic monitoring and analysis, on-site emergency response, and laboratory testing. Community nurses are vital to emergency medical rescue for emergency public health events. Nurses must have following conditions and skills to be competent during emergencies.

(1) Conditions: With a background in general medicine, possessing first aid skills, a good physique and strong willpower, good psychological qualities, and having received health emergency training and being qualified.

(2) Skills: a. On-site assessment and first aid. b. Transportation and supervision of injured personnel. c. Psychological support techniques. d. Health education. e. Evaluation and judgment ability. f. Other rescue skills. g. Ability to collaborate with personnel from other departments.

III. Prevention, Surveillance, Early Warning, and Reporting of Community Emergency Public Health Events

i. Prevention

1. Assess Potential Hazards and Rescue Approaches in the Community　Community nurses should be familiar with the environment and work with relevant departments to address traffic, health, diet, safety, and other community risks, take timely measures to eliminate these factors, and prevent emergencies. Rescuer agencies and routes should be known to assist with evacuation when needed.

2. Health Education　Promote residents' knowledge of relevant laws and regulations such as *Regulation on the Urgent Handling of Emergency Public Health Events*; carry out targeted health education and training on personal protective skills

保障,如引进急需专业人才;建立公共卫生培训和突发事件应急演练基地;以能力建设为中心大力开展全员培训,重点提升疫情监测分析能力、现场应急处置能力和实验室检验能力。社区护士是突发公共卫生事件医疗救护的重要成员,参与救护的社区护士必须具备以下条件和能力,才能胜任突发事件的护理工作。

(1) 条件:具有全科医学背景、急救技能、良好体魄与坚强意志、良好的心理素质,接受过卫生应急培训并合格。

(2) 能力:①现场评估和急救;②伤员转运与监护;③心理支持技术;④健康教育;⑤评估和判断能力;⑥其他救护技能;⑦与其他部门人员的协作能力。

三、社区突发公共卫生事件预防、监测、预警和报告

(一) 社区突发公共卫生事件预防

1. **评估社区存在的隐患和救援途径**　社区护士应熟悉周边环境,在相关部门的配合下,了解社区在交通、卫生、饮食、安全等方面存在的隐患,及时采取措施,杜绝这些危险因素,预防各种突发事件的发生;熟悉可利用的救援机构、救援路径,在事件发生时能及时取得联系,帮助居民疏散。

2. **健康教育**　对居民进行《突发公共卫生事件应急条例》等相关法律法规知识的宣传;根据事件发生的季节性、人群特征,开展针对性的健康教育和自救、互救、避险、逃生等个人防护技能的培训;提高居民的自我防范意识和保护

such as self-help, mutual rescue, risk avoidance, and evacuation according to the seasonality and population of the event; enhance residents' self-protection awareness and skills, eliminate panic psychology, and reduce losses.

3. Daily Drills　The community conducts drills on emergency plans for common emergency public health events, such as establishing emergency teams, preparing materials, staffing, and carrying out on-site rescue, hygiene disposal, epidemic prevention, etc., to strengthen the awareness and management of community emergency response, and improve the ability of medical staff to take preventive and emergency measures.

ii. Surveillance and Early Warning of Community Emergency Public Health Events

1. Surveillance　It is a long-term, continuous and systematic collection of data on changing trends and influencing factors of disease, health, injury (disability) or death in the population, and timely feedback through analysis, in order to take effective interventions and evaluate the results. Surveillance is an important method of epidemiology, which plays an important role in preventing and controlling the further spread and exacerbation of emergencies. Surveillance is an important task for grassroots health institutions to prevent and respond to emergency public health events.

2. Early Warning　Emergency warning is a preventive measure for crisis management. Establishing an effective and feasible early warning management mechanism can prevent emergencies. Early warning of emergency public health events is to take appropriate emergency responses timely and minimize the harm to emergencies.

(1) The Basic Methods of Early Warning:

1) Direct warning: It refers to the direct warning report for the occurrence of highly

技能,消除恐慌心理,减少损失。

3.日常演练　社区针对常见突发公共卫生事件应急预案进行演练,如建立应急小组、物资准备、人员配备等,并开展现场救护、卫生处置、疫情防范等,加强社区突发事件应对意识和管理,提高医护人员采取预防和急救措施的能力。

(二)社区突发公共卫生事件监测与预警

1.监测　是长期、连续、系统地收集人群中有关疾病、健康、伤害(残)或死亡的变化趋势及其影响因素的资料,经过分析,及时反馈信息,以便采取有效干预措施并评价其结果。监测是流行病学的重要方法与手段,对预防和控制突发事件进一步扩散和危害加剧具有重要作用。监测是基层卫生机构预防与应对突发公共卫生事件的重要工作。

2.预警　突发事件预警是应对危机的预防措施,建立高效可行的预警管理机制,能够避免突发事件发生。突发公共卫生事件的早期预警是为了及时采取相应的应急反应,将突发事件的危害降到最低。

(1)预警的基本方式:

1)直接预警:指对发生烈性传染病或易传播疾病、原因不明性疾病、重大食物中毒等直接

infectious or easily communicable diseases, unexplained diseases, major food poisoning, etc.

2) Qualitative warning: It uses statistical methods, computerized for the qualitative estimation of the development trend and intensity of the disease to clarify whether it is increasing or decreasing, epidemic or sporadic. Methods include comprehensive prediction, control chart, Bayes probability, and stepwise discriminant analysis, etc.

3) Quantitative warning: It refers to using linear and exponential curve prediction models, multiple stepwise regression analysis, simple time series, seasonal cycle regression models, and other methods to quantitatively warn of diseases.

4) Long term warning: It adopts expert consultation method to alert the long-term epidemic trend of diseases.

(2) Warning Response: According to the predicted analysis results, the classification of epidemic warning response is shown in Table 11-1.

进行预警报告。

2）定性预警：指采用多种统计方法，借助计算机完成对疾病的发展趋势和强度的定性估计，明确是上升还是下降，是流行还是散发。采用的统计方法包括：综合预测法、控制图法、Bayes 概率法、逐步判别分析等。

3）定量预警：指采用直线预测模型、指数曲线预测模型、多元逐步回归分析、简易时间序列、季节周期回归模型等预测方法对疾病进行定量预警。

4）长期预警：采用专家咨询法对疾病的长期流行趋势进行预警。

（2）预警响应：根据预测分析结果，进行疫情预警响应分级，如表 11-1 所示。

Table 11-1　Classification of Epidemic Warning Response

Graded	Warning color	Epidemic description	Response measures
Level I	Red	It was confirmed that the emergency had the ability of human-to-human transmission and an outbreak occurred	Under the command of the provincial Center for Disease Control and Prevention (CDC), carry out on-site disposal
Level II	Orange	3 or more confirmed cases have occurred within a certain range, or 1 or more confirmed cases have died	The provincial CDC provides on-site technical guidance, and the epidemic site is responsible for on-site disposal
Level III	Yellow	1 confirmed case occurred within a certain range	The county-level CDC provided on-site technical guidance, and the place where the epidemic occurred was responsible for on-site disposal
Level IV	Blue	A certain disease epidemic occurs within a certain range	The CDC in the place where the epidemic occurred is responsible for medical observation and on-site disposal of contacts

表 11-1　疫情预警响应分级

分级	预警颜色	疫情描述	响应措施
Ⅰ级	红色	证实突发事件具备人传人的能力，出现暴发流行	在省级疾病预防控制中心的指挥下，开展现场处置
Ⅱ级	橙色	一定范围内发生 3 例以上确诊病例，或发生 1 例或 1 例以上确诊病例死亡	省级疾病预防控制中心给予现场技术指导，疫情发生地负责现场处置
Ⅲ级	黄色	一定范围内发生 1 例确诊病例	县级疾病预防控制中心现场技术指导，疫情发生地负责现场处置
Ⅳ级	蓝色	一定范围内发生某种疾病疫情	由疫情发生地的疾病预防控制中心负责接触者的医学观察和现场处置

(3) Early Warning Information Release: According to various emergency plans for emergency public health events, warning information is released based on the possible occurrence, development trend, and harm degree. The main contents include: the name, category, warning level, starting time, possible impact scope, warning items, response measures and issuing authorities of public emergencies. In the process of dealing with emergencies, a timely, transparent and credible information system should be established. Make full use of media tools such as television and newspapers to release the latest information and facts timely, ensuring accuracy, timeliness, and openness, and ensuring the credibility and authority of the information.

iii. Report of Community Emergency Public Health Events

1. Report Deadline　The initial report must be submitted within 24h after the emergency public health events are verified and confirmed, the stage report must be submitted daily, and the summary report must be submitted within 10 working days after the incident is handled. Under any of the following circumstances, all community health institutions (including health centers and clinics in towns) must report to higher level institutions/bureaus within 2h via network：

(1) Occurrence or possibility of outbreak or epidemic of infectious diseases.

（3）预警信息发布：根据各类突发公共卫生事件应急预案，按照突发公共卫生事件发生可能、发展趋势和危害程度，发布预警信息。预警信息的主要内容包括：突发公共卫生事件的名称、类别、预警级别、起始时间、可能影响范围、警示事项、应对措施和发布机关等。在突发事件处置过程中，应建立一个及时、透明、可信的信息系统，充分利用电视、报刊等媒体工具，在第一时间发布最新信息和事实，保证准确、及时、公开，确保信息的可信度和权威性。

（三）社区突发公共卫生事件报告

1. 报告时限　初次报告必须在核实确认发生突发公共卫生事件后 24 小时内上报，阶段报告可按每日上报，总结报告在事件处理结束后 10 个工作日内上报。有下列情形之一的，各社区卫生机构（含乡镇卫生院、诊所）应当在 2 小时内通过网络向上一级卫生机构及卫生局上报：

（1）发生或可能发生传染病暴发、流行。

(2) Occurrence or discovery of unexplained group diseases.

(3) The bacteria species and virus species of infectious diseases are lost.

(4) Major food and occupational poisoning incidents have occurred or may occur.

2. Reporting Procedures and Methods Institutions with the conditions for direct network reporting shall carry out direct network reporting of information related to infectious diseases and/or emergency public health events within a specified time. Those without the conditions for direct reporting via the internet shall report by telephone, fax, and other means in accordance with the relevant requirements, and at the same time submit the infectious disease report card and/or emergency public health events information report card to the county-level CDC.

3. Report Content It includes the event name, preliminarily determined category and nature, location and time of occurrence, number of cases and deaths, main clinical symptoms, possible causes, measures taken, reporting unit, reporting personnel, and communication methods.

Section 3 Management of Community Emergency Infectious Diseases

I. Overview of Infectious Diseases

i. Concept

Infectious diseases are caused by various pathogens that spread from human to human, animal to animal, or human to animal. Pathogens are mainly microorganisms and a few parasites, also known as parasitic diseases. For some infectious diseases, the epidemic prevention department must timely grasp incidence and countermeasures. Therefore, once discovered, it should be reported timely according to the

（2）发生或发现不明原因的群体性疾病。

（3）发生传染病菌种、毒种丢失。

（4）发生或者可能发生重大食物和职业中毒事件。

2. 报告程序与方式　具备网络直报条件的机构，在规定时间内进行传染病和 / 或突发公共卫生事件相关信息的网络直报；不具备网络直报条件的，按相关要求通过电话、传真等方式进行报告，同时向辖区县级疾病预防控制机构报送传染病报告卡和 / 或突发公共卫生事件相关信息报告卡。

3. 报告内容　包括事件名称、初步判定的事件类别和性质、发生地点、发生时间、发病人数、死亡人数、主要的临床症状、可能原因、已采取的措施、报告单位、报告人员及通信方式等。

第三节　社区突发传染病的管理

一、传染病的概述

（一）概念

传染病是由各种病原体引起的能在人与人、动物与动物或人与动物之间相互传播的一类疾病。病原体中大部分是微生物，小部分为寄生虫，由寄生虫引起的疾病又称寄生虫病。对于有些传染病，防疫部门必须及时掌握其发病情况并采取对策，发现后应按规定时间及时报告，这类传染病称为法定传染病。目前，我国法定传染病共41种，分为甲、乙、丙3类。

prescribed time, which is called notifiable disease. At present, there are 41 notifiable diseases in China, divided into 3 categories: A, B and C.

ii. Characteristics of Infectious Diseases

1. Pathogens Present   Every infectious disease has its specific pathogen, including microorganisms and parasites, with bacteria and virus being the most common.

2. Infectious   The pathogen of infectious diseases can be transmitted from one person to another through certain channels.

3. Post Infection Immunity   Most patients can develop varying degrees of immunity after recovering from the disease. After being infected with pathogens, the body can produce specific immunity.

4. Epidemiological Characteristics   Infectious diseases can spread among the population, and their epidemic process is influenced by natural and social factors, exhibiting various epidemic characteristics.

iii. Infectious Disease Transmission

Pathogens spread through routes and infect susceptible individuals, forming new infections. Infection requires three links: source of infection, route of transmission and susceptible population.

1. Source of Infection   Refers to people and animals who have pathogens growing and reproducing in their bodies, and can excrete pathogens, that is, people and animals who are infected with infectious diseases or carry pathogens.

2. Route of Transmission   The pathway through which pathogens pass in the external environment before invading new susceptible hosts after being discharged from the infectious source. The route of transmission of an infectious disease can be single or multiple. The main routes of transmission include air transmission, water source transmission, food transmission, contact transmission, soil-borne transmission, vertical

（二）传染病的特点

1. **有病原体**   每一种传染病都有它特异的病原体，包括微生物和寄生虫，其中以细菌和病毒最常见。

2. **有传染性**   传染病的病原体可以从一个人经过一定的途径传染给另一个人。

3. **感染后有免疫性**   大多数患者在疾病痊愈后，都可产生不同程度的免疫力。机体感染病原体后可以产生特异性免疫。

4. **有流行病学特征**   传染病能在人群中流行，其流行过程受自然因素和社会因素的影响，并表现出多方面的流行特征。

（三）传染病传播

指病原体被已感染者排出，经过一定的传播途径，传入易感者而形成新的感染的全部过程。传染病得以在某一人群中发生和传播，必须具备传染源、传播途径和易感人群3个基本环节。

1. **传染源**   指在体内有病原体生长繁殖，并可将病原体排出的人和动物，即患传染病或携带病原体的人和动物。

2. **传播途径**   指病原体自传染源排出后，在侵入新的易感宿主前，在外界环境中所行经的途径。一种传染病的传播途径可以是单一的，也可以是多个的。主要的传播途径有空气传播、水源传播、食物传播、接触传播、经土壤传播、垂直传播（母婴传播）、体液传播、粪 - 口传播等。

transmission (mother to child transmission), body fluid transmission, fecal-oral transmission, etc.

3. Susceptible Population　People who lack immunity to a certain infectious disease and are susceptible to the disease, as well as those who lack specific immunity to infectious disease pathogens and are susceptible to infection.

II. Reporting and Classification Management of Infectious Diseases

i. Report of Infectious Diseases

According to the Regulations on Public Health Emergency and Epidemic Surveillance Reporting, reporting entities shall implement the following protocols:

1. 2-hour digital reporting via the national web-based system for　Confirmed/suspected cases of Category A diseases (plague, cholera), Category B diseases requiring Category A management (e.g., pulmonary anthrax, SARS), Emerging infectious disease outbreaks or unexplained disease clusters.

2. 24-hour digital reporting for　Other notifiable Category B/C diseases (confirmed/suspected cases and designated pathogen carriers).

3. Offline reporting mechanisms Facilities without digital capacity must notify local primary health institutions (township health centers/community health centers) or county CDC within 24 hours, concurrently submitting physical case report forms.

ii. Classification Management of Infectious Diseases

According to the *Law of the People's Republic of China on the Prevention and Treatment of Infectious Diseases*, China implements classified management of infectious diseases.

1. Category A Infectious Diseases Refers to infectious diseases that pose a particularly serious threat to human health and safety, may cause significant economic losses and social impacts, and require mandatory management, isolation, treatment, health quarantine, and control

3．易感人群　指对某种传染病缺乏免疫力、易受该病感染的人群和对传染病病原体缺乏特异性免疫力、易受感染的人群。

二、传染病的报告及分类管理

（一）传染病的报告

根据《突发公共卫生事件与传染病疫情监测信息报告管理办法》，责任报告机构及人员发现以下情形应立即启动疫情报告程序：

1．2 小时网络直报　确诊或疑似甲类传染病（鼠疫、霍乱）、乙类传染病中按甲类管理的病种（如肺炭疽、传染性非典型肺炎），以及其他传染病暴发或不明原因疾病聚集性病例。

2．24 小时网络直报　其他法定乙类、丙类传染病的确诊 / 疑似病例及规定报告的病原携带者。

3．无网络直报条件的机构　须在 24 小时内向属地基层卫生机构（乡镇卫生院 / 社区卫生服务中心）或县级疾控中心进行代报，同步寄送纸质报告卡。

（二）传染病的分类管理

依照《中华人民共和国传染病防治法》规定，我国传染病实施分类管理。

1．甲类传染病　指对人体健康和生命安全危害特别严重，可能造成重大经济损失和社会影响，需要采取强制管理、强制隔离治疗、强制卫生检疫，控制疫情蔓延的传染病。甲类传染病共 2 种，包括霍乱、鼠疫。

of the spread of the epidemic. There are 2 species in total, including cholera and plague.

2. Category B Infectious Disease
Refers to the infectious diseases that cause serious harm to human health and life safety and may cause considerable economic loss and social impact, and require strict management, implement various prevention and control measures, reduce the incidence rate and harm. There are 28 species, including: novel coronavirus infection (COVID-19), SARS, AIDS, viral hepatitis, poliomyelitis, HPAI, measles, epidemic hemorrhagic fever, rabies, epidemic encephalitis B, dengue fever, anthrax, bacterial dysentery and amebic dysentery, tuberculosis, typhoid and paratyphoid fever, epidemic cerebrospinal meningitis, pertussis, diphtheria, neonatal tetanus, scarlet fever, brucellosis, gonorrhea, syphilis, leptospirosis, schistosomiasis, malaria, human infection with H7N9 avian influenza, monkeypox.

In addition, the infectious diseases classified as category B, such as SARS, and pulmonary anthrax of anthrax, are subject to the prevention and control measures of category A infectious diseases.

3. Category C Infectious Diseases
Refers to the common and frequent, cause harm to human health and life safety, may cause a certain degree of economic losses and social impact, need to monitor and manage, pay attention to the epidemic trend, control the outbreak of epidemic infectious diseases. There are 11 species, including: filariasis, echinococcosis, leprosy, influenza, mumps, rubella, hand, foot and mouth disease, epidemic and endemic typhus, kala-azar, acute hemorrhagic conjunctivitis, infectious diarrhoeal diseases other than cholera, dysentery, typhoid and paratyphoid fever.

III. Prevention and Emergency Management of Community Emergency Infectious Diseases

The prevention and control of infectious

2. 乙类传染病　指对人体健康和生命安全危害严重，可能造成较大经济损失和社会影响，需要采取严格管理，落实各项防控措施，降低发病率，减少危害的传染病。乙类传染病共28种，包括：传染性非典型肺炎、艾滋病、病毒性肝炎、脊髓灰质炎、人感染高致病性禽流感、麻疹、流行性出血热、狂犬病、流行性乙型脑炎、登革热、炭疽、细菌性和阿米巴痢疾、结核病、伤寒和副伤寒、流行性脑脊髓膜炎、百日咳、白喉、新生儿破伤风、猩红热、布鲁氏菌病、淋病、梅毒、钩端螺旋体病、血吸虫病、疟疾、人感染H7N9禽流感、新型冠状病毒感染、猴痘。

此外，乙类传染病中的传染性非典型肺炎和炭疽中的肺炭疽，采取甲类传染病的预防、控制措施。

3. 丙类传染病　指常见多发、对人体健康和生命安全造成危害，可能造成一定程度的经济损失和社会影响，需要监测管理，关注流行趋势，控制暴发流行的传染病。丙类传染病共11种，包括：丝虫病、包虫病、麻风病、流行性感冒、流行性腮腺炎、风疹、手足口病、流行性和地方性斑疹伤寒、黑热病、急性出血性结膜炎，除霍乱、痢疾、伤寒和副伤寒以外的其他感染性腹泻病。

三、社区突发传染病的防控与应急管理

传染性疾病预防和控制是社区传染病管理

diseases is the most crucial aspect of community infectious disease management and epidemic prevention and control. Emphasize social and community interaction and coordination, and conduct infectious disease monitoring, publicity, and education, etc. Comprehensively carry out community joint prevention and control, as well as mass prevention and governance.

i. Basic Principles and Measures

1. Basic Principles　Adhere to "prevention first, prevention and treatment combined, scientific and legal, and graded classification", standardize precision prevention and control with local emergency response, and fulfill epidemic prevention and control tasks in accordance with "timely detection, rapid disposal, precise control, and effective treatment".

2. Basic Measures　The "4 early" measures should be implemented, namely "early detection, early reporting, early isolation, and early treatment" measures. Strengthen community prevention and control precision, expand the detection range, timely detection of sporadic cases and clusters of outbreaks, continuously consolidate the epidemic prevention and control, to safeguard people's life safety and body health.

ii. Management of Infectious Diseases

1. Treatment and Management of Patients　Isolation, medical observation and other measures were taken for infectious disease patients and suspected patients in accordance with relevant standards. Especially, personal protection and infection control should be done according to regulations to prevent the spread of the epidemic.

2. Management of Close Contacts of Infectious Diseases and Individuals Exposed to Health Hazards　Assist in tracking and searching for individuals who have been exposed to infectious diseases or other health hazards, and provide necessary basic medical and preventive services to centralized or home-based medical observers.

和疫情防控最重要的环节。充分发挥社会、社区联动与协同作用，切实做好传染病的监测、宣传教育等工作，全面做好社区联防联控、群防群治。

（一）基本原则与措施

1. **基本原则**　坚持"预防为主、防治结合、依法科学、分级分类"的原则，坚持常态化精准防控和局部应急处置有机结合，按照"及时发现、快速处置、精准管控、有效救治"的工作要求，全力做好常态化疫情防控工作。

2. **基本措施**　做好"四早"措施落实。即开展"早发现、早报告、早隔离、早治疗"的措施，加强社区精准防控，扩大检测范围，及时发现散发病例和聚集性疫情，不断巩固疫情防控成果，切实维护人民群众生命安全和身体健康。

（二）传染病的处理

1. **患者医疗救治和管理**　按照有关规范要求，对传染病患者、疑似患者采取隔离、医学观察等措施，尤其是要按规定做好个人防护和感染控制，严防疫情传播。

2. **传染病密切接触者和健康危害暴露人员的管理**　协助开展传染病接触者或其他健康危害暴露人员的追踪、查找，对集中或居家医学观察者提供必要的基本医疗和预防服务。

3. Epidemiological Investigation

Assist in conducting epidemiological investigations on patients and suspected patients in the jurisdiction, collect and provide relevant information on patients, close contacts, and other individuals exposed to health hazards.

4. Management of Epidemic Focuses and Areas

Carry out on-site control, disinfection and isolation, personal protection, and management of medical waste and sewage within medical institutions. Assist in the sanitation of contaminated areas, carry out insecticidal and rodent control work.

5. Emergency Vaccination and Preventive Medication

Assist in carrying out emergency vaccination, preventive medication, distribution of emergency drugs and protective equipment, and provide guidance.

6. Propaganda and Education

Carry out publicity and education on relevant knowledge, skills, laws and regulations based on the nature and characteristics of infectious diseases in the jurisdiction.

Section 4   Management of Community Emergency Disaster Events

I. Overview of Disasters

i. Concept of Disasters

The World Health Organization defines disasters as any event that causes facility damage, severe economic damage, casualties, or deterioration of health conditions, and its scale and severity have exceeded regional capacity, spreads and develops externally, requiring assistance. The United Nations International Decade for Natural Disaster Reduction expert group defines disasters as the destruction of the human ecological environment beyond the existing resource capacity of affected communities.

3. 流行病学调查　协助对本辖区患者、疑似患者开展流行病学调查，收集和提供患者、密切接触者、其他健康危害暴露人员的相关信息。

4. 疫点疫区处理　做好医疗机构内现场控制、消毒隔离、个人防护、医疗垃圾和污水的处理工作。协助对被污染的场所进行卫生处理，开展杀虫、灭鼠等工作。

5. 应急接种和预防性服药　协助开展应急接种、预防性服药、应急药品和防护用品分发等工作，并提供指导。

6. 宣传教育　根据辖区传染病的性质和特点，开展相关知识技能和法律法规的宣传教育。

第四节　社区突发灾害性事件的管理

一、灾害的概述

（一）灾害的概念

灾害又称灾难，世界卫生组织对灾害的定义为：任何能引起设施破坏、经济严重受损、人员伤亡、健康状况恶化的事件，其规模、严重程度已超出区域承受能力并向外部扩散和发展，需要寻求援助。联合国"国际减灾十年"专家组定义为：灾害是一种超出受影响社区现有资源承受能力的人类生态环境的破坏。

Disasters can be seen as referring to the collective term for things that can cause devastating effects on humans and the environment they depend on for survival. When the scale and severity of public emergency exceeds the area's capacity to withstand, continuously spread and develop, it can evolve into a disaster event.

ii. Classification of Disasters

There are many methods for categorizing disasters, according to their causes can be divided into:

1. **Natural Disasters** It is a natural phenomenon that causes damage and harm to the natural ecological environment, human living environment, and human life and property, such as meteorological disasters, earthquake-induced geological disasters, and biological disasters.

2. **Artificial Disasters** It refers to the disaster-causing processes and results caused by unreasonable human activities, such as technical accidents, environmental hazards, artificial terrorist incidents, etc.

Disasters of any kind are sudden and destructive, their scale and intensity exceed the self-rescue abilities or bearing capacity of the disaster community. Disaster is the most serious event in public emergencies, which will pose a serious threat to human health, life and property safety. It is necessary to reconstruct life, society and people's mental psychology after disasters.

iii. Characteristics of Disasters

1. **Suddenness** Suddenness means something happens suddenly and unexpectedly. Suddenness is the most basic feature of disaster occurrence, including two aspects: accidental occurrence and rapid progression. It can be seen that disasters often occur without warning or clear signs, making it difficult to detect, leaving people with insufficient time to analyze, prepare, and respond, and without rich information as a basis for making correct judgments.

2. **Harmfulness** Harmfulness refers to the wide-ranging and influential nature of a disaster

可见，灾害是指能够给人类和人类赖以生存的环境造成破坏性影响的事物总称，当突发公共事件的规模和严重程度超出发生区域的承受能力，不断扩散和发展，可演变成灾害事件。

（二）灾害的分类

灾害的分类方法很多，按照其发生原因可分为：

1. **自然灾害** 是对自然生态环境、人类居住环境、人类及其生命财产造成破坏与危害的自然现象，如气象灾害、地震地质灾害、生物灾害。

2. **人为灾害** 指人类不合理活动引起的致灾过程和结果，如技术事故、环境公害、人为恐怖事件等。

无论是何种灾害都具有突发性和破坏性，其规模和强度超出发生灾害社区的自救能力或承受能力。灾害是突发公共事件中最为严重的事件，会对人类健康及生命财产安全构成严重威胁，灾后都需要对生活、社会及人们的精神心理进行重建。

（三）灾害的特点

1. **突发性** 是指发生突然，出乎人们的意料。突发性是灾害发生最基本的特点，包含两方面意思：发生的偶然性和进展的迅速性。可见，灾害发生往往没有征兆或者征兆不明显，很难被察觉，使人们没有充足的时间来分析、准备和应对，同时也没有丰富的信息作为做出正确判断的依据。

2. **危害性** 是指灾害性事件的危害涉及面广、影响力大，可以是一个区域、地区甚至整个

event, which can affect a region, or even the entire country and the world. If not timely response, it will cause a comprehensive social crisis involving various impacts. The harmfulness of catastrophic events makes it more difficult for people to cope with crises, such as terrorist attacks, which have a wide range of impacts and can even cause catastrophic effects.

3. Unconventionality   Unconventionality refers to a catastrophic event that goes beyond the general pattern of events, exhibits variability, and even develops in a leapfrog manner. This unconventional behavior disrupts people's habitual thinking, making it difficult to manage according to its regularity and characteristics, forcing people to take emergency measures to respond to disaster events.

iv. Classification of Disasters

Under China's four-tier disaster response framework established by the *National Natural Disaster Relief Emergency Plan* and the *National Overall Emergency Response Plan for Public Incidents*, disasters are classified into four levels (Ⅰ–Ⅳ) based on three key parameters: geographical scope, severity of impact, and controllability. This classification system utilizes a color-coded alert mechanism with red, orange, yellow, and blue corresponding to each respective disaster level.

1. Level Ⅰ Disasters (Extremely Severe Disasters)   The disaster has a wide-ranging impact, affecting several provinces and cities, and hundreds of counties, resulting in significant casualties and economic losses. It has a serious impact on the social and economic development of a region and requires the central government to organize and direct disaster relief work. For example, the 8.0-magnitude Wenchuan earthquake in Sichuan Province in 2008 belongs to level Ⅰ disasters. They are usually represented in red.

2. Level Ⅱ Disasters (Severe Disasters) The scope of the disaster involves 1–2 provinces

国家及全世界，若没有及时应对，会造成涉及多方面影响的综合性社会危机。灾害性事件的危害性增加了人们处理危机的难度，如"恐怖袭击事件"影响范围很大，甚至可能造成灾难性的影响。

3. 非常规性　是指灾害性事件超出了一般事件规律，呈现出易变性，甚至呈"跳跃式"发展。这种非常规性打乱了人们的惯性思维，难以按照其常规性和特征性进行管理，迫使人们不得不采取紧急措施应对灾害性事件的发生。

（四）灾害的分级

根据中国《国家自然灾害救助应急预案》和《国家突发公共事件总体应急预案》构建的四级灾害响应体系，灾害按其范围、损害程度和可控性分为4级，并用红、橙、黄、蓝4种颜色分别代表不同的灾害级别。

1. Ⅰ级灾害（特大灾害）　灾害范围广，涉及多个省市、几百个县，人员伤亡和经济损失巨大，对一定区域社会经济造成严重影响，需要中央政府组织指挥救灾工作。如2008年四川汶川8.0级大地震属于特大灾害。特大灾害通常用红色表示。

2. Ⅱ级灾害（大灾害）　灾害范围涉及1~2省、几十个县，造成人员伤亡和经济损失严重，

and dozens of counties, causing serious casualties and economic losses, and seriously affecting the lives and economic development of the people in the disaster area. The relevant central departments and provincial governments are responsible for organizing and leading the disaster response. Level Ⅱ disasters are usually represented in orange.

3. Level Ⅲ Disasters (Relatively Severe Disasters) The scope of the disaster is one province, causing certain casualties and economic losses, and seriously affecting the lives and economic development of the people in the disaster-affected areas. Disaster relief is supported by the central government and other provinces, and the provincial government relies on local organizations for disaster relief. Level Ⅲ disasters are usually represented in yellow.

4. Level Ⅳ Disasters (General Disasters) Occurred in local areas, causing casualties and affecting the lives and economies of the people in the disaster area, supported by provincial governments, mainly relying on local organizations for disaster relief. Level Ⅳ disasters are usually represented in blue.

Ⅱ. On-Site Rescue of Community Emergency Disaster Events

i. Principles and Techniques of On-site Rescue

1. Principles of On-site Rescue Community on-site rescue is different from hospital first aid. It requires the use of limited resources on site in emergency situations to maximize the rescue of injured patients and reduce the incidence of casualties. Therefore, its rescue principles are saving lives, stabilizing the condition, and rapid transportation.

2. Basic Rescue Techniques On-site rescue techniques include cardiopulmonary resuscitation (CPR), ensuring airway patency, providing effective breathing, maintaining circulatory function, controlling external hemorrhage, protecting injured cervical vertebra, and bone fixation.

对灾区人民生活和经济发展造成严重影响，由中央有关部门和省政府组织领导抗灾。通常用橙色表示。

3. Ⅲ级灾害（较大灾害） 成灾范围为1个省，造成一定人员伤亡和经济损失，对成灾区域人民生活和经济发展造成严重影响，由中央及他省支援、省政府依靠当地组织进行抗灾救灾。通常用黄色表示。

4. Ⅳ级灾害（一般灾害） 在局部地区发生，造成一定人员伤亡，灾区人民生活和经济受到一定影响，由省级政府支援，主要依靠当地组织进行抗灾救灾。通常用蓝色表示。

二、社区突发灾害性事件的现场救护

（一）现场救护原则与技术

1. 救护原则 社区现场救护不同于医院院内急救，要求在紧急情况下，利用现场有限资源，最大限度地救护伤员，减少伤亡率，因此其救护原则为抢救生命、稳定病情和迅速转运。

2. 基本救护技术 现场救护技术主要包括心肺复苏、保证气道通畅、提供有效呼吸、维持循环功能、控制外出血、保护受伤的颈椎和骨折固定。

Early emergency treatment for severe multiple injuries generally follows the VICSO procedure:

(1) Get the Injured Out of Danger Immediately: Assess the environment before rescue, and help the injured out of danger before rescue.

(2) V Stands for Ventilation, Which Means Ventilation to Maintain Airway Patency: Provide timely and sufficient oxygen, quickly relieve respiratory obstruction, remove foreign matters such as active dentures, broken teeth, and blood clots in the oral cavity, and aspirate respiratory secretions.

(3) I Stands for Injection, Which Means Infusion for Shock Resistance: Establishing the vein passage, rapidly supplementing blood volume, and increasing effective blood volume are important measures to rescue traumatic shock. According to the degree of shock, 2–3 venous passages should be established, and large blood vessels should be selected. 16–20G intravenous cannula needle can be used to quickly input a large amount of fluid. One of the venous passages should be used as a blood transfusion device to prepare for possible blood transfusion.

(4) C Stands for Control Bleeding, Which Means Controlling Active Bleeding: Emergency control of active massive bleeding caused by trauma to avoid shock and death due to sharp reduction of blood volume in a short period of time. If there is a wound, the surface should be immediately compressed and wrapped with dressing, and should cooperate with the doctor's debridement and suturing to stop bleeding. If there is a fracture, it should be fixed with a splint.

(5) S Stands for Supervision, Which Means Multi-functional Monitoring: Monitor vital signs, ECG, respiration, blood pressure and oxygen saturation continuously with a multifunctional monitor. Put in an urethral catheter and record urine volume per hour. According to the monitoring results, timely take corresponding rescue measures.

(6) O Stands for Operation, Which Means Surgical Treatment: For patients with indications of

严重多发伤早期急救一般按 VICSO 程序进行：

（1）立即使伤者脱离危险区：救护前先评估环境，帮助伤员脱离危险区再施救。

（2）V（ventilation），通气，保持呼吸道通畅：及时充分给氧，迅速解除呼吸道阻塞，取出口腔内活动性义齿、碎牙、血块等异物，吸净呼吸道分泌物。

（3）I（injection），输液抗休克：建立静脉通道，迅速补充血容量，增加有效血容量是抢救创伤性休克的重要措施。根据休克程度建立 2~3 条静脉通道，宜选用大血管，可用 16~20G 静脉留置针，以便快速输入大量液体，其中一条静脉通道用输血器，为可能的输血做好准备。

（4）C（control bleeding），控制活动性出血：紧急控制创伤引起的活动性大出血，以免因短时间内血容量锐减而发生休克和死亡。有伤口的，其表面立即用敷料加压包扎并配合医师清创缝合止血，骨折用夹板固定。

（5）S（supervise），多功能监护：监测生命体征，用多功能监护仪持续监测心电图、呼吸、血压、血氧饱和度。留置导尿管，记录每小时尿量。根据监测结果，及时采取相应抢救措施。

（6）O（operation），手术治疗：对有紧急手术指征的患者，及时做好采血、配血、备皮、药物

emergency surgery, make preoperative preparations such as blood collection, blood matching, skin preparation, and drug testing, inform the operating room and anesthesiology department to make corresponding preparations, escort the patient into the operating room, and make detailed handovers with the operating room nurse.

ii. Content of On-site Disaster Rescue Work

The rescue work of community nurses at disaster sites mainly includes the following aspects:

1. **Assess Casualties On-site** It includes the time, location, number and type of casualties; the main injuries of the wounded, the measures taken and the medical resources invested; and the urgent medical problems that need to be solved.

2. **Classification of On-site Injuries and Patients** According to the injury situation of the victim, classify them into light, medium, severe, and death, and mark them with green, yellow, red, and black injury cards respectively. Place the injury cards on the chest, wrist, or ankle of the injured person for easy identification by rescue personnel and corresponding emergency measures.

BOX 11-1 Learning More

Color-coded Triage and Treatment Priorities in On-site Assessment

According to the *Emergency Medical Response Work Management Method (Trial Edition)* issued by the National Health Commission of China in December 2023, the on-site triage classification is divided into four levels. The injury identification card uses a uniform color code to facilitate the identification of patients with different degrees of injury and enable quick action to be taken.

1. **Red** First priority for treatment and transfer. Indicates that the patient's condition is critical and life-threatening. If they receive

试验等术前准备，通知手术室、麻醉科作好相应准备，护送患者进手术室，并与手术室护士作详细交接。

（二）灾害救护现场救护工作内容

社区护士在灾害现场中的救护工作内容主要包括以下几个方面：

1. **评价现场伤亡情况** 包括事件发生的时间、地点、伤亡人数及种类；伤员主要的伤情、采取的措施及投入的医疗资源；急需解决的医疗救护问题。

2. **现场伤员的分类** 依据受害者的伤病情况，按轻、中、重、死亡分类，并分别用绿、黄、红、黑色的伤病卡做出标识，将伤病卡置于伤病员的胸部、手腕或脚踝部位，便于救护人员辨认并采取相应的急救措施。

BOX 11-1 知识拓展

现场检伤分类中的颜色标识及救治顺序

按照 2023 年 12 月我国国家卫生健康委颁布的《突发事件医疗应急工作管理办法（试行）》规定，现场检伤分类划分为四个等级，伤情识别卡使用统一的颜色标识，便于识别不同程度伤情的患者，并快速采取相应措施。

1. **红色** 第一优先处置、转送。表示伤病员情况危重，有生命危险，如果得到紧急救治则有生存的可能。常见于收缩压小于 60mmHg、

emergency treatment, there is a chance of survival. Common symptoms include a systolic blood pressure of less than 60mmHg, unconsciousness, sudden cardiac and , respiratory arrest, or dyspnea, upper airway obstruction, tension pneumothorax, massive hemorrhage, coma, etc.

2. Yellow   Second priority for treatment and transfer. Indicates that the patient's condition is serious but relatively stable, allowing for treatment within a certain time frame. Common symptoms include severe scald, scalp avulsion, humerus fracture, shoulder dislocation, stable drug poisoning, mild consciousness disorder, etc.

3. Green   Third priority for treatment and transfer. Indicates that the patient's injury is relatively minor, conscious and alert, with normal vital signs, able to cooperate with examination, and able to walk independently. No need for transfer to a hospital for treatment, on-site first aid. Common symptoms include simple wound ruptures, sprains, etc.

4. Black   Deceased or injured patients with extremely severe injuries who have no chance of survival. Such as trunk separation, severe trauma and internal organs prolapse caused by falling from a great height.

3. Transfer the Wounded   Fill out the blood type, severity of the injury, first aid treatment, precautions, etc. of the injured person one by one on the injured person's information sheet and place it in the injured person's pocket. In the transportation process, scientifically carry the injured according to their condition and choose appropriate transportation to avoid secondary damage, such as massive hemorrhage, fracture, etc., should be treated first before transport.

4. Reporting and Management of Relevant Information   According to the reporting procedures stipulated by the relevant laws and regulations, timely report new cases, severe patients, and other situations that occur on site.

意识丧失、心搏和呼吸骤停或呼吸困难、上呼吸道梗阻、张力性气胸、大出血、昏迷等。

2. 黄色   第二优先处置、转送。表示伤病员情况严重但相对稳定，允许在一定时间内救治。常见于严重烫伤、头皮撕脱伤、肱骨骨折、肩关节脱位、稳定性的药物中毒、轻度意识障碍等。

3. 绿色   第三优先处置、转送。表示患者伤情较轻，意识清醒，生命体征正常，能配合检查，可自行走动，不需转诊医院治疗，可现场救护。常见有单纯伤口破裂、扭伤等。

4. 黑色   表示已死亡者或损伤非常严重，没有存活希望的伤员。如躯干分离、高空坠落致严重创伤及内脏脱出者。

3. 转送伤员   将经治伤员的血型、伤情、急救处置、注意事项等逐一填写在伤员情况单上，并置于伤员衣袋内。转运过程中，根据伤员的伤情科学搬运，并选择合适的交通工具，避免造成二次损伤，如大出血、骨折等应先处理再转运。

4. 相关信息的报告与管理   按照相关法律法规规定的报告程序，对现场发生的新病例、重症患者等情况及时报告。

5. On-site Epidemiological Investigation and Population Management Cooperate with professional prevention and control institutions to implement measures such as isolation and medical observation for infectious disease patients and suspected patients; regular follow-up of isolated individuals and guide the patient's home disinfection; carry out health education, popularize rescue knowledge, and answer relevant questions; distribute emergency drugs and protective equipment, and guide residents to use them correctly.

6. Command and Dispatch Other On-site Medical Rescue Forces Dispatch other personnel involved in medical assistance as needed.

III. Recovery Period Management of Community Emergency Disaster Events

Disasters have the characteristics of suddenness, unpredictability, and severity of harm. They not only cause huge economic losses and serious casualties, but also cause physical and psychological problems for people. Post-disaster management focuses on managing the impact of sudden disaster events on people, with psychological issues being more important.

i. Common Psychological Problems After Community Disaster

1. Psychological Stress Reaction It is the body's adaptive response to various stressors. The stress response caused by catastrophic events manifests as emotional reactions, physiological reactions, cognitive disorders, and behavioral abnormalities.

(1) Emotional reactions, such as sadness, anger, fear, depression, anxiety, and unease.

(2) Physiological reactions, such as fatigue, headache, dizziness, insomnia, nightmares, palpitations, asthma, muscle twitching, and other symptoms.

(3) Cognitive disorders, such as abnormal

5. 现场流行病学调查与人群管理　配合专业防治机构对传染病患者、疑似患者采取隔离、医学观察等措施；对隔离者进行定期随访，指导患者家庭消毒；开展健康教育，普及救护知识，解答相关问题；发放应急药品和防护用品，并指导居民正确使用。

6. 指挥、调遣现场其他医疗救助力量　根据需要，对参与医疗救助的其他人员进行调遣。

三、社区突发灾害性事件的恢复期管理

灾害发生具有突发性、不可预料性、危害严重性等特点，不仅会造成巨大的经济损失和严重的人员伤亡，还会造成人们的躯体健康问题和心理问题。灾后管理主要是针对突发灾害性事件影响的管理，其中心理问题的管理更为重要。

（一）社区灾后常见心理问题

1. 心理应激反应　是人的身体对各种紧张刺激产生的适应性反应。灾害性事件造成的应激反应表现为情绪反应、生理反应、认知障碍及行为异常等。

（1）情绪反应，如悲痛、愤怒、恐惧、忧郁、焦虑不安等。

（2）生理反应，如疲乏、头痛、头晕、失眠、噩梦、心慌、气喘、肌肉抽搐等症状。

（3）认知障碍，如感知异常、记忆力下降、

perception, memory loss, difficulty concentrating, difficulty thinking and understanding, poor judgment, loss of interest in work and life.

(4) Behavioral abnormalities, such as restlessness, coercion, avoidance, verbal abuse, liking to be alone, excessive dependence, stiff behavior, refusal to eat or drink or excessively, alcoholism, etc., can even lead to mental breakdown, self-injury, and suicide.

2. Psychological Stress Disorder

The strong psychological stress caused by disasters not only leads to short-term psychological disorders in individuals, such as acute stress disorder (ASD), but also long-term psychological trauma, such as post-traumatic stress disorder (PTSD), which may worsen or trigger diseases in some individuals. In severe cases, psychological crises such as loss of control and emotional disorders may occur.

(1) ASD: Also known as acute stress reaction (ASR), is a clinical syndrome characterized by a series of physiological and psychological reactions, mainly including fear, increased alertness, avoidance, and irritability, which are directly caused by a sharp and severe mental impact and occur from a few minutes to a few hours after being stimulated.

ASD usually occurs within 4 weeks after a traumatic event and lasts for at least 2d. ASD has a higher incidence in the post-traumatic population and has a significant impact on social and economic life. If not handled properly, 20%–50% of people may transition from ASD to PTSD, which can be painful and difficult to treat for a long time. The duration of ASD is up to 4 weeks, and more than 4 weeks should be considered PTSD.

(2) PTSD: Refers to an abnormal psychological response to severe stress factors such as trauma, also known as delayed psychogenic reaction. It often occurs several months or years after a sudden event, and refers to the long-term anxiety and excitement of victims after experiencing emergency, life-threatening, or dangerous physical

精神不易集中、思考与理解困难、判断失误、对工作和生活失去兴趣等。

（4）行为异常，如坐立不安、强迫、回避、骂人、喜欢独处、过度依赖、举止僵硬、拒食或暴饮暴食、酗酒等，严重的甚至精神崩溃，出现自伤、自杀。

2. 心理应激障碍

灾害造成的强烈的心理应激不仅会导致个体出现短时的心理障碍，如急性应激障碍（acute stress disorder，ASD），还会导致长期的心理创伤，如创伤后应激障碍（post-traumatic stress disorder，PTSD），也可能加重或诱发疾病，严重时发生意志失控、情感紊乱等心理危机。

（1）急性应激障碍：又称急性应激反应（acute stress reaction，ASR），以急剧、严重的精神打击为直接原因，在受刺激后几分钟至几小时发病，症状表现为一系列生理心理反应的临床综合征，主要包括恐惧、警觉性增高、回避和易激惹等症状。

ASD一般发生于创伤事件后4周以内，持续至少2d。ASD在创伤后人群中发生率较高，对社会经济生活影响较大。如果处理不当，可有20%~50%的人由ASD转为PTSD，长期存在痛苦，难以矫治。ASD持续时间至多4周，超过4周应考虑为PTSD。

（2）创伤后应激障碍：指对创伤等严重应激因素的一种异常精神反应，又称延迟性心因性反应，常于突发事件发生后的数月或数年后发生，指受灾人由于经历紧急的、威胁生命的或对身心健康有危险的事件，导致在创伤之后出现长期的焦虑与激动情绪。根据美国《精神障碍诊断与统计手册》（DSM-Ⅳ），PTSD的诊断标准

and mental health. According to the *Diagnostic and Statistical Manual of Mental Disorders* (DSM-Ⅳ) in the United States, the diagnostic criteria for PTSD are: a. Individuals must have experienced severe, life-threatening traumatic stressors. b. Manifesting as a sustained reproduction of traumatic experiences, repeated painful memories, nightmares, fantasies, and corresponding physiological reactions. c. Individuals have persistent avoidance and overall emotional numbness. d. There is a sustained increase in alertness, such as emotional irritability, difficulty initiating asleep, etc. e. The above symptoms persist for at least one month and lead to significant subjective pain and social dysfunction in individuals.

3. Psychological and Behavioral Reactions of Different Groups Due to differences in factors such as gender, knowledge, personal coping skills, education, degree of exposure to disasters, disaster experience, and role in disaster events, the degree of psychological trauma suffered by each person varies; in addition, due to social support and other reasons, the same degree of disaster damage can also cause different psychological damage.

(1) Psychological and Behavioral Reactions of Survivors: After experiencing life and death disasters, many people have lingering palpitations. In the beginning, survivors may have a sense of unreality, not believing that what is happening, thinking it is a nightmare. After realizing the harsh reality, they will go through a period of depression, indifferent to everything around them. Finally, once they realize that these tragedies are real, they will develop serious psychological problems, and if not guided in a timely and effective manner, they may gradually develop PTSD.

(2) Psychological and Behavioral Reactions of the Victims' Families: When their loved ones die, they will fall into immense grief, experiencing varying degrees of emotional and physiological abnormalities, cognitive impairment, abnormal

为：①个体必须经历过严重的、危及生命的创伤性应激源；②表现为持续性的重现创伤体验，反复痛苦回忆、噩梦、幻想以及相应的生理反应；③个体有持续性的回避与整体感情反应麻木；④有持续性的警觉性增高，如情绪烦躁、入睡困难等；⑤以上症状持续至少 1 个月，并导致个体明显的主观痛苦及社会功能受损。

3. 不同群体的心理行为反应 每个人由于性别、知识能力、个人应对方式、所受教育程度、受灾程度、灾害经历、灾害性事件中所处角色等因素的不同，所承受的心理创伤的程度不同；由于社会支持等原因，相同的灾害破坏程度也能造成不同的心理伤害。

（1）幸存者的心理行为反应：经历过生死劫难后，很多人心有余悸。一开始，幸存者会有"不真实感"，不相信发生的一切是真的，认为是场噩梦；在意识到残酷的现实之后，他们会经历一段消沉期，对周围的一切漠不关心；最后，一旦他们认识到这些悲剧是真实的，便会产生严重的心理问题，如果得不到及时、有效的疏导，有可能逐渐发展为 PTSD。

（2）罹难者家属的心理行为反应：当自己的亲人遇难时，亲属会陷入无比悲痛中，不同程度地出现情绪和生理异常反应、认知障碍、异常行为，甚至出现精神崩溃、自伤、自杀的倾向。尤其是与罹难者关系越亲近的家属其症状越明显，

behavior, and even a tendency towards mental breakdown, self-injury, and suicide. Especially for family members who have a closer relationship with the victim, their symptoms become more apparent. The victim's family often blames themselves, leading to feelings of guilt and self-blame.

(3) Psychological and Behavioral Reactions of Rescuers: After a disaster occurs, rescuers will immediately engage in rescue work. Because of the special nature of their work environment, facing heavy casualties and their roles in disasters, they will experience a series of psychological stresses, such as fear, anxiety, helplessness, and frustration.

(4) Psychological and Behavioral Reactions of the General Public: A major disaster not only leaves serious psychological trauma for survivors, victims' families, and rescuers, but also causes potential psychological damage to the entire society, making ordinary people who receive information about the event feel anxious, fearful, helpless, and even anxious all day long. In severe cases, it can cause social chaos.

ii. Health Management during Post-disaster Recovery Period in Communities

1. Provide Medical Rehabilitation Services for Injured Patients Disaster events often lead to physical and mental disabilities for many people, requiring long-term training, treatment, and care. In particular, home visits and disease management should be provided for bereaved, unattended patients and those with limited transportation.

2. Community Public Health Management During the recovery period from emergencies, communities establish special epidemic prevention organizations, and community nurses assist health and epidemic prevention personnel in health education, environmental management, and health improvement. a. Centralized disinfection and sterilization, pay attention to food hygiene, and prevent the occurrence of infectious diseases. b. If it is a group infectious disease, assist

遇难者家属经常会把责任归咎到自己身上，而产生内疚、自责心理。

（3）救援人员的心理行为反应：灾害发生后，救援人员会立刻投入到抢救工作中去，由于他们工作环境的特殊性，面对惨重的伤亡情况以及他们在灾难中所担任的角色，他们会产生一系列的心理应激，如恐惧、焦虑、无助、挫败感。

（4）一般公众的心理行为反应：一场重大的灾害不仅给幸存者、遇难者家属、救援人员留下严重的心理创伤，也会对社会公众造成潜在的心理损伤，得知事件信息的普通群众会感到焦虑不安、恐惧、无助，甚至惶惶不可终日，严重者会引发社会混乱。

（二）社区灾后恢复期的健康管理

1. 为伤、病者提供康复期医疗护理服务 灾害性事件常导致很多人肢体残疾、精神障碍，需接受长时间的训练、治疗和护理，尤其是要为失去亲人、无人照顾的患者以及交通不便者提供上门服务，进行家庭访视和疾病管理。

2. 社区公共卫生管理 突发事件恢复期，社区专门成立防疫组织，社区护士要协助卫生防疫人员进行卫生宣教，管理环境和改善卫生条件。包括：①集中消毒灭菌，注意食物卫生，预防传染病的发生；②若是群体性传染病，协助防疫人员找出传染源，监控事件动态，早发现、早隔离、早治疗；③对集体居住的和可能感染的居民进行相应疫苗接种。

epidemic prevention personnel to identify the source of infection, monitor the dynamics of the event, detect early, isolate early, and treat early. c. Vaccinate those who live in groups and may be infected.

3. Psychological Intervention for Key Populations

While providing material relief after an emergency, psychological disaster relief is also an indispensable part of the disaster relief process. Psychological intervention is the timely and effective psychological assistance provided to individuals in a psychological crisis, enabling them to quickly overcome difficulties and crises, and readjust to life. Psychological intervention workers are generally trained psychologists, social workers, psychiatrists and other professionals, as well as the involvement of organizational management.

(1) Psychological Intervention Measures： When conducting psychological intervention, different measures should be taken according to different objects, as shown in Table 11-2.

3. 重点人群的心理干预　突发事件后进行物资救灾的同时，心理救灾也是救灾过程中不可缺少的组成部分。心理干预是对处在心理危机状态下的个人及时给予有效的心理援助，使之尽快摆脱困境，战胜危机，重新适应生活。心理干预工作者一般是经过专门训练的心理学家、社会工作者、精神科医生等专业人员，同时也需要组织管理人员的参与。

（1）心理干预措施：进行心理干预时，应根据不同的对象采取不同的措施，详见表11-2。

Table 11-2　Psychological Intervention Measures for Different Objects

Intervention targets	Intervention measures
Survivors	a. Create a secure environment. b. Maintain close contact with survivors, establish communication relationships, encourage them to vent their inner pain, and give them positive suggestions. c. Help them objectively and realistically analyze and judge the nature and consequences of events, correct unreasonable cognition, and guide them to adopt positive coping strategies. d. Help them solve some practical life problems, such as providing food, repairing houses, etc
Victims' families	a. Provide meticulous care in daily life and physiology, reflecting personalization and detail. b. Guide them to vent negative emotions such as depression and anxiety, patiently listen, and help the families of the victims accept the facts. c. Maintain smooth communication between the families of the victims and enable them to obtain psychological support from each other
Rescuers	a. Before executing the task, develop a corresponding organizational plan, clarify the task, reduce expected anxiety, and establish team confidence. b. When carrying out tasks, arrange work positions and working hours reasonably ($< 12h$) to ensure communication with family members. c. Timely arrange psychological intervention methods such as stress reduction, report sharing, and crisis intervention. d. After the task is completed, arrange a break to relax
General public	a. Provide accurate and authoritative information to help the public understand the truth, identify sources of pressure, and block unnecessary panic caused by rumors. b. Strengthen education on disaster related knowledge, popularize mental health knowledge, and methods for responding to disasters. c. Provide a psychological counseling hotline

表 11-2　不同对象的心理干预措施

干预对象	干预措施
幸存者	①营造有安全感的环境；②保持与幸存者密切接触，建立沟通关系，鼓励其宣泄心中的痛苦，给予积极的暗示；③帮助其客观地、现实地分析和判断事件的性质和后果，纠正不合理的认知，采用积极的应对策略；④帮助解决一些生活实际问题，比如提供食品、修葺房屋等
罹难者家属	①给予生活、生理上精心的照顾，体现个性化、细节化；②引导其宣泄抑郁、焦虑等负性情绪，耐心倾听，帮助罹难者家属接受事实；③保持罹难者家属之间信息通畅，使他们相互心理支持
救援人员	①执行任务前，制订应对的组织计划，明确任务，减轻预期焦虑，建立团队自信心；②执行任务时，合理安排工作岗位与工作时间（< 12 小时），保证其与家人之间的交流；③适时安排减压、分享报告、危机干预等心理干预措施；④任务结束后，安排休息放松
一般公众	①提供准确、权威的信息，使公众了解实情，明确压力源，阻断谣言带来的不必要的恐慌；②加强灾害相关知识教育，普及精神卫生知识、应对灾害的方法；③提供心理咨询热线电话

(2) Psychological Intervention Precautions:

1) Serious and sincere attitude: Obtain the trust of the disaster victims through a serious and sincere attitude, make them willing to confide, and maintain a continuous support relationship.

2) Pay attention to communication skills: Express understanding and support through eye contact and body movements. If the disaster victims are unwilling to say more, keep silent and patient to avoid increasing their sense of compulsion; don't express too much sympathy to avoid aggravating their negative emotions; use more open communication methods to allow the disaster victims to fully express their emotions.

3) Being able to grasp the main psychological problems of disaster victims: In sudden events, the psychological problems of disaster victims are more complex. Some people keep confiding and venting their emotions, while others remain silent. Therefore, in order to understand what they want to express, grasp the key points to communicate and solve, it is necessary to observe carefully, listen sincerely, and empathize.

(Wen Guimin)

（2）心理干预注意事项

1）态度认真、真诚：通过认真、真诚的态度取得受灾者的信赖，使其愿意倾诉，保持持续的支持关系。

2）注意沟通技巧：通过眼神交流、肢体动作表达理解和支持，若对方不愿多说，则保持沉默，不要急躁，以免增加对方的强迫感；不要过多地表达同情，以免加重对方的负性情绪；多用开放式交流法，使对方能完全表达自己的情感。

3）能及时抓住受灾者的主要心理问题：突发事件中受灾者的心理问题较复杂，有的人一直在倾诉、发泄情绪，有的人则默不作声，因此，要能明白其想表达的内容，抓住要沟通、解决的重点，需要细致地观察、真诚地倾听和"共情"。

（温桂敏）

Key Points

1. Emergency public health events refer to major infectious disease outbreaks, group

内容摘要

1. 突发公共卫生事件是指突然发生，造成或者可能造成社会公众健康严重损害的重大传

diseases of unknown causes, major food and occupational poisoning, and other sudden events that cause or may cause serious damage to public health.

2. American crisis management expert Robert Heath's crisis management theory divides crisis management into four stages, namely the 4R model of crisis management, including: reduction, readiness, response, and recovery.

3. The principles of emergency management for emergency public health events include 5 aspects: prevention-oriented, quick response, classification guidance, timely handling, territorial management.

4. Early warning of emergency public health events is to take appropriate emergency responses timely and minimize the harm to emergencies.

5. Measures to deal with sudden outbreaks of infectious diseases and emergency public health events in the community include: medical treatment and management of patients; management of close contacts of infectious diseases and individuals exposed to health hazards; epidemiological investigation; management of epidemic focuses and areas; emergency vaccination and preventive medication; and propaganda and education.

6. The WHO defines disasters as any event that causes facility damage, severe economic damage, casualties, or deterioration of health conditions, and its scale and severity exceeds regional capacity and spreads and develops externally, requiring assistance.

7. The rescue work of community nurses at disaster sites mainly includes: assessment of casualties on site; classification of on-site injuries and patients; transfer of the wounded; reporting and management of relevant information; on-site epidemiological investigation and population management; command and dispatch other on-site medical rescue forces.

染病疫情、群体性不明原因疾病、重大食物和职业中毒以及其他严重影响公众健康的事件。

2. 美国危机管理专家 Robert Heath 的危机管理理论将危机管理分为 4 个阶段，即危机管理的 4R 模式，包括：缩减力、预备力、反应力、恢复力。

3. 突发公共卫生事件应急管理原则包括 5 个方面：预防为主、快速反应、分类指导、及时处理、属地管理。

4. 突发公共卫生事件的早期预警是为了及时采取相应的应急反应，将突发事件的危害降到最低。

5. 社区突发传染病和突发公共卫生事件的处理措施包括：患者医疗救治和管理；传染病密切接触者和健康危害暴露人员的管理；流行病学调查；疫点疫区处理；应急接种和预防性服药；宣传教育。

6. 灾害又称灾难，世界卫生组织对灾害的定义为：任何能引起设施破坏、经济严重受损、人员伤亡、健康状况恶化的事件，其规模、严重程度已超出区域承受能力并向外部扩散和发展，需要寻求援助。

7. 社区护士在灾害现场中的救护工作内容主要包括：评价现场伤亡情况；现场伤病员的分类；转送伤员；相关信息的报告与管理；现场流行病学调查与人群管理；指挥、调遣现场其他医疗救助力量。

| 思 考 题

(Questions 1 to 2 share the same question stem)

In early 2003, the SARS epidemic ravaged the globe, and China was also severely affected. Initially, due to a lack of understanding of its pathogen and routes of transmission, the epidemic spread rapidly. With the deepening of scientific research, it was gradually clarified that the pathogen was a variant of the coronavirus, and effective prevention and control measures were taken, ultimately controlling the epidemic.

1. According to *Law of the People's Republic of China on the Prevention and Treatment of Infectious Diseases*, which category of infectious diseases does SARS belong to? How should this epidemic be reported according to the regulations?

2. What are the measures for handling infectious diseases?

(Questions 3 to 4 share the same question stem)

On May 12, 2008, a magnitude 8.0 earthquake occurred in Wenchuan County, Aba Tibetan and Qiang Autonomous Prefecture, Sichuan Province. The earthquake severely damaged an area of about 500,000 square kilometers, with a total population of 46.256 million, resulting in direct economic losses of 845.14 billion yuan.

3. Based on the disaster's scope, degree of impairment, and controllability, to which level of disaster does this incident belong?

4. If the crisis management theory proposed by American crisis management expert Robert Heath were applied to the emergency management of this public emergency, what specific management steps would be involved?

（1~2 题共用题干）

2003 年初，"非典"疫情肆虐全球，我国也受到严重影响。初期，由于对其病原体和传播途径认识不清，疫情迅速扩散。随着科学研究的深入，逐步明确其病原体为冠状病毒的一种变种，并采取了有效的防控措施，最终控制了疫情。

1. 依照《中华人民共和国传染病防治法》规定，"非典"属于哪一类传染病？应当如何针对这一疫情进行相关信息报告？

2. 传染病的处理措施包括哪些内容？

（3~4 题共用题干）

2008 年 5 月 12 日，四川省阿坝藏族羌族自治州汶川县发生里氏 8.0 级大地震，地震严重破坏地区约 50 万平方千米，受灾总人口达 4 625.6 万人，造成直接经济损失 8 451.4 亿元。

3. 按灾害范围、损害程度和可控性分级，这一灾害属于几级灾害？

4. 如运用美国危机管理专家 Robert Heath 的危机管理理论，对该突发公共事件进行应急管理，具体管理步骤包括哪些？

［1］ 姜丽萍. 社区护理学［M］. 5 版. 北京：人民卫生出版社，2021.

［2］ 王爱红，张先庚. 社区护理学［M］. 3 版. 北京：人民卫生出版社，2021.

［3］ 吴冬晓，胡翠环. 英国社区护理的现状及对我国的启示［J］. 智慧健康，2019，5（15）：54-55.

［4］ 李立明. 公共卫生与预防医学导论［M］. 北京：人民卫生出版社，2017.

［5］ 徐亮，李军. 社区护士岗位培训教程［M］. 北京：人民卫生出版社，2013.

［6］ 泮昱钦. 社区护理［M］. 杭州：浙江大学出版社，2011.

［7］ BARNES E，BROWN G，KERR D J. The UK benefits from a truly National Health Service［J］. Lancet，2022，400（10346）：78-80.

［8］ HEDLEY-WHYTE J，MILAMED D R. Planning of the UK's National Health Service［J］. Ulster Med J，2022，91（1）：39-44.

［9］ ROY D，WEYMAN A K，PLUGOR R，et al. Institutional commitment and aging among allied health care professionals in the British National Health Service［J］. Health Serv Manage Res，2021，34（2）：54-61.

［10］ 卫生部. 卫生部关于规范城乡居民健康档案管理的指导意见［EB/OL］. (2009-12-03)［2024-05-20］. ttps://www.gov.cn/gzdt/2009-12/03/content_1479764.htm.

［11］ 国家卫生健康委，国家中医药管理局. 关于规范家庭医生签约服务管理的指导意见［EB/OL］. (2018-09-29)［2024-05-20］. https://www.gov.cn/zhengce/zhengceku/2018-12/31/content_5435461.htm.

［12］ 上海市卫生健康委员会. 关于印发《上海市居民电子健康档案服务规范（2020 版）》的通知［EB/OL］. (2020-04-26)［2024-05-20］. https://wsjkw.sh.gov.cn/jcws2/20200426/36c5d78b475b473abebf63e9a2432ec4.html.

［13］ 中华人民共和国中央人民政府. 中华人民共和国基本医疗卫生与健康促进法［EB/OL］. (2019-12-29)［2024-05-20］. https://www.gov.cn/xinwen/2019-12/29/content_5464861.htm.

［14］ 国家卫生计生委，国家中医药管理局. 关于进一步规范社区卫生服务管理和提升服务质量的指导意见［EB/OL］. (2015-11-25)［2024-05-20］. http://www.nhc.gov.cn/jws/s3581r/201511/1742007746a64005a16e32de00cc5fc5.shtml.

［15］ 卫生部，国家发展计划委员会，教育部，等. 关于印发《关于发展城市社区卫生服务的若干意见》的通知［EB/OL］. (1999-07-16)［2024-05-20］. http://www.nhc.gov.cn/wjw/gfxwj/201304/198b4a75380c45dd9dd4ad486e206be5.shtml.

［16］ 卫生部，国务院体改办，国家计委，等. 关于印发《关于加快发展城市社区卫生服务的意见》的通知［EB/OL］. (2002-08-22)［2024-05-20］. http://www.nhc.gov.cn/wjw/gfxwj/201304/5d6de93afb4b45e0b180b0b47976f1a5.shtml.

［17］ 国家卫生健康委，财政部，国家中医药局，等. 关于做好 2023 年基本公共卫生服务工作的通知［EB/OL］.

（2023-07-06）[2024-05-20]. https：//www.gov.cn/zhengce/zhengceku/202307/content_6891440.htm.

[18] 世界卫生组织. 初级卫生保健 [EB/OL]. （2023-11-15）[2024-05-20]. https：//www.who.int/zh/news-room/fact-sheets/detail/primary-health-care.

[19] 陈园，王珂，史赤天，等. 日本《全球健康战略》的实施及其对我国的启示 [J]. 现代药物与临床，2023，38（12）：3145-3149.

[20] 黄锦玲，曾志嵘. 我国城市社区卫生服务政策演进逻辑及走向研究 [J]. 中国全科医学，2023，26（34）：4239-4245.

[21] 宋徽江，秦卫，黄熙涯，等. 上海市浦东新区社区全科医疗质量控制测评分析 [J]. 中华全科医学，2022，20（5）：812-815.

[22] 杨辉，韩建军，许岩丽，等. 中国全科医学行业十年发展：机会和挑战并存 [J]. 中国全科医学，2022，25（1）：1-13，28.

[23] 崔小琴，张志梁，马雪萍，等. 社区卫生服务机构注册护士配置现状分析 [J]. 中国农村卫生事业管理，2021，41（12）：879-882.

[24] 张倩倩，金花，于德华. 国内外社区卫生服务质量评价内容差异的系统综述 [J]. 中国全科医学，2022，25（1）：20-28.

[25] 金花，易春涛，史玲，等. 基层医疗卫生机构全科临床质量管理实践探索：以上海市全科医学临床质量控制中心建设为例 [J]. 中国全科医学，2022，25（1）：29-34，42.

[26] 孙梦. "健康云"构建整合型服务体系 [J]. 中国卫生，2020（10）：34.

[27] 王扣柱，杨薇娜，马学东，等. 上海市闵行区社区卫生服务综合标准化建设的主要做法和成效 [J]. 中国全科医学，2020，23（16）：2020-2024.

[28] 孙延红. 社区卫生服务信息系统之健康档案研究 [J]. 知识文库，2020（2）：47，49.

[29] 何秋平，陈发钦. 国内外社区卫生服务发展现状研究 [J]. 中国农村卫生事业管理，2016，36（3）：328-332.

[30] BRAMWELL D，CHECKLAND K，SHIELDS J，et al. Community nursing services in England：an historical policy analysis[M]. London：Palgrave Macmillan，2023.

[31] LEESEBERG STAMLER L，YIU L，DOSANI A，et al. Community health nursing：a Canadian perspective [M]. 5th ed. Toronto：Pearson Canada Inc，2020.

[32] BROOK J，MCGRAW C，THURTLE V. Oxford handbook of primary care and community nursing[M]. 3rd ed. Oxford：Oxford University Press，2021.

[33] PEDERSEN JF，EGILSTRØD B，OVERGAARD C，et al. Public involvement in the planning，development and implementation of community health services：a scoping review of public involvement methods[J]. Health Soc Care Community，2022，30（3）：809-835.

[34] LI B，CHEN J. Barriers to community-based primary health care delivery in urban China：a systematic mapping review[J]. Int J Environ Res Public Health，2022，19（19）：12701.

[35] GADEKA DD，AKWEONGO P，WHYLE E，et al. Role of actor networks in primary health care implementation in low- and middle-income countries：a scoping review[J]. Glob Health Action. 2023，16（1）：2206684.

[36] BLAY N，SOUSA MS，ROWLES M，et al. The community nurse in Australia. Who are they? A rapid systematic review[J]. J Nurs Manag，2022，30（1）：154-168.

[37] 郭清. 健康管理学 [M]. 2 版. 北京：人民卫生出版社，2023.

[38] 郭姣. 健康管理学 [M]. 北京：人民卫生出版社，2020.

[39] 王健，马军，王翔. 健康教育学 [M]. 3 版. 北京：高等教育出版社，2021.

[40] 何国平，赵秋利. 社区护理理论与实践 [M]. 2 版. 北京：人民卫生出版社，2018.

[41] World Health Organization. Bending the trends to promote health and well-being：a strategic foresight on the future of health promotion[EB/OL].（2022-10-06）[2024-08-04]. https：//www.who.int/publications-detail-redirect/9789240053793.

[42] World Health Organization. Community engagement：a health promotion guide for universal health coverage

in the hands of the people[EB/OL].（2020-10-05）[2024-08-04]. https：//www.who.int/publications-detail-redirect/9789240010529.

[43] World Health Organization. WHO guideline on school health services[EB/OL].（2021-06-22）[2024-08-04]. https：//www.who.int/publications-detail-redirect/9789240029392.

[44] World Health Organization. Community empowerment[EB/OL].[2024-08-04]. https：//www.who.int/teams/health-promotion/enhanced-wellbeing/seventh-global-conference/community-empowerment.

[45] World Health Organization. Health promotion[EB/OL].（2016-08-20）[2024-08-04]. https：//www.who.int/news-room/questions-and-answers/item/health-promotion.

[46] World Health Organization. A healthy lifestyle - WHO recommendations[EB/OL].（2010-05-06）[2024-08-04]. https：//www.who.int/europe/news-room/fact-sheets/item/a-healthy-lifestyle---who-recommendations.

[47] LAMORTE，WAYNE W. The health belief model[EB/OL].（2022-11-03）[2024-08-04]. https：//sphweb.bumc.bu.edu/otlt/MPH-Modules/SB/BehavioralChangeTheories/BehavioralChangeTheories2.html.

[48] Global Burden of Disease Collaborative Network. Global burden of disease study 2019（GBD 2019）results[EB/OL].[2024-08-04]. https：//vizhub.healthdata.org/gbd-results/.

[49] Agency for Toxic Substances and Disease Registry. Models and frameworks for the practice of community engagement[EB/OL].（2015-06-25）[2024-08-04]. http：//medbox.iiab.me/modules/en-cdc/www.atsdr.cdc.gov/communityengagement/pce_models.html.

[50] Community Tool Box. Precede/Proceed[EB/OL].[2024-08-04]. https：//ctb.ku.edu/en/table-contents/overview/other-models-promoting-community-health-and-development/preceder-proceder/main.

[51] 李春玉，姜丽萍. 社区护理学[M]. 4 版. 北京：人民卫生出版社，2017.

[52] 胡朋，周建芳. 代际支持对老年人口健康影响研究[J]. 中国卫生事业管理，2024，41（1）：95-100.

[53] 杨臻华. 基于家庭弹性视角的痴呆患者家庭照顾者负担研究[D]. 济南：山东大学，2021.

[54] 洪伊荣，何朝珠，谢春燕，等. 老年患者家庭照顾者喘息服务研究进展[J]. 中国老年学杂志，2022，42（7）：1783-1787.

[55] 代莉莉，段艳芹，张梅，等. 社区老年人居家护理服务需求结构性研究[J]. 中国全科医学，2021，24（25）：3238-3243.

[56] 李雅岑，刘宁宁，肖云霞，等. "互联网 +"母婴居家护理服务中的安全管理实践[J]. 中国护理管理，2023，23（7）：984-988.

[57] YAMAGUCHI Y，GREINER C，NAKAMURA M，et al. Caregiver burden and psychological status and their associations with sleep quality among family caregivers living with older people with dementia：a mixed method study[J]. Geriatric Nursing，2024，60：504-510.

[58] SMEEKES O S，DE BOER T R，VAN DER MEi R D，et al. Differentiating between home care types to identify older adults at risk of adverse health outcomes in the community[J]. Journal of the American Medical Directors Association，2024，25（11）：105257.

[59] PALACIOS-NAVARRO G，SANTAMARÍA R，Del Río D，et al. Effects of a home care community-dwelling intervention on cognition，mental health，loneliness and quality of life in elder people：the VERA study[J]. International Journal of Medical Informatics，2024，185：105378.

[60] YANG J，MA B，CHEN S，et al. Nurses' preferences for working in Uber-style 'Internet plus' nursing services：a discrete choice experiment[J]. International Journal of Nursing Studies，2025，161：104920.

[61] WANG F，WU Y，SUN X，et al. Reliability and validity of the Chinese version of a short form of the family health scale[J]. BMC Prim Care，2022，23（1）：108.

[62] CRANDALL A，WEISS-LAXER NS，BROADBENT E，et al. The family health scale：reliability and validity of a short- and long-form[J]. Front Public Health，2020，8：587125.

[63] 国家卫生健康委办公厅. 关于印发儿童青少年近视防控适宜技术指南的通知[EB/OL].（2019-10-15）[2025-04-18]. http：//www.nhc.gov.cn/jkj/s5898bm/201910/c475e0bd2de444379402f157523f03fe.shtml.

[64] SMITH JD, FU E, KOBAYASHI MA. Prevention and management of childhood obesity and its psychological and health comorbidities[J]. Annu Rev Clin Psychol, 2020, 16: 351-378.

[65] HUANG J, ZHOU X, LI X, et al. Regional disparity in epidemiological characteristics of adolescent scoliosis in China: data from a screening program[J]. Front Public Health, 2022, 10: 935040.

[66] 孔北华, 马丁, 段涛. 妇产科学 [M]. 10 版. 北京: 人民卫生出版社, 2024.

[67] 郁琦. 绝经学 [M]. 北京: 人民卫生出版社, 2013.

[68] 安力彬, 陆虹. 妇产科护理学 [M]. 7 版. 北京: 人民卫生出版社, 2022.

[69] 中国营养学会. 中国居民膳食指南 (2022) [M]. 北京: 人民卫生出版社, 2022.

[70] 卡伦·万巴赫. 母乳喂养与人类泌乳学 [M]. 6 版. 高雪莲, 孙瑜, 张美华, 译. 北京: 人民卫生出版社, 2021.

[71] 中华医学会妇产科学分会产科学组. 孕前和孕期保健指南 (2018) [J]. 中华妇产科杂志, 2018, 53 (1): 7-13.

[72] 刘洪妍, 王晓娇, 孙丽萍, 等. 育龄妇女孕期体重管理的最佳证据总结 [J]. 护士进修杂志, 2023, 38 (19): 1779-1784.

[73] 中国营养学会"中国产褥期(月子)妇女膳食"工作组. 中国产褥期(月子)妇女膳食建议 [J]. 营养学报, 2020, 42 (1): 3-6.

[74] 庄云婷, 翟巾帼, 张莉等. 妊娠期孕妇下肢痉挛管理的最佳证据总结 [J]. 中华护理杂志, 2022, 57 (18): 2276-2282.

[75] 石志宜, 卢颖, 邢丽媛, 等. 妊娠相关下腰痛预防与管理的最佳证据总结 [J]. 中华护理杂志, 2021, 56 (6): 934-941.

[76] 耿小婷, 李淑英, 张金燕, 等. 产后身体活动最佳证据研究 [J]. 中国康复理论与实践, 2022, 28 (7): 809-815.

[77] 马乐, 刘娟, 李环, 等. 产后盆底康复流程第一部分——产后盆底康复意义及基本原则 [J]. 中国实用妇科与产科杂志, 2015, 31 (4): 314-321.

[78] 刘娟, 葛环, 李环, 等. 产后盆底康复流程第二部分: 康复评估——病史收集、盆底组织损伤及盆底功能评估 [J]. 中国实用妇科与产科杂志, 2015, 31 (5): 426-432.

[79] 李环, 龙腾飞, 李丹彦, 等. 产后盆底康复流程第三部分——产后盆底康复措施及实施方案 [J]. 中国实用妇科与产科杂志, 2015, 31 (6): 522-529.

[80] 中华医学会围产医学分会, 中华护理学会妇产科护理专业委员会, 中国疾病预防控制中心妇幼保健中心. 新生儿早期基本保健技术的临床实施建议 (2017 年, 北京) [J]. 中华围产医学杂志, 2017, 20 (9): 625-629.

[81] 中华医学会围产医学分会, 中华医学会妇产科学分会产科学组, 中华护理学会产科护理专业委员会, 等. 中国新生儿早期基本保健技术专家共识 (2020) [J]. 中华围产医学杂志, 2020, 23 (7): 433-440.

[82] World Health Organization. Early essential newborn care clinical practice pocket guide, 2nd edition[R/OL]. (2022-08-02) [2025-04-18]. https://www.who.int/publications/i/item/9789290619659.

[83] World Health Organization. Adolescent pregnancy: evidence brief[R/OL]. (2019-04-08) [2025-04-18]. https://www.who.int/publications/i/item/WHO-RHR-19.15.

[84] 徐桂华, 何桂娟. 老年护理学 [M]. 2 版. 北京: 人民卫生出版社, 2022.

[85] 曾渝, 王中男. 社区健康服务与管理 [M]. 北京: 人民卫生出版社, 2020.

[86] 周郁秋, 张会君. 老年健康照护与促进 [M]. 北京: 人民卫生出版社, 2018.

[87] 杨莘, 程云. 老年专科护理 [M]. 北京: 人民卫生出版社, 2019.

[88] 中华医学会老年医学分会, 《中华老年医学杂志》编辑委员会. 老年人衰弱预防中国专家共识 (2022) [J]. 中华老年医学杂志, 2022, 41 (5): 503-511.

[89] 皮红英, 高远, 候惠如, 等. 老年人跌倒风险综合管理专家共识 [J]. 中华保健医学杂志, 2022, 24 (6): 439-441.

[90] 《中国老年骨质疏松症诊疗指南 (2023)》工作组, 中国老年学和老年医学学会骨质疏松分会, 中国医疗保健国际交流促进会骨质疏松病学分会, 等. 中国老年骨质疏松症诊疗指南 (2023) [J]. 中华骨与关节外科

杂志，2023，16（10）：865-885.

[91] GANZ DA，LATHAM NK. Prevention of falls in community-dwelling older adults[J]. N Engl J Med，2020，382（8）：734-743.

[92] PIERCY KL，TROIANO RP，BALLARD RM，et al. The physical activity guidelines for Americans[J]. JAMA，2018，320（19）：2020-2028.

[93] PINTO TCC，MACHADO L，BULGACOV TM，et al. Is the Montreal Cognitive Assessment（MoCA）screening superior to the Mini-Mental State Examination（MMSE）in the detection of mild cognitive impairment（MCI）and Alzheimer's Disease（AD）in the elderly?[J]. Int Psychogeriatr，2019，31（4）：491-504.

[94] 公共安全科学技术学会公共卫生安全与健康专业委员会，中国医师协会全科医师分会. 基层健康治理专家共识2024[J]. 中国全科医学，2024：1-4.

[95] 北京高血压防治协会，中国老年学和老年医学学会，北京市社区卫生协会，等. 成人高血压合并2型糖尿病和血脂异常基层防治中国专家共识（2024年版）[J]. 中国全科医学，2024，27（28）：3453-3475，3482.

[96] 王继光. 社区高血压防治与规范化管理[J]. 中华全科医师杂志，2023，22（6）：553-556.

[97] NGUYEN TNM，WHITEHEAD L，SAUNDERS R，et al. Systematic review of perception of barriers and facilitators to chronic disease self-management among older adults: implications for evidence-based practice[J]. Worldviews Evid Based Nurs，2022，19（3）：191-200.

[98] HE R，WEI F，HU Z，et al. Self-management in young and middle-aged patients with hypertension: a systematic review and meta-synthesis of qualitative studies[J]. Syst Rev，2024，13（1）：254.

[99] 王刚. 社区康复学[M]. 2版. 北京：人民卫生出版社，2018.

[100] 朱天民. 社区康复[M]. 2版. 北京：人民卫生出版社，2018.

[101] 王玉龙. 康复功能评定学[M]. 3版. 北京：人民卫生出版社，2018.

[102] World Health Organization. Community-based rehabilitation: CBR guidelines[EB/OL]. （2010-05-12）[2024-03-25]. https://www.who.int/publications/i/item/9789241548052.

[103] World Health Organization. International Day of Persons with Disabilities 2023[EB/OL]. （2023-03-07）[2024-03-25]. https://www.who.int/campaigns/international-day-of-persons-with-disabilities/2023.

[104] 谌永毅，吴欣娟，李旭英，等. 健康中国建设背景下安宁疗护事业的发展[J]. 中国护理管理，2019，19（6）：801-806.

[105] 陆宇晗. 我国安宁疗护的现状及发展方向. 中华护理杂志，2017，52（6）：659-664.

[106] 谌永毅，刘翔宇. 安宁疗护专科护理[M]. 北京：人民卫生出版社，2020.

[107] Worldwide Hospice Palliative Care Alliance. Global atlas of palliative care，2nd ed 2020[EB/OL]. （2020-10-07）[2025-04-18]. http://www.thewhpca.org/resources/global-atlas-on-end-of-life-care.

[108] 海峡两岸医药卫生交流协会全科医学分会. 姑息治疗与安宁疗护基本用药指南[J]. 中国全科医学，2021，24（14）：1717-1734.

[109] National Comprehensive Cancer Network. NCCN clinical practice guidelines in oncology: adult cancer pain[EB/OL]. （2025-03-12）[2025-04-18]. https://www.nccn.org/guidelines/guidelines-detail?category=3&id=1413.

[110] 中华人民共和国国家卫生健康委员会. 癌症疼痛诊疗规范（2018年版）[J]. 临床肿瘤学杂志，2018，23（10）：937-944.

[111] 王昆，金毅. 难治性癌痛专家共识（2017年版）[J]. 中国肿瘤临床，2017，44（16）：787-793.

[112] 中国抗癌协会肿瘤营养专业委员会，中华医学会肠外肠内营养学分会. 中国肿瘤营养治疗指南（2020）[M]. 北京：人民卫生出版社，2020.

[113] National Comprehensive Cancer Network. NCCN clinical practice guidelines in oncology: cancer related fatigue[EB/OL]. [2025-04-18]. https://www.nccn.org/guidelines/guidelines-detail?category=3&id=1424.

[114] National Comprehensive Cancer Network. NCCN clinical practice guidelines in oncology: distress management[EB/OL]. （2024-11-18）[2025-04-18]. https://www.nccn.org/guidelines/guidelines-detail?category=3&id=1431.

［115］陆宇晗，陈钒．肿瘤姑息护理实践指导［M］．北京：北京大学医学出版社，2017．

［116］樊代明．中国肿瘤整合诊治技术指南：安宁疗护［M］．天津：天津科学技术出版社，2023．

［117］许可怡，贾婧琪，胡馨，等．中国现行法律制度下生前预嘱的实现路径探讨［J/OL］．中国医学伦理学，2024：1-15［2024-11-11］．http://kns.cnki.net/kcms/detail/61.1203.R.20241106.0949.010.html．

［118］周春鹤，李惠艳，高巍，等．晚期癌症患者基于共享决策理论的预立医疗照护计划干预［J］．护理学杂志，2024，39（10）：1-5．

［119］王心茹，绳宇．生前预嘱、预立医疗指示和预立医疗照护计划的概念关系辨析［J］．医学与哲学，2020，41（24）：1-4，14．

［120］李秀华．灾害护理学［M］．北京：人民卫生出版社，2015．

［121］ZHANG S，CHU-KE C，KIM H，et al. Public view of public health emergencies based on artificial intelligence data［J］. Journal of Environmental and Public Health，2022，2022（1）：5162840.

［122］THAKUR A，CHOUDHARY D，KUMAR B，et al. A review on post-traumatic stress disorder（PTSD）：symptoms，therapies and recent case studies［J］. Current molecular pharmacology，2022，15（3）：502-516.